Merger Control, National Security, and Foreign Direct Investment Screening

Merger Control, National Security, and Foreign Direct Investment Screening

A Comparative Perspective

IOANNIS KOKKORIS

OXFORD
UNIVERSITY PRESS

OXFORD
UNIVERSITY PRESS

Great Clarendon Street, Oxford, OX2 6DP,
United Kingdom

Oxford University Press is a department of the University of Oxford.
It furthers the University's objective of excellence in research, scholarship,
and education by publishing worldwide. Oxford is a registered trade mark of
Oxford University Press in the UK and in certain other countries

Published in the United States of America by Oxford University Press
198 Madison Avenue, New York, NY 10016, United States of America

British Library Cataloguing in Publication Data
Data available

Library of Congress Control Number: 2024931048

ISBN 978–0–19–883734–3

DOI: 10.1093/law-ocl/9780198837343.001.0001

Printed and bound by
CPI Group (UK) Ltd, Croydon, CR0 4YY

Preface

Throughout the twentieth century and into the twenty-first there have been a number of occasions where measures were adopted aiming at protecting national economies from foreign economic interests. Such protectionist measures are accentuated at times of crisis, such as the financial crisis of 2007, or the Covid-19 pandemic. Although the importance of market integration has now been recognized, which may resist the strengthening of protectionist policies, an increasing number of stakeholders are advocating a renewed emphasis on nationalist policies in relation to FDI and merger control.

This trend has led to merger control assessment becoming subject to factors that are not merger-specific per se. Such factors relate to national security considerations, which competition and other government authorities take into account in the assessment of foreign direct investment (FDI) and thus of mergers and acquisitions (M&A) transactions. This trend has been intensifying across many jurisdictions, and from the perspective of businesses and private practitioners, the most important factors of national security FDI regimes are predictability, decreasing the level of complexity, and guaranteeing specificity. All of these factors are at risk, as this book illustrates, when we assess the approach various regimes globally adopt in assessing FDI.

The book adopts a comparative perspective. The analysis will follow a two-pronged perspective for each jurisdiction it analyses. The first prong is the institutional regime for assessing national security concerns in FDI. This perspective is broadly similar across jurisdictions. The second prong is the assessment of decision-making in these jurisdictions in relation to FDI and the identification of sectors or entities of priority.

We are only at the beginning of a global proliferation of national security and FDI screening regimes. The pace of development will be rapid, and authorities globally will on the one hand need to adapt to changing business models and investment strategies, while enhancing the accuracy, effectiveness, and transparency of the regimes on the other.

I would like to acknowledge the commitment and dedication shown by Dr Claudia Lemus, my colleague at Queen Mary University of London. In addition to Claudia, I was blessed with a stellar group of research assistants, including Stefanos Merikas, Athanassios Skourtis, Micaela Duffau, Nicoletta Triantafillou, Yajie Gao, Massimiliano Trovato, Anton Dinev, Muhammad Safa Uygur, and Anik Bhaduri.

I would also like to express my gratitude to Imogen Hill, Charlotte Kershaw, and the whole team at Oxford University Press, for their foresightedness and continuous support in this book. The views expressed in this book are my own and do represent any views of the UK Competition Appeals Tribunal.

Professor Ioannis Kokkoris
London, October 2023

Contents

Table of Legislation

CHINA

Primary and Secondary Legislation

Official Guidance

EUROPEAN UNION

Primary and Secondary Legislation

Official Guidance

INDIA

Primary and Secondary Legislation

Official Guidance

JAPAN

Primary and Secondary Legislation

Official Guidance

RUSSIAN FEDERATION

Primary and Secondary Legislation

SOUTH AFRICA

Primary and Secondary Legislation

Official Guidance

UNITED KINGDOM

Primary and Secondary Legislation

Official Guidance

UNITED STATES

Primary and Secondary Legislation

Official Guidance

OTHER JURISDICTIONS

Australia

Austria

Canada

1
Introduction

1.1 Economic Nationalism, Protectionism, and the Notion of National Security

In the context of global markets, the notion of economic nationalism refers to measures that can be adopted to protect national economies from foreign economic interests.[1] Nations have adopted a wide range of policies, including controlling imports and direct foreign investment, and strengthening state-owned companies.[2] Friedrich List, the nineteenth-century thinker whose ideas influenced the rise of economic nationalism, proclaimed that the only way to attain prosperity was industrialization, and to that end it was necessary to protect domestic industry against foreign competition.[3] Protectionist policies have been adopted with vigour throughout history, particularly during the Great Depression (1929–34)—when policies oriented to replacing goods which were formerly imported with domestically produced, known as import substitution,[4] were introduced in the 1930s across Asia, Africa, and Latin America (sometimes accompanied by expropriation of foreign companies and sequestration)[5]—and during the financial crisis of 2008–09.[6] It seems that these protectionist measures are accentuated in times of crisis, which in present times can be perceived as the Covid-19 pandemic and the exponential expansion of certain countries investment abroad. Although the importance of market integration has now been recognized as countering the strengthening of protectionist policies, an increasing number of stakeholders are advocating renewed emphasis on nationalist policies in relation to foreign direct investment (FDI) and in particular to mergers and acquisitions (M&A) assessment, especially from sovereign wealth funds and state-owned enterprises.

[1] Sam Pryke, 'Economic Nationalism: Theory, History and Prospects' (2012) 3(3) Global Policy 281; Anthony D Smith, *Nationalism and Modernism: A Critical Survey of Recent Theories of Nations and Nationalism* (Routledge 1998) 49.

[2] Pryke (n 1) 285.

[3] Jeromin Zettelmeyer, 'The Return of Economic Nationalism in Germany' (March 2019) Peterson Institute for International Economics Policy Briefs 19-4, https://www.piie.com/publications/policy-briefs/return-economic-nationalism-germany accessed 15 September 2023.

[4] For an interesting background and discussions about import substitution, see Werner Baer, 'Import Substitution and Industrialization in Latin America: Experiences and Interpretations' (1972) 7(1) Latin American Research Review 95; Albert O Hirschman, 'The Political Economy of Import-Substituting Industrialization in Latin America' (1968) 82(1) The Quarterly Journal of Economics 1; David Felix, 'Import Substitution and Late Industrialization: Latin America and Asia Compared' (1989) 17(9) World Development 1455.

[5] Geoffrey Jones, *Multinational Companies and Global Capitalism* (OUP 2005) 244.

[6] For further analysis see Pryke (n 1) 285–89.

Figures 1.1 and 1.2 illustrate the average FDI stocks and flows, respectively, to and from the European Union (EU), the United Kingdom (UK), the United States (US), China, Russia, Japan, India, and South Africa between 2013 and 2022. This provides very useful context for the assessment of the screening regimes in place in the jurisdictions that we will analyse in this book.

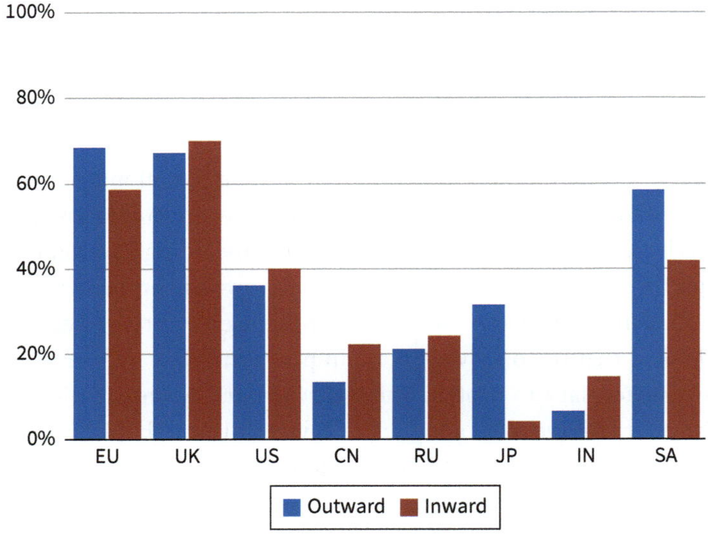

Figure 1.1 FDI stocks as % of GDP in several jurisdictions (2013–22 average)
Source: Data from OECD, 'FDI Stocks' <https://data.oecd.org/fdi/fdi-stocks.htm> accessed 15 September 2023

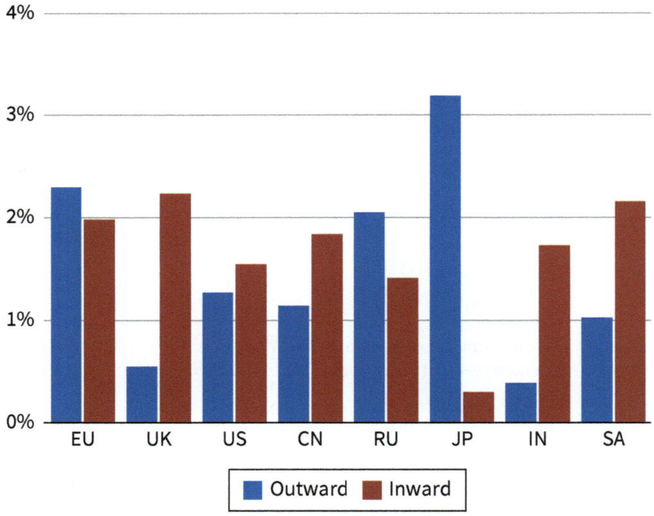

Figure 1.2 FDI flows as % of GDP in several jurisdictions (2013–22 average)
Source: Data from OECD, 'FDI Flows' <https://data.oecd.org/fdi/fdi-flows.htm> accessed 15 September 2023

More recently, the Covid-19 pandemic has reinvigorated the debate about the need to reassess the global trade model. The outbreak made governments reflect on the merits of globalized supply chains and the security of supply.[7] In response to the pandemic, several jurisdictions seeking to protect their economic sovereignty either introduced or updated screening regimes for foreign investment on national security grounds.

Indeed, the United Nations Conference on Trade and Development (UNCTAD)'s 2021 *World Investment Report* indicated that in 2020, sixty-seven countries adopted policy measures related to foreign investment, most of which took place in developed economies, largely as a response to the pandemic, and mainly restrictive.[8] The report noted that the number of restrictive policy measures in reaction to the pandemic exceeded those that were adopted during the financial crisis of 2008–09.[9] It also outlined that even if the vast majority of FDI measures have been generally adopted by developed economies (81 per cent), an important number of developing and emerging economies are mirroring the movement.[10]

Figure 1.3 shows the Organisation for Economic Cooperation and Development (OECD) assessment of FDI restrictiveness for the UK, the US, China, Russia, Japan, India, South Africa, Germany, Spain, France, and Italy. The OECD's data webpage defines restrictiveness based on 'four main types of restrictions: foreign equity restrictions; discriminatory screening or approval mechanisms; restrictions on key foreign personnel and operational restrictions' and assigns a score between 0 (open) and 1 (closed). The book will analyse in detail the regimes in place in the first seven countries, plus the European Union, and we will assess the approach they take to national security assessment of FDI.

[7] Philip Lowe, Adam Kidane, and Alec Burnside, 'Industrial Policy and EU Merger Control: Finding the Right Tools' in Ioannis Kokkoris and Nicholas Levy (eds), *Research Handbook on Global Merger Control* (Edward Elgar 2023) 273; Ioannis Kokkoris, 'EU Merger Control and National Security Assessment: A Moving Target', in ibid 328; K Fountoukakos, V Roberts, and R Allen, 'Addressing National Security Concerns in the Merger Context', in Ioannis Kokkoris and Claudia Lemus (eds), *Research Handbook on the Law and Economics of Competition Enforcement* (Edward Elgar 2022) 217.

[8] United Nations Conference on Trade and Development (UNCTAD), 'World Investment Report 2021: Investing in Sustainable Recovery' 109 https://unctad.org/system/files/official-document/wir2021_en.pdf accessed 15 September 2023.

[9] ibid.

[10] ibid 109, 111.

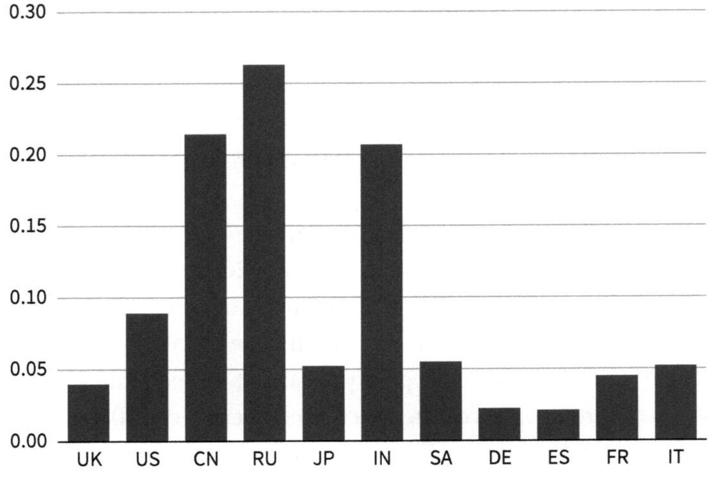

Figure 1.3 OECD FDI Restrictiveness Indicator (2020)
Source: Data from OECD, 'FDI Restrictiveness' (indicator) <*https://data.oecd.org/fdi/fdi-restrictiveness.htm*> accessed 15 September 2023
There was no data available for the EU. Germany, Spain, France, and Italy were used as proxy instead.

The types of measures vary from country to country: some are temporary and others are permanent, some have lowered the thresholds that trigger intervention, some have expanded the prior approval requirements for FDI, and others have established strategic sectors where the special power regime is applied strictly.[11]

FDI has both economic and security implications. This book will focus on the latter, which are generally disregarded by economic models.[12] As we will illustrate in detail in this book, the concept of national security varies considerably from jurisdiction to jurisdiction. There is a wide diversity of what jurisdictions consider to be national security. The concept of national security differs from one legal system to the other: some jurisdictions use a narrow definition, while others use an open and vague definition of what national security considerations entail. There is no exact definition of what national security is, and, therefore, the interpretation is left to the relevant authority.

The book will focus on jurisdictions that are influential in the assessment of transactions globally, including countries which account for significant inflows and outflows of FDI, and for a significant number of important FDI and merger control decisions. The aim of the book is to illustrate the fast-developing and expanding approach in the assessment of national security considerations in FDI. The book will mainly cover the EU, UK, US, and China, but also discuss other jurisdictions such as Japan, India, Russia, and South Africa.

[11] ibid 111–13.
[12] Jaeger M, *A More Strategic Approach to Foreign Direct Investment Policy* (German Council on Foreign Relations, 2023).

1.2 The Approach to the Assessment of National Security in the EU

The EU has been recognized as a leading recipient of FDI[13] and as one of the most open investment regimes in the world.[14] This approach derives from the notion that FDI stimulates the emergence of capital, the transfer of technology, the integration of societies, the improvement of employment conditions, and advances in research and product development.[15] The referred openness tendency was bolstered with the entry into force of the Lisbon Treaty, in which article 207(1) of the Treaty on the Functioning of the European Union (TFEU) incorporated FDI into the EU's common commercial policy (CCP),[16] translating the elimination of restrictions on international trade and investments in a constitutional obligation for the EU's common commercial policy.[17] As a result, the number of cross-border M&As, through FDI, has gradually increased in the EU by attracting the attention of US investors during the 1960s, later during the 1990s from Japanese and Korean firms, and most recently from the People's Republic of China (PRC).[18]

It has been argued that the flow of Chinese FDI was also prompted by the financial crisis that afflicted the globe in 2008–09, accompanied by the sovereign debt crisis in Europe.[19] The statistics show that Chinese investment expanded by 155 per cent between 2009 and 2011. By 2012 China had become one of the most important investors in Germany, and by 2012 Europe was the most attractive destination for Chinese outbound FDI.[20] This staggering surge raised concerns among different stakeholders, who were suspicious that this foreign control would compromise the national security

[13] According to the OECD, a direct investment is 'a category of cross-border investment made by a resident in one economy (the direct investor) with the objective of establishing a lasting interest in an enterprise (the direct investment enterprise) that is resident in an economy other than that of the direct investor. The motivation of the direct investor is a strategic long-term relationship with the direct investment enterprise to ensure a significant degree of influence by the direct investor in the management of the direct investment enterprise. The "lasting interest" is evidenced when the direct investor owns at least 10% of the voting power of the direct invest enterprise.' See OECD, *Benchmark Definition of Foreign Direct Investment (BMD4)* (4th edn, 2008) https://www.oecd.org/investment/fdibenchmarkdefinition.htm accessed 15 September 2023. M&As are a form of FDI in which companies either associate operations or where one company acquires stakes in another company. See Dustin Tingley and others, 'The Political Economy of Inward FDI: Opposition to Chinese Mergers and Acquisitions' (2015) 8(1) Chinese Journal of International Politics 27, 28.

[14] See OECD, FDI Regulatory Restrictiveness Index (2013) https://www.oecd.org/investment/fdiindex.htm accessed 16 August 2023; European Commission, Communication 'Towards a Comprehensive European International Investment Policy' COM (2010) 343 final, 3–4.

[15] European Commission, 'Reflection Paper on Harnessing Globalisation' (2017) 8 https://commission.europa.eu/publications/reflection-paper-harnessing-globalisation_en accessed 15 September 2023.

[16] Catherine Titi, 'International Investment Law and the European Union: Towards a New Generation of International Investment Agreements' (2015) 26(3) European Journal of International Law 639.

[17] Stephan W Schill, 'The European Union's Foreign Direct Investment Screening Paradox: Tightening Inward Investment Control to Further External Investment Liberalization' (2019) Amsterdam Law School Legal Studies Research Paper No. 2019-17, 10–11; see also arts 119 and 206 TFEU.

[18] Carlos Esplugues, 'Towards a Common Screening System of Foreign Direct Investment on National Interest Grounds in the European Union' (2018) 11(2) Culture, Media and Entertainment Law 3 https://ssrn.com/abstract=3267386 accessed 15 September 2023.

[19] Sophie Meunier, '"Beggars Can't Be Choosers": The European Crisis and Chinese Direct Investment in the European Union'(2014) 36(3) Journal of European Integration 283, 284.

[20] ibid.

of the EU Member States and their degree of control over key sectors.[21] In response, some Member States introduced measures aiming to interfere with Community-dimension transactions, a reaction that was described as a 'renaissance of protectionism'.[22] Under the EU Merger Regulation (EUMR), the European Commission has exclusive jurisdiction to review Community-dimension transactions,[23] which correspond to those that satisfy the thresholds indicated in article 1(2)[24] or (3) EUMR[25] or referred to the Commission pursuant articles 4(5)[26] or 22[27] EUMR. Notably, article 21(3) EUMR (known as the 'exclusivity principle') provides that 'No Member State shall apply its national legislation on competition to any concentration that has a Community dimension', which contrasts with the competence that Member States enjoy with regard to concentrations that do not have a Community dimension.[28] This Community dimension, or supranational jurisdiction, was adopted under the presumption that it would offer some benefits to the firms operating in the European single market, such as a one-stop shop, the prevalence of long-term policy objectives rather than the short-term inclinations of Member States, and the fact that a supranational institution would develop capacity expertise in a faster and more efficient manner, among others.[29]

In the EU regime, article 21 of the EU Merger Regulation allows Member States to adopt, with regard to concentrations with an EU dimension, measures to protect certain interests other than competition, as long as these measures are necessary and proportionate to their aim and compatible with EU law. Article 21 EUMR distinguishes between 'recognized interests'—namely security of supply, plurality of the media, and

[21] Alison Jones and John Davies, 'Merger Control and the Public Interest: Balancing EU and National Law in the Protectionist Debate' (2014) 10(3) European Competition Journal 453, 455.

[22] Neelie Kroes, 'European competition policy facing a renaissance of protectionism—which strategy for the future?' (St Gallen International Competition Law Forum, St Gallen, 11 May 2007) https://ec.europa.eu/commission/presscorner/detail/en/SPEECH_07_301 accessed 15 September 2023.

[23] Art 21(2) EUMR states that the Commission 'shall have sole jurisdiction' to control the compatibility of concentrations of a Community dimension.

[24] Art 1(2) EUMR indicates that a concentration has a Community dimension where: (a) the aggregate worldwide turnover of all the undertakings concerned is more than €5,000 million, and (b) the aggregate Community-wide turnover of each of at least two of the undertakings concerned is more than €250 million.

[25] Art 1(3) EUMR provides that a concentration that does not meet the thresholds laid down in para 2 has Community decision where: (a) the combined aggregate worldwide turnover of all the undertakings concerned is more than €2,500 million; (b) in each of at least three Member States, the combined aggregate turnover of all undertakings concerned is more than €100 million; (c) in each of at least three Member States included for the purpose of point (b), the aggregate turnover of each of at least two of the undertakings concerned is more than €25 million; and (d) the aggregate Community-wide turnover of each of at least two of the undertakings concerned is more than €100 million. Unless each of the undertakings concerned achieves more than two-thirds of its aggregate Community-wide turnover with one and the same Member State (known as the 'two-thirds rule').

[26] Art 4(5) EUMR refers to a mechanism for merging parties to make a reasoned submission that the Commission should review the concentration which does not have a Community dimension, and which is capable of being examined under the national competition laws of at least three Member States.

[27] Art 22 EUMR gives power to the Commission to examine a concentration without Community dimension when one or more Member States request the Commission to examine any concentration as defined in art 3 that does not have a Community dimension within the meaning of art 1 but affects trade between Member States and threatens to significantly affect competition within the territory of the Member State or States making the request.

[28] Art 21(1) EUMR. As a general rule, the national law only applies to concentrations which do not have Community dimension.

[29] Michael Harker, *'Cross-Border Mergers in the EU: The Commission v the Member States'* (2007) 3(2) European Competition Journal 503, 507.

prudential rules, all of which are considered prima facie legitimate—and 'other public interests', which require an *ex ante* review by the Commission.

Examples of Member States attempting to intervene under article 21 in the Commission's review of a proposed merger include the following:

- Spain cited article 21 as justification for imposing certain conditions on E.ON's bid for Endesa (Case COMP/M.4110), as well as on Enel and Acciona's bid for Endesa (Case COMP/M.4685), although both transactions had already been cleared unconditionally by the Commission.
- Poland imposed divestment conditions on the Unicredito/HVB merger (Case COMP/M.3894) under article 21, despite the fact that the full transaction had already been authorized by the Commission.
- Italy cited article 21 as justification for refusing to authorize the Abertis/Autostrade merger (Case COMP/M.4249), based on public concerns unrelated to competition law. This occurred during the Commission's review of the transaction, which was subsequently cleared.

Almost all Member States (except Cyprus and Bulgaria)[30] have screening mechanisms in place or have initiated the introduction of screening mechanisms to assess non-competition law considerations of concentrations. Moreover, the existing screening mechanisms are characterized by differences in scope and procedure: some operate *ex ante*, some *ex post*; notification can be voluntary or mandatory; general/sectoral coverage; companies/assets; applicable to investments from other Member States and third countries or third countries only, etc.[31]

The Commission published a Regulation in 2021 in order to establish a framework for the Member States, and in certain cases the Commission, to screen foreign direct investments in the European Union, while allowing Member States to take into account their individual situations and national circumstances.[32] The Regulation provides that the Commission may carry out a screening on grounds of security and public order, in case where a foreign direct investment may affect projects or programmes of Union interest.

[30] European Commission, Staff Working Document accompanying the Proposal for a Regulation establishing a framework for screening of foreign direct investments in the European Union, SWD (2017) 297, 2.

[31] ibid.

[32] The specific objectives to be achieved are the following:

> provide a coherent framework to screen foreign direct investment in the EU on grounds of security or public order, without impinging on Member States' national prerogatives;
>
> facilitate close and systematic cooperation among Member States and between Member States and the Commission with regard to the screening of certain foreign direct investment when these raise security or public order concerns, including strengthened exchange of information;
>
> increase transparency of foreign direct investment that may have an impact on security or public order;
>
> effectively address cases of foreign direct investment raising security or public order concerns in relation to projects or programmes of Union interest;
>
> prevent circumvention of national foreign direct investment screening mechanisms.

In addition, the EU Commission has taken further concrete steps to screen certain foreign direct investments into the EU.[33] It has set out a proposal for the abovementioned Regulation that establishes a framework to screen foreign direct investments from third countries on grounds of security and public order in the EU, together with a cooperation mechanism among Member States as well as a framework for screening at the EU level.

The chapter on the EU will present the approach of the Commission in previous cases where public interest in general and national security in particular was invoked. In addition, the chapter will discuss the recent changes in the EU regulatory framework as it relates to the assessment of national security concerns arising from various FDI initiatives and M&A transactions, and will discuss the annual reports the EU Commission has published, showcasing its approach in this controversial and sensitive areas.

1.3 The Approach to the Assessment of National Security in the UK

In the UK, prior to the entry into force of the Enterprise Act in 2002, mergers were reviewed under a broad public interest test. With the adoption of the Enterprise Act, two significant changes took place. Firstly, the primacy of a competition-based test was stated. Secondly, a list of public interest considerations that could be taken into account in merger assessment was included in the Act. The UK merger control regime allows for intervention in mergers by the Secretary of State on national security and media plurality grounds; also, there is a safeguard procedure, under which ministers can give notice of an additional public interest ground, should this arise in a particular case, seeking the approval of Parliament to use it. The Secretary of State can also intervene in a very limited number of cases on public interest grounds where the jurisdictional thresholds are not met.

In one of the most recent cases involving national security considerations, Hytera's proposed acquisition of digital radio manufacturer Sepura, a public interest intervention notice on national security grounds was invoked. There have been six other such interventions on national security grounds, including the defence merger cases *General Dynamics/Alvis, Finmeccanica/AgustaWestland, Finmeccanica/BAE Systems, Lockheed Martin/Insys,* and *General Electric/Smiths Aerospace,* under the pre-existing national security regime. Those transactions were ultimately cleared by the Office of Fair Trading after the parties offered remedies.

In a recent significant legislative development,[34] the UK government has expanded its national security regime. This followed the example of other developed countries

[33] European Commission, Communication 'Welcoming Foreign Direct Investment while Protecting Essential Interests' COM (2017) 494 final.

[34] Department for Business, Energy and Industrial Strategy (BEIS), 'National Security and Infrastructure Investment Review: The Government's Review of the National Security Implications of Foreign Ownership or Control' (October 2017) https://www.gov.uk/government/uploads/system/uploads/attachment_data/file/652505/2017_10_16_NSII_Green_Paper_final.pdf accessed 15 September 2023.

and made more substantive changes to how the national security implications of foreign investment are scrutinized. The reforms have a particular focus on ensuring adequate scrutiny of whether significant foreign investment in critical businesses raises any national security concerns and providing the ability to act in circumstances where this might be the case. The expectation is that the need to act will be relatively rare, but the risk that this can turn into a tool to implement industrial policy considerations does exist.

The reforms are concerned only with national security, and arguably are designed to be focused and proportionate in their scope and application. The reforms in the UK regime include:

- an expanded version of the 'call-in' power, modelled on the existing power within the Enterprise Act 2002, to allow government to scrutinize a broader range of transactions for national security concerns within a voluntary notification regime, and/or
- a mandatory notification regime for foreign investment into the provision of a focused set of 'essential functions' in key parts of the economy. Mandatory notification could also be required for new projects that could reasonably be expected in future to provide essential functions and/or foreign investment in specific businesses or assets.

The book will analyse these proposals and will also incorporate all M&A assessments made under the new regime. The impact of Brexit will also have a bearing on the approach of the Competition and Markets Authority and the government under the new regime, and the book will endeavour to assess whether Brexit is likely to contribute to an insular and protectionist approach by the UK regime.

This chapter discusses in detail the legal framework that currently governs inward FDI in the UK. The timing of the recent reforms to the UK national security regime, half a year after the end of the transition period from the UK's exit from the European Union and its free-trade area, marks the importance of this framework for the UK economy. With the effects of Brexit on inward FDI as yet uncertain, the UK government's focus on national security preoccupation with its regulation has been more intense than ever. While inward investment remains of vital importance to the UK economy, the new regime is expected to affect inward investment and scrutinize the participation of foreign investors in some key industries.

1.4 The Approach to the Assessment of National Security in the US

The Committee on Foreign Investment in the United States (CFIUS) is an inter-agency committee authorized to review transactions that could result in the control of a US business by a foreign person in order to determine the effect of such transactions on the national security of the US. During the review period, CFIUS members examine the transaction in order to identify and address, as appropriate, any national security concerns that arise as a result of the transaction. CFIUS can decide within an initial thirty-day review period, but in certain circumstances CFIUS may initiate a subsequent investigation, which must be completed within forty-five days.[35] These deadlines affect the timing of the approval of transactions.

If CFIUS finds that the transaction does not present any national security risks, or that other provisions of law provide adequate and appropriate authority to address the risks, then CFIUS will advise the parties in writing. If CFIUS finds that a covered transaction presents national security risks and that other provisions of law do not provide adequate authority to address the risks, then CFIUS may enter into an agreement with, or impose conditions on, parties to mitigate such risks, or may refer the case to the President for action.

Where CFIUS has completed all action with respect to a covered transaction, or the President has announced a decision not to exercise his authority with respect to the covered transaction, then the parties receive a 'safe harbour' with respect to that transaction.

The chapter on the US regime assesses the enforcement goals and structure of regulatory framework related to national security assessment in the US. The book describes the extensive US regulatory framework that is relevant for this assessment. The analysis will focus on the composition, legislation, the relevant national security interest considerations that CFIUS takes into account, and the respective decision-making process, and will present some seminal cases that illustrate not only the enforcement approach of CFIUS but also critically discuss the impact of CFIUS on legal and investment certainty.

1.5 The Approach to the Assessment of National Security in China

Since the Chinese Antimonopoly Law (AML) came into force in 2008, the Ministry of Commerce (MOFCOM, which became the State Administration for Market Regulation, SAMR) has reviewed over 750 merger cases. Separate to the AML and to merger control enforcement by SAMR, all foreign investment in China is subject to discretionary approval by MOFCOM or one of its local branches. In some sectors, special regulatory approval may be required by other administrative agencies also. Foreign investment is also regulated on a sector-by-sector basis by MOFCOM, as outlined in the Foreign Investment Industrial Guidance Catalogue, which has been revised periodically in recent years. Under the Foreign Investment Industrial Guidance Catalogue,

[35] CFIUS may also refer a transaction to the President for decision and the President has to announce a decision with respect to a transaction within fifteen days of CFIUS's completion of the investigation.

some sectors are closed to foreign investment or subject to foreign ownership restrictions, while foreign investment in certain industries is encouraged through preferential policies.[36]

The approval that needs to be considered under the national security review regime is relevant if the transaction involves the military sector (including enterprises located near key and sensitive military facilities, and other enterprises active in connection with national defence), key agricultural products, as well as sectors involving key energy infrastructure, transport, technology and equipment manufacturing, and the transaction will result in the acquisition of 'actual control' by the foreign investor over the Chinese domestic business. If a transaction needs to be reviewed on national security grounds, it will be conducted by an inter-ministerial committee, led by the National Development and Reform Commission (NDRC) as well as MOFCOM (the Committee).

The following four main types of structures are caught:

- A foreign investor acquires equity interests in a non-foreign-invested enterprise in China ('domestic enterprise'), or subscribes for an increase in the registered capital of a domestic enterprise, thereby converting the domestic enterprise into an FIE.
- A foreign investor acquires the equity interests of the Chinese shareholder in a foreign-invested enterprise (FIE) in China, or subscribes to an increase in the capital of such enterprise.
- A foreign investor establishes an FIE and agrees by contract to acquire and operate the assets of a domestic enterprise through such FIE; or the foreign investor acquires equity interests in a domestic enterprise through such FIE.
- A foreign investor directly acquires the assets of a domestic enterprise and uses such assets to invest in, and establish, an FIE to operate said assets.

In addition, the Rules on Mergers with and Acquisitions of Domestic Enterprises by Foreign Investors (the M&A Rules) also require a notification to MOFCOM where a transaction will result in a foreign investor obtaining a controlling equity interest in a domestic Chinese enterprise under any of the following circumstances:

- the domestic target operates in a 'key industry';
- the transaction has an impact on state 'economic security'; or
- the domestic target possesses a well-known trademark or established Chinese brand.

[36] Yuxin Shen and others, 'The Foreign Investment Regulation Review: China' (The Law Reviews, 21 October 2022) https://thelawreviews.co.uk/title/the-foreign-investment-regulation-review/china accessed 15 September 2023.

Under the Security Review Circular,[37] whether a proposed M&A transaction constitutes a threat to national security will be determined by looking at its potential impact on the following:

- the production and supply of products and services and the relevant facilities necessary for national defence within China;
- national economic stability;
- order within society;
- China's ability to research and develop key technologies relating to national security.[38]

The national security review is conducted in two phases: a 'general review' (Phase I), which lasts up to thirty working days, and a 'special review' (Phase II), which lasts up to sixty working days. Where the Committee cannot reach consensus, the transaction may be referred to the State Council for final determination, for which there is no time limit for a decision. Where the Committee determines that a transaction gives rise to national security concerns, parties may be required to abandon or (in cases where completion has already occurred) unwind the transaction, or to put in place remedial measures to address the concern.

1.6 The Approach to the Assessment of National Security in Other Jurisdictions: Japan, India, Russia, and South Africa

The aim of the chapter is to discuss the main features of the regimes, the historical background that led to the specific protectionist stance each regime took and the challenges they entail for the legal and investment communities.

The chapter will focus on the measures that have been adopted in Russia, Japan, India, and South Africa. These jurisdictions are pertinent case studies as their unique characteristics offer us the opportunity to provide some reflections. For instance, the collapse of the Soviet Union was a watershed moment for liberal thinkers, who have sought to keep governments separated from business. Despite the expectations, the Russian regime has seen in the FDI rules a useful tool to advance its aspirations of greater oversight of the government on business activity.

Like other countries, Japan has expanded the scope of review, lowering the equity thresholds from 10 per cent to 1 per cent and by classifying more than 500 companies

[37] General Office of the State Council of China, Circular on Security Review System of Merger and Acquisition by Foreign Investors (3 February 2011) https://investmentpolicy.unctad.org/investment-laws/laws/229/china-circular-on-security-review-system-of-merger-and-acquisition-by-foreign-investors accessed 15 September 2023.

[38] Lehman Brown, 'China's New National Security Review Procedures for Mergers and Acquisitions Involving Foreign Investors' (18 March 2011) https://www.lehmanbrown.com/wp-content/uploads/2014/12/Insights-2011-4.pdf accessed 15 September 2023.

in twelve industries as relevant to national security. Unlike most jurisdictions, Japan has incorporated some foreign investment screening exemptions.

India has crafted its national security measures grounded on land borders. This tactic was devised to protect its companies from opportunistic takeovers during the pandemic.

In South Africa, a screening mechanism of foreign investments was introduced in 2018 but is not yet in force.

In this context, this chapter suggests that for the business community, it is difficult to navigate all these distinctive rules, that foreign investment rules have proven to be reciprocal tools, and if applied without sufficient caution, governments are putting the benefits of free markets in peril.

As this book explains, the world has experienced the effects of economic globalization, a trend once seen as irreversible.[39] Progressively, this tendency that once was fervently embraced under the presumed notion that it would boost worldwide prosperity,[40] is facing increased opposition. The first signs of this wave against globalization and free markets emerged when the financial crisis of 2007–09 hit the global economy.[41] This upheaval cast doubt on whether liberalized businesses without government oversight was a safe approach. Hence, governments responded in a synchronized manner, implementing different regulations to prevent future financial crises.[42] More recently, the debate about the virtues of globalization have been refuelled by developed economies. As an illustration, Donald Trump during his election campaign pledged that he would raise trade barriers, withdraw from some trade agreements, limit imports, among other measures, arguing that globalization helped 'the financial elite', while leaving 'millions of our workers with nothing but poverty and heartache'.[43] In the UK, Brexit was a clear sign that globalization was no longer perceived as a panacea[44] and, having left the European Union, the UK sought to protect its companies from unattractive foreign investors by widening the national security rules.[45]

[39] Gao Shangquan, 'Economic Globalization: Trends, Risks and Risk Prevention' (2000) CDP Background Paper No 1 https://www.un.org/en/development/desa/policy/cdp/cdp_background_papers/bp2000_1.pdf accessed 15 September 2023.

[40] See Adam Smith, *An Inquiry into the Nature and Causes of the Wealth of Nations* (first published 1776, OUP 2008). In his work, Smith explains that in integrated world markets there is a better division of labour, an essential factor for technological progress that promotes global prosperity.

[41] Anjan V Thakor, 'The Financial Crisis of 2007–2009: Why Did It Happen and What Did We Learn' (2015) 4(2) Review of Corporate Finance Studies 155.

[42] For an interesting analysis of the fragmented regulatory responses see Sumit Agarwal and others, 'Inconsistent Regulators: Evidence from Banking' (2014) 129 Quarterly Journal of Economics 889.

[43] Nick Corasaniti, Alexander Burns, and Binyamin Appelbaum, 'Donald Trump Vows to Rip Up Trade Deals and Confront China' *New York Times* (28 June 2016) https://www.nytimes.com/2016/06/29/us/politics/donald-trump-trade-speech.html accessed 15 September 2023.

[44] For a good discussion about why most British people voted for Brexit, see Harold D Clarke, Matthew Goodwin, and Paul Whiteley, *Brexit: Why Britain Voted to Leave the European Union* (CUP 2017).

[45] Liz Alderman, 'Its Eye on China, Britain Pushes Back on Foreign Takeovers' *New York Times* (24 July 2018) https://www.nytimes.com/2018/07/24/business/uk-china-takeovers-national-security.html accessed 15 September 2023. For a comprehensive overview of the legal framework that was adopted to tighten foreign direct investment rules in the UK, see chapter 4 of this book, 'National Security and FDI Screening in the UK'; and Ioannis Kokkoris, 'National Security as a Public Interest Consideration in UK Merger Control' (2021) 14(2) Journal of Strategic Security 47.

The Covid pandemic fuelled additional protectionism, especially in relation to sensitive supply chains. Similar concerns to the above have also been prevalent in countries such as Russia, South Africa, India, and Japan. We will look into all these developments and the continuous strengthening of protectionism in a number of major jurisdictions globally.

2
Merger Control Regimes Around the World

2.1 Introduction

The enactment of new merger control regimes around the world in recent decades has been staggering. It has gone from just three in the early 1990s, to eighty in 2008, reaching its highest level of more than 140 in 2019.[1] Besides the enactment of new merger provisions, there has also been a marked interest in enforcing previously ignored merger control, because of an increase in the number of multi-jurisdictional mergers.[2] This endeavour has produced both positive and negative outcomes. From a positive perspective, there has been the promotion of economic performance and the safeguarding of consumer welfare.[3] Less welcome, though, is the heightened possibility of conflicting decisions over the same transaction, an increment of the costs associated with the transaction for businesses and regulators, excessive scrutiny, duplicative proceedings, sometimes the risk of proceedings when the transaction does not have a nexus with the jurisdiction, and the imposition of inconsistent remedies.[4]

In an attempt to alleviate these difficulties, a considerable body of literature has been produced with the aim of exploring their origins, to offer some solutions or to explain why harmonization of merger assessment is a 'noble but utopian aspiration'.[5] Some authors have indicated that the starting point of any debate should be to answer two fundamental questions: (i) why do we have antitrust laws, and (ii) for whose benefit do we enforce them?[6] Continuing with the same type of basic enquiry, others like Stucke have indicated that the central issue lies in clearly defining the antitrust goals—for instance, consumer welfare is often cited as a policy goal, but there is no consensus as to what it exactly means, or who the consumers are.[7] Another interesting, and perhaps

[1] Nicholas Levy, Alexander Waksman, and Lanto Sheridan, 'Global Merger Control—Where to Now?' (2020) 8 Journal of Antitrust Enforcement 319, 320.

[2] Former US Assistant Attorney General Thomas Barnett, 31 May 2007, at the Sixth Annual ICN Conference, Moscow.

[3] Ariel Ezrachi, 'The Role of Voluntary Frameworks in Multinational Cooperation over Merger Control' (2004) 36(2) George Washington International Law Review 433.

[4] ibid; Daniel Sokol and William Blumenthal, 'Merger Control: Key International Norms and Differences', in A Ezrachi (ed), *Research Handbook on International Competition Law* (Edward Elgar 2012) 319, 320; Jonathan Galloway, 'Convergence in International Merger Control' (2009) 5(2) Competition Law Review 181; Ioulia Kampouridi, 'Arguments for the EU-US Convergence and against Global Merger Control Regime' (2015) 38(1) World Competition 107; Anu Piilola, 'Assessing Theories of Global Governance: A Case Study of International Antitrust Regulation' (2003) 39 Stanford Journal of International Law 207, 225.

[5] Daniel A Crane, 'Substance, Procedure, and Institutions in the International Harmonization of Competition Policy' (2009) 10 Chicago Journal of International Law 143.

[6] ibid.

[7] Maurice E Stucke, 'Reconsidering Antitrust's Goals' (2012) 53(2) Boston College Law Review 551, 577. Joseph F Brodley, 'The Economic Goals of Antitrust: Efficiency, Consumer Welfare, and Technological Progress' (1987)

less existential view, is that merger control requires the use of economic analysis which is often centred on limited data, leading regulators to very different conclusions based on the same facts.[8] A very optimistic approach claims that, since the number of cases in which convergence has been reached among different competition authorities over the same transaction surpasses the number of divergences, it is clear that we are going in the right direction; while the observed contradictions are in response to differences in market conditions, which could be overcome if an economically based competition policy, both at home and internationally, was adopted.[9] In contrast, Gerber has predicted that extensive convergence is unlikely to happen, at least soon, given the insurmountable obstacles that convergence entails.[10]

If the examination of the foundations of the issue has been controversial, the formulation of possible solutions has been no less contentious. As an illustration, the enactment of a global antitrust system has been proposed,[11] but is seen as unworkable, considering that the attainment of a code that encapsulates the private interests of all countries is a very ambitious project, and even if it was achieved, interpretation issues would be unavoidable.[12] The creation of an international court or central authority responsible for solving global competition cases has also been suggested;[13] the main criticism of this proposal is that it seems very unlikely that countries would be willing to compromise their sovereignty. Bilateral agreements have also been advocated, yet their implementation has not eliminated the appearance of conflicting decisions.[14] Harmonization has repeatedly been recommended; however, it has been said that the lack of enforceability makes this proposal futile.[15] In examining in more detail the harmonization option, it has been indicated that it would be advisable to begin by harmonizing the procedural aspects of merger control, which in terms of sovereignty is less invasive, and the benefits would be immediate.[16] Nonetheless, it has been warned that the alignment of procedural rules is not a straightforward task, given that they are a

62 New York University Law Review 1020, 1032, indicated that consumer welfare 'is the most abused term in modern antitrust analysis'; see also Barak Orbach, 'The Antitrust Consumer Welfare Paradox' (2011) 7(1) Journal of Competition Law & Economics 133, 134.

[8] Frederic Jenny, 'Substantive Convergence in Merger Control: An Assessment' (2015) 1(1) Concurrences 21, 23.

[9] John J Parisi, 'International Regulation of Mergers: More Convergence, Less Conflict' (2005) 61 NYU Annual Survey of American Law 509, 518. Rachel Brandenburger and Joseph Matelis have also argued that there is already a state of convergence 'of merger policy around the world'. See Rachel Brandenburger and Joseph Matelis, 'The 2010 U.S. Horizontal Merger Guidelines: A Historical and International Perspective' (2011) 25(3) Antitrust Magazine https://www.justice.gov/atr/page/file/1382881/download accessed 15 September 2023.

[10] David J Gerber, *Global Competition: Law, Markets, and Globalization* (Oxford University Press 2010) 289.

[11] Eleanor Fox, 'Mergers in Global Markets: GE/Honeywell and the Future of Merger Control' (2002) 23 University of Pennsylvania Journal of International Law 457.

[12] Sara Holloway, 'International Merger Control: Globalization or Global Failure' (2006) 34 Denver Journal of International Law and Policy 353, 369. Michal S Gal and Inbal Faibish Wassmer have claimed that setting a common standard for review might not be beneficial to all member states; see 'Regional Agreements of Developing Jurisdictions: Unleashing the Potential' in Josef Drexl and others (eds), *Competition Policy and Regional Integration in Developing Countries* (Edward Elgar 2012) 291.

[13] Alen Balde, 'Competition on the Global Market: A Way towards an Autonomous International court for Global Competition Cases' (2008) 6 Managing Global Transitions: International Research Journal 207; Crane (n 5).

[14] Ezrachi (n 3).

[15] Holloway (n 12) 370.

[16] Crane (n 5) 157.

reflection of the divergent nature of judicial and administrative structures in each jurisdiction, whose reform is even more daunting.[17]

Despite the hurdles that every proposed solution faces, efforts have been put together to reach consensus, at least informally. In this regard, the role played by the Organisation for Economic Cooperation and Development (OECD) and the International Competition Network (ICN) has been significant. These organizations have given important guidance and produced recommended practice in both procedural and substantive merger control that are observed by many jurisdictions and are used to shape the design of new merger regimes, although compliance is voluntary, and progress depends on the will of each country. Another important contribution has been the creation of a merger working group to facilitate greater convergence between the European Union (EU) and the United States (US) through a set of best practices on cooperation in merger investigations.[18] Similarly, bilateral agreements have been signed with the aim of increasing coordination and cooperation between competition authorities.[19] Against this backdrop, the purpose of the next section is to examine in further detail some merger regimes across the world with the goal to highlight their main differences and similarities, and thereby to contribute to the debate.

2.2 Foundations, Goals, and Development

The antitrust regimes that have been created across multiple jurisdictions have differing goals. In the US, the Sherman Act was enacted in 1890 to enhance economic efficiency and consumer welfare.[20] Later, the Clayton Act was enacted in 1914,[21] initially to control stock acquisitions, with a subsequent pre-merger notification regime enacted in 1978.[22] Both were in response to economic goals. In Europe, on the other hand, the emergence of competition law coincided with the reaction to two devastating world wars and the urge to prevent a future one, which led in 1957 to the establishment of the European Economic Community in the pursuit of political goals including distributional effects, fairness, and market integration.[23] Later, in 1990, the first merger

[17] Robert Pitofsky, 'EU and US Approaches to International Mergers—View from the US Federal Trade Commission', in International Bar Association, *EC Merger Control: Ten Years On—Papers from the EC Merger Control 10th Anniversary Conference held in Brussels in September 2000 under the auspices of the European Commission Directorate General for Competition and the International Bar Association* (2000) 47.

[18] US-EU Merger Working Group, 'Best Practices on Cooperation in Merger Investigations' (2011) http://ec.europa.eu/competition/mergers/legislation/best_practices_2011_en.pdf accessed 15 September 2023.

[19] Parisi (n 9) 515.

[20] Sherman Act, 26 Stat 209-10 (1890), codified as amended at 15 USC §§ 1–7. Sections 1 and 2 of the Sherman Act provide that mergers may be challenged if they place unreasonable restraints on trade or create a potential monopoly: Sherman Act, ch 647, § 1, 2, 26 Stat 209 (1890), current version at 15 USC § 1, 2.

[21] 15 USC § 18, prohibiting mergers and acquisitions that might substantially lessen competition or tend to create a monopoly.

[22] Federal Trade Commission (FTC), 'Introductory Guide I to the Premerger Notification Program' (2002), reprinted in William C Holmes and Dawn E Holmes, *Antitrust Law Sourcebook for the United States and Europe* (Thomson West 2005) I–475.

[23] Treaty of Rome (25 March 1957), art 2, 298 UN Treaty Ser 11, 15, stating that: 'It shall be the aim of the Community, by establishing a Common Market and progressively approximating the economic policies of Member States, to promote throughout the Community a harmonious development of economic activities, a

regulation (European Community Merger Regulation) was enacted,[24] which has been mirrored by many jurisdictions.[25]

Some other countries have also shaped their antitrust regimes according to their own historical circumstances. Specifically, Russia as part of a liberalization process initially used competition law to regulate natural monopolies,[26] China has seen antitrust law as a tool to achieve economic growth[27] and to promote 'the healthy development of the socialist market economy',[28] Canada as a driver to promote small and medium-sized enterprises,[29] and South Africa as a means to protect historically disadvantaged people.[30] These noteworthy differences in basic approaches to antitrust law, which have been modified and adapted over time, have inevitably impacted the primary purpose of merger control. So, even if it has been noted that there is a large consensus that the main purpose of merger control is to protect competition by impeding the creation and enhancement of market power and to protect consumers,[31] there are notorious differences in the fundamental principles incorporated in some merger review provisions. Among them: the protection of employment, encouragement of enterprise, and achievement of industrial policy objectives such as the promotion of international competitiveness of the local economy and the creation of strong national firms.[32] Particularly, industrial policy and national security considerations have featured most prominently in recent years, a fact that, according to a study presented by Neven and Roller, inevitably will create conflict under the presumption that convergence is likely if competition authorities have as a common objective the protection of consumers' interest and the market definition is global, and almost impossible if other objectives like promotion of national champions prevail.[33]

In evaluating mergers it is widely accepted that the consumer welfare standard should be applied by agencies, a position that has been recognized by the US and the EU, who have insisted that their merger reviews rest on an economically based analytical

continuous and balanced expansion, an increased stability, and accelerated raising of the standard of living and closer relations between its Member States.'

[24] Council Regulation (EEC) No 4064/89 of 21 December 1989 on the control of concentrations between undertakings OJ L35/1.

[25] OECD, Report on Country Experiences with the 2005 OECD Recommendation on Merger Review, 2013.

[26] OECD, 'Competition Law and Policy in Russia: An OECD Peer Review' (2004) 11, 14 http://www.oecd.org/dataoecd/10/60/32005515.pdf accessed 15 September 2023.

[27] Zhenguo Wu, 'Perspectives on the Chinese Anti-Monopoly Law' (2008) 75 Antitrust Law Journal 73, 79.

[28] Antimonopoly Law of the People's Republic of China, art 1, unofficial English translation available at https://www.chinalawtranslate.com/en/anti-monopoly-law-2022/ accessed 15 September 2023.

[29] Andrew T Guzman, 'Is International Antitrust Possible?' (1998) 73 NYU Law Review 1501, 1539.

[30] Competition Act 89 of 1998, as amended by Competition Amendment Act 18 of 2018, ch 1 § 2 https://www.compcom.co.za/wp-content/uploads/2021/03/Competition-Act-A6.pdf accessed 15 September 2023.

[31] Larry Fullerton and Megan Alvarez, 'Convergence in International Merger Control' (2012) 26(2) Antitrust 20; Sokol and Blumenthal (n 4) 326.

[32] OECD, 'Roundtable on Cross-Border Merger Control: Challenges for Developing and Emerging Economies—Background Note' (2011) 1 DAF/COMP/GF https://one.oecd.org/document/DAF/COMP/GF(2011)1/en/pdf accessed 15 September 2023. For further discussion, see Stefan Thomas, 'Normative Goals in Merger Control—Why Merger Control Should Not Attempt to Achieve "Better" Outcomes than Competition', in Ioannis Kokkoris and Claudia Lemus (eds), *Research Handbook on the Law and Economics of Competition Enforcement* (Edward Elgar 2022) 143.

[33] Damien J Neven and Lars-Hendrik Roller, 'The Scope of Conflict in International Merger Control' (2000) Social Science Research Center Berlin Discussion Paper FS IV 00-14, 13.

framework in which consumer welfare is a well-established standard.[34] Having indicated earlier that there is a lack of consensus about the meaning of consumer welfare, and falling beyond the scope of this book to enrich the debate, it would be enough to mention that the consumer surplus is a common methodology adopted to measure consumer welfare. Consumer surplus referring to the 'excess of social valuation of a product over the price actually paid', a concept that is illustrated by Stucke using the following example: if after a long hike, a person is willing to pay $2 for a cold Diet Coke, and at the local store the price was 50 cents, then the consumer surplus was $1.50.[35] Another common way to gauge consumer welfare is by looking at total surplus, which takes into account the perceived welfare of buyers and sellers (the latter refers to the total amount that a producer actually takes and the lowest total amount at which he would be prepared to sell).[36] There are other methodologies oriented to measure consumer welfare as including social welfare, such that at the end it will affect the outcomes of merger reviews, given their marked differences.[37] This assertion has been confirmed by the International Competition Network (ICN), which after analysing the answers provided by fifty-seven agencies in relation to their understanding and application of the consumer welfare standard, found that the lack of agreement about the meaning of the concept and its assessment has resulted in different outcomes.[38]

2.3 Merger Review: Substantive Issues

2.3.1 Market Definition

In most jurisdictions, market definition is used as a first step to investigate market power and to assess mergers with the main purpose to identify key players and to establish relevant market shares in a particular market.[39] In the US, however, market definition is not necessarily the first step in merger analysis to establish if a merger is anticompetitive; instead, there is an explicit reference in the Horizontal Merger Guidelines of 2010[40] (hereinafter the '2010 Merger Guidelines') to the use of the Upward Pricing

[34] Levy and others (n 1) 321; Ken Heyer, 'Consumer Welfare and the Legacy of Robert Bork' (2014) 57(S3) Journal of Law & Economics S19. See also Neelie Kroes, 'European Competition Policy—Delivering Better Markets and Better Choices', Speech at European Consumer and Competition Day (London, 15 September 2005) ('Consumer welfare is now well established as the standard the Commission applies when assessing mergers and infringements of the Treaty rules on cartels and monopolies'); Steven C Salop, 'Question: What Is the Real and Proper Antitrust Welfare Standard? Answer: The True Consumer Welfare Standard' (2010) 22 Loyola Consumer Law Review 336.

[35] Stucke (n 7).

[36] Sokol and Blumenthal (n 4) 329.

[37] Orbach (n 7).

[38] International Competition Network (ICN), 'Competition Enforcement and Consumer Welfare' (2011) 17 https://www.internationalcompetitionnetwork.org/wp-content/uploads/2019/11/SP_CWelfare2011.pdf accessed 15 September 2023.

[39] Andrea Calef and others, 'Response to CMA Consultation (CMA 129): Draft Revised Merger Assessment Guidelines' (University of East Anglia Centre for Competition Policy, 8 January 2021) https://research-portal.uea.ac.uk/en/publications/response-to-cma-consultation-cma-129-draft-revised-merger-assessm accessed 15 September 2023.

[40] US DOJ and FTC, 'Horizontal Merger Guidelines' (2010) para 6.1.

Pressure test (UPP), seeking to determine the extent of the incentives that a merged entity might have to increase price above pre-merger levels.[41] While market definition is not ineludibly the starting point in merger review in the US, product market has long been defined in that country under the Hypothetical Monopolist Test (HMT)—also known as the Small but Significant Non-transitory Increase in Price (SSNIP) test—introduced in the Horizontal Merger Guidelines 1982, and now applied in most jurisdictions.[42] Under the SSNIP, two products are estimated to be in the same market if a hypothetical non-transitory '5–10 percent increase for product A would cause sufficient numbers of customers to switch to product B to make the price increase unprofitable for the supplier of product A'.[43] Importantly, the EU expressly adopted the SSNIP test by indicating that the purpose of defining the relevant market is to anticipate the possibility that a merged entity would have to increase prices to anti-competitive levels.[44] Some other countries like Mexico have moved in the same direction by legally requiring the definition of the market, whereas in others like Chile there is no such obligation.[45] Other models, like the Compensating Marginal-Cost Reduction (CMCR)[46] or the Gross Upward Price Pressure Index (GUPPI), have been developed with the purpose of replacing the market definition; however, the use of the HMT with the aid of defining relevant markets remains prevalent in many jurisdictions.

Although the application of market definition is widely accepted in most jurisdictions, there are voices calling for the advance of new instruments, in particular in digital markets in which market shares or concentration measures would be insufficient to anticipate the potential effects of the merger.[47] The argument is that the traditional tools to review mergers are appropriate for markets that can be clearly defined, where market players and market shares can be determined, which is not the case in the digital space. This shortfall, according to this argumentation, has allowed the acquisition of small start-ups by large platforms: 'not a single one has been blocked anywhere'.[48] To illustrate this phenomenon, it has been reported that during the past ten years, Google has bought on average one company every three weeks.[49] The explanation is that, particularly in big data mergers, it is unlikely that agencies, under the traditional market definition standard, can conclude that such deals are anticompetitive, given the ubiquity and non-rivalry nature of data, which makes it unfeasible that a merger could affect

[41] Carl Shapiro and Joseph Farrell, 'Antitrust Evaluation of Horizontal Mergers: An Economic Alternative to Market Definition' (2010) 10 The BE Journal of Theoretical Economics 1.

[42] Jenny (n 8) 30.

[43] James S Venit and William J Kolasky, 'Substantive Convergence and Procedural Dissonance in Merger Review', in SJ Evenett, A Lehmann, and B Steil, *Antitrust Goes Global: What Future for Transatlantic Cooperation?* (Royal Institute of International Affairs/Brookings Institution 2000) 79.

[44] [1997] OJ C372/5.

[45] OECD, Policy Roundtables: Market Definition (2012) 12 http://www.oecd.org/daf/competition/Marketdefinition2012.pdf accessed 15 September 2023.

[46] The CMCR involves prices, quantities, and demand elasticities; see Greg Werden, Luke Froeb, and Steve Tschantz, 'The Effects of Merger Efficiencies on Consumers of Differentiated Products' (2005) 1(2) European Competition Journal 245, 255.

[47] Luis Cabral and others, 'The EU Digital Markets Act: A Report from a Panel of Economic Experts' (2021) https://dx.doi.org/10.2760/139337 accessed 15 September 2023.

[48] ibid.

[49] Luis Cabral, 'Merger Policy in Digital Industries' (2021) 54 Information Economics and Policy 100866.

the obtainability of data to the extent of foreclosing the market.[50] While the debate and number of proposals to address these concerns increase with time, some commentators contend that the existing tools are adequate.[51] In the end, what remains certain is that merging parties need to be aware of the legal developments in each jurisdiction and to support their deals according to the prevailing requirements.

2.3.2 Substantive Assessment

A theory of harm is used to anticipate possible changes that a concentration might create and to compare the impact on rivalry and expected harm to consumer welfare, as compared with the competitive situation likely to arise in the absence of the merger.[52] Among the various theories of harm, most jurisdictions focus their merger reviews on determining the likelihood of unilateral price effects affecting consumers.[53] Other theories look at adverse coordinated effects,[54] vertical effects,[55] and conglomerate effects.[56] In predicting the competitive situation without the merger, also known as the counterfactual, competition agencies usually evaluate the effects of the deal against the existing conditions at the time of the merger—the 'status quo ante'.[57] These are the most common conditions: (i) entry, in which the counterfactual holds that the buyer would enter the market on its own in the absence of the merger; (ii) increased competition in the future compared to competition levels before the merger; (iii) decreased competition, in which the acquired firm would become a much less important competitor in the future; and (v) exit, where the acquired firm would leave the market without the merger.[58] It has been reported that competition agencies diverge in their assessment of these conditions, and that countries like the UK includes the analysis of the counterfactuals all merger inquiries.[59]

At the same time, merger control systems apply a substantive test against which they establish whether a transaction should be approved, modified, or prohibited. Three tests are more generally used: (i) the dominance test; (ii) the Significant Lessening

[50] Jörg Hoffmann and Germán Johannsen, 'EU-Merger Control & Big Data—On Data-specific Theories of Harm and Remedies' (2019) Max Planck Institute for Innovation and Competition Research Paper No 19-05, 52. https://ssrn.com/abstract=3364792 accessed 15 September 2023.

[51] Maurits Dolmans, Henry Mostyn, and Patrick F Todd, 'Competition Enforcement: Is the Abuse Toolbox Adequate?' in Ioannis Kokkoris and Claudia Lemus (eds), *Research Handbook on the Law and Economics of Competition Enforcement* (Edward Elgar 2022) 76.

[52] Richard Whish and David Bailey, *Competition Law* (7th edn, Oxford University Press 2012) 818.

[53] Greg Werden, 'Unilateral Effects of Horizontal Mergers I: Basic Concepts and Models' in Wayne D Collins (ed), *Issues in Competition Law and Policy* (ABA Section of Antitrust Law 2008) 1319.

[54] Janusz Ordover 'Coordinated Effects' in Wayne D Collins (ed), *Issues in Competition Law and Policy* (ABA Section of Antitrust Law 2008) 1359.

[55] Whish and Bailey (n 52) 819.

[56] Ariel Ezrachi, *EU Competition Law: An Analytical Guide to the Leading Cases* (3rd edn, Hart 2012) 344.

[57] European Commission, 'Guidelines on the assessment of horizontal mergers under the Council Regulation on the control of concentrations between undertakings' (2004/C 31/03) para 9.

[58] Mathew Johnson and Ilaria Fanton, 'The Economic of Merger Control in a Dynamic World: A Focus on the Relevant Counterfactual', in Ioannis Kokkoris and Claudia Lemus (eds), *Research Handbook on the Law and Economics of Competition Enforcement* (Edward Elgar 2022) 280.

[59] Whish and Bailey (n 52) 822.

of Competition (SLC) test; and (iii) the Significantly Impede Effective Competition (SIEC) test. Under the dominance test, a merger can be prohibited if a dominant position is created or strengthened, but it is important to note that, among competition authorities, there is no unified understanding of the dominant position concept.[60] Conversely, the SLC test does not focus on market shares but rather on the competitive effects of the merger and the loss of competition.[61] The SIEC revolves around the concern that anticompetitive effects may arise even in the absence of dominance or collective dominance, as would be the case of non-coordinated effects in oligopolistic markets.[62]

Market shares and concentration levels provide useful first indications of the market structure. Increases in market shares or market concentration can be measured using a Herfindahl-Hirschman Index (HHI), which in jurisdictions like in the US and Russia provides a presumption that once a pre-established threshold is met, this needs to be rebutted by the merging parties providing convincing evidence that the transaction will not produce anticompetitive effects.[63] The HHI results also imply that if the threshold is not satisfied, it is very unlikely that the transaction will be challenged, as it is within safe harbours.[64] In contrast, the EU does not apply such a presumption based on the HHI numbers,[65] and Canada indicates that even if high levels of concentration are present, it can be necessary to undertake further investigation.[66] Thus, given the variety of options to establish possible unilateral effects and coordinated effects from which a jurisdiction can choose, it is unsurprising that we can have divergence in merger assessments. In relation to vertical and conglomerate mergers, the policy approach is also dissonant.[67] While in the EU there are more conceptual possibilities for intervention, the US is less concerned about this type of transaction.[68]

2.3.3 Efficiencies

Efficiencies are also part of the overall assessment of the mergers. In the EU, efficiency claims have rarely been accepted as part of the defence, partly because, as some commentators have argued, efficiency may be regarded as a sign of dominance.[69] With the EUMR the EU clarified that efficiency claims would be taken into account in merger

[60] Jenny (n 8) 31–32.
[61] ibid 31.
[62] Whish and Bailey (n 52) 866–67.
[63] 2010 Guidelines § 5.3.
[64] Fullerton and Alvarez (n 31) 22.
[65] EC (n 57) para 21.
[66] Competition Bureau of Canada (CBC), Merger Enforcement Guidelines (2011) paras 5.9–5.10 https://ised-isde.canada.ca/site/competition-bureau-canada/sites/default/files/attachments/2022/cb-meg-2011-e.pdf accessed 15 September 2023.
[67] See OECD, Vertical Mergers (2007) DAF/COMP(2007)21 15 https://www.oecd.org/competition/mergers/39891031.pdf accessed 15 September 2023, indicating that 'there is not a consensus regarding appropriate enforcement policy with respect to vertical mergers'.
[68] Sokol and Blumenthal (n 4) 331.
[69] Venit and Kolasky (n 43) 85.

analysis,[70] stipulating three conditions that the merging parties need to observe: efficiencies need to (i) benefit consumers, that is, the merger must have a direct positive effect on consumers; (ii) be merger specific, so the efficiency cannot be obtained in the absence of the merger; and (iii) be verifiable, in other words, attainable within a reasonable period of time, and not merely speculative.[71] Regarding this verification factor, is has been argued that when innovation is the alleged benefit, it is difficult to demonstrate that the predicted advance will become real within the timeframe of two or four years, given that by nature, research and development (R&D) is uncertain, a fact that complicates the efficiency defence in the EU, considering that the Commission has an inclination to overestimate potential efficiency loses and to underestimate potential efficiency gains.[72]

In contrast, in the US, the attitude towards efficiencies is more lenient and its assessment is fully integrated as part of the likely competitive effects of the mergers.[73] The US framework provides that merging parties need to demonstrate that the efficiencies are merger-specific, cognizable, verifiable, do not emerge from anticompetitive restrictions of output or service, and sufficient to reverse the merger's potential to harm consumers in the relevant market.[74] The US agencies then undertake a balancing exercise, comparing the degree of the cognizable efficiencies against the degree of likely harm to competition absent the efficiencies.[75] Contrary to the EU approach, the US's attitude towards efficiencies has become too permissive, this is true particularly in the banking sector where approvals have been granted largely because the merging parties were experiencing financial difficulties, and despite recognizing that the merger would supress competition between them, the regulator recognized that by avoiding the deterioration of the financial condition of the applicants, the community would automatically induce benefits.[76] Hence, the premise that the efficiencies need to be passed on to the consumer for the agencies to conclude that they would be necessary to prevent the merger from being anticompetitive, loses credibility.[77] The merger control rules in Canada also demand that the CCB contrasts the efficiencies gained from a merger and balances them against any potential harm to competition, exercise in which the merging parties must provide sufficient evidence about the alleged efficiencies.[78] Other jurisdictions that also accept efficiencies as part of competitive analysis or as a defence are the UK, Australia, and Brazil.[79]

[70] EC (n 57).

[71] ibid para 77.

[72] Justus Haucap, 'Merger Effects on Innovation: A Rationale for Stricter Merger Control?' DICE Discussion Paper, No 268, 10 (September 2017) https://www.econstor.eu/bitstream/10419/168579/1/898417104.pdf.

[73] US Department of Justice (DOJ) and Federal Trade Commission (FTC), Horizontal Merger Guidelines (2023).

[74] ibid.

[75] ibid.

[76] *Alaska Mutual Bancorporation*, 73 Fed Res Bull 921 (1987).

[77] US Horizontal Merger Guidelines (n 73).

[78] CBC, 'Review of s. 11 of the Competition Act' (12 August 2008) https://ised-isde.canada.ca/site/competition-bureau-canada/en/how-we-foster-competition/education-and-outreach/publications/review-s-11-competition-act accessed 15 September 2023.

[79] Peter Alexiadis, Elsa Sependa, and Laura Vlachos, 'Merger Control: "Around the World in 80 Days: Management of the Merger Review Process of Global Deals"' (2018) 19 Business Law International 201, 235.

Generally, the ICN has identified that the treatment of efficiencies across jurisdictions varies according to the state of development of their economy, the goals of their competition laws, their levels of enforcement experience, and the extent of regulation and deregulation, among other factors.[80] Likewise, among competition authorities there is a discrepancy in how they deal with merger efficiencies, the level of evidence required to substantiate them, and whether they should be considered in cases with high concentration levels.[81] In this context, the incorporation of one-size-fits-all solution seems unreasonable, as, if jurisdictions choose an approach neither too strict nor too benevolent, convergence might arise.

2.3.4 Ancillary Restraints

Ancillary restraints that are vital to enable the merged entity to obtain its economic objectives and its expected efficiencies are permissible in the merger control context, although they could be seen as anti-competitive in a different context. Examples of these limitations are non-compete and non-solicitation clauses, licensing agreements, and exclusive purchase and supply obligations.[82] Traditionally, these restrictions are accepted when there is evidence that they are merger-related, objectively necessary and effective within a reasonable time, and subject to geographic and scope considerations.[83] The EUMR rules that 'a decision declaring a concentration compatible shall be deemed to cover restrictions directly related and necessary to the implementation of the concentration',[84] which are covered by the Commission's clearance decision.[85] Whereas, in Ukraine, ancillary restraints are not automatically covered by the AMC merger approval decision, and as they are seen as concerted practices (eg non-compete clauses), a separate antitrust clearance is required.[86]

In Brazil, the ancillary restraints that are submitted with the filing are covered by CADE's approval decision, and often those not exceeding five years and effective solely in the markets relevant to the concentration are approved.[87] In Japan, whether ancillary restraints are approved as part of the final decision is a matter that is decided on a case-by-case basis by the Japan Fair Trade Commission (JFTC).[88] In the US, under the HSR

[80] ICN Merger Working Group: Analytical Framework Subgroup, 'Project on Merger Guidelines' (3rd ICN Annual Conference, Seoul, April 2004), https://www.internationalcompetitionnetwork.org/wp-content/uploads/2018/05/MWG_MergerGuidelinesReport.pdf accessed 15 September 2023.

[81] ibid.

[82] George Metaxas and Hector Armengod, 'EC Merger Regulation and the Status of Ancillary Restrictions: Evolution of the European Commission's Policy' [2005] 9 European Competition Law Review 500.

[83] Alexiadis and others (n 79) 242.

[84] EUMR, arts 6(1)(b), 8(1) and 8(2). See also Recital 21.

[85] Ancillary Restraints Notice, para 2.

[86] Igor Svechkar and others, 'Merger Control in Ukraine: Overview' (Thomson Reuters Practical Law, 1 February 2022) https://uk.practicallaw.thomsonreuters.com/1-570-0010 accessed 15 September 2023.

[87] Luis Nagalli and others, 'Merger Control 2020: Brazil' (Chambers and Partners Practice Guides, 11 July 2023) https://practiceguides.chambers.com/practice-guides/comparison/726/11625/18072-18076-18092-18104-18112-18121-18123-18128-18132-18134 accessed 15 September 2023.

[88] Kozo Kawai, Kazumaro Kobayashi, and Tatsuya Tsunoda, 'Merger Control in Japan: Overview' (Thomson Reuters Practical Law, 1 January 2022) https://uk.practicallaw.thomsonreuters.com/8-504-3670 accessed 15 September 2023.

filing procedure, merging parties must report the existence of ancillary agreements between them, yet the agencies might not examine them during the HSR waiting period, and still have the authority to challenge them at a later stage.[89] In terms of scope, in South Africa it is common for the Commission to approve ancillary restraints such as trade restrictions, whose duration does not exceed three years.[90] In this context, it is noticeable that there is a good variety of approaches in relation to the approval of ancillary restraints agreements as part of merger clearance decisions. Against this divergence, however, there is also a great convergence in most jurisdictions where it is expected that the merging parties perform their own self-assessment and provide evidence about the need for and legitimacy of the ancillary restraints, which in countries like Canada, Colombia, Albania, and Argentina must be done as part of the formal notification.[91] Hence, merging parties need to show great diligence in substantiating and supporting the need for any ancillary restraints, a task that needs to be planned and progressed well in advance of the notification of the deal, and parties also need to be careful not to implement these restraints before approval, in order to avoid gun-jumping sanctions.

2.4 Merger Review: Procedural Issues

2.4.1 Notifiable Transactions

The type of transaction is essential in determining whether approval is required or not. It has been claimed that one important aspect is that the operation has a material local nexus with the reviewing jurisdiction, and that could be a minimum level of sales or assets.[92] In this regard, the ICN has reported that many jurisdictions do not have a local nexus requirement as part of the notification threshold.[93] Kenya is an example of a country where deals that do not have a local nexus are not notifiable.[94] In Austria, the local nexus in the digital economy derives from the number of monthly active users or unique visits, which are used to measure the domestic activity requirement.[95] For other jurisdictions, aspects such as a material change in the identity of the undertaking triggers approval; this is the case in Nigeria and Kenya, whereas in the US the attention lies in the involvement of specific contractual rights and corporate arrangements.[96]

[89] James Fishkin and others, 'Merger Control—USA: Law & Practice' (Chambers Global Practice Guide, 2020) https://www.dechert.com/content/dam/dechert%20files/knowledge/publication/2020/7/Chambers-Merger-Control-2021-USA-EU-Chapters.pdf accessed 15 September 2023.

[90] Burton Phillips and Shawn van der Meulen, 'Merger Control in South Africa' (Lexology, 8 August 2019), https://www.lexology.com/library/detail.aspx?g=bcbbca02-7fca-49cd-a930-1ce39aee3c69 accessed 15 September 2023.

[91] Alexiadis and others (n 79) 242.

[92] Galloway (n 4).

[93] ICN, 'Implementation of the ICN recommended practices for merger notification and review procedures' (April 2005) Annex B, RP I https://www.internationalcompetitionnetwork.org/wp-content/uploads/2018/05/MWG_ImplementationRPsMergerNotification.pdf accessed 15 September 2023.

[94] Alexiadis and others (n 79) 214.

[95] Dieter Zandler and Vanessa Horaceck, 'The Merger Control Review: Austria' (The Law Reviews, 16 August 2023) https://thelawreviews.co.uk/title/the-merger-control-review/austria accessed 15 September 2023.

[96] Alexiadis and others (n 79) 207.

In the EU the focus is on the concept of control, which can be obtained by different means such as through contracts or rights that confer decisive influence exercised by one undertaking (sole control) or two or more undertakings (joint control).[97] In the UK there are three different levels of control: legal, de facto and material influence, and any change on the level of control prompts assessment.[98]

Some jurisdictions like the EU, Austria, Germany, and the UK review acquisitions of non-controlling minority shareholdings to ensure that they will not harm competition or consumers.[99] In the US, the US Horizontal Merger Guidelines 2010 give jurisdiction to the antitrust agencies to review full and partial mergers of competitors in which cross- or common shareholdings are involved.[100] Similarly, the creation of full function joint ventures (JVs) is notifiable in jurisdictions like the EU, although this is not though the case when the JV is created to perform a single specific activity during a certain period of time, and if the JV does not have its own access to or presence on the market.[101] Some other countries apply different rules to review JVs, as in Israel, where new JVs are required to be notified.[102]

Other factors that are applied to determine whether a transaction is notifiable are the size of the transaction (or the size of the company, as in the US); a turnover-based threshold is applied in the EU; a share of supply and target turnover threshold is used in the UK; a turnover-based and transaction value threshold is exercised in Germany; and a combination of assets and turnover-based test is observed in South Africa.[103] Also, some countries combine the threshold test by looking at the revenues, assets, and market shares. Furthermore, it is important to note that indexation mechanisms are also used to update the respective revenue thresholds, as is the case in Canada, Italy, and the US.[104] In other countries like Colombia, multiples of the prevailing minimum wage are used to calculate the operational income and assets test.[105] In addition, some jurisdictions have created specific calculation methods to review particular sectors, such as the insurance industry in the EU and online gambling in Ireland.[106]

[97] EUMR, art 3(2).

[98] CMA, 'Merger Assessment Guidelines' (CMA129) (revised 18 March 2021) para 3.2.5 https://assets.publishing.service.gov.uk/government/uploads/system/uploads/attachment_data/file/1051823/MAGs_for_publication_2021_--_.pdf accessed 15 September 2023.

[99] EC, Commission Staff Working Document: 'White Paper Towards more Effective EU Merger Control' SWD (2014) 221 final.

[100] US Horizontal Merger Guidelines 2010 § 13, stating that: 'In most horizontal mergers, two competitors come under common ownership and control, completely and permanently eliminating competition between them. This elimination of competition is a basic element of merger analysis. However, the statutory provisions referenced in Section 1 also apply to one firm's partial acquisition of a competitor. The Agencies therefore also review acquisitions of minority positions involving competing firms, even if such minority positions do not necessarily or completely eliminate competition between the parties to the transaction.'

[101] EC, Consolidated Jurisdictional Notice under Council Regulation (EC) No 139/2004 on the control of concentrations between undertakings [2008] OJ C95/01.

[102] Alexiadis and others (n 79) 210.

[103] Levy and others (n 1) 323.

[104] Alexiadis and others (n 79) 212.

[105] For 2019, the threshold was set at 60,000 CLMMW (about $15 million), See Competition Exchange, 'The Republic of Colombia, Superintendence of Industry and Commerce' (February 2021) https://web.archive.org/web/20210728210713/https://www.compex.org/en/agency_details.php?id=20210118105800631011 accessed 15 September 2023.

[106] Alexiadis and others (n 79) 213.

Likewise, the jurisdictional thresholds for merger assessment are constantly modified by the competition agencies in response to their desire to either amplify or limit their review powers, and therefore to devote greater or fewer resources. The amplification means that more transactions will meet the lower thresholds and will require clearance, a circumstance that has been observed in Latvia and Colombia, whereas in jurisdictions like Russia, Ukraine, Hungary, Korea, and South Africa the thresholds have been significantly increased, resulting in a smaller number of transactions subject to review.[107] Lately, Germany amended its merger control rules by increasing the annual sales in Germany of one of the companies involved from €25 million to at least €50 million, and the annual sales in Germany of another company involved from €5 million to €17.5 million, with the intention of freeing resources that can be allocated to other competition proceedings.[108]

It has been argued that higher notification thresholds are more appropriate as antitrust agencies will then review only those deals large enough to raise serious anticompetitive concerns, as is the case in the EU, and thus justify the burden imposed on the merging parties and the resources of the competition authorities and other relevant stakeholders.[109] Another complication is that when using the asset test, there is no unified definition of 'asset' across jurisdictions, whether it refers to just the buyer or one merging party, or to both buyer and seller (or both merging parties), as is the case in Brazil and Ukraine.[110] The same applies for the market share test, as in some countries the threshold is met by taking into account all parties involved, while in some others it is satisfied by just looking at one party.[111]

Additionally, some jurisdictions like the EU offer a simplified procedure for mergers that are unlikely to raise anti-competitive concerns, including mergers in which the combined market share of the competing merging parties is below 20 per cent; in vertically related markets if the combined market share is below 30 per cent; and in cases where the combined market shares of the merging companies are between 20 per cent and 50 per cent but the post-merger market share is small. Under the simplified procedure the Commission will not undertake a market investigation.[112] A similar approach is applied in other countries like Colombia, where parties need only provide notice of the transaction prior to closing if the combined market share is more than 20 per cent, which allows for smaller transactions to escape scrutiny.[113]

An additional variance in terms of notification requirements is that some countries request a pre-merger notification, while others have post-merger notification requirements. The pre-merger notification implies that approval is a preceding requirement to

107 ibid 205–06.

108 See the 10th Amendment Act to the German Act Against Restraints of Competition (ARC) that entered into force on 19 January 2021.

109 Venit and Kolasky (n 43) 89–90.

110 Alexiadis and others (n 79) 213.

111 ibid 214.

112 See European Commission, Notice on a Simplified Procedure for Treatment of Certain Concentrations Under Council Regulation (EC) No 139/2004 (2013/C 366/04).

113 See Superintendence of Industry and Commerce (SIC), 'Integraciones Empresariales' https://www.sic.gov.co/las-integraciones-empresariales accessed 15 September 2023.

close a transaction, an approach that is followed in jurisdictions like the US and EU.[114] In the post-merger scenario, the transaction can be reviewed after it closes, as is the case in Costa Rica, Indonesia, Paraguay, Japan, and Korea.[115] For multi-jurisdictional transactions this disparity offers a great risk considering that even if approvals have already been obtained in countries with pre-merger requirements, there is no certainty that it would be the same in those jurisdictions where there is a post-merger filing requirement.[116] Some commentators have advocated for the adoption of a uniform interjurisdictional rule where the pre-merger notification be applied worldwide.[117]

There is another fundamental difference in terms of notification that relates to the triggering event for notifications. In the EU, for instance, the merging parties must notify prior to any of the following occurring: (i) the conclusion of the agreement creating a concentration, (ii) the announcement of the public bid, or (iii) the acquisition of a controlling interest by one firm over another.[118] In the US, approval is also a prerequisite to implementation of the deal where a memorandum of understanding may be notified without a legal deadline.[119] Equally, jurisdictions that have adopted a mandatory notification system contemplate the imposition of sanctions for not notifying, or notifying late a proposed transaction to the competition agency, an aspect that will be explored in more detail later. In other countries like the UK, Australia, New Zealand, Singapore, Venezuela, Mauritius, and Panama, notification is voluntary. These regimes assume that any potential competition concerns can be adequately addressed after the merger is consummated. This has the advantage that these agencies enjoy the discretion to investigate only mergers that raise significant concerns, resulting in savings by reducing the number of merger reviews.[120]

Besides the range of events that could trigger the need to notify, merging parties need to be aware of the filing deadlines to avoid sanctions. These deadlines are present in both pre-merger and post-merger regimes.[121]

2.4.2 Pre-notification Discussions

Another aspect related to the notification process is the existence of pre-notification discussions. In general terms, the purpose is to discuss aspects such as the nature of the transaction, the identification of the undertakings involved, determination of the turnover thresholds, issues related to the identification of the respective markets, and potential competitive concerns, among many others. Once the discussions have taken

[114] ICN, 'Merger Notification and Procedures Templates' https://www.internationalcompetitionnetwork.org/working-groups/merger/templates accessed 15 September 2023.
[115] Crane (n 5) 147.
[116] ibid.
[117] ibid.
[118] See EUMR, art 4(1).
[119] Venit and Kolasky (n 43) 89.
[120] Sokol and Blumenthal (n 4) 335.
[121] Alexiadis and others (n 79) 219.

place, a smooth and quick process review is expected, but by no means guaranteed. On 1 January 2021, the Bulgarian Commission for Protection of Competition (CPC) introduced this type of procedure for communicating with applicants before the notification for a concentration is made. The meeting is initiated at least two weeks before the notification for concentration, is confidential, and if the parties agree, the documents provided in these pre-notification contacts would be used by the national authority when evaluating the proposed notification.[122]

In the US, given that the DOJ and FTC have concurrent jurisdiction to review mergers, sometimes it is difficult to anticipate which agency will assess the deal, and therefore the merging parties cannot start pre-notification until the authority that will assess the transaction has been decided.[123] Although pre-merger discussions seem beneficial, Kress has identified that in the US banking sector, where regulators are responsible for the review decision, these private meetings between the merging parties and the regulators have undermined the reliability of the merger enforcement.[124] This practice, according to Kress, has resulted in: (i) a large number of withdrawals when issues are identified by the reviewing agency, or simply to avoid a prohibition decision; (ii) large number of approvals because after pre-notification discussions, regulators are expected to approve the deals that have been previously analysed; and (iii) a low level of judicial review, considering that the number of prohibitions is insignificant. For instance, in 2018 the Federal Reserve approved 95 per cent of the merger applications and zero prohibitions.[125]

The pre-notification discussions that take place in the EU seek to establish the type of quantitative data and the specific amount of information that will be required once a formal notification is filed, and to provide merging parties with the opportunity to informally discuss the intended concentration.[126] Nevertheless, it has been reported that the pre-notification period can last many months, considering that during the meetings, aspects such as theories of harm or potential efficiencies are also discussed and supported with substantive submissions.[127] Thus, the broad discretion enjoyed by the Commission during the pre-notification discussion period as well as its duration have been the object of criticism.[128] By contrast, in Mexico there are strict rules that prevent parties from contacting case handlers or decision-making officials, a restriction that

[122] Lexology, 'Bulgarian Competition Commission Introduces Pre-Merger Notification Discussion' (10 February 2021) https://www.lexology.com/library/detail.aspx?g=7c716338-4388-463f-9b97-92941be29d45 accessed 15 September 2023.

[123] William E Kovacic, Petros C Mavroidis, and Damien J Neven 'Merger Control Procedures and Institutions: A Comparison of the EU and US Practice' (2014) Robert Schuman Centre for Advanced Studies Working Paper No 476, 24.

[124] Jeremy C Kress, 'Modernizing Bank Merger Review' (2020) 37 Yale Journal on Regulation 435, 454.

[125] ibid 454–58.

[126] Commission Regulation 139/2004. See also Commission Regulation 802/2004, Preamble §11, stating that 'the Commission shall give the notifying parties and other parties involved in the proposed concentration, if they so request, an opportunity before notification to discuss the intended concentration and in strict confidence'.

[127] Kovacic and others 476, 20–21 (1 February 2014).

[128] ibid 21.

makes sense in antitrust cases but perhaps is less appropriate in merger cases, where aspects such as remedies need to be discussed at an early stage.[129]

2.4.3 Gun-jumping

Gun-jumping refers to the situation where an undertaking which is obliged to notify a transaction, fails to do so or notifies it too late.[130] It also signifies that, in those regimes that have adopted pre-merger notification requirements, the merging parties breached the obligation to suspend the implementation of the concentration until approval is granted.[131] In both cases, what is penalized is the fact that the competition authority did not have the ability to assess the transaction prior to completion. In relation to the standstill or non-implementation requirement, some jurisdictions, eg Algeria and Tunisia, do not explicitly impose such a suspensory obligation; however, the merging parties cannot implement parts of the transaction which are irreversible or measures that would alter the market situation on a lasting basis.[132] The EU demands that merging parties wait for its approval before the implementation of the transaction, and the following examples are considered a breach of such an obligation: (i) coordination between merging parties on prices or terms to be offered to customers; (ii) allocating customers for sales; (iii) coordination of negotiations with customers for sales to be made after the merger is approved (eg negotiations of long-term contracts); (iv) plans made regarding products, distributors or employees (eg appointment of new directors); and (v) the exchange of detailed information concerning customers, prices and product plans.[133]

In the UK, where the notification system is voluntary, the Competition and Markets Authority (CMA) has the power to impose financial penalties where without reasonable excuse an interim enforcement order (IEO), is not observed.[134] In South Africa, the Competition Agency has prosecuted gun-jumping cases where prior to approval a number of events occurred that indicate the parties closed the transaction, such as access to strategic information, interaction with customers and suppliers, and a change of the business name that has been communicated to the public.[135] The enforcement

[129] American Bar Association (ABA)—Section of Antitrust Law, 'Assessment of Global Competition Agency Implementation of ABA Best Practices for Antitrust Procedure' (29 April 2019) https://www.americanbar.org/content/dam/aba/administrative/antitrust_law/comments/april-2019/sal-procedural-transparency-2019-04-29.pdf accessed 15 September 2023.

[130] Vincent Power, 'Gun-Jumping in European Union Merger Control: The Law and Practice' (2020) 22 Irish Journal of European Law 66, 68.

[131] ibid.

[132] Baker McKenzie, 'An Overview of Competition and Antitrust Regulations' (August 2019) https://www.bakermckenzie.com/-/media/files/insight/guides/2019/overview-of-competition-and-antitrust-regulations-in-africa.pdf accessed 15 September 2023.

[133] EUMR, art 7.

[134] Enterprise Act 2002, s 94A.

[135] Baker McKenzie (n 132).

activity against gun-jumping has increased significantly in recent years, as well as the amount of the fines.[136]

Sanctions for gun-jumping vary across countries. In the EU, the Commission can impose a fine of up to 10 per cent of the turnover of the undertaking concerned.[137] In the UK, the CMA is entitled to impose fines up to 5 per cent of the total value of the global turnover of the undertaking concerned, where the undertaking is responsible for providing evidence of an objectively reasonable excuse for the failure to comply with the IEO.[138] Besides the imposition of fines, some agencies have the power to order that the transaction be voided or reversed.[139] Also, it is worth mentioning that in many jurisdictions there is a time limit within which the competition authorities should make a decision about the transaction, and once the time has expired, there is a presumption of approval, therefore the merging parties can proceed with consummating the transaction without the risk of a gun-jumping investigation. A common theme regarding gun-jumping sanctions is the lack of precise guidance about what comprises proper and improper implementation, and a lack of clarity about the circumstances in which notification is necessary, aspects relevant considering the huge sanctions that undertakings might confront in case of failure to fulfil these obligations.[140]

2.4.4 Documents

The documentation that needs to be submitted with the notification filing is not a trivial matter. A great number of jurisdictions, including the US, EU, Brazil, Mexico, South Africa, China, and others, require an extensive amount of data to substantiate the rationale of the merger, to define the relevant market, to establish how the market operates, including the market players.[141] Beyond the amount of data that merging parties have to provide, some countries, like Colombia, North Macedonia, and Costa Rica, request that certain submitted documents follow notarizations, apostilles, and translations rules.[142] A more complicated scenario is observed in the review process of mergers in regulated markets in the US, in sectors where there is a concurrent regime, which signifies that merging parties endure substantial expenses in responding to coinciding requests for information by the antitrust agency and the sectoral regulator.[143] Moreover, it has been claimed that because the US antitrust agencies have twenty days to make a decision following the parties' full compliance with a second request for

[136] Authority for Consumers and Markets (ACM), 'ACM imposed fines of EUR 12.5 million on cold-storage firms' (Press release, 23 March 2016) https://www.acm.nl/en/publications/publication/15609/ACM-imposed-fines-of-EUR-125-million-on-cold-storage-firms accessed 15 September 2023.

[137] EUMR, art 7.

[138] Enterprise Act 2002, s 94A.

[139] Law 1340/2009, art 13.

[140] Power (n 130).

[141] Craig Lee and others, 'The Stories Merger Documents Tell: The US, EU, Asia, Brazil, Mexico, and South Africa Perspectives' (2018) 39(4) European Competition Law Review 161.

[142] Alexiadis and others (n 79) 219–20.

[143] James R Weiss and Martin L Stern, 'Serving Two Masters: The Dual Jurisdiction of the FCC and the Justice Department Over Telecommunications Transactions', 6 CommLaw Conspectus, 206 (1998).

information, this 'unrealistic' short period of time has served as an incentive to demand huge amounts of information, costing millions of dollars to collect and file.[144] The Canadian Competition Bureau (CCB) has also been criticized over the extensive amount of data that merging parties need to provide.[145]

The costs and the practical implications of collecting the information that a review process involves are not the only issues that merging parties should consider. Experience has shown that the information collected in a merger assessment process could be used by antitrust agencies to trigger civil and criminal investigations as well. As an example, the review process of the merger between Telefonica and Portugal Telecom exposed an existing anticompetitive agreement, which ended in a fine imposed by the Commission of €66,894,000 on the former and €12,290,000 on the latter.[146] In China, the merger review process is also used to ensure compliance with other regimes.[147] Equally, merging parties in South Africa need to be ready to deliver documents that are not merger-specific, as it has been the case of providing franchise agreements in which the Competition Commission had concerns about possible restrictive effects on competition, or lease agreements that in another merger process led to similar concerns.[148]

A high degree of diligence is also indispensable in relation to the accuracy of the information provided. As an illustration, Facebook received a fine of €110 million imposed by the European Commission for providing misleading information in relation to the acquisition of WhatsApp. According to the information provided by Facebook, the exchange of data between the merging parties was not possible, but two years later WhatsApp announced updates to its terms of service and privacy policy, whereby user phone numbers could be linked to Facebook users' identities.[149] In this context, it is important that merging parties be prepared to provide timely, accurate, and sufficient levels of data, but at the same time, agencies should make use of this power wisely, as the burden could be troublesome not just for the merging parties but also for the agency staff who might need to navigate through massive amounts of data, a task that could become insurmountable. Finally, it should be mentioned that some jurisdictions issue interim decisions regarding the completeness of the filing process, indicating whether the totality of the information has been provided or not, as is the case in Denmark, Bulgaria, and Costa Rica. Finally, a notification fee is imposed in a number of jurisdictions on the merging parties.[150]

144 Venit and Kolasky (n 43) 94.

145 It has been reported that the specific way the data needs to be provided can be extremely expensive and cumbersome. See Michael Laskey and Susan M Hutton, 'Competition Bureau Bulks Up Electronic Production Guidelines' (Stikeman Elliott, 11 September 2015) http://www.stikeman.com/en-ca/kh/competitor/competition-bureau-bulks-up-electronic-production-guidelines accessed 15 September 2023.

146 See EC, 'Antitrust: Commission fines Telefonica and Portugal Telecom €79 million for illegal non-compete contract' (Press Release, 23 January 2013) https://ec.europa.eu/commission/presscorner/detail/en/IP_13_39 accessed 15 September 2023.

147 Lee (n 141).

148 ibid 161–66.

149 See EC, 'Mergers: Commission fines Facebook €110 million for providing misleading information about WhatsApp takeover' (Press Release, 18 May 2017) https://ec.europa.eu/commission/presscorner/detail/en/IP_17_1369 accessed 15 September 2023.

150 Alexiadis and others (n 79) 222.

2.4.5 Review Timeline

As mentioned earlier, some jurisdictions apply a simplified or fast-track procedure to mergers with modest market shares, or restricted vertical links that are unlikely to raise anticompetitive concerns, and in those cases usually a decision is made in fifteen to thirty working days (in most jurisdictions).[151] Procedures that do not fall within the simplified or fast-track procedure, are generally reviewed in two steps or phases. Phase I covers unproblematic transactions that in jurisdictions like the EU could take up to 25 working days (more than 90 per cent of the cases are resolved in Phase I),[152] whereas in other countries like Brazil, Phase I takes around six months.[153] A Phase II assessment is relevant for more challenging transactions, where more time is given to the agencies to assess them in terms of effects on competition. For instance, in the EU the Commission has ninety working days to make a final decision,[154] an approach that has been mirrored by the Danish merger control regime.[155] Lastly, it is important to note that some jurisdictions contemplate the possibility of requests for additional information being issued which stops the review deadlines, whereas in countries like Austria this 'stop-the-clock' mechanism does not apply when additional information is required or remedies are submitted, therefore if the merging parties need more time, they must request an extension.[156]

An interesting case study in relation to the merger review deadlines relates to the telecommunications sector in the US. In this sector, the regulator—the Federal Communications Commission (FCC)—which jointly with the antitrust agencies is responsible for the assessment of M&As, has a voluntary deadline of 180 days to make a decision, which however is not frequently observed.[157] It has been reported that in most cases, even if the antitrust agency did not have any concerns, as in *Comcast/NBCU*, the merging parties had to wait over a year to obtain clearance from the FCC.[158] The same delay was observed in *SBC/Ameritech*, where a year after the application was filed, the merging parties received a letter from the FCC warning them that in the absence of commitments, a hearing would occur.[159] Such a discretionary timeline does

[151] ibid 223.

[152] EC, 'Competition: Merger Control Procedures' https://ec.europa.eu/competition/publications/factsheets/merger_control_procedures_en.pdf accessed 15 September 2023.

[153] Leonardo Canabrava and others, 'Merger Control in Brazil: Overview' (Thomson Reuters Practical Law, 1 January 2022) https://uk.practicallaw.thomsonreuters.com/4-501-1911 accessed 15 September 2023.

[154] EC (n 152).

[155] See Olaf Koktvedgaard, Søren Zinck, and Frederik André Bork, 'Denmark: Merger Control' (Global Competition Review, 8 July 2020) https://globalcompetitionreview.com/review/the-european-middle-eastern-and-african-antitrust-review/2021/article/denmark-merger-control accessed 15 September 2023.

[156] Zandler and Horaceck (n 95).

[157] See FCC, 'Overview of the FCC's Review of Significant Transactions' https://www.fcc.gov/reports-research/guides/review-of-significant-transactions accessed 15 September 2023. See also Victoria Peng, 'Astroturf Campaigns: Transparency in Telecom Merger Review' (2016) 49 University of Michigan Journal of Law Reform 525, 528.

[158] Christopher S Yoo, 'Merger Review by the Federal Communications Commission: Comcast-NBC Universal' (2014) 45(3) Review of Industrial Organization 295, 313.

[159] William J Kolasky, 'The FCC's Review of the Bell Atlantic/NYNEX and SBC/Ameritech Mergers: Regulatory Overreach in the Name of Promoting Competition' (2001) 68(3) Antitrust Law Journal 771, 799; SBC/Ameritech, Memorandum Opinion and Order, Docket 98-141, app C.

not enhance certainty and predictability, aspects that are relevant particularly in sectors that evolve so rapidly. For this reason, it is advisable that merger control regulations globally consider binding review timelines that should be observed by the respective agencies.

2.4.6 Sector-specific Regimes

Many countries have exclusive merger control rules for specific sectors of the economy. The rules vary in terms of scope of intervention, levels of jurisdictional thresholds, and application of tailored substantive tests to assess the transactions in these sectors. At the EU level, for example, Member States are entitled to retain jurisdiction over concentrations in the media sector under standards that allow their prohibition based on broad concerns, rather than exclusively competition ones.[160] In the most recent amendment of the merger control rules in Germany, companies in certain sectors of the economy can now be asked to notify mergers that do not meet the pre-established notification thresholds, and the Federal Cartel Office (FCO) can consider aspects such as access to competition-relevant data and intermediation power to assess market power.[161] The same approach has recently been adopted in China, where undertakings in the online and sharing economy sectors have been advised to voluntary notify their deals, even if they do not reach the mandatory notification threshold, with the aim to allow the State Administration for Market Regulation (SAMR) to verify that they are compatible with the competitive market environment.[162] Austria has introduced new rules for the review of mergers in the digital economy, in addition to the existing ones in the banking, insurance, utilities, gambling, telecommunications, and aviation industries, in which a new threshold based on the 'value of consideration' is applied (for instance, the value of data collected by the acquired undertaking triggers a review even if the merging parties' turnover is very low).[163]

In regulated sectors, the differences are remarkably more pronounced, to such an extent that the decision is transferred to the regulators or is shared concurrently between the regulators and the antitrust agencies. The latter scenario is observed in the US, where for instance in the financial sector and according to the Bank Merger Act of 1960, before merging, a bank requires approval from its regulator, that is: for national banks, the Office of the Comptroller of the Currency (OCC); for state member banks, the Federal Reserve Board (FRB or the Board); and for non-member banks, the Federal Deposit Insurance Corporation (FDIC). Likewise, the Act provides three indicators

160 EUMR, art 21(4).

161 See the 10th Amendment Act to the German Act Against Restraints of Competition (ARC) that entered into force on 19 January 2021.

162 See Yajie Gao and Wei Han, 'The Chinese Anti-Monopoly Commission of the State Council Publishes Anti-Monopoly Guidelines on Platform Economy' (e-Competitions 7 February 2021).

163 Zandler and Horaceck (n 95); Christian Herbst, 'Public Mergers and Acquisitions in Austria: Overview' (Thomson Reuters Practical Law, 1 September 2021) https://uk.practicallaw.thomsonreuters.com/6-501-9614 accessed 15 September 2023.

that the agencies must examine during the merger review: 1) the effect on competition, 2) the convenience and needs of the community to be served, and 3) the financial conditions of the banks seeking to merge, and the general character of their management.[164] Simultaneously, the DOJ conducts a separate competition-based assessment of the transactions. The two agencies' assessment fits into the different filing instructions and process overview that rules the review of each regulator. This shared jurisdiction among multiple regulators and antitrust agencies creates at times an intricate assessment process that leads to uncertainty with respect to process and outcomes, as well as to excessive costs, and often contradictory decisions.

Moving to another jurisdiction, in the UK the following regulated sectors have specific rule in relation to merger assessment: water and sewerage; energy, rail, airports, and aviation; financial services, and healthcare. Specifically, in the water sector a substantive test different from the Substantial Lessening of Competition test is applied, in which the CMA verifies if after the merger, enough water businesses would remain for the Water Services Regulation Authority (OFWAT) to be able to perform its role of making comparisons. As OFWAT uses comparative information across different regional water companies to determine whether water prices are fair, and whether those regulated companies are performing well, when a merger in this sector is filed, the regulator ensures that the proposed combination would not impair its benchmarking capacity.[165] In the health sector, the CMA must inform the regulator (NHS Improvement) about concentrations involving NHS hospitals or ambulance services, and the regulator will provide advice in relation to the potential customer/patient benefits for people who use those services. Against this backdrop, merging parties need to be aware of the different policy considerations involving specific sectors, as well as the procedural matters and the bodies which have jurisdiction to review them.

2.4.7 Remedies

Remedies can be imposed in order to prevent any competitive harm that a merger might cause, or to restore the structure of the market in the event that a concentration would distort it.[166] Merger remedies could be structural, usually designed to have an immediate impact, irreversible by nature, not demanding continuous monitoring, and often consisting of the divestiture of assets or the transfer of intellectual property rights.[167] Agencies can also impose behavioural remedies that involve adhering to specific rules

[164] 12 USC § 1828(c)(2).

[165] Nigel Parr, Duncan Liddell, and Stefen Vaz, 'Merger Control Laws and Regulations: United Kingdom 2023' (ICLG, 13 December 2022) https://iclg.com/practice-areas/merger-control-laws-and-regulations/united-kingdom accessed 15 September 2023. See also 'Ofwat's Approach to Mergers and Statement of Methods' (October 2015) https://www.ofwat.gov.uk/wp-content/uploads/2015/11/pap_pos20151021mergers.pdf accessed 15 September 2023.

[166] OECD, 'Remedies in Merger Cases' (2012) DAF/COMP(2011)13, http://www.oecd.org/daf/competition/RemediesinMergerCases2011.pdf accessed 15 September 2023.

[167] ibid.

for a specific period of time under monitoring, such as non-discriminatory provisions or contracting restraints.[168] Generally, the imposition of remedies responds to the following principles: assessment, proportionality, effectiveness, potential remedy of burdens and costs, and transparency and consistency.[169] Contrary to the approach observed in antitrust investigations, the process of discussing remedies seems to be more consensual in merger reviews.[170] At least this is the case in the EU, where in order to conditionally clear a transaction, the European Commission has the power to accept commitments proportionate to the competition concerns and capable of eliminating them.[171]

The same is not true in the US, considering that, for instance in the telecommunications sector, merging parties frequently offer conditions that fall beyond the scope of the regulator's functions.[172] As an illustration, the Federal Communications Commission (FCC) negotiated with Comcast/NBCU more than 100 commitments that were not merger-specific,[173] contrary to what some scholars had anticipated, that 'the merger should and likely will be passed with few conditions'.[174] In another merger case the FCC imposed thirty conditions with penalties of over $1 billion and performance requirements in twenty categories and payments of $1.25 billion over three years to the US Treasury for a shortfall.[175] Yet, even if the merging parties willingly negotiate obligations that are outside the scope of judicial review[176] and frequently are difficult to monitor and enforce, that does not mean that the process is any less arbitrary. A further complication is that in the regulated sectors in the US, where there is concurrent jurisdiction with DOJ/FTC, the type of remedies that are imposed is divergent. In the energy sector, for example, while the DOJ and FTC prefer the imposition of structural remedies,[177] the Federal Energy Regulatory Commission (FERC) is inclined to impose behavioural remedies, and in the end the merging parties need to conform with both sets of remedies resulting in elevated costs for them.[178]

[168] ibid.

[169] ICN Merger Working Group: Analytical Framework Subgroup, 'Merger Remedies Review Project' (4th ICN Annual Conference, Bonn, June 2005), https://www.uni-goettingen.de/de/document/download/b1dcf3398b09292b5ae557095337f655.pdf/ICN_Remedies_StudyFINAL5-10.pdf accessed 15 September 2023.

[170] Ioannis Lianos, 'Competition Law Remedies in Europe', in Ioannis Lianos and Damien Geradin (eds), *Handbook of Competition Law: Enforcement and Procedure*' (Edward Elgar 2013) 362, 364.

[171] ECMR, Recital 30.

[172] Bryan N Tramont, 'Too Much Power, Too Little Restraint: How the FCC Expands Its Reach through Unenforceable and Unwieldy Voluntary Agreements' (2000) 53 Federal Communications Law Journal 49, 54.

[173] Yoo (n 158) 314.

[174] Thomas Curtin, 'Achieving "The Franchise": The Comcast—NBC Universal Merger and the New Media Marketplace' (2010) 19 CommLaw Conspectus 149, 178.

[175] Kolasky (n 159) 799–800; see also Tramont (n 172) 54–5.

[176] Rachel E Barkow and Peter W Huber, 'A Tale of Two Agencies: A Comparative Analysis of FCC and DOJ Review of Telecommunications Mergers' [2000] University of Chicago Legal Forum 29, 73.

[177] The DOJ 2004 Remedies Policy Guide, Sec 3.1, https://www.justice.gov/d9/pages/attachments/2019/07/30/205108.pdf accessed 15 September 2023, indicates that: 'Structural remedies are preferred to conduct remedies in merger cases because they are relatively clean and certain, and generally avoid costly government entanglement in the market. A carefully crafted divestiture decree is simple, relatively easy to administer, and sure to preserve competition. A conduct remedy, on the other hand, typically is more difficult to craft, more cumbersome and costly to administer, and easier than a structural remedy to circumvent.'

[178] Diana L Moss, 'Antitrust versus Regulatory Merger Review: The Case of Electricity in Review of Industrial Organization' (2008) 32 Review of Industrial Organization 241, 254.

A similar issue is observed at an international level when multi-jurisdictional transactions are affected by inconsistent remedies imposed by different countries as a result of the nature of the divergent competitive tests applied.[179] To illustrate the extent of the divergence, it has been reported that the EU, US, Germany, and UK tend to impose more structural remedies, whereas jurisdictions like France, Austria, Ireland, Turkey, COMESA, and Singapore normally include behavioural obligations in their commitment decisions.[180] Seeking to mitigate the risk of divergence, jurisdictions like the EU and US have adopted 'Best Practices' aiming to reach some consensus in relation to which remedy proposals are more appropriate to satisfy their respective concerns, arising from an M&A transaction.[181] Furthermore, jurisdictions with a marked preference for structural remedies will accept divestment of assets located outside national borders.[182]

Currently, there is an ongoing debate regarding the flexibility that agencies should show in terms of the types of remedies to be imposed. Some are advocating embracing remedies that fit into the market realities.[183] Specifically, in big data mergers the use of conditional or precautionary measures such as 'sunrise clauses' has been suggested, meaning that a merger could be cleared even if a potential anti-competitive outcome is identified by which a pre-established remedy will take effect in the future if the competition concern materializes.[184]

2.4.8 Third Parties

In both the EU and UK, where the merger review process contemplates formal consultations with a range of stakeholders, third parties are invited to a hearing where they can offer their views about the potential competitive outcomes of the merger, and customers, suppliers, and competitors have the right to submit comments during the assessment process.[185] The fact that in the EU, competitors are given a considerable amount of time during the hearings to dispute a proposed merger,[186] has led to comments that the role of competitors is far more significant than in the role they have in the US merger assessment system.[187] This assertion is confirmed in the US financial sector in relation to the Federal Reserve Board (FRB), where the merger control rules

179 ICN Merger Working Group: Analytical Framework Subgroup (n 170).

180 Thomas Wilson, 'Merger Remedies—Is it time to go more behavioural?' (Kluwer Competition Law Blog, 21 February 2020) https://competitionlawblog.kluwercompetitionlaw.com/2020/02/21/merger-remedies-is-it-time-to-go-more-behavioural/ accessed 15 September 2023.

181 European Commission, Press Release IP(02) 1591 of 30 Oct. 2002.

182 OECD (n 166) 22.

183 Wilson (n 180).

184 Hoffmann and Johannsen (n 50) 52–56.

185 Alexiadis and others (n 79) 229; see also UK Competition Commission, 'Chairman's Guidance on Disclosure of Information in Merger Inquiries, Market Investigations and Reviews of Undertakings and Orders accepted or made under the Enterprise Act 2002 and Fair Trading Act 1973' (April 2013) www.gov.uk/government/uploads/system/uploads/attachment_data/file/284387/cc7_revised_.pdf accessed 15 September 2023.

186 Regulation 802/2004, arts 16 and 18.

187 Venit and Kolasky (n 43) 87–88.

do not provide a stage for public comments; however, the FRB considers all written public comments and, at its discretion, schedules hearings.

Another criticism is that the ability that states, community groups, and public officials at state and federal level enjoy, to challenge merger approvals in the banking sector, has permitted them to negotiate and exert from merging parties, unwilling to endure a long litigation process, remedies that are not always merger-related.[188] In the US, merging parties are less worried about competitors trying to challenge the merger or sue for damages, as the Supreme Court has repeatedly denied standing to competitors,[189] an approach that reflects how reserved the US system has been in granting rights to competitors in merger proceedings. The fact that the EU accords greater weight to competitors, while the US seems less prone to outsiders' influence, has led to the theory that the EU inquisitorial system is more open to competitors' views than the US adversarial system.[190] This theory seems to be supported by looking at Brazil, where customers, suppliers, and competitors, following a publication of merger proceedings in an Official Gazette, submit to the Conselho Administrativo de Defesa Economica (CADE) with arguments, studies and evidence that are usually considered when deciding the merger cases.[191]

A worrying case of third-party intervention relates to South Africa, where, it has been reported, the Minister of Economic Development openly influences the decision-making of the Competition Commission (SACC), to such an extent that merging parties on some occasions, rather than engaging in discussions with the agency, prefer to lobby the Minister. Likewise, the types and number of conditions imposed in certain merger cases are previously recommended by the Minister.[192] It is undeniable that third parties contribute greatly to the merger review by offering data and views that are valuable; however, it is important that agencies evaluate them neutrally and maintain an appropriate degree of independence.

2.4.9 Appeals

The institutional design and the merger control rules shape the judicial review of merger decisions across the world. In the EU, for instance, the EU Commission acts as an investigator, prosecutor, judge, and jury.[193] Once the EU Commission has come to a conclusion, its decision is written and made public, with a detailed explanation of the legal and economic considerations that have led to the respective result of its assessment, an aspect that has enhanced a rich body of precedents that parties can use to

[188] Brian W Smith and Laura R Biddle, 'Is the Bank Merger Regulatory Review Process Ripe for Change?' (2005) 18 Bank Accounting & Finance 9, 13–14.

[189] *Cargill v Monfort of Colorado, Inc*, 107 SCt 484 (1986).

[190] Thomas Giebe and Miyu Lee, 'Competitors in Merger Control: Shall They Be Merely Heard or Also Listened To?' (2020) 49 European Journal of Law and Economics 431.

[191] ABA—Section of Antitrust Law (n 129).

[192] ibid 89.

[193] Kampouridi (n 4).

predict likely outcomes, and facilitates parties with the preparation of comprehensive judicial review before the European Courts.[194] The opposite occurs in the US, where merger cases are not determined by the antitrust agencies, whose main task is to decide whether to challenge transactions in Court,[195] and whose decisions do not contain detailed explanations of the legal or economic reasoning, just a brief summary of the analysis supporting their decisions, a shortfall that has compromised the existence of an important body of valuable precedents.[196] Thus, a limited description of the analysis is presented by the DOJ through a 'Competitive Impact Statement' in federal courts and by the FTC seeking a preliminary injunction through an 'Analysis of Aid Public Comment' in district courts.[197] Parties can appeal an adverse decision and to petition the US Supreme Court to review the appeal decision; yet, if the number of litigated cases is low, the appeals heard by the Supreme Court is even lower.[198]

As an example of this low litigation rate, it has been reported that since 1985, the DOJ has not challenged a single bank merger.[199] Worryingly, the few cases that are litigated suffer long delays, thus, in 2016 on average 179 days passed between the complaint and the first day of the trial, which lasted 34 days.[200] Another jurisdiction that provides a limited explanation of its decisions, is Taiwan, where the Fair Trade Commission of Taiwan (TFTC) has tried to address criticisms of its failures to issue decisions with detailed reasoning, particularly if the decision is to reject a filing.[201] In spite of these efforts, merging parties do not benefit from having decisions that include the evidence that was relevant to the agency's decision, as the TFTC by law enjoys great deference when reviewing merger cases and therefore its decisions are not frequently challenged.[202]

In Ukraine, a reform in 2017 introduced new procedural rules in relation to judicial review, establishing that the decisions of the Antimonopoly Committee of Ukraine (AMC) can be appealed to commercial courts, which need to make their decisions within the following deadlines: first instance, up to 135 calendar days; appeal, up to seventy-five calendar days; and cassation, up to eighty calendar days.[203] It has been indicated that these short timeframes have compromised the quality of the judgments as the courts dispose the cases mostly based on procedural issues, showing great deference to the AMC.[204] Appeals in Austria are decided by the Supreme Court of Justice (OGH)

194 ABA—Section of Antitrust Law (n 129) 111.

195 15 USC §18.

196 Venit and Kolasky (n 43) 95–96.

197 ABA—Section of Antitrust Law (n 129) 112.

198 ibid 119.

199 Kress (n 124) 453; Aaron C Stine and Eric D Gorman, 'Ebbing the Tide of Local Bank Concentration: Granting Sole Authority to the Department of Justice to Review the Competitive Effects of Bank Mergers' (2012) 62 Syracuse Law Review 405, 417.

200 Dechert, 'DAMITT 2016 Year in Review: Significant Antitrust Merger Investigations Longer Than Ever; Deal Agreements Reflect Expected delays' (January 2017) https://info.dechert.com/10/7980/January-2017/damitt-2016-year-in-review.asp accessed 15 September 2023.

201 Joshua D Wright, 'The Taiwan Fair Trade Commission's Problematic Qualcomm Decision Highlights the Urgent Need for the U.S. Leadership in International Antitrust' (Federalist Society Blog, 13 December 2017) https://fedsoc.org/commentary/blog-posts/the-taiwan-fair-trade-commission-s-problematic-qualcomm-decision-highlights-the-urgent-need-for-u-s-leadership-in-international-antitrust accessed 15 September 2023.

202 ABA—Section of Antitrust Law (n 129) 109.

203 Svechkar and others (n 86).

204 ABA—Section of Antitrust Law (n 129) 121.

within two months of receipt of the files from the Cartel Court, and if the OGH orders that a new decision needs to be made, the Cartel Court has five months to do so.[205]

South Africa offers an interesting case study, as there is an important distinction between intermediate and large mergers.[206] Intermediate mergers are examined by the Competition Commission (SACC) in a timeline of sixty business days, and its decision does not provide sufficient information about the evidence that has been considered, leaving the merging parties in a position where either they accept multiple and onerous conditions, or request that the Tribunal reviews the decision, which is usually costly and time-consuming. Large mergers are investigated by the SACC, which recommends approval or prohibition of the merger to the Competition Tribunal. The Tribunal makes the final decision and the Competition Appeal Court decides the appeals.[207]

In Belgium, merging parties and third parties are entitled to appeal the decision of the Competition College within thirty days of notification of the decision. The Market Court, a specialized chamber of the Brussels Court of Appeal, is responsible for reviewing merger control decisions. In turn, judgments made by the Market Court can be subject to revision by the Supreme Court on points of law and procedure.[208] Interestingly, in Brazil, parties do not need to appeal prohibition or conditional merger approvals made by the General Superintendence, as they are automatically sent to CADE's Tribunal for review, and final decision, which in turn and in practice are rare, can be reviewed by a federal court.[209]

Considering the above, it appears that some reforms on a global scale are required. It is important that agencies provide sufficient information in their final decisions about the legal and economic reasons that have been considered in order to facilitate preparation of the appeals. At the same time, courts would benefit from having written decisions in which relevant aspects such as theories of harm, market studies and relevant markets, among many others, are contained in the challenged decisions. Similarly, even if short timelines are vital, especially in merger cases, they cannot come at the expense of quality. Also, if extensive deference is given to competition agencies, then the purpose of the judicial review becomes superfluous. Finally, merging parties need to pay close attention to the diverse appeal procedures among jurisdictions, and take the respective time and costs into account.

[205] Zandler and Horaceck (n 95).

[206] An intermediate merger meets any of the following thresholds: (i) the combined annual turnover in, into, or from South Africa of the acquiring firm/s and the target firm/s is valued at ZAR 600 million or more; (ii) the combined assets in South Africa of the acquiring firm/s and the target firm/s are valued at ZAR 600 million or more; (iii) the annual turnover in, into, or from South Africa of the acquiring firm/s plus the assets in South Africa of the target firm/s is valued at ZAR 600 million or more; (iv) the annual turnover in, into, or from South Africa of the target firm/s plus the asset/s in South Africa of the acquiring firms is valued at ZAR 600 million or more, and (v) the annual turnover in, into, or from South Africa, or the asset value of the target firm/s in South Africa, must be ZAR 100 million or more. A larger merger exceeds ZAR 6.6 billion and the turnover or asset value of the target firm/s equals or exceeds ZAR 190 million. See Xolani Nyaly and Lital Avivi, 'Merger Control in South Africa: Overview' (Thomson Reuters Practical Law, 1 February 2022) https://uk.practicallaw.thomsonreuters.com/2-504-5969 accessed 15 September 2023.

[207] ABA—Section of Antitrust Law (n 129) 135.

[208] Annick Vroninks and Antoine Accarain, 'Merger Control in Belgium: Overview' (Thomson Reuters Practical Law, 1 December 2020) https://uk.practicallaw.thomsonreuters.com/w-020-3331 accessed 15 September 2023.

[209] Nagalli and others (n 87) para 8.1.

2.5 Conclusion

This chapter has sought to examine and identify the prevailing substantive and procedural rules in merger control across different jurisdictions. Although the examination covers a limited number of countries, the sample has been sufficient to provide us with key elements that have been used to establish the major differences and similarities among them, to elaborate on how merger enforcement is taking place and to identify main challenges. In comparing the various systems, the realization is that even if there are some commonalities, the most acute difficulty lies in the extend of discrepancies. In substantive terms, the origin of the variance resides in the overarching purposes that inform merger control. Yet even in those jurisdictions where consumer welfare has been adopted as a policy goal, its meaning remains unclear and its application distinctive. The issue becomes more complex when non-economic goals are accommodated within the merger frameworks. As each country has its own view as to what social considerations are of potential interest to merger control, assessment and enforcement take place largely on a national basis.

We have also seen how the variety of goals combined with the dissimilar nature of the administrative and judicial bodies in charge of enforcing the merger control rules in every jurisdiction, has resulted in heterogeneous procedural terms. The inconsistency of the procedures ranges from diverse notification requirements, volumes of information accompanying the applications, different timelines, and pre-merger vis-à-vis post-merger model, among many others. In consequence, merging parties subject to multi-jurisdictional merger reviews carry the burden of increased transaction costs, unnecessary delays, and reduced certainty. In addition, the excessive scrutiny of cross-border mergers runs the risk of overlapping decisions over the same transaction, making the enforcement efforts ineffective. Further, competition authorities impose remedies according to the domestic interests, and merging parties need to conform with all of them. In a nutshell, more consistent merger frameworks and merger procedures would alleviate the unjustified costs that merging parties need to endure and would mitigate the chances of contradictory merger decisions. Nonetheless, as we will explore in more detail in the next chapters, this renewed enthusiasm for industrial policy guided by a desire to promote jobs or secure inputs needed for national security is at odds with harmonization. Therefore, we do not expect to see greater levels of consistency in the future direction of merger control, not only in 'sensitive' areas that can raise national security concerns but also in sectors of the economy, such as digital sector.

3

National Security and FDI Screening in the EU

3.1 Introduction

The European Union (EU) has been recognized as a leading recipient of foreign direct investment (FDI)[1] and as one of the most open investment regimes in the world.[2] This approach derives from the notion that FDI stimulates the emergence of capital, the transference of technology, the integration of societies, the improvement of employment conditions, and the advance in research and product development.[3] The referred openness tendency was bolstered with the entry into force of the Lisbon Treaty, in which article 207(1) of the Treaty on the Functioning of the European Union (TFEU) incorporated FDI into the EU's common commercial policy,[4] translating the elimination of restrictions on international trade and investments in a constitutional obligation for the EU's common commercial policy.[5] As a result, the number of cross-border mergers and acquisitions (M&As), through FDI, has gradually increased by the EU attracting the attention of United States (US) investors during the 1960s, later during the 1990s from Japanese and Korean firms, and most recently from the People's Republic of China (PRC).[6]

[1] According to the Organisation for Economic Cooperation and Development (OECD), a direct investment is 'a category of cross-border investment made by a resident in one economy (the direct investor) with the objective of establishing a lasting interest in an enterprise (the direct investment enterprise) that is resident in an economy other than that of the direct investor. The motivation of the direct investor is a strategic long-term relationship with the direct investment enterprise to ensure a significant degree of influence by the direct investor in the management of the direct investment enterprise. The "lasting interest" is evidenced when the direct investor owns at least 10% of the voting power of the direct investment enterprise.' See OECD Benchmark Definition of Foreign Direct Investment (4th edn 2008), 17, https://www.oecd.org/investment/fdibenchmarkdefinition.htm accessed 15 September 2023. Mergers and acquisitions (M&A) are a form of FDI in which companies either combine operations or where one company acquires stakes in another company. See Dustin Tingley and others, 'The Political Economy of Inward FDI: Opposition to Chinese Mergers and Acquisitions' (2015) 8(1) Chinese Journal of International Politics 27, 28.

[2] See OECD, FDI Regulatory Restrictiveness Index, https://www.oecd.org/investment/fdiindex.htm accessed 15 September 2023; European Commission, Communication from the Commission to the Council, the European Parliament, the European Economic and Social Committee, and the Committee of the Regions: Towards a comprehensive European international investment policy. COM (2010) 343 final, Brussels 7 July 2010, 3–4.

[3] European Commission, 'Reflection Paper on Harnessing Globalisation' (2017) 8 https://commission.europa.eu/publications/reflection-paper-harnessing-globalisation_en accessed 15 September 2023.

[4] Catherine Titi, 'International Investment Law and the European Union: Towards a New Generation of International Investment Agreements' (2015) 26(3) European Journal of International Law 639.

[5] Stephan W Schill, 'The European Union's Foreign Direct Investment Screening Paradox: Tightening Inward Investment Control to Further External Investment Liberalization', Amsterdam Law School Legal Studies Research Paper No 2019-17, Amsterdam Centre for International Law No 2019-06, pp 10–11; See also arts 119 and 206 TFEU.

[6] Carlos Esplugues, 'Towards a Common Screening System of Foreign Direct Investment on National Interest Grounds in the European Union' (2018) 11(2) Culture, Media and Entertainment Law 3 https://ssrn.com/abstract=3267386 accessed 15 September 2023.

It has been argued that the flow of Chinese FDI was also prompted by the financial crisis that afflicted the globe in 2008, accompanied by the sovereign debt crisis in Europe.[7] The statistics show that Chinese investment expanded by 155 per cent between 2009 and 2011. By 2012, China became one of the most important investors in Germany, and by 2012, Europe was the most attractive destination for Chinese outbound FDI.[8] This staggering surge raised concerns among different stakeholders, who were suspicious that this foreign control would compromise the national security of the Member States and their degree of control over key sectors.[9] In response, some Member States introduced some measures orientated to interfere with Community dimension transactions, a reaction that was known as the 'renaissance of protectionism'.[10] Under the EU Merger Regulation (EUMR), the European Commission has exclusive jurisdiction to review Community dimension transactions,[11] which correspond to those that satisfy the thresholds indicated in article 1(2)[12] or (3) EUMR[13] or referred to the Commission pursuant to article 4(5)[14] or 22[15] EUMR. Notably, article 21(3) EUMR provides that 'No Member State shall apply its national legislation on competition to any concentration that has a Community dimension' (known as the 'exclusivity principle') which contrasts with the competence that Member States enjoy with regard to concentrations that do not have a Community dimension.[16] This Community dimension or supranational jurisdiction was adopted under the presumption that it would offer some benefits to the firms operating in the European single market, such as a one-stop shop, the prevalence of long-term policy objectives rather than short-term

[7] Sophie Meunier, '"Beggars Can't Be Choosers": The European Crisis and Chinese Direct Investment in the European Union' (2014) 36(3) Journal of European Integration 233, 284.
[8] ibid.
[9] Alison Jones and John Davies, 'Merger Control and the Public Interest: Balancing EU and National Law in the Protectionist Debate' (2014) 10(3) European Competition Journal 453, 455.
[10] Neelie Kroes (European Commissioner for Competition Policy), 'European Competition Policy Facing a Renaissance of Protectionism—Which Strategy for the Future?', St Gallen International Competition Law Forum, 11 May 2007, https://ec.europa.eu/commission/presscorner/detail/en/SPEECH_07_301 accessed 15 September 2023.
[11] Art 21(2) EUMR states that the Commission 'shall have sole jurisdiction' to control the compatibility of concentrations of a Community dimension.
[12] Art 1(2) EUMR indicates that a concentration has a Community dimension where (a) the combined aggregate worldwide turnover of all the undertakings concerned is more than €5,000 million, and (b) the aggregate Community-wide turnover of each of at least two of the undertakings concerned is more than €250 million.
[13] Art 1(3) provides that a concentration that does not meet the thresholds laid down in para 2 has a Community decision where: (a) the combined aggregate worldwide turnover of all the undertakings concerned is more than €2,500 million; (b) in each of at least three Member States, the combined aggregate turnover of all undertakings concerned is more than €100 million; (c) in each of at least three Member States included for the purpose of point (b), the aggregate turnover of each of at least two of the undertakings concerned is more than €25 million; and (d) the aggregate Community-wide turnover of each of at least two of the undertakings concerned is more than €100 million unless each of the undertakings concerned achieves more than two-thirds of its aggregate Community-wide turnover with the same Member State (known as the 'two-thirds rule').
[14] Art 4(5) refers to a mechanism for merging parties to make a reasoned submission that the Commission should review the concentration that does not have a Community dimension, and is capable of being examined under the national competition laws of at least three Member States.
[15] Art 22 EUMR gives power to the Commission to examine a concentration without a Community dimension when one or more Member States request the Commission to examine any concentration as defined in art 3 that does not have a Community dimension within the meaning of art 1 but affects trade between Member States and threatens to significantly affect competition within the territory of the Member State or states making the request.
[16] Art 21(1) EUMR. As a general rule, the national law only applies to concentrations which do not have a Community dimension.

inclinations of Member States, and the fact that a supranational institution would develop capacity expertise more quickly and efficiently, among others.[17]

3.2 Application of the EUMR to Public Interest Cases

The application of the EUMR needs to strike a balance between the competition goals and other public policy objectives pursued by EU law and related constitutional provisions.[18] Thus, Recital 23 of the EUMR indicates that 'the Commission must place its appraisal within the general framework of the achievement of the fundamental objectives referred to in article 2 of the Treaty establishing the European Community and article 2 of the Treaty on European Union' taking into account other objectives such as the 'balanced and sustainable development of economic activities'. This provision reflects the approach contained in article 7 TFEU that states 'The Union shall ensure consistency between its policies and activities, taking all of its objectives into account and in accordance with the principle of conferral of powers.'

Hence, the EUMR permits the consideration of other public policies and, therefore, the Member States reserved some measures to protect their legitimate interests. Thus Article 24(4) distinguishes between 'recognized interests' and 'other public interests':

> Member States may take appropriate measures to protect legitimate interests other than those taken into consideration by this Regulation and compatible with the general principles and other provision of Community law. Public security, plurality of the media and prudential rules shall be regarded as legitimate interests ... Any other public interest must be communicated to the Commission by the Member State concerned and shall be recognised by the Commission after an assessment of its compatibility with the general principles and other provisions of Community law before the measures referred to above may be taken. The Commission shall inform the Member State concerned of its decision within 25 working days of that communication.

According to the above provision, public security, plurality or media, and prudential rules are expressly recognized as legitimate interests. Other public interests, which are unspecified, require an *ex ante* procedural requirement and involve a standstill obligation until the Commission resolves the matter. The Commission, through the 'Notes on Council Regulation 4064/89',[19] has clarified that the plurality of media refers to the right to 'maintain diversified sources of information for the sake of plurality of media and multiplicity of views', and that the prudential rules involve the reputation 'of individuals, the honesty of transactions and, the rules of solvency, in the banking and

[17] Michael Harker, 'Cross-Border Mergers in the EU: *The Commission v the Member States*' (2007) 3 European Competition Journal 503.

[18] Council Regulation (EC) 139/2004 on the control of concentrations between undertakings (EUMR) [2004] OJ L24/1.

[19] European Commission, 'Notes on Council Regulation (EEC) 4064/89' (1998) https://ec.europa.eu/competition/mergers/legislation/notes_reg4064_89_en.pdf accessed 15 September 2023.

insurance sectors'.[20] With regard to the public security, the Commission has specified that aspects concerning 'the production of or trade in arms, munitions and war material' give Member States the right to intervene.[21] The Commission has also tried to provide more clarity about the scope of the public security consideration across the case law by asserting that 'public security may be relied on only if there is a genuine and sufficiently serious threat to a fundamental interest of society',[22] and that is justified 'to ensure a minimum level of energy supplies in the event of a crisis'.[23] In this context, some commentators have indicated that given the nature of the plurality of media and the prudential rules interests, those are unlikely to be used as an industrial policy,[24] whereas the vagueness of the concept of public security may be exercised arbitrarily, by which the proportionality principle could dictate whether the alleged interest could have been safeguarded in a less restrictive way.[25] Even if a merger satisfies the Community dimension it is possible for a Member State to try to prohibit it by invoking the protection of the legitimate interests contained in article 21(4), so the next part explores the analysis carried out by the Commission in this respect.

The first step is to determine that the alleged interest is not already protected by the EUMR; otherwise, the application of this regulation should be enough to overcome the relevant concerns.[26] The second step is to ensure that the intended measures do not contravene the EU law, in particular, articles 49 TFEU[27] that refers to the freedom of establishment and 63 TFEU[28] that states the freedom of movement of capital. A third step is to undertake an internal market analysis aimed at identifying whether the measure constitutes an obstacle to trade, whether that obstacle is reasonable, and whether that reason is proportionate and non-discriminatory.[29] The Commission's analysis covers the different sectors of the economy and the decisions made by diverse types of national authorities, such as ministers and regulators.[30] The results of the analysis could result in the approval of the invoked measure, as it responds to a legitimate public interest that require to be protected or in the denial of the intended measure. Member States are entitled to oppose a merger on public interest grounds, but they cannot approve a merger

[20] ibid. Prudential rules are also understood as the supervision by a public authority of the ownership, control, and financial stability of companies involved in the financial services industry. See Mark Furse, *The Law of Merger Control in the EC and the UK* (Hart Publishing 2007) 60.

[21] European Commission (n 19).

[22] Case COMP/M.4685 *Enel/Accional/Endesa*, para 58.

[23] ibid.

[24] Edurne Navarro and others, *Merger Control in the EU* (2nd edn, Oxford University Press 2005) 14.66.

[25] Jonathan Galloway, 'The Pursuit of National Champions: The Intersection of Competition Law and Industrial Policy' (2007) 28(3) European Competition Law Review 172.

[26] Jones and Davies (n 9) 255.

[27] Art 49 TFEU provides that 'restrictions on the freedom of establishment of nationals of a Member State in the territory of another Member State shall be prohibited. Such prohibition shall also apply to restrictions on the setting-up of agencies, branches or subsidiaries by nationals of any Member State established in the territory of any Member State.'

[28] Art 63 TFEU indicates that 'all restrictions on the movement of capital between Member States and between Member States and third countries shall be prohibited'.

[29] Damien MB Gerard, 'Protectionist Threats against Cross-Border Mergers: Unexplored Avenues to Strengthen the Effectiveness of Article 21 EUMR' (2008) 45 Common Market Law Review23.

[30] ibid 24.

that has been already blocked by the Commission.[31] However, the outcome is different if the Member State omits the obligation to notify a public interest other than the ones outlined in the EUMR (ie, media plurality, public security, prudential rules). In this case, the validity of such an obligation resides in the *effet utile* principle, which prevents Member States from escaping the application of the rules contained in article 21(4) by, for instance, arguing that their domestic laws prevent them from notifying.[32]

At the same time, the European Court of Justice (ECJ) has outlined that if the Member State fails to notify, that does not mean that the Commission is not entitled to assess the respective measure.[33] Therefore, the respective outcome would be that if the adopted measures are not compatible with article 21(4), the Member State will be required to remove them, and eventually, if the non-observance persists the Commission can start an infringement procedure.[34]

There is a large number of measures that Member States can adopt to prevent a cross-border transaction, among them:

1) 'Golden shares' which give greater powers to governments, such as the right to dissent from corporate changes or to have the final say about acquisition plans.[35] 'Golden shares' could also take the form of *ex ante* domestic legislation or private corporate rules aiming at ensuring inward investment control and management of key strategic industries.[36] The European Commission takes a specific approach to appreciate the validity of a 'golden share'. Thus, it must be non-discriminatory, based on objective criteria that are made public in advance, subject to judicial review, the least restrictive means of protecting a legitimate public interest.[37]
2) 'Moral persuasion' consists of warnings that the new merged entity will face acute regulatory rules. In spite of this appearing to be a lenient interference, a study has revealed that government support greatly defines the likelihood of success of a merger bid.[38]
3) 'White knight' refers to tactics that delay the opposed bid until a more welcome bidder for the target is found.[39]

[31] See Public Interest Considerations in Merger Control—Note by the European Union (2016) DAF/COMP/WP3/WD(2016)11 https://one.oecd.org/document/DAF/COMP/WP3/WD(2016)11/En/pdf accessed 15 September 2023.

[32] The Commission has clarified that a Member State 'cannot rely on lacunae in its own legal order or, in any event, on questions concerning its administrative organisation to justify the violation of the communication obligation provided for by Article 21(4) of the Merger Regulation'. See Commission Case COMP/M.4197 *E.ON/Endesa* § 35 and 116.

[33] In the *Commission/Spain* [2008] case, the ECJ declared that 'in the absence of notification it was inevitable for the Commission to assess *ex-officio* the compliance of the measures at issue with the Community law'.

[34] Art 258 TFEU states 'If the Commission considers that a Member State has failed to fulfil an obligation under the Treaties, it shall deliver a reasoned opinion on the matter after giving the State concerned the opportunity to submit its observations. If the State concerned does not comply with the opinion within the period laid down by the Commission, the latter may bring the matter before the Court of Justice of the European Union.'

[35] Serdar Dinc and Isil Erel, 'Economic Nationalism in Mergers and Acquisitions' (2013) 68 Journal of Finance 2471, 2477.

[36] Harker (n 17) 520.

[37] Communication of the Commission on certain legal aspects concerning intra-EU investment, 19 July 1997.

[38] Dinc and Erel (n 35) 2476, 2496.

[39] ibid 2477.

4) 'Public funding' whereby governments offer financial support to domestic bidders to finalize the transaction, often through public pension funds or lends approved by public banks.[40]
5) 'Creation of National Champions', in which two or more domestic companies merge with the ambition to create a considerably sized firm that will not be easy to acquire by foreign investors.[41]

The duty of the Commission is to ensure that any of these measures are proportionate and non-discriminatory. In relation to the mentioned proportionality, the measure must (i) be suitable for securing the objective that it pursues and (ii) must not go beyond what is necessary to attain it.[42] It follows from these requirements that it is indispensable that the objective be easily identifiable and that there are no other less anti-competitive means to achieve it. As for the latter, the measure should not favour one bidder at the expense of the unwelcomed bidder, which implies that the application of uneven or obscure requirements will not be tolerated by the Commission.

Notwithstanding the apparent narrow scope for the valid application of protectionist measures at national level and the concomitant potential outcomes in case of non-observance, the reality is that Member States frequently implement them to discourage foreign acquisitions and to promote nationalism instead, disregarding the Commission's authority.[43] One plausible explanation for this is that it is almost impossible to isolate antitrust enforcement from the involvement of other stakeholders, such as politicians and public officials, who, through legislation or any other means, try to advance non-competition goals that clash with those pursued by the competition law.[44] The literature has also devoted some efforts in understanding this approach, and from a trade theory perspective there is a notion that by increasing the domestic firms' profits, for instance, by decreasing their costs through subsidies, there will be an immediate increase in the national welfare.[45] From an innovation perspective, the view is that governmental intervention, in exceptional cases and for very short periods of time, may benefit small jurisdictions afflicted by precarious technological development.[46] In direct contrast to the apparent benefits that intervention may offer, some commentators have also warned that there is a high risk that governments choose to help unprofitable and inefficient firms.[47] This risk derives from biases such as the preference for supporting projects that generate more voters' acceptance regardless of the gains from competition, or the inclination to maintain natural monopolies under the presumption

[40] ibid; see also Gerard (n 29) 24.
[41] Dinc and Erel (n 35) 2477.
[42] See Case C-483/99, *Commission/France* [2002] ECR I-4781, para 45.
[43] Andrew Scott, 'Last Rites for the Two-Thirds Rule in EC Merger Control?' [2006] Journal of Business Law 619.
[44] Galloway (n 25) 7.
[45] Barbara J Spencer and James A Brander, 'International R&D Rivalry and Industrial Strategy' (1983) 50(4) Review of Economic Studies 702.
[46] Philippe Aghion, 'Some Thoughts on Industrial Policy and Growth', in Oliver Falck, Christian Gollier, and Ludger Woessmann (eds) *Industrial Policy for National Champions* (CESifo Seminar Series, the MIT Press 2011): 19–23.
[47] ibid 94.

that they are indisputably indispensable, or the proclivity to impede that firms cease to exist, a step that has been recognized as an important part of the course of productivity growth, by injecting funding to struggling firms in an attempt to resurrect them.[48]

Against this backdrop, the following section examines some cases to identify the types of measures adopted by different Member States, the most significant substantive aspects in assessing their validity, and identify the evolution of the assessment of public interest concerns.[49]

3.3 Discussion of Seminal Cases Pursuant to Article 21 EUMR

3.3.1 *BSCH/A. Champalimaud*, 1999

In this case, the third largest financial institution in Portugal—the financial group Champalimaud—and the largest bank in Spain—Banco Santander Central Hispano (BSCH)—announced a transaction in which BSCH would acquire joint control over Champalimaud.[50] As part of Champalimaud's portfolio there was an insurance company—Mundial Confianca SA (MC), which had business with different Portuguese banks. In Portugal, as part of a privatization process, a legal provision was enacted giving the government the power to restrict a foreign firm from acquiring holdings in privatized firms or voting rights; as MC was a reprivatized firm, the then Minister for Finance tried to exercise the bestowed power to block the deal.[51] In addition, there was a specific provision stating some prudential rules in the insurance sector whereby foreign firms were prohibited from acquiring in excess of 20 per cent of domestic insurance firms. Despite satisfying the Community dimension requirement, the Portuguese government did not notify the Commission about the public interest surrounding the transaction but instead displayed great publicity across the country about its intention to defend the national economy by prohibiting the transaction.[52]

Before the Commission resolved the cross-border merger in August 1999, a Portuguese bank—Banco Commercial Português (BCP)—announced its interest in acquiring MC and two other banks that belong to the Champalimaud group, a bidder that was seen as friendly by the government but that raised concerns that it was acting as a 'white knight'.[53] Then, the Commission authorized the BSCH/Champalimaud merger and ordered the Portuguese government to terminate the decision based on

[48] Oliver Falck and Stephan Heblich, 'Do We Need National Champions: If So, Do We Need A Champions-Related Industrial Policy? An Evolutionary Perspective', Jena Economic Research Papers, No 2007, 088, 7–10; Paul Seabright, 'National and European Champions - Burden or Blessing?' CESifo Forum 2/2005, pp. 52–55.

[49] Appendix 1 presents the main factual context, arguments, and decisions of the Commission in these cases.

[50] See Cases M.1616, M.1680, and M.1724 *BSCH/A. Champalimaud* (1999), IP/99/669, IP/99/772, IP/99/774, IP/99/818, and IP/00/296.

[51] Case IV/M.1616 (1999).

[52] Al Goodman, 'Banco Santander of Spain Will Acquire 2 Portuguese Banks' *New York Times* (12 November 1999) https://www.nytimes.com/1999/11/12/business/international-business-banco-santander-of-spain-will-acquire-2-portuguese-banks.html accessed 15 September 2023.

[53] Harker (n 17) 510.

the prudential rules in the insurance sector limiting the voting rights of BSCH, which in its view, did not respond to a legitimate interest according to the meaning of article 21(4) and were unsubstantiated.[54] Given that a month later the Portuguese government ignored the referred order, the Commission was forced to request the ECJ for interim measures.[55] However, under the watch of a new Minister of Finance, the merging parties agreed a new deal making further action from the ECJ or the Commission unnecessary.[56]

This case was used by Competition Commissioner Mario Monti to illustrate the enormous authority that the Commission exerts over mergers with a Community dimension and to prevent the other Member States from incurring actions to prevent non-nationals from entering their markets.[57] The same position has been shared by some commentators, who have expressed that this case has served to confirm that the Commission is 'the final arbiter on cross-border mergers and acquisitions in the EU'.[58] However, one might argue that the case also serves to exemplify to what extent the Member States are willing to challenge the authority of the Commission to protect their national interests, and how the use of moral persuasion and 'white knight' measures can prove to be effective in repealing undesirable investors.

3.3.2 *Secil/Holderbank/Cimpor*, 2000

In July 2000, the Portuguese company Secil Companhia Geral de Cal e Cimentos SA (Secil) and the Swiss Holderbank group (Holderbank) requested the Commission's approval to acquire the Portuguese cement manufacturer Cimpor Cimentos de Portugal SGPS (Cimpor), a company nationalized in the 1970s and then privatized in the 1990s.[59] According to a public bid revealed in June 2000, that post-merger Cimpor's assets would be divided geographically, the part purchased by Holderbank had a Community dimension whereas Secil's did not. Following the notification of the transaction to the Commission, the Portuguese government applied the Decree-Law 380/93, which states that the acquisition of shares representing more than 10 per cent of the share capital with voting rights in companies to be privatized requires prior authorization by the Ministry of Finance, rejected the deal through two decisions.[60] In consequence, the Portuguese government received a letter in September 2000 in which the Commission inquired about the reasons for such rejection. As a response, Portugal indicated that the transaction was refused because it opposed the aims of privatization by subtracting

[54] See Cases M.1616, M.1680, and M.1724 *BSCH/A. Champalimaud* (1999), IP/99/669, IP/99/772, IP/99/774, IP/99/818, and IP/00/296.

[55] IP/99/818, 3 November 1999.

[56] Harker (n 17) 511.

[57] IP/00/296, 27 March 2000.

[58] S Mohamed, 'National Interest Limiting EU Cross-Border Bank Mergers' (2000) 21 European Competition Law Review 248, 256.

[59] Case COMP/M.2054 *Secil/Holderbank/Cimpor*.

[60] ibid.

Cimpor from the Portuguese capital markets, by deterring the government's efforts to restructure the sector, and by precluding the transfer of the state's holding in Cimpor under ideal economic and financial conditions.[61] The Commission found that the two decisions made by the Portuguese Minister of Finance that prevented the acquisition of Cimpor underpinned in national economic policy guidelines, which were not notified to the Commission, did not satisfy any of the public interests contemplated by the Merger Regulation, and therefore ordered their withdrawal.[62] For instance, by looking at the prudential rules, the Commission indicated that they were inapplicable in this case as the merging parties were not involved in activities in the field of banking or provision of insurance services.[63] The Commission also held that the rules enacted by the Portuguese government constituted barriers to the freedom of establishment and free movement of capital.[64]

Next, the Portuguese authorities failed to comply with the Commission's order; in January 2001, the merging parties discharged their merger plans, and in February 2001, Portugal initiated an action for annulment of the Commission decision under article 21 EUMR before the Court of Justice.[65] Portugal alleged that the Commission did not have authority under article 21 EUMR to rule on the compatibility of public interest grounds that were not notified and that as a result, the Commission should have started proceedings under article 226 EC instead. The court rejected these arguments, noting that proceedings under article 226 EC did not encompass the short time limits contained in the Merger Regulation; this is that by the time a decision was made concerning the failure to fulfil the obligation under article 226 of the Treaty, the measures adopted by the Member State concerned would have produced irreversible effects. It was also added that if the arguments presented by the Portuguese authorities were embraced, that would encourage Member States not to notify, the court concluded that even in the absence of communication of the interests by Member States, the Commission still has the power to review whether they are compatible with the general principles and other provisions.[66]

The following implications can be drawn from this case. First, national financial interests cannot override the general principles of freedom of establishment and free movement of capital. Second, when Member States fail to notify the Commission of their interests, such an omission does not mean the Commission's authority is removed.

[61] ibid.

[62] The Commission noted that the 'development of... shareholding structures in companies undergoing privatisation with a view to reinforcing the corporate capacity and the efficiency of the national production apparatus in a way that is consistent with [national] ... economic policy guidelines' did not justify the restrictions to the freedom of establishment and free movement of capital. C(2000)3543 Final, 22 November 2000.

[63] Case COMP/M.2054 *Secil/Holderbank/Cimpor*.

[64] Tea Makela, Directorate-General Competition, unit E-3, 'The Court of Justice rules for the first time on Article 21(3) of the Merger Regulation in case C-42/01 *Portuguese Republic v Commission*', Competition Policy Newsletter, No 1 Spring 2005, 19–20. On 4 June 2002, the Court indicated that the provisions under examination were manifestly discriminatory, and the argument that the measures were necessary to protect the financial interests of the country reiterated that such economic reasons could not be used to justify restrictions on freedom of movement. See Case C-367/98 *Commission v Portugal*.

[65] ibid.

[66] Case C-42/01, *Portuguese Republic v Commission*, Judgment of 22 June 2004.

Indeed, the court ratified that the Commission enjoys full jurisdiction to safeguard the rules that govern mergers with Community dimension, by which infringement proceedings under article 21(4) (ex-article 21(3)) prevail over article 226 of the Treaty. Third, it confirms that even if the Commission and the Court of Justice declared the illegality of the measures taken by the Portuguese authorities, the truth is that the merging parties abandoned their merging plans as a direct result of these tactics, which for Portugal still represented a triumph.

3.3.3 'Golden Shares'—*Commission v France*, 2002

On 4 June 2002, the court decided the action initiated by the Commission under article 226 EC to declare that articles 2(1) and (3) of Decree No 93-1298 of 13 December 1993, which bestowed the state with golden shares in Societe Nationale Elf-Aquitaine (Elf), a firm present in the petroleum market, were incompatible with the Treaty.

According to the referred Decree, the French Minister for Economic Affairs had to approve any transaction involving Elf if certain conditions were met and had the right to deny a transfer of capital decision.[67] Before the Commission started the infringement proceeding under article 226, it issued a formal notice to the French government who consider that the legal provisions were necessary to ensure the permanency of energy supplies but expressed its willingness to modify them. Following some amendments, the Commission was dissatisfied given that intervention was still justified in cases that 'might threaten to disrupt France's supplies of petroleum products', a consideration that, in the French authorities' view, forced the approval decision of a non-community company acquiring control of Societe National Elf-Aquitaine to be made by a local authority.[68]

In deciding the matter, the court considered that safeguarding supplies of petroleum products in times of crisis was a legitimate public interest. Nonetheless, it clarified that such an interest must be a genuine and sufficiently serious threat to a fundamental interest of society and that any obstacle to repealing it must be proportionate. These conditions that were not present in this case. In relation to article 2(1) of Decree 93-1298, the court denoted that such provisions did not indicate under which circumstances prior approval would be granted or refused, an omission that violated the principle of legal certainty contained in article 73(b) of the Treaty. As per article 2(3) of Decree 93-1298, the court found that the broad right to oppose transfers of capital was unrelated to the concern of maintaining a minimum supply of petroleum products and, therefore, regarded the measure as disproportionate.

Thus, the Court of Justice struck down the so-called 'golden share' regime in France in a sense that these kinds of state measures that prevent or dissuade cross-border

[67] Case C-483/99, *Commission v France*, Judgment of 4 June 2002.
[68] ibid.

investment may be in breach of the fundamental EC Treaty provisions on the free movement of capital and the freedom of establishment.[69]

3.3.4 *BBVA/BNL* and *ABN AMRO/Banca Antonveneta*, 2005

On 29 March 2005, the Spanish bank Banco Bilbao Vizcaya Argentaria (BBVA) announced the acquisition of the Italian bank Banca Nazionale de Lavoro (BNL), and a day after, the Dutch bank ABN AMRO also revealed its intention to purchase the Italian bank Banca Antonveneta (BA).[70] On 27 April 2005, the Commission authorized the two operations after finding that they did not raise any competition concerns.[71] However, considering that under Italian law both transactions require approval from the Bank of Italy,[72] they were blocked for apparently contravening prudential rules.[73] Simultaneously, the Bank of Italy tactfully encouraged the Italian bank Banca Popolare di Lodi (BPL) to bid for BA and the Italian insurer Unipol for BNL.[74] These actions triggered complaints from ABN who argued that the Bank of Italy violated article 21 EUMR by favouring the BPL's counter-bid, a claim that the Commission did not support.

Finally, after facing severe delays in adopting an approval decision and dealing with high levels of uncertainty, the Bank of Italy allowed the acquisition of BA by ABN AMRO to proceed.[75] Regarding BBVA, it complained that some of the conditions imposed by the Bank of Italy upon the acquisition of BNL did not respond to justifiable prudential rules and therefore were contrary to article 21 EUMR. In this case, the delay tactics used to find a more suitable buyer, the Italian insurer Unipol, who counter-bid for BNL, provoked the subsequent abandonment of the merger plans by BBVA, and the Commission did not act further under article 21 EUMR, purportedly because the lack of an active response from the Italian authorities to obstruct the operation.[76] At a later stage, it became public that the real reason that supported the rejection of the discussed foreign investments was a preference for a 'national consolidation' of the banking sector.[77]

This latest development provoked the Commission under article 226 to issue a letter to the Italian government in which it expressed that 'an exercise of supervisory authority which lacks procedural transparency and can create legal uncertainty' might

[69] Cleary Gottlieb Steen and Hamilton, 'ECJ Rules on Golden Shares' (Thomson Reuters Practical Law, 5 July 2022) https://uk.practicallaw.thomsonreuters.com/3-106-9737.

[70] Cases COMP/M. 3768 and COMP/M.3780, respectively.

[71] ibid.

[72] Elisa Zaera Cuadrado, 'Italian Cross-Border Banking Mergers: A Case for Article 21 of the Merger Regulation?' Directorate-General Competition, Unit D-4, Competition Policy Newsletter, No 3 Autumn 2005, 95, https://ec.europa.eu/competition/publications/cpn/2005_3_95.pdf accessed 15 September 2023.

[73] Mathias Koehler, 'Merger Control as Barrier to EU Banking Market Integration', Centre for European Economic Research, Discussion Paper No 07-082 (December 2009): 7, https://www.econstor.eu/bitstream/10419/29640/1/616485557.pdf accessed 15 September 2023.

[74] ibid 7.

[75] Cuadrado (n 72) 95.

[76] ibid; Koehler (n 73) 5; Gerard (n 29) 28.

[77] Koehler (n 73) 5; OECD (n 31) 7.

result in 'a disincentive to investment from other Member States in the Italian banking industry, in violation of EC Treaty rules on the free movement of capital (article 56) and the right of establishment (Article 43)'.[78] The Commission's decision to act under article 226 instead of article 21 EUMR contrasts with the approach observed in the Cimpor case, where the Commission and the court highlighted that the establishment of possible infringements to mergers with Community dimension is most suitable under article 21 in light of the short timelines that characterize merger procedures and that if they are not observed, the harm can be irreversible. Certainly, in this case the damage was witnessed when BBVA withdrew its bid, and ABN AMRO had to deal with great uncertainty. Indeed, the fact that the Bank of Italy as a national supervisory authority did not specify the criteria used to deny the operations, reducing its reasoning to ambiguous concerns such as the stability of governance, demonstrated the lack of procedural transparency, and the breadth of uncertainty afflicting the prudential assessment.[79] All these circumstances took place under the watch of the Commission who decided not to act in the face of the apparent Member State's inactivity.[80] Gerard has explained that the existence of EU secondary law, article 16 of Directive 2000/12/EC of March 2000, that gave *ex ante* powers to Member States to assess operations involving credit institutions, refrained the Commission from taking a more active role in this case and at the same time, generated a new regulatory framework governing the financial sector aimed at preventing similar situations in the future.[81]

The Commission supported the terms of the new regulatory framework in the results shown by a survey that revealed that the mishandling of supervisory powers, in this case, was not just confined to Italy but rather present in other EU countries.[82] Yet even if the new policy regime tried to improve the EU prudential framework, it has been noted that there is still a divergent approach amidst the Member States and that the procedures are not fully transparent.[83] In light of these remaining issues, it seems appropriate to advocate for more certainty, as in the view of the ECJ national measures that do not provide certainty are equivalent to unjustifiable restrictions on free movement.[84]

3.3.5 *Unicredit/HVB*, 2006

In June 2005, the Italian bank Unicredit sought to acquire the German bank Bayerische Hypo-und Vereinsbank AG (HVB), a transaction approved by the Commission in

[78] IP/05/1595, 14 December 2005.

[79] ibid.

[80] The ECJ has clarified that the inaction of a Member State is 'as likely to obstruct intra-Community trade as is a positive act'. See Case C-265/95, *Commission/France* [1997] ECR I-6959, para 31.

[81] Gerard (n 29) 28.

[82] Koehler (n 73) 1.

[83] Anna Gardella, Massimiliano Rimarchi, and Davide Stroppa, 'Potential Regulatory Obstacles to Cross-Border Mergers and Acquisitions in the EU Banking Sector' European Banking Authority Staff Paper, No 7 (February 2020) 2, https://www.eba.europa.eu/sites/default/documents/files/document_library/844126/Potential%20obstacles%20M&A.pdf accessed 15 September 2023.

[84] Case C-118/96, *Safir* [1998] ECR I-1897, para 29.

October 2005.[85] Nevertheless, it is relevant to refer to an important precedent to understand the issues at stake. During the 1990s, Poland entered a privatization process resulting in the acquisition of many public assets, including the Polish bank, BPH SA (BPH), which in 1998 was acquired by HVB subject to some non-compete clauses valid for a ten-year period. These clauses included the following prohibitions: (i) opening subsidiaries and/or branches in Poland, (ii) acquiring control of banks active in Poland, and (iii) investing in any company active in the Polish banking sector.[86] Similarly, in 1999, another state-owned bank Polska Kasa Opieki SA (Pekao) was acquired by Unicredit under the same non-compete clauses described earlier.[87]

In this context, the Polish government reacted vigorously against the Commission's decision to approve it. Firstly, by claiming that the supranational authority had diminished the reliability of the Polish privatization process. Secondly, by demanding the fulfilment of the non-compete clauses through the order that in February 2006 the Polish Treasury had given to Unicredit, to sell BPH's shares in three months—an order accompanied by the warning that failure to comply would result in the annulment of the whole Pekao privatization agreement.[88] However, the Polish government failed to request the Commission's assessment of its legitimate interests under article 21(4). Thirdly, by filing an action against the Commission, accusing it of breaching article 10 EC that refers to the duty of loyal cooperation, which in the Polish government's view was transgressed when its legitimate interests of de-monopolization and privatization were ignored.[89]

Subsequently, in 2006, the Commission initiated infringement proceedings against Poland for considering that the restraints contained in the privatization agreements prevented the free movement of capital.[90] At the same time, under article 21 EUMR rules, the Commission launched a procedure arguing that the enforcement of the non-compete clauses, that were part of the privatization agreements, constituted measures taken by the Polish government capable of impeding the consummation of the already approved Unicredit/HVB merger. Adding, they were disproportional, and no other hypothetical interests had been communicated, which led it to determine that they appeared to be incompatible with the EC law.[91] Before the period that the Commission gave to the Polish authorities to justify their actions expired, an agreement between the Member State and Unicredit/HVB was announced, in which the merger was endorsed subject to the commitment to sell the BPH brand, the divestiture of 200 of the 480 BPH's branches, and the promise not to eliminate jobs from BPH or Pekao until March 2008.[92]

[85] Case COMP/M.3894 *Unicredit/HVB*.
[86] IP/06/277, 8 March 2006.
[87] ibid.
[88] Harker (n 17) 519.
[89] [2006] OJ C96/18.
[90] IP/06/276, 8 March 2006.
[91] ibid.
[92] Mark Landler, 'Unicredit and Poland Reach Deal on 2 Banks' *New York Times* (5 April 2006), https://www.nytimes.com/2006/04/05/business/worldbusiness/unicredit-and-poland-reach-deal-on-2-banks.html accessed 15 September 2023.

This case exemplifies the adoption of *ex ante* measures contained in privatization provisions envisaged to secure that foreign deals would not expand beyond the boundaries admitted by the national authorities, in this case, non-compete clauses. Restraints that were unduly enforced to prevent a deal already approved by the Commission but rejected by the Member State, under the unsupported claim to protect competition. The case shows again that Member States choose not to follow article 21(4) rules, carrying the risks of possible infringement outcomes, as their desire to protect their interests is more predominant. Perhaps most importantly, it also demonstrates that the intervention was so effective that the Member State finally succeeded in defending its position. A circumstance that contrasts with the perception regarding this case that was publicly expressed by the Competition Commissioner, Neelie Kroes, to whom the Commission was prepared to impede that Member States do not 'stand in the way of mergers falling within the Commission's exclusive competence'.[93]

3.3.6 *Endesa*, 2006

In September 2005, Gas Natural, a Spanish energy company announced a bid for Endesa, a Spanish electricity undertaking one of the largest utility companies in Spain.[94] Endesa's board rejected the bid after finding it inadequate and contrary to the interests of its shareholders, so they committed to defend the self-government of the company.[95] Then, Endesa requested the Commission's authority to review the merger by arguing that it had a Community dimension, which was denied according to the 'two-thirds rule',[96] and instead the jurisdiction rested with the Spanish government which in February 2006 approved the transaction subject to some conditions,[97] in spite of the opinion provided by the Spanish Competition Defence Tribunal (CDT) that the deal should be prohibited as it would have an anticompetitive impact on the energy markets.[98] It is important to note that while the national authorities were reviewing the deal, Endesa filed a claim before a commercial court in Madrid alleging an anticompetitive conspiracy derived from the bid, which was substantiated resulting in a court order to suspend the Gas Natural bid for some months, a decision that months later was reversed by a Provincial Court of Appeals.[99]

[93] IP/06/277, 8 March 2006.

[94] Francisco Marcos, 'When Competition is the Last Concern: The Battle for the Control of ENDESA', Working Paper IE Law School AJ8-189 (Sept. 3, 2012): 8.

[95] ibid 9.

[96] Case COMP/M.3986 *Gas Natural/Endesa*. Decision declaring the lack of a Community dimension, 15 November 2005 (C(2005) 4468). Endesa argued that less than two-thirds of its Community-wide turnover was located within Spain. Endesa then challenged the Commission's decision and requested some interim measures that were denied and later, in July 2006, confirmed by the General Court. See [2006] OJ C22/20–21; *Endesa/Commission* T-417/05 R order 1 February 2006 and *Endesa/Commission* T-417/05, Judgment 14 July 2006.

[97] Economy and Treasury Ministry Order EHA/193/2006, 3 February 2006.

[98] CDC Report C-94/05, *Gas Natural/Endesa*.

[99] Judicial Decree of the Commercial Judge No 8, 21 March 2006 and Judicial Decree of the Madrid Provincial Court No 28, 15 January 2007 (Proc 523/2005).

In the middle of Endesa's resistance, on 21 February 2006, E.ON, the largest German energy group at that time, made a competing bid for all Endesa's shares welcomed by Endesa's board, who apparently encouraged the offer but was rejected by the Spanish government who immediately enacted a regulation so-called the 'anti-E.ON Decree'.[100] This regulation incremented the powers of the regulator by requiring its prior approval if more than 10 per cent of share capital of a regulated company was involved and set specific conditions to grant it, applicable to all ongoing transactions, including E.ON, that acted accordingly and in June 2006, the regulator approved the deal subject to multiple conditions,[101] a decision that was appealed before the Minister for Industry, Tourism and Commerce who held some of the conditions.[102] At this point, it is important to highlight that on 25 April 2006, the Commission had already approved the transaction according to the EUMR.[103] In response, the Commission initiated two infringement procedures, one related to article 226 EC in which it was declared that the Decree 4/2006 violated the freedoms of capital and establishment,[104] and another referred to article 21(4) EUMR where the Commission declared the illegality of the conditions imposed to E.ON by the Spanish government to allegedly protect public security concerns, which in the Commission's view were unsubstantiated, discriminatory, and disproportionate, and requested their suspension, an order that was not followed and ended up in the EU Court of Justice, that in March 2008 coincided with the Commission's position and asserted that Spain failed to observe the EC Treaty.[105] The court said that at the time the Spanish government imposed them it was unlikely to anticipate the effects of the transaction in terms of security of supply, and that in any case the regulator had the power to repeal any possible threat at any time.[106]

A further development took place in April 2007 when E.ON announced the abandonment of its intention to bid for Endesa, an event preceded by the acquirement of some of Endesa's shares by the Italian State-Owned Enterprise ENEL and the Spanish construction firm Acciona, who together launched a bid for Endesa and who offered some assets to E.ON in exchange for the withdrawal of its bid.[107] This Acciona/ENEL offer was approved by the Spanish regulator subject to certain conditions and simultaneously unconditionally approved by the Commission.[108]

[100] Decree 4/2006; see Marcos (n 94) 22.

[101] Among the conditions, the obligation that Endesa would continue to be the parent of the group for ten years, the suspension of voting rights in case the conditions were not observed, the divestiture of assets located outside Spain, the commitment to ensure the investment plans of Endesa in tactical assets, the guarantee to allocate dividends restrictively, and that their members of the board would remain located in Madrid. In relation to the latter, Endesa argued that by keeping these members in Madrid, it would be easy to ensure the security of supply, including assets and transfers of income. See Harker (n 17) 514.

[102] Case COMP/M. 4197 *E.ON/Endesa*.

[103] Case COMP/M. 4110 *E.ON/Endesa*, 25 April 2006.

[104] See IP/07/1374, 21 September 2007.

[105] See Judgments of the Court (Third Chamber) 6 March 2008, *Commission of the EC v Kingdom of Spain*, Case C-196/07 [ECR 2008 I-00041] and of 17 July 2008, *Commission of the EC v Kingdom of Spain*, Case C-207/07 [ECR 2008 I-00111].

[106] See Judgments of the Court (Third Chamber) 6 March 2008, *Commission of the EC v Kingdom of Spain*, Case C-196/07 [ECR 2008 I-00041] and of 17 July 2008, *Commission of the EC v Kingdom of Spain*, Case C-207/07 [ECR 2008 I-00111].

[107] Marcos (n 94) 26–27; Harker (n 17) 517.

[108] Case COMP/M.4685 *Enel/Acciona/Endesa*; Case COMP/M. 5171 *Enel/Acciona/Endesa*.

Undoubtedly, this case offers important lessons. Firstly, the Commission had the opportunity to shed some light on the meaning of public security as a legitimate interest, which can be invoked when there are authentic and sufficient hazards that could compromise, as in the *Endesa* case, the supply of energy. Secondly, it has shown that national interests are well embedded among public and private stakeholders and as a result, they play a key role in guiding their actions despite the legal consequences for breaching the rules of the Union. Thirdly, it confirms the effectiveness of the Member States' measures to hinder transactions not aligned with their interests. In the *Endesa* case, the tender offer presented in September 2005 by Gas Natural was finally concluded in July 2007 with the approval of the acquisition by Acciona/Enel, thanks to diverse strategies implemented to dilate the process.

3.3.7 *Abertis/Autostrade*, 2006

In September 2006, the Commission approved the merger between Abertis, a Spanish company present in the controlling of toll motorways in Spain and some other countries, and Autostrade, the holding company of Autostrade per I'Italia SpA, the holder of the concession for the management and maintenance of the Italian toll motorway network, as the transaction did not raise concerns.[109] Before the Commission reached a decision about this cross-border merger, on 4 August 2006, the Italian Infrastructure Minister made public a negative opinion about the transaction, alleging a conflict of interest and distrust about Abertis' ability to undertake the necessary investment to conserve and develop the Italian motorway network under the qualitative and security standards.[110] A day later, on 5 August 2006, the public authority in charge of granting motorway concessions in Italy (ANAS) issued a decision rejecting Autostrade's request to merge with Abertis.[111] Shortly after the merger was cleared, the Commission reached a preliminary conclusion that the Minister's opinion and ANAS's rejection violated article 21 of the EUMR after finding the factual and legal basis on which the concerns were based unclear, the public interest that was supposedly harmful vague, that the concession itself was sufficient to address any public interest and that Italy did not communicate the taken measures to the Commission.[112]

Later, on 7 November 2006, a meeting between the Italian Minister for Public Works and the European Commissioner for Competition took place, resulting in the commitment from the Italian government to remove any unjustified obstacle regarding the Abertis/Autostrade merger and its unconditional cooperation with the Commission 'in ensuring that this cross-border merger can take place without unjustified hindrance', a position that the Commission welcomed.[113] In spite of the good spirit, the

[109] IP/06/1244, 22 September 2006.
[110] IP/06/1418, 18 October 2006.
[111] ibid.
[112] ibid.
[113] MEMO/06/414, 7 November 2006.

Italian government adopted an urgent legal provision altering the rules applicable to motorway concession operators, including the power to unilaterally modify the terms and conditions of the current concession contracts, the limitation on voting rights, and the increment of the fee concessions from 1 per cent to 2.4 per cent, subject to a withdrawal of the existing concession in case of a disagreement between the concessionaries and the Italian authorities.[114]

In light of this latest development, the merging parties suspended the transaction until a solution was reached. In the meantime, the Commission opened infringement proceedings against Italy in relation to the new regime for motorway concession, in which it expressed its concerns that the uncertainty that the reform entailed could discourage investors. At the same time, it was found that the regulation infringed on the free movement of capital and the right of establishment, given the lack of clarity about its pursued objectives and the lack of validation of the measures. Likewise, the Commission considered that the threat of withdrawal of the existing concessions enlarged the restrictive effects of the provision.[115]

On 5 January 2007, the Italian Minister for Infrastructure and the Commissioner for Competition met again to discuss the Italian authorization procedure for transferring Autostrade motorway concessions. The Commissioner stated disappointment regarding the lack of cooperation from the Italian authorities and clarified that while any action to confirm whether concession holders remain financially viable does not deserve to be condemned; any further actions orientated at extracting far-reaching outcomes to solve past or future issues emerging from existing concessions remain questionable.[116] Afterwards, on 31 January 2007, the Commission concluded that Italy had violated article 21 EUMR by not authorizing the transfer of the motorway concession to the newly merged entity.[117] Lastly, in July 2007, the Commission accepted the rules that the Italian government introduced to clarify the regulatory framework for the authorization of the transfer of motorway concessions, and closed its case under article 21 EUMR. In particular, the Commission was satisfied with the two limited requirements of the proposed rules involving mergers with a Community dimension; this is that the new concessionaire (i) undertakes all the existing obligations of the previous concessionaire and (ii) enjoys all the financial and technical resources to fulfil those obligations.[118] Additionally, the Competition Commissioner Neelie Kroes stressed:

> I trust that the changes being introduced by the Italian authorities will ensure that there is no recurrence of the issues that the Commission raised in its preliminary assessments. I will continue monitoring the situation to ensure that in cases of future cross-border mergers in this sector, companies will be treated fairly and in compliance with Community rules.[119]

[114] See Decree-Law No 262/2006 of 29 September 2006, as amended.
[115] IP/06/1561, 14 November 2006.
[116] MEMO/07/01, 5 January 2007.
[117] IP/07/117, 31 January 2007.
[118] IP/07/1119, 18 July 2007.
[119] ibid.

In the *Abertis/Autostrade* case, the Italian government quickly moved from exercising moral persuasion to effectively using 'golden shares' measures that took the form of *ex post* domestic regulation, indisputably targeting the approved merger. The purpose that surrounded the enactment of this new regulatory framework was so evident that it was almost impossible for the Member State to convince the Commission otherwise, especially considering the involved threat of ending the concession, an aspect that emphasized how discriminatory and disproportionate the measures were. In the aftermath, even if the Italian government amended the scrutinized regulation, the consummation of the merger was hampered, and the initial promises made to the Commission were flagrantly ignored.

The analysis of the case law shows that the Commission holds a narrow view that the protection of national interests and key sectors of the national economies usually results in the violation of the principles of freedom of establishment and free movement of capital in the EU.

It is also clear that solely economic factors are inadequate to justify such fundamental rights. Likewise, Member States are prepared to challenge the authority of the Commission if their alleged legitimate interests are threatened, and the adoption of a broad range of measures has proven effective. Unsurprisingly, there is an increased concern that among Member States, the promotion of nationalism objectives through restricting foreign acquisitions is widespread. Even if there have been a number of cases in which Member States have tried to rely on recognized interests to review a merger, recognition of other legitimate interests has been rare.

Besides the examined EUMR, another important regulation allows the control of inward FDI via FDI screening mechanisms, which have recently been reformed at the EU level. The next part will explore the main modifications in more detail.

3.4 The EU Framework Regulation for the Screening of Foreign Direct Investment

3.4.1 Regulation 2019/452 of 19 March 2019 Establishing a Framework for the Screening of Foreign Direct Investments into the EU

As indicated in the previous section, the staggering increase of Chinese FDI across almost all EU Member States alerted the European governments who perceived this M&A activity as a threat to their national security. Consequently, some Member States tried to interfere with Community dimension transactions, a tendency described as the 'renaissance of protectionism'.[120] However, as this chapter has shown, the measures adopted by Member States under the legitimate interests contained in article 21(4) targeted operations between Member States rather than those from non-EU acquirers.

[120] Kroes (n 10).

Also, Member States have long been requesting the adoption of a common system of evaluation on national security grounds.[121]

As an illustration, as early as in 2007, Germany requested the development of a system orientated to assess FDI plans on national security-based grounds, resembling the existing CFIUS scheme already adopted in the US for the same purpose.[122] This suggestion that was echoed by the EU Commissioner Michel Barnier who also mentioned that such a scheme adopted in the US could be a workable solution in the EU, whereby an EU authority with the power to prohibit operations involving advanced technology seemed necessary.[123] Most recently, in 2017, the governments of Germany, France, and Italy sent a letter to the EU Trade Commissioner promoting the creation of a mechanism to oppose the acquisition of EU companies by foreign firms involved in the technological sector, following concerns that the existing tools were ineffective.[124] These concerns, it has been reported, derived from the scarce number of occasions in which the Commission has endorsed the legitimate interests put forward by Member States in an attempt to repeal foreign investors.[125] Unsurprisingly, in July 2017, Germany announced a reform to its FDI screening regime, reinforcing the powers to veto foreign takeovers, and few months later the UK made a similar announcement regarding the acquisition of military and high-tech firms on the grounds of national security and France has extended the existing FDI rules to include other sectors.[126] In particular, the French President Emmanuel Macron referred to the permissive approach towards the fast acquisition of EU infrastructure by China as a 'strategic error'.[127] The pressure has also amounted from the media who has extensively covered China's outward foreign direct investment (OFDI) in a wide range of sectors across the EU, politicians, and the academia.[128]

Gradually, the European Commission started devoting more attention to the matter. Thus, in May 2017, while recognizing that FDI fosters growth, it also admitted the common concern that European firms developing key technologies were at risk of vanishing into the hands of foreign investors, particularly non-EU state-owned businesses, concerns that, it added, 'need careful analysis and appropriate action'.[129] On

[121] Jost Wubbeke and others, 'Made in China 2025: The Making of a High-tech Superpower and Consequences for Industrial Countries' (2016) Merics Papers on China No 2, December 2016, 61 https://merics.org/en/report/made-china-2025 https://www.merics.org/en/papers-on-china/made-china-2025 accessed 15 September 2023.

[122] Esplugues (n 6).

[123] Haiyan Zhang and Daniel Van Den Bulcke, 'China's Direct Investment in the European Union: A New Regulatory Change?' (2014) 12 Asia Europe Journal, 159–177, 162.

[124] Reuters, 'Italy, France, Germany ask EU to Boost Powers to Block Foreign Acquisitions—Reports' (22 August 2017) https://www.reuters.com/article/us-europe-m-a-regulations-idUSKCN1B20IP accessed 15 September 2023.

[125] Angela Huyue Zhang, 'The Single Entity Theory: An Antitrust Time-Bomb for Chinese State-Owned Enterprises?' (2012) 8(4) Journal of Competition Law and Economics 805, 807.

[126] Kyriakos Fountoukakos, Veronica Roberts, and Ruth Allen, 'Addressing National Security Concerns in the Merger Context', in Ioannis Kokkoris and Claudia Lemus (eds), *Research Handbook on the Law and Economics of Competition Enforcement* (Edward Elgar 2022) 217.

[127] Philip Blenkinsop and Robin Emmott, 'EU Leaders Call for End to "Naivety" in Relations with China' (Reuters, 22 March 2019) https://www.reuters.com/article/us-eu-china-idUSKCN1R31H3 accessed 15 September 2023.

[128] Zhang and Van Den Bulcke (n 123), 161–62 (2014); Esplugues (n 6).

[129] European Commission, Reflection Paper on Harnessing Globalisation, 15 (2017).

13 September 2017, the Commission proposed a Regulation determining a framework for screening FDI into the EU.[130] The announcement of the regulation was accompanied by a more manifest sense of nationalism observed in the welcoming FDI document in which the European Commission stated that one of the two main objectives of the regulation was to defend EU assets from transactions against the essential interests of the Union or its members,[131] and in the President of the European Commission's speech, who expressed that 'Europe must always defend its strategic interests and that is precisely what this new framework will help us to do. This is what I mean when I say we are not naïve free traders.' The proposal acknowledged that while some countries have adopted proper FDI screening mechanisms, the EU has failed to afford the same importance to the subject. Broadly, the proposal contemplated that the Commission would have the authority to carry out the screening of FDI affecting projects or programmes of Union interest; it proposed a framework for coordination between the Member States and the Member States and the Commission, it provided a set of basic procedural standards for national FDI screenings governed by the principles of transparency, non-discrimination, and confidentiality, and it enabled the Commission to issue non-binding opinions to the Member States concerned.[132]

As part of the proposal, in March 2019, the European Commission presented a working document on foreign investment in the EU, containing an analysis of FDI flows into the EU.[133] Among the most salient findings in this FDI working document, the European Commission noted the fact that between 2007 and 2017 the number of acquisitions by state-owned entities (SOEs), particularly from China, Russia, and the United Arab Emirates, was three times higher, that the number of acquisitions involving individuals or families had increased from thirty-one to 197, and that in the period 2012–16, EU assets owned by the Chinese state soared from almost €16 billion to around €160 billion.[134] The document also admitted that the majority of Chinese operations could be associated with the Chinese government as they normally require its authorization and usually receive loans approved by Chinese banks, which are mostly controlled by the government.[135]

Some commentators who have attentively been examining the relationship between the Chinese state and the SOEs, have extended these two aspects indicated by the European Commission, with the fact that China's Communist Party (CCP) controls

[130] European Commission, 'Proposal for a Regulation of the European Parliament and of the Council establishing a framework for screening of foreign direct investments into the European Union' COM(2017) 487 final.

[131] European Commission, Communication 'Welcoming Foreign Direct Investment while Protecting Essential Interests' COM (2017) 494 final.

[132] European Commission, 'Proposal for a Regulation of the European Parliament and of the Council establishing a framework for screening of foreign direct investments into the European Union', COM(2017) 487 final (13 September 2017).

[133] European Commission, Commission Staff Working Document on Foreign Direct Investment in the EU: Following up on the Commission Communication 'Welcoming Foreign Direct Investment while Protecting Essential Interests' of 13 September 2017, SWD(2019) 108 final.

[134] ibid 57. Hanemann and others have noted that since 2000, almost 60 per cent of Chinese FDI in Europe came from SOEs or sovereign entities in China. See Thilo Hanmann, Mikko Huotari, and Agatha Kratz, 'Chinese FDI in Europe: 2018 Trends and Impact of New Screening Policies', Merics Papers on China, 18 (March 2019).

[135] European Commission (n 133), 56.

the Chinese economy and within it the SOEs, including the control over the SOEs' personnel, meaning that the management of these entities are designated by the CCP, who are expected to follow the party's policies; an assumption that remains valid despite some observed intentions to recruit global talent, which does not remove the incontrovertible strong ties between the CCP and the SOEs management.[136] Indeed, it has been indicated that SOEs are a crucial part of the most recent Chinese economic strategy aimed at becoming a 'globally competitive manufacturing superpower largely independent of foreign technology', as revealed in the 'Made in China 2025' strategy.[137] According to China's plan, this will be achieved by modernizing the following targeted industries: aviation, machinery, robotics, railway equipment, energy-saving vehicles, among others.[138] This approach, Meunier has noted, is not new as historically Chinese investments have been influenced by the aspiration to acquire superior technology companies rather than allocating huge amounts of money into developing new ones. Furthermore, it has been argued that Chinese FDI has been characterized by the desire to exploit managerial know-how by building the reputation of recognized brands instead of creating them from scratch, by the need to expand the service of Chinese companies abroad, and by evading trade barriers.[139]

In this context, Regulation (EU) 2019/452 of the European Parliament and of the Council of March 2019 (the Regulation) established a framework for screening FDI into the Union that came into force in October 2020.[140] The latter does not apply to intra-EU investments.[141] By adopting this Regulation, the EU sought to establish Union-wide coordination and cooperation mechanisms on screening, including through a set of recommendations and principles governing the screening of investments.[142]

Unlike the EUMR, the Regulation does not give the European Commission the power to disapprove the FDI, and instead, the final decision still rests solely in the Member State where the FDI screening is taking place. However, it is worth noting that this is the first time that the European Commission will have a role in the assessment of FDI, a matter that was entirely reserved for Member States.[143] The scope of the regulation covers FDI into the Union on the grounds of security or public order, restricting the intervention of the European Commission to just issuing opinions, and it covers only M&A to be reviewed, omitting greenfield or portfolio investments.[144] Likewise, the Regulation does not establish a united EU-wide screening mechanism, leaving it up to the Member States to adopt their own national screening instruments.[145]

[136] Zhang (n 125) 813.

[137] Max J Zenglein, Anna Holzmann, 'Evolving Made in China 2025 China's Industrial Policy in the Quest for Global Tech Leadership', Merics Papers on China No 8 (2019): p 7, https://www.merics.org/sites/default/files/2019-07/MPOC_8_MadeinChina_2025_final_3.pdf accessed 15 September 2023.

[138] Wubbeke and others (n 121) 5.

[139] Meunier (n 7).

[140] [2019] OJ L 79/I 1.

[141] Kyriakos Fountoukakos, Daniel Vowden, and Daniel Barrio, 'European Union: Foreign Direct Investment Regulations', Global Competition Review, 6 December 2022

[142] UNCTAD, 'The Evolution of FDI Screening Mechanism', Key Trends and Features, Issue 25, February 2023.

[143] Regulation (EU) 2019/452, art 6(9).

[144] ibid art 1(1).

[145] ibid art 3(1).

The notions of 'security' and 'public order' are not defined under the Regulation. However, the provision includes five factors likely to trigger security or public order concerns if acquired by foreign investors:

1) critical infrastructure, counting a wide range of sectors from health to electoral or financial infrastructure;
2) critical technologies and dual-use items;
3) supply of critical inputs, comprising energy or raw materials, as well as food security;
4) access to sensitive information, including personal data, or the ability to control such information; and
5) the freedom and pluralism of media.[146]

In this regard, it is noted that it is likely that Member States do not enjoy the appropriate amount of information to assess the deals or the capacity to identify the threats within the array of designated sectors.[147] Further, some commentators have indicated the lack of reasoning behind the inclusion of some sectors such as media or food security, which according to the statistics, do not attract the interest of Chinese investors.[148]

Article 4(2) further provides that, in determining whether FDI is likely to affect security or public order, the Member States and the Commission may also take into account whether the foreign investor is directly or indirectly controlled by the government of a third country, including through significant state-backed funding rather than direct ownership[149].

Also, the Regulation imposes a duty on the Member States to annually inform the Commission about the FDI taking place in their territory,[150] a measure envisaged to promote convergence. Equally, the Regulation establishes a rather cumbersome co-operation mechanism in which the Member State concerned needs to notify the Commission and the other Member States of any FDI that could raise any security or public order concerns so that the Commission can issue an opinion and the other Member States can provide comments. The Member State where the FDI is taking place is responsible for the final decision.[151] With this complicated regime, it is possible to envisage a situation in which information needs to be shared among twenty-eight countries and the European Commission, all of them entitled to provide comments, not to mention the possibility to request additional information. This situation does

[146] ibid art 4(1).

[147] Wolf Zwartkruis and Bas De Jong, 'The EU Regulation on Screening of Foreign Direct Investment: A Game Changer?' (2020) 31(3) European Business Law Review 447, 469.

[148] Pawet Mateusz Gadocha, 'Assessing the EU Framework Regulation for the Screening of Foreign Direct Investment—What is the Effect on Chinese Investors?' (2020) 6 The Chinese Journal of Global Governance 57.

[149] Regulation (EU) 2019/452, art 4(2)

[150] ibid art 5(1).

[151] ibid art 6 states that once the Member State has notified the Commission and the other Member States of any FDI, the Member States have fifteen calendar days to inform the Member State concerned about their intention to provide comments; this needs to be within thirty-five calendar days following receipt of the initial notice. The Commission has an extra five calendar days beyond the thirty-five to deliver its opinion.

not favour the short timelines in an M&A transaction and can impact the merger control process. As an illustration, Austria has expanded Phase I of its merger assessment from one to two months to accommodate the duration of the European FDI screening, a change that some other Member States might also need to consider.[152]

Another unclear aspect is whether foreign investors will have access to the comments and opinions delivered by the Member States and the Commission. Overall, it is questionable how this intricate mechanism of collaboration would improve the FDI decision-making process at a national level. It makes one wonder why the Regulation did not increase the Commission's capacity to oppose FDI, as initially contemplated in the proposal. The next section examines the reasons behind this segregated approach.

The fundamental cause that impeded the adoption of a unified FDI screening authority and mechanism within the EU was divergent views among Member States about the benefits of Chinese investments.

On one side, Germany and France called for a more stringent approach supporting the idea of having a centralized authority as they perceive Chinese investment as a threat, and on the other side, the Nordic and Mediterranean countries see Chinese investment as a crucial part of their economies. This latter coalition successfully influenced the adoption of a weak FDI screening device.[153] Interestingly, during the discussions prior to the adoption of the regulation, Finland described the proposal as the emergence of protectionism from EU's 'major players' and Greece requested compensation for the harm that its economy would suffer if the Chinese investment was banished.[154] This concern from Greece arose from the Belt and Road Initiative (BRI), an idea conceived by Chinese firms that consists of building a cross-border transport corridor from the Mediterranean to Central Europe aiming at decreasing transportation costs and facilitating entry to the European market,[155] combined with the development of a logistics hub in the city of Pireaus by Huawei and ZTE.[156] This increased inflow of Chinese investments in Greece explains why some Member States were more interested in preserving their macroeconomic domestic benefits rather than supporting the adoption of a common EU-wide screening regime that 'would have effectively removed their authority over certain key transactions'.[157] In short, the regulation did not

[152] Samantha J Mobley, Anita Lukaschek, and Luca Montani, 'The EU Foreign Investment Mechanism is Now Operational' (Baker McKenzie, 14 October 2020) https://insightplus.bakermckenzie.com/bm/antitrust-competition_1/eu-the-eu-foreign-investment-mechanism-is-now-operational accessed 15 September 2023.

[153] Ethan Kable, 'Buying Influence? An Analysis of the Political and Economic Impacts of Chinese Foreign Direct Investment in the European Union', CMC Senior Thesis 2510 (2020) 61–63, https://scholarship.claremont.edu/cmc_theses/2510 accessed 15 September 2023.

[154] Laurens Cerulus and Jakob Hanke Vela, 'Enter the Dragon', POLITICO (4 October 2017) https://www.politico.eu/article/china-and-the-troika-portugal-foreign-investment-screening-takeovers-europe/ accessed 15 September 2023.

[155] Plamen Tonchev, 'China's Road: Into the Western Balkans' (European Union Institute for Security Studies, 15 February 2017) https://css.ethz.ch/content/dam/ethz/special-interest/gess/cis/center-for-securities-studies/resources/docs/EUISS-Brief_3_China_Western_Balkans.pdf accessed 15 September 2023.

[156] John Seaman, Mikko Huotari, and Miguel Otero-Iglesias, 'Chinese Investment in Europe. A Country-Level Approach', A Report by the European Think-tank Network on China (ETNC) December 2017, 73, https://merics.org/sites/default/files/2020-04/171216_ETNC%20Report%202017_0.pdf accessed 15 September 2023.

[157] It has been reported that they are welcomed 'without asking some necessary questions', see ibid 74. This report also covers Chinese Investments in other European countries like Portugal, Romania, Slovakia, Spain, Hungary, and the Netherlands.

accomplish harmonization among the national screening provisions, which differ in terms of scope (some cover just transactions from non-EU countries, others also include EU countries), nature (France covers the gambling sector and Greece the acquisition of land), procedures (some have adopted *ex ante* reviews, others *ex post*), and level of development, leaving non-EU business interested in investing in the EU facing significant levels of uncertainty that arise from the unrestricted flexibility and the divergence of the Member States' FDI regimes.[158]

This is a situation that becomes even more complex when one considers that not every Member State has a national screening system and that, according to the Regulation, are not compelled to adopt one, such as Bulgaria and Cyprus, which have not shown any intention to implement them,[159] but that in any case still has the choice to consider comments and opinions in their 'broader policy making'.[160]

However, in line with international progress, there is a rising number of FDI screening regimes. The legislative developments in 2021 will be studied later in this section. In 2020, the government of Malta announced that it had established a National Office for FDI Screening as an implementing entity for the EU Regulations on FDI screening.[161] Furthermore, Luxembourg has recently announced that it was ready to launch a foreign investment screening regime meant to catch investments by non-EEA investors. More specifically, this new regime will apply to companies governed by Luxembourg law and that carry out 'critical activities', such as the aerospace sector, the communication sector, the energy sector, and others.[162] The Estonian Parliament adopted the Foreign Investment Reliability Assessment Act on 25 January 2023 which will enter into force on 1 September 2023.[163] The Irish government has proposed to introduce a new foreign investment screening regime in Ireland. An initial draft of the Screening of Third Country Transactions Bill 2022 was published on 2 August 2022, and an updated draft was published on 25 January 2023. This new tool will enable the Minister for Enterprise, Trade and Employment to review, for the first time, transactions involving foreign investment that may impact on security or public order in Ireland.[164]

In May 2022, the Dutch Senate adopted the Investments, Mergers and Acquisitions Security Screening Bill (ISSB), introducing a mandatory and suspensory review mechanism for investments that may affect Dutch national security. The latter will apply regardless of the acquirer's country of origin. The Dutch Minister of Defence is also

[158] Catriona Hatton, Brian R Byrne, and Alexandre Lichy, 'The EU's FDI Proposal. What Does it Mean and How Will it Interact with EU Merger Control?' Competition Law Insight, Business Intelligence/Informa, Vol 17, 3 (March 2018), 1.

[159] Information relevant by 2019, see Thilo Hanmann, Mikko Huotari, Agatha Kratz, 'Chinese FDI in Europe: 2018 Trends and Impact of New Screening Policies', Merics Papers on China, 16–17 (March 2019).

[160] See the Commission's explanation of art 8 in the Explanatory Memorandum accompanying the Proposal.

[161] UNCTAD, Investment Policy Hub, 'Malta establishes the National Office for Foreign Direct Investment Screening', 12 June 2020.

[162] Linklaters, 'Foreign investment control in the Benelux ... Part 3—Luxembourg set to launch foreign investment screening regime', 22 October 2022.

[163] Tonis Tamme, 'Estonia to Start Reviewing the Credibility of Foreign Investments', https://triniti.eu/insights/estonia-to-start-reviewing-the-credibility-of-foreign-investments accessed 15 September 2023.

[164] Arthur Cox, 'An Overview of the Proposed Foreign Investment Screening Regime in Ireland', 10 February 2023

preparing a bill to protect the Dutch defence technological and industrial sector. It will introduce a sector-specific test which will also entail *ex ante* screening.[165]

On 1 June 2022, the federal and regional governments in Belgium agreed a draft legislative text for a Belgian FI screening regime, expected to enter into force on 1 July 2023.[166] The draft proposed mandatory and suspensory FDI filing requirement for investments by non-EU businesses in existing Belgian entities active in key sectors, including critical infrastructure, defence, supply of critical inputs, digital infrastructure, and cybersecurity.[167] The new regime was expected to enter into force on 1 January 2023 and will principally affect investors from outside the EU. The regime will apply to investments that have not yet closed at the time the rules enter into force.[168] At the end of 2022, the National Council of the Slovak Republic adopted Act No 497/2022 Coll. on Screening Foreign Investments.[169]

In relation to FDI that potentially could affect projects or programmes of Union interest, the Regulation indicates that the Commission can conduct a security review of the related transaction and provide the Member State concerned with an opinion, which is non-binding but that triggers an explanation in case of deviation.[170] Even if the Member State needs to provide a justification if the final decision is contrary to the Commission's opinion, the power to decide rests with the Member State. At the moment, the Regulation includes eight European-funded projects, among them: Galileo and EGNOS, Copernicus, Horizon 2020, Trans-European Networks for Transport, Trans-European Networks for Energy, Trans-European Networks for Telecommunications, European Defence Industrial Development Programme, and Permanent Structured Cooperation (PESCO).[171]

In procedural terms, the Regulation establishes some information requirement principles[172] and ensures that any exchanged information should be treated as confidential and protected as such.[173] However, it is important to remember that the Treaty contemplates that no Member State is bound to provide information 'contrary to the essential interests of its security' and is entitled to take the required measures aimed at protecting themselves.[174] Another relevant aspect covered by the Regulation, is the right granted to foreign investors and concerned undertakings to seek recourse against a screening decision adopted by a national authority.[175] Yet, the framework does not provide for a

165 Gerrit Oosterhuis and others, 'Foreign Direct Investment Regimes Netherlands', 30 November 2022, https://iclg.com/practice-areas/foreign-direct-investment-regimes-laws-and-regulations/netherlands accessed 15 September 2023.

166 Lodewick Prompers, Sari Corrijn, Florian Jonniaux, and Lucas Macharis, 'Foreign Investment Control in the Benelux... Part 1—Belgium to Start Screening Foreign Investments', 28 September 2022.

167 Christopher Kimball, Christine Graham, Anna Caro, and Penelope Hale, 'Global Developments in Foreign Direct Investment Screening Regimes', 30 November 2022.

168 Ashurst, 'Proposals for new FDI regimes in Belgium, Ireland and the Netherlands', 3 October 2022.

169 Zuzana Nikodemova and Oliver Göndör, 'The New Act on Screening Foreign Investments Due to Come into Force from 1 March 2023', 28 February 2023.

170 Regulation (EU) 2019/452, art 8.

171 ibid, annex.

172 ibid, art 9.

173 ibid, art 10.

174 Martin Trybus, 'The EC Treaty as an Instrument of European Defence Integration: Judicial Scrutiny of Defence and Security Exceptions' (2002) 39 Common Market Law Review 6, 1369, 1354.

175 Regulation (EU) 2019/452, Art 3(5).

specific procedure to make use of this right of defence, which implies that the parties could effectively enjoy this legal instrument in those Member States where it is available. At the same time, the Regulation imposes the obligation to maintain, amend or adopt measures required to ensure the effectiveness of the national screening mechanisms, a duty that the Member States without them do not need to assume.[176]

Considering the above assessment, the EU FDI screening mechanism raises more questions than answers. Primarily, it remains doubtful whether the new scheme would become an effective tool to block Chinese investments given that some Member States rely heavily on them, which might suggest that their reviews could be lenient or that the rules would be applied without much rigour. In this sense, the reference made by the European Commissioner for Trade in 2012 about the adoption of a new common FDI scheme, which in his view was 'neither desirable nor feasible',[177] seems to have been premonitory. The former Danish Prime Minister and former Secretary General of NATO, Anders Fogh Rasmussen, later reiterated this view, saying that 'a Europe-wide early warning system will not make up for the lack of national screening rules in 15 EU states. The measures are discretionary and far less stringent than those in any other G7 nation'.[178] Indeed, according to the terms of the Regulation, neither the Member States nor the Commission have the power to block the FDI or enforce remedies to prevent them from happening.

From a legal perspective, the Commission has stated that the Regulation is consistent with article 63 TFEU that prohibits any restrictions on the free of movement of capital or payments, either foreign or domestic, between Member States and between them and third countries, as well as the related case law of the Court of Justice.[179] Certainly, Recital 4 of the Regulation notes that Member States are entitled to restrict this freedom of movement on public security and public policy grounds, according to article 65(1)(b) TFEU.[180] Here, it is important to bear in mind that the ECJ has validated the view that capital movements originating from outside the EU may receive different treatment than those originating from inside the EU and has recognized that under article 49 TFEU some investors have the right of establishment in the EU so they cannot be assessed under article 63, considering that:

> [S]ince the Treaty does not extend freedom of establishment to third countries, it is important to ensure that the interpretation of Article 63(1) TFEU as regards relations with third countries does not enable economic operators who do not fall within the limits of the territorial scope of freedom of establishment to profit from that freedom. Such a risk does not exist in a situation as that at issue in the main proceedings. The legislation of the Member State in question does not relate to the conditions of access

176 ibid, art 3(6).

177 Karel De Gucht, 'EU-China Investment: A Partnership of Equals Bruegel Debate' (Brussels, 7 June 2012).

178 Anders Fogh Rasmussen, 'China's Investment in Europe Offers Opportunities—and Threats' *Financial Times* (20 November 2017) https://www.ft.com/content/9e7428cc-c963-11e7-8536-d321d0d897a3 accessed 15 September 2023.

179 Explanatory Memorandum, p 4.

180 Regulation (EU) 2019/452, Rec 4.

of a company from that Member State to the market in a third country or of a company from a third country to the market in that Member State.[181]

The issue at stake is to establish when an FDI contravenes the freedom of establishment or when it falls within the scope of the freedom of capital.[182]

Once the Member State starts assessing the transaction under articles 63 and 65 TFEU, the next step is establishing whether any potential restriction would be justified. This step involves a significant level of complexity given the vagueness of the concepts of public policy and public security, combined with the guidance provided by the ECJ that demands a strict interpretation of public policy and public security concerns, meaning that they need to be 'genuine and sufficiently serious threat to a fundamental interest of society', in which pure economic or administrative concerns do not fit,[183] as well as proportionate, a concept that according to Barnard, relates to legal certainty.[184] In terms of proportionate authorization systems, the ECJ has established a set of principles, among them, the need to establish timelines, narrow powers, *ex ante* requirements when *ex post* is insufficient, and clear assessment criteria based on specific and objective conditions.[185] Additionally, the Regulation is based on the exclusive competence for constraining FDI in the EU contained in the common commercial policy under article 207(1) TFEU. Although the scope of FDI in light of article 207(1) is unclear, it has been said that the Commission has followed Opinion 2/15 of the ECJ regarding the Free Trade Agreement EU-Singapore, where it was clarified that the agreed conditions with Singapore investors had to be necessary and unrestrictive and that they did not have to observe public order, public security or other public interests considerations, and recognized that Member States enjoy some discretion when negotiating trade agreements.[186] In other words, the Regulation reaffirms that the EU is entitled to limit the access of FDI, and therefore the Union delegates the exclusive competence awarded by article 207(1) to the Member States under article 3(1) of the Regulation.[187]

Article 3 of the Regulation establishes certain minimum requirements for Member States' screening mechanisms:[188]

a. rules and procedures shall be transparent and non-discriminatory between third countries (paragraph 2);

[181] CJEU, Case C-35/11, *Test Claimants (ii)*, ECLI:EU:C:2012:707, para 100; CJEU, Case C-47/12, *Kronos*, ECLI:EU:C:2014:2200, paras 53–54.

[182] Schill (n 5) 13–14.

[183] ECJ C-54/99 (*Eglise de Scientology*), para 17.

[184] Catherine Barnard, *The Substantive Law of the EU: The Four Freedoms* (OUP 2016) 541.

[185] Zwartkruis and De Jong (n 147) 458.

[186] Opinion 2/15 of the Court, *FTA EU-Singapore*, EU:C:2017:376, paras 99–103.

[187] Schill (n 5) 19–20.

[188] Frank Röhling and Uwe Salaschek, 'The Foreign Investment Regulation Review: EU Overview' (The Law Reviews, 21 October 2022), https://thelawreviews.co.uk/title/the-foreign-investment-regulation-review/eu-overview accessed 15 September 2023.

b. screening mechanisms shall set out triggering events for the screening, the ground for screening and detailed procedural rules, including time frames (paragraphs 2 and 3);
c. confidential information made available to the Member States shall be protected (paragraph 4);
d. foreign investors and undertakings concerned shall have the possibility to seek recourse against screening decisions of national authorities (paragraph 5); and
e. the screening mechanisms shall include measures necessary to identify and prevent circumvention of the screening mechanism and screening decisions (paragraph 6).

Some commentators have indicated that as the Regulation does not impose specific conditions about the terms or scope of the different national screening mechanisms, then it fulfils the discretion principle stated in Opinion 2/15.[189] In this context, what remains unclear is whether any decision to prohibit an FDI transaction according to the terms of the Regulation would easily comply with the rest of provisions examined above.

In addition, the Regulation relates to the EUMR if the transaction falls within the scope of both. In this sense, the Member State assessing the merger under the national screening system should observe article 21(4) EUMR so that the transaction can be impeded on the grounds of public security, plurality of media or prudential rules (if these are relevant), as examined in the previous section of this chapter. Recital 36 of the Regulation indicates that it should be applied in a consistent manner with article 21(4) EUMR and that in the event of overlap between them, then the foundations for screening included in article 1 of the Regulation and the notion of legitimate interests covered in article 21(4) EUMR should be interpreted coherently, also taking into account the compatibility of the measures envisaged to protect those interests with other EU law provisions.[190] In the event that Member States do not comply with the rules contained in article 21(4) and article 65 TFEU, then they will be exposed to a possible infringement procedure before the European Courts.

Currently, it is still difficult to anticipate the implications of this new Regulation, a shortfall that was recognized by the Commission itself when, by the time the proposal was presented, indicated that 'in view of the rapidly changing economic reality, growing concerns of citizens and Member States, the proposal is exceptionally presented without an accompanying impact assessment'.[191] Nevertheless, some commentators are expecting that the Commission will act more flexibly in challenging FDI restrictions underpinned on security and public order, particularly if the transaction relates to non-EU jurisdictions.[192] Whereas others assume that the Commission will

[189] Zwartkruis and De Jong (n 147) 459.
[190] Regulation (EU) 2019/452, Rec 36.
[191] European Commission, 'Proposal for a Regulation of the European Parliament and of the Council establishing a framework for screening of foreign direct investments into the European Union', COM(2017) 487 final, p 10 (13 September 2017).
[192] Zwartkruis and De Jong (n 147) 472.

follow its established narrow approach towards the application of article 21(4), especially after announcing that the Regulation will be applied in a consistent manner with the EUMR.[193] In relation to bilateral investment treaties, it has been said that the Regulation could become a bargaining tool but that article 63 TFEU might undermine its effectiveness and result in an internal obstacle.[194] Accordingly, Schill has indicated that despite the relative weakness of the Regulations, it signals a great determination to achieve reciprocity in bilateral negotiations, especially with powerful economic countries like the US and China, rather than just protecting national interests.[195] This view on the lack of protectionism contrasts with other authors who consider that it is very likely that national concerns could be used so broadly that Chinese investments would be effectively hindered and with them the benefits of such investment such as financing, employment, research, and innovation.[196] Particularly in times of crisis, European countries have found a good alternative in Chinese investment, if not the only, and as Meunier has reported, a good number of those transactions have involved the payment of the full price of the assets or even more.[197] However, this argument might not be enough to overcome the concerns that hostile Chinese takeovers in fragile European economies can be used to exert great economic and political power.[198]

In November 2021, the European Commission published its first annual report on the screening of FDI into the Union.[199] It highlighted the fact that:

> the FDI Screening Regulation—and individual EU Member State screening legislation and mechanisms—reflect a strong focus on protecting security or public order, and a strong awareness of the criticality of certain investment targets, eg, critical infrastructure and inputs, including certain technologies, certain sectors such as the health sector, and the risks that investments by certain investors may pose.[200]

The report noted that 2020 saw a decrease in FDI inflows almost everywhere in the EU, with the exception of Belgium, Hungary, Luxembourg, Spain, and Sweden, which saw increased flows but a decline in the number of deals.[201] The opposite was true in 2022, as the net FDI inflow in the EU fell to €140 billion, amidst a global reduction of 14 per cent.[202] However, it should be pointed that this is largely affected by the poor

[193] Hatton, Byrne, and Lichy (n 158).

[194] Gadocha (n 148) 48–49.

[195] Schill (n 5) 4.

[196] Miguel Otero-Iglesias and Manuel Weissenegger, 'Motivations, Security Threats and Geopolitical Implications of Chinese Investment in the EU Energy Sector: the Case of CDP Reti' (2020) 26 (2) European Journal of International Relations 594–620, 598.

[197] Meunier (n 7) 293.

[198] Tomasz Kamiski, 'Sovereign Wealth Fund Investments in Europe as an Instrument of Chinese Energy Policy' (2017) 101 Energy Policy 735.

[199] European Commission, 'First Annual Report on the screening of foreign direct investments into the Union First Annual Report on the screening of foreign direct investments into the Union' COM(2021)714 final.

[200] ibid 1.

[201] Emily Xueref-Poviac, 'FDI Screening in the EU: European Commission publishes its first annual report on the Screening Regulation' (Clifford Chance, 16 December 2021) https://www.cliffordchance.com/briefings/2021/12/fdi-screening-in-the-eu--european-commission-publishes-its-first.html accessed 15 September 2023.

[202] European Commission, Third Annual Report on the Screening of FDI into the EU COM(2023) 590 final, 2.

performance of Luxembourg—excluding which, the inflow of FDI in the EU would have grown by 22 per cent.[203]

Turning to the decisional practice at the Member State level, in 2020, 91 per cent of the dossiers formally screened were approved, the majority without conditions (79 per cent) and some with conditions (12 per cent). A minimal portion (2 per cent) was prohibited, and 7 per cent were aborted by the parties for unknown reasons, hence not requiring any decision by the national authorities. The second annual report, issued in September 2022,[204] covers 2021 and presents comparable data: the authorizations rose to 96 per cent, with most issued without any conditions; the share of conditional approvals, however, almost doubled to 23 per cent. Prohibitions and withdrawals both halved to 1 per cent and 3 per cent, respectively. Finally, in 2022, as documented by the third annual report, released in late 2023, unconditional authorizations rose to 86 per cent, while the deal approved with remedies fell to 9 per cent. These numbers, summarized by Figure 3.1, clearly illustrate that the EU remains open to FDI, although the Member States appear to be becoming more familiar with these new legal prerogatives and more confident in using them.

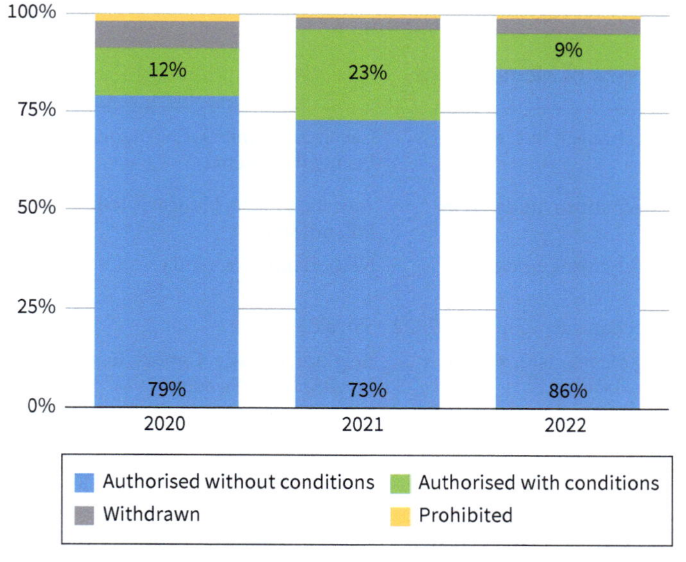

Figure 3.1 Breakdown of the outcomes of FDI dossiers formally screened (2020–22)
Adapted from European Commission, First Annual Report on the Screening of FDI into the EU, COM(2021) 714 final, page 11, figure 6; Second Annual Report on the Screening of FDI into the EU, COM(2022) 433 final, page 12, figure 7; Third Annual Report on the Screening of FDI into the EU COM(2023) 590 final, page 12, figure 7 © European Union, 1995-2023. Reproduced here under the terms of the Creative Commons Attribution 4.0 International (CC BY 4.0) licence

The Commission has been actively encouraging Member States at political and technical levels to adopt, adapt, and implement national screening mechanisms. These

[203] Commission Staff Working Document 'Screening of FDI into the Union and its Member States' SWD(2023) 329 final, 3.

[204] European Commission, 'Second Annual Report on the screening of foreign direct investments into the Union' COM(2022)433 final.

calls have indeed resulted in intense legislative activity at the national level. Until 2017, Portugal was the only Member State which employed a screening mechanism; when the Regulation came into force, the number rose to eleven; as of 2022, two-thirds of the Member States (eighteen out of twenty-seven) had one in place, and the number of notified regimes has now reached twenty-one,[205] which will be reflected in the next annual report. Furthermore, several Member States have been taking steps to adapt or expand their screening mechanisms or to introduce one if they still do not have one on the books. This trend has doubtless accelerated in the wake of the Covid-19 pandemic and the geopolitical tensions that followed. In 2021, three Member States adopted a new screening mechanism, six Member States expanded existing regimes, and seven initiated consultative or legislative processes to introduce new regimes.[206] Out of the nine EU Member States that did not have any FDI screening tool in place, only two—Bulgaria and Cyprus—still had not taken any steps to fill the gap. The 2022 developments, illustrated in Table 3.1, follow the same direction: eight Member States updated their screening mechanisms (and two more were in the process of doing so), Slovakia introduced a new one, and Cyprus joined the group of Member States which are introducing such regimes.

Table 3.1 Overview of Member States' Legislative Situation and Developments (2022)

FDI screening mechanism in place	Czechia, Denmark, Germany, Finland, Malta, Portugal, Slovenia
FDI screening mechanism, updated in 2022	Austria, France, Hungary, Italy, Latvia, Lithuania, Poland, Spain
FDI screening mechanism, update underway	Netherlands, Romania
FDI screening mechanism, adopted in 2022	Slovakia
No FDI screening mechanism, adoption underway	Belgium, Croatia, Cyprus, Estonia, Greece, Ireland, Luxembourg, Sweden
No FDI screening mechanism, adoption not underway	Bulgaria

Source: Data from European Commission, Third Annual Report on the Screening of foreign direct investments into the Union, pages 9-10 *© European Union, 1995-2023. Reproduced here under the terms of the Creative Commons Attribution 4.0 International (CC BY 4.0) licence.*

Table 3.2 illustrates the list of sectors that fall within the national security assessment in EU and non-EU countries.[207]

205 ibid 10.

206 Tilman Kuhn and others, 'The EU Releases its Second Annual FDI Report Showing Increased Momentum in FDI Regulation and Screening in the EU27' (White and Case, 7 September 2022) https://www.whitecase.com/insight-alert/eu-releases-its-second-annual-fdi-report-showing-increased-momentum-fdi-regulation accessed 15 September 2023.

207 ibid.

Table 3.2 Overview of Countries' Focus on National Security Assessment of FDI (2023)

Country	Defence	Healthcare	Energy	Telecom	Agriculture/ Food production	Transportation	Real estate	Other
Austria	□	□	□	□	□	□		Food, IT, water
Bulgaria	□		□				□	Finance
Bosnia & Herzegovina	□							Media
Croatia								Finance
Czech Republic	□	□	□			□		Finance, data, critical technologies
Denmark	□		□					
Estonia	□		□	□			□	Finance, media
Finland	□							
France	□	□	□	□	□	□	□	Data, media
Germany	□	□	□	□	□	□	□	Media, cloud computing, telematics, finance, dual-use goods, crypto-tech, etc.
Hungary	□	□	□	□	□	□		
Italy	□	□	□	□	□	□	□	Finance, data, media, critical technologies
Latvia			□	□	□		□	Gambling
Malta	□	□	□	□		□	□	
Montenegro	□							
North Macedonia	□							
Norway	□						□	Fundamental national functions
Poland	□	□	□	□	□	□	□	
Romania	□		□	□		□	□	Finance

(*continued*)

Table 3.2 Continued

Country	Defence	Healthcare	Energy	Telecom	Agriculture/ Food production	Transportation	Real estate	Other
Russia	☐		☐	☐		☐		Media, insurance
Serbia	☐							
Slovenia	☐	☐	☐	☐	☐	☐	☐	Finance, Insurance, data, critical technologies
Spain	☐	☐	☐	☐	☐	☐	☐	Finance, data, critical technologies
Türkiye			☐	☐		☐	☐	
United Kingdom*	☐							Finance, media

Reproduced from Tobias Heinrich et al, 'Foreign direct investment reviews 2023: Europe' (White Case, 20 March 2023) https://www.whitecase.com/insight-our-thinking/foreign-direct-investment-reviews-2023-europe accessed 15 September 2023 @ White & Case.

As mentioned, the second annual report highlights the fact that only 1 per cent of the transactions were blocked by Member States (compared to slightly more before, ie, 2 per cent in the first report), confirming that the EU remains open to foreign direct investments and Member States only deny cases that pose very serious threats to security and public order. The document also reveals that the vast majority of FDI poses no problem from a public security point of view and is approved swiftly (both at a national level and under the Regulation).[208] The small proportion of prohibitions in the EU is comparable to that observed in the other major jurisdictions analysed in this book.

The report also provides an overview of sector-specific FDI trends. For instance, the top sectors for acquisitions, after information and communications technology (ICT) (28 per cent), were manufacturing (24.7 per cent), professional, scientific and technical services (8.9 per cent), financial services (7.3 per cent), and retail (7 per cent).[209] Table 3.3 shows, by sector, the number of foreign acquisitions and greenfield investments into the EU in 2021.

Table 3.3 Foreign Acquisitions and Greenfield Investments by Sector: Share Over Total (2022)

Equity stakes	Share (%)	Year-on-year (% change)		Greenfield	Share (%)	Year-on-year (% change)	
	2022	21/22	20/22		*2022*	21/22	20/22
ICT	28.0	−18.6	13.4	Retail	29.9	2.0	26.3
Manufacturing	24.7	−17.9	18.6	ICT	19.4	17.6	53.9
PST	8.9	-7.6	33.6	Financ. Insur.	10.8	33.2	56.3
Financ. Insur.	7.3	-5.8	10.2	PST	10.5	26.6	35.5
Retail	7.0	−15.1	−0.8	Manufacturing	10.4	−13.1	4.0
Electricity	4.3	−10.5	8.5	Accommodation	6.5	−29.4	−11.8
Transport	3.5	24.0	40.9	Transport	5.1	−44.0	-26.2
Admin. support	2.9	18.6	82.1	Admin. support	2.7	5.8	43.1
Construction	2.5	−32.3	83.3	Real estate	1.2	−10.8	0.0
Real estate	2.4	−34.8	13.2	Electricity	0.9	−33.3	50.0
Accommodation	2.1	−24.5	164.3	Arts. Entert.	0.7	−35.5	66.7
Health	1.9	−17.1	−22.7	Water supply	0.7	0.0	125.0
Arts. Entert.	1.5	-6.9	22.7	Health	0.7	0.0	125.0
Mining	1.0	−21.7	20.0	Education	0.3	0.0	−42.9
Education	0.8	−17.6	7.7	Construction	0.3	−46.2	-63.2
Agriculture	0.7	−25.0	20.0	Other services	0.1	−33.3	−42.9
Remaining sections	0.6	−38.9	10.0	Remaining sections	0.1	−57.1	−75.0

Reproduced from Commission Staff Working Document 'Screening of FDI into the Union and its Member States' SWD(2023) 329 final, page 8, Table 2 © European Union, 1995-2023. Reproduced here under the terms of the Creative Commons Attribution 4.0 International (CC BY 4.0) licence.

Note: Detail by target sector (NACE-Rev.2).

[208] European Commission, 'EU investment screening and export control rules effectively safeguard EU security', Press release, 2 September 2022.

[209] Report from the Commission to the European Parliament and the Council, Second Annual Report on the screening of foreign direct investments into the Union, Brussels, 1 September 2022, COM(2022) 433 final.

At a national level, as shown by Figure 3.2, the five sectors with the highest number of transactions were manufacturing, ICT (down from 36 per cent to 24 per cent), financial activities, wholesale and retail, and professional activities. The first three sectors are the same ones as in the first annual report but in a different order.[210]

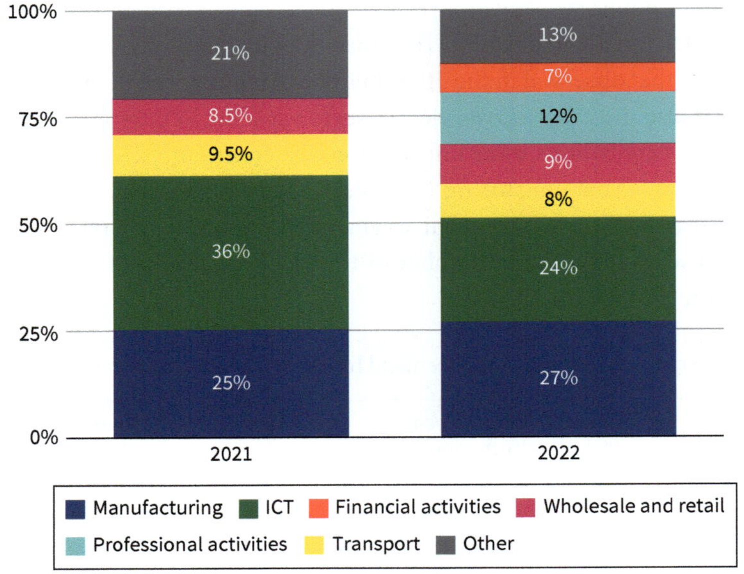

Figure 3.2 Breakdown of notified transactions by sector (2021)

Reproduced from European Commission, 'Second Annual Report on the Screening of foreign direct investments into the Union', figure 8; and Third Annual Report on the Screening of foreign direct investments into the Union, figure 8 © European Union, 1995-2023. Reproduced here under the terms of the Creative Commons Attribution 4.0 International (CC BY 4.0) licence

Note: As cases can encompass several sectors (i.e. NACE codes), the total in the graph is higher than the total number of cases notified in 2021. The category 'other' encompass all other sectors below 4%, for example, electricity, gas, steam and air conditioning supply; transporting and storage.

In addition, it should be noted that the European Commission published, in April 2022, 'Guidance to the Member States concerning foreign direct investment from Russia and Belarus' where it urged EU Member States to implement the FDI Screening Regulation to address risks related to security or public order related to FDI from the Russian Federation and Belarus.[211] Notably, the European Commission calls upon Member States to: 'implement fully the FDI Screening Regulation, including through active participation in the cooperation mechanism between Member States and between them and the Commission, to address risks related to security or public order related to FDI from Russia and Belarus'.[212]

[210] ibid 14.

[211] UNCTAD, 'The Evolution of FDI Screening Mechanism' (2023) 25 *Key Trends and Features*.

[212] European Commission, Guidance to the Member States concerning foreign direct investment from Russia and Belarus in view of the military aggression against Ukraine and the restrictive measures laid down in recent Council Regulations on sanctions (2022/C 151 I/01), 6 April 2022

Finally, according to the Commission Work Programme 2023, the Commission will examine whether additional tools are necessary with respect to outbound strategic investment controls similar to the US Revised National Critical Capabilities Defense Act, which, if enacted, would create a similar regime to CFIUS with the important differentiation that it would apply to outbound investments. [213]

3.4.2 Regulation (EU) 2022/2560 of the European Parliament and of the Council of 14 December 2022 on Foreign Subsidies Distorting the Internal Market and the Digital Markets Act

There have been increasing concerns that foreign companies, such as state-owned companies, receive funding support from their governments and may be influenced by foreign government's intentions to pursue non-economic goals. 'They may engage in uncompetitive, politically motivated behavior, which can cause security risks and technological leakage.'[214]

In addition to the FDI screening regime, the EU expanded its remit in other areas of competition enforcement and some highly sensitive sectors. The EU has now formally adopted its new Foreign Subsidies Regulation[215] (FSR), which will apply from 12 July 2023. Guidelines are now awaited to clarify what must be included in notifications under the FSR and to provide further procedural details (in February 2023, the European Commission invited stakeholders to give feedback on the implementation of the FSR). In particular, the Draft Implementing Regulation contains detailed rules on the submission of notifications concerning: mergers, acquisitions or other concentrations; foreign financial contributions in the context of public procurement procedures; the conduct of inspections and interviews in the context of in-depth investigations; the offer of proposed remedies to address potential distortions of the internal market; and access to the Commission's file, and rights of defence more generally.[216] The draft also provides standardized notification forms. The China Chamber of Commerce to the EU (CCCEU) expressed deep concerns over the draft on implementing the FSR. Indeed, in its written feedback, the CCCEU said that the FSR:

> poses multiple challenges, including the market openness of the EU towards foreign investments, the sound justification for any new and separate legal framework in

[213] European Commission, Communication 'Commission work programme 2023: A Union standing firm and united' COM(2022) 548 final.

[214] Jaeger M, *A More Strategic Approach to Foreign Direct Investment Policy* (German Council on Foreign Relations, 2023).

[215] Regulation (EU) 2022/2560 of the European Parliament and of the Council of 14 December 2022 on foreign subsidies distorting the internal market.

[216] Andrea Pomana and others, 'European Commission Publishes Draft Implementing Rules for EU Foreign Subsidies Regulation: Another Layer of Complexity', 8 February 2023, https://www.mayerbrown.com/en/perspectives-events/publications/2023/02/european-commission-publishes-draft-implementing-rules-for-eu-foreign-subsidies-regulation-another-layer-of-complexity accessed 15 September 2023.

addition to the existing mechanisms, the legal certainty that the new instrument could provide, the disproportional burdens the new instrument would impose, and most importantly, the potential discriminatory implementation of new instrument towards Chinese businesses, which in turn distorts the level playing field.[217]

Article 44 of the new Regulation provides that the latter is without prejudice to the application of Regulation 2019/452. The FSR is meant to 'level the playing field' between EU operators and their competitors from non-EU Member States, which are not subject to the same kind of strict subsidy disciplines as EU Member States.[218]

In this context, the notification obligations are now triggered not by foreign 'subsidies' but by foreign 'financial contributions', which have a broader scope. Indeed, a financial contribution is 'provided directly or indirectly by a third country, it confers a benefit and is limited to one or more undertakings or industries'.[219] Inspired by EU state aid rules, foreign subsidies include the transfer of state funds/liabilities (capital injections, grants, loans, fiscal incentives, guarantees, etc), forgoing of state revenue (tax exemptions, etc.), and provision or purchase of goods or services.[220] The financial contribution must be provided by: (i) the central government; or (ii) any other authority at other levels of government; or (iii) public or private entities whose actions can be attributed to the central government of a non-EU country (which may target sovereign wealth funds or publicly backed PE houses).[221] Thus, the FSR will target EU and non-EU based multinational companies that are active in the EU and have received direct or indirect financial contributions from a non-EU government, including the UK.

FSR introduces three new subsidy control tools for the European Commission to address foreign subsidies:

- A general *ex-officio* tool: this new tool enables the European Commission to investigate any market situation regardless of thresholds, for instance, when it suspects that a distorting foreign subsidy may be involved.[222] According to Recital 61 of the Regulation, 'for reasons of legal certainty, it is appropriate to limit the period within which it is possible for the Commission to investigate a foreign subsidy to ten years from the date of granting that foreign subsidy'.
- A notification-based tool in relation to potentially subsidized M&As: concentrations will trigger an *ex ante* notification obligation if at least one of the merging undertakings, the acquired undertaking or the joint venture is established in the Union and generates an aggregate turnover in the Union of at least €500 million

[217] China Chamber of Commerce to the EU, 'CCCEU Expresses Deep Concerns over Draft Implementing Rules for EU's Foreign Subsidies Regulation', March 9 2023, http://en.ccceu.eu/2023-03/09/c_2900.htm accessed 15 September 2023.

[218] Kyriakos Fountoukakos, Lode Van Den Hende, and Morris Schonberg, 'EU Foreign Subsidies Regulation Adopted—Draft Implementing Regulation to be Published Beginning of 2023', Herbert Smith Freehills, 21 December 2022

[219] Regulation (EU) 2022/2560, Rec 11 Regulation.

[220] ibid art 3.

[221] ibid art 3.

[222] ibid art 9.

and the following undertakings were granted combined aggregate financial contributions of more than €50 million from third countries in the three years preceding the conclusion of the agreement, the announcement of the public bid, or the acquisition of a controlling interest.[223] While the review periods provided for in the FSR follow the timelines under the EUMR, the review procedures under the FSR and EUMR will be completely independent.[224]
- A notification-based tool in relation to potentially subsidized public procurement bids: a notifiable foreign financial contribution in a public procurement procedure shall be deemed to arise where the estimated contract value is equal to or exceeds €250 million, and the bidder, its group or main subcontractors/suppliers were granted a financial contribution of at least €4 million per third country.[225]

Once the Commission determines the existence of a subsidy, it will assess (i) whether the subsidy has distortive effects on the internal market and (ii) whether positive effects can counterbalance this distortion. The FSR provides a few legal presumptions to determine the existence of distortion or lack thereof.[226]

- Subsidies likely to be distortive: (i) supporting failing business (without a long-term plan to restructure); (ii) unlimited guarantees; (iii) facilitating a concentration; (iv) an export financing measure that is not in line with the OECD Arrangement on officially supported export credits; and (v) enabling a company to submit an unduly advantageous tender.
- Subsidies unlikely to be distortive: the FSR considers that foreign subsidies to SMEs could cause distortions compared with foreign subsidies to large undertakings. Also, the FSR states that a foreign subsidy to a beneficiary that shows a low degree of activity in the internal market, measured, for instance, in terms of turnover achieved in the Union, is less likely to cause distortions than a foreign subsidy to a beneficiary that has a more significant level of activity in the internal market. Also, foreign subsidies not exceeding €4 million over a consecutive period of three years should be deemed, as a general rule, unlikely to distort the internal market.
- Non-distortive subsidies (*de minimis*): below €200,000 per the third country in the previous three years.

Following an in-depth investigation, the European Commission can issue (i) a no objection decision, (ii) a commitments/redressive measures decision, or (iii) a prohibition decision.[227] Similar to merger control remedies, redressive measures and commitments

[223] ibid art 20.
[224] Blomstein, 'Foreign Subsidies Regulation—ready, set, go', 14 December 2022.
[225] Regulation (EU) 2022/2560, art 28.
[226] ibid Rec 19–20.
[227] ibid art 11.

can be structural (divestment) or behavioural (such as licensing under FRAND conditions or repaying the foreign subsidy with an interest rate).

Pursuant to article 17 of the Regulation, if the parties breach the standstill suspensory obligation or fail to notify a notifiable transaction (which are two distinct infringements), the EC may impose a fine of up to 10 per cent of the parties' worldwide aggregate turnover. Where a company supplies incorrect, incomplete, or misleading information, it may be subject to fines of up to 1 per cent of its worldwide turnover and periodic penalty payments of up to 5 per cent of its average daily aggregate turnover for each working day of delay. These levels of fines have the same theoretical limits as under the EUMR.

The foreign subsidy control is closely modelled on the EU merger control procedure; indeed, the FSR established a two-step procedure: as a first step, there is the preliminary review (akin to Phase I for merger control), where the European Commission will determine whether there is a foreign subsidy distorting the internal market.[228] As a second step, the European Commission will launch an in-depth investigation (akin to Phase II for merger control) to gather additional relevant information to assess the foreign subsidy.[229] Following an in-depth investigation, the Commission can adopt: (i) a no objection decision; (ii) a commitments/redressive measure decision; or (iii) a decision prohibiting a concentration or the award of the contract.[230]

The Regulation also enables undertakings to request 'pre-notification consultations with the Commission based on good faith, with the aim of receiving guidance on whether the thresholds for notification are met'.[231]

As far as the rules of proceeding are concerned, the FSR review process is modelled on the EUMR. After the formal notification, the European Commission has an initial twenty-five working-day period (same as Phase 1 of EUMR filings) to check if there are indications that the parties have been granted a foreign subsidy that distorts the internal market. If so, the European Commission can open an in-depth investigation (Phase 2) of up to ninety additional working days (extendable by fifteen working days in case of remedies) (same as Phase 2 of EUMR filings). This alignment with EU merger control should allow parties to coordinate their FSR and EUMR filings.[232]

Thus, from now on, investments in the EU can go through three different mechanisms (merger control, FDI, and FSR), and one cannot but wonder how the two sets of rules on foreign investments coexist.[233] Recital 3 of the FSR provides that 'This Regulation covers all economic sectors, including those that are of strategic interest to the Union and critical

[228] ibid art 10.
[229] ibid art 11.
[230] ibid art 25.
[231] ibid Rec 38.
[232] Camille Paulhac, Juliette Hua, Jade-Alexandra Fearns, and others, 'Dealmakers Beware of a New Regulatory Hurdle: the European Foreign Subsidies Regulation is Here', 22 February 2023, https://www.paulhastings.com/insights/client-alerts/dealmakers-beware-of-a-new-regulatory-hurdle-the-european-foreign-subsidies accessed 1 February 2024.
[233] Pablo Figueroa and Julia M Böhme, 'The Foreign Subsidies Regulation and Foreign Direct Investment: How to Reconcile', 9 January 2023, competitionlawblog.kluwercompetitionlaw.com/2023/01/09/the-foreign-subsidies-regulation-and-foreign-direct-investment-how-to-reconcile/ accessed 1 February 2024.

infrastructures, such as those mentioned in article 4(1), point (a), of Regulation (EU) 2019/452 of the European Parliament and of the Council.'[234]

Finally, we should also note the Digital Markets Act (DMA), which imposes a significant regulatory burden on digital firms designated as gatekeepers due to the size of their operations. Providing Recital 71 of the DMA, 'the gatekeepers should inform the Commission of all of their intended acquisitions, prior to their implementation, of other undertakings providing core platform services or any other services provided within the digital sector or other services that enable the collection of data.'[235] Article 14 of the Regulation states that 'A gatekeeper shall inform the Commission of any intended concentration within the meaning of article 3 of Regulation (EC) No 139/2004, where the merging entities or the target of concentration provide core platform services or any other services in the digital sector or enable the collection of data, irrespective of whether it is notifiable to the Commission under that Regulation or to a competent national competition authority under national merger rules.'[236]

3.5 Conclusion

The above analysis reveals that the views around the implications of the European FDI scheme are divided, and it is still too early to predict them. Even if there have been significant advances since 2019, the articulation between the screening carried out by national authorities and the EC remains a challenge. In its report,[237] the European Commission firmly expects additional Member States to adopt and strengthen their FDI screening regime soon. The interplay of EUMR and FDI will also be a key challenge. Indeed, fourteen years after its last article 21 decision, this is the first time that the Commission has applied this provision within the FDI context.[238]

Nonetheless, it appears important that the Commission and the Member States carefully deal with FDI transactions as they will either facilitate or obstruct international agreements, considering that reciprocity plays a key role in this type of negotiation. Equally, the Member States must apply the FDI rules in accordance with the EU principles and laws, otherwise the predominance of nationalism and protectionism goals could undermine the trust of the proceedings, provoking undesirable consequences at a national and international level. Indeed, the extent to which Member States can obstruct FDI transactions without infringing the EU law is still unclear.

In addition, Member States should be willing to cooperate, adopt rigorous standards of review, and try to reach similar approaches, as this is the best way to make this FDI

[234] Regulation (EU) 2022/2560, Rec 3.
[235] ibid Rec 71.
[236] ibid art 14.
[237] European Commission, 'Report From the Commission to the European Parliament and the Council on the Screening of Foreign Direct Investments into the Union', 1 September 2022
[238] Clifford Chance, 'Interplay of EU Merger Control and FDI Review: Implementation of National FDI Screening Regimes have to Comply with EU Law (VIG/AEGON Joint Venture)', March 2022

framework enforceable. As for the investment community, they need to undertake a thorough analysis of their FDI plans, examining not just the sector and the activities to which the investment relates but also the Member States that the transaction might impact. Also, with time, the EU and the Member States will identify specific procedural challenges of the Regulation and can address them and improve the underlying infrastructure of the cooperation mechanism.

Finally, even more recently, the European Commission indicated in its 2023 Work Programme that it will 'examine whether additional tools are necessary in respect of outbound strategic investments controls' and is 'prepared to revise the EU's FDI screening regulation'.[239]

In an interesting comment published in a widely circulated newspaper in China (China Daily), the commentator perceives the wide-ranging risks listed as strong protectionist measures despite the EU's claim to preserve 'maximum levels of economic openness and dynamism'. Such a strategy risks violating World Trade Organization rules of non-discrimination. The commentator adds that 'national security and economic security have become the most abused terms since the Donald Trump administration unleashed various protectionist and unilateral trade measures'.[240] This denotes the polemic nature of national security assessment amidst a worsening geopolitical environment.

Appendix 1: Public Interest Cases Under Article 21 EUMR

Case IV/M.567 *Lyonnaise des Eaux/Northumbrian Water*

One of the illustrative cases in which an EU Member State intervened in relation to a proposed merger scrutinized by the EU Commission under the EUMR is represented by the *Lyonnaise de Eaux/ Northumbrian Water* case. The proposed concentration involved the acquisition of Northumbrian Water by the French company Lyonnaise des Eaux present in the market for a water supply in the United Kingdom (UK). The operation had a Community dimension; therefore, the EC Commission had jurisdiction to assess the concentration. At the time of the decision, the water industry in the UK was regulated by the Water Industry Act 1991 (the WIA) leading the UK authorities to request the Commission to authorize the application of the sectoral legislation to the merger at stake.

Under the framework of the sectoral regulation, the Monopolies and Mergers Commission (MMC) was required to assess whether a water merger is against the public interest by applying a qualified test provided in sections 32 to 34 of WIA. Under this test, the MCC had to establish whether the merger in question would prejudice the industry regulator's ability to make comparisons between different water enterprises. The underlying rationale of this test is to enable the industry regulator (Director General of Water Services—DGWS) to fulfil one of its functions under the WIA, that is, to control the prices for the services provided by the enterprises by imposing price caps in each company licence.

Thus, the UK requested the Commission to recognize its legitimate interest in applying the public interest test provided in sections 32 to 34 of the WIA. The Commission issued a decision recognizing that the objective of the UK sectoral legislation is to ensure the proper functioning of a vital service

[239] European Commission, Commission Work Programme 2023: 'A Union standing firm and united', 18 October 2022.

[240] Chen Weihua, 'EU's Economic Security Strategy Misguided and Self-Damaging' (China Daily, 30 June 2023) https://www.chinadaily.com.cn/a/202306/30/WS649e0d79a310bf8a75d6c6a9.html accessed 15 September 2023.

and protection of consumers.[241] Also, it stated that although such an interest is not one of those particularly described by article 21(4) EUMR and requires thus a specific authorization, it is compatible with the general principles and other provisions of EU law.[242] Therefore, the Commission authorized the application of the public interest test provided by the sectoral legislation, provided that the UK Competition Authority will communicate in each case the expected measures to enable the Commission to verify that the measures are appropriate, proportional, and non-discriminatory.[243] Consequently, the UK authorities communicated the proposed measures: a) tightening of price control in respect of the merged firms' water business by comparison with the existing price control with a given cumulative effect over six years, and b) an obligation on Lyonnaise to list all its UK water interests on the stock exchange by 2005.[244] The Commission had not raised any objections in relation to these measures.

The decision recognized the legitimate interest of the UK in applying the sectoral regulation not only in the merger at stake but in all cases involving a water merger having a Union dimension, provided that the measures taken under the industry's regulatory framework are compliant with the Commission's decision (ie, the measures are non-discriminatory, appropriate, and proportionate according to the underlying objectives of the legislation and in compliance with the general principles and other provisions of EU law).

Case IV/M.1346 *EDF/London Electricity*

The operation involved the acquisition of London Electricity, controlled by the Entergy Corporation, by EdF, a French state-owned company that generates, distributes, and supplies electricity in several Member States. During the notification proceedings of the transaction, the UK authorities filed a request to the Commission that the merger be referred to them to be assessed under the national competition law in accordance with article 9 of the EUMR.[245] The UK asserted jurisdiction on the grounds that the merger would create or strengthen a dominant position which would significantly impede effective competition on a distinct market within the UK, which did not constitute a substantial part of the internal market.[246] However, the Commission considered that the conditions laid down in article 9 for referral were not met and therefore rejected the UK authorities' request.

Concurrently, the UK authorities made a request pursuant to article 21(3) EUMR for the recognition of certain public interests as legitimate interests other than those prescribed by the EUMR.[247] The Commission examined the request and concluded that the measures put forward by the UK authorities in the request were taken in accordance with the existing regulatory environment in the UK for the ongoing regulation of the electricity industry and not directed at the merger itself.[248] Thus, the Commission took the view that such regulatory activity was not prohibited by the Merger Regulation and concluded that was not necessary to issue a decision authorizing the measures that could be taken by the UK authorities. Therefore, the industry regulator (OGES) imposed certain licence conditions on the notifying party, which informed the Commission of the measures thereof. The Commission considered the measures concluding that they are part of the regulatory provisions governing the industry and even though the UK authorities will be responsible for the implementation and monitoring of these measures, they do not constitute an application of the national competition law to a concentration having Community dimension, nor measures to protect legitimate interests other than those specified by the EUMR.

241 European Commission, Article 21(3) Decision of 29 March 1995, para 2.
242 ibid para 5.
243 ibid para 6.
244 Case IV/M567 *Lyonnaise des Eaux/Northumbrian Water*, para 8.
245 Case IV/M.1346 *EDF/London Electricity*, para 7.
246 ibid.
247 ibid para 8.
248 ibid.

Case IV/M.1616 *BSCH/A. Champalimaud*

The case involved the acquisition of joint control of several Portuguese banks by BSCH, which was notified to the Commission in June 1999. Following the notification of the operation to the Commission, the Portuguese Ministry of Finance issued a decision blocking the merger on prudential grounds.

Portuguese authorities justified its opposition decision to the merger by mentioning that an assessment of whether, in the light of the relevant legislation and available information, the specific conditions of the merger will guarantee a 'sound and prudent management'[249] of the acquired undertaking. Furthermore, the Commission identified two reasons for standing behind the opposition's decision. The first one refers to the infringement of rules of a procedural nature, namely 'that BSCH acquired a qualified participation in MC without previously notifying it to the Minister of Finance, as foreseen in article 43 of Decreto-Lei 94B/98 of 17 April'.[250] Secondly, that the concentration strictly interferes with the national interest and with strategic sectors which are essential to the Portuguese economy and financial system.[251] Of particular interest is a statement made by the Portuguese Minister of Finance to the local press stating that:

> there are strategic sectors that we want to be kept in Portuguese hands, but we will never use illegal methods to achieve this. Several times the government talked to financial institutions and expressed to all of them, including to the Champalimaud group, the wish that the decision power in large financial Portuguese institutions would remain in Portuguese hands. ... The policy of this government is that strategic sectors should be kept in Portuguese hands.[252]

A similar statement had been made by the Portuguese Prime Minister.

The Commission assessed the compatibility of the measures taken by the Portuguese authorities with article 21 EUMR. In relation to the national and strategic interests asserted by the Portuguese state, the Commission noted that such interests breach the principle of non-discrimination because of nationality laid down in article 12 of the Treaty.[253]

Moreover, the Commission considered that measures of such kind would inevitably constitute an infringement of the principles of freedom of establishment and free movement of capital within the EU.[254] Regarding the argument related to the breach of procedural rules invoked by the Portuguese authorities, the Commission noted that such an argument cannot stand as valid because the interest in avoiding a violation of procedural rules does not form part of the interests explicitly mentioned in article 21(3) EUMR. Thus, the Commission concluded, citing the interpretative notes on EUMR adopted by the Council, that compliance with formal or procedural rules is not included in the list of interests considered prudent, nor are they included under the headings of the other two legitimate interests mentioned in article 21(3) EUMR, that is, public security and plurality of media.[255] Furthermore, the Commission went on to consider that the decision taken by the Portuguese authorities is not compatible with the general principle of proportionality which requires that measures taken by a Member State should be kept at a minimum of action necessary to afford protection of the interest at stake. Hence, a decision to block a merger with a Community dimension to ensure that the operation in question is notified to the national authorities constitutes a breach of this principle as there are less restrictive alternatives to oblige the parties to inform the competent authorities.[256]

In relation to the concerns invoked by the Portuguese authorities in its decision, that is, sound and careful management of the insurance undertaking MC and appropriate supervision by the authorities, the Commission held that considering the particular circumstances of the case that none of these

[249] Para 7 of the decision issued by the Portuguese Minister of Finance quoted in the Commission Decision in Case IV/M.1616 *BSCH/A. Champalimaud* at para 16.
[250] ibid para 17.
[251] ibid para 18.
[252] ibid para 21.
[253] ibid para 28.
[254] ibid.
[255] ibid para 30.
[256] ibid para 33.

motives formed the basis of the decision.[257] Also, the Commission mentioned several other mergers in the financial sector having similar structures notified to receive an assessment under EUMR and the Portuguese Republic did not block the operations on grounds of protection of legitimate prudential interests.[258] Thus, the Commission adopted the decision requiring the Republic of Portugal to immediately suspend the measures adopted in relation to the notified concentration.

Case COMP/M.2054 *Secil/Holderbank/Cimpor*

The case concerned an operation involving the acquisition by Holderbank (Switzerland) and Secil (Portugal) of shares in the Portuguese company Cimpor—a former state-owned company that was privatized during the 1990s. The Portuguese government held around 12 per cent of the shares, and 10 per cent had the status of golden shares. Pursuant to Cimpor's by-laws, the Portuguese government had a veto right over Cimpor's strategic decisions and any amendments to the its by-laws. The acquiring parties designed their offer in such a way as to make the Portuguese state waive its special rights in Cimpor.

The offer made by the acquiring parties was subject to, *inter alia*, the following conditions:

1. The acquisition of a minimum of 67 per cent of the total issued share capital of Cimpor.
2. Obtaining the authorization by the Minister of Finance under Decree Law No 380/93.
3. Acceptance by the Portuguese state, in any form, to waive prior to the offer closing all the special privileges and rights of its shares in Cimpor.
4. Adopting an irrevocable resolution of Cimpor's General Meeting of Shareholders before the offer registration, amending Cimpor's by-laws to remove all current voting limitations (ie, no shareholder other than the state can vote in excess of 10 per cent of all the votes).

Measures Adopted by the Portuguese Authorities Relating to the Notified Concentration

The notifying parties applied for prior authorization from the Minister of Finance to acquire through a public bid offer a minimum of 67 per cent of the share capital of Cimpor in accordance with the provisions of the Decree-Law No 380/93. Pursuant to article 1 of the Decree-Law, the acquisition of more than 10 per cent of the share capital in companies which have not yet been privatized is subject to authorization of the Minister of Finance.[259] Consequently, the Minister of Finance adopted a decision through which opposed the notified concentration declaring that the Portuguese government did not intend to relinquish its shares in Cimpor[260] being requested to inform the public about the government's decision. As a result, the parties applied for a new authorization from the Minister of Finance presenting the amended version of the initial offer to the effect that the state should: (i) waive its special rights granted to the state under Cimpor's by-laws; (ii) dispose of its shares in Cimpor outside the mechanism provided in Law 11/90; or (iii) vote in favour of an amendment to Cimpor's by-laws at the General Meeting of Shareholders.[261]

Cimpor's General Meeting of Shareholders, including the state in its capacity as a shareholder, voted against the proposal to eliminate the limitations on exercise of voting rights. At the same time, the Minister of Finance issued the second decision relating to the renewed application refusing to authorize the operation. Following this decision, the Lisbon Stock Exchange requested the parties withdraw their public offer. However, the parties refused to do so, and they modified

[257] ibid para 46.
[258] ibid para 57.
[259] Case COMP/M.2054 *Secil/Holderbank/Cimpor*, para 15.
[260] ibid para 16.
[261] ibid para 18.

their bid by raising the price offered per share by 15 per cent and proposed to strengthen the state's shareholding in the resulting company and meet the government requirements. Thus, the modified offer presupposes the acquisition of 51 per cent of the share capital of Cimpor as well as maintaining the company listed on the Lisbon Stock Exchange. The Lisbon Stock Exchange refused to register the modified bid, justifying its decision by citing the Minister of Finance's decision stating that the acquisition of more than 10 per cent of the capital of Cimpor shall not be authorized pending the privatization of the company.[262]

The First Decision

The first decision issued by the Minister of Finance is based on Decree-Law 380/93, which provides that the acquisition of more than 10 per cent of the capital in companies to be reprivatized is subject to the prior authorization of the Minister of Finance. According to the law, the approval should be based on the objectives pursued by article 3 of Law No 11/90.[263] Paragraph 5 of the Decision states that the Decree-Law aims to allow the state to control the corporate structure of companies of which privatization has not yet been finalized.[264] Thus, the Decree-Law grants the government the right to control who would acquire control in Cimpor and this goes beyond the mere disposal of the government shares in the company.[265]

In paragraph 2 of the decision, the Minister of Finance states that the notifying parties linked their application with the exercise by the state of its shareholding rights and modifying its position in the company. Therefore, the decision notes that such a situation leads to privatization in the form of a direct sale, which needs to be completed under article 13 of the Framework Law for Privatization and carrying out this operation under the circumstances of the present case would lead to possible legal conflicts with the rules governing the privatization procedures.[266]

The Minister of Finance based the decision on three main arguments. Firstly, it states that the privatization process should be undertaken at the initiative of the Portuguese government.[267] The second argument points to the constitutional principle of equal treatment, mentioning that the Framework Law for Privatization materializes this principle by providing as the main forms of privatization the public offers and public auctions. Thus, if the state decides to sell shares in a company, which at the time of the sale was already in the process of privatization to another company even though other buyers were in a similar position, this would represent a violation of the principle of equal treatment.[268] Finally, the decision refers to the exceptional nature of direct sales and restricted tenders/auctions as means of privatization,[269] noting that the Portuguese constitution establishes that it should be carried out as a general rule and preferably through public auction or offering on the stock exchange. Therefore, privatization through direct sale of shares or assets could be pursued only where the national interest or the economic and financial situation requires it of the company. Finally, the decision concluded that the government does not intend to pursue the final stage of the Cimpor's privatization process through the direct sale of the shares or at least without entering into a contract with several other potentially interested parties.[270]

262 ibid para 22.
263 ibid para 24.
264 ibid para 25.
265 ibid para 26.
266 ibid para 28.
267 ibid para 30.
268 ibid para 31.
269 ibid para 32.
270 ibid para 33.

The Second Decision

The second decision came as a result of the unfavourable vote of the General Meeting of Shareholders, where the elimination of article 7 of Cimpor's by-laws was proposed, which stated that no shareholder other than that state or similar entities has the right to vote in excess of 10 per cent of all votes. Thus, the decision finds the parties' offer unenforceable.[271].

However, the decision went on to the substance of the application and concluded that the parties' objectives conflicted with the objectives pursued by the Framework Law for Privatization.[272]

Firstly, it is argued that full implementation of the parties' acquisition would lead to the withdrawal of Cimpor from the capital market and thus hinder the company's contribution to the development of the national capital market, as well as the possibility of Portuguese citizens having access to the company's share capital.[273] Secondly, the parties' corporate project is not compatible with the government's reorganization strategy for the sector at stake, in particular considering the division of assets as envisaged by the parties. Thirdly, the implementation of the concentration would go against the state's interests as it would make the disposal of the remaining share of the state unviable under fair economic and financial conditions.[274] Lastly, the decision finds that accepting the parties' bid would be contrary to the principle of equal treatment which governs the privatization transaction draft of the last phase of Cimpor's privatization process as already prepared by the government.[275]

Compatibility of the Measures with Article 21 of EUMR

The Portuguese authorities failed to communicate to the Commission the public interests considered necessary to protect by the decisions blocking the concentration.[276] There was, in fact, a single letter sent to the Commissioner in charge of competition policy after the Portuguese authorities opposed the operation, but the Commission did not consider such a letter as constituting a communication pursuant to article 21 EUMR.[277]

In assessing the compatibility of the measures taken by the Portuguese authorities, the Commission went on to consider the reasons on which the government based its decision to block the parties' transaction (ie, the development of the corporate structure in companies in ongoing privatization aiming at re-establishing the corporate capacity and efficiency of the national production apparatus consistent with the economic policy guidelines of the Portuguese government[278] and which the decisions mentioned as being the cornerstone objective pursued by the Decree-Law 380/93).

Then, the Commission concluded that such an objective does not constitute an interest falling under the headings of public security, plurality of the media, and prudential rules.[279] Firstly, the Commission noted that in accordance with the interpretative Notes on the EUMR 'prudential rules' relate to financial services and concern, *inter alia*, the good reputation of individuals managing such companies, the honesty of transactions, and rules on solvency.[280] Further, the Commission noted that the parties to the concentration are present neither in the banking sector nor in the provision of insurance services, and it is clear from the second decision that the authorization system provided by the national legislation is not related to the supervision of banking or insurance sectors.[281] Thus, the Minister of Finance's decisions to oppose the concentration as designed by the parties is not included under the heading of 'prudential rules' listed in article 21 EUMR.

[271] ibid para 35.
[272] ibid para 36.
[273] ibid para 40.
[274] ibid para 42.
[275] ibid para 43.
[276] ibid para 49.
[277] ibid.
[278] ibid para 50.
[279] ibid para 51.
[280] ibid para 52.
[281] ibid.

Secondly, the Commission assessed whether the government's actions could be justified by a legitimate interest represented by the 'plurality of media'. Obviously, it concluded that this was not the case.

Lastly, the Commission analysed whether the exception concerning the protection of public security was applicable. In this respect, the Commission relied on the fact that the Court of Justice has not accepted that industrial or economic policy falls within the meaning of 'public security'.[282] Thus, the interest invoked by the Portuguese authorities does not constitute an interest justifying a measure under the concept of public security.[283] Hence, the Commission concluded that the Republic of Portugal should have applied for an authorization under article 21 EUMR to successfully rely on the interest mentioned in the blocking decisions.[284]

Therefore, the Commission determined that the two decisions adopted by the Minister of Finance constituted an infringement of the rules on freedom of establishment and free movement of capital within the EU and thus could not be warranted under any public interest reasons established in the case law of the ECJ.[285]

Case COMP/M.3768 *BBVA/BNL* and Case COMP/M.3780 *ABN AMRO/Banca Antonveneta*

The cases involved the notification to the Commission of two acquisition operations: the first concerned the acquisition by the Spanish bank BBVA of the Italian bank BNL and the acquisition by the Dutch bank ABN AMRO of the Italian bank Antonveneta by way of public bids. Apart from the notification made before the Commission, the bids were also notified the by Bank of Italy, which is responsible for assessing the compatibility of the takeover bids with prudential rules. Similarly, the Bank of Italy is also responsible for authorizing the increase in the shareholdings in an Italian bank above certain levels. The Commission cleared the two concentrations through a simplified procedure as none of them raised any competitive concerns.

However, after the clearance, the acquiring parties accused the Bank of Italy of infringing article 21 EUMR by creating certain obstacles to their bids.

Firstly, ABN AMRO considered that the Bank of Italy infringed article 21 EUMR because it treated ABN in a discriminatory manner by favouring a counteroffer from the part of an Italian bank BPI, and thus created serious obstacles to ABN's offer.[286] Nevertheless, after requesting information from the Bank of Italy and BPI and examining the ABN's complaint, the Commission decided not to open a formal investigation in relation to the allegation thereof.

Secondly, BBVA claimed that the Bank of Italy infringed article 21(4) EUMR because the approval of BBVA's bid was made conditional upon the acquisition of a shareholding above 50 per cent in BNL.[287] BBVA declared that this requirement could not be justified on the grounds of respect of prudential rules, and it constituted an obstacle to the takeover of control which could be realized with a shareholding of below 50 per cent.[288]

The Commission made known its position on this matter, declaring that conditioning the approval of the bid upon the acquisition of a shareholding above 50 per cent would constitute an infringement of article 21 EUMR. However, following this statement, the Bank of Italy declared that it has not made the approval conditional upon the acquisition of a shareholding above 50 per cent, but that in the case of an acquisition below the 50 per cent threshold, supplementary verification as to the BBVA ability to exercise effective control should be made.[289]

282 ibid para 54.
283 ibid.
284 ibid para 56.
285 ibid para 58.
286 Cuadrado (n 72).
287 ibid.
288 ibid.
289 ibid.

Case COMP/M.3894 *Unicredito/HVB*

The case involved the acquisition by the Italian bank Unicredito Italiano (UCI) of the control of the German bank Bayerische Hypo-und Vereinsbank AG (HBV) by way of a public bid. After examining the concentration's compatibility with the internal market, the Commission decided to clear the merger unconditionally.

However, despite the Commission clearance of the concentration, the Polish government requested UCI to divest its shares in the Polish bank BHP (Unicredito acquired control over the Polish branch through the acquisition of the German bank HVB) justifying this measure on the grounds of a 'non-compete' obligation contained in the Privatization Agreement concluded in 1999 between Unicredit and the Polish Treasury for the privatization of a Polish bank Pekao.[290] The 'non-compete' clause prevented Unicredit for ten years from:

(i) opening subsidiaries/branches in Poland;
(ii) acquiring control of banks in Poland;
(iii) making any capital investment in any company active in the banking sector in Poland.[291]

Therefore, given that Unicredito indirectly acquired control over a Polish bank, the Polish auditing authority declared that the non-compete obligation inserted in the Privatization Agreement had been infringed and invited thus Unicredito to divest its newly acquired shares to another company with the consequence of the Privatization Agreement being revoked. The Polish authorities justified the insertion of the non-compete clause preventing Unicredito from acquiring or investing in any of Pekao's competitors on the Polish market by reasons of protection of competition.[292]

The Commission intervened reaching a preliminary conclusion that the measures imposed by the Polish authorities constitute a violation of article 21 EUMR and an infringement of the right of establishment and free movement of capital within the EU. The Commission expressed its concerns in detail concerning the fact that the decision to invoke and enforce the non-compete obligation of the Privatization Agreement can de facto prevent the Unicredito/HVB concentration.[293] However, the Commission had not proceeded with the case further as ultimately a settlement was reached.[294]

Case COMP/M.4197 *E.ON/Endesa*

The case concerned a concentration arising from a cash offer made by E.ON, a German company active in the electricity and gas sectors throughout Europe and the USA, to acquire the entire share capital of Endesa. The latter is a Spanish company active in the energy sector in Europe and in both South and North America. Prior to the notification made to the Commission, E.ON registered its bid to the Spanish Stock Markets Authority (CNMV), which informed E.ON that its bid was in competition with a bid already launched by a Spanish energy company, Gas Natural.

The Commission analysed the operation and concluded that the notified operation constitutes a concentration within the meaning of EUMR and decided to clear the merger without conditions.

Before the Commission clearance of the concentration, the Spanish government adopted a series of legislative measures aimed at increasing the national energy regulator's (CNE) supervisory powers—Royal Decree-Law 4/2006 under an urgent procedure. According to the Decree-Law, in the case of an acquisition of more than 10 per cent of the share capital, or any participation ensuring the acquiring party the ability to impose significant influence in a company active in a regulated sector (eg, transport and distribution of electricity and gas), is subject to the prior approval by CNE. Also, the law

[290] European Commission, 'Mergers: Commission launches procedure against Poland for preventing Unicredit/HVB merger' (Press release IP/06/277, 8 March 2006).
[291] ibid.
[292] ibid.
[293] ibid.
[294] OECD (n 31).

provides that the approval is made pursuant to the application of a legal test, which is comprised, *inter alia*, of the following grounds:

(i) the existence of significant risks or negative effects on the activities in a regulated sector;
(ii) the protection of public interest in the energy sector and particularly the proper maintenance of sector policy objectives, especially concerning the strategic assets (ie, electricity and gas infrastructure, nuclear power plants, thermal plants using domestic coal);
(iii) the possibility that a company carrying out regulated activities cannot ensure the exercise of such activities as a result of other activities carried out by the acquirer of the target entity;
(iv) public security.[295]

The law also establishes that its provisions apply to all pending operations except those CNE has already issued authorization decisions. In fact, at the time of its adoption, the only pending concentration covered by this provision was E.ON's offer, which initially was not subject to any approval from CNE.[296]

Simultaneously, the Commission launched an infringement action pursuant to article 226 of the Treaty alleging that the Royal Decree's provisions are contrary to the principles of free movement of capital and freedom of establishment within the EU. The Commission considered that the CNE's right to grant or refuse authorization is based on grounds that lack clarity and, therefore, give rise to wide discretionary powers on the part of the CNE, raising concerns in relation to the proportionality of the potential measures taken by the authority.[297]

Measures Taken by Spain Directed Towards the E.ON/ Endesa Concentration

In compliance with the newly adopted Decree-Law, E.ON filed an application requesting CNE to authorize its operation. CNE analysed the measure and adopted a decision to impose nineteen conditions on the concentration. These conditions are varied, including corporate requirements, financial and investment requirements, reporting requirements, requirements related to the management of assets, divestiture requirements, and compliance requirements.

Regarding the corporate requirements (first condition), E.ON was required:

1. to enable Endesa to remain the parent company of its group for ten years following the merger; and
2. to maintain the corporate structure of Endesa as it was before the concentration, that is, meaning that E.ON was not allowed after the concentration to merge any of the companies in Endesa's group with any of the divisions of the E.ON group as well as restructuring Endesa's group.[298]

The CNE justified this requirement by considering that potential changes in Endesa's corporate structure would negatively affect the Spanish public interest regarding the security of supply.[299] Nevertheless, the Commission considered that these requirements limit E.ON's economic freedom relating to the exercise of its control over Endesa constituting thus a restriction of the freedom of establishment and the principle of free movement of capital within the EU.[300] In particular, the Commission considered that cross-border mergers represent specific exercise means of the freedom of establishment essential to the proper functioning of the internal market, and by limiting E.ON's

[295] Case COMP/M.4197 *E.ON/Endesa*, para 12.
[296] ibid, para 13.
[297] ibid para 15.
[298] ibid para 42.
[299] ibid para 43.
[300] ibid para 44.

liberty to merge some companies of its group with companies of Endesa's group after the concentration, the measures in question infringe the principle of freedom of establishment within the EU.[301]

Regarding the financial and investment requirements (second to fifth conditions), E.ON was required to maintain and undertake certain measures to satisfy CNE that Endesa's financial stability and investment plans would continue following the merger. CNE justifies the imposition of these requirements by stating that E.ON could reduce investments in order to increase the dividends and recoup its initial expenses made for the acquisition of Endesa.[302] However, the Commission considered that these requirements constitute barriers to the free movement of capital and freedom of establishment.[303]

In relation to the requirements concerning the management of power plants and the supply of gas, CNE imposed on E.ON an obligation to maintain the marginal operative lives of Endesa's generation plants and to ensure the natural gas supply plans as planned by Endesa. CNE had not specifically justified the imposition of the requirement relating to the operative life of the power plants, but it aimed at mitigating the risks raised by the concentration for the security of supply.[304] Regarding the requirement to continue Endesa's gas supply commitments, CNE explained that such a requirement aims at ensuring the security of supply. However, the Commission disagreed with CNE and concluded that the imposition of these requirements represents a violation of the same principles of freedom of establishment and free movement of capital within the EU It also considered that this requirement is not a necessary and proportionate measure to ensure the security of supply because the Spanish legislation already requires suppliers to guarantee production capacity, foreseeing severe sanctions in this respect.[305]

As with the requirements related to the disposal of assets and the transfer of management (ninth to thirteenth conditions), CNE required E.ON to assign the management of the nuclear plants in which Endesa holds shares to the co-owner of those plants to refrain from involvement in the decision-making relating to the provision of services and supply of fuel to nuclear power plants as well as divesting the only nuclear plant solely owned by Endesa.[306] CNE argued that the acquisition of control over Endesa by E.ON could create the risk that the business decisions made in relation to the power plants would pursue short-run business interests that may be in conflict with the Spanish public interest and sectoral policy raising concerns for the security of electricity supply and public security.[307] CNE argued that the legal safety requirements in Spain and Germany differ and considered the risk that E.ON would find it difficult to adhere to the safety standards in Spain.[308] Finally, CNE noted that the national security interest could be safeguarded only by requiring the foreign owners of the nuclear assets to dispose of the management of the assets converting their shareholding into a financial investment only.[309]

The Commission disagreed with the arguments put forward by CNE and argued that these requirements violate the rules on free movement of capital and freedom of establishment inside the EU.[310] The Commission argued that the CNE's arguments on nuclear safety cannot stand as valid because it is the community which has an exclusive competence on this matter and that the users of nuclear installations and fuels have to abide to specialized controls from the Euratom Supply Agency and the Commission's Safeguards Inspectors.[311] The Commission did not consider that the E.ON's acquisition of control over Endesa would raise serious concerns for nuclear security, safety or for the security of electricity supply[312] because after the merger the nuclear plants concerned will continue to be owned/co-owned and managed/co-managed by Endesa and the Commission's and Spanish

301 ibid para 45.
302 ibid para 62.
303 ibid para 63.
304 ibid para 78.
305 ibid para 79.
306 ibid para 86.
307 ibid para 87.
308 ibid.
309 ibid.
310 ibid para 88.
311 ibid para 89.
312 ibid para 90.

authorities' control would not change after the concentration.[313] Moreover, the Commission cited several examples illustrating that foreign ownership and management nuclear power plants in other Member States did not raise any concerns regarding the security of electricity supply other than the inherent risks present in the industry which could be addressed by general sectoral measures.[314]

In relation to the requirement of disposal of assets outside the mainland territory of Spain as well as disposal of power plants using domestic coal, the Commission considered that the main reason behind these requirements is represented by Spain's energy policy considerations requiring the maintaining of strategic assets under the control of a Spanish company and it represents a means of arbitrary discrimination and a disguised limitation to the free movement of capital and freedom of establishment within the EU.[315]

Finally, the Commission analysed the compatibility of the last conditions imposed by CNE, that is, the requirement of prior authorization for the acquisition of participations in Endesa and the establishment of the power of CNE to review or withdraw its approval in certain cases, especially whereby a third party will acquire more than 50 per cent of E.ON's share capital or voting rights.[316] The Commission cited the case law of the ECJ in *Commission v United Kingdom*[317] and *Commission v Spain*,[318] where the court concluded that state measures that prevent the acquisition of shares in companies restricting investors from other Member States to make direct investments constitute a breach of the fundamental EU law principle of free movement of capital and therefore, they are prohibited. Further, the Commission puts forward the argument that the measures in question are disproportionate as potential risks related to the security of energy supply could be addressed using general sectoral rules applicable to all undertakings in the industry.[319] It also argued that the condition requiring not to give preference to E.ON's interests when adopting strategic corporate decisions regarding Endesa is discriminatory in nature since there is no similar requirement imposed on any other energy company active in Spain.[320]

In light of the above, the Commission adopted the decision concluding that Spain infringed article 21 EUMR by adopting a decision without prior communication and authorization by the Commission as well as the imposition of a number of requirements going against the EU rules on free movement of capital and freedom of establishment interfering with the Commission's exclusive competence to assess and authorize concentrations having an EU dimension.[321]

Case COMP/M.4685 *Enel/Acciona/Endesa*

The case concerned a concentration involving the acquisition of joint control by the Italian company Enel and the Spanish company Acciona of the Spanish energy operator Endesa. The operation consisted of a joint public offer to acquire shares in Endesa that were not already under their ownership or control.[322] After the launching of the offer, Enel, Acciona, and Endesa decided to transfer to E.ON certain assets and rights, including Enel's electricity production, distribution, and supply business in Spain, some of Endesa's assets located in Spain as well as its business in several countries.[323]

The parties notified the Commission concerning their intention to acquire joint control over Endesa, but the scope of their notification was limited to the net assets of Endesa without including the assets to be transferred to E.ON. Pursuant to this notification, the Commission adopted a decision

[313] ibid para 91.
[314] ibid para 96.
[315] ibid para 104 and 111.
[316] ibid para 118.
[317] Case C-98/01 *Commission v United Kingdom* [2003] ECR I-4641 para 47.
[318] Case C-463/00 *Commission v Spain* [2003] ECR I-4581 paras 61–62.
[319] Case COMP/M.4197 *E.ON/Endesa*, para 130.
[320] ibid para 131.
[321] ibid para 132.
[322] Case COMP/M.4685 *Enel/Acciona/Endesa*, C(2007)5913 final, para 8.
[323] ibid para 9.

whereby declared that the concentration is one having a Community dimension and declared it compatible with the internal market.[324]

After the Commission cleared the operation, the CNE adopted a decision imposing several conditions on the party's concentration, giving rise to the Commission decision discussed in the following.

In the text of the decision, the Commission referred to its decisions concerning the measures taken by the Spanish authorities in relation to the E.ON/Endesa concentration and the infringement procedure brought against Spain concerning the provisions of the Royal Decree-Law 4/2006. Regarding the Commission decision finding that Spain violated article 21 EUMR, in the first instance, the Spanish authorities lowered the conditions imposed on E.ON rather than eliminating them, which led the Commission to adopt a second decision finding that Spain failed to comply with its duties under article 21 EUMR.[325] And, in the second instance, the Spanish authorities refused to abide the Commission's decisions which lead the latter to bring proceedings against Spain before the Court of Justice.

The Court concluded that Spain failed to fulfil its obligations under each of the two decisions.[326] The Commission also recalled that it brought proceedings against Spain in an action for infringement under article 226 of the Treaty, alleging that Spain failed to comply with its duties under the Treaty by adopting legislative measures (ie, the Royal Decree-Law 4/2006) that are contrary to the rules on free movement of capital and freedom of establishment within the community. The Court of Justice concluded that by adopting the provision in the Royal Decree-Law 4/2006, which confer CNE the power to authorize the acquisition of shareholding above 10 per cent in companies carrying on certain regulated activities in the energy sector, Spain failed to fulfil its obligations under articles 43 EC and 56 EC concerning the free movement of capital and freedom of establishment.[327]

Measures Adopted by the Spanish Authorities in Relation to Enel/Acciona/Endesa Concentration

In accordance with the provisions of the Royal Decree-Law, the Spanish authorities adopted the following decisions concerning the parties' operation:

(i) CNE authorized Enel's intention to raise its stake in Endesa beyond the 10 per cent threshold following the acquisition of a non-controlling 24.99 per cent stake in Endesa, subject to certain conditions.
(ii) CNE authorized Enel and Acciona to take over the joint control of Endesa, imposing certain conditions.
(iii) The Minister of Industry modified the conditions imposed by CNE following the appeals made by Enel against the decision adopted by the latter authority.

The Commission did not act against the CNE's first decision since the acquisition of a non-controlling interest by Enel did not involve a concentration with a Community dimension, but nevertheless, it decided to take action against the CNE's second decision since this second decision involved a concentration with a Community dimension (ie, the joint acquisition of control of Endesa by Enel and Acciona).[328]

Initially, CNE imposed twelve conditions on Enel/Acciona's concentration; however, the Minister of Industry removed five conditions and modified a further four. The Commission assessed the compatibility of the conditions as modified by the Minister of Industry, noting that the text of the modified conditions is identical with that of the conditions imposed on E.ON and found by the Commission to be contrary to community law.[329]

[324] ibid para 10.
[325] Press Release IP/07/296 of 7 March 2007.
[326] Case C-196/07 *Kingdom of Spain v European Commission* [2008] ECR I-41.
[327] Case C-207/07 *Commission v Kingdom of Spain*, ECLI:EU:C:2008:428.
[328] Case COMP/M.4685 *ENEL/Acciona/Endesa*, paras 29 and 30.
[329] ibid para 38.

The conditions analysed by the Commission are the following:

1) ACCIONA and ENEL will maintain ENDESA, S.A. as an independent company, with full operating responsibility in implementing its business plan, and as head of its group. Its brand, registered office, governing body and effective management and decision-making centre will remain in Spain.[330]
2) The applicants must maintain ENDESA duly capitalised. ENDESA must comply with a debt service ratio (net financial debt/EBITDA) of less than 5.25 for a minimum of three years from the takeover of ENDESA. The applicants must inform CNE of the evolution of this ratio each quarter from the date of the takeover of ENDESA.
3) Acciona and ENEL will assume and carry out, through their control over ENDESA, all the investments in regulated gas and electricity activities (both transmission and distribution) in both sectors (as defined in Function 14 of Additional Provision No 11(3)(1) of Law 34/98) included in: (1) the latest investment plans announced by ENDESA for 2006-2011 described in this Decision, (2) the document Planning of the gas and electricity sectors. Development of the transmission networks 2002-2012 approved by the Council of Ministers and submitted to the Parliament, and (3) the CNE's Framework report on the demand for electricity and natural gas and its coverage.
4) In view of the special nature of nuclear assets with respect to public security, ACCIONA and ENEL in the exercise of their control over ENDESA must comply with the obligations and regulations concerning nuclear energy, specifically compliance with all the codes and agreements with the other partners concerning management of nuclear plants as regards security and supply of uranium.
5) ACCIONA and ENEL will, for a period of five years from acquisition of ENDESA, ensure that the aggregate annual consumption of each plant owned by ENDESA currently consuming national coal is not less that the aggregate annual amounts specified for consumption by these plants in the 2006–2012 National Coal Mining Plan, in so far as the current conditions and circumstances are maintained.
6) ACCIONA and ENEL will, during a period of five years from the acquisition of ENDESA, maintain the companies that currently manage the transmission, distribution and generation assets of the mainland and non-mainland electricity systems within the ENDESA Group.[331]

Compatibility of the Measures with Article 21 EUMR

Regarding the first condition imposed on Enel and Acciona, that is, maintaining Endesa as an independent company as well as its brand (the first condition), the Commission reiterates its findings in the E.ON decision, where it concluded that such requirements significantly limit the parties' freedom to establish the corporate structure of its group after the merger and, thus, represent an unreasonable interference with the parties' freedom of establishment and free movement of capital.[332] Further, the Commission reminded that the existence of such restriction is not necessary and proportionate for the protection of legitimate public interest, and it also does not comply with the principle of non-discrimination.[333] The Commission argued that such a condition is discriminatory in nature because CNE would not have the power to impose a similar requirement as an industry regulator on undertakings outside the control procedure of the concentrations of regulated assets.[334]

It finally concluded that in the absence of an objective justification, the imposition of such corporate conditions led to the situation in which, for reasons of economic policy, Endesa's business centres remained inside the Spanish territory and could not be transferred to another Member State,

[330] ibid para 35.
[331] ibid para 38.
[332] ibid para 61.
[333] ibid para 68.
[334] ibid para 75.

which therefore represents a way of arbitrary discrimination and restricts the free movement of capital and freedom of establishment.[335]

Similarly, as with the requirement to maintain Endesa's brand after the concentration, the Commission argues that this condition acts as a significant limitation on the parties' economic freedom to establish their business strategies after the merger, as the use of brands represents an important part of the business strategies post-merger limiting thus the parties' freedom of establishment and free movement of capital.[336]

Regarding the second and third conditions (ie, reporting capitalization and investment obligation), the Commission recalls the argument made in the E.ON decisions stating that the imposition of such financial requirements significantly limits the parties' economic freedom after the merger being contrary to the rules on free movement of capital as well as freedom of establishment and they are neither necessary nor proportionate for the protection of the public interest to safeguard public security and security of electricity supply giving rise to a discriminatory treatment.[337]

As with the condition that Enel and Acciona should ensure that Endesa's power plants using domestic coal will use such fuel as foreseen in the national mining plans for the years 2006–12, the Commission noted that the mining plan does not oblige the companies to consume fixed amounts of coal, but it only encourages the operators to maintain their consumption at fixed levels.[338] Therefore, the Commission concluded that CNE through this condition imposed an additional obligation which is not foreseen by the Spanish general legislation, and which limits the economic freedom of the parties interfering with their right of free movement of goods.[339]

The Commission considered that the obligation on Endesa to use domestic coal could not be justified on grounds of protection of public interest and goes against the principles of proportionality and non-discrimination.[340] In particular, the Commission mentioned that as in the case of the Minister's decision in *E.ON/Endesa*, the imposition of such an obligation is necessary to ensure the use of domestic coal to reduce Spain's dependency on foreign energy resources, but stated that Spanish authorities did not indicate any element leading to the conclusion that the Enel/Acciona's acquisition of Endesa will pose a genuine and sufficient threat for the security of supply or that after the operation the merged entity will reduce its demand of domestic coal.[341]

Regarding the sixth condition (ie, the obligation to maintain within Endesa's companies which own assets outside mainland Spain for five years), the Commission recalled that a similar condition imposed by the Spanish authorities on E.ON was found to be liable to restrict the economic freedom of E.ON to decide the corporate structure of its group and sell businesses after the merger representing, therefore, a barrier of cross-border concentration violating the rules on the free movement of capital and freedom of establishment.[342] Moreover, it considered that such an obligation could not be justified for the protection of the legitimate interests recognized by the first sentence of article 21(4) EUMR (ie, public security, plurality of media and prudential rules).[343]

Thus, in light of the above, the Commission concluded that Spain failed to comply with its obligations under article 21 EUMR by imposing a number of conditions which could not be justified by the legitimate interests listed in paragraph 4 of article 21 as they are contrary to the EU law on the free movement of capital and goods and freedom of establishment interfering with the Commission's exclusive competence to deal with concentrations having a Community dimension.[344]

335 ibid para 76.
336 ibid para 78.
337 ibid para 83.
338 ibid para 100.
339 ibid paras 101 and 102.
340 ibid para 103.
341 ibid para 104.
342 ibid paras 114 and 115.
343 ibid.
344 ibid para 124.

Case COMP/M. 4685 *Abertis/Autostrade*

The case concerned a concentration between the Spanish company Abertis and the Italian company Autostrade by way of exchange of shares. The Commission cleared the concentration without conditions.

Following the concentration, the Italian national body responsible for granting motorway concessions refused to transfer the concession to the newly formed entity because of the concerns relating to Abertis's financial ability to invest in the Italian motorway infrastructure network. The Commission intervened and reached a preliminary conclusion that the actions taken by the Italian authorities violated article 21(4) EUMR because they failed to fix in advance and in a sufficiently clear manner the public interest criteria for the conduct of the authorization procedure and to adopt an authorization decision for the transfer of the concession contributing to de facto blocking or seriously affecting the completion of a concentration with a Community dimension.[345]

The Commission also stated that by implementing such measures without requesting its authorization, the Italian authorities breached the notification and stand-still obligation provided by article 21 EUMR, and the measures are contrary to the principle of legal certainty and may constitute an unjustified limitation of the principles of free movement of capital and freedom of establishment enshrined in articles 43 and 56 of the EC Treaty[346].

Case M.10102 *Vienna Insurance Group (VIG)/Aegon*

VIG is an international insurance group based in Austria. It conducts its business through subsidiaries in several countries, mainly the Central and Eastern Europe region (CEE). Aegon Group specializes in life and non-life insurance, pension funds, asset management, and ancillary services businesses.

In 2020, Aegon decided to sell several subsidiaries in the CEE region (Hungary, Poland, Romania, and Turkey) to one buyer. The best offer was made by VIG. The two parties quickly entered into negotiations. Just the day before the signing of the transaction, the Hungarian government amended its 'permanent' FDI regime by including insurance activities in the scope of activities deemed sensitive to national security.

As a result, the planned transaction was suddenly subject to the 'permanent' FDI screening regime. Thus, Hungarian authorities argued that the acquisition threatened Hungary's legitimate interests and issued their veto on 6 April 2021.

The parties decided to submit an application for a judicial review against the veto decision and filed a complaint to the Commission. Subsequently, the latter opened an investigation to assess whether the veto complied with the EUMR, giving the Commission an exclusive competence to assess concentration with an EU dimension.

In this case, the transaction could threaten the internal market in the sense that it would result in horizontal overlaps in the field of insurance products in different countries, including Hungary.

Following its investigation, the Commission had reasonable doubts as to whether the veto genuinely aimed to protect Hungary's legitimate interests within the meaning of the EUMR. In particular, it was unclear how the acquisition by VIG of Aegon's Hungarian assets would pose a threat to a fundamental interest of society, given that the merged entity will be a moderately sized competitor and will continue to face sufficient competitive pressure and that the parties are not particularly close competitors.[347] As a reminder, the Commission stated that Member States can only take appropriate measures to protect legitimate interests if (i) such measures are compatible with the general principles and other provisions of EU law and if (ii) the measures are genuinely aimed at protecting a legitimate interest.[348]

[345] Press Release IP/07/117 of 31 January 2007.

[346] ibid.

[347] European Commission, Case M.10102 *VIG/Aegon CEE.*

[348] 'The Relationship between FDI screening and Merger Control Reviews'—Note by Hungary (2022) DAF/COMP/WD(2022)104 https://one.oecd.org/document/DAF/COMP/WD(2022)104/en/pdf accessed 15 September 2023.

Therefore, the European Commission concluded that Hungarian authorities infringed article 21 EUMR. More especially, the European Commission stated that the veto was incompatible with the freedom of establishment.[349]

Finally, in 2022, an agreement was signed between the two parties. Indeed, in a press release, Aegon announced that it had completed the divestment of its Hungarian businesses to VIG. The transaction amounted to €620 million.[350]

Appendix 2: Recent Public Interest Cases in Member States

Carrefour and Couche-Tard, France, 2021

In 2021, one of Canada's biggest companies, Alimentation Couche-Tard, bid €16.2 billion for French supermarket chain Carrefour.

France's FDI control regime provides that FDI in sensitive sectors are subject to prior approval by the Minister of the Economy. Among these 'strategic sectors', one may find defence-related activities and the army. This list has never stopped expanding and now includes activities relating to agricultural products that 'contribute to national food security objectives'.

In the Carrefour-Couche-Tard operation, the Minister of the Economy, Bruno Le Maire, expressed his position even before an official referral was made by the relevant parties.[351] He signalled his intention to block the transaction in the name of 'food security'.

Syngenta and Verisem, Italy, 2021

In 2021, China-backed Swiss group Syngenta offered c. €200 million to acquire seed producer Verisem from US fund Paine Schwartz Partners. Verisem originated in Italy in the 1970s and, by 2021, had a global footprint, including facilities in Europe, North America, and Asia.

In October 2021, Italian Prime Minister Mario Draghi and Minister of Agriculture Stefano Patuanelli, using the special 'golden power' rules that apply to attempts by non-EU groups to buy strategic companies, including banks and insurers,[352] vetoed the acquisition under the Italian foreign investment control legislation.[353]

The deal had already drawn the attention of—and raised criticism from—the agricultural lobby Coldiretti (which advocates for an all-Italian agricultural supply chain). According to the Italian press, the reason behind the veto is that the acquisition of Verisem would have shifted the control of seed for producing vegetables and aromatic herbs entirely to Asia. In this context, 'agri-food' is considered to be a strategic sector according to the investment control regime.[354]

This represented the first and, so far, the only time the Italian government has relied on FI rules to block a transaction in the agri-food sector.

[349] European Commission, 'Mergers: Commission finds that Hungary's veto over the acquisition of AEGON's Hungarian subsidiaries by VIG breached Article 21 of the EU Merger Regulation', Press release, 21 February 2022.

[350] AEGON, 'Aegon Completes Sale of Hungarian Businesses and Announces Debt Tender Offer and Share Buyback' (Press release, 23 March 2022) https://www.aegon.com/investors/press-releases/2022/aegon-completes-sale-of-hungarian-businesses-and-announces-debt-tender-offer-and-share-buyback accessed 15 September 2023.

[351] Raphaël Dalmas and Alma Nicolaï, 'Foreign Investment Controls in France: Curfew for Couche Tard!', 28 January 2021, https://astura.fr/wp-content/uploads/Astura-28012021-FDI-controls-in-France-curfew-for-Couche-Tard-1.pdf, https://portolano.it/en/newsletter/portolano-cavallo-inform-corporate/italian-government-vetoes-acquisition-of-italian-seeds-producer-by-chinese-multinational-group accessed 1 February 2024.

[352] Global Times, 'Italy's Blocking of Chinese Deal Hurts Agricultural Cooperation', 14 April 2022.

[353] Daniel Joseph Giuliano, Francesco Portolano, 'Italian Government Vetoes Acquisition of Italian Seed Producer by Chinese Multinational Group', 15 November 2021.

[354] ibid.

Heyer Medical/Aeonmed, Germany, 2022

On 27 April 2022, the German government blocked the acquisition of German medical products manufacturer Heyer Medical AG by the Chinese Aeonmed Group. More particularly, Heyer is a manufacturer of ventilators for the treatment of respiratory diseases and anaesthesia. Beijing-based Aeonmed Group produces similar anaesthesia and mechanical ventilation medical devices.

The BMWK became aware of this transaction after it had closed. After two years of review, BMWK found that the acquisition of Heyer Medical by Aenomed would impair Germany's public order and security with regard to the supply of essential medical products for the healthcare sector. The government also expressed its concerns about the political influence of the Chinese government in the German economy by creating economic and technological dependencies in a key sector.[355]

This decision should be seen as a strong indication that the German government is able and willing to use the tools it has gained by the tightened German FDI rules.[356]

Cosco/Port of Hamburg, Germany, 2022

Cosco Shipping is a state-owned multinational based in Shanghai. It focuses on marine transportation services. The company intended to take over 35 per cent of the port terminal operator. The transaction quickly became the subject of FDI screening initiated by the German Ministry of Economics on the basis of the Foreign Trade and Payments Ordinance.

In October 2022, the government only allowed Cosco to acquire a company share of less than 25 per cent. Even if the details of the decision remain confidential, the Federal Ministry of Economics justified the step by saying that the takeover would otherwise pose a 'threat to public order and security'. The government also prevented Cosco from acquiring atypical control through special rights. Among other things, the Chinese group is prohibited from 'contractually granting itself veto rights over strategic business or personnel decisions'. Cosco is also not allowed to appoint members of the management or persons in operative management positions who make decisions independently.[357]

According to BMWK's press release, the partial prohibition decision prevents Cosco from acquiring a 'strategic' shareholding and reduces the acquisition to mere financial participation.[358]

Elmos/Silex, Germany, 2022

This case involved Elmos Semiconductor SE, based in Dortmund, which develops, produces and markets semiconductors mainly for use in the automotive industry and Swedish Silex Microsystems, a subsidiary of Chinese Sai Microelectronics.

In November 2022, the government prohibited the operation stating that any mitigation measures, such as an approval of the acquisition with conditions, were not suitable to remedy these concerns.

[355] Christoph H Seibt, 'China?—Thanks But No Thanks' (Manager Magazine, 3 May 2022) https://www.manager-magazin.de/politik/weltwirtschaft/china-thanks-but-no-thanks-a-5b019b4d-405a-4854-9b1b-bb0e2fbd0027 accessed 15 September 2023.

[356] Mirko von Bieberstein, 'Germany Prohibits Acquisition of Heyer Medical by Chinese Investor', 9 May 2022, https://www.clearygottlieb.com/news-and-insights/publication-listing/germany-prohibits-acquisition-of-heyer-medical-by-chinese-investor, accessed 1 February 2024.

[357] Dr Sandra Schuh, 'Cosco Case Shows: Foreign Direct Investments are Under Increased Scrutiny in Germany', 28 October 2022, https://www.pinsentmasons.com/out-law/news/investoren-aus-dem-ausland-werden-haeufiger-ueberprueft, accessed 1 February 2024.

[358] Peter Camesasca, Horst Henschen, Katherine Kingsbury, Martin Juhasz, and Ron Thoma, 'COSCO FDI Review: Germany Partially Prohibits Chinese Investment in a Hamburg Container Terminal—Spotlight on Minority Investments', 8 November 2022, https://www.lexology.com/library/detail.aspx?g=4ecb8bc6-6f66-4cd9-932b-c5f5b7640d9f, accessed 1 February 2024.

According to the Federal Cabinet, the transaction would have endangered Germany's public order and security. Indeed, Minister Habeck identified the following national security risk: 'we need to take a close look at take-overs involving significant infrastructure or where there is a risk that technology will transfer across to buyers from non-EU countries. It is particularly important for us that Germany's and Europe's technological sovereignty be protected in the semiconductor industry'.[359]

[359] Federal Ministry for Economic Affairs and Climate Action, 'Elmos Chip Factory Cannot be Sold to Chinese Investor—Cabinet Blocks Sale' (Press Release, 9 November 2022).

4
National Security and FDI Screening in the UK

4.1 Introduction

This chapter discusses the legal framework currently governing inward foreign direct investment (FDI) in the United Kingdom (UK). The timing of the recent reforms to the UK national security regime in this chapter, more than two years after the end of the transition period from the UK's exit from the European Union (EU) and its free trade area, marks the importance of this framework for the UK economy. With the effects of Brexit on inward FDI still uncertain, the UK government's focus on national security preoccupation with its regulation has been more intense than ever. While inward investment remains of vital importance to the UK economy, the new regime is expected to affect inward investment and scrutinize the participation of foreign investors in some key industries.

The structure of this chapter is the following: section 4.2 sets the scene for the topic by providing some basic information on the evolution of the regulation of FDI. It also introduces the key concerns most often cited in relation to foreign investment. Section 4.3 provides an extensive background on the assessment of national security in the UK prior to the recent legislative initiatives and the overhaul of the national security regime. Section 4.4 gives a detailed description of the existing legislative framework for government intervention in UK transactions. Additionally, it includes an overview of other mechanisms used to intervene in transactions to protect national security and sets the background for the National Security and Investment Act 2021 (NSIA). Section 4.5 describes the new regime for government intervention and provides a summary of the key provisions of the new Act. Finally, section 4.6 proceeds to evaluate the new UK regime, on the basis of a comparative analysis of other European FDI regimes.

4.2 Setting the Scene

4.2.1 Modern History of Foreign Direct Investment

Foreign direct investment (FDI) can be described as an investment made by a person or company resident of one country into business interests located in another country. In practice, FDI takes place when a non-resident investor establishes business operations in a foreign country or acquires business assets in a foreign company. In contrast to portfolio investment, FDI is not established by a mere purchase of equity in a foreign company.[1] The key distinctive feature of FDI is that it is undertaken with the intention of obtaining effective control of or at least substantial influence over the decision-making of a foreign business. For this reason, FDI usually involves the acquisition of lasting management interests or technology assets in addition to or as an alternative to capital investment.

Since the early 1990s, there has been an increasing global trend of trade liberalization and privatization of key service industries, aiming to create a welcoming environment for foreign investors. Both established and emerging economies sought to attract foreign investors and secure favourable terms for them by either deregulating some of their former state-controlled sectors or entering into international investment agreements. The creation of free trade areas and the expansion of the EU contributed to the progressive removal of policy and regulatory obstacles governing investment flows.

The effect of FDI on the host economy has attracted much research and literature, with economic theory and policymakers frequently emphasizing its benefits.[2] For the past few decades, FDI has been an integral part of an open and effective international economic system and a major catalyst to development.[3] In particular, FDI has been a prominent driver of economic growth for both developed and developing countries, especially with respect to employment creation, capital accumulation, transfer of technology, improved provision of services, and increased competition.[4]

Despite ongoing investment liberalization, many countries continue to maintain or introduce protective barriers to foreign investment, including sector-specific restrictions, FDI screening frameworks, and a regulatory framework for inward FDI.[5] It is, therefore, apparent that many countries consider inward foreign investment flows as a source of serious risks and challenges for the host country.

[1] According to the Organisation for Economic Cooperation and Development (OECD) and its World Investment Report 2009, an operative rule for the distinction between a portfolio investment and a FDI is that FDI must relate to at least 10 per cent of the shares or the voting power in the foreign-based company.

[2] Among others, see Pierre-Olivier Gourinchas and Olivier Jeanne, 'Capital Flows to Developing Countries: The Allocation Puzzle' (2013) 80(4) Review of Economic Studies 1484.

[3] OECD, 'Foreign Direct Investment for Development: Maximising Benefits, Minimising Costs' (2002) 3 https://www.oecd.org/investment/investmentfordevelopment/1959815.pdf accessed 15 September 2023.

[4] UNCTAD, 'Investment and Technology Policies for Competitiveness: Review of Successful Country Experiences' (2003) https://unctad.org/system/files/official-document/iteipc20032_en.pdf accessed 15 September 2023; and Federico Carril-Caccia and Elena Pavlova, 'Foreign Direct Investment and its Drivers: A Global and EU Perspective' (2018) European Central Bank Economic Bulletin, Issue 4/2018 https://www.ecb.europa.eu/pub/economic-bulletin/articles/2018/html/ecb.ebart201804_01.en.html accessed 15 September 2023.

[5] Among these countries, Australia tightened its investment screening procedures in the energy and agricultural sectors, Belgium introduced a new screening mechanism to intervene in foreign acquisitions, China set up national security review procedures for inward FDI, while France and Germany extended the scopes of their existing FDI regimes to cover several new strategic technology activities.

4.2.2 The Broader Context for National Security Considerations and FDI

The technological facilitation of foreign investment inflows has intensified the host countries' concerns, most of which relate to excessive foreign control in the domestic economy and adverse effects on their national security.

Some of the concerns related to FDI refer to the displacement of business activities and workers, transfer of research and development (R&D) and possible monopolistic practices, as well as cyber-security and terrorist threats and the rise of state-owned foreign enterprises.[6]

Additionally, there has been a widespread focus on safeguarding sectors of strategic importance, such as the defence and energy sector, critical infrastructure, and core technologies, where the takeover of domestic firms could create or reinforce foreign dependence or otherwise impair national security. Such concerns were mainly provoked in cases of large multinational corporations acquiring controlling stakes in businesses that domestic governments considered sensitive. Finally, other geopolitical factors are also relevant in assessing national security concerns arising from FDI, including the widespread economic nationalism and, more recently, the economic volatility created by the Covid-19 pandemic.

All these factors have played an important role in the adoption of an interventionist tendency by many developed countries (including Germany, France, Australia, and now the UK), which have recently sought to emphasize national sovereignty and promote national interests over FDI. Indeed, in its *World Investment Report 2022*, the United Nations Conference on Trade and Development (UNCTAD) highlights the fact that nearly all of the policy measures less favourable to investment adopted in 2021 were adopted by developed countries.[7] At the same time, however, numerous countries with emerging economies are adopting other policy measures to promote and facilitate investment. Notably, developing countries in Asia are now taking the lead in adopting investment liberalization measures.

4.2.3 The UK's Strategy on the Assessment of National Security Considerations for FDI

Traditionally, the UK has operated a relatively liberal regime and FDI-oriented economic development policy, encouraging foreign investors to participate and contribute to its national economy.

[6] Hogan Lovells, 'The rise of FDI regimes and their impact on M&A transactions' (January 2021) https://www.engage.hoganlovells.com/knowledgeservices/news/the-rise-of-fdi-regimes-and-their-impact-on-ma-transactions accessed 15 September 2023.

[7] UNCTAD, *World Investment Report 2022: International Tax Reforms and Sustainable Investment*, https://unctad.org/system/files/official-document/wir2022_en.pdf accessed 15 September 2023.

The 'open for business' stance has come under public scrutiny on several occasions in the past, including in 2014, after US-domiciled Pfizer's failed bid for its UK-listed counterpart AstraZeneca, the Softbank/ARM takeover in 2016,[8] and in 2020, after it was announced that the Chinese telecommunications firm Huawei's equipment would be banned from the UK's 5G networks.[9]

In response to this scepticism, the then Prime Minster, Theresa May, confirmed her plans for a 'proper industrial strategy' that would allow the government to step in to defend strategically important sectors from unwanted foreign investment.[10]

In the past two decades, the UK government's powers to intervene in proposed foreign investment have been limited by the Enterprise Act 2002 to transactions that meet strict criteria and exceed certain thresholds. However, recent developments in the UK's national security policy and regulation (in particular, the new National Security and Investment Act) mean that greater scrutiny is expected in the near future for transactions that raise national security concerns.

After changes in the political scenery and a long period of review and consultation of the UK's approach to national security matters, several short-term reforms were implemented in anticipation of long-term changes to the screening process of FDI. The proposed reforms sought to update the existing legal framework in order to respond to advances in technology in industries where, in the government's view, there is an increased risk of foreign investors (i) engaging in espionage (due to increased access to assets, personnel and data), (ii) undertaking sabotage, and (iii) using their control over important British enterprises to promote their interest in negotiations towards other deals.[11]

Long-term changes were brought forward by the UK National Security and Investment Bill (NSI Bill), which received Royal Assent on 29 April 2021, becoming the NSIA. The NSIA will introduce a new regime for FDI screening in the UK, separate from the merger control regime, to address acquisitions of British companies and assets and include a mandatory notification and pre-approval requirement for the most sensitive sectors of the economy, backed up by a voluntary notification option for the rest of the economy and a call-in power for transactions that have not been notified. The UK government has repeatedly stated that it is determined 'to protect the country's national

[8] SoftBank's £24.3 bn acquisition of ARM Holdings was announced in the weeks following the Brexit vote in June 2016. The large acquisition of a British technology company faced strong opposition from the media and public. SoftBank sought to deal with potential concerns about the takeover by becoming the first bidder to give legally binding post-offer undertakings under the UK Takeover Code. See Herbert Smith Freehills, 'UK Takeover Code—Bidder Elects to Give Post-Offer Undertakings for the First Time' (Oxford Business Law Blog, 30 September 2016) https://blogs.law.ox.ac.uk/business-law-blog/blog/2016/09/uk-takeover-code---bidder-elects-give-post-offer-undertakings-first accessed 15 September 2023.

[9] Department for Digital, Culture, Media, and Sports (DCMS), 'Huawei to be removed from UK 5G networks by 2027' (14 July 2020) https://www.gov.uk/government/news/huawei-to-be-removed-from-uk-5g-networks-by-2027 accessed 15 September 2023; DCMS, 'UK Telecoms Supply Chain Review Report' (July 2019) https://www.gov.uk/government/publications/telecoms-supply-chain-review-terms-of-reference accessed 15 September 2023.

[10] Theresa May, Speech at Conservative Leadership Campaign Launch (Birmingham, 11 July 2016) https://www.wlrk.com/docs/TheresaMayJuly11Speech.pdf accessed 15 September 2023.

[11] Department for Business, Energy, and Industrial Strategy (BEIS), National Security and Infrastructure Investment Review (October 2017) para 47 https://assets.publishing.service.gov.uk/government/uploads/system/uploads/attachment_data/file/652505/2017_10_16_NSII_Green_Paper_final.pdf accessed 15 September 2023.

security from potentially hostile foreign direct investment, while ensuring the UK remains a global champion of free trade and an attractive place to invest'.[12] The NSIA came into force on 4 January 2022, and the regime has retroactive application in that the government will have the power to call in for review transactions which closed on or after 12 November 2020.[13]

Nevertheless, the market reaction has been mostly critical of the new regime, with many commentators expressing concerns about its potential negative effects on foreign investment inflows. The new screening regime is expected to significantly expand the range of circumstances in which the government can investigate and assess national security concerns. Therefore, it is anticipated that a far greater number of transactions will fall under the thresholds for review than at present, with corresponding consequences in terms of timeline and uncertainty for investors and businesses. Finally, significant sanctions will be available for non-compliance, including fines on a turnover basis and criminal liability. Further commentary on the potential implications of the new regime are given in greater detail in section 4.3.

4.3 The Evolution of the Assessment of National Security and Public Interest

4.3.1 From the 1965 Monopolies and Mergers Act to the 1973 Fair Trading Act

This section will start by discussing the approach of the UK regime to public interest considerations, and in particular, it will focus on cases that raised national security concerns and discuss how the assessment of these transactions was conducted. This will then lead us to discuss in the next section the recent legislative and policy developments in the UK that aim to expand the remit of the UK government in assessing concentrations that potentially raise national security concerns.

The idea of controlling merger and acquisition activities based on public interest considerations was not incorporated into the British legal system until the 1965 Monopolies and Mergers Act (1965 Act). Although certain rules had been introduced earlier to address the creation and abuse of market power by the 1948 Monopolies and Restrictive Practices Act and the subsequent 1956 Restrictive Practices Act (1956 Act), 'merger path to market power' was not a significant public concern until the early 1960s.[14] Nevertheless, public debate on the restrictive characteristics of merger

[12] BEIS, 'New Powers to Protect UK from Malicious Investment and Strengthen Economic Resilience' (11 November 2020) https://www.gov.uk/government/news/new-powers-to-protect-uk-from-malicious-investment-and-strengthen-economic-resilience accessed 15 September 2023.

[13] NSIA, Part 1, Ch 1, s 2.

[14] AS Gilbert, 'System of Enforcement: the United Kingdom—the Monopolies Commission' (1963) 6 International and Comparative Law Quarterly Supplementary Publication 57, 58; CK Rowley, 'Mergers and Public Policy in Great Britain' (1968) 11 Journal of Law and Economics 75, 77.

activities on trade gained momentum from the beginning of 1960s. Those debates essentially paved the way for the adoption of the 1965 Act. Pass and Sparkes describe the road to the 1965 Act as follows:

> The introduction of merger legislation in 1965 was motivated by a number of factors: a growing concern with the increased scale of merger activity by large companies in the early 1960s and the effects of mergers in increasing industrial concentration; a recognition of the fact that many mergers were undertaken to reduce competitive pressures rather than to promote economic efficiency; and the difficulties involved in ensuring a more efficient market performance solely by 'conduct' remedies in industries where effective competition was lacking.[15]

The 1965 Act was mainly seen as a 'bipartisan measure', allowing it to have a smooth passage through the legislative process.[16] The Act entrusted the then Monopolies Commission and Board of Trade with powers to control mergers that 'operate or may be expected to operate against the public interest'.[17] From an institutional point, the Monopolies Commission was responsible for conducting inquiries upon receiving referrals from the Board of Trade, which held the powers to impose standstill obligations, prohibit or restrict acquisitions, order dissolution or impose conditions on relevant parties.[18] Only twenty cases out of 798 notified mergers had been referred to the Monopolies Commission, from the passage of the 1965 Act to the adoption of 1973 Fair Trading Act (1973 Act).[19] The number illustrates that the referral power was considered as an important one, sometimes even a 'political' one as Vanderver suggested.[20]

Any guidelines with regard to the content of public interest criteria, however, were not issued at the time, which made the Act open to several criticisms on certainty and predictability fronts.[21] The 1965 Act provided that the Monopolies Commission should take into account 'all the matters which appear in the particular circumstances to be relevant and have regard (amongst other things) to any matter to which the Board may from time to time direct them to have regard'.[22] However, no such significant clearance or direction by the authorities had been issued during the period 1965–73.

The 1973 Act again introduced a broad public interest test, elaborating its considerations under five categories.[23] These categories comprise: i) maintaining and promoting

[15] CL Pass and JR Sparkes, 'Control of Horizontal Mergers in Britain' (1980) 14 Journal of World Trade 135, 138.
[16] DG Goyder, 'Monopolies and Mergers Act, 1965' (1965) 28 The Modern Law Review 693.
[17] JB Heath, 'United Kingdom: Monopolies and Mergers Bill Foreign Antitrust Section' (1965) 10 Antitrust Bulletin 175, 176.
[18] Monopolies and Mergers Act 1965, s 6.
[19] Pass and Sparkes (n 15) 141.
[20] Timothy Vanderver, 'Competition and British Merger Regulation' (1970) 11 Harvard International Law Journal 126, 136.
[21] Rowley (n 14) 83; CY Pass, 'Horizontal Mergers and the Control of Market Power in the U.K. Foreign Antitrust' (1972) 17 Antitrust Bulletin 811, 812; Bruce Lyons, David Reader, and Andreas Stephan, 'UK Competition Policy Post-Brexit: In the Public Interest?' (2016) https://ssrn.com/abstract=2864461 accessed 15 September 2023.
[22] Monopolies and Mergers Act 1965, s 7(10).
[23] Fair Trading Act 1973, ss 84(1)(a)–(e).

effective competition, ii) price, quality, and variety considerations, iii) innovation, potential competition and reduction of costs, iv) balanced distribution of the industry and employment, and finally, v) international competitiveness. In that regard, 'effective competition' was only a part of the public interest criteria under the Act.[24] Furthermore, the power to refer cases to the Monopolies and Mergers Commission, established by the 1973 Act, resided with the Secretary of State, whereas the Director General of the then newly set-up Office of Fair Trading (OFT) shared with the Secretary of State, the powers to refer cases involving monopoly situations or restrictive agreements to Monopolies and Mergers Commission. Gribbin explains the difference between monopoly and merger procedures by the arguably political character of the latter, particularly by emphasizing its effects on unemployment and the need to remedy the harmful effects of the 1930s, the 1939–45 war, pervasiveness of cartels and to prevent asset-stripping.[25] He concludes his analysis with the following words: 'it is not surprising that Ministers should wish to retain the power to refer to the Monopolies Commission where regional employment or other social considerations might be affected by important merger transactions'.[26]

In fact, however, competition-related considerations were decisive by far in cases between 1974 and 1983.[27] Moreover, competition criteria became more prominent with a statement from the then Secretary of State, Norman Tebbit, in 1984 (also referred to as the 'Tebbit Doctrine').[28] In his statement, Mr Tebbit indicated that 'references to the Monopolies & Mergers Commission would be made primarily, but not exclusively, on competition grounds, taking into account the international dimension of competition'.[29] The Tebbit Doctrine had been the dominant political approach to merger control in the UK until the passage of 2002 Enterprise Act (2002 Act), which also designated the competition criteria as the primary test for merger control.[30]

[24] David Reader, 'Revisiting the Role of the Public Interest in Merger Control' (Doctoral Thesis, University of East Anglia 2015) 23.

[25] JD Gribbin, 'Recent Antitrust Developments in the United Kingdom Foreign Antitrust' (1975) 20 Antitrust Bulletin 397, 398.

[26] ibid 398.

[27] Charlie Weir, 'The Implementation of Merger Policy in the U.K. 1984–1990 Foreign Antitrust' (1993) 38 Antitrust Bulletin 943, 960.

[28] John Fingleton, 'Mergers and the Public Interest: A Wolf in Sheep's Clothing?' (2018) https://fingleton.com/wp-content/uploads/2018/10/John-Fingleton-Mergers-and-the-public-interest-a-wolf-in-sheeps-clothing-Oct-2018.pdf accessed 15 September 2023.

[29] Federico Mor and Steve Browning, 'Contested Mergers and Takeovers' (2018) Commons Library Briefing No 5374 https://researchbriefings.files.parliament.uk/documents/SN05374/SN05374.pdf accessed 15 September 2023.

[30] Georgine M Kryda, 'The Competition Criterion in British Merger Control Policy' (2002) 30 Policy Studies Journal 252, 266.

Mention must be made, for the sake of completeness, that the then Secretary of State Peter Lilley (1990–92) sought to prevent mergers which he saw as 'nationalization by the back door'. Under Lilley Doctrine, acquisitions of British companies by the state-owned foreign companies were actively pursued at the time. Mor (n 16) 11–12. See for a political and socio-economic analysis of British merger control throughout its history: Hubert Buch-Hansen, 'The Political Economy of Regulatory Change: The Case of British Merger Control' (2012) 6 Regulation and Governance 101.

4.3.2 From the 1973 Fair Trading Act to the 2002 Enterprise Act

In the UK, prior to the entry into force of the Enterprise Act,[31] mergers were reviewed under a broad public interest test, which included competition considerations. With the adoption of the Act in 2002, two significant changes took place. Firstly, the primacy of a competition-based test was made explicit. Secondly, a list of public interest considerations to be taken into account in merger assessment was included in the Act. The UK merger control regime allows for intervention in mergers by the Secretary of State on national security and media plurality grounds; also, there is a safeguard procedure under which ministers can give notice of an additional public interest ground if it happens to arise in a particular case, and seek the approval of Parliament to use it. The Secretary of State can also intervene in a very limited number of cases on public interest grounds where the jurisdictional thresholds are not met.

The provision to assess concentrations based on public interest considerations was not incorporated into the British legal system until the 1965 Monopolies and Mergers Act (1965 Act).

The public interest regime created by the 2002 Act represents a paradigm shift in several respects.

- Firstly, the notion of public interest under the 2002 Act basically excludes the competition law-based ‘substantial lessening of competition’ (SLC) test from its scope. In other words, the Act draws a clear distinction between competition law considerations and other ‘public interest considerations’ in merger control instead of an overarching notion of public interest.
- Secondly, from an institutional point of view, while the Act leaves no room for political intervention with respect to SLC-based merger assessments, it mainly preserves the former institutional approach regarding public interest mergers. Arguably, the earlier institutional setting ‘protects’ the competition law regime from political interventions.[32] However, it also strengthens the idea that public interest interventions are mainly political, thereby not objective.[33] Finally, the Act sets public interest criteria as an exceptional intervention mechanism. The latter is two-fold. Firstly, the Act limits its public interest considerations to particular concerns specifically listed under it. Secondly, it confers an exceptional power to Secretary of State subject to subsequent parliamentary approval to add a new public interest.

[31] UK Enterprise Act 2002.

[32] Mor and Browning (n 29) 7; John Fingleton, ‘Mergers and the Public Interest: A Wolf in Sheep's Clothing?’ (2018) 3 http://www.fingletonassociates.com/publications/mergers-and-the-public-interest-a-wolf-in-sheeps-clothing/, 3–4; Andreas Stephan, ‘Did Lloyds/HBOS Mark the Failure of an Enduring Economics Based System of Merger Regulation?’ (Social Science Research Network 2011) SSRN Scholarly Paper ID 1931007 2 https://papers.ssrn.com/abstract=1931007 accessed 25 January 2019; David Reader, ‘Revisiting the Role of the Public Interest in Merger Control’ (Doctoral Thesis, University of East Anglia 2015), 93.

[33] ibid 106.

4.3.3 The 2002 Enterprise Act: Procedural Aspects of Assessment

The 2002 Act lays out the administrative procedure for the public interest regime in Part III. As stated in section 42(2) of the Act, the Secretary of State has the power to make references to the CMA or a sectoral regulator[34] in case '... he believes that it is or may be the case that one or more than one public interest consideration is relevant ...'.

The existing legislation provides for three types of public interest notices. The Public Interest Intervention Notice (PIIN) is the main power for the Secretary of State to intervene in 'relevant merger situations' which raise certain public interest concerns (section 42). Secondly, a European Intervention Notice (EIN) applies when a 'concentration with a community dimension' is in place (section 67).[35] Finally, a Special Intervention Notice (SPIN) may be issued by the Secretary of State when a 'special merger situation', as set out in Chapter 3 of the Act, is concerned (section 59).[36]

The difference between the types of notices purely relates to jurisdictional issues. For example, PIIN might be issued only where a 'relevant merger situation' has been created. To be qualified as a relevant merger situation, a merger activity should satisfy the conditions laid down in section 23 of the Act, which basically provides for two tests, respectively, the 'ceasing to be distinct test' and either the 'turnover test' or the 'share of supply test'. In contrast, in the case of special merger situations, the Secretary of State may intervene even when the turnover or share of supply thresholds are not satisfied. EINs, in return, require the satisfaction of certain jurisdictional thresholds set out in the European Union Merger Regulation (EUMR).[37]

According to the jurisdictional test in the UK, the 'ceasing to be distinct' test, as set out in section 26, applies where 'any two enterprises cease to be distinct enterprises if they are brought under common ownership or common control'.[38] Either the 'turnover test' or the 'share of supply test' must also be satisfied alongside the 'ceasing to be distinct test' to trigger a PIIN. According to section 23 of the 2002 Act, the turnover test is satisfied where 'the value of the turnover in the United Kingdom of the enterprise being taken over exceeds £70 million'. In addition to that, subsection 3 provides that the share

[34] Eg, in the case of media mergers, the Office of Communications (Ofcom) may be required to give a report to the Secretary of State on public interest aspects of the case concerned (s 44A).

[35] These are also referred to as 'legitimate interest cases'.

[36] The term 'special merger situation', as laid down in the s 59 of the Act, is basically designed to capture certain mergers which do not satisfy the turnover or share of supply tests and therefore do not qualify as a 'relevant merger situation'. However, the Act limits special merger situations to mergers where 'a person carrying on one or more of the enterprises concerned was a relevant government contractor' in the defence sector or where suppliers of newspaper/broadcasting enterprises which supply at least one quarter of the newspapers/broadcasting of any description are involved. Furthermore, the 'ceasing to be distinct' test still applies to special merger situations.

[37] Council Regulation (EC) No 139/2004 of 20 January 2004 on the control of concentrations between undertakings, [2004] OJ L 024/0001–0022. EUMR basically provides for two turnover tests. The worldwide turnover test requires that the combined turnover of the undertakings must be above €5,000 million. Alternatively, each of at least two undertakings concerned must have an EU-wide turnover of more than €250 million. However, there is no EU dimension if each of the undertakings concerned achieved at least two-thirds of its turnover in one and the same Member State.

[38] It is stated in s 26(3) that: 'A person or group of persons able, directly or indirectly, to control or materially to influence the policy of a body corporate, or the policy of any person in carrying on an enterprise but without having a controlling interest in that body corporate or in that enterprise, may ... be treated as having control of it.'

of supply test is satisfied where 'in relation to the supply of goods of any description, at least one-quarter of all the goods of that description which are supplied in the United Kingdom, or in a substantial part of the United Kingdom... are supplied by one and the same person'. Apart from these provisions, current proposals to change the thresholds for national security matters are of significance. In brief, the proposed changes significantly reduce the threshold for some mergers regarding national security concerns.[39]

Issuing of a PIIN serves as a trigger to start the Phase 1 procedure. PIINs must include the relevant merger situation, public interest considerations related to the relevant merger situation, and a proposed timetable if the public interest consideration is not finalized (section 43). Upon receiving a PIIN, the CMA is tasked to give a report to the Secretary of State (section 44(2)). The report by the CMA should contain its assessment and recommendations on jurisdictional and substantive issues and a summary of any representations about the case which relate to any public interest consideration (eg, the national security consideration) mentioned in the PIIN or which may be relevant to the Secretary of State's decision as to whether to refer (section 44(3)). It should in particular include an assessment on whether there is a relevant merger situation, the merger results in SLC, whether the markets concerned are of sufficient importance, whether the arrangements are sufficiently far advanced, whether there are outweighing benefits which offset the adverse effects of substantially lessening of competition, and whether it would be appropriate to deal with the matter by way of undertakings (section 44(4)). The CMA, at this point, is not required to decide on public interest considerations.[40]

The Secretary of State holds the power to refer the case for a Phase 2 investigation if the conditions under section 45 of the Act are satisfied. Under this section, a merger is referred for a Phase 2 investigation to the CMA if, *inter alia*, 'the relevant public interest consideration or considerations concerned operates or may be expected to operate against the public interest' (section 45(2)/(5)). The Secretary of State shall accept the assessment of the CMA on competition law matters.[41]

The Phase 2 procedure for national security cases is similar to that of ordinary merger procedures of the CMA.[42] The main difference is that at the end of the process, the CMA submits the final report to the Secretary of State who then takes the final decision on the issue of national security. The Secretary of State may make an 'adverse public interest finding' or 'no finding' (section 54(2)) decision. If the Secretary of State makes a no finding decision, the transaction is cleared on public interest grounds. If the Secretary of State makes an adverse public interest finding, then the transaction is prohibited. Alternatively, the Secretary of State might decide to request remedies for

[39] See below 2.2.1.

[40] However, in case of a media merger PIIN, Ofcom should provide a report to the Secretary of State on 'the effects of the on the effect of the consideration or considerations concerned on the case' (s 44A). 'Mergers: Guidance on the CMA's Jurisdiction and Procedure' (no 23) para 16.7. https://assets.publishing.service.gov.uk/government/uploads/system/uploads/attachment_data/file/1044636/CMA2_guidance.pdf accessed 15 September 2023.

[41] S 46(2). One exception to this rule is Lloyds/HBOS where the Secretary of State decided to clear the transaction on financial stability grounds, while the CMA had recommended a prohibition on competition law grounds.

[42] CMA (n 40).

the adverse effects of the merger on the public interest. There is also the possibility that an anti-competitive merger could be allowed in the presence of outweighing benefits to public interest. Such authorization under public interest was used only once in *Lloyds/ HBOS* merger by the Secretary of State.[43] In such a case, the Secretary of State did not refer the relevant case for a Phase 2 investigation. The Secretary of State concluded 'that ensuring the stability of the UK financial system justifies the anti-competitive outcome which the Office of Fair Trading has identified and that the public interest is best served by clearing the merger'.[44]

4.3.4 The 2002 Enterprise Act: Institutional Aspects of Assessment

Before Brexit, in case of a concentration, the European Commission was the sole authority for allowing a merger on competition law grounds (EUMR, art 21). As a result, the CMA could not decide on the competition law aspects of the case.[45] It was only supposed to assess the public interest considerations and make the appropriate recommendation to the Secretary of State. The Secretary of State could not allow a merger to take place on public interest grounds in cases where the Commission had already prohibited the transaction due to its merger inquiry. Thirdly, apart from public security, plurality of media, and prudential rules, which are explicitly mentioned in the EUMR, the adoption of any other public interest test must be approved by the Commission in the case of a concentration with a community dimension.[46]

Overall, the UK public interest procedure represents a complex mechanism involving a regulator and a political decisionmaker.[47] The CMA's duty in Phase 1 is to collect, summarize, and publish all representations from the relevant parties. In a Phase 2 investigation, in contrast, the CMA has wide powers to investigate the public interest implications of the relevant merger case (sections 47 and 50).[48] In practice, it is argued that the aforementioned joint decision-making mechanism brings along a transparent

[43] Decision by Lord Mandelson, the Secretary of State for Business, not to refer to the Competition Commission the merger between Lloyds TSB Group plc and HBOS plc under s 45 of the Enterprise Act 2002. http://data.parliament.uk/DepositedPapers/Files/DEP2008-2685/DEP2008-2685.pdf accessed 15 September 2023.

[44] ibid.

[45] CMA (n 40) para 16.19.

[46] EUMR, art 21(4).

[47] A diagram for the UK's public interest merger procedure where a PIIN is issued is shown in Appendix 1. Since the adoption of the 2002 Act, 'Office of Fair Trading' (1973–2014), 'Competition Commission' (1998–2014), and CMA (2014–) respectively played their part in the assessment of public interest mergers alongside several Secretaries of State such as 'Secretary of State for Trade and Industry', 'Secretary of State for Business, Innovation and Skills' and 'Secretary of State for Culture, Media and Sport'.

[48] In the past, eleven cases out of fourteen were cleared after CMA's Phase 1 assessment without being referred to the second stage while two cases were referred to Phase 2 and in one case, the parties announced the withdrawal of the bid (Appendix 2). As will be explored further below, in the BSkyB/ITV merger, the then Competition Commission (CC) did not find any adverse public interest while in the Sky/Fox merger CMA recommended that the proposed transaction should be allowed with a divestiture remedy because of public interest concerns at the end of its Phase 2 inquiry.

process compared to a sole ministerial decision-making process due to the autonomous nature of the competition authority and that of its assessment.[49]

The institutional setting of the public interest regime provided in the Act is not without criticisms. The common criticism of the CMA's assignment on public interest cases is that the CMA does not have extensive expertise in national security cases.[50] It must also be borne in mind that the CMA builds its expertise upon receiving Phase 2 referrals. CMA's media merger inquiries are perfect examples of that argument. Notably, the 411-page *Fox/Sky* final report, illustrates CMA's maturity in conducting a Phase 2 public interest inquiry and its ability to build upon insights from the previous case law in media mergers.

A second criticism is that the CMA's role in the public interest regime contradicts its statutory duty to promote competition.[51] The balancing act of competition concerns and other public interest considerations is not a straightforward task.[52] However, it must be emphasized that the CMA does not make the final decision on the public interest considerations. It is for the Secretary of State to balance the various public interests at stake. Furthermore, setting aside financial stability grounds, media plurality grounds, and national security grounds does not necessitate a balancing exercise, as will be explained further below.[53]

The Secretary of State's decision-making role in public interest mergers is criticized on multiple grounds. The first and most obvious problem is the high risk of politically biased decision-making. NewsCorp's bid to acquire full control of BSkyB in 2010 was highly illustrative of that point. The immediate comments after the announcement of NewsCorp's bid to acquire 60.9 per cent of BSkyB shares[54] suggested that the bid was problematic, at least on political grounds.[55] The initial concern for the regulators was on cross-media ownership issues. This was mainly because NewsCorp was then the biggest newspaper company in the UK, accounting for one-third of the whole market, and Sky was the biggest broadcaster.

However, eventually, two other incidents determined the fate of the case. Firstly, the then Secretary of State Vincent Cable stepped down because of a statement to some reporters indicating that he had 'declared war on Rupert Murdoch' just after he issued an

[49] Andreas Stephan, 'Did Lloyds/HBOS Mark the Failure of an Enduring Economics Based System of Merger Regulation?' (Social Science Research Network 2011) SSRN Scholarly Paper ID 1931007 2 https://papers.ssrn.com/abstract=1931007 accessed 25 January 2019; 16.

[50] Bruce Lyons, David Reader, and Andreas Stephan, 'UK Competition Policy Post-Brexit: In the Public Interest?' (Social Science Research Network 2016) SSRN Scholarly Paper ID 28644614 11.

[51] ibid.

[52] The *Lloyds/HBOS* case illustrates the difficulties associated with the mentioned balancing exercise.

[53] See below 2.2.3.

[54] At the time of the bid, Murdoch had already owned 39.1 per cent of the BSkyB shares and 40 per cent of the NewsCorp shares.

[55] Mail Online, 16 June 2010 https://www.dailymail.co.uk/news/article-1286957/Murdoch-unveils-plan-control-BSkyB.html accessed 14 June 2019; BBC, 15 June 2010 https://www.bbc.com/news/10316087 accessed 14 June 2019; *Daily Telegraph* (14 June 2010) https://www.telegraph.co.uk/finance/newsbysector/epic/bsy/7827991/BSkyB-takeover-Rupert-Murdoch-moves-towards-full-BSkyB-takeover.html accessed 14 June 2019. Eg, BBC editor's opinion on the bid was as following: '... any agreed deal between News Corporation and BSkyB may cause problems for the UK's coalition government. ... because while the Conservatives had benefited from the support of News Corporation's newspapers during the general election, the Liberal Democrats were far more hostile to Mr Murdoch's media empire'.

EIN on 4 November 2010.[56] Secondly, a phone-hacking scandal within the *News of the World*, a subsidiary of NewsCorp, was uncovered during the investigation which eventually led to the withdrawal of the bid.[57] The latter also led to a public inquiry led by the Lord Justice Leveson ('Leveson Inquiry').[58]

Secondly, it can be argued to a certain degree that the appointment of the CMA to assess public interest cases creates a certain amount of consistency and continuity,[59] therefore alleviating concerns of unpredictability in political decision-making to a degree. However, predictability is still imperfect because of political decision-making itself.[60] Moreover, the lack of extensive precedents on national security mitigates the required degree of consistency that would be very welcome for the legal and business community.

The above-mentioned challenges are not identical for all public interest considerations. For example, the existing system seems to be the best solution for financial stability grounds. This is mainly because CMA's duties are very relevant to the balancing exercise of the competition consideration and financial stability consideration.[61] Moreover, it also seems sensible for the Secretary of State to intervene and make a decision at the Phase 1 stage, instead of a lengthy Phase 2 review, because of the significance of the implications of financial instability.

However, as regards national security concerns, the situation is quite different. First, a politically independent market authority such as the CMA would have little legitimacy in deciding on national security matters. Furthermore, disclosure of national security concerns to CMA could pose challenges for national security. This was illustrated in *Hytera/Sepura*, where the Home Office presented directly to the Secretary of State regarding the security concerns raised by the transaction.[62] The CMA, in its report to the Secretary of State, stated that it was not 'expert in national security matters and therefore, in Phase 1, it only summarises the representations made to it' and added that it had 'no reason to doubt any representations made by the Home Office on the appropriateness of the undertakings to remedy or prevent the specific effects adverse to the public interest identified'.[63] Thirdly, there is limited room for conflict of interest for political decision-makers with respect to national security matters. An additional concern also relates to instances where national security considerations mask considerations related to industrial policy and the former is used as a tool to promote the latter.

[56] BBC, 21 December 2010 https://www.bbc.com/news/av/business-12053175/cable-i-have-declared-war-on-murdoch.

[57] BBC, 13 July 2011 https://www.bbc.com/news/business-14142307 accessed 14 June 2019.

[58] https://webarchive.nationalarchives.gov.uk/20140122144906/http://www.levesoninquiry.org.uk/ accessed 25 January 2019.

[59] David Reader, 'Accommodating Public Interest Considerations in Domestic Merger Control: Empirical Insights' [2016] SSRN Electronic Journal 45 https://papers.ssrn.com/abstract=2736917 accessed 25 January 2019.

[60] David Reader, 'Revisiting the Role of the Public Interest in Merger Control' (Doctoral Thesis, University of East Anglia 2015) 105.

[61] The Financial Conduct Authority has a similar competition objective.

[62] *Hytera/Sepura* (BEIS). https://www.gov.uk/cma-cases/hytera-sepura-public-interest-intervention-notice.

[63] CMA, 'Hytera-Sepura: A report to the Secretary of State for Business, Energy and Industrial Strategy on the anticipated acquisition by Hytera Communications Corporation Limited of Sepura PLC', 4 May 2017, https://assets.publishing.service.gov.uk/government/uploads/system/uploads/attachment_data/file/613459/sepura-hytera-cma-report-redacted.pdf.

4.3.5 The 2002 Enterprise Act: Substantive Aspects of Assessment

Section 58 of the 2002 Act specified considerations that currently consist of national security, media plurality, and the stability of the UK's financial system. Originally, national security was the only public interest consideration in the 2002 Act. Subsequently, media plurality was added as a public interest consideration by the Communication Act in 2003 (CA 2003). Finally, the stability of the financial system has been added by order as a public interest concern during the Lloyds/HBOS merger in 2008.[64]

Substantive public interest considerations are listed *numerus clausus* in section 58 of the 2002 Act. However, section 58(3) provides for an exceptional mechanism that allows for the Secretary of State to introduce new public interest concerns. Section 58(3) states that: 'the Secretary of State may by order modify this section for the purpose of specifying in this section a new consideration or removing or amending any consideration which is for the time being specified in this section'. The newly added public interest consideration then has to be approved by the two Houses of Parliament.[65]

The existence of such a power in the Act is subject to criticism as it may allow an influx of new public interest grounds.[66] In particular, Parliament's inability to revise the proposed public interest is regarded as a weakness for parliamentary scrutiny of that power.[67] Nevertheless, as Reader points out, justification for the existence of such a provision could be that it might be essential when time is of significance.[68] Out of consideration and respect for the cautious use of such a power, it has been used only twice since the enactment of the 2002 Act. As far as the 'stability of the UK financial system' is concerned, it took Parliament only nine days to approve the new public interest concern in *Lloyds/HBOS*.[69] In June 2020, the government, in exercise of the powers conferred by section 58(3), introduced a fourth public interest consideration which consists in 'the need to maintain in the United Kingdom the capability to combat, and to mitigate the effects of, public health emergencies'.[70]

4.3.6 The Assessment of National Security as Public Interest in UK Case Law

As we show in Appendix 2, there have been fifteen national security interventions since the adoption of the 2002 Act. Most of those cases were cleared at the Phase 1 stage with

[64] *Lloyds TSB plc/HBOS plc Final Report* (Office of Fair Trading). https://www.gov.uk/cma-cases/lloyds-tsb-plc-hbos-plc.

[65] David Reader, 'Revisiting the Role of the Public Interest in Merger Control' (Doctoral Thesis, University of East Anglia 2015) 96.

[66] ibid 95.

[67] ibid 103.

[68] ibid 104.

[69] Howard Cartlidge and Dervla Broderick, 'BSkyB/ITV: Competition Appeal Tribunal Dismisses BSkyB's Appeal' 17 Utilities Law Review 13.

[70] S 58(2E), Enterprise Act 2002 https://www.legislation.gov.uk/ukpga/2002/40/section/58.

undertakings *in lieu* of references (UILs) by the parties, although four cases were closed after the parties abandoned the deal, either in Phase 1 or Phase 2.

While there is no clear definition for the term, the eleven decisions suggest that national security concerns have been construed very narrowly, adopting a restricted view that particularly focused on defence issues. The Ministry of Defence (MoD) has generally raised three particular concerns in previous cases: (i) the maintenance of the UK's strategic capabilities, (ii) the protection of classified information and technology, and (iii) the transfer of ownership.

The earliest decision regarding national security aspects as a public interest consideration under the 2002 Act relates to the *General Dynamics/Alvis* case.[71] The case concerned the acquisition of Alvis, a company involved in the design, development, and production of armoured fighting vehicles and military land systems, by US-based General Dynamics which operated in aerospace, combat systems, information systems and technology, and marine systems. The MoD, in this case, expressed two concerns: the maintenance of the UK's strategic capabilities and the protection of classified information. The Ministry first said Alvis was the 'design authority' for the British Army's armoured fighting vehicles. In that regard, the MoD said it could not update the said equipment without Alvis's expertise. Secondly, the Ministry indicated that some of these capabilities related to highly classified technology and information. The Secretary of State allowed the merger to proceed upon UIL's from General Dynamics. The company undertook that it would continue to manage military programmes in which it is a contractor or subcontractor. It also committed to ensure the continuity and development of its UK operations. Moreover, it agreed to operate in line with the UK National Security Regulations regarding the security aspects of classified information. The MoD stipulated that the company must appoint both a compliance and a security officer and hold inspection powers to be used by its representatives. In the *Finmeccanica/AgustaWestland* case, the parties had to give UILs, similar to those in *General Dynamics/Alvis*, to proceed with the merger.

The *Finmeccanica/AgustaWestland* case related to an acquisition by an Italian holding company, Finmeccanica, of a Dutch company, AgustaWestland, which was formed by GKN and Finmeccanica as a joint venture.[72] The MoD put forward the same concerns as in the *General Dynamics/Alvis* case. It was stated in the decision that AgustaWestland was the design authority for the UK Armed Forces helicopter fleet and had unique skills and knowledge regarding the said equipment.[73] In the *Lockheed Martin Corporation/Insys Ltd* case, the MoD stated that Lockheed Martin Corporation (LMC) might 'choose to rationalise its defence activities with the potential consequence that these essential UK capabilities could be either run down or sold off or transferred abroad to be combined with LMC's other activities in these areas'.[74] Moreover, the MoD

[71] *General Dynamics/Alvis* https://www.gov.uk/cma-cases/general-dynamics-alvis.

[72] *Finmeccanica/AgustaWestland*, https://www.gov.uk/cma-cases/finmeccanica-s-p-a-agustawestland-n-v.

[73] In the *Finmeccanica/BAE* case, similar concerns were raised, https://www.gov.uk/cma-cases/finmeccanica-bae.

[74] *Lockheed Martin Corporation/Insys Ltd* (Department of Trade and Industry), https://www.gov.uk/cma-cases/lockheed-martin-insys.

said that the transaction could raise concerns because LMC could have the incentives to complement and improve their own capabilities with Insys' unique capabilities. The Ministry argued that combining information and technology without the UK approval could have constituted a significant risk to the UK security of supply due to the US International Traffic in Arms Regulations.

In the *General Electric Company/Smiths Aerospace* case, the MoD identified a third concern: the transfer of ownership.[75] The case involved the acquisition of a British company, Smiths Aerospace (SA), by a US-based company, General Electric (GE). The MoD stated that the said acquisition could enable GE to influence SA in a way that could affect national security. This concern was also raised in the *Atlas Elektronik GmBH UK/ Qinetiq's UWs Winfrith Division* merger.[76] The OFT's report stated that 'independence and impartiality of research outputs and advice' could be compromised by the transaction.[77] The MoD's confidence in the independence and impartiality of such outputs and advice was based on three factors: (i) the fact that Qinetiq is not a major manufacturer or supplier of weapons systems, (ii) a rigid compliance regime, and (iii) government's share in the company which offsets potential conflicts of interest. In that connection, the MoD called the independence and impartiality of the merged entity into question as the company would favour its own products post-merger. To address these specific concerns, the MoD stipulated that there should be firewalls between business compartments and that the merged entity must handle conflicts of interest that would conform with the published MoD commercial policy.

The CMA's first case where national security concerns were raised is *Hytera/ Sepura*.[78] This is the first intervention notice under section 42 of the Enterprise Act that the Secretary of State has issued on national security grounds. Other public interest interventions under section 42 have been on media plurality grounds and to protect the stability of the financial system.

The case concerned the acquisition of the UK-based Sepura by a Chinese company, Hytera. Sepura operated in the market for digital radios and related products for public sector and commercial customers. The Home Office put forward two concerns: protection of sensitive information and technology, and maintenance of UK capabilities in servicing and maintaining radio devices used by emergency services and other agencies in the UK. Of particular significance was that some national security concerns related to the acquisition were directly presented to the Secretary of State by the Home Office. In that respect, the CMA left any decision to propose remedies to the Home Office. The CMA's competitive assessment focused on the products the parties currently produce, supply, distribute or service and on new devices in the parties' pipelines or under consideration.[79]

[75] *General Dynamics/Alvis*, https://www.gov.uk/cma-cases/general-dynamics-alvis.

[76] *Atlas Elektronik GmBH UK/Qinetiq's UWs Winfrith Division* (Department for Business, Innovation and Skills), https://www.gov.uk/cma-cases/atlas-elektronik-gmbh-uk-qinetiq-s-uws-winfrith-division.

[77] Para 11.

[78] *Hytera/Sepura* (BEIS). https://www.gov.uk/cma-cases/hytera-sepura-public-interest-intervention-notice.

[79] These include: Airwave-accredited TETRA devices (Airwave-TETRA devices), TETRA devices for use on private networks other than Airwave (non-Airwave TETRA devices), and dual- or single-mode devices for use on

The Home Office advised CMA that national security is relevant to the merger in order to protect sensitive information and technology and maintain UK capabilities in servicing and maintaining radio devices used by emergency services and other agencies in the UK. Sepura's devices use sensitive technology and are used by the UK's emergency services and other UK authorities to transmit and store sensitive information. In the Home Office's view, unauthorized access to this technology and information or insufficient security controls on access could directly prejudice the operations and security of the emergency services and other authorities.[80]

The Home Office had advised the Secretary of State separately as to specific risks identified in relation to national security matters and possible remedies to address those risks and had engaged with the parties on possible undertakings to resolve the national security concerns arising from the transaction. As the CMA itself noted, the CMA is not expert in national security matters and therefore, in Phase 1, it only summarizes the representations made to it. Nonetheless, the CMA has given advice on features which might, in general, strengthen the effectiveness of any suitable remedies. The CMA accepted the representations made by the Home Office on the appropriateness of the undertakings to remedy or prevent the specific effects adverse to the public interest identified by it. Consistent with its Phase 1 role, CMA did not provide any recommendations on the national security public interest consideration under section 44(6) of the Enterprise Act. In light of the CMA's report and the advice provided by the Home Office on security concerns, the Secretary of State referred the transaction to the CMA under section 45 of the Enterprise Act for a detailed Phase 2 investigation.

The undertakings[81] were intended to provide assurance that sensitive information and technology is protected and ensure the maintenance of UK capabilities in servicing and maintaining radio devices used by the emergency services in the UK. The Secretary

LTE networks. This encompassed potential products that the CMA considered it possible the parties might supply in the future.

80 In particular, the Home Office told the CMA that:

> It was concerned about physical security in relation to company processes and premises, system security in IT systems, and personnel security in relation to employees and company management as a result of the transaction. Therefore, it would be necessary under any new ownership arrangements to ensure that such information and technology was protected and access limited.

Sepura was a key supplier of radio devices to the UK's emergency services and other UK authorities. The work of the UK emergency services and other government agencies is central to the protection of public safety and national security, and relied on the availability of functioning radio devices.

Although Sepura Airwave-TETRA devices currently used by the emergency services were due to be phased out, there is a risk that, under new ownership, the repair and maintenance currently provided by Sepura could cease to operate or be sold or transferred abroad before the end of that period. The Home Office therefore considered that it would be necessary under any new ownership arrangements to include some provision for ongoing UK maintenance and repair of existing Sepura devices used by the emergency services.

https://assets.publishing.service.gov.uk/government/uploads/system/uploads/attachment_data/file/613459/sepura-hytera-cma-report-redacted.pdf.

81 The proposed undertakings require Hytera and Sepura to:

> Implement enhanced controls to protect sensitive information and technology from unauthorised access. In particular, Sepura must maintain its certification and will maintain the necessary security controls required by the Home Office. One member of Sepura's board of directors must be a British citizen with appropriate security clearance. Only personnel with security clearance will have access to a secure area. Sepura will employ a security controller (who must be a British citizen) responsible for facilitating and overseeing compliance with the security requirements.

of State considered the proposed undertakings are appropriate to remedy, mitigate or prevent any of the effects adverse to the public interest and accepted the undertakings offered by Hytera and Sepura instead of making a reference to the CMA.

In *Gardner Aerospace Holdings/Northern Aerospace*, CMA examined a merger case in the aerospace industry.[82] In its advice to the Secretary of State, CMA stated that the parties had undertaken to implement certain measures in cooperation with the MoD to satisfy the national security concerns raised by the UK government in a related merger that took place before the proposed transaction. The case was cleared on those grounds by the Secretary of State.

A balancing exercise between national security considerations and competition considerations, would illustrate that competitive concerns could not overrule national security concerns. Therefore, there would be no balancing exercise with respect to these aspects as national security would always supersede competition law concerns. The challenge would therefore be to determine the procedural and substantial procedure of national security in a way that would create a sufficiently transparent, predictable, and certain environment for the businesses.

In a recent case which concerned satellite communication services, the MoD identified two concerns.[83] The first concern was that the transaction might have created a potential for parties to have access MoD-related sensitive information. Secondly, MoD stated that the transaction could affect the continuity of supply as it would take a significant time switch to another supplier.

In 2019, Advent notified the acquisition of Cobham and on 17 September 2019, the Secretary of State for Business, Energy, and Industrial Strategy (BEIS) announced that she would intervene in the transaction. The UK MoD identified Cobham as a supplier and subcontractor of services such as air-to-air refuelling, electronic warfare systems, and training in relation to software used in combat aircraft. This transaction raised national security concerns and on 20 December 2019, the Secretary of State announced that the undertakings were offered by the merging parties to mitigate the national security risks and cleared the merger:

a. Sensitive UK government information to be protected, and the new Advent board will comply with national security requirements.

Provide rights of access to premises and information so that relevant agencies, including the Home Office, the Ministry of Defence and GCHQ, can audit compliance with the security measures. The parties must provide the Home Office with information and allow entry to their premises and access to information to representatives of the Home Office, the Ministry of Defence and GCHQ.

Continue the UK repair and maintenance service for the relevant radio devices as long as is required by the Home Office (as long as the Airwave Service is operational). The capability to provide repair services must continue to be directly controlled by a company or companies incorporated in the UK under the laws of England, unless agreed otherwise by the Home Office.

[82] *Gardner Aerospace Holdings/Northern Aerospace* (Department for Business, Energy and Industrial Strategy). https://www.gov.uk/government/publications/proposed-acquisition-of-northern-aerospace-limited-by-gardner-aerospace-holdings-limited-decision-notice.

[83] *Connect Bidco/Inmarsat*, https://www.gov.uk/government/publications/proposed-acquisition-of-inmarsat-plc-by-connect-bidco-ltd-public-interest-intervention.

b. The new owners of Cobham are to fulfil the terms of the existing contracts and notify any material change that could affect the ability to supply key services.
c. The new owners are to inform the Ministry of Defence and Home Office of any plans to sell all or parts of Cobham's business to protect national security interests in future transactions.

Separate from the public interest intervention and the mitigation of national security concerns, the parties agreed to maintain Cobham's headquarters in the UK, to continue the use of Cobham as a registered name in the UK, to significantly protect jobs.[84]

Overall, it can be said the MoD intervened in cases where an acquisition put unique strategic capabilities or sensitive information were put at risk. The strategic capabilities were put at risk mainly where the target was an 'authority' to provide such capabilities, meaning there would have been no viable alternative arrangement if that supplier stopped supplying. Similar concerns were also present where the supplier was not such authority, but switching to another supplier would take time. Additionally, the loss of impartiality of a supplier was considered an important element in cases where these strategic capabilities were related to research and advice services.

In almost all cases, concerns regarding the protection of sensitive information followed the former concern. Distinctively, in *Hytera/Sepura, Connect Bidco/Immarsat,* and *Cobham/Advent,* the security of sensitive information was the primary concern. Both cases concerned communication services. While this is not the case in the above-mentioned cases, it is also plausible to think that protecting sensitive information could be a national security concern even where the target could easily be substituted by another supplier.

On 20 December 2019, the Secretary of State issued a PIIN under section 42 of the Enterprise Act in the context of the acquisition of Mettis Aerospace Limited by a Chinese company known as Aerostar. In this case, the CMA had not received representations from the MoD, and neither did the Secretary of State from the Secretary of State for Defence regarding the national security implications of the merger. In its report, the CMA acknowledged that the parties had abandoned the deal,[85] and consequently, on 26 February 2020, the Secretary of State closed the intervention.[86]

In the *Ultra Electronics Holdings/Cobham Ultra Acquisitions* case, on 18 August 2021, the Secretary of State issued a PIIN in relation to the acquisition of Ultra Electronics

[84] At the time of writing this chapter, Cobham has notified its intention to buy UK company Ultra. 'Cobham, which was taken private by U.S. private equity firm Advent last year, said it will safeguard and support the UK's national security and create new manufacturing and engineering jobs and apprenticeships. It will also protect existing jobs, maintain a UK headquarters and boost investment. In order to protect Ultra's businesses and stakeholders, Cobham said it will engage with the British government to agree details of its binding commitments - including their duration and form.' https://www.reuters.com/business/aerospace-defense/defence-group-cobham-buy-british-rival-ultra-36-bln-2021-08-16/ accessed 17 December 2021.

[85] Competition and Markets Authority, Proposed acquisition of Mettis Aerospace Limited by Aerostar: CMA report, para 2.10, https://assets.publishing.service.gov.uk/government/uploads/system/uploads/attachment_data/file/868639/mettis-aerostar-cma-report-redacted.pdf.

[86] BEIS, 'Anticipated acquisition of Mettis Aerospace Limited by Aerostar—reference decision', https://assets.publishing.service.gov.uk/government/uploads/system/uploads/attachment_data/file/868717/mettis-aerostar-decision-notice.pdf.

Holdings Plc by Cobham Ultra Acquisitions Limited. Under section 44 of the Act, the Secretary of State instructed the Competition and Markets Authority to investigate the proposed acquisition and to report its findings by 18 January 2022. Thus, the CMA reported that the transaction at hand would create a relevant merger situation and summarized the representations it received relating to the national security public interest consideration specified in the intervention notice. Indeed, section 44(3)(b) of the Act requires the CMA to provide a summary of representations it has received about the transaction, which particularly relate; the MoD considered that the transaction would raise a number of national security concerns including risks related to: assured capabilities, to UK security of supply, and unauthorized access to classified material.[87] Finally, the Secretary of State considered that the proposed undertakings would mitigate the national security risks identified to an acceptable level and therefore proposes to accept the undertakings instead of making a reference to a Phase 2 inquiry.[88]

Lastly, on 18 October 2021, the Secretary of State issued a PIIN in relation to the acquisition of Meggitt by Parker Hannifin. The Secretary of State later concluded, having taken into account the CMA's view of the matter, that by committing to divesting Parker's entire AWB business (aircraft wheels and brakes division), the parties would remove any overlap between their respective activities and would thus address the outstanding competitive issues in a satisfactory way.

4.3.7 Should We Broaden the Public Interest Criteria Post-Brexit?

Over years after the adoption of the 2002 Act, a few cases led to a debate on whether a broader public interest regime was necessary.[89] For example, energy security grounds were discussed during the *Gazprom/Centrica* takeover.[90] Food security was put forward as a new public interest criteria during the *Craft/Cadbury* takeover in 2010.[91] In *Pfizer/AstraZeneca*, 'national interests' were discussed as part of the broader public interest debate.[92]

The current discourse on broadening the public interest criteria reflects a degree of suspicion towards FDIs. These concerns, in part, are covered by the government by its aforementioned steps to implement a new national security framework.[93] However, issues such as employment, scientific advancement or food security remain unresolved.

[87] Competition and Markets Authority, 'Cobham—Ultra Electronics A report to the Secretary of State for Business, Energy and Industrial Strategy on the anticipated acquisition by Cobham Ultra Acquisitions Limited of Ultra Electronics Holdings plc', 13 January 2022.

[88] BEIS, Notice of acceptance of undertakings given by Cobham Ultra Acquisitions Limited and Ultra Electronics Holdings Plc pursuant to para 3(2) of sch 7 to the Enterprise Act 2002, 6 July 2022, https://assets.publishing.service.gov.uk/government/uploads/system/uploads/attachment_data/file/1088799/Doc_3_-_Redacted_Decision_Notice.pdf.

[89] https://www.competitionpolicyinternational.com/consideration-of-public-interest-factors-in-antitrust-merger-control/ accessed 13 February 2019.

[90] Mor and Browning (n 29) 17.

[91] ibid 20.

[92] ibid 31.

[93] See above 2.2.1.

At this point, it is essential to remember that even the Tebbit Doctrine, which gave prominence to competition law-based assessment, was not seen as sufficient to provide certainty and predictability for undertakings. Therefore, as Stephan suggests, 'a return to broader political interventions on public interest grounds would risk creating inconsistency in merger regulation and uncertainty for firms'.[94] That is indeed true considering the evolution of the merger control regime. Secondly, corporate governance[95] and the City Code on Takeovers and Mergers ('City Code') could be an alternative way to address these problems. An example of that was the *Arm/Softbank* takeover, where the government demanded post-offer undertakings relating to employment and the location of HQs.[96] Thirdly, given the highly politicized nature of issues such as employment, there is a high risk of politically biased decision-making when balancing the interests at stake. Therefore, for example, it would not be surprising to observe political decisionmakers favour their own constituency over others.

Post-Brexit, several changes to the public interest regime would be expected to materialize. First of all, the concentrations with an EU dimension would fall under the sole jurisdiction of the relevant UK authorities. In that regard, any procedural requirement to communicate the cases with the EU would cease to exist (eg, EIN). Furthermore, as the EUMR will not be applicable anymore, adopting public interest considerations other than national security, financial stability, and media plurality will be possible.[97] Thirdly, it will be possible for the Secretary of State to allow mergers which have anti-competitive effects but also balancing benefits to public interest since the EU will not have the sole jurisdiction over these mergers.

As we have seen above, public interest scrutiny in merger control has existed in the UK since the adoption of the 1965 Act. In its very first forms, it covered a broad array of public interest grounds such as competition, employment, innovation, international competitiveness, and industrial strategy. However, competition criteria became the dominant test over the years. Along with the adoption of the 2002 Act, the latter became the primary criterion, leaving a little room for other public interest grounds. In its current state, the Act only allows for national security, media plurality, BSOs and FEGs, and financial stability grounds as overwhelming public interests. Nevertheless, it also leaves room for possibly introducing a new public interest by the Secretary of State, subject to parliamentary approval.

There are a number of cases in the UK merger control regime where public interest and national security considerations were taken into account by the competition authorities and the Secretary of State. These cases range from the media sector and media plurality concerns to recent cases in the high tech sector and national security concerns.

[94] Stephan (n 18) 15.

[95] ibid 14.

[96] *Financial Times* http://markets.ft.com/data/announce/detail?dockey=1323-13388096-728F8DM5IK1U80P5726H93PDNO accessed 12 July 2019.

[97] Leigh M Davison, 'Envisaging the Post-Brexit Landscape: An Articulation of the Likely Changes to the EU–UK Competition Policy Relationship' (2018) 39 Liverpool Law Review 99, 110.

There have been fifteen interventions and eleven decisions on the grounds of national security grounds, including defence mergers *General Dynamics/Alvis*,[98] *Finmeccanica/AgustaWestland*,[99] *Finmeccanica/BAE Systems*,[100] *Lockheed Martin/Insys*,[101] *General Electric/Smiths Aerospace*,[102] and *Cobham/Ultra Electronics*.[103] Those transactions were ultimately cleared by the CMA after the parties offered remedies.

UK's public interest legislation appoints a regulator (the CMA) and a politician (Secretary of State) as part of its dual decision-making mechanism. In doing that, it does not distinguish between the nature of the public interest consideration in question. However, significant differences in that regard exist. Therefore, from an institutional point of view, a distinction between the types of public interest grounds is recommended as a more efficient approach.

The recent legislative initiative by the UK government to extend national security grounds reflects a new approach towards FDIs as we will see in the following sections. It shows that the concept of national security is broadened to include critical infrastructure and advanced technologies. As the proposals in that respect would potentially affect a wide range of markets where dual use of the facilities or technologies are involved, transparency and effective judicial review are of utmost importance to provide certainty and safety. It also seems to be a positive step to remove CMA from the aforementioned assessment of national security concerns since sole ministerial decision-making could decrease the level of bureaucracy.

While it is often stressed by the government that the UK will remain an investment-friendly environment for FDIs, there is a strong possibility that mergers in a broader range of industries, compared to the current situation, will be subject to national security checks. As we will see below, the UK government intends to follow the example of other developed countries and make more substantive changes to how it scrutinizes the national security implications of foreign investment. The reforms focus on ensuring adequate scrutiny of whether significant foreign investment in critical businesses raises any national security concerns and the ability to act in circumstances where this might be the case. The expectation is that the need to act would be relatively rare, but the risk that this can become a tool to implement industrial policy considerations does exist.

[98] *General Dynamics/Alvis*, https://www.gov.uk/cma-cases/general-dynamics-alvis accessed 15 September 2023.

[99] *Finmeccanica/AgustaWestland*, https://www.gov.uk/cma-cases/finmeccanica-s-p-a-agustawestland-n-v accessed 15 September 2023.

[100] *Finmeccanica/BAE Systems*, https://www.gov.uk/cma-cases/finmeccanica-bae accessed 15 September 2023.

[101] *Lockheed Martin Corporation/Insys Ltd* (Department of Trade and Industry), https://www.gov.uk/cma-cases/lockheed-martin-insys accessed 15 September 2023.

[102] *General Electric Company/Smiths Aerospace* (Department of Trade and Industry), https://www.gov.uk/cma-cases/general-electric-company-smiths-aerospace accessed 15 September 2023.

[103] *Cobham/Ultra Electronics* https://www.gov.uk/cma-cases/cobham-slash-ultra-electronics-merger-inquiry accessed 15 September 2023.

4.4 Current Legal Framework in the UK

As discussed above, traditionally, the UK had no standalone foreign investment screening regime, but the powers to assess national security considerations were provided for in the public interest test of the Enterprise Act 2002. The government's powers to intervene in foreign investment are primarily founded upon the national merger control regime and supplemented by specific sector regulations.

This section sets out the statutory powers and other means currently available to the UK government to protect national interests from being undermined by FDI. It begins with a detailed description of the ministers' intervening powers under the Enterprise Act 2002, then explores other sector-specific and emergency powers, and finally summarizes the use of 'golden shares' for the purposes of maintaining state control of several strictly regulated businesses.

4.4.1 Role of Ministers in Public Interest Cases

The Enterprise Act limited the government's ability to intervene in merger decisions where a strictly defined 'public interest' is at stake. As a result, the Secretary of State can only intervene in mergers once the CMA has established jurisdiction using the same thresholds as for competition-related grounds.[104] The only exception is given in relation to very limited circumstances prescribed by the Special Public Interest Regime, which is briefly described below.

4.4.2 The Public Interest Grounds

The only public interest considerations that the Secretary of State may take into account are specified in section 58 of the Enterprise Act:

a. national security (including public security);[105]
b. financial stability;[106]

[104] In addition, before the UK's exit from the EU, the government's intervention powers were also subject to the European Commission's approval on merger cases under its exclusive jurisdiction.

[105] Transactions reviewed by the MoD on the basis of national security were mostly defence mergers, with public security concerns often dealt with through a range of undertakings, including the maintenance of strategic capabilities domestically and the protection of classified information and technology. See *General Dynamics/Alvis PLC* (2004), *Lockheed Martin Corporation/Stasys Ltd* (2005), *General Electric Company/Smiths Aerospace* (2007), *Atlas Elektronik GmbH UK/Qinetiq's Underwater Systems Winfrith Division* (2009). Also see *Gardner Aerospace Holdings/Northern Aerospace* (2018), MoD undertakings referred to in the CMA report.

[106] The Enterprise Act 2002 (Specification of Additional s 58 Consideration) Order 2008 (SI 2008/2645) added a new s 58(2D) to the Enterprise Act that classifies 'the interest of maintaining the stability of the UK financial system' as a new public interest consideration. The need for this addition became apparent when, in September 2008, the Secretary of State decided to intervene in the proposed acquisition by Lloyds TSB of HBOS on the basis that they believed that the stability of the UK financial system ought to be specified as a public interest consideration in s 58

c. media plurality;[107]
d. capability to combat and to mitigate the effects of public health emergencies.[108]

Aside from the named public interests listed under the Enterprise Act 2002, the Secretary of State also retains a residual power to propose new public interest criteria not specified under the statute.[109] If at the time that the Secretary of State wishes to intervene in a particular transaction, the relevant public interest consideration has not been specified, then the consideration can be added by way of an order, which must be approved by the UK Parliament.[110]

4.4.3 Procedure for Assessment of National Security Concerns Under the Enterprise Act

The process for government intervention, as set out in section 42, the Enterprise Act 2002, is initiated with the Secretary of State issuing a public intervention notice (PIIN) on the basis of one or more statutory public interest grounds.[111]

Following the issue of an intervention notice, the CMA must prepare a report advising the Secretary of State on competition and jurisdictional issues, including whether a particular merger qualifies as a relevant merger situation, as described above. The CMA does not provide its own advice on public interest issues at this stage, as it is admittedly not an expert on national security issues. Therefore, the report will generally provide a summary of any representations received by the relevant parties, including those of other governmental departments where relevant.[112]

The Secretary of State is bound by the CMA's findings on competition issues but can decide on whether any public interest concerns are raised and, if so, decide on the appropriate remedial action to address the issues identified. If further investigation on a merger is required, the Secretary of State can refer it back to the CMA, which will

of the Enterprise Act and that the stability of the UK financial system may be relevant to the consideration of the merger.

[107] The Communications Act 2003 introduced new media public interest considerations involving the need to ensure plurality of ownership of broadcasting companies and the need for high quality and diversified broadcasting in media mergers and considerations relating to the need for accurate presentation of news and free expression in newspaper mergers (ss 375–77, Communications Act 2003).

[108] On 23 June 2020, the Enterprise Act 2002 (Specification of Additional s 58 Consideration) Order 2020 added s 58 (2E) to the Enterprise Act to allow a further public interest consideration: 'The need to maintain in the UK the capability to combat, and to mitigate the effects, of public health emergencies'. More details are provided later in this chapter.

[109] See ss 58(3) and 58(4) of the Act.

[110] ibid 11. On the Lloyds TSB/HBOS merger, the Secretary of State intervened on the basis of a public interest consideration that has not been 'finalized' and was therefore required to take action as soon as practicable to finalize it. For this reason, the Secretary of State made an affirmative resolution in Parliament after its summer recess.

[111] The relevant Secretary of State, in most cases, is the Secretary of State for Business, Innovation, and Skills. However, since December 2010, the Secretary of State for Media, Culture, and Sport has been responsible for media and communications policy, including merger control.

[112] In particular, for media public interest cases, the sector regulator (Ofcom) will provide a separate report to the Secretary of State on the issues of media plurality and diversity.

call an independent Inquiry Group to conduct a Phase 2 investigation.[113] The Phase 2 Group of the CMA will conduct a thorough investigation and report to the Secretary of State on whether the merger operates or is expected to operate against the public interest. The Phase 2 Group has twenty-four weeks to prepare the report, but this period may be extended by eight weeks.

After receiving the Phase 2 report, the Secretary of State would decide whether the transaction may proceed and, if so, whether any remedial action must be taken. The government would either accept undertakings by the parties or impose remedies, and where this is considered insufficient to protect national security, it can block a deal altogether. The Secretary of State must publish the decision within thirty days of receipt of the CMA's report. The Secretary of State must accept the CMA's conclusions as to the competition-related effects of the transaction and its jurisdictional assessment. However, the Secretary of State will only have regard to and is not bound by the CMA's recommendations on remedies or the assessment of public interest issues.

Finally, the concerned parties can appeal to the Competition Appeal Tribunal (CAT).[114] A 'decision' includes a failure to take a decision permitted or required by the Enterprise Act. The CAT has the power to quash the whole or part of the relevant decision or dismiss the appeal. Decisions given by the CAT may be further appealed before the Court of Appeal.

It is important to note that the government has never used the power to block transactions in national security-related interventions, and overall, there have been very few public interest interventions on national security grounds since the Enterprise Act was enacted.[115]

4.4.4 The Special Public Interest Regime

In certain limited circumstances, the Secretary of State may intervene in a transaction in the absence of the requirements for a 'relevant merger situation' being met in full, so long as certain other conditions are satisfied.[116] This exceptional power relates to circumstances where either:

[113] The threshold for referral is low, and the Secretary of State has a wide margin for exercising its discretion. The power to make a referral should be exercised if they believe there is a risk not 'purely fanciful' that the merger 'might be expected to operate' against the public interest. See the statements of the Secretary of State in *Fox/Sky* (2017) at www.gov.uk/government/news/statement-from-the-culture-secretary-on-the-proposed-sky-plc-21st-century-fox-inc-merger.

[114] The Competition Appeal Tribunal is an independent judicial body established by s 12 and Sch 2 of the Enterprise Act 2002.

[115] The first public interest intervention notice was issued in February 2007 in relation to BSkyB's acquisition of a 17.9 per cent stake in ITV. In August 2012, the Secretary of State for Culture, Media, and Sport issued an intervention on media plurality public interest grounds in relation to the acquisition by Global Radio Holdings Limited of Guardian Media Group's radio stations. In April 2017, an intervention was made on national security grounds regarding the acquisition of Sepura by Hytera Communications.

[116] Ss 59(3) and 59(3A)–(3D), Enterprise Act 2002, as amended by s 378, Communications Act 2003.

- at least one of the enterprises is carried on in the UK, and one of the parties is a 'relevant government contractor', a person who has been notified by the Secretary of State that they, or their employees, holds information or documents relating to defence and of a confidential nature; or
- the merger involves the supply of at least 25 per cent of a particular type of newspaper or broadcasting in the UK or a part of the UK.

In such cases, although no competition assessment is involved, the procedure for referral to the CMA remains the same as with other public interest reasons. The Secretary of State makes the final decision on the public interest issue and any appropriate remedies.

4.4.5 Amendments to the National Security Regime

In October 2017, the government published the National Security and Infrastructure Investment Green Paper, reviewing the national security implications arising from foreign investment and control. The Green Paper introduced a set of short- and long-term proposals to reform and strengthen its powers to scrutinize these national security implications of foreign investment.[117]

The first consultation focused on the short-term proposals that resulted in the first significant amendments to the UK merger control regime since the Enterprise Act 2002 came into force.[118]

The second consultation set out broad options for longer-term, more far-reaching reforms. This was followed by the National Security and Investment White Paper in July 2018, which set out even more detailed proposals. These far-reaching reforms were later brought forward by the NSI Bill, which will be discussed in detail below.

Additional short-term measures were later added by way of two statutory instruments[119] as a way of mitigating urgent risks pending the implementation of more comprehensive powers in the forthcoming new FDI regime in the UK.[120]

[117] National Security and Infrastructure Review: 'The Government's Review of National Security Implications of Foreign Ownership or Control' (October 2017) para 75 https://www.gov.uk/government/uploads/system/uploads/attachment_data/file/652505/2017_10_16_NSII_Green_Paper_final.pdf accessed 15 September 2023.

[118] The Enterprise Act 2002 (Share of Supply Test) (Amendment) Order 2018 and the Enterprise Act 2002 (Turnover Test) (Amendment) Order 2018, which came into force on 11 June 2018.

[119] Enterprise Act 2002 by the Enterprise Act 2002 (Share of Supply Test) (Amendment) Order 2020 and the Enterprise Act 2002 (Turnover Test) (Amendment) Order 2020.

[120] See Press release from the BEIS and The Rt Hon Alok Sharma MP, titled 'New protections for UK businesses key to national security and fight against coronavirus' published on 21 June 2020, available at https://www.gov.uk/government/news/new-protections-for-uk-businesses-key-to-national-security-and-fight-against-coronavirus accessed 15 September 2023.

4.4.6 Lower Thresholds for Certain Sectors

In 2018, there were amendments to the Enterprise Act 2002, which changed the thresholds for the turnover and share of supply tests within the Act for two sectors:

(i) The military and dual-use sector.[121]
(ii) The advanced technology sector. The key areas where the amended thresholds apply are:
- computing hardware, defined as enterprises that own or create intellectual property rights in the functional capability of multi-purpose computing hardware, or design, maintain or support the secure provisioning or management of roots of trust of multi-purpose computing hardware; and
- quantum-based technology, defined as enterprises that research, develop, design or manufacture goods for use in, or supply services based on, quantum computing or quantum communications technologies. This would include the creation of relevant intellectual property or components.

In practice, the 2018 reforms extended the scope of deals qualifying for national security review only in the above areas by lowering the relevant thresholds for review.

For transactions in the above sectors, the turnover threshold and share of supply tests were amended as follows:

(a) the business being taken over must have a UK turnover of over £1 million rather than £70 million; and
(b) the target business must supply at least one-quarter of all goods or services of a particular description. Thus, while there is no longer a requirement for a merger to increase the share of supply, the test continues to operate by reference to the commercial strength arising out of the transaction.[122]

Finally, mergers within the scope of the amended thresholds will follow the same statutory process as those in any other area of the economy. In other words, the existing public interest considerations listed in the Act were not extended or amended, and the procedure for referrals to the CMA remains the same.

[121] Enterprises in this sector design and manufacture military items (such as arms, military, and paramilitary equipment) and so-called dual-use items, which could have both military and civilian uses.

[122] The Enterprise Act 2002 (Share of Supply Test) (Amendment) Order 2018 and the Enterprise Act 2002 (Turnover Test) (Amendment) Order 2018, which came into force on 11 June 2018.

4.4.7 Public Health Emergencies

In light of the Covid-19 pandemic, the UK government introduced a new public interest ground on which it can intervene in mergers, namely 'to maintain UK capability to combat and mitigate public health emergencies'.[123] This measure was taken in response to the growing concern of the economic implications of the global pandemic and the risk of opportunistic and hostile investments by foreign state-aided stakeholders.[124]

The UK government showed a clear intention to facilitate state intervention in proposed M&As involving businesses relevant to the pandemic response, such as vaccine research companies and personal protective equipment (PPE) manufacturers. However, the reforms were designed to address mergers or acquisitions of enterprises whose financial stability is adversely affected due to the economic implications of a pandemic. Therefore, the new public interest ground can be interpreted as widely as to include transactions in any sector of the economy, given that they have the potential to raise suspicions of unfairly benefiting from the economic implications of the pandemic.

4.4.8 Artificial Intelligence, Cryptography, and Advanced Materials

With effect from 21 July 2020, the Enterprise Act's scope was extended to cover three further sectors to which the lower thresholds introduced by the 2018 amendments would also apply.[125] The additional sectors related to advanced technology:

a. artificial intelligence;
b. cryptographic authentication technology;
c. advanced materials.

The recent addition of these sectors shows that the UK government acknowledges the emergence of new technologies as a prominent financial arena and intends to send an important message to those seeking to take advantage of smaller companies in these critical sectors that can affect the UK's national security.[126]

[123] The Enterprise Act 2002 (Specification of Additional Section 58 Consideration) Order 2020.

[124] Similar measures and other tactical changes to the FDI regime have been made other jurisdictions, including France, Germany, Australia, and Canada, among others for the purposes of enabling the protection of critical healthcare infrastructure.

[125] Enterprise Act 2002 (Share of Supply) (Amendment) Order 2020.

[126] Reference from the Statement of the Secretary of State for Business, Energy, and Industrial Strategy (Alok Sharma), made before the House of Commons on 22 June 2020, Statement UIN HCWS305, can be found at https://questions-statements.parliament.uk/written-statements/detail/2020-06-22/hcws305.

4.4.9 Other Mechanisms to Protect National Security

In addition to the above-mentioned regime, several other statutory grounds enable the government to intervene in UK companies' activities that raise national security risks and concerns.[127] Alongside these statutory grounds, the use of certain contractual terms or 'golden shares' is often opted by the government to ensure that control is retained in certain companies.

4.4.10 Sector-Specific Regulations

The main sectors in which such intervention powers of the UK government may arise include energy, civil nuclear and manufacturing, health, water, and communications. In particular:

- The Civil Contingencies Act 2004 contains an extensive set of powers for state intervention to impose emergency regulations to address an actual or threatened 'catastrophic emergency', such as a serious disruption to the supply of money, food, water, energy or fuel, or a threat to communication or transport systems.
- Under section 13 of the Industry Act 1975, the Secretary of State has the broad power to block an acquisition by a non-UK-based entity of an 'important manufacturing undertaking' when it appears that there is a serious and immediate probability of a change of control contrary to the interests of the UK.
- Section 208 of the Water Industry Act 1991 allows the government to issue directions to water supply/sewerage undertakers and licensees in the interests of national security or to mitigate the effects of a civil emergency.
- Section 132 of the Communications Act 2003 provides that the Secretary of State can require the Office of Communications to suspend or restrict a provider's entitlement to provide networks, services or associated facilities in the interests of national security or to protect the public from any threat to public safety or health.
- The Energy Act 1976 permits the government to control the production, supply, acquisition, and use of fuels and electricity.

Moreover, in some sectors of the economy, the government or independent regulators operate licensing or authorization schemes, allowing for certain control over the individuals and entities participating in the relevant activities. Despite these regulatory schemes not being specifically applicable to foreign investors, in some cases, the nationality of an investor will play a part in the authorization process.[128]

[127] National Security and Infrastructure Review (n 117) 26.

[128] Eg, with regards to airline licensing, it is required that an entity operating an airline within the EEA must be majority-owned and effectively controlled by an EEA Member State or nationals of such Member States. https://www.caa.co.uk/Commercial-industry/Airlines/Licensing/Requirements-and-guidance/Airline-licensing/.

Despite the sector-operational regulation, only limited oversight or powers relate to ownership or control of corporations, and these are not necessarily focused on national security concerns. Further details of these sector-specific regulations are outside the scope of this section.

4.4.11 The Takeover Code

The independent Takeover Panel administers the City Code on Takeovers and Mergers ('Takeover Code'), which determines the process and timetable for takeovers of a UK public company.[129] The Takeover Code requires companies to set out their plans in a timely manner and explain how they will handle the target company, in the event of a successful takeover bid.[130]

Notably, bidding companies are required to make statements in the takeover offer document on their post-offer intentions with regard to matters affecting the target company, including the future business direction, employment changes, strategic plans, pension schemes, and fixed assets. A similar statement is required by the target company's board, setting out its opinion on the offer's long-term effects on the company's and the shareholders' interests.[131] Any unreasonable or unexplained deviation from the statements may lead to severe sanctions, including disciplinary action by the Takeover Panel.

In addition to intention statements, the Takeover Code, as amended in 2015, allows the companies involved to voluntarily make legally binding commitments, known as post-offer undertakings, in which they commit to or refrain from taking specified action. The reason behind such undertakings is to ensure that bidders comply with commitments made concerning the operation of the target business and alleviate any fears of significant changes being made to the company post-takeover.[132] The undertakings are enforceable by the Takeover Panel, which in the event of a breach can either take disciplinary action, impose financial penalties, or seek a court order securing compliance.[133]

[129] Pursuant to Part 28 of the Companies Act 2006, the Panel on Takeovers and Mergers is the supervisory and regulatory authority in respect of UK public companies' takeovers.

[130] While the merger control regime seeks to review the competition and (on occasion) public interest implications of a transaction, the City Code on Takeovers and Mergers outlines a broad range of behavioural and procedural standards for the merging parties to adhere to during and after the offer period.

[131] Furthermore, the Code complements other relevant legal duties of the board, especially the duty to promote the success of the company under s 172 of the Companies Act 2006

[132] A high-profile example of the use of such undertakings was the takeover of ARM by Softbank in 2016, which effectively guaranteed (i) to at least double ARM's UK employees to enable ARM to continue to develop leading-edge technology in the UK; (ii) to increase ARM's non-UK employees; (iii) to maintain ARM's global headquarters in the UK; and (iv) to maintain the proportion of technical employees to non-technical employees broadly in line with historical trends experienced by ARM.

[133] Ss 11(a) and (b) of the Takeover Code and s 952 of Companies Act 2006 provide that rules may confer power on the Panel to take disciplinary action or impose sanctions on a person who has breached a rule or failed to comply with a direction given by the Panel. Finally, s 10(d) of the Code and s 955 of the Companies Act 2006 provides that the Panel may seek enforcement by the courts.

The Takeover Code provides important safeguards with respect to adherence to timing and disclosure requirements during a takeover while engaging the bidders to be proactive to avoid public and media scrutiny. Nevertheless, there appears to be room for improvement, especially towards more detailed post-takeover plans given by the bidder and provisions for informed and timely public debate on the likely impact of the takeover.[134]

Notably, the current regime has been recognized as insufficient by both the Takeover Panel and the UK government, while further amendments are due to be incorporated into the Takeover Code.[135] A detailed account of the Takeover Code and the forthcoming changes is outside the scope of this section.

In December 2022, the Code Committee of the Takeover Panel set out several amendments to the presumptions of the definition of 'acting in concert'. In short, persons acting in concert are treated under the Code as a single person. These amendments will take effect from 20 February 2023.[136]

4.4.12 Contractual Clauses and Golden Shares

The UK government often utilizes contractual terms and other commercial arrangements to further ensure its key interests are defended in certain sectors.

One of the ways it can do this is by inserting 'change of control' clauses in funding agreements with companies in receipt of public funds, for example, for research and development, to support innovation, and the development of cutting-edge technologies. These clauses can be enforced in the event of a takeover and will allow the government to claim back the funding if the takeover renders the new company ineligible to receive the grant, or the government takes issue with the intentions of the acquirer with regard to the use of the funding.[137] Other government procurement policies require similar contractual clauses to be adhered to by governmental contractors undertaking projects, in which they hold sensitive information.[138]

Another instrument often employed by the government to defend a domestic company against unsolicited takeovers is the issuance and acquisition of 'golden shares'.[139]

[134] The Takeover Panel, 'Consultation paper issued by the Code Committee of the Panel: statements of intention and related matters', 2017, and the government's review of the national security implications of foreign ownership or control, 'National Security and Infrastructure Investment Review', October 2017.

[135] The UK's Takeover Panel has published the final text changes to the Takeover Code (the Code) and confirmed that they will take effect on 5 July 2021. The changes relate to the offer timetable and conditions to offer. The Takeover Panel Response Statement 2020/2021.

[136] Evershed Sutherland, 'Keeping You Informed Changes to the Takeover Code', February 2023, https://www.eversheds-sutherland.com/documents/services/commercial/client-update-takeover-code-changes-february-2023.pdf accessed 15 September 2023.

[137] National Security and Infrastructure Review (n 117) 18.

[138] Eg, contractors of the MoD must notify the MoD of any 'intended, planned or actual change in control of the contractor', even where there is no change in the company's ultimate beneficial owner. The clause is known as DEFCON 566 'Change of Control of Contractor'.

[139] For analysis of the golden shares case law, see: M Andenas and F Wooldridge, *European Comparative Company Law* (CUP 2009) 14–20, S Grundmann and F Moslein, *Golden Shares-State Control in Privatized Companies: Comparative Law, European Law and Policy Aspects* (EBFLJ (EUREDIA) 2004) 623, N De Luca, *European Company Law* (CUP 2017) 352–64.

This mechanism was first founded by the UK government in the privatization movement in the 1980s and followed later by many other European countries, as it allowed governments to retain control over privatized entities and implement certain policy objectives in the name of public interest.[140]

In the UK, many former state monopolies in strategic industries were privatized, such as energy, aerospace, telecommunications, and the utilities sector.[141] Due to the importance of these sectors for public security and national independence, the UK government sought to retain some control in their businesses activities.[142]

A 'golden share' is a special class share designed to remain the property of the state, granting it special powers and allowing it to exercise control over the company's management. Essentially, the state holds classes of shares with varying rights attached to them, which often provide a level of control disproportionate to the actual value of the shares.[143] The 'golden' nature of the shares stems from the fact that the board of the concerned company is required to obtain the 'golden shareholder's' written consent before acting on any of certain pre-determined events, such as large disposals, dilution of shareholdings, blocking foreign investors from acquiring shares, and controlling the appointment of directors.[144] Thus, the holder of 'golden shares' can act as a majority shareholder and outvote other shareholders or veto any major corporate action.[145]

However, the use of 'golden shares' has been traditionally an issue of debate at an international level. Under the free movement of capital principle, as enshrined in EU law, such state interventions could only be justified by the existence of overriding public interests and must be applied in a legally certain and proportional way.[146] The European Commission has brought a series of infringement proceedings against Member States, whose public authorities were granted disproportionate power in companies by way of golden shares, without valid justification.[147]

140 OECD, 'A Policy Maker's Guide to Privatisation' (March 2019) https://www.oecd.org/corporate/a-policy-maker-s-guide-to-privatisation-ea4eff68-en.htm accessed 15 September 2023.

141 Among others, British Aerospace, British Airways, Rolls-Royce plc, British Gas and British Petroleum, Brit Oil plc, Enterprise Oil plc, and Cable and Wireless plc.

142 See OECD (n 143) 56.

143 Jelena Ganza, 'Free Movement of Capital and Golden Shares in Volkswagen: Unexpected Twist or Foreseeable Outcome?' (KSLR EU Law Blog, 7 April 2014) https://blogs.kcl.ac.uk/kslreuropeanlawblog/?p=678 accessed 15 September 2023.

144 Hogan Lovells, 'Going for Gold: How Golden Shares can Help Lock in Mission for Social Enterprises' (15 December 2015) https://www.hoganlovells.com/en/publications/going-for-gold-how-golden-shares-can-help-lock-in-mission-for-social-enterprises accessed 15 September 2023.

145 Heinemann Andreas, 'Government Control of Cross-border MA: Legitimate Regulation or Protectionism?' 15(3) Journal of International Economic Law 843–70.

146 Art 63 Treaty of the Functioning of the EU prohibits, with certain exceptions, restrictions on the movement of capital between EU Member States.

147 Fifteen cases of the use of golden shares have been evaluated by the CJEU: *Commission v Italy*, C-58/99, judgment of the CJEU of 23 May 2000; *Commission v France*, C-483/99, 4 June 2002; *Commission v Belgium*, C-503/99, 4 June 2002 (justified); *Commission v Portugal*, C-367/98, 4 June 2002; *Commission v United Kingdom*, C-98/01, 13 May 2003; *Commission v Spain*, C-463/00, 13 May 2003; *Commission v Italy* C-174/04, 2 June 2005; Joined cases C-282/04 and C-283/04, *Commission v Netherlands*, 28 September 2006; *Federconsumatori v Commune di Milano*, C-463/04 and C-464/04, referred to the Court for preliminary ruling, 6 December 2007; *Commission v Germany*, C-112/05, 23 October 2007; *Commission v Spain*, C-274/06, 14 February 2008; *Commission v Spain*, C-207/07, 17 July 2008; *Commission v Italy*, C-326/07, 26 March 2009; *Commission v Portugal*, C-171/06, 8 July 2010; *Commission v Portugal*, C-543/08, 11 November 2010. In all of the above, the use of golden shares was found unjustified and thus illegal, the only exception being *Commission v Belgium* case C-503/99.

The Court of Justice has consistently held that a golden share can be justified if it aims to grant Member States a degree of influence on undertakings that were initially public and subsequently privatized, where those undertakings are active in sectors involving the provision of services in the public interest or strategic services. The striking majority of cases where EU Member State governments sought to use their golden shares to block a corporate decision failed to pass this justification test set by the Court of Justice and were declared illegal.

Despite their controversial nature, the use of golden shares has often been deployed by many EU Member States, including the UK.[148] In the UK, the generally accepted view is that the use of 'golden shares' is sanctioned by common law and permitted under Companies Act 2006.[149]

Finally, according to the Guidelines on Corporate Governance of State-Owned Enterprises of the OECD, the use of golden shares should be limited to cases where they are strictly necessary to protect certain essential public interests, such as public security and proportionate to the pursuit of these objectives.[150]

4.4.13 Some Interim Concluding Thoughts

After examining the existing regimes for state involvement and intervention in mergers and takeovers, it is apparent that they are poorly structured and perplexing for a potential investor. While improvements have recently been made towards adapting the regimes to modern national security priorities, several weaknesses can still be identified.

Firstly, due to technological advancements of the last two decades, the Enterprise Act jurisdictional tests and thresholds may no longer be appropriate for governmental intervention in mergers on national security grounds. Until now, the primary legislative focus has been on mergers and takeovers of large corporations in certain key sectors. However, the presence of smaller companies in critical infrastructure sectors is growing along with the need for measures to protect the sectors inherently susceptible to national security risks. Moreover, the nature of potential national security risks has evolved, and it has become apparent that threats are not necessarily confined to specific regulated sectors. To this end, the government has recognized the need to extend the scope of assessment of national security risks.

It has also been recognized that risks may arise in relation to foreign involvement in UK businesses in forms distinct from ownership, such as by way of control in, access

[148] The UK government holds golden shares in a number of companies, particularly in the defence sector, includingRolls-Royce, BAE Systems, and Qinetiq, see The Economist, 'Take your Partners' (7 April 2016) www.economist.com/news/britain/21696551-defence-firms-look-joint-ventures-boost-exports-and-profits-take-your-partners accessed 15 September 2023. Also, in August 2017, the UK government completed the sale of the state-backed Green Investment Bank (GIB) to private parties. Following the sale, five independent trustees will hold 'special shares', giving them the power to approve or reject any changes in GIB's green purposes in the future. See www.gov.uk/government/news/uk-governments-sale-of-green-investment-bank-completed.

[149] Hogan Lovells (n 144).

[150] OECD (n 140).

to or influence in corporate decision-making. Currently, none of the powers in the Enterprise Act can be used to intervene in asset acquisitions or investment in new projects. It is thus important that all direct and indirect foreign control in UK companies is subject to monitoring.

Another major weakness of the public interest merger review procedure lies in the decision-making process. On the one hand, the CMA, an independent authority, coordinates the whole process, even where no competition concerns exist. Despite its admitted lack of expertise in assessing public interests' considerations, the CMA is responsible for making recommendations on such issues.

On the other hand, the final decision rests with a single individual, the Secretary of State , who must balance both competition and public interest considerations, even in cases where these are not necessarily compatible or comparable. This exclusive power has been commented as problematic mainly for reasons that relate to the consistency between decisions, transparency of reasoning, and, crucially, the ability of the Secretary of State to afford adequate consideration to all interests at stake. Finally, there is an inherent risk that the relevant Secretary of State would take into consideration political interests and short-term strategies, which do not align with the quasi-judicial decision-making role.

After a long period of consultation, the UK government has recently taken some important steps towards introducing a standalone FDI review system, which aims to create a robust and comprehensive policy for state intervention. The following section describes the new regime before concluding whether it appears to adequately address the current limitations and meet the market's expectations.

4.5 The New UK National Security Regime for FDI

4.5.1 The National Security and Investment Act

The UK government brought the Bill on NSI Bill before the UK Parliament in November 2020. On 5 May 2021, the NSIA was published after receiving Royal Asset on 29 April 2021. The NSIA entered into force on 4 January 2022, while parts of the regime, such as the Secretary of State's 'call-in powers', apply to transactions that are completed even before that time. In other words, in addition to transactions where a trigger event occurs on or after 4 January 2022, relevant deals where a trigger event occurred during the period 12 November 2020 to 3 January 2022 can be called-in for review now the regime has commenced.[151]

The NSIA launched an investment screening regime based on national security criteria, separate from the existing merger screening by the CMA. Under the Enterprise Act 2002, the existing regime will continue to run in parallel, with the CMA remaining the competent authority for competition law purposes only. Therefore, when the new

[151] Norton Rose Fulbright, 'The UK's New NSI Regime: What Do You Need to Know?', June 2022

regime is implemented, the national security considerations will effectively be removed from the public interest and special public interest regimes under the Enterprise Act 2002. However, the government's statutory powers to intervene in investments for the purposes of protecting media plurality, financial stability, and public health emergencies will be preserved.

Whereas the scope of the Enterprise Act 2002 is largely defined by the size of the transaction (through the turnover and share of supply thresholds), the new national security screening system focuses on how an investor could acquire the ability to undermine national security. The UK government will be able to scrutinize, impose conditions on or, as a last resort, block a deal if it is concluded that there is an unacceptable risk to Britain's national security.

Principal features of the new regime include:

i. the establishment of a dedicated governmental unit,
ii. a mandatory notification and pre-approval system for transactions in specific sectors of the economy,
iii. a voluntary notification system available to investors,
iv. 'call-in powers' of the Secretary of State for unnotified investments,
v. a specific time limit for intervention,
vi. the application of remedies to address risks to national security and sanctions for non-compliance with the regime, and
vii. a mechanism for legal challenge of governmental decisions.

4.5.1.1 Investment Security Unit

A new operational unit, namely the Investment Security Unit (ISU), was established within the Department for BEIS and later moved to the cabinet office. The ISU is responsible for identifying, assessing, and mitigating national security risks arising when a person gains control of a qualifying asset or qualifying entity as set out in the Act. Under the auspices of the ISU, a digital portal will operate, which investors and businesses will use to notify of their proposals.

The ISU has already begun its operations and has called businesses to engage with it at this preliminary stage. For investors who are already involved in or plan on being involved in transactions that may fall under the requirements of the NSIA, the ISU is providing informal advice on a non-binding basis until the NSIA is fully in effect.

4.5.1.2 Mandatory Notification System for Key Sectors

The UK government has introduced a mandatory notification system for M&A transactions, pursuant to which certain business acquisitions must obtain government clearance before they can take place. These acquisitions are known as 'notifiable acquisitions' under the NSIA.

The mandatory notification system, however, only applies to proposed transactions that meet all of the following necessary criteria:

(a) the acquirer obtains control in the target company in excess of defined thresholds ('trigger events');
(b) they relate to companies and other entities undertaking specified activities in the UK ('qualifying entities'); and
(c) the target entities are operating in sensitive sectors of the economy.

We will discuss what exactly a 'notifiable acquisition' is by exploring each of the above elements to understand which transactions fall under the mandatory regime.

4.5.1.3 Qualifying Entities

The regime has a comprehensive UK nexus test. Non-UK-based target entities can be caught. The mandatory notification regime applies to specified categories of transactions that involve the acquisition of control over certain 'qualifying entities'.

According to the Act, a 'qualifying entity' is:

(i) any UK entity (body corporate, partnership, unincorporated association or trust);
(ii) any entity that carries on activities in the UK; or
(iii) any entity that supplies goods or services to persons in the UK.

It is important to emphasize that the Act applies to a wide range of entities, whether or not they have legal personality. In addition, investments in entities supplying goods and services to, or carrying on activities in, the UK could be caught under the new regime, even where the investment is through a vehicle incorporated outside the UK. Thus, the new law also applies to 'foreign-to-foreign' transactions where there is a change of control over the target business that carries on activities in the UK or supplies goods or services to persons in the UK.[152]

4.5.1.4 Trigger Events

For the purposes of the NSIA, acquisitions of control of a 'qualifying entity' are known as 'trigger events'. The acquisitions that require a mandatory notification system include those where:

a. the acquirer gains or increases its interest in the entity by virtue of the percentage of the voting rights or shares that the acquirer holds increasing:
   - from 25 per cent or less to more than 25 per cent;[153]

[152] Ashurst, 'UK National Security and Investment Control Regime' (4 February 2022) https://www.ashurst.com/en/insights/quickguide-uk-national-security-and-investment-control-regime/ accessed 15 September 2023.

[153] In an earlier iteration of the Bill, before it became an Act, the acquisition of a right or interest crossing a threshold of 15 per cent in a qualifying entity would be a 'notifiable acquisition'—not a 'trigger event' in itself, but one which must be notified so that an assessment could be made of whether there was a trigger event. However, this 15 per cent threshold was removed from the Bill shortly before it received Royal Assent, so transactions at this level do not require mandatory notification under the Act. It has been commented that this change was prompted by a concern that the threshold was disproportionate, noting that similar mandatory notification systems, eg, under the US CFIUS regime, use the threshold of 25 per cent as a starting point.

- from 50 per cent or less to more than 50 per cent; or
- from less than 75 per cent to 75 per cent or more;[154]

b. the acquirer obtains voting rights in the entity that, whether alone or with other voting rights held by it, enables it to secure or prevent the passing of any corporate resolution.

Therefore, if an investor already holds shares or voting rights in an entity, an increase in that shareholding, however small, which takes the investor over any of the thresholds listed above (ie, 25 per cent, 50 per cent or 75 per cent), will require a mandatory notification. Thus, transactions involving the acquisition of minority shareholdings will be subject to mandatory notification. This means that investors cannot avoid the obligation to notify by staggering the acquisition of a larger shareholding across several separate transactions.

It must be emphasized that the mandatory notification obligation is not limited to acquisitions of particular shareholdings. It is sufficient for a trigger event for the acquirer to obtain special voting rights or veto rights, enabling it to secure or block the passage of any corporate resolution.

Finally, the NSIA also grants the Secretary of State the power to specify and amend the scope of what may be considered a 'notifiable acquisition'. The reason behind this provision, which mirrors the one under the Enterprise Act 2002, was to enable the new national security regime to remain up to date as the nature of national security threats to the UK evolves. It further allows for the possibility of subsequent regulations bringing the acquisition of control over qualifying assets within the mandatory notification regime, which would significantly broaden the scope of transactions that must be notified.

4.5.1.5 Sensitive Sectors for National Security

The Act provides that mandatory notification will only be required for certain types of transactions in seventeen key sectors, regarded as being the most sensitive areas of the economy based on their susceptibility to national security threats.

These sectors are as follows:

- advanced materials
- advanced robotics
- artificial intelligence
- civil nuclear
- communications
- computing hardware
- critical suppliers to the government
- critical suppliers to the emergency services
- cryptographic authentication

[154] Notably, this aligns with the figures used by the CMA when assessing whether a merger may raise competition concerns.

- data infrastructure
- defence
- energy
- synthetic biology
- military and dual use
- quantum technologies
- satellite and space technologies
- and transport.

If a transaction falls within one of the specified sectors, it will be subject to a mandatory notification obligation if it involves one of the specified 'trigger events', as outlined above.

The definitions of these sectors have yet to be confirmed, while it remains possible that the focus of certain core sectors, including artificial intelligence and synthetic biology, will be narrowed. The government has consulted on that matter with businesses and organizations operating in the relevant sectors, and some important revisions were proposed in an interim publication in March 2021.[155]

Finally, at the end of 2021, the government published further guidance to assist businesses. It explains when activities are caught by the regulations and circumstances that fall outside its scope. For instance, regarding the artificial intelligence sector is concerned, the new guidance provides details on what is meant by 'identification': identification can include human identification, object identification and event identification.[156]

In its Annual Report 2022–23, the first to take into account a full year's worth of data, the UK government provided helpful statistics on the mechanism.[157] Between April 2022 and March 2023, the Secretary of State received 866 notifications (671 mandatory, 180 voluntary, and fifteen retrospective validation applications); 806 of these were accepted, while forty-three were rejected (seventeen were still pending at the end of the reporting period).

4.5.2 The Mandatory Notification Procedure

According to Chapter 4, section 14 of the NSIA, it is the acquirer's responsibility to notify of the proposed transaction. Notifications need to be made to the ISU via a new

[155] BEIS, 'National Security and Investment: Sectors in Scope of the Mandatory Regime', March 2021.

[156] UK Government, 'Guidance: National Security and Investment Act: Details of the 17 types of notifiable acquisitions', Updated 20 July 2022, https://www.gov.uk/government/publications/national-security-and-investment-act-guidance-on-notifiable-acquisitions/national-security-and-investment-act-guidance-on-notifiable-acquisitions#ai

[157] BEIS, 'National Security and Investment Act 2021: Annual Report 2022–23' (July 2023) https://assets.publishing.service.gov.uk/government/uploads/system/uploads/attachment_data/file/1169054/National_Security_and_Investment_Act_2021_annual_report_2022-23__PDF_.pdf accessed 15 September 2023. The First annual report only covered January–March 2022; see BEIS, 'National Security and Investment Act 2021: Annual Report 2022' (June 2022) https://assets.publishing.service.gov.uk/government/uploads/system/uploads/attachment_data/file/1083295/E02757792-nsi-annual-report-2022.pdf accessed 15 September 2023.

digital portal. The exact form and contents of the mandatory notice will be prescribed by regulations, which are yet to be issued by the government.

If the mandatory notice is accepted, the Secretary of State must respond to the relevant persons 'as soon as reasonably practicable'.[158] Notably, no time limit is specified regarding initial notification of acceptance. However, once the notification has been accepted, the Secretary of State has thirty working days to decide whether a thorough assessment of the transaction will be necessary. Before the end of the statutory review period, the Secretary of State must either give a call-in notice in relation to the proposed notifiable acquisition or notify each relevant person that no further action will be taken under the Act.[159] In the latter event, the proposed transaction is cleared and proceed to carry out their business plans.

On the other hand, the mandatory notice may be rejected on the grounds that it does not meet the requirements of the Act or the relevant regulations or does not contain sufficient information to allow the Secretary of State to decide how to proceed. If the mandatory notice is rejected, the Secretary of State must, as soon as practicable, provide reasons in writing for that decision to the person who gave the notice.

Figure 4.1 illustrates the breakdown of mandatory notifications by sector. Defence was the most common area by a wide margin, with 47 per cent of the mandatory notifications, followed by critical suppliers to government, data infrastructure, military and dual use, and artificial intelligence.

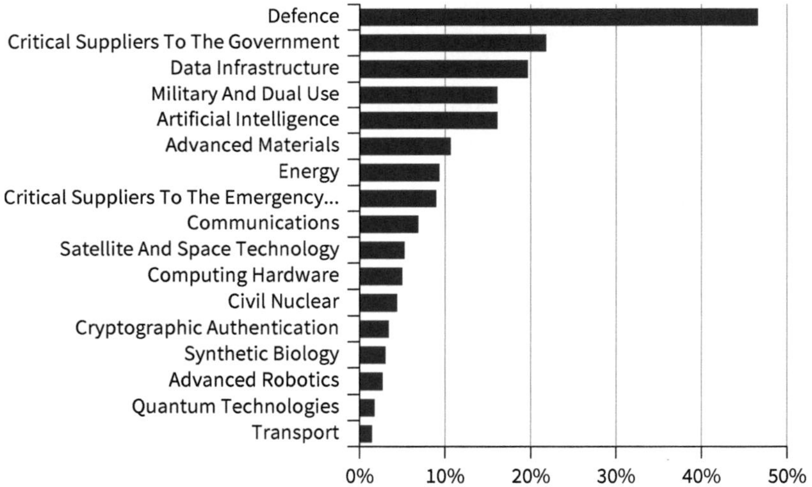

Figure 4.1 Breakdown of mandatory notifications by sector (April 2022–March 2023)

Reproduced from Department for Business, Energy and Industrial Strategy, 'National Security and Investment Act 2021: Annual Report 2022-23', page 15, figure 6, under the terms of the Open Government Licence © Crown Copyright 2022

Note: each notification can be associated with more than one area, hence the total number of notifications associated with each area is higher than the total number of notifications; mandatory notifications have been received for acquisitions taking place in each of the 17 sensitive areas of the economy

[158] NSIA, Part 1, Ch 4, s 14 para 5

[159] NSIA, Part 1, Ch 4, s 14 para 8.

4.5.2.1 Void Transactions

The most draconian provision of the new regime relates to the consequences of non-compliance with the mandatory notification regime. Transactions that fall under the mandatory regime cannot be completed until clearance is granted, and transactions without clearance will be void. In addition, when parties fail to notify the ISU of a notifiable acquisition, the Secretary of State could use its call-in powers to initiate an investigation. However, this power may only be exercised until the end of six months, beginning with the day the Secretary of State becomes aware of the transaction.

Effectively, notifiable acquisitions for which no notification has been made may remain subject to government intervention for an indefinite period following completion. Further details on potential sanctions for non-compliance with the notification requirement and process are provided later in this section.

4.5.2.2 Retrospective Validation

As seen above, notifiable acquisitions, for which no mandatory notice is given before completion, will be legally void and control in the relevant entity will be unaffected. This harsh legislative position is mitigated by the provision for an application to validate the acquisition retrospectively. Any person materially affected by the nullification of a notifiable acquisition may apply for a validation notice in relation to the acquisition.[160] On acceptance of such application, the Secretary of State must respond as soon as practicable, notifying the concerned person of its decision to accept or reject the application. If the application is accepted, the Secretary of State must act before the end of the review period by giving each relevant person a call-in notice concerning the acquisition or a validation notice, rendering the acquisition retrospectively valid and cleared.

Alternatively, in the absence of the relevant application, section 15 of the NSIA provides that the Secretary of State must consider issuing a validation notice before the end of the period of six months, beginning with the day on which it becomes aware of the notifiable acquisition.

4.5.3 The Voluntary Notification System

Alongside the mandatory notification requirement of the regime, a voluntary notification system is also introduced to encourage notification from parties who consider that their proposed transaction may have implications for national security.

The rules and processes for the voluntary system are more lenient, with lower thresholds comprising the 'trigger events'. Essentially, the voluntary part of the regime will be triggered on:

i. The acquisition of control of a qualifying entity or the ability to materially influence the policy of a 'qualifying entity'.

[160] For details on retrospective applications, see NSIA, Part 1, Ch 4, s 16.

ii. The acquisition of a right or interest in, or in relation to, a 'qualifying asset' providing the ability to use or control the asset (either entirely or to a greater extent).

In this context, 'material influence' has the same meaning in the UK merger control case law[161] and arises from the acquirer's ability to materially influence the strategic, commercial policy of the target business that is relevant to its behaviour in the marketplace.[162] It could, thus, be triggered by the acquisition of looser forms of control, such as acquisitions of minority shareholdings as low as 10–15 per cent or transactions where an individual or entity influences the 'direction of the entity'.[163] For example, if a minority shareholder's recommendations are followed by other key shareholders, then this is envisaged to be sufficient to trigger the proposed regime. The regime appears to seek to capture even the most extreme scenario, where a hostile party obtains material influence over the target business' affairs by way of coercion.

Additionally, the voluntary regime can be triggered by acquisitions or other transactions giving control over certain assets, including land, tangible movable property, and intellectual property. In the absence of any *de minimis* rules applying with respect to 'qualifying assets', it is yet possible that a simple transfer of information or commercial techniques of an economic value may qualify for voluntary notification and national security assessment.

It is important to highlight that the voluntary part of the regime applies to any sector of the economy and thus is not restricted to the seventeen key sectors, as outlined above. This, certainly, significantly expands the list of transactions, of which a voluntary notification may be prudent. Thus, parties involved in a deal with the potential to result in a significant change of control of the target entity or its assets will need to consider whether a voluntary notification is advisable.

As shown by Figure 4.2, the breakdown of voluntary notifications by area of the economy looks quite different from that of mandatory notifications: the latter was dominated by one sector—defence—with almost half of the notifications, while in this case, five sectors each account for 15–18 per cent of the notifications, including one—academic research and development in higher education—which is not included in the already mentioned list of seventeen key sectors.

[161] In considering whether material influence may be present in a particular case, the CMA considers not only whether the acquiring party has the right to block special resolutions but also whether, given other factors, it can do so as a practical matter. See CMA Decision: Anticipated acquisition by RWE AG of a 16.67 per cent minority stake in E.ON SE (5 April 2019); CMA Decision: Anticipated acquisition by Prosafe SE of Floatel International Limited (5 September 2019); OFT Report: Acquisition by British Sky Broadcasting Group plc of a 17.9 per cent in ITV plc; Report to the Secretary of State for Trade and Industry (14 December 2007) and *British Sky Broadcasting Group plc v the CC* and the Secretary of State [2008] CAT 25; and OFT Decision: Anticipated acquisition by Centrica plc of a 20 per cent stake in Lake Acquisitions Limited (a wholly owned subsidiary of EDF SA) (7 August 2009).

[162] On the definition of 'material influence', see the CMA's 'Mergers: Guidance on the CMA's jurisdiction and procedure', December 2020.

[163] According to the CMA, the term 'material influence' means the general management of the entity's business and thus includes the strategic direction of a company and its ability to define and achieve its commercial objectives.

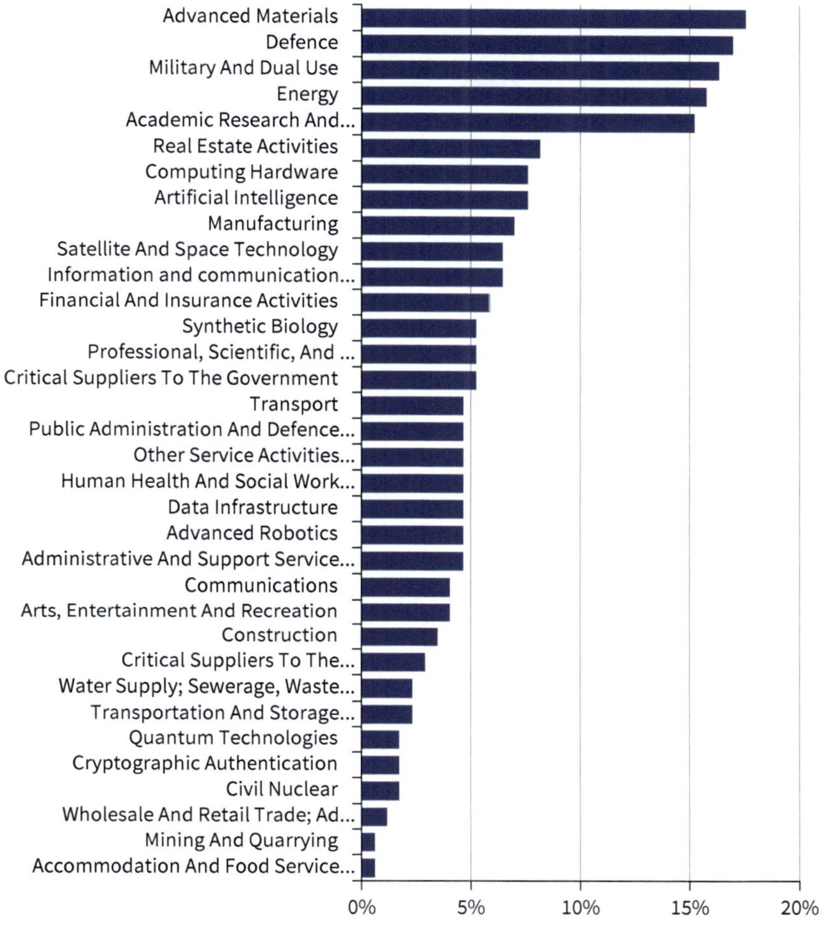

Figure 4.2 Breakdown of voluntary notifications by sector (April 2022–March 2023)

Reproduced from Department for Business, Energy and Industrial Strategy, 'National Security and Investment Act 2021: Annual Report 2022-2023', page 17, figure 7 under the terms of the Open Government Licence © Crown Copyright 2022

Notes: Some names are too long to display in the chart. These are: 'Other Service Activities (Membership Organisations, Repair, Personal Services, etc)'; 'Academic Research and Development in Higher Education'; 'Water Supply; Sewerage, Waste Management, and Remediation Activities'; Each notification can be associated with more than one area, hence the total number of notifications associated with each area is higher than the total number of notifications.

4.5.3.1 Call-in Powers

The NSIA grants the Secretary of State for Business, Energy, and Industrial Strategy an expansive 'call-in' power, enabling it to review transactions in the wider economy, which were not mandatorily notifiable but may raise national security concerns ('qualifying transactions'). Essentially, this provision was made so that the UK government could preserve its intervening rights (previously under the public interest regime) without relying on the goodwill of the parties involved.[164]

A 'call-in' situation may occur for one of two reasons:

a. when the parties have not voluntarily submitted a notification, but the government's market monitoring suggests the transaction should be called in; and
b. when a transaction has been voluntarily notified, but the Secretary of State requires further assessment to be undertaken beyond the initial notification screening.

The events triggering the exercise of call-in powers concerning the acquisition of rights or interests in qualifying entities or assets are the same as for the voluntary notification regime.

Therefore, as seen above, a 'qualifying transaction' is broadly defined to include acquisitions of 'material influence'. The definition of what constitutes 'material influence' over a target company is not yet clear, but if the CMA's approach to the term is followed, it could potentially bring within review thresholds investments in which less than a 25 per cent interest is acquired. Consequently, the call-in provisions could apply to transactions resulting in percentages of ownership or levels of control way below the 'mandatory notification' triggers. In such cases, the surrounding facts and particular circumstances of the transaction should be taken into account on a case-by-case risk assessment.

Additionally, the Secretary of State for BEIS is able to call-in transactions resulting in the acquisition of control of 'qualifying assets'. It must be noted that acquiring control of a qualifying asset is not exhausted in acquiring ownership but also includes acquiring a right or interest in relation to it and being able to use it, or direct or control its use, to a greater extent than prior to its acquisition.[165] For instance, obtaining a licence of an asset is capable of triggering the Secretary of State's power to 'call-in' a transaction. As seen above, the Act provides several examples of 'qualifying assets', such as land, tangible movable property, and ideas, information or techniques which have industrial, commercial or other economic value, such as trade secrets, databases, designs, specifications, and software.[166]

[164] BEIS, 'Impact Assessment on the National Security and Investment Bill', on 9 November 2020, available at https://assets.publishing.service.gov.uk/government/uploads/system/uploads/attachment_data/file/934276/nsi-impact-assessment-beis.pdf.

[165] NSIA, Part 1, Ch 2, s 9 para 1.

[166] NSIA, Part 1, Ch 2, s 7 describes the term 'qualifying assets' with examples of such assets. To give an example of what kind of transactions of assets might qualify for call-in, during the Parliamentary debates, Nadhim Zahawi (the then Under-Secretary of State for BEIS) stated that 'sales of software products to consumers by a software company would not be caught by the regime, but it would not prevent a transaction involving the software company selling the underlying code base supporting that software to a buyer acting in a professional capacity from the possibility of call-in under the regime, where that might give rise to a national security risk'.

Notably, the government's draft Statement of Policy Intent, published alongside the draft NSI Bill, emphasized that the Secretary of State rarely expects to intervene in asset transactions. Moreover, a key factor for pursuing an intervention would be the asset's 'proximity to a sensitive site'.[167] What is meant by 'proximity to a sensitive site' is not clearly defined, but it can be expected that transactions of land which are situated or are proximate to critical national infrastructure sites or government buildings are more likely to be called-in.[168]

It needs to be highlighted that this reserved power is not limited to oversight of transactions occurring in the seventeen core sectors but covers transactions in the wider UK economy. Furthermore, under its new powers, the Secretary of State is authorized to call-in and review transactions with minimal connection to the UK as long as the target company is undertaking business in, or supplying services or goods to, the UK. Thus, certain extra-territorial deals with tenuous connections with the UK are expected to fall under the government's scrutiny for the first time.

Finally, the call-in regime will capture transactions that are in progress or contemplation as well as those completed on or after the date the Bill was published (ie, 12 November 2020), where they have given rise or may give rise to a national security risk.

Between April 2022 and March 2023, sixty-five call-in notices were issued, including ten concerning acquisitions that had not been notified. Considering only the notifications (and the retrospective validations), fifty-five acquisitions out of the 766 notified, or about 7 per cent, warranted a call-in notice. It should be noted that these figures are below the government estimates (1,000–1,800 notifications and 70–95 call-ins) published prior to the NSIA coming into force, and these estimates were generally considered to be conservative at the time;[169] however, it is difficult to draw reliable conclusions from the first full year of operation of the NSIA.

Figure 4.3 sums up the breakdown of call-ins by sector. The data are not as dispersed as voluntary notifications no as concentrated as for mandatory notifications. Military and dual-use accounts for 37 per cent of the notices, with Defence and Advanced materials slightly below 30 per cent. Academic research is still the most concerned non-key area of the economy, but it's in the single digits.

[167] The concept of 'proximity to sensitive site' is already applied in the US, as seen in CFIUS' intervention in Ralls Corporation's acquisition of a wind farm project near to a Department of Defense site.

[168] BEIS, 'National Security and Investment: Statement About Exercise of the Call-in Power' (2 November 2021) https://www.gov.uk/government/publications/national-security-and-investment-statement-about-exercise-of-the-call-in-power accessed 15 September 2023.

[169] Simon Ward, Marie Bates, and Charlie Court, 'Could the UK's National Security and Investment Act affect your business?', Farrer and Co, 4 October 2022

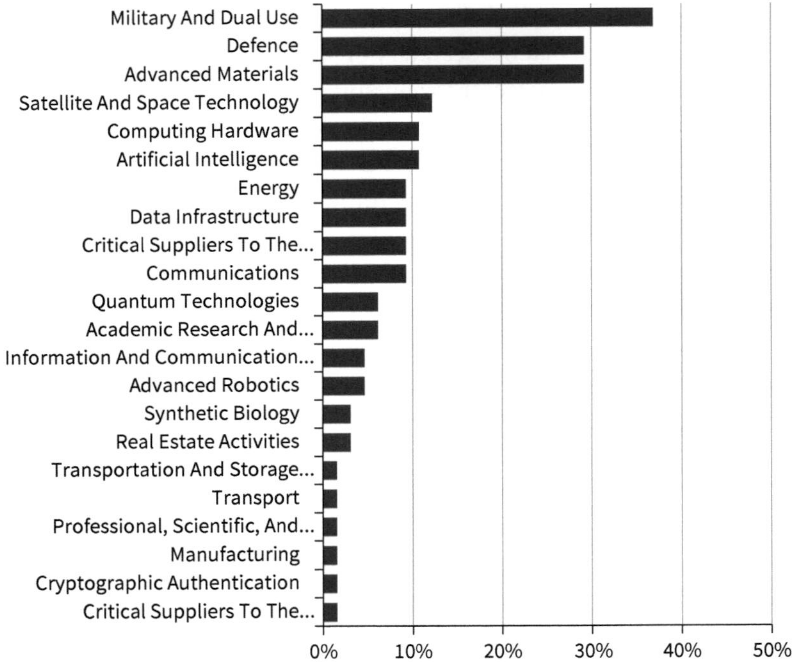

Figure 4.3 Breakdown of call-ins by sector (April 2022–March 2023)

Reproduced from Department for Business, Energy and Industrial Strategy, 'National Security and Investment Act 2021: Annual Report 2022-23', page 24, figure 10, under the terms of the Open Government Licence © Crown Copyright 2022

Note: each notification can be associated with more than one area, hence the total number of notifications associated with each area is higher than the total number of notifications; mandatory notifications have been received for acquisitions taking place in each of the seventeen sensitive areas of the economy

4.5.3.2 Call-in Considerations

When exercising their powers, the Secretary of State, as the ultimate decisionmaker, must consider the following risk factors:

a. the 'target risk', including the nature of the target and whether it is in an area of the economy where the government considers risks more likely to arise;[170]
b. the 'trigger event risk', meaning the type and level of control being acquired (as seen above) and how this could be used in practice;
c. the 'acquirer risk', being the extent to which the acquirer raises national security concerns.[171]

[170] To that end, the government considers that the economy can be split into three levels of risk: the 'core areas', the 'core activities', and the 'wider economy'. The risk assessment of a transaction, thus, highly depends on the category of national security risk in which it can be placed.

[171] In particular, the Secretary of State will look into the person having the ultimate control of the acquiring entity, his track record and whether the acquirer has committed any relevant criminal offences or has known affiliations with any parties directly involved in the transaction.

4.5.3.3 Call-in Procedure and Timeline

In practice, under its newly established powers, the Secretary of State may review specific acquisitions of control of legal entities and assets by issuing 'call-in notices'. The call-in notice must include a description of the trigger event to which it relates and state the names of the persons to whom the notice is given.

The notice may be issued up to five years after a trigger event has taken place, so long as that five-year period does not extend back before 12 November 2020. However, it cannot be issued after the end of the period of six months beginning with the day on which the Secretary of State became aware of the trigger event.[172] Especially with regards to trigger events taking place after 12 November 2020 but before the date on which the NSIA comes into force ('commencement day'), the six-month period begins on commencement day, rather than the day on which the Secretary of State becomes aware of it.[173] It is therefore possible that the NSIA will be applied to transactions concluded before the Bill was passed.

While there are similar powers in place under the French, German, and Italian FDI regimes, the five-year post-completion application is considerably longer than the retrospective period provided in the new EU-wide regime, under which transactions can be subject to review for up to fifteen months after completion.

Overall, the government's scope for intervention under its call-in powers appears considerably wide, leaving no room for potentially dangerous deals to slip through the net unchecked. In some respects, the call-in regime appears even broader than many comparable European regimes; however, further guidance is expected to clarify how the call-in powers will be exercised in practice and how excess burdens to businesses can be avoided.

At the time of writing, the UK government has issued a total of seventeen final orders on whether to prohibit or permit a transaction subject to remedies. This practice stands in stark contrast to the previous regime.

In the first few months of the operation of the new regime, a number of transactions have been prohibited by the UK government. On 15 July 2022, the government prohibited Beijing Infinite Vision Technology Company's acquisition of know-how related to SCAMP-5 and SCAMP-7 vision sensing technology from the University of Manchester. The technology in question had been developed to enable the next generation of autonomous robots and was thus related to IP rights.[174] According to the UK government, the technology concerned could be used 'to build defence or technological capabilities which may present national security risk to the United Kingdom'.[175]

[172] The government's draft statement of policy intent indicates that coverage of a deal in a national news publication may be sufficient for the government to be deemed aware of the deal.

[173] NSIA, Part 1, Ch 1, s 2.

[174] Debevoise and Plimpton, 'UK Government Prohibits Third Deal Under Its New National Security and Investment Act', 21 November 2022, https://www.debevoise.com/insights/publications/2022/11/uk-government-prohibits-third-deal, accessed 1 February 2024.

[175] BEIS, 'National Security and Investment Act 2021: Publication of Notice of Final Order' (20 July 2022) https://assets.publishing.service.gov.uk/government/uploads/system/uploads/attachment_data/file/1092802/aquisition-scamp5-scamp7-know-how-final-order-notice-20220720.pdf accessed 15 September 2023.

The transaction did not trigger a mandatory notification but highlights the ISU's wide remit for review and confirms that the ISU will take a keen interest in transactions that involve politically sensitive foreign investors.[176]

Less than a month later, another transaction was blocked on national security grounds in relation to the acquisition of UK-based Pulsic by Super Orange HK, a Shanghai-based developer of chip-design software. The UK government was concerned that a risk to national security would arise from the application of the intellectual property, knowledge, processes, and techniques for software developed and owned by the target for the electronic design automation products to facilitate the building of cutting-edge integrated circuits that could be used in a civilian or military supply chain.[177]

In December 2022, the Secretary of State prevented SiLight (Shanghai) Semiconductor Limited from acquiring a 100 per cent shareholding in HiLight Research Limited. The administration considered that a risk to national security arises relating to the potential for HiLight Research Limited's technology to be used to build technological capabilities, which may present national security risks to the UK.

In addition to the above prohibitions, there were transactions that were approved subject to conditions. In July 2022, the UK government, in its decision regarding the acquisition of Sepura by Epiris (emergency services), required the parties to 'implement enhanced controls to protect sensitive information and technology from unauthorised access, and to provide rights of access to premises and information so that relevant agencies are able to audit compliance with the security measures'.[178] These conditions aim to 'provide assurance that sensitive information and technology is protected and to ensure the maintenance of UK capabilities in repairing, servicing and maintaining the devices used in the TETRA Airwave network and Emergency Services Network used by emergency services in the UK'.[179]

On 2 September 2022, the UK government published a decision stating it has imposed conditions in the context of the acquisition of shares in Reaction Engines Limited by Tawazun Strategic Development Fund LLC, a venture capital firm based in Abu Dhabi. The Minister considered that the technology developed by Reaction Engines Limited has dual-use applications and that there is potential for sensitive IP be covertly accessed by hostile actors, leading to a military uplift which may present a national security threat to the UK. Unfortunately, no more information was given regarding the conditions to mitigate the risk to national security in the final order.[180]

176 Jennifer PM Marsh, Gabriela da Costa, Niall J Lavery, and Ryan Mullen, 'The UK National Security Regime Wets Its Feet: UK Government Publishes New Guidance', 26 June 2022, https://www.klgates.com/The-UK-National-Security-Regime-Wets-Its-Feet-UK-Government-Publishes-New-Guidance-8-26-2022, accessed 1 February 2024.

177 BEIS, 'Acquisition of Pulsic Ltd by Super Orange HK Holding Ltd: Notice of Final Order' https://www.gov.uk/government/publications/acquisition-of-pulsic-ltd-by-super-orange-hk-holding-ltd-notice-of-final-order/acquisition-of-pulsic-ltd-by-super-orange-hk-holding-ltd-notice-of-final-order (17 August 2022) accessed 15 September 2023..

178 ibid.

179 ibid.

180 BEIS, Acquisition of shares in Reaction Engines Limited by Tawazun Strategic Development Fund LLC: Notice of Final Order (2 September 2022) https://www.gov.uk/government/publications/acquisition-of-sha

On 14 September 2022, the UK government imposed a set of conditions in the context of the acquisition of the Stonehill project asset development rights by Stonehill Energy Storage Ltd. The 'Stonehill project' aims to improve the UK Power Grid's ability to use renewable energy. The Secretary of State identified potential national security risks relating to the security of an important UK electricity asset and services provided to the National Grid and imposed two conditions: (i) a requirement on the acquirer to obtain government approval before appointing a power offtake operator; and (ii) a restriction on the sharing of information from the power offtake operator to the acquirer.[181]

On 16 September 2022, in the sector of satellite and space technologies, the UK government approved the acquisition of Connect Topco Limited by Viasat, Inc. Two national security risks were identified: the protection of information and the maintenance of strategic capabilities. The approval was subject to the following two conditions: (i) controls are in place to protect information from unauthorized access, and (ii) strategic capabilities continue to be provided by Inmarsat and Viasat to the UK government.[182]

On 29 September 2022, in the energy sector, the government imposed information access on Chinese investors Redrock Investment's indirect acquisition of a 35 per cent stake in Electricity North West. It notably imposed restrictions on sharing information from the Target to the Acquirer.[183] Indeed, the Secretary of State identified a national security risk related the to the security of an important UK electricity asset. However, on 20 December 2022, the Secretary of State revoked the final order because of the Acquirer's decision not to proceed with the acquisition.

Also, on the same day, the UK government approved the acquisition of CPI Intermediate Holdings, INC by Iceman Acquisition Corporation (100 per cent) subject to the following remedy: it required the Acquirer to 'to keep CPI TMD's research, development and manufacturing capabilities in relation to atomic clocks in the United Kingdom'.[184]

On 10 October 2022, a final order was released by the government in the context of the acquisition of Ligeance Aerospace Technology Co Ltd by Sichuan Development Holding Co Ltd. The government cleared the transaction but imposed a set of five conditions concerning information sharing, security measures, board appointments, board appointment of HM government observer, and notification of asset transfers. According to the Secretary of State, these conditions were necessary in order to mitigate a national security risk related to the security of a UK aerospace company.

res-in-reaction-engines-limited-by-tawazun-strategic-development-fund-llc/acquisition-of-shares-in-reaction-engines-limited-by-tawazun-strategic-development-fund-llc-notice-of-final-order.

[181] Clifford Chance, Global Antitrust/FDI Energy Sector Newsletter, October 2022, https://www.cliffordchance.com/content/dam/cliffordchance/briefings/2022/10/global_antitrust_fdi_energy_newsletter_oct-2022.pdf accessed 15 September 2023.

[182] BEIS (n 179).

[183] ibid.

[184] ibid.

In November 2022, the UK government undid the acquisition of Newport Wafer Fab (UK's largest silicon wafer producer) by China-backed Nexperia, which closed in July 2021 and was called-in retrospectively for review on 25 May 2022. Some of NWF's work was highly sensitive in a sense that it has over a dozen UK government research contracts which involved developing chip technology for a radar system that would be used in fighter jets.[185] The review was lengthy, with the initial thirty-day review period initially being extended by the statutory maximum of forty-five days, again by four weeks and then for an indefinite period on 3 October 2022.[186] Finally, on 16 November 2022, the government required 'Nexperia BV to sell at least 86% of NNL within a specified period and by following a specified process' noting that a national security risk arises from the 'technology and know-how that could result from a potential reintroduction of compound semiconductor activities at the Newport site', which may 'undermine UK capabilities' and adding that 'the location of the site could facilitate access to technology and expertise in the South Wales Cluster' (a group of major industrial companies in the region), which could 'prevent the Cluster being engaged in future projects relevant to national security'.[187]

We should note that this case is the first use of BEIS' retroactive powers to review a transaction that closed prior to the entry into force of the NSI (January 2022). On 5 December 2022, the Secretary of State imposed conditions on the transaction between Truphone Limited and TP Global Operations Limited (both English companies). TP Global Operations Limited would acquire the assets and subsidiaries of Truphone Limited. The government had concerns regarding the disruption of UK mobile services and the potential to exploit Truphone UK user data. This is why it required the acquirer (i) to appoint a Chief Information Security Officer (CISO) approved by the Secretary of State and (ii) to put in place telecoms information security measures on the acquirer and require the acquirer to carry out a security audit by an HMG approved auditor to produce a report setting out any new security measures.[188]

Also, on the 5 December 2022, the UK government imposed conditions in the context of the acquisition of XRE Alpha Limited by China Power International Holding Limited (a state-owned company). According to the administration, the operation would raise national risk in relation to the power system. Thus, the conditions imposed by the Business Secretary restrict the management of certain services to

[185] Tom Jowitt, 'UK Government Blocks Newport Wafer Fab Acquisition, Citing National Security', 17 November 2022, https://www.silicon.co.uk/workspace/components/uk-government-blocks-newport-wafer-fab-acquisition-citing-national-security-486643, accessed 1 February 2024.

[186] Debevoise and Plimpton, 'UK Government Prohibits Third Deal Under Its New National Security and Investment Act', 21 November 2022, https://www.debevoise.com/insights/publications/2022/11/uk-government-prohibits-third-deal accessed 1 February 2024.

[187] BEIS, Acquisition of Newport Wafer Fab by Nexperia BV: Notice of Final Order https://www.gov.uk/government/publications/acquisition-of-newport-wafer-fab-by-nexperia-bv-notice-of-final-order accessed 15 September 2023.

[188] BEIS, 'Acquisition of the assets and subsidiaries of Truphone Limited by TP Global Operations Limited: Notice of Final Order' (5 December 2022) https://www.gov.uk/government/publications/acquisition-of-the-assets-and-subsidiaries-of-truphone-limited-by-tp-global-operations-limited-notice-of-final-order/acquisition-of-the-assets-and-subsidiaries-of-truphone-limited-by-tp-global-operations-limited-notice-of-final-order accessed 15 September 2023.

government-approved operators. The final order also limits the information that can be shared with China Power International Holding.[189]

On 19 December 2022, in the context of the purchase of a 100 per cent stake in Upp Corporation Ltd by L1T FM Holdings UK Ltd (which includes the parent company LetterOne Core Investment Sàrl), the Secretary of State considered a national security risk to arise from Upp's indirect ownership by certain beneficial owners of LetterOne, a number of whom are subject to sanctions under the UK's Russia sanctions regime. Thus, it required LetterOne to sell 100 per cent of Upp within a specified period and following a specified process, and Upp to complete a security audit of the Upp network before the sale.[190] In the final order, no more information was given as far as the 'specified process' is concerned.

On 22 February 2023, the Secretary of State expressed his concerns about an operation where Stellex Capital Management LLC would gain control of the qualifying entity, David Brown Santasalo Sàrl, via its wholly owned subsidiary Gear Bidco Sàrl by increasing the percentage of shares held in David Brown Santasalo Sàrl from less than 75 per cent to 75 per cent or more. The government required the acquirer to 'maintain continuity of supply in respect of critical Ministry of Defence programmes and ensures that the capability necessary to maintain that continuity of supply is retained in the UK'.[191]

On 8 June 2023, the Secretary of State issued a final order concerning the transaction between Canada-based underwater scanning company Voyis Imaging and the University of Southampton for the sale of undisclosed assets. The government argued that 'a risk to national security will arise from this trigger event as a result of potential military uplift to foreign states through gaining access to the licensed' asset. Ultimately, the transaction was approved on the condition that the acquirer must 'carry out due diligence checks on all new customers' and report their details to the government annually.[192] It can be observed that the deal looks a lot like the one between China-based Beijing Infinite Vision and the University of Manchester, but the final outcome was quite different.

On 7 August 2023, France-owned EDF Energy was conditionally allowed to acquire GE Oil and Gas Marine and Industrial and GE Steam Power. The Secretary of State observed that the transaction might affect 'the critical national security and defence

[189] BEIS, 'Acquisition of XRE Alpha Limited by China Power International Holdings Limited: Notice of Final Order' (5 December 2022) https://assets.publishing.service.gov.uk/government/uploads/system/uploads/attachment_data/file/1122010/XRE_Alpha_-_Final_Order.pdf accessed 15 September 2023.

[190] BEIS, NSIA, Publication of Notice of Final Order, https://www.gov.uk/government/publications/acquisition-of-upp-corporation-ltd-by-l1t-fm-holdings-uk-ltd-notice-of-final-order/acquisition-of-upp-corporation-ltd-by-l1t-fm-holdings-uk-ltd-notice-of-final-order accessed 15 September 2023.

[191] BEIS, NSIA, Publication of Notice of Final Order, https://www.gov.uk/government/publications/acquisition-of-david-brown-santasalo-sarl-by-stellex-capital-management-llc-via-its-subsidiary-gear-bidco-sarl-notice-of-final-order/acquisition-of-david-brown-santasalo-sarl-by-stellex-capital-management-llc-via-its-wholly-owned-subsidiary-gear-bidco-sarl-notice-of-final-order accessed 15 September 2023.

[192] BEIS, Notice of Final Order 'Acquisition of assets belonging to the University of Southampton by Voyis Imaging Inc' https://www.gov.uk/government/publications/acquisition-of-assets-belonging-to-the-university-of-southampton-by-voyis-imaging-inc-notice-of-final-order/acquisition-of-assets-belonging-to-the-university-of-southampton-by-voyis-imaging-inc-notice-of-final-order accessed 15 September 2023.

capabilities relating to naval propulsion systems' and imposed a number of commitments on the acquirer: physical and information security requirements; governance arrangements adequate to protect sensitive information; the appointment of a government observer to the boards of the companies concerned; the establishment of a steering committee to oversee compliance with said security requirements; and significantly the obligation to 'maintain capacity and capability in respect of critical Ministry of Defence programmes in the UK'.[193]

Finally, in another operation in the telecom industry, the French group Altice's increased stake in British Telecom (BT) plc (from 12 per cent shareholding to 18 per cent), the government decided not to take further action under the NSIA,[194] but this call-in is nonetheless a sign that the UK government will not hesitate to call-in relatively low minority shareholdings for review where the target is a UK entity of major strategic importance.

Regarding these recent developments, it is noticeable that the main sectors of focus continue to be the 'traditional' sectors (ie, military, defence, dual use). We should note that most of the final orders are broad and that it is too early to identify any trends.[195] Even if the regime is still fairly new, it is obvious that the UK government will not hesitate to call-in deals with possible national security implications and particularly those with investors from certain countries.[196] Moreover, the final orders reflect that even UK investors are not immune from the imposition of remedies.

4.5.4 Timeframe for Assessments

The NSIA is introducing, for the first time, a standard timetable, with each stage of review requiring notice from the Secretary of State before the next stage commences.

At the first stage, once a transaction has been notified or called-in, the government will be required to undertake its review within a thirty-working day period ('initial period'). If, during that initial period, the transaction is called-in for a detailed national security assessment, this will need to be completed within the thirty-working

[193] BEIS, Notice of Final Order 'Acquisition of GE Oil and Gas Marine and Industrial UK Ltd and GE Steam Power Ltd by EDF Energy Holdings Ltd via its wholly owned subsidiary, GEAST UK Ltd' https://www.gov.uk/government/publications/acquisition-of-ge-oil-gas-marine-industrial-uk-ltd-and-ge-steam-power-ltd-by-edf-energy-holdings-ltd-via-its-wholly-owned-subsidiary-geast-uk-ltd/acquisition-of-ge-oil-gas-marine-industrial-uk-ltd-and-ge-steam-power-ltd-by-edf-energy-holdings-ltd-via-its-wholly-owned-subsidiary-geast-uk-ltd accessed 15 September 2023.

[194] BEIS and The Rt Hon Kwasi Kwarteng MP, 'Government to Take No Further action Under National Security and Investment Act on BT Share Acquisition' 23 August 2022, https://www.gov.uk/government/news/government-to-take-no-further-action-under-national-security-and-investment-act-on-bt-share-acquisition, accessed 1 February 2024.

[195] Cooley Alert, 'UK NSI Regime—A New Dawn for UK National Security?', 8 November 2022, https://www.cooley.com/news/insight/2022/2022-11-08-uk-nsi-regime-a-new-dawn-for-uk-national-security, accessed 1 February 2024.

[196] Debevoise and Plimpton, 'UK Government Prohibits Third Deal Under Its New National Security and Investment Act', 21 November 2022, https://www.debevoise.com/insights/publications/2022/11/uk-government-prohibits-third-deal, accessed 1 February 2024.

day deadline unless, before the end of the initial period, the Secretary of State gives an 'additional period notice' to the parties.

An 'additional period notice' may be served if the Secretary of State reasonably believes that:

(i) a trigger event has taken place or that arrangements are in progress or contemplation which, if carried into effect, will result in a trigger event;
(ii) a risk to national security has arisen from the trigger event or would arise from the trigger event if carried into effect; and
(iii) an additional period is required to assess the trigger event further.

If these conditions are met, the initial review period may be extended by a further forty-five working days (ie, totalling seventy-five working days from notification or call-in), beyond which further extensions may be agreed between the Secretary of State and the acquirer.

Moreover, should additional information be requested, or the attendance of the concerned parties be considered essential, the 'clock will stop', extending the total review period further. When issuing either information or attendance notice, a time limit for compliance with their requirements will be specified. If that time limit elapses or the Secretary of State is satisfied that the requirements have been complied with (if earlier), the concerned persons will be notified accordingly. The period between the information or attendance notice being served and the specified time limit expiry (or earlier compliance) does not count towards the initial, additional, or voluntary period, as discussed above.[197]

Therefore, it appears that the statutory review timelines allow some scope for flexibility, which may be appropriate when reviewing complex cases. Nevertheless, the Act guarantees that the parties would have an initial response within thirty working days of notification. Certainly, this statutory provision should be much appreciated by prospective investors, enabling them to account for time for the notification process into deal timetables. This contrasts with the existing public interest regime, under which timelines are set on a case-by-case and, at times, on a rather unpredictable basis.

The Annual Report published by the UK government provides statistics, shown in Table 4.1, on the time in which notifications were accepted or rejected and the timeframe within which notifications were assessed once accepted.[198]

[197] NSIA, Part 2, s 24.

[198] Samantha J Mobley and Zeyang Gao, 'UK Government Publishes First NSIA Annual Report' (Baker McKenzie, 27 June 2022)

Table 4.1 Average Time in Which Notifications were Treated (April 2022–March 2023)

Average number of working days ...	Median		Mean	
	Mandatory	Voluntary	Mandatory	Voluntary
... from receiving a notification to informing parties of acceptance	4		5	
... from receiving a notification to giving written reasons for rejection	10	7	12	9
... from accepting a notification to calling in the acquisition	28	27	27	25
... from calling in an acquisition to issuing a final notification	25		31	

Author's elaboration based on Department for Business, Energy and Industrial Strategy, 'National Security and Investment Act 2021: Annual Report 2022–23', pages 19–20, 27, and 32, under the terms of the Open Government Licence © Crown Copyright 2022

4.5.5 Remedies and Sanctions

Under the Act, the UK government grants itself powers to impose remedies where deals are found to create national security risks and to administer sanctions for non-compliance with the regime.

The government will have the power to impose mitigation measures to address any national security concerns identified. Following a national security assessment, the government could decide to approve the transaction, make the approval conditional on undertakings or prohibit the whole transaction. Possible conditions include adjusting the shareholding or control an investor is permitted to acquire, restricting access to commercial information, or controlling access to certain operational sites or works.[199] These may include, for example, conditions restricting access to sensitive sites, access to confidential information and prohibiting intellectual property transfers. Where a transaction is already implemented, the government will have alternative powers to order the transaction that has taken place to be divested or unwound. Finally, the government will have the power to amend their terms and even block deals altogether.

On the other hand, a comprehensive penalty framework is set to address failures to comply with the new regime. Sanctions can be expected to be severe, with serious economic harm being a real possibility for deviant investors.

An automatic consequence of failing to obtain clearance for a mandatorily notifiable transaction is that the transaction will be void. Furthermore, both criminal and

[199] James Marshall and others, 'UK FDI: National Security and Investment Bill is Published', 13 November 2020 https://www.covcompetition.com/2020/11/uk-fdi-national-security-and-investment-bill-is-published/ accessed 15 September 2023.

civil sanctions will apply for non-compliance with the mandatory aspects of the regime, including:

- financial penalties in the greater amount of (a) up to 5 per cent of the worldwide turnover of the business in question and (b) £10 million;
- corporate criminal penalties;
- imprisonment of up to five years; and
- director disqualification for up to fifteen years for specified directors and officers.

In a memorandum of understanding published in June 2022, the UK government has helpfully clarified that: 'in order to avoid potential conflicts between remedies imposed (or accepted) under the NSIA 21 and EA 02, BEIS will, where appropriate, consider aligning the review processes of BEIS and the CMA should it be judged helpful in certain cases, by requesting a voluntary extension period with the merger parties to ensure that remedies are effective and that BEIS and CMA avoid any clash in remedies. This will in general follow the application of an interim order' but it added that 'for national security reasons, it may not always be appropriate to align review processes'.[200] It remains to be seen how this will be implemented.

4.5.6 Transitional Provisions

The NSIA has a degree of retroactive effect on specific aspects of its regime. At the time of writing, transactions completed on or after 12 November 2020 (the date after the publication of the Bill) can be retrospectively reviewed by the Secretary of State using the call-in regime. Essentially, the retrospective call-in power applies to transactions on or after 12 November 2020 and conditional deals entered into before that date but for which a 'trigger event' meeting the tests for notification occurs later.

Nevertheless, the Act provides a long stop, as the government will only be able to review transactions completed after the Bill is introduced but before the Act is in force for up to five years after completion.

Notably, the merger control provisions of the Enterprise Act 2002 will continue to apply in the interim period, so it is likely that the government will only use its new call-in powers where transactions fall outside the existing national security provisions of the Enterprise Act.

Much to the relief of many investors, the mandatory notification element of the regime is not retrospective and would rather take effect once the new regime is officially up and running. Nevertheless, as seen above, deals signed before the Act comes into force may be called-in by the Secretary of State if a trigger event occurs later. To that

[200] 'MoU between BEIS and the CMA on the operation of the National Security and Investment Act 2021' (16 June 2022), https://www.gov.uk/government/publications/operation-of-the-national-security-and-investment-act-2021-memorandum-of-understanding/mou-between-beis-and-the-cma-on-the-operation-of-the-national-security-and-investment-act-2021 accessed 15 September 2023.

end, parties involved in deals that could give rise to situations triggering a subsequent national security review should consider approaching the Investment and Security Unit for guidance.

4.6 Initial Evaluation and Market Reaction

The recent developments in the UK legislative landscape are signalling the beginning of a new era for investment screening. The need for a coherent regime that would focus directly on national security considerations has been recognized by most academics, while many UK businesses have been longing for a change to the outmoded merger review system.[201]

Without a doubt, the new regime seems able to stand up to the expectation of enhancing the government's ability to intervene in cases where national security concerns are raised while providing a range of remedies to mitigate such concerns. At the same time, certain defects in the previous system will be resolved, especially concerning the contentious coexistence of competition law and national security criteria, under the same review process. However, it is difficult to quantify the potential benefits as numerous and complex interlinkages between investments and national security considerations exist.

Without debating the merits of these developments, there are reasons to believe that the new legislative system could prove particularly challenging for UK businesses, creating new regulatory hurdles to investment in the wider economy.

Since the first proposals of the Bill, there have been conflicting reactions in the UK markets, with companies participating in the selected sectors vocal about their concerns about the potential negative effects of the new law on their activities. Some perceived weaknesses of the new regime relate to the abstract term of 'national security', its potential scope for political interference, and the ultimate economic impact on domestic and foreign investment. Each of these concerns will be discussed separately with a view to establishing whether there is room for further improvement.

4.6.1 National Security Definition

A major concern for investors is presented by the absence of a definition for 'national security', potentially allowing the UK government considerable discretion in the

[201] See Dr Ashley Thomas Lenihan, LSE, 'Foreign Investment Regimes: Three Things the West Needs to Better Protect National Security', 1 March 2021, available at https://blogs.lse.ac.uk/businessreview/2021/03/01/foreign-investment-regimes-three-things-the-west-needs-to-better-protect-national-security/ accessed 15 September 2023, where it is highlighted that best practice with respect to FDI regulation should ensure that the focus is only on national security, rather than national interest or other protectionist considerations.

application of the new regime.[202] As with the merger control regime, state intervention in national security reasons comes with an important degree of flexibility.

The importance of legal certainty and predictability cannot be underestimated in the context of FDI screening. Since international competitiveness is now a priority for the UK economy more than ever, establishing a transparent, open, and enabling policy environment for investment remains pivotal.

Despite its initial commitments to addressing the lack of consistency and unpredictability of the previous regime,[203] at this point, the UK government has avoided defining what national security considerations are to be taken into account when reviewing proposed transactions, perpetuating uncertainty for businesses and investors.

Given the high upfront costs of some qualifying transactions, such as negotiating an M&A transaction, firms would need to be confident that their transaction will be subjected to a consistent and predictable assessment process.[204] A regime which lacks these qualities is likely to undermine business confidence, which may lead investment activity to stagnate.[205]

Therefore, the new reforms would need to warrant high standards of transparency and predictability to mitigate any adverse effects they might have on investor confidence and alleviate any fears of political discretion.[206] To that end, guidance should be provided on how national security risks are to be identified and assessed so that parties can respond accordingly and take measures to prevent their deals giving ground to such risks.[207] In addition, the criteria against which a deal will be assessed should

[202] Covington and Burling LLP, 'UK National Security and Investment Law is Approved by Parliament', under Global Policy Watch, available at https://www.globalpolicywatch.com/2021/05/uk-national-security-investment-law-is-approved-by-parliament/ accessed 15 September 2023. Amongst other academics, Dr Roger Barker (Director of Policy and Corporate Governance, Institute of Directors) expressed such concerns at the Foreign Affairs Committee, 'Oral evidence: The FCDO's role in blocking foreign asset stripping in the UK', HC 296, Qq231 and 234, 24 November 2020. BT expressed similar concerns on its 'Written evidence submission from BT (BFA0026)' while emphasizing that the Act should provide for a 'clear, transparent, predictable process'; available at https://committees.parliament.uk/writtenevidence/18448/pdf/ accessed 15 September 2023. However, the dynamism of threats faced by the UK and the consequent need for flexibility in responding to them have also been recognized by commentators.

[203] National Security and Infrastructure Review (n 117).

[204] On the commercial effect of this unpredictability, see Roger Barron's (Paul Hastings) and Veronica Robert's (Herbert Smith Freehills) comments before the Foreign Affairs Committee 'Oral evidence: The FCDO's role in blocking foreign asset stripping in the UK', HC 296, 24 November 2020, Q245–Q250.

[205] Dr David Reader, 'UK Merger Control: finely tailored but time for a new suit?', in Barry Rodger, Peter Whelan, and Angus MacCulloch (eds), *The UK Competition Regime: A Twenty-Year Retrospective* (OUP 2021) Ch 7. According to Dr Reader, by choosing not to narrow the definition of 'national security', the government risks 'inflicting irreputable damage on the UK's ability to attract "welcome" investment, as well as that which is unwanted'. See also John Fingleton, 'Mergers and the Public Interest: A Wolf in Sheep's Clothing?' (Fingleton Associates, 16 October 2018) https://fingleton.com/news/mergers-and-the-public-interest-a-wolf-in-sheeps-clothing accessed 15 September 2023.

[206] See witness evidence given before the Foreign Affairs Committee, 'Oral evidence: The FCDO's role in blocking foreign asset stripping in the UK', HC 296, 24 November 2020. In particular. see Roger Barker (Director of Policy and Corporate Governance, Institute of Directors) commenting that there would be much greater confidence in the whole process if there was transparency about how the procedure is working, the result and the rationale of decisions that are made in respect of notifications on particular transactions', Q234.

[207] See witness evidence given by Dr Christopher Mackmurdo (Former Head of National Security Research, Foreign and Commonwealth Office and Founder at Legatus) and Sophia Gaston (Director at British Foreign Policy Group), before the Foreign Affairs Committee, 'Oral evidence: The FCDO's role in blocking foreign asset stripping in the UK', HC 296, 1 December 2020, Q262–268.

be expressly named, where possible, and their scope provided within the legislation to avoid inconsistent interpretations by decision-makers.

However, it must be taken into consideration that the level and type of threat that the UK faces in relation to its national security changes in a way, that is, by its nature, difficult to predict, but it is essential that there is enough flexibility to allow the government to pre-empt future risks. The underlying concept of national security is abstract and fluid while interlinked to other policy considerations, which are ever-evolving.[208] Notably, the Covid-19 pandemic has highlighted the difficulty in predicting the types of considerations that the broad term of 'national security' may give rise to in the future. Therefore, investors need to keep in mind that the list of national security risks and the sectors to which the national security regime will apply can be adapted depending on the developments in the UK economy and the priorities of the UK government.

4.6.2 Political Interference

Some commentators have expressed concern about the potential for political interference in business activities under the new regime and, more specifically, under the exercise of call-in powers.[209]

Concerns are raised with regards to the ministers' new powers to intervene to, and even unwind, deals retrospectively, even when the transaction was not subject to mandatory notification.[210] This is perceived as a potentially intrusive power, adding to the existing uncertainty of the new regulatory regime.[211] It further means that parties to qualifying transactions cannot rely on an initial assessment for the purposes of the mandatory regime but will need to be alert to potential trigger events taking place a long time after completion of the deal. This essentially perpetuates the risks and costs of complying with the new law.

Furthermore, it is claimed that the current uncertainty in terms of what constitutes a national security issue can also be used as an interventionist tool by the government to influence the development of a number of sectors in the UK

[208] Freshfields Bruckhaus Deringer, Report on 'Public interest or protectionism? Navigating the new normal', 2018. Highlighting the challenge of achieving this balance, the Centre for Competition Policy stated that 'constraining the definition of national security in advance may be difficult, due to the breadth and unpredictable nature of national security interests; yet the instrument should not become one that can be unduly applied'. Centre for Competition Policy, Written evidence submitted to House of Commons Foreign Affairs Committee—blocking foreign asset stripping of UK companies (BFA0014), September 2020.

[209] ibid 67, see comments by Dr Roger Barker and Andy Sellars (Strategic Development Director, Compound Semiconductor Applications Catapult), with the latter arguing that 'a slightly worrying feature of the Bill in its current form is that the final arbiter is the Secretary of State. There is a concern that the decision becomes politicised in a particular situation'. QU230.

[210] The uncertainty created by the five-year 'call-in' period has been a central concern raised by many commentators giving oral evidence on the NSI Bill before the Foreign Affairs Committee. Among others, note Hazel Moore (Chair and Co-Founder at FirstCapital) and Russ Shaw (Founder of Global Tech Advocates), who claimed that five years is 'too long' and risks disincentivizing investors.

[211] 'Considering the U.K.'s permissive starting point, with no formal foreign investment regime and only limited instances where the government could intervene, investors are being asked to place an unusually high degree of trust in the current U.K. Government.' See J Webber, S Ashall, M Readings, E Rodriguez, and E Rarity, Shearman & Sterling LLP 'UK: The UK National Investment and Security Bill is Published', 13 November 2020.

economy.[212] As the concept of national security evolves and expands, the line between protecting national security and establishing industrial policy is increasingly blurred.[213] While national security criteria ostensibly serve the legitimate purpose of protecting the safety and security of citizens, there is nonetheless a risk that these criteria can be abused by governments, that may adopt a broad definition to the concept of 'national security' in order to accommodate other political interests and implement an industrial strategy.[214] In particular, national security may be used as a pretext to pursue other industrial policy objectives such as restriction of foreign investment in sectors of strategic importance in order to achieve technological leadership and greater domestic production.[215]

However, as discussed in section 3, the UK government already has a range of tools at its disposal to safeguard its political interests in such sectors, from tax and procurement policy, to investment in domestic infrastructure, and R&D. It is thus claimed that a greater political interference to investment would raise concerns of an emerging national protectionism[216],

[212] The risk of inconsistent approaches by successive Secretaries of State is inherently higher when there is no established process to assess national security threats. See Andy Sellars (ibid 74): 'The way to mitigate the process of politicisation is to have a good technical definition of security.' Also, Roger Barker (ibid 67) suggested that the Bill should include measures providing greater transparency regarding the basis for decisions. More precisely, he noted that in order to avoid politicization, 'there should be a very clear definition of national security that can be interpreted and understood in a very transparent way that is applied consistently by independent experts'. ibid 67, QU231-133.

[213] Freshfields Bruckhaus Deringer, Report on 'Public interest or protectionism? Navigating the new normal', 2018, p. 15.

[214] According to Dr Ashley Lenihan of the London School of Economics (LSE), 'on the whole, in the Bill as written ... it is very clear that the powers for review and intervention should be used only for an identified risk of national security, and not on the grounds of national interest. ... The concern is if we see the UK blocking deals where it could mitigate because a deal has become a political hockey puck. In today's world, ... any case has the potential to be discussed widely in the political debate. The question is how it is treated by Government and how other countries perceive that treatment.' Public Bill Committees, 'National Security and Investment Bill (Second sitting)', 24 November 2020, Col 36–37. Also, M&A lawyer Roger Barron, giving oral evidence to the Committee, stated that 'defence and national security are political in many ways' (Q246). In addition, similar opinions have been raised by others before the Foreign Affairs Committee (FAC). It has been claimed that the new regime allows for interpretations of 'national security' in the context of specific investments to be driven or influenced by political or economic considerations. FAC, 'Oral evidence: The FCO's role in blocking foreign asset stripping in the UK', HC 296, Q149, 8 September 2020. In particular, John Fingleton noted a 'huge amount of political lobbying about which cases get looked at and how they are determined' (Q297). The 2018 takeover of GKN by Melrose and the attempted bid for AstraZeneca by Pfizer in 2014 were given as examples of such politicization of the review process. See Department for Business, Energy, and Industrial Strategy, 'Government Response: Government responds to GKN/Melrose takeover', 29 March 2019; and Melrose, 'Post-offer undertakings in relation to the acquisition of GKN plc (GKN) by Melrose Industries PLC (Melrose)', 1 April 2019.

[215] House of Commons, Foreign Affairs Committee (FAC), 'Striking the balance: Protecting national security through foreign investment legislation', Sixth Report of Session 2019–21, 19 January 2021. While setting clear parameters around national security is admittedly difficult, greater clarity on how 'national security' will be characterized in the context of a transaction should be provided. The FAC highlights that the government should distinguish between 'national security' and the broader 'public interest' or 'solely economic' concerns that are not within scope to prevent undue uncertainty for businesses and avoid any misuse of the term 'national security'. John Fingleton, commenting on the Bill before the FAC, highlighted the risk of private interest pressure on a Minister and pointed to the need for remedies available to a minister being directly related to the overall objective, aka national security, and no other considerations (ie, keeping employment in a certain region of the country). FAC, 'Oral evidence: The FCO's role in blocking foreign asset stripping in the UK', HC 296, Q149, 8 September 2020.

[216] ibid 79, On protectionism in merger review regimes, see article by Margaret Vestager (Commissioner for Competition, European Commission), 'Enforcing Competition Rules in the Global Village', NYU Law Address, New York, 20 April 2015, claiming that 'Political protectionism in merger control may trigger long-term adverse effects and "poison the well" of international antitrust cooperation'. Also, Jonathan Galloway points out that while

which could have profound side effects to the post-pandemic and post-Brexit UK economy.[217]

While the national security strategy is yet to be fully developed, it remains to be seen how robustly the new regime will be insulated from short-term political pressure.[218] At the same time, commentary that substantive state intervention will increase in the UK economy should be read with caution. The new regime essentially sanctions intervention powers that have been in existence for quite some time. Although the regime is more expansive than initially proposed, the new review system does not go much further than codifying existing government practice.[219] Therefore, the government would no longer need to rely on other practices such as 'change of control' clauses and post-offer commitments under the Takeover Code to safeguard its interests.

4.6.3 Applicability

4.6.3.1 No *de Minimis* Thresholds

In contrast to the current system under the Enterprise Act, the new national security regime is designed so as to cover a wide range of business activities that were outside the scope of the UK government until now. The government has broadened its focus beyond full mergers and acquisitions and granted itself powers to scrutinize and evaluate a much wider range of transactions, including minority investments, acquisitions of voting rights, and the sale of bare assets.[220]

the shift away from public interest criteria and political decision-making has reduced the scope for direct protectionism, this has had the effect of increasing the visibility of protectionism by forcing industrial policy considerations 'out from the shadows of opaque public interest tests'; Jonathan Galloway, 'The Pursuit of National Champions: The Intersection of Competition Law and Industrial Policy' (2007) 28(3) European Competition Law Review 172, 182.

[217] David Reader: 'A protectionist act is not necessarily illegitimate, but a culture where states regularly afford favourable treatment to domestic undertakings, at the expense of foreign firms, can be extremely harmful to interstate trade and development of the global economy.' David Michael Reader 'Revisiting the Role of the Public Interest in Merger Control', PhD Thesis University of East Anglia, September 2015, p 45. A recent study by UCL and LSE economists estimate a 37 per cent fall in foreign investment into the UK post-Brexit due to leaving the EU single market and customs union. Randolph Luca Bruno, Nauro Ferreira Campos, and Saul Estrin, 'The Effect on Foreign Direct Investment of Membership in the European Union', 6 January 2021, available at: https://doi.org/10.1111/jcms.13131. See also EY UK Attractiveness Survey, June 2019: 'Tipping point', which reported a further decline (from 2017) pp 8, 9, and 15 in predicted foreign investor sentiment towards the UK in the long term, available at www.ey.com/uk/en/issues/business-environment/ey-uk-attractiveness-survey accessed 15 September 2023. Finally, among other commentators, Max von Thun, 'The Government's National Security and Investment Bill Could Close the Door on Global Britain', 11 November 2020, article in *CityAM*, available at https://www.cityam.com/the-governments-national-security-and-investment-bill-could-close-the-door-on-global-britain/ accessed 15 September 2023.

[218] Ashley Thomas Lenihan, 'Foreign Investment Regimes: Three Things the West Needs to Better Protect National Security', LSE Business Review, 1 March 2021, available at: https://bit.ly/3qkwmG3, where it is stated that a strong institutional culture and deep institutional capacity is needed in order for strong institutions, like the Committee on Foreign Investment in the United States (CFIUS), to be able to withstand outside political pressures and focus on national security remits. Particular focus should be given to intelligence cooperation among agencies: training and funding.

[219] See J Webber, S Ashall, M Readings, E Rodriguez, and E Rarity, Shearman and Sterling LLP 'UK: The UK National Investment and Security Bill is Published', 13 November 2020.

[220] On the scope and (mis-)direction of the legislation, see John Fingleton on 'Britain must rethink its "national security" law', Financial Times, 23 January 2021. In particular, the former Chief Executive of the Office of Fair Trading claims that 'national security risks lie more with people and knowhow than with capital'. For this

While the range of transactions caught by the regime is wider than expected, the NSIA does not provide for any exemptions based on economic criteria, such as the transaction value or target turnover. This means that no automatic exclusion from review is afforded to trigger events merely because they involve a small, newly formed 'qualifying entity' or a 'qualifying asset' of limited monetary value. This indicates a change of approach from the merger review regime, which limits government intervention to transactions that exceed size and market share thresholds determined by the CMA, as discussed in section 3.

Despite the absence of exemptions applying to small-sized transactions, the NSIA has created safe harbours for certain types of transactions in which a party acquires less than a 25 per cent interest in a 'qualifying entity' and no 'material influence' over the policy of the entity or effective control of the corporate decision-making. Although some comfort is provided to minority investors and private equity sponsors, this inclusion clearly does not go as far as to exclude certain types of transactions with a degree of certainty.

Given that transactions of any size may be caught under the NSIA, it is estimated that a large number of deals will have to be notified to the ISU. The government is anticipating around 1,000 to 1,830 notifications and seventy to ninety-five national security assessments per year.[221] Thus, the newly formed ISU will be expected to assess numerous more transactions than were previously investigated for national security by the CMA.

However, the Department for BEIS estimates that the vast majority of transactions will be able to proceed unhindered, and investments will be screened much faster than under the current process of the Enterprise Act.[222] Moreover, it is said that most transactions are expected to be assessed within the initial review period of thirty working days, as adherence to statutory timelines will be, for the first time, a vital component of the review process.

Consequently, although the NSIA could potentially capture a broad range of transactions, it is not anticipated to cause many issues in terms of conditions being imposed or deals being blocked. Nevertheless, this heavy workload may lead to long waiting times between notification and final approval, with a significant impact on deal timetables.[223]

reason, he suggests that the interests of national security are better served by steps that target the risk directly, such as monitoring access to academic information and protecting key employees who carry valuable intellectual property.

[221] Department for Business, Energy and Industrial Strategy (BEIS), 'Impact Assessment on National Security and Investment Act', 9 November 2020.

[222] See BEIS Press release 'New and Improved National Security and Investment Act Set to Be Up and Running', 20 July 2021, where it is claimed that 'investments will be screened much more quickly than the current regime, assessing transactions within thirty working days—and often faster—with timelines now set out in law, rather than by the government on a case-by-case basis as is currently the case'.

[223] The issue of burdensome and protracted merger review processes is seen in the US, where extensive assessment of business planning documents is frequent. See Nicholas Levy, Alexander Waksman, and Lanto Sheridan, 'Global Merger Control—Where to Now?' (2020) 8 Journal of Antitrust Enforcement 319.

4.6.3.2 Limited Jurisdictional Barriers

On a similar note, no exceptions are provided based on the investor's characteristics, such as identity or nationality.[224] Unlike many other FDI review mechanisms, the NSIA, as drafted, covers acquisitions by any acquirer without reference to their origins. Therefore, the new regime applies equally to UK-based and foreign investors. This is consistent with the UK merger review regime, under which no distinction is made based on the parties' nationality, but it has been commented as 'truly-rare' in comparison to similar legislation in other countries.[225] Further, the inclusion of domestic investors is expected to 'lead to a much larger volume of mandatory notifications than most other national security FDI regimes',[226] resulting in greater delays for deal completion.

Despite the initial promotion of the UK's 'first foreign investment screening regime',[227] the UK government later sifted its approach by recognizing that an acquirer does not necessarily need to be foreign in order to be hostile to national security and to give rise to concerns.[228] According to the government, national security risks are most likely to arise 'when acquirers are hostile to the UK's national security, or when they owe allegiance to hostile states or organisations'. Interestingly, the government has emphasized that 'it does not regard state-owned entities, sovereign wealth funds, or other entities affiliated with foreign states as being inherently more likely to pose a national security risk'.[229] It has been, therefore, clarified that when exercising its call-in powers, the Secretary of State will take into account the entity's affiliations to hostile parties, rather than the existence of a relationship with foreign states in principle, or their nationality.

To that end, we argued that a more targeted and proportionate approach, providing exemptions for investments by UK nationals or entities that are ultimately controlled by UK nationals, would better reflect where national security risks are most likely to lie without adding to the existing regulatory hurdles for UK businesses.[230]

224 While the NSIA allows for exemptions for certain types of acquirers to be created by statutory instruments, it is not expected that any acquirer-specific exemptions will be introduced at this initial stage.

225 The US, German, and Chinese regimes are all designed to screen 'foreign investment' defined by reference to residency, nationality, and place of incorporation. For example, the sector-specific review under the German regime applies to all acquisitions by non-German resident investors. Under the Chinese national security review regime ('Foreign Investment Law'), a person will be regarded as a 'foreign' investor if their nationality or place of incorporation (for entities) is outside mainland China.

226 Intervention by Dr Ashley Lenihan from the London School of Economics, Official Report, Commons, National Security and Investment Bill Committee, 24 November 2020; col 33.

227 ibid 68.

228 BEIS, 'Draft Statement of Policy Intent', updated 2 March 2021, available at https://www.gov.uk/government/publications/national-security-and-investment-bill-2020/statement-of-policy-intent accessed 15 September 2023.

229 ibid 93.

230 See also comment by Lord Vaizey of Didcot on Committee Debate on National Security and Investment Bill on Tuesday, 9 March 2021, Col 586GC ('A more targeted and proportionate approach, which would better reflect where national security risks are most likely to lie, would be to exempt from the mandatory filing requirement acquisitions and investments by UK nationals or entities ultimately controlled by UK nationals'). He then proposed further exemptions for investors from countries which are closely allied to the UK, such as Australia, Canada, New Zealand, and the US. A similar intervention was made by Michael Leiter from Skadden Arpson in Official Report, Commons, National Security and Investment Bill Committee, 24 November 2020, col 42 ('I think trying to take a slightly smaller bite of the apple and not including current UK businesses in the scheme would be well advised.').

4.6.3.3 Timing Challenges for Dealmakers

The NSIA contains a prescribed schedule for reviewing trigger events and carrying out national security risk assessments. However, as described thoroughly in section 4, the timeline for reviews may be less certain in practice and could ultimately result in a lengthy and unpredictable procedure. This could, in turn, have a significant impact on deal timetables and the parties' financing arrangements, reducing deal certainty, and creating new challenges for investors.[231] In particular, the issuing of a call-in notice can have important timing implications as certain parts of the process are not subject to statutory deadlines. Consequently, compliance with the new process would be a new consideration to be factored into the timing and completion risk analysis of current and new investments in businesses with a UK nexus.[232]

Acting proactively, investors should assess early in the negotiation process how the new legislative system may implicate a contemplated transaction and decide whether notifying the ISU is required or at least advisable. Moreover, prospective investors should also analyse the potential threats to national security that may arise after completing a particular transaction and assess whether the government will have jurisdiction to review a transaction under its call-in powers for five years post-completion. Depending on the likelihood of a call-in notice being issued, the parties may need to take steps to ensure that appropriate contractual protections are in place to deal with any relevant national security issues. In particular, deal documentation should address the need and risk associated with the relevant regulatory processes or approvals, in particular by:

i. having assurances for cooperation from both the target and the seller during the review process;
ii. providing how risk and cost will be allocated between the parties;
iii. covering required approvals under contractual covenants.[233]

Alternatively, the parties may wish to make the transaction conditional on the Secretary of State not having referred the transaction for a thorough assessment under the NSIA by a certain date.

Furthermore, transactions subject to the mandatory regime may attract more publicity than usual during the screening process, which could lead to media or public scrutiny and a greater risk of reputational damage. This means that a coordinated public affairs and communications strategy will be vital for businesses operating in sensitive sectors. For that reason, they may need to consider whether it would be appropriate to

[231] J Webber, S Ashall, M Readings, E Rodriguez, and E Rarity, Shearman & Sterling LLP 'UK: The UK National Investment and Security Bill is Published', 13 November 2020.

[232] Article by Joanna Valentine, Michael Sholem, and Dmitry Morgan of Cadwalader, Wickersham, and Taft LLP, 'The UK's National Security and Investment Act' (2021) XI(132) National Law Review.

[233] Alex Potter, 'The Foreign Investment Regulation Review: United Kingdom' (The Law Reviews, 20 October 2020) https://thelawreviews.co.uk/title/the-foreign-investment-regulation-review/united-kingdom accessed 15 September 2023.

instruct public relations advisers and make public undertakings regarding their post-completion intentions.[234]

Finally, businesses may want to consider engaging with the Secretary of State for BEIS or the ISU before entering into new deals to help determine whether a call-in notice is likely to be issued concerning a particular transaction and to proactively discuss any potential concerns. It may be possible to avoid an intervention or in-depth review if an agreement can be reached directly with the Secretary of State regarding suitable undertakings to remedy any potential national security concerns presented by the transaction. It should be noted that the Secretary of State and the CMA have accepted this option in a number of cases reviewed for public interest issues under the merger review process.

4.6.3.4 Compliance Costs

As discussed above, the vast majority of transactions are expected to have no implications for national security and should receive clearance on completion of the initial review. However, it can be argued that the new regime may place undue financial burden on hundreds of businesses, whether or not they participate in the sensitive sectors. In particular, it is anticipated that additional costs will be incurred by UK businesses by familiarizing themselves with the new regime, engaging with the government prior to notification, making a notification, and formalizing the detailed national security reviews. At this point, however, the estimated costs associated with complying with the new legislative requirements are uncertain, while this uncertainty should ease with the first few cases reviewed.

4.6.3.5 Economic Impact

The introduction of a mandatory and 'suspensory' review regime with a significantly broad scope of application has been causing uneasiness among UK businesses and investors.[235] This change in approach has led to concern that the NSI law will act to deter investment in the UK in the long term.[236] In particular, it has been claimed that the new regime will slow down the flow of FDI at a particularly critical juncture for the country while creating unnecessary hurdles to domestic business deals.[237]

[234] ibid 95.

[235] Gregory Lascelles and others, 'The UK Parliament approves the National Security and Investment Act', Concurrences, e-Competitions News Issue April 2021, N°100852, p 2.

[236] Among others, see Lord Peter Mandelson (former Business Secretary) describing the NSI Bill as 'a powerful deterrent to foreign direct investment', 'Mandelson criticises new security and investment bill as "chaotic"' *The Guardian* (27 November 2020).

[237] See also criticism by John Fingleton, 'Mergers and the Public Interest: A Wolf in Sheep's Clothing?' (2018) https://fingleton.com/wp-content/uploads/2018/10/John-Fingleton-Mergers-and-the-public-interest-a-wolf-in-sheeps-clothing-Oct-2018.pdf accessed 15 September 2023, 85, who claimed that the regime was 'over-expansive' and dismissed its benefits as 'very illusory'. Amongst others, he raised the concern that such an FDI regime could ruin the City's reputation as a global business hub, 'a reputation which is more crucial than ever with looming end of the Brexit Transition period, and the need to rejuvenate the U.K. economy post-COVID-19'. According to the government's Impact Assessment, 'some studies have pointed out that in the short-term uncertainty about the new regime could have adverse effects on investments and M&A activity'. see BEIS, 'Impact Assessment on the National Security and Investment Bill', on 9 November 2020, para 11.

Despite the additional regulatory burdens that may be caused for investors, it seems unlikely to the author that inward foreign investment in the UK will be significantly harmed since most developed countries have successfully followed similar strategies for quite some time. It could even be stated that while FDI regimes proliferating worldwide, investors should now be beginning to adjust to the new normal.

Finally, according to the government's Impact Assessment of the new law, there is evidence that the potential negative impact of regulatory hurdles on investments may be offset by the increased security and economic stability in the country as a result of the regime.[238] Without a doubt, there are many factors that need to be taken into account when assessing the potential impact that the regime will have on the UK economy. A thorough economic approach to the new regime is beyond the scope of this chapter.

4.6.3.6 Competition on the Sidelines

The separation of competition policy from FDI screening means that transactions may be subject to both regimes, which may bring different and contrasting outcomes. While being assessed on competition or public interest grounds in accordance with the merger control procedure,[239] a transaction may still be subject to the sector-specific mandatory notification system, prompting a new holistic assessment of its characteristics and effects.

This may result in transactions being blocked on national security grounds despite being found not to raise any competition issues and even having pro-competitive effects. This can lead to transactions with pro-competitive benefits relating to efficiencies and innovation.

It is, thus, essential that wherever an intervention on national security grounds is made, the assessment takes into account the potential impact on competition alongside the national security concerns before any decision is reached on whether or not to approve the transaction.[240] If a thorough consideration is not conducted, competition may be rendered a lesser priority. For this purpose, it might be necessary that the new regime promotes close cooperation between the BEIS and the CMA.

4.6.3.7 Government's Commitments

In response to the above concerns, the UK government has repeatedly stated that it aims to preserve the UK's status as an attractive place to invest while providing efficient clearance processes for transactions, certainty and transparency for investors and

[238] BEIS, 'Impact Assessment on the National Security and Investment Bill', on 9 November 2020, para 111, which also refers to A Bonaime, H Gulen, and M Ion, 'Does Policy Uncertainty Affect Mergers and Acquisitions?' (2018) Journal of Financial Economics.

[239] As discussed above, the public interest provisions of the Enterprise Act will continue in force, but the NSIA replaces the national security consideration of the Enterprise Act 2002.

[240] David Michael Reader 'Revisiting the Role of the Public Interest in Merger Control', PhD Thesis University of East Anglia, September 2015, pp 117–24.

businesses.[241] Moreover, the Department of Business, Energy and Industrial Strategy has further emphasized the government's key commitments:

1. to provide clearance for the vast majority of transactions promptly and within the initial review period of thirty working days from notification;
2. to limit its interest to issues of national security and not broader economic concerns;[242] and
3. to provide adequate and suitably trained staff with cross-government expertise to deliver the work of the ISU.

To that end, the government launched the newly established Office for Investment, which is comprised of public and private sector experts and sits within the Department for International Trade.[243] The Office for Investment is aiming at playing the role of driving investment in the UK and balancing the counter-effects of regulatory hurdles.

4.7 Conclusion

The NSIA is expected to present new challenges for UK-based companies and private equity investors. The UK Prime Minister Rishi Sunak, in his speech in the *Integrated Review Refresh 2023: Responding to a more contested and volatile World*,[244] presented to the UK Parliament in March 2023 and updated in May 2023, stated that the government will use the NSIA to prevent high-risk investment in critical infrastructure and sensitive technologies.

Looking at crude numbers, the new regime appears more interventionist than the public interest one. However, there can be multiple reasons for this increase, but one that is clear is the increased focus on certain countries and sectors. As of 15 October 2023, there have been seventeen interventions, which resulted in five prohibitions and twelve approvals with conditions—one of these was later revoked due to the acquirer's withdrawal. Interestingly, fourteen of the seventeen orders were issued between July–December 2022. As evidenced by Table 4.2, the most common sectors were military and dual use (five transactions), Communications, Advanced materials (four each),

241 BEIS, Press release 'National security bolstered as Bill to protect against malicious investment granted Royal Assent', 29 April 2021, available at https://www.gov.uk/government/news/national-security-bolstered-as-bill-to-protect-against-malicious-investment-granted-royal-assent accessed 15 September 2023.

242 Statement of Policy Intent, states: 'The power to address national security risks will be governed by the principles of necessity and proportionality, and will not be used arbitrarily to interfere with investment. Its use will not be designed to limit market access for individual countries; the transparency, predictability, and clarity of the legislation surrounding the call-in power is designed to support foreign direct investment in the UK, not to limit it.'

243 Department for International Trade, Press release: 'New Office for Investment to Drive Foreign Investment into the UK', 9 November 2020.

244 *Integrated Review Refresh 2023: Responding to a more contested and volatile World*, https://www.gov.uk/government/publications/integrated-review-refresh-2023-responding-to-a-more-contested-and-volatile-world/integrated-review-refresh-2023-responding-to-a-more-contested-and-volatile-world accessed 15 September 2023.

followed by Energy and Communications (three each). As to the countries of the origins of the prospective buyer, in half of the cases considered, the acquirer was based in China—one transaction was approved without conditions, four with conditions, and four were blocked; the only other blocked transaction so far concerned a Russia-based acquirer. The remaining transactions involved acquirers from the US (three), Canada, France, Germany, the United Arab Emirates, and the UK. All of these were approved with conditions. Typical mitigation measures varied widely according to the specificities of the cases, but they included:[245]

- government approval for certain decisions made by the acquired entity;
- restrictions on the sharing of sensitive information by the target with the acquirer;
- appointment of certain personnel in the acquired entity, such as board members or key staff members;
- board observers to be appointed by the government;
- the continued provision of services to the government;
- maintenance of R&D and other capabilities in the UK; and
- the performance of due diligence checks on new customers, with the further obligation to share the outcome with the government.

Table 4.2 NSIA Final Orders (July 2022–September 2023)

Transaction	Sectors	Acquirer Country	Outcome	Date
Sepura/Epiris	Communications Supplier to emergency services	UK	Approved w/conditions	14 Jul 2022
Beijing Infinite Vision/ University of Manchester	Computing hardware Military and dual use	China	Blocked	20 Jul 2022
Super Orange/Pulsic	Advanced materials Computing hardware Military and dual use	China	Blocked	17 Aug 2022
Tawazun/Reaction Engines	Defence Military and dual use	UAE	Approved w/conditions	2 Sep 2022
Stonehill Energy Storage/ Stonehill project	Energy	China	Approved w/conditions	14 Sep 2022
Viasat/Inmarsat (Connect Topco)	Communications Satellite and space technologies	US	Approved w/conditions	15 Sep 2022

(*continued*)

[245] Levy N and others, UK National Security Regime: Enforcement Practice and Updated Guidance, Cleary Gottlieb Steen Hamilton https://www.clearygottlieb.com/news-and-insights/publication-listing/uk-national-security-regime-enforcement-practice-and-updated-guidance accessed 15 September 2023.

Table 4.2 Continued

Transaction	Sectors	Acquirer Country	Outcome	Date
Redrock Investment/ Electricity North West	Energy	China	Approved w/conditions	29 Sep 2022
Iceman/CPI	Quantum technologies	US	Approved w/conditions	29 Sep 2022
Sichuan Development/ Ligeance Aerospace	Satellite and space technologies	China	Approved w/conditions	10 Oct 2022
Nexperia/Newport Wafer Fab	Advanced materials Computing hardware	China	Blocked	16 Nov 2022
China Power/XRE Alpha	Energy	China	Approved w/conditions	5 Dec 2022
TP Global Operations/ Truphone	Communications	German	Approved w/conditions	5 Dec 2022
SiLight Semiconductor/ HiLight Research	Advanced materials Military and dual use	China	Blocked	19 Dec 2022
L1T FM/Upp	Communications	Russia	Blocked	19 Dec 2022
Stellex Capital/David Brown Santasalo	Defence Critical supplier to gov't	US	Approved w/conditions	22 Feb 2023
Voyis Imaging/University of Southampton	Military and dual use	Canada	Approved w/conditions	8 Jun 2023
EDF Energy/GE Oil & Gas Marine/GE Steam Power	Defence Critical supplier to gov't	France	Approved w/conditions	7 Aug 2023

Author's elaboration based on BEIS, 'Notice of Final Orders under the National Security and Investment Act 2021' https://www.gov.uk/government/collections/notice-of-final-orders-made-under-the-national-security-and-investment-act-2021 accessed 15 September 2023
Note: The government doesn't disclose its classification of individual cases by sector, so the data presented in this table might not match the official figures exactly

Careful consideration and a proactive approach would be essential to mitigate the concerns associated with the new regime. Overall, the regime is in line with many of those administered by countries worldwide (USA, Canada, Australia, France, Italy), so international investors are expected to be broadly familiar with the rationale, the notification requirement, and the assessment process of such regimes.

While the ISU is actively consulting with practitioners and companies regarding the notification requirements, further guidelines are expected to be developed soon, shedding some light on the operation of the new review system. In the coming months, we should expect secondary implementing legislation to be passed, providing important details of the new regime.

At the time of writing, several key regulations have already been published, including:

- guidance on the intended use of the call-in power;[246]
- regulation settling the definitions of the seventeen core sectors[247] (finally published at the end of 2021) with further guidance to assist businesses in the interpretation of their practical application;[248]
- guidance on how the NSIA could affect people or acquisition outside the UK;[249]
- guidance on how the new Act will work alongside other regulators and codes, including the Enterprise Act 2002, the CMA and the Takeover Code;[250]
- guidance on how to prepare for the new rules;[251]
- guidance on completing and registering a notification form;[252]
- guidance for the higher education and research-intensive sectors;[253]
- guidance on 'if you need to tell the government about an acquisition that could harm the UK's national security';[254]

In addition, a number of policy documents were published in 2023 illustrating the government's priorities in sectors such as semiconductors, quantum technologies, AI, critical minerals, telecoms, synthetic, and engineering biology.[255]

It remains to be seen how the government will find the fine balance between enabling sufficient control over hostile investors and avoiding deterring investment when reviewing transactions in practice.

[246] BEIS 'National Security and Investment Act 2021: Draft statement for the purposes of section 3' July 2021; the statement sets out how the Secretary of State expects to exercise the power to give a call-in notice.

[247] Draft Regulations laid before Parliament under s 63(5) of the NSIA for approval by resolution of each House of Parliament: 'The National Security and Investment Act 2021 (Notifiable Acquisition) (Specification of Qualifying Entities) Regulations 2021'.

[248] BEIS, Guidance, 'National Security and Investment Act: details of the 17 types of notifiable acquisitions', Updated 20 July 2022

[249] BEIS, Guidance: 'How the National Security and Investment Act could affect people or acquisitions outside the UK; 20 July 2021.

[250] BEIS Guidance 'The National Security and Investment Act alongside regulatory requirements' published on 20 July 2021.

[251] BEIS, Guidance 'National Security and Investment Act: prepare for new rules about acquisitions which could harm the UK's national security', published 20 July 2021. Also, see Guidance: 'National Security and Investment Act: guidance for the higher education and research-intensive sectors'.

[252] BEIS Guidance, 'National Security and Investment: market guidance notes July 2022', Updated January 2023, published 19 July 2022.

[253] ibid.

[254] ibid.

[255] *Integrated Review Refresh 2023: Responding to a more contested and volatile World*, https://www.gov.uk/government/publications/integrated-review-refresh-2023-responding-to-a-more-contested-and-volatile-world/integrated-review-refresh-2023-responding-to-a-more-contested-and-volatile-world accessed 15 September 2023; UK Science and Technology Framework, https://www.gov.uk/government/publications/uk-science-and-technology-framework accessed 15 September 2023; Critical Minerals Refresh: Delivering Resilience in a Changing Global Environment https://www.gov.uk/government/publications/uk-critical-mineral-strategy/critical-minerals-refresh-delivering-resilience-in-a-changing-global-environment-published-13-march-2023 accessed 15 September 2023; UK's International Technology Strategy https://www.gov.uk/government/publications/uk-international-technology-strategy/the-uks-international-technology-strategy accessed 15 September 2023.

Appendix 1: UK's Public Interest Merger Procedure (PIIN)

Author's elaboration

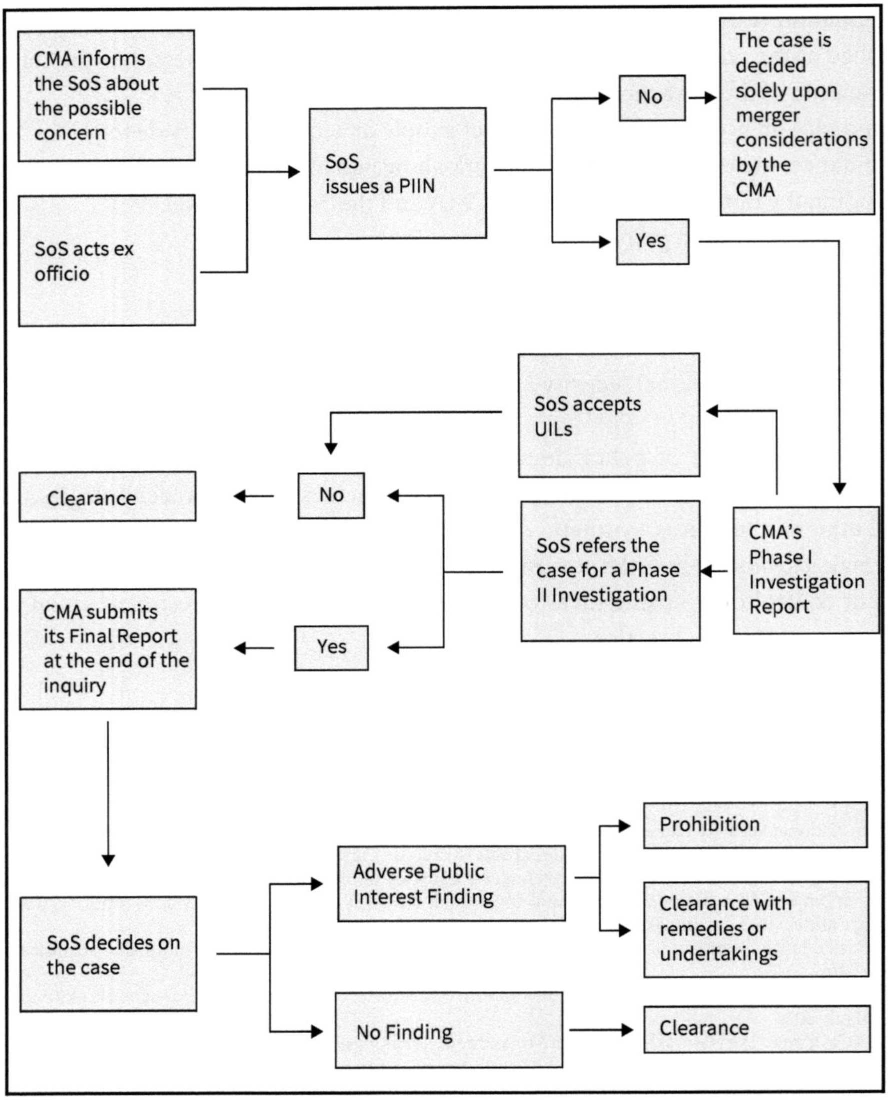

Appendix 2: Notices Issued by the Secretary of State on National Security Grounds 2002–21

Date	Case	Notice	Sector	Phase	Outcome
11 Mar 2004	*General Dynamics/Alvis*	EIN	Defence	Phase 1	Cleared w/UILs
26 Aug 2004	*Finmeccanica/ AgustaWestland*	EIN	Defence	Phase 1	Cleared w/UILs
7 Feb 2005	*Finmeccanica/BAE*	EIN	Defence	Phase 1	Cleared w/UILs
17 Aug 2005	*Lockheed Martin/Insys*	SPIN	Defence	Phase 1	Cleared w/UILs
20 Mar 2007	*General Electric/Smiths Aerospace*	EIN	Defence	Phase 1	Cleared w/UILs
15 May 2009	*Atlas Elektronik UK/ UWs Winfrith*	SPIN	Defence	Phase 1	Cleared w/UILs
10 Apr 2017	*Hytera/Sepura*	PIIN	Communications	Phase 1	Cleared w/UILs
17 Jun 2018	*Gardner Aerospace/ Northern Aerospace*	PIIN	Defence	Phase 1	Cleared w/UILs
22 Jul 2019	*Connect Bidco/Inmarsat*	PIIN	Communications	Phase 1	Cleared w/UILs
5 Dec 2019	*Gardner Aerospace/ Impcross*	PIIN	Aerospace	Phase 1	Abandoned
20 Dec 2019	*Aerostar/Mettis*	PIIN	Aerospace	Phase 1	Abandoned
19 Apr 2021	*NVIDIA/Arm*	PIIN	Electronics	Phase 2	Abandoned
18 Aug 2021	*Cobham/Ultra Electronics*	PIIN	Defence	Phase 1	Cleared w/UILs
5 Sep 2021	*Shanghai Kington Technology/Perpetuus*	PIIN	Engineering	Phase 2	Abandoned
18 Oct 2021	*Parker-Hannifin/ Meggitt*	PIIN	Aerospace	Phase 1	Cleared w/UILs

Author's elaboration

5

National Security and FDI Screening in the US

5.1 Introduction

Merger control cannot be analysed in a vacuum, since it is subject to wider policy considerations as well as political influence, especially in certain sectors of the economy. However, these may vary from one sector to another. A visible way of how politics influence competition enforcement concerns is 'the manner in which the application of competition law is handled and the way competition cases are decided'.[1] It follows, then, that politics plays a double role in United States (US) competition law enforcement, namely: in the legislative process (bearing in mind that US competition laws were passed at first to address the trusts phenomenon, breaking up powerful firms and monopolies) as well as in the enforcement of US competition and regulatory authorities.[2] According to Doern and Wilks there are three modes in which such political expression could exist: 'the core of competition policy and its objectives; the extent and nature of non-competition policy goals that are allowed by statute to be considered in decision-making; and exemption provisions.'[3]

The approach of merger control in the US is to achieve efficiency.[4] In principle, US competition agencies[5] do not consider national security or other public interest factors

[1] Eyad Maher Dabbah, *International and Comparative Competition Law* (CUP 2010) 57.

[2] ibid 256.

[3] B Doern and S Wilks, *Comparative Competition Policy* (OUP 1996).

[4] OECD, Directorate for Financial and Enterprise Affairs, Competition Committee, Public Interest Considerations in Merger Control—Note by the United States (2016) 2 https://www.ftc.gov/system/files/attachments/us-submissions-oecd-other-international-competition-fora/1606public_interest_merger-us.pdf accessed 15 September 2023. Consumer welfare as the dominant paradigm emerged in US antitrust law in the 1970s. It is not the purpose of the present chapter to engage in detail with the emergence of consumer welfare as the prevalent aim in US antitrust law, the presentation of the historical context and the development of the concept of consumer welfare having been well documented in literature. See further Barak Orbach, 'How Antitrust Lost Its Goal' (2013) 81 Fordham Law Review 2253, 2257 et seq, 2268 et seq. It has been pointed out that the link made by Robert Bork (*The Antitrust Paradox* (Free Press 1993)) between the intent of the historical legislator with regard to the Sherman Act and consumer welfare as the intended aim of that Act is more than doubtful. Nevertheless, US courts and primarily the Supreme Court seem to have been willing to adopt consumer welfare as the new paradigm in US antitrust law. (Kenneth Heyer, 'Consumer Welfare and the Legacy of Robert Bork' (2014) 57 The Journal of Law & Economics S19–32, doi:10.1086/676463; Barak Orbach, 'How Antitrust Lost Its Goal' (2013) 81 Fordham Law Review 2253, 2257 et seq). Consumer welfare has been credited with a switch to an approach that has moved away from adhering to structuralist considerations and bringing competitive assessment closer to market actuality. Notwithstanding the ongoing discussion regarding the contours of the paradigm, consumer welfare has brought to the fore of competition law enforcement the focus on economic goals, and has thus rationalized to a significant extent the identification of harm to competition in enforcement, particularly in light of the measurability and hence predictability that it entails. In the context of European Union (EU) competition law, consumer welfare has been identified as a competition objective at a later stage compared to the US, alongside the move towards a more economic approach, and has been applied by the European Commission with considerably more flexibility compared to enforcement policy in the US.

[5] Technically, only the Federal Trade Commission (FTC) is an independent agency, while the Antitrust Division of the US Department of Justice (DOJ) is part of the executive branch of government. However, for the purposes of this chapter they are referred to together as 'agencies'.

in the enforcement of antitrust laws. They note that decisions should be based solely on the competitive effects and consumer benefits of the transaction under review.[6] It was even explained by academics at the beginning of the 1960s that:

> using antitrust law to achieve non-competition goals, which often resulted in the protection of inefficient competitors, was inimical to consumer welfare and was not Congress's intent in enacting the U.S. statutes.[7]

The overall objective of this chapter is to assess how US government authorities assess national security considerations in mergers and acquisitions (M&A) transactions, and more broadly in foreign direct investment (FDI) involving such transactions. To achieve this objective, the chapter will focus on the role that national security considerations play, and will describe the extensive US regulatory framework and case law.

The chapter will analyse the role and regulatory framework of the Committee on Foreign Investment (CFIUS), discuss the concept of national security, analyse recent legislative developments to strengthen the regime, and engage in detail with CFIUS' enforcement record. It will conclude by reviewing the activity of different US Presidents in this area.

5.2 The Role and Regulatory Framework of the Committee on Foreign Investment (CFIUS)

5.2.1 Composition, Legislation, and Regulation

The CFIUS, established by Executive Order 11888(b) ('Executive Order') in 1975,[8] is an interagency body, which consists of nine Cabinet members, comprising the Departments of the Treasury (chair), Justice, Homeland Security, Commerce, Defense, State, Energy, and the Offices of the US Trade Representative, and Science & Technology Policy.[9] The Secretary of Labor and the Director of National Intelligence (DNI) serving as *ex officio* members.[10] Notices to CFIUS for the assessment of transactions are received and considered by the Director of the Office of Investment Security in the Department of the Treasury.[11]

The Executive Order added five executive office members to CFIUS in order to 'observe and, as appropriate, participate in and report to the President': the Director of the Office of Management and Budget, the Chairman of the Council of Economic

[6] Organisation for Economic Cooperation and Development (OECD), 'Public Interest Considerations in Merger Control—Note by the United States' 2.

[7] ibid 4.

[8] Executive Order 11858 (b), 7 May 1975, 40 FR 20263.

[9] US Department of the Treasury, 'The Committee on Foreign Investment in the United States (CFIUS)' https://home.treasury.gov/policy-issues/international/the-committee-on-foreign-investment-in-the-united-states-cfius accessed 15 September 2023.

[10] Congressional Research Service, 'The Committee on Foreign Investment in the United States (CFIUS)' RL33388 (26 February 2020) 14.

[11] US Department of the Treasury (n 9).

Advisors, the Assistant to the President for National Security Affairs, the Assistant to the President for Economic Policy, and the Assistant to the President for Homeland Security and Counterterrorism. The President can appoint members on a temporary basis to the Committee as well.[12]

The law requires CFIUS to review all 'covered foreign investment transactions' in order to determine whether they threaten to impair US national security, if the foreign entity involved is controlled by a foreign government, or if the transaction would result in control of any 'critical infrastructure that could impair national security'.[13] According to the Department of the Treasury,[14] a 'covered transaction' is any transaction that could result in foreign control of a person engaged in interstate commerce in the US. Transactions that lead to less than a 7 per cent shareholding, bought in a stock exchange or other open market, and are aimed at being merely a passive investment can be excluded from the CFIUS review.

CFIUS is required annually[15] to assess whether there is credible evidence of: (i) a coordinated strategy by one or more countries to acquire US companies involved in research, development, or production of 'critical technologies',[16] or (ii) industrial espionage activities assisted by foreign governments against US companies aimed at obtaining commercial secrets related to such critical technologies.[17]

In 2018 President Trump enacted into law[18] the Foreign Investment Risk Review Modernization Act of 2018 (FIRRMA), which broadened the scope of CFIUS by explicitly adding four new types of 'covered transactions':[19]

i) a purchase, lease, or concession by or to a foreign person of real estate located in proximity to sensitive government facilities;
ii) 'other investments' in certain US businesses that afford a foreign person access to material non-public technical information in the possession of the US business, membership on the board of directors, or other decision-making rights, other than through voting of shares;
iii) any change in a foreign investor's rights resulting in foreign control of a US business or an 'other investment' in certain US businesses; and
iv) any other transaction, transfer, agreement, or arrangement designed to circumvent CFIUS jurisdiction.

[12] ibid.

[13] Congressional Research Service (n 10) 14.

[14] Federal Register, Vol 73, No 226, Rules and Regulations, 21 November 2008.

[15] Through its annual report issued to the Congress.

[16] '[T]he so-called America COMPETES ACT of 2022 … testifies to the US's policy to ensure that the US is leading the innovation of critical and emerging technologies, such as next-generation telecommunications, artificial intelligence, quantum computing, semiconductors, and biotechnology, by modernizing export controls and investment screening regimes and associated policies and regulations.' A Strohoff and S Schuh, 'Outbound foreign investment regime on the horizon in the EU', 2023 https://www.pinsentmasons.com/out-law/analysis/outbound-foreign-investment-regime-on-the-horizon-in-the-eu accessed 15 September 2023.

[17] CFIUS, 'Annual Report to Congress CY 2015' 27–31 https://home.treasury.gov/system/files/206/Unclassified-CFIUS-Annual-Report-report-period-CY-2015.pdf accessed 15 September 2023. The Report from CY 2015 concluded that there is a high likelihood of espionage activity but, given the Report's unclassified nature, declined to provide an assessment of whether a 'coordinated strategy' exists.

[18] Effective since 13 August 2018.

[19] A covered transaction is defined by FINSA as 'any merger, acquisition, or takeover … by or with any foreign person which could result in foreign control of any person engaged in interstate commerce in the United States.'

The amendments brought in by the FIRRMA have been called 'the most substantial changes to CFIUS have come with the Congress and the White House working in unison'.[20]

The authority of the President to suspend or prohibit certain transactions was initially provided by the addition of the Exon-Florio amendment in 1988, which was itself substantially revised by the 1993 Byrd amendment which further expanded CFIUS's scope to include a specific focus on the threat from foreign government investment, including state-owned and controlled entities,[21] then the Foreign Investment and National Security Act of 2007 (FINSA),[22] which expanded the list of national security concerns relevant to a CFIUS review beyond the traditional defence and military activities, to include, for instance, potential foreign government control, non-proliferation, counterterrorism cooperation, trans-shipment or diversion risk, and energy security,[23] and FIRRMA in 2018 which established mandatory filing for twenty-seven specifically enumerated industries identified by reference to their North American Industry Classification System ('NAICS') codes deemed to be 'critical technologies'.[24] Moreover, FIRRMA also introduced a relevant change, since henceforth it is permitted to share:

> [i]nformation important to the national security analysis or actions of the Committee [CFIUS] to any domestic governmental entity, or to any foreign governmental entity of a United States ally or partner, under the exclusive direction and authorization of the chairperson, only to the extent necessary for national security purposes, and subject to appropriate confidentiality and classification requirements.[25]

The disclosure of information is to an unlimited list of countries, since FIRRMA states that information-sharing could be to any domestic or foreign 'governmental entity of a United States ally or partner'. Definitions of 'ally' and 'partner' have not been included, either in FIRRMA or in any other legislative text.

As the chapter shows in the next section, CFIUS processes and assessment process is not impervious to the political agenda of the US Administration. However, there are commentators who argue that in principle the CFIUS process seems to be isolated from politics,[26] as CFIUS never discloses whether a transaction is pending review, not even cases where the parties disclose this information to the press. The President of the United States (POTUS) is entitled to be the decision-maker on the approval of concentrations, when delegated such decision-making power by CFIUS.

[20] Harry G Broadman, 'U.S. Foreign Investment Policy Gets A Tougher But More Transparent CFIUS' (Forbes, 2019) https://www.forbes.com/sites/harrybroadman/2019/01/04/u-s-foreign-investment-policy-gets-a-tougher-but-more-transparent-cfius/#2e5302e21fe6 accessed 15 September 2023.

[21] Emily Xueref-Poviac and others, 'The Evolving Concept of National Security', The Global Competition Review, 6 December 2022.

[22] Effective since 24 October 2007.

[23] Xueref-Poviac and others (n 21).

[24] ibid.

[25] S 2098—115th Congress: Foreign Investment Risk Review Modernization Act of 2018, s 1713.

[26] Neal Wolin, 'Wolin on CFIUS' Brunswick Review (8 February 2018) https://www.brunswickgroup.com/neal-wolin-on-cfius-committee-on-foreign-investment-in-the-united-states-i7159/ accessed 15 September 2023.

5.2.2 An Overview of the CFIUS Process

The regulations governing the CFIUS review process[27] were wholly revised by FIRRMA which clarified and broadened the scope and process of CFIUS, as Figure 5.1 shows.

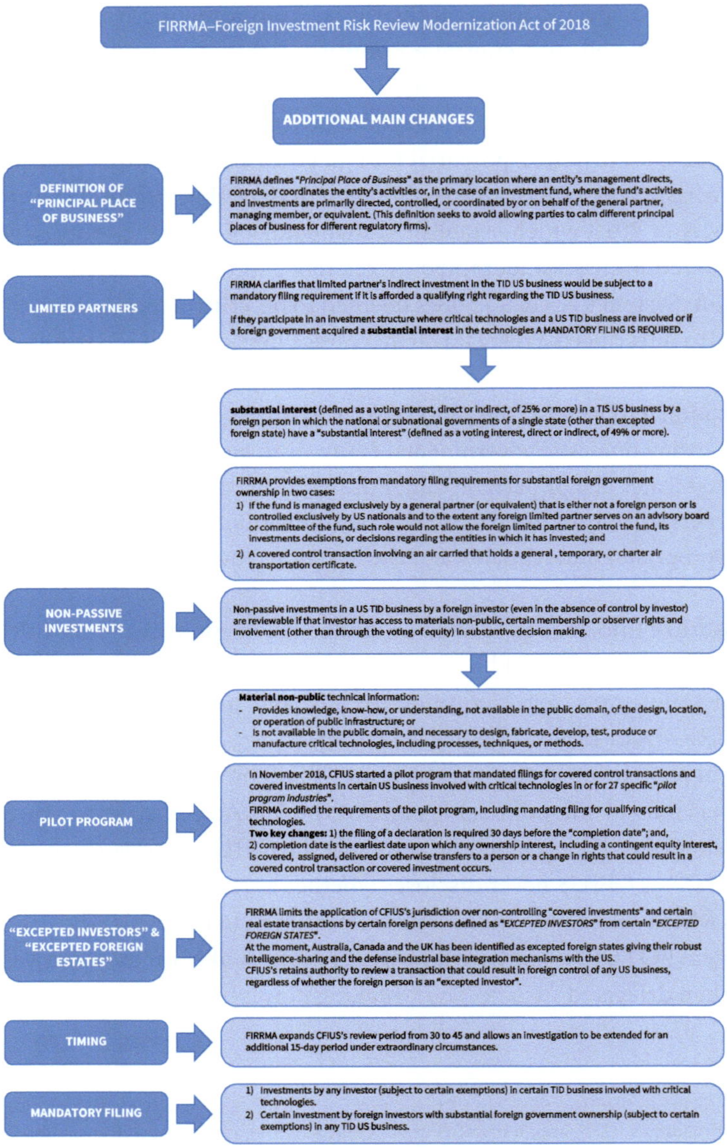

Figure 5.1 Main changes introduced by FIRRMA
Author's elaboration

[27] Codified at 31 CFR Part 800 and 31 CFR Part 801.

Over the years, the CFIUS process has evolved and currently it includes an informal stage with no deadline that comprises an unofficial CFIUS determination prior to the formal filing.[28] The parties to a transaction are encouraged to file a draft notice and other appropriate documents describing the transaction. This informal review, which can last for a non-binding length of time, serves the interests of CFIUS (which manages to achieve a better understanding of the transaction) as well as the companies involved in the proposed transaction. It's worth noting that Treasury Department officials have acknowledged that this informal contact enabled CFIUS staff 'to identify potential issues before the review process formally begins'.[29] Once this informal stage has been completed, it is followed by the formal stages of the CFIUS assessment.

FIRRMA provides for an abbreviated, or 'light', filing process through a new 'declaration' procedure,[30] where CFIUS has thirty days to review the declaration and to determine if the transaction involves a foreign person in which a foreign government has a substantial interest.[31] The national security review must be completed within forty-five days of the filing of the declaration, and entails also a review by the Director of National Intelligence ('DNI'), which can send requests for information to different government departments. Notably, the majority of transactions are cleared at the initial stage.

CFIUS may initiate a forty-five-day investigation of the transaction, that can be extended for an additional fifteen-day period under extraordinary circumstances[32] if:[33]

(i) CFIUS believes that the transaction threatens national security and the threat has not been mitigated through an agreement with the parties;
(ii) the lead CFIUS agency reviewing the transaction recommends that an investigation be conducted;
(iii) the transaction is a 'foreign government-controlled transaction';[34] or
(iv) the transaction would result in foreign control of any 'critical infrastructure' of the US.[35]

Should such national security investigation take place because the national security concerns are not addressed, CFIUS, acting on behalf of the President and based on a 'risk-based analysis' of the threat posed by the transaction,[36] has the authority to

[28] Congressional Research Service (n 10) 11.

[29] Testimony of Robert Kimmett, Briefing on the Dubai Ports World deal before the Senate Armed Services Committee, 23 February 2006.

[30] FIRRMA § 1706.

[31] Congressional Research Service (n 10).

[32] FIRRMA § 1709. What constitutes extraordinary circumstances will be defined by regulation, see s 1709, § I (ii) (I).

[33] FIRRMA revised the procedures and timetables governing filings with CFIUS. Under this new law, unless investors choose to file a formal 'long-form' notice with CFIUS, they are obligated to file a 'short-form' declaration forty-five days before the transaction is completed.

[34] CFIUS will continue to consider all relevant facts and circumstances, rather than applying a bright-line test to determine whether a transaction results in foreign control (see CFIUS reform, 14 November 2008).

[35] Exon-Florio amendment.

[36] Daniel C Schwartz and Jennifer K Mammen, 'The Role of CFIUS in International Business Transactions' (2017) 2 International Business Law Journal 115–31..

negotiate, impose, or enforce any conditions on the parties in order to mitigate any threat to US national security.[37] These conditions are often instrumented as contracts 'between the US government and the transaction parties and typically contains enforcement clauses'.[38] The US government has stated these contracts impose 'strict compliance backed by the threat of court-imposed injunctive relief to compel performance. However … CFIUS agencies are reportedly seeking very high monetary penalties for breaches.'[39] It should be noted that a great number of deals do not proceed due to national security concerns and the required conditions imposed by CFIUS, but only a small percentage become publicly known.[40]

At the end of the investigation, if a CFIUS member recommends that the transaction be prohibited, or that a Presidential determination is appropriate, it may refer the matter to POTUS, who has fifteen days to make a decision.[41] POTUS has the authority—granted by FINSA—to block transactions that threaten to impair the national security. However, POTUS is under no obligation to follow the recommendation of CFIUS to suspend or prohibit a transaction. The President must conclude that US laws are inadequate to protect the national security, and must have 'credible evidence' that the transaction will impair national security.[42]

In deciding whether to block a transaction, POTUS can take into account a non-exhaustive list of twelve criteria:

(i) domestic production needed for projected national defence requirements;
(ii) capability and capacity of domestic industries to meet national defence requirements, including the availability of human resources, products, technology, materials, and other supplies and services;
(iii) control of domestic industries and commercial activity by foreign citizens as it affects the capability and capacity of the US to meet the requirements of national security;
(iv) potential effects of the transactions on the sales of military goods, equipment, or technology to a country that supports terrorism or proliferates missile technology or chemical and biological weapons; and transactions identified by the Secretary of Defence as 'posing a regional military threat' to the interests of the US;

[37] Congressional Research Service (n 10) 13.
[38] Jeanne Archibald and Jeremy Zucker, 'Exon-Florio "Safe Harbour" Threatened' (2007) 68 European Lawyer 14.
[39] ibid.
[40] Wolin (n 26).
[41] According to Executive Order 11858, section 6: a) any member of the CFIUS may conduct its own enquiry with respect to the potential national security risk posed by a transaction, but communication with the parties to a transaction shall occur through or in the presence of the lead agency, or the chairperson if no lead agency has been designated.

b) The CFIUS shall undertake an investigation of a transaction in any case, in addition to the circumstances described in the Act, in which following a review a member of the CFIUS advises the chairperson that the member believes that the transaction threatens to impair the national security of the US and that the threat has not been mitigated.

[42] Congressional Research Service (n 10) 13.

(v) potential effects of the transaction on US technological leadership in areas affecting US national security;
(vi) whether semiconductor deals or the transaction has a security-related impact on critical infrastructure in the US;
(vii) potential effects on US critical infrastructure, including major energy assets;
(viii) potential effects on US critical technologies;
(ix) whether the transaction is a foreign government-controlled transaction;
(x) in cases involving a government-controlled transaction, a review of: (A) the adherence of the foreign country to non-proliferation control regimes, (B) the foreign country's record on cooperating in counter-terrorism efforts, (C) the potential for transhipment or diversion of technologies with military applications;
(xi) long-term projection of the US requirements for sources of energy and other critical resources and materials; and
(xii) such other factors as the President or CFIUS determine to be appropriate.[43], [44]

However, it should be noted that none of the of the criteria has been invoked explicitly in any of the Executive Orders relating to the five deals that have been blocked by US Presidents so far. Instead, they were mentioned only in some of the press releases from the President's staff in the framework of each transaction.[45]

Notwithstanding that the CFIUS process is voluntary, the advantage of filing a notice before CFIUS outweighs the risk of not doing so. This is because a transaction that has been reviewed by CFIUS is then placed under a 'safe harbour', which means that it cannot be challenged as infringing the Exon-Florio thereafter.[46] Conversely, not filing a foreign transaction before CFIUS puts the transaction at an open-ended risk, since it could be deemed contrary to national security, thus having a sword of Damocles hanging over it, at any time after its completion.

Figure 5.2 shows the proportion of deals that were submitted to CFIUS scrutiny, and requested further investigation and mitigation measures between 2013 and 2022.

[43] The last requirement under factors iv and vi–xii were added by PL 110-49.

[44] Congressional Research Service (n 10) 18–19.

[45] As an example, see Treasury Secretary Mnuchin's sayings regarding the *Lattice Semiconductor* deal (and https://www.herbertsmithfreehills.com/latest-thinking/president-trump-blocks-chinese-firms-acquisition-of-us-semiconductor-company accessed 15 September 2023) or CFIUS statements regarding the *Qualcomm/Broadcom* deal (https://www.reuters.com/article/us-qualcomm-m-a-broadcom-merger/president-trump-halts-broadcom-takeover-of-qualcomm-idUSKCN1GO1Q4 accessed 15 September 2023), among many others.

[46] Archibald and Zucker (n 39) 15; and Gregory Husisian, 'The Future of CFIUS Reviews under the Trump Administration' (2017) 23(2) *International Trade Law & Regulation* 68, 69. However, it should be noted that '[a]lthough it is possible the new [Trump] administration might try to undo previously approved transactions, it is unlikely. The statute provides for undoing previous approvals only if information submitted turns out to be false, misleading or to have had material omissions' (ibid 73).

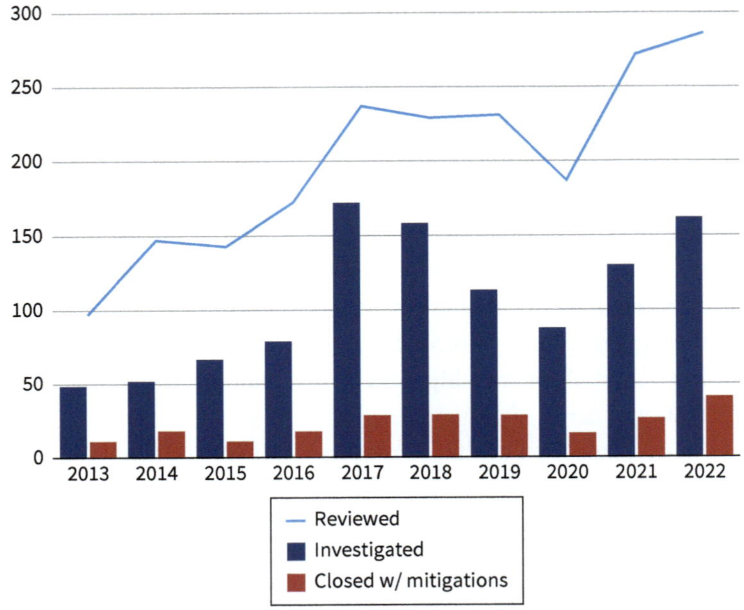

Figure 5.2 Transactions reviewed, investigated, closed with mitigations by CFIUS (2013–22)

Based on data from Committee on Foreign Investment in the United States, Annual Report CY 2013, CY 2014, CY 2015, CY 2016-17, CY 2018, CY 2019, CY 2020, CY 2021, CY 2022

Note: The figures relate to notices, not transactions (eg they don't discount notices that were withdrawn and later refiled)

Despite the significant number of CFIUS investigations and the number of deals where mitigation conditions either were imposed or were withdrawn by the parties, only one transaction was rejected by CFIUS each year between 2016 and 2020. Irrespective of the burdensome nature of the CFIUS review, and its uncertain outcome, this ratio of less than 1 per cent of CFIUS reviews is actually encouraging, for foreign companies looking to invest in the US.[47]

The share of actions that the CFIUS concludes after adopting mitigation measures to resolve national security concerns hit a peak of forty-one in 2022, having been below thirty for a few years (with a Covid-19 dip in 2020). In addition, the CFIUS may adopt mitigation measures to address residual national security concerns even when a transaction has been voluntarily withdrawn and abandoned—for instance, it did so twice in 2021 and three times in 2022.[48]

[47] In FY 2015, for instance, 1,801 transactions were reported under the HSR Act. The DOJ brought twenty-two merger enforcement challenges, of which in only three cases did it initiate administrative litigation (less than 0.20 per cent of transactions where the competition authorities were against the deal occurring). See https://www.ftc.gov/system/files/documents/reports/federal-trade-commission-bureau-competition-department-justice-antitrust-division-hart-scott-rodino/160801hsrreport.pdf accessed 15 September 2023.

[48] CFIUS, Annual Report CY 2021, 15 https://home.treasury.gov/system/files/206/CFIUS-Public-AnnualReporttoCongressCY2021.pdf accessed 15 September 2023; CFIUS, Annual Report CY 2022, 19 https://home.treasury.gov/system/files/206/CFIUS%20-%20Annual%20Report%20to%20Congress%20CY%202022_0.pdf accessed 15 September 2023 .

We can infer from its Annual Report that CFIUS is reviewing an increasing number of cases, but mitigation remains more common than blocking.

5.2.3 CFIUS National Security Assessment

Throughout the CFIUS assessment process, the analysis of the capability or intention of a foreign entity to cause national security harm is at the core of the CFIUS assessment of the transaction. The focus is on whether the nature of the US business can lead to an impairment of US national security. The concept of 'national security' has resulted in a significant transformation of the US government's foreign investment regime. Today, twenty-seven industries are deemed to be 'critical technologies'.

The CFIUS assessment is grounded on information provided by the parties, public and government sources, including the classified 'National Security Threat Assessment' that, as required by section 721, the DNI prepares for CFIUS within 20 days after a notice of a transaction is accepted.[49] However, it must be stressed that the requirement is not only that the transaction imposes a mere threat, but that it can also lead to a vulnerability in US national security.[50] There is a statutory list of national security factors included in section 721(f),[51] which focus on the nature of the US business over which control is being acquired[52] as well as on the identity of the foreign person acquiring control of a US business.[53]

[49] Federal Register, Vol 73, No 226, Rules and Regulations, 21 November 2008.

[50] David N Fagan, *The US Regulatory and Institutional Framework for* FDI, in Karl P Sauvant (ed), *Investing in the United States: Is the US Ready for FDI from China?* (Edward Elgar Publishing 2009) 59.

[51] CFIUS operates pursuant to s 721 of the Defense Production Act of 1950, as amended.

[52] Transactions that CFIUS has reviewed and have presented national security considerations usually involve foreign control of US businesses that provide products and services to agencies of the US government and state and local authorities.

[53] S 721(f) sets out the following factors:

(1) domestic production needed for projected national defense requirements,
(2) the capability and capacity of domestic industries to meet national defense requirements, including the availability of human resources, products, technology, materials, and other supplies and services,
(3) the control of domestic industries and commercial activity by foreign citizens as it affects the capability and capacity of the United States to meet the requirements of national security,
(4) the potential effects of the proposed or pending transaction on sales of military goods, equipment, or technology to any country—
   (A) identified by the Secretary of State—
      (i) … as a country that supports terrorism;
      (ii) … as a country of concern regarding missile proliferation; or
      (iii) … as a country of concern regarding the proliferation of chemical and biological weapons;
   (B) identified by the Secretary of Defense as posing a potential regional military threat to the interests of the United States; or'
   (C) listed under … the 'Nuclear Non-Proliferation-Special Country List' … or any successor list;
(5) the potential effects of the proposed or pending transaction on United States international technological leadership in areas affecting United States national security;
(6) the potential national security-related effects on United States critical infrastructure, including major energy assets;
(7) the potential national security-related effects on United States critical technologies;

In the 2015 Annual Report, CFIUS identified three national security risks that were not included in past practice, namely: (i) the potential disclosure of substantial pools of personal information; (ii) the potential loss of one of only a few US suppliers; and (iii) the potential loss of US technological advantages.[54] Concerning these three risks, the first one entails that any acquisition of a US business, which comprises a great deal of private information, may pose a national security risk (including in relation to transactions in the financial, healthcare, and insurance sectors). The second one, pertaining to deals where there are few alternative suppliers operating, evidences the relevance awarded by the US government to US supply chain issues. The third risk, comprising the loss of US technological advantages to foreign acquirers that also develop technology, would seem to be the key to pass FIRRMA, on the basis of which the CFIUS' authority to review transactions was strengthened.[55]

The CFIUS annual reports include an assessment by the US Intelligence Community (USIC). While the 2012 report indicated that the USIC found coordination among foreign entities 'to acquire companies involved in US critical technologies',[56] the 2014 report acknowledged that the USIC just anticipated a possible 'effort among foreign governments or companies to acquire US companies involved in research, development, or production of critical technologies for which the United States is a leading producer'.[57] This observation was emphasized in the 2015 Annual Report, where the USIC noted that 'foreign governments are extremely likely to use a range of collection methods to obtain critical US technologies'.[58] Based on these findings, that have moved from 'vague' concerns to 'severe' concerns in a matter of only three years, it is not a surprise that the scope of CFIUS expanded over the years, culminating in the FIRRMA Act

(8) whether the covered transaction is a foreign government-controlled transaction …
(9) as appropriate, and particularly with respect to transactions requiring an investigation … a review of the current assessment of—
    (A) the adherence of the subject country to non-proliferation control regimes, including treaties and multilateral supply guidelines, which shall draw on, but not be limited to, the annual report on 'Adherence to and Compliance with Arms Control, Nonproliferation and Disarmament Agreements and Commitments' required by section 403 of the Arms Control and Disarmament Act;
    (B) the relationship of such country with the United States, specifically on its record on cooperating in counter-terrorism efforts, which shall draw on, but not be limited to, the report of the President to Congress under section 7120 of the Intelligence Reform and Terrorism Prevention Act of 2004; and
    (C) the potential for transshipment or diversion of technologies with military applications, including an analysis of national export control laws and regulations;
(10) the long-term projection of United States requirements for sources of energy and other critical resources and material; and
(11) such other factors as the President or the Committee may determine to be appropriate, generally or in connection with a specific review or investigation.

[54] CFIUS, Annual Report CY 2015 (n 17).
[55] The 'loss of emerging technologies and personal information' was added to the list of national security threats.
[56] William R Vigdor and Daniel J Gerkin, 'CFIUS Annual Report Confirms Recent Trends and Highlights Factors to be Considered when Notifying Transactions to CFIUS' (Lexology, 2018) https://www.lexology.com/library/detail.aspx?g=d1e42bfe-e4cc-4b9a-b40a-6deaeb21a2a4 accessed 15 September 2023.
[57] CFIUS, Annual Report to Congress CY 2014, 29 https://home.treasury.gov/system/files/206/CFIUS-Annual-Report-to-Congress-for-CY2014.pdf accessed 15 September 2023.
[58] CFIUS, Annual Report CY 2015 (n 17), 31.

on the one hand, and in the increase in the number of CFIUS cases between 2015 and 2017, a trend unlikely to be reversed.

Previous CFIUS Annual Reports show an increased scrutiny of semiconductor deals. In 2015 at least two semiconductor-related transactions with Chinese parties were cleared by CFIUS,[59] followed by adverse outcomes for Chinese acquirers in 2016 and 2017, and a strong setback in 2017 with President Trump's blocking of the proposed acquisition of Lattice Semiconductor Corporation by a US-headquartered private equity fund whose sole investor was owned and controlled by the Chinese government.

Furthermore, the CFIUS approach illustrates the increasing use of mitigation measures, which comprise:

> conditions as restricting which persons can access certain technologies/information, establishing procedures regarding US government contracting, establishing corporate security committees to oversee classified or export-controlled products or technical data, requiring divestments of critical business units, providing periodic monitoring reports to the US Government regarding national security issues, or giving the US Government the right to review future business decisions that implicate national security.[60]

Given the growth in the imposition of these mitigation measures, it is likely that 'an increasingly stringent review process will result in more companies backing off of transactions that encounter resistance from the committee'.[61] The outcome of such a trend could be the diversion of incoming foreign direct investments (FDI) and the exclusion of particular countries. In 2021, there were not significant increases in the percentage of transaction requiring mitigation based on CFIUS concerns, though some cases requiring mitigation took longer to resolve.[62]

5.2.4 Proposals for Changes to CFIUS

The strengthening of the scope of CFIUS was advocated for quite some time prior to FIRRMA coming into effect.

Commentators have noted that 'Republicans in Congress have been trying for years to alter the scope of the CFIUS review process and are likely to view the election of Mr Trump as an opportunity to enact this agenda.'[63] The chapter discusses below some of

[59] Namely, OmniVision Technologies, Inc (acquired by a consortium composed of Hua Capital Management Co Ltd, CITIC Capital Holdings Limited, and GoldStone Investment Co Ltd) and Integrated Silicon Solution, Inc (acquired by Uphill Investment Co).

[60] Husisian (n 47) 69–70.

[61] ibid 70.

[62] Farhad Jalinous, 'CFIUS continues its watchful eye on foreign investment', White & Case, 22 August 2022.

[63] Husisian (n 47) 72.

the most recent concerns of Congress in relation to the CFIUS remit, and the proposed legislation to address these concerns.

These concerns have focused on: (1) the increase in foreign investment activity by Chinese state-owned companies; (2) the perception that such investment is part of a government-coordinated approach that serves official strategic purposes; and (3) the fact that investments from Chinese companies are receiving government support, giving them an 'unfair' competitive advantage over other private investors.[64]

Consequently, there are several amendments to the CFIUS remit that are put forward. The amendments aim to broaden the scope of the review and also its mandate to adopt a more holistic approach in the assessment of transactions. In addition, a mandatory filing process is being put forward. The proposals include leveraging access to the US market to gain reciprocal access in foreign markets; applying penalties to foreign firms that receive subsidized financing or preferential domestic regulations; and discriminating among foreign investors based on membership in certain organizations.[65]

5.2.4.1 HR 2810, National Defense Authorization Act for Fiscal Year 2018

This Act[66] enables the Secretary of Defense to offer recommendations to agencies in order to improve the effectiveness of the interagency vetting of foreign investments that could impair the national security of the US;[67] to establish a process for enhancing the ability of the Defense Department to analyse and monitor foreign investments in the defence industrial base;[68] to allow for the development of a programme to assess the feasibility of increasing the capability of the defence industrial base to support production needs to meet military requirements and the manufacturing and production of emerging and commercial technologies;[69] and to allow for the 'exemption of organizations whose ownership or majority control is based in a country that is part of the national technology and industrial base from one or more of the foreign ownership, control, or influence requirements of the National Industrial Security Program'.[70] Moreover, the Act also requires the Commander of the Air Force Space and Missile Systems Centre to establish and maintain a watch list of contractors under the criteria of 'security or foreign ownership and control issues'.[71]

5.2.4.2 HR 2932, the Foreign Investment and Economic Security Act of 2017

This Act is intended to 'alter the composition of CFIUS and require a "net benefits" (cost-benefit) test, as part of a CFIUS national security review of a proposed foreign

[64] Congressional Research Service (n 10) 41.
[65] Congressional Research Service (n 10) 42–44. Notably, greenfield investments are also not covered by CFIUS, so there is a gap in coverage that Congress could seek to fill by amending the statute. However, it does not currently seem to be a priority on Congress's agenda.
[66] The measure was signed by President Trump on 12 December 2017, and designated PL 115-91.
[67] HR 2810, National Defense Authorization Act for Fiscal Year 2018, s 1069.
[68] ibid s 1071.
[69] ibid s 1711.
[70] ibid s 1712.
[71] ibid s 1612.

investment transaction'.[72] This test provides that the President 'shall' consider the overall effects on the level of economic activity in the US and the effect of the proposed investment transaction on productivity, industrial efficiency, technology transfers, product innovation, and competition within the US and with other countries.[73] Thus, the scope of the analysis is expanded by introducing an additional criterion in the assessment of the national security risks that a transaction may pose. This Act grants the net benefit test an important role in determining whether a transaction can be approved from a national security perspective.

5.2.4.3 S 616, the Food Security is National Security Act of 2017

This Act includes the Secretaries of Agriculture and Health and Human Services as permanent members of CFIUS and, by doing so incorporates the impact of foreign investment in the food and agriculture systems on national security, as part of the CFIUS criteria for its assessment of a transaction.[74]

5.2.4.4 S 1722, the True Reciprocity Investment Act of 2017

This Act requires CFIUS to consider the reciprocity of foreign investment; that is, whether an investor's home country would allow a reciprocal investment of US interests in the same industry.[75]

5.2.4.5 S 2987/HR 5515, the Foreign Investment Risk Review Modernization Act of 2018 (FIRRMA)

FIRRMA represents a comprehensive revision of the foreign investment review process under CFIUS, modifying the Act's defensive approach into a more assertive role that emphasizes US economic, as well as national security interests.[76] This piece of legislation, that was incorporated and enacted as part of the 2019 National Defense Authorization Act, addresses concerns arising from certain foreign non-controlling investments involved with critical technology, critical infrastructure, or sensitive personal data[77] and real estate transactions that previously fell outside CFIUS's jurisdiction.[78]

Besides broadening the scope of transactions subject to CFIUS's review, this Act introduces some changes aiming to make the assessment process more effective by adding a definition for 'principal place of business'; clarifying the application of the 'incremental acquisition rule'; adjusting the treatment of genetic data within the definition of 'sensitive personal data'; amending the definition of 'substantial interest'; modifying the exceptions for certain real estate transactions in airports and maritime ports; and refining the geographic coverage relating to certain

[72] Congressional Research Service (n 10) 48.
[73] ibid.
[74] ibid.
[75] <https://www.congress.gov/bill/115th-congress/senate-bill/1722/text> accessed 15 September 2023.
[76] Congressional Research Service (n 10) 49.
[77] Known as TID US business and by which FIRRMA now provides some examples of these types of transactions.
[78] <https://home.treasury.gov/system/files/206/Summary-of-FIRRMA.pdf> accessed 15 September 2023.

military installations.[79] An additional development responds to the limitation of CFIUS's jurisdiction over non-controlling 'covered investments' and certain real estate transactions by certain 'excepted investors' from certain 'excepted foreign estates'.[80] Such limitation is not absolute though, as even if a foreign person meets the modified criteria to qualify as an 'excepted investor', CFIUS shall retain authority to review a transaction that could result in foreign control of any US business.[81]

Pursuant to FIRRMA, while CFIUS continues as a voluntary process, there are two categories of foreign investment where mandatory filing is required: (i) investments by an investor (subject to certain exemptions) in certain TID businesses involved with critical technologies, and (ii) certain investments by foreign investors with substantial government ownership (subject to certain exemptions) in any TID US business.[82] In light of the recent expansion of CFIUS's authority, it seems that almost any foreign person or entity is potentially within its regulatory reach.

FIRRMA strengthens the role of CFIUS by on the one hand providing clarity to a number of considerations that are relevant for its assessment, and on the other clarifying the criteria of what would be considered an 'excepted investor', while maintaining its power to assess all transactions involving foreign acquirers and US domestic assets.

Under the Biden Administration, the committee remains steadfast in its comprehensive approach to deal reviews by focusing on a wide range or areas of interest such as supply chains. CFIUS has broadened its involvement in certain sectors, on the grounds of national security, such as real estate.

In March 2022, US Secretary of Commerce Gina Raimondo expressed support for a screening regime to review outbound investment.[83] More recently, in December 2022, President Biden signed into law the Consolidated Appropriations Act, 2023 which allocated approximately $1.7 trillion in federal funding to various government agencies, including the US Department of Commerce and the US Department of the Treasury.[84] As far as outbound investment are concerned, it is said in the explanatory statements that:

> the Department is encouraged. in coordination with the Department of the Treasury, to consider its role in the establishment of a program to address the national security threats emanating from outbound investments from the United States in certain sectors that are critical for U.S. national security. Not later than 60 days after enactment of this act. the Department shall submit a report describing its efforts and identifying the resources that would be required to establish and implement it.[85]

[79] <https://home.treasury.gov/system/files/206/Final-FIRRMA-Regulations-FAQs.pdf> accessed 15 September 2023.

[80] ibid. The provision has identified Australia, Canada, and the UK as 'excepted foreign estates', given their robust intelligence-sharing, and defence industrial base integration mechanisms with the US.

[81] ibid.

[82] FIRRMA, s 1706, § (v)(IV)(bb)(AA)(cc).

[83] Farhad Jalinous, 'CFIUS continues its watchful eye on foreign investment', White & Case, 22 August 2022

[84] US Government, HR 2471 Consolidated Appropriations Act, 2022 117th Congress (2021–22), 19 December 2022.

[85] US Government, Division B-Commerce, Justice, Science and Related Agencies Appropriation Act, 2023, <https://www.appropriations.senate.gov/imo/media/doc/Division%20B%20-%20CJS%20Statement%20FY23.pdf> accessed 15 September 2023.

This development confirms that an outbound investment screening regime is, at this point, inevitable, and we will see how its establishment will affect future outward investment by US companies.[86] Interestingly, in a visit of Treasury Secretary Yellen to China in July 2023, the Secretary stated that US controls on investment into China would only target sensitive national security sectors, in an attempt to mitigate the negative reaction of China to this new regime.[87]

A recent initiative in the US also relates to the expansion of CFIUS power in real estate transactions. This need arose from the acquisition in 2022 by Fufeng USA, part of the Chinese Fufeng Group, of land near a military installation (Grand Forks Air base). CFIUS considered the issue of jurisdiction and decided it did not have jurisdiction to review this transaction, most likely because it did not involve an existing business but was a greenfield investment.[88] Even though in 2020, CFIUS implemented significant changes pursuant to the FIRRMA that expanded CFIUS's jurisdiction to include certain real estate transactions by foreign persons, in response to the criticism of curtailed jurisdiction of CFIUS, additional proposals were put forward to expand its jurisdiction. In May 2023, the US Department of the Treasury proposed a rule that adds eight military installations to the list of sites around which the Committee on Foreign Investment in the US has jurisdiction to review real estate transactions.[89] This is the first expansion of CFIUS's real estate authority since it came into effect in 2020.

5.3 National Security Assessment by CFIUS

In relation to the state's involvement in assessing foreign takeovers, US law generally does not restrict foreign ownership of, or investment in, US companies.[90] However, cross-border mergers could require not only an antitrust review, but also a review by CFIUS, to determine whether they are harmful to national interest or national security.[91]

[86] Chase D Kaniecki, Pete Young, 'Potential Outbound Investment Screening Regime Receives Federal Funding', 4 January 2023, https://www.clearytradewatch.com/author/ckaniecki/page/2/ accessed 1 February 2024.

[87] 'US controls on investment will not harm China, Yellen tells Beijing', *Financial Times*, 9 July 2023, https://www.ft.com/content/29fc010c-13db-4489-8101-259fc69955c9 accessed 15 September 2023.

[88] Akin Gump Strauss Hauer and Feld LLP, 'Foreign Investment In Real Estate Is Getting More Complicated', https://www.lexology.com/library/detail.aspx?g=0405c0f3-229f-47b3-ad1c-16da8b1efba5 accessed 15 September 2023.

[89] Squire Patton Boggs, 'CFIUS Determines It Lacks Jurisdiction To Review Chinese Land Acquisition', https://www.tradepractitioner.com/2023/06/cfius-determines-it-lacks-jurisdiction-to-review-chinese-land-acquisition/ accessed 15 September 2023.

[90] Marvin Goldman, 'United States: Doing Business In The USA: Regulation Of Foreign Investment' (Mondaq, 2006) <http://www.mondaq.com/unitedstates/x/45120/Compliance/Doing+Business+In+The+USA+Regulation+Of+Foreign+Investment> accessed 15 September 2023.

[91] CFIUS operates pursuant to s 721 of the Defense Production Act of 1950, as amended ('section 721'), and as implemented by Executive Order 11858, as amended, and the regulations at chapter VIII of title 31 of the Code of Federal Regulations. The authority of the President to suspend or prohibit certain transactions was initially provided by the addition of s 721 to the Defense Production Act of 1950 by a 1988 amendment commonly known as the Exon-Florio amendment. https://home.treasury.gov/policy-issues/international/the-committee-on-foreign-investment-in-the-united-states-cfius/cfius-laws-and-guidance accessed 15 September 2023.

Notwithstanding that US policy has been open to foreign direct investments, there have been many cases over the last forty years where attempts by foreign companies have been received with caution by CFIUS in relation to the impact of these transactions on national security, a concept as ambiguous if not more, as the impact of the transaction on competition. Instead, political opposition has led to legislation and executive orders, which created a legal framework for CFIUS to review proposed transactions.

According to UNCTAD's 2022 *World Investment Report*, flows to the US rebounded strongly by 143.6 per cent, from $151 billion in 2020 to $367 billion in 2021, mainly due to a surge in cross-border M&As making the United States the largest recipient of FDI.[92]

5.3.1 Trends in CFIUS Enforcement

CFIUS has been criticized for operating 'in the shadows', far from the public eye,[93] and its 'reviews have always been something of a black box'.[94] Yet, following the 9/11 terrorist attacks of 2001 and the proposed acquisition of commercial operations at six US ports by Dubai Ports World in 2006, CFIUS's procedures began to draw the attention of the Members of Congress and the public.[95] Since 2008 CFIUS has been publishing annual reports showcasing its enforcement record. As is shown in Table 5.1, the number of notices filed grew significantly, almost tripling between 2013 and 2022, while investigations more than tripled in the same timespan. Prohibitions, however, remain extremely rare—only 5 out of more than 2,000 cases.

Table 5.1 Covered Transactions, Withdrawals, and Presidential Decisions (2013–22)

Year	Filed	Withdrawn (during Review)	Investigated	Withdrawn (during Investigation)	Presidential decisions
2013	97	3	49	5	0
2014	147	3	52	9	0
2015	143	3	67	10	0
2016	172	6	79	21	1
2017	237	4	172	70	1
2018	229	2	158	64	1
2019	231	0	113	30	1
2020	187	1	88	28	1
2021	272	2	130	72	0
2022	286	1	162	87	0
Total	**2001**	**25**	**1070**	**396**	**5**

Based on data from CFIUS Annual Report CY 2022, 21

[92] UNCTAD, *World Investment Report 2022*.
[93] Archibald and Zucker (n 39) 14.
[94] Husisian (n 47) 68.
[95] Congressional Research Service (n 10).

Declarations grew even more rapidly, going from 20 to 164 in a mere four-year period, as evidenced in Table 5.2. That's understandable since, as already mentioned, filing a declaration seems to afford companies legal certainty without increasing their regulatory risk significantly.

Table 5.2 Declarations and Withdrawals (2018–22)

	Filed	Withdrawn
2018	20	1
2019	94	1
2020	126	1
2021	164	0
2022	154	0
Total	558	3

Based on data from CFIUS, Annual Report CY 2022, table I-1, page 5

Finally, Table 5.3 illustrates that there has been a gradual but clear change in the countries whose firms being acquirers of US domestic assets notify CFIUS of their transactions. As former Deputy US Treasury Secretary Neal Wolin explains, '[p]reviously, there were many transactions from the UK, from Canada and from other NATO allies. And increasingly there are now transactions that originate from other countries that have more complicated national security relationships with the US.'[96] Over the past decade, Chinese investors have established themselves as the most significant source of CFIUS filings, with 365 covered notices out of a total of 2001—or a share of around 18 per cent—in the 2013–22 period. Over the same timespan, China has been the largest contributor every year except in 2019, 2020, and 2022. The increase may indicate Chinese investors do not view the CFIUS process as an impediment to investment.[97] This trend likely reflects the intense scrutiny to which Chinese investments are subject by the Committee.[98]

Table 5.3 Covered Transactions by Acquirer Home Country or Economy (2013–22)

Country/ Economy	2013	2014	2015	2016	2017	2018	2019	2020	2021	2022	Total
Australia	0	4	4	4	5	4	11	10	4	6	52
Austria	0	0	0	1	2	1	4	0	3	4	15
Bahamas	0	0	0	0	0	0	1	0	0	0	1
Bahrain	0	0	0	0	0	0	0	0	0	1	1
Belgium	0	0	1	0	3	1	0	0	1	1	7
Bermuda	0	0	0	1	0	2	2	1	0	1	7

(continued)

[96] Wolin (n 26).

[97] Morrison Foerster, 'Key Points from the CFIUS Annual Report for Calendar Year 2021', 15 September 2022, https://www.mofo.com/resources/insights/220915-key-points-from-the-cfius-annual-report

[98] David Mortlock and others, '2021 CFIUS Annual Report Reveals Key Trends in Reviews of Foreign Investment', Willkie Farr & Gallagher, 22 August 2022

Table 5.3 Continued

Country/ Economy	2013	2014	2015	2016	2017	2018	2019	2020	2021	2022	Total
Brazil	1	0	0	1	1	0	0	2	2	3	10
British Virgin Islands	0	1	0	6	4	0	0	1	1	4	17
Canada	12	15	22	22	22	29	23	11	28	17	201
Cayman Islands	1	3	8	5	8	2	2	5	18	10	62
Chile	1	0	0	0	0	0	0	1	1	1	4
China	21	24	29	54	60	55	25	17	44	36	365
Colombia	0	0	0	0	0	0	1	0	0	0	1
Croatia	0	0	0	0	0	0	0	0	0	1	1
Czech Republic	0	0	0	0	0	0	0	1	3	2	6
Denmark	0	0	1	0	0	3	2	2	5	2	15
Dominican Republic	0	0	0	0	0	0	0	0	0	1	1
Finland	0	1	2	3	0	0	0	2	1	2	11
Fiji	0	0	0	0	0	2	0	0	0	0	2
France	7	6	8	8	14	21	13	11	13	14	115
Germany	4	9	1	6	7	12	13	7	10	10	79
Guernsey	0	0	0	0	1	1	4	3	3	6	18
Hong Kong	1	6	2	3	0	0	4	3	0	0	19
Hungary	0	0	0	0	1	0	0	0	0	0	1
India	1	2	0	1	3	4	3	6	1	3	24
Indonesia	0	1	2	0	0	0	0	0	0	0	3
Ireland	1	1	2	3	3	9	1	2	2	9	33
Isle of Man	0	0	0	0	0	0	0	0	0	1	1
Israel	1	5	3	3	4	5	2	6	12	9	50
Italy	0	0	2	0	2	3	3	3	4	3	20
Japan	18	10	12	13	20	31	46	19	26	15	210
Jersey	0	0	0	1	3	1	0	3	2	2	12
Kuwait	0	0	0	1	2	0	0	1	0	2	6
Lebanon	0	0	0	1	0	0	0	1	2	0	4
Liechtenstein	0	1	0	0	1	0	0	0	1	1	4
Luxembourg	1	0	2	5	2	0	1	5	4	5	25
Malaysia	0	0	0	0	0	1	0	1	0	0	2
Malta	0	0	0	1	0	0	0	0	0	1	2
Mauritius	0	0	0	0	0	0	0	0	0	1	1
Mexico	2	0	0	1	2	0	0	0	2	2	9
Netherlands	1	8	5	3	7	5	6	6	5	1	47
New Zealand	0	0	0	0	0	0	0	0	0	3	3
Norway	1	1	0	2	2	0	0	1	2	1	10
Philippines	0	0	0	0	0	0	0	1	0	0	1
Papua New Guinea	0	0	0	0	1	0	0	0	0	0	1
Portugal	0	0	1	0	5	0	1	4	7	2	20
Qatar	0	1	0	0	0	1	1	2	2	1	8

Table 5.3 Continued

Country/ Economy	2013	2014	2015	2016	2017	2018	2019	2020	2021	2022	Total
Russian Federation	1	1	0	0	3	6	1	0	7	1	20
Saudi Arabia	2	1	1	0	1	1	3	0	3	4	16
Seychelles	0	0	0	1	0	0	0	0	0	0	1
Singapore	3	6	3	2	6	5	10	10	13	37	95
South Africa	0	0	2	0	2	1	0	1	1	1	8
South Korea	1	7	1	7	6	4	10	2	13	14	65
Spain	1	2	2	1	1	2	2	3	0	4	18
Sweden	2	2	3	1	6	9	7	10	5	9	54
Switzerland	3	7	2	0	7	2	4	2	1	1	29
Taiwan	1	0	0	1	0	4	4	4	4	3	21
Thailand	0	0	0	0	0	0	1	0	2	2	5
Turkey	0	0	2	2	0	2	2	1	0	1	10
Ukraine	0	0	0	0	0	0	0	0	1	1	2
United Arab Emirates	2	1	1	1	2	3	4	2	0	6	22
United Kingdom	7	21	19	7	18	5	13	14	13	18	135
Vietnam	0	0	0	0	0	0	1	0	0	0	1
Total	97	147	143	172	237	229	231	187	272	286	2001

Based on data from CFIUS, Annual Reports (CY 2015, 16–17; CY 2018, 20–21; CY 2021, 32–33; CY 2022, 39–40)

The debate concerning CFIUS's approach and scope of intervention is intense. There are those who argue that CFIUS's involvement in deals is increasing each year, a view supported by the data illustrated above.[99] On the other hand, there are commentators who strongly argue that CFIUS attempts to mitigate national security issues and 'get to a place where the deal can be approved with modifications'.[100] In particular, Wolin firmly sustains that '[t]he basic policy judgment of the Obama Administration, and of many administrations before it, was favourably disposed to inward foreign investment because it is good for the US economy.'[101] It is only by the analysis of case law in the next section of this chapter that one can get a flavour of CFIUS's criteria and enforcement trend.

[99] 'Nearly 250 cases in 2017, an increase of approximately 40 percent in the number of cases reviewed by CFIUS over the high-water mark that occurred in 2016; this increased case volume contributed significantly to the longer process [of review], because the case volume made it harder for CFIUS to accept and dispose of cases quickly.' (See Wilson Sonsini Goodrich & Rosati Professional Corporation, *CFIUS in 2017: A Momentous Year*, 1.)

[100] Wolin (n 26).

[101] ibid.

5.3.2 Concept of National Security in Law and Practice

According to the Exon-Florio amendment ('Exon-Florio'),[102] 'the term "national security" shall be construed so as to include those issues relating to "homeland security", including its application to critical infrastructure'. The latter term in this definition implies 'systems and assets, whether physical or virtual, so vital to the United States that the incapacity or destruction of such systems or assets would have a debilitating impact on national security'. However, the scope of such a scenario has never been precisely defined since national security considerations are not listed, and thus are currently subject to different interpretations even within Congress.[103] Instead of offering a clear-cut definition, the law regulating foreign investments in the US defines 'national security sensitive industries' as those that implicate 'critical infrastructure', 'critical technology', 'critical resources', and the presence of any other factors the executive branch deems appropriate.[104] Such an open-ended and broad definition results in ambiguity and legal uncertainty, and grants political actors the ability to block proposed transactions under the pretence of national security concerns.

FIRMMA has tried to fill the gap by providing some examples of businesses that involve national security considerations, that is, for 'critical technology' (defence articles, defence services, nuclear-related facilities), for 'critical infrastructure' (telecoms, power, oil and gas, water, finance) and, for 'sensitive personal data' (health data, geolocation, biometric enrolment, etc).

The CFIUS enforcement record provides a somewhat clear picture to the concept of national security and the sectors of interest from a national security perspective. The majority of the reviewed transactions involve 'dual-use technologies or artificial intelligence or semiconductors or big sets of personal data ... [a]nd those transactions have tended to raise greater national security sensitivity'.[105]

Figures 5.3 and 5.4 illustrate the breakdown of covered transactions by area of the economy between 2013 and 2022. While both the finance, information, and services sector and the manufacturing sector grew significantly in absolute terms over the period considered, the former now accounts for more than half of the notices (up from a third in 2013), while the latter went from about 36 per cent to less than 30 per cent. The remaining two sectors (Mining, Utilities, and Construction; and Wholesale Trade, Retail Trade, and Transportation) almost halved their total share in the ten-year period, falling from more than 30 per cent to around 18 per cent.

[102] An amendment from 1988 which added s 721 to the Defense Production Act of 1950 (codified at 50 USC 4565), codifying the process CFIUS used to review foreign investment transactions. The actual introduction of national security into the US regime came a few years before, on 7 May 1975, when CFIUS was established by Executive Order 11858 (b), 40 FR 20263.

[103] FINSA tried to fill the gap by including threats to homeland security and critical infrastructure as part of the definition of national security. 50 USC §4565(a)(5).

[104] Paul Marquardt, Chinyelu Lee, and Nathanael Kurcab, 'Foreign Investment Review, United States', in *Getting the Deal Through*, 2019, https://www.clearygottlieb.com/-/media/files/getting-the-deal-through-foreign-investment-review-2019--united-states-pdf.pdf> accessed 15 September 2023.

[105] Wolin (n 26).

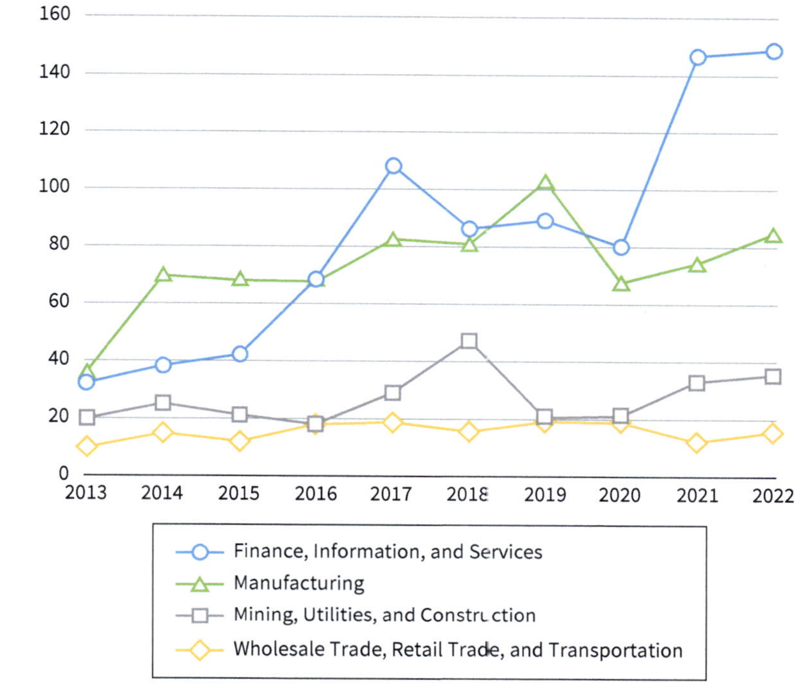

Figure 5.3 Covered Notices by Sector (2013–22)
Based on data from CFIUS, Annual Report CY 2022, page 24

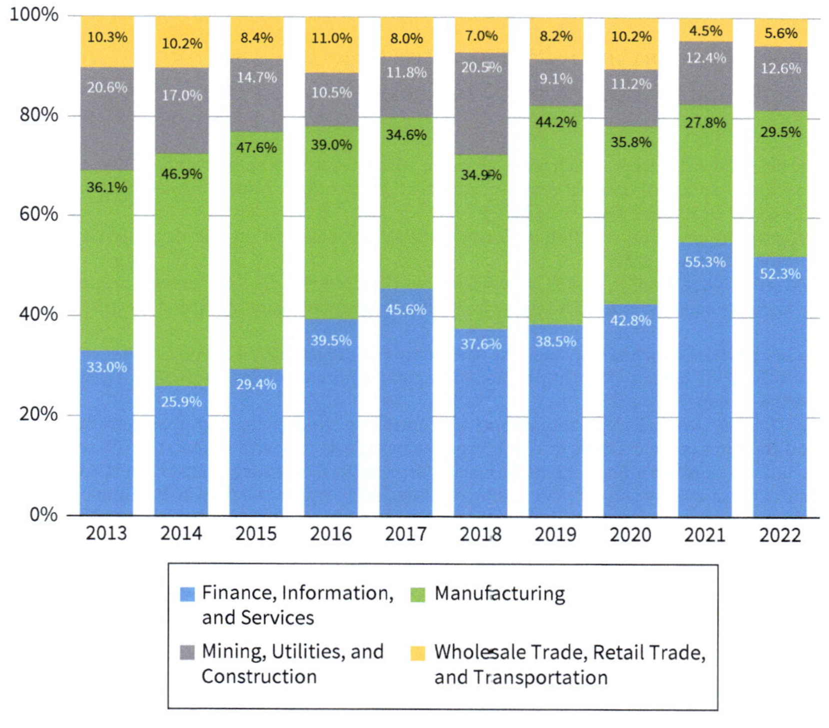

Figure 5.4 Covered notices by sector as a percentage of all covered notices (2013–22)
Based on data from CFIUS, Annual Report CY 2022, page 24

In September 2022, President Biden issued an Executive Order on ensuring Robust Consideration of Evolving National Security Risks by the CFIUS. This is the first time in the Committee's history that a president has directed CFIUS to prioritize certain national security risks when reviewing covered transactions.[106] Until now, the national security factors that form CFIUS's mandate have been defined by Congress in the Defense Product Act of 1950 and more recent legislation including the Foreign Investment Risk Review Modernization Act of 2018.

This Executive Order does not change the Committee's review process or legal jurisdiction; it mostly provides details on existing factors and adds new national security factors. Specifically, the Executive Order requires CFIUS to consider five national security factors in its review: domestic supply capacity and supply chain resilience, US technological leadership in critical sectors, aggregate industry investment trends, cybersecurity risks, and sensitive data on US persons.[107] The new Executive Order also highlights CFIUS's increasing attention to the cumulative threat posed by a pattern of investment by a specific foreign investor. Thus, it confirms this ongoing trend by the Committee of viewing transaction in a broader investment context.[108]

In addition, the Executive Order highlights that CFIUS considers not only the foreign persons who are acquiring interest in US businesses, but also foreign investors' third-party ties, including commercial ties, to foreign adversaries or countries of special concern, which can be understood to include China as well as Russia.[109]

The general trajectory of strengthening the national security regime in the US has received bipartisan support. This led not only to the Executive Order mentioned above but also to the Enforcement and Penalty Guidelines, the CHIPS Act, and to new restrictions under US export control[110] authorities targeting China as well as a new regime to review outbound investments by US businesses.[111]

[106] Michael J Lowell, Lizbeth Rodriguez-Johnson, Manasi Venkatesh, and others, 'Executive order directs CFIUS to expand review of national security factors', 5 October 2022, https://www.lexology.com/library/detail.aspx?g=806ad227-2c3d-4ab0-b8ca-682d7b6f93d6.

[107] Executive Order on Ensuring Robust Consideration of Evolving National Security Risks by the CFIUS in the USA, EO 14083 15 September 2022.

[108] Kirkland & Ellis, 'President Biden Issues First-Ever Directive to CFIUS on National Security Considerations in Transactions', 21 September 2022, https://www.kirkland.com/publications/kirkland-alert/2022/09/cfius-executive-order.

[109] Christian C Davis, Davina Garrod, Clete R Willems, and others, '2022 Foreign Investment Review and What to Expect in 2023', 31 January 2023, https://www.akingump.com/en/insights/alerts/2022-foreign-investment-review-and-what-to-expect-in-2023.

[110] The USA has two main legal frameworks for controlling exports: the Export Administration Regulations (EAR) and the International Traffic in Arms Regulations (ITAR). Under the EAR, the BIS regulates exports of 'dual-use and less sensitive military items' by placing them on its Commerce Control List (CCL). In contrast, the ITAR restrict those articles and services with explicit defence purposes on the US Munitions List (USML). The most recent reforms under the Obama Administration resulted in many items being moved from the USML to the CCL in order to expedite their approval processes. ECRA functions as an addition to the EAR. In August 2018, the USA enacted the Export Control Reform Act (ECRA), as part of the John S McCain National Defense Authorization Act for Fiscal Year 2019. Introduced as bi-partisan legislation, ECRA enables increased controls on 'emerging and foundational technologies [that are] essential to the national security of the United States'. It mandates that the President 'shall establish and maintain lists published by the Secretary of Commerce of items that are controlled under [ECRA]'. Controls, in this context, refer to 'export, reexport, or transfer'. Export is defined as 'the shipment or transmission of the item out of the US, including the sending or taking of the item out of the US, in any manner; and the release or transfer of technology or source code relating to the item to a foreign person in the US'. https://www.europarl.europa.eu/cmsdata/210523/EPRS_BRI(2019)644187_EN.pdf accessed 15 September 2023.

[111] Revised National Critical Capabilities Defense Act of 2022.

In October 2022, the US Department of the Treasury published its first enforcement and penalty guidelines regarding mandatory filing requirements, including those related to US businesses critical technologies,[112] and compliance with mitigation agreements, and Assistant Secretary for Investment Security Paul Rosen stated that CFIUS 'will not hesitate to use all of its tools and take enforcement action'.[113]

The 'Creating Helpful Incentives to Produce Semiconductors' (CHIPS) Act,[114] is aimed at reducing US dependence on Chinese critical technologies by implementing an industrial strategy to revitalize domestic manufacturing, create good-paying American jobs, strengthen American supply chains, and accelerate the industries of the future.[115]

Similar to the EU Foreign Subsidies Regulation Regime, the 2023 Omnibus Bill requires merging parties to disclose foreign subsidies from 'foreign entities of concern' that include China. The Federal Trade Commission will work with the Department of Justice, CFIUS, the International Trade Commission, and the Office of the United States Trade Representative to assess whether foreign subsidies raise concerns.

The Revised National Critical Capabilities Defense Act, if it is enacted would create a similar regime to CFIUS with the important differentiation that it would apply to outbound investments. A Committee on National Critical Capabilities would review outbound investment initiatives by US and, very interestingly, foreign entities that engage in 'covered activity' and could require such initiatives to be notified to the Committee in writing at least forty-five days before undertaking the activity.[116] The Committee would assess whether the covered activity raises national security concerns and if it does, it can impose mitigation measures, or recommend to POTUS certain actions, including blocking the envisaged investment.[117]

Finally, in August 2023, President Biden issued a new executive order aiming to constrain the ability of US companies which handle technologies relevant to national security to invest in 'countries of concern'.[118] The order names three such technologies—semiconductors, artificial intelligence, and quantum computing—and identifies China as the only country of concern. The measure had been expected for some time and addresses the widespread concern that the free flow of American capital, financial as well as human, might be helping China enhance its military capabilities. And while the details are still being worked out by the Treasury Department, it's not premature to note

[112] US Department of the Treasury, CFIUS Enforcement and Penalty Guidelines, October 2022

[113] US Department of the Treasury, 'Treasury Releases CFIUS Enforcement and Penalty Guidelines', Press Release, 20 October 2022.

[114] CHIPS Act, Pub Law No 117-167, 2022

[115] Joe Biden, The White House, 'FACT SHEET: CHIPS and Science Act Will Lower Costs, Create Jobs, Strengthen Supply Chains, and Counter China', 9 August 2022.

[116] The EU may take a similar approach, as outlined in the Communication 'Commission Work Programme 2023', COM (2022) 548 final https://commission.europa.eu/system/files/2022-10/Commission%20work%20programme%202023.pdf accessed 15 September 2023.

[117] https://www.cov.com/en/news-and-insights/insights/2022/06/revised-national-critical-capabilities-defense-act-of-2022-proposes-expansive-outbound-investment-review-regime accessed 15 September 2023.

[118] Executive Order 14105 of 9 August 2023 on Addressing United States Investments in Certain National Security Technologies and Products in Countries of Concern, 88 FR54867 https://www.whitehouse.gov/briefing-room/presidential-actions/2023/08/09/executive-order-on-addressing-united-states-investments-in-certain-national-security-technologies-and-products-in-countries-of-concern/ accessed 15 September 2023.

that the order signals a major shift, by setting out to regulate outbound investment, and by relying on broad rules rather than a case-by-case approach.[119] The policy has already proven quite controversial: US-based investors are concerned with the many uncertainties that still surround the order and are figuring out how to adapt to the new rules as seamlessly as possible;[120] meanwhile, China officials have made it clear that they're not impressed with the latest development.[121]

5.4 CFIUS Enforcement Record: Some Seminal Cases

After reviewing the structure, scope of CFIUS, and the procedure in assessing foreign investments, this section will present some of the main CFIUS investigations in order to showcase the approach CFIUS takes in assessing national security concerns and the measures CFIUS has taken to address them.

A review of the CFIUS enforcement record that the chapter will present below, portrays three clear observations. The first is the increasing number of CFIUS notifications over the last few years. The second observation is the increasing severity of concerns that CFIUS has identified, which led to the FIRRMA Act strengthening CFIUS's remit. The third observation is that CFIUS has been approving a larger number of cases with mitigations. In addition, the CFIUS enforcement record illustrates an increased scrutiny of semiconductor deals, particularly for Chinese acquirers, as well as a tendency for more transactions that are notified to CFIUS to require lengthier investigations and mitigation conditions in order to be approved.[122]

5.4.1 *Verio/NTT Communications*

One of the first important cases that CFIUS assessed was in the telecommunications sector. The envisaged transaction was the acquisition of Verio, Inc—a US company that operates websites for businesses and provides Internet services—by NTT Communications—a Japanese telecommunications company.[123] The FBI instigated the lengthy CFIUS review that took place in 2000. CFIUS's intervention led to a fall in Verio's stock price as a result

[119] Farhad Jalinous and others, 'President Biden Orders Establishment of New Program to Restrict US Outbound Investment in Certain Tech Sectors in China' (White & Case, 16 August 2023) https://www.whitecase.com/insight-alert/president-biden-orders-establishment-new-program-restrict-us-outbound-investment accessed 15 September 2023.

[120] Pete Schroeder, Michelle Price, and Carolina Mandl, 'US investors want clarity on Biden's vague curbs on China tech' (Reuters, 27 September 2023) https://www.reuters.com/technology/us-investors-want-clarity-bidens-vague-curbs-china-tech-2023-09-27/ accessed 27 September 2023.

[121] Competition Policy International, 'Governments React to Biden's Executive Order on Chinese Tech' (14 August 2023) https://www.pymnts.com/cpi_posts/governments-react-to-bidens-executive-order-on-chinese-tech/ accessed 15 September 2023.

[122] Vigdor and Gerkin (n 57).

[123] The case also passed through the FTC's jurisdiction, who ordered an early termination of the merger review, given that the 'waiting period' ended on 14 June 2000. https://www.ftc.gov/enforcement/premerger-notification-program/early-termination-notices/20003430 accessed 15 September 2023.

of uncertainty in the market regarding the outcome of the transaction.[124] Concerns had arisen related to the fact that the majority interest of the Japanese government in the acquiring company could grant it access to information regarding surveillance that was being conducted on email and other web-based traffic crossing Verio's computer system.[125] Certain government officials even 'expressed deep reservations that NTT's ownership of Verio's extensive telecommunications would raise foreign espionage risks by giving the Japanese state-controlled company access to US wiretapping activities'.[126]

Notwithstanding the concerns raised by the transaction, CFIUS recommended President Clinton not to intervene in the process.[127] POTUS decided not to intervene, claiming that all national security concerns related to the merger had been resolved.[128]

5.4.2 *SoftBank/Sprint Nextel*

A few years later, in 2013, CFIUS reviewed and approved another transaction in the telecommunications sector. SoftBank filed to acquire Sprint Nextel for $21.6 billion.[129] CFIUS found that there were no unresolved national security issues associated with the proposed acquisition,[130] but required that 'SoftBank and Sprint enter into a National Security Agreement with the Department of Defense, the Department of Homeland Security and the Department of Justice (the "USG Parties")'.[131] The national security issue that was raised was that '[w]ithout US ownership and control of Sprint, SoftBank's reliance on Chinese equipment manufacturers raises significant national security concerns'.[132] The National Security Agreement addressed this problem and comprised, inter alia, that (i) SoftBank and Sprint had to appoint an independent member for Sprint's new board of directors, which had to be approved by the USG Parties; (ii) when Sprint either obtained operational control of Clearwire[133] or consummated its proposed acquisition of Clearwire, USG Parties had a one-time right to require the former to remove certain equipment deployed in the latter's network; and (iii) the USG Parties had the right to review and approve certain network equipment vendors and managed

[124] EveryCRSReport.com, available at <www.everycrsreport.com> accessed 15 September 2023.

[125] ibid.

[126] CNN Money, 'Clinton OK's NTT/Verio Deal' (23 August 2000) <https://money.cnn.com/2000/08/23/deals/ntt_verio/> accessed 15 September 2023.

[127] ibid.

[128] ibid.

[129] Given that the 'waiting period' had ended, the FTC ordered an early termination of the merger review on 6 December 2012. https://www.ftc.gov/enforcement/premerger-notification-program/early-termination-notices/20130159 accessed 15 September 2023.

[130] SEC, Form 8-K dated May 29, 2013, Sprint Nextel Corporation, Commission file number 1-04721, available at <https://www.sec.gov/Archives/edgar/data/101830/000119312513238554/d545797d8k.htm> accessed 15 September 2023.

[131] SEC, Form 8-K dated May 29, 2013, Sprint Nextel Corporation

[132] Michael J de la Merced, *SoftBank and Sprint Win National Security Clearance for Deal* (DealBook, 2013) <https://dealbook.nytimes.com/2013/05/28/softbank-and-sprint-said-to-win-national-security-clearance-for-deal> accessed 15 September 2023.

[133] Clearwire was a telecommunications operator which provided mobile and fixed wireless broadband communications services to retail and wholesale customers in the US, Belgium, and Spain. After being acquired by Sprint Nextel, it changed its name to Sprint Corporation.

services providers of Sprint, as well as of Clearwire, once the former completed its proposed acquisition.[134]

5.4.3 *Smithfield Foods/Shuanghui International Holdings*

Also in 2013, in the food sector, a Hong Kong-based company that owns a variety of businesses in the food and logistics sectors—Shuanghui International Holdings Ltd—proposed to acquire the world's largest hog producer and pork processor, US company Smithfield Foods Inc, for $4.7 bn, in the largest acquisition of a US firm by a Chinese company up to that time.

The significance of this case was due to the public interest arrogated to 'food security'. The National Strategy for Critical Infrastructures and Key Assets identified the latter as a fundamental part of the country's core infrastructure, which makes the assurance of its safety a high priority.[135] Even though the meat industry is not as sensitive as the natural resources one, the transaction still received much criticism from politicians. For instance, while the review by CFIUS was taking place, the US Senate Committee on Agriculture, Nutrition and Forestry held a hearing where several concerns regarding the transaction were raised, including those about the security and safety of food supplies in the country, the potential impact of the transaction on jobs and food prices, and the restrictions on reciprocal investment opportunities into China.[136] Iowa Senator Chuck Grassley expressly pointed out that 'the deal might further consolidate the agriculture industries ... [since] it will be more difficult for market participants to buy pork products with a fair price ... [and] consumers [will have] fewer choices and higher costs.'[137]

The fact that Smithfields was going to be a vertically integrated company not only raised concerns related to the effect of the merger in 'different markets and different parts of the food production infrastructure in ways that might not have been considered in a CFIUS review',[138] but it also provided a 'future competitor with the necessary resources to mount a competitive challenge to other U.S. food producers'.[139] Notwithstanding all of the above, the transaction was approved by CFIUS.

[134] Since Clearwire relied on the Chinese firm Huawei for equipment and for cell tower base stations, SoftBank agreed to remove Huawei as a supplier when the acquisition of Sprint was finalized. See also SEC, Form 8-K dated 29 May 2013, Sprint Nextel Corporation.

[135] The National Strategy for the Physical Protection of Critical Infrastructure and Key Assets, February 2003, at 36.

[136] Francis J Aquila and others, 'Sullivan & Cromwell discusses Shuanghui International's CFIUS Clearance for its Purchase of Smithfield Foods' (CLS Blue Sky Blog, 20 September 2013) https://clsbluesky.law.columbia.edu/2013/09/20/sullivan-cromwell-discusses-shuanghui-internationals-cfius-clearance-for-its-purchase-of-smithfield-foods/ accessed 15 September 2023.

[137] Chanting Chen, 'A National Security Study of the Shuanghui-Smithfield Case' [2017] *DEStech Transactions on Social Science, Education and Human Science* 439 http://dx.doi.org/10.12783/dtssehs/hsmet2017/16534 accessed 15 September 2023.

[138] Congressional Research Service (n 10).

[139] ibid.

5.4.4 *ChemChina/Syngenta*

Chinese state-owned enterprise (SOE) ChemChina proposed to acquire Syngenta—an agrochemical Swiss company—in 2016 for $43 billion, which would lead to the creation of the largest acquisition of a US entity by a Chinese firm. This created turmoil among US lawmakers and groups of farmers, who feared a Chinese SOE being in a position to influence the country's food supply.[140] As US Senator Chuck Grassley, chairman of the US Senate Judiciary Committee[141] stated, '[t]he fact that a state-owned enterprise may have yet another stake in US agriculture is alarming'.[142]

CFIUS cleared the transaction, but Syngenta refused to provide details to the public as to the envisaged requested mitigating measures imposed to the parties, stating it was 'not disclosing the details of the agreement with CFIUS ... [since] mitigation measures are not material to Syngenta's business'.[143] This emphasizes the secrecy of CFIUS' decision making process and assessment, and creates uncertainty amongst foreign investors as well as uncertainty in the legal and business community.

In April 2017 the FTC cleared the acquisition,[144] imposing on the buyer a requirement to divest several pesticides from its portfolio that were manufactured by Adama Agricultural Solutions Ltd, an Israeli-based ChemChina subsidiary. American Vanguard Corp. was set to acquire the pesticides, although the terms of this transaction were not disclosed.[145]

5.4.5 *Chicago Stock Exchange/Chongqing Casin Enterprise Group*

In 2016 CFIUS was asked to intervene once again in a merger where the Chinese government was involved. The case related to the envisaged acquisition of the Chicago Stock Exchange by the Chinese-led consortium Chongqing Casin Enterprise Group for a value of about $22 million.[146] Since the ties between the acquirer and Chinese government officials could grant China's government influence over US equity markets, some Congress Members sent a letter to the US Administration expressing their concerns regarding how such influence could potentially enhance the acquirers' ability

[140] Michael Shields and Greg Roumeliotis, 'U.S. clearance of ChemChina's Syngenta deal removes key hurdle' (Reuters, 22 August 2016) https://www.reuters.com/article/us-syngenta-ag-m-a-chemchina-approval-idUSKCN10X0DS accessed 15 September 2023.

[141] US Senator Chuck Grassley is sponsoring a bill to permanently add the US Department of Agriculture to the CFIUS review process.

[142] Shields and Roumeliotis (n 145).

[143] https://www.reuters.com/article/syngenta-ag-ma-chemchina-measureschina-n/syngenta-says-wont-disclose-details-of-cfius-clearance-any-mitigation-measures-not-material-to-its-business-idUSZ8N135028 accessed 15 September 2023.

[144] https://www.ftc.gov/system/files/documents/cases/1610093_china_national_syngenta_decision_and_order.pdf accessed 15 September 2023.

[145] Schwartz and Mammen (n 37).

[146] Congressional Research Service (n 10) 64.

to manipulate the markets to the advantage of Chinese companies or the Chinese economy.[147]

Although CFIUS approved the merger by the end of 2016, the SEC was requested by the concerned Members of the Congress to block the acquisition.[148] After a lengthy review period, the SEC blocked the transaction, given that the 'lack of information on the would-be buyers threatened the ability to properly monitor the exchange after the deal.'[149]

5.4.6 *Alibaba/MoneyGram*

In the financial services sector, CFIUS decided to block the proposed acquisition of MoneyGram International—worldwide provider of financial services—by Ant Financial, a Chinese company owned by the Alibaba Group, in 2018.[150] In this case CFIUS intervened even though MoneyGram did not deal with particularly sensitive information from a national security perspective, did not operate in the defence sector, nor did it deal with critical infrastructure.

The parties tried to address the concerns that CFIUS had raised in relation to the envisaged transaction, and offered various commitments. Notwithstanding their intention to mitigate national security, approval 'was denied because the Chinese government holds a 15% stake in Ant Financial, and it was feared the data held by MoneyGram could be used by the Chinese government to target activists, journalists, and others'.[151]

5.4.7 *Aleris/Zhongwang*

In the defence industry, Zhongwang USA, an investment firm, cancelled its planned acquisition of US aluminium maker Aleris Corp after failing to receive approval on national security grounds.[152] Aleris produced specialized alloys used by the defence industry. Its research and technology were so critical to US economic and national security interests that the US Commerce Department initiated an investigation to

[147] Rogin, Josh, 'Congress Wary of National Security Implications of Chinese Deal for Chicago Stock Exchange' *Chicago Tribune* (17 February 2016).

[148] On antitrust grounds, on the other hand, the DOJ signed off on November 2016, finding that deal did not violate any antitrust laws. See https://www.houstonchronicle.com/business/article/In-brief-Chinese-group-buying-Chicago-exchange-6811059.php accessed 15 September 2023.

[149] John McCrank, 'SEC blocks Chicago Stock Exchange sale to China-based investors' (Reuters, 16 February 2018) https://www.reuters.com/article/us-sec-chicagostockexchange/sec-blocks-chicago-stock-exchange-sale-to-china-based-investors-idUKKCN1G000H accessed 15 September 2023.

[150] Notwithstanding that the merger obtained antitrust clearance in the US. See http://ir.moneygram.com/news-releases/news-release-details/moneygram-and-ant-financial-enter-amended-merger-agreement.

[151] Olga Torres and Jonathan Creek, 'United States: 2018 Trends For CFIUS Reviews' (Mondaq, 2018), http://www.mondaq.com/unitedstates/x/675886/Inward+Foreign+Investment/2018+Trends+For+CFIUS+Reviews accessed 15 September 2023.

[152] However, it did obtain the antitrust clearance. Once the 'waiting period' ended, the FTC ordered an early termination of the merger review, on 13 October 2016. https://www.ftc.gov/enforcement/premerger-notification-program/early-termination-notices/20161823 accessed 15 September 2023.

determine whether an import of aluminium from either China or any other country could compromise US national security.

After two failed attempts to get CFIUS approval, and since this agency continued to raise national security concerns with the merger, the parties withdrew their request for approval.[153]

5.4.8 *Cree/Infineon*

CFIUS was reluctant to grant clearance on the grounds of national security concerns, in the proposed acquisition by German chipmaker Infineon Technologies AG of US LED lighting maker Cree Inc's Wolfspeed Power unit. Notably, the latter 'makes devices using gallium nitride, a sensitive powdery compound that can have military applications', which has been the reason for 'US blocking acquisitions in the past'.[154] According to a press release issued by Cree Inc, 'Cree and Infineon have been unable to identify alternatives which would address the national security concerns of [CFIUS], and as a result, the proposed transaction will be terminated.'[155]

Although the parties did not specify the nature of the national security concerns, it was argued that the main reason for the CFIUS concerns related to the Chinese ability to obtain Cree technology via the German acquirer.[156] Even though Infineon is based in Germany, it has significant engineering and manufacturing resources in China.[157]

5.4.9 *NavInfo/HERE*

Showing the comprehensive scope of the US national security review process, in 2017 CFIUS withheld another approval to a merger involving Chinese parties. Chinese investors led by digital map and software provider NavInfo Co called off plans to buy a 10 per cent minority stake in the digital mapping service and software company HERE International BV.[158] The latter is a German company whose controlling shareholders are BMW, Daimler AG and VW's Audi business, and is developing high-resolution maps to enable autonomous driving,[159] and has assets in the US, thereby triggering the CFIUS review.

[153] Aleris Reports Second Quarter 2017 Results. https://www.sec.gov/Archives/edgar/data/1518587/000151858717000029/a2q17earningsrelease.htm accessed 15 September 2023.

[154] Christoph Steitz, Liana B Baker, 'Infineon, Cree warn U.S. might block Wolfspeed deal' (Reuters, 2017) https://www.reuters.com/article/us-cree-m-a-infineon-technol-idUSKBN15N2U1 accessed 15 September 2023.

[155] Cree Inc, Press Release, Ex-99.1, Form 8-K, 16 February 2017, SEC Filing.

[156] Steitz and Baker (n 159).

[157] https://www.ledsmagazine.com/leds-ssl-design/article/16700750/cree-cancels-wolfspeed-deal-with-infineon-based-on-us-government-concerns accessed 15 September 2023.

[158] HERE Press Release, 'HERE expands into China; provides update on shareholders', 26 September 2017.

[159] Eric Auchard, 'Chinese drop investment in maps firm HERE after U.S. resistance' (Reuters, 2017) https://www.reuters.com/article/us-china-autos-security-idUSKCN1C11H4 accessed 15 September 2023.

This rejection was characterized as an indication of the Trump Administration's caution toward Chinese acquisitions.[160] US analysts familiar with CFIUS had acknowledged that '[y]ou get the sense that this US administration would just rather have these transactions fall off, just run out the clock on the transactions', which can explain the trend of CFIUS in leaving recent Chinese transactions 'in limbo' instead of explicitly requesting mitigation measures or recommending POTUS to prohibit it.[161]

NavInfo official statements stated that there had been changes in CFIUS's approach after the latest US elections 'at a time when China–US relations have been strained by Mr. Trump's harsh rhetoric against Chinese trade',[162] stating that CFIUS continuously required them to change their application, and revealed that 'even the emails they gave us were very vague, and just mentioned "national security reasons".'[163]

5.4.10 *Ekso Bionics*

In 2019, Ekso Bionic, Inc, a US company manufacturing robotic exoskeletons for medical and industrial use, entered into a joint venture with two Chinese parties in order to develop and service the exoskeleton market in China and in other Asian markets. The main aim of the transaction was to create a global manufacturing centre.

The Department of Defense requested information regarding the export classification of Ekso's products and whether Ekso intended to notify CFIUS of the joint venture. The operation was notified to CFIUS in December 2019 even if Ekso had publicly disclosed that the transaction was outside the CFIUS' jurisdiction. Following its review, CFIUS concluded that its national security concerns regarding the joint venture could not be mitigated and required that Ekso terminate its role with the joint venture.

One may argue that the CFIUS has significantly expanded its jurisdiction in a sense that it only has jurisdiction over acquisition of 'control' over a US business.[164] Indeed, in this case, it appears that the joint venture acquired no assets in the United States. Thus, with this case, US companies engaged in manufacturing R&D may be aware that any equity investment may trigger CFIUS jurisdiction as far as 'critical technologies' are concerned and licensed to the joint venture.

[160] Chris Reiter and David McLaughlin, 'Chinese Bid for Stake in Mapping Firm Denied by U.S. Panel' *Bloomberg* (2017) https://www.bloomberg.com/news/articles/2017-09-26/chinese-bid-for-stake-in-here-maps-denied-by-u-s-security-panel accessed 15 September 2023.

[161] Auchard (n 164).

[162] Yung Yang, 'Chinese bid for mapping company falls at US hurdle' *Financial Times* (2017) https://www.ft.com/content/6f0e519c-a33f-11e7-9e4f-7f5e6a7c98a2 accessed 15 September 2023.

[163] ibid.

[164] Olivier J Borgers, 'Foreign Investment Review, USA', McCarthy Tétrault LLP 2 February 2022.

5.4.11 *Magnachip*

In this operation, Wise Road Capital, a Chinese private equity firm, agreed to indirectly acquire Magnachip Corp, a New York Stock Exchange (NYSE) listed company with operations in Asia, for $1.4 bn. The latter design and manufactures analogue and mixed signal semiconductors.[165]

However, in December 2021, Wise Road Capital and Magnachip Corp announced that they had to abandon their planned merger in the face of CFIUS disapproval.

Even if is it well established that CFIUS views the semidconductor sector as very sensitive from a US national security perspective, here again, the parties believed that a CFIUS review was not mandatory or recommended, because of Magnachip's limited US presence. In this context, they did not notify the transaction. However, a few months later, CFIUS blocked the operation, concluding that the deal posed '"risk to national security" and that the parties failed to adequately mitigate the identified risks'.[166] This case highlights the fact that the Committee pays more attention to non-notified transactions which could present risks for national security.

This case exemplifies the fact that CFIUS has broad discretion in interpreting its rules and is willing to use that discretion as needed in order to review transactions in which it may have a substantive interest. In the case of Magnachip, the transaction involved China and semiconductors, both of which are hot buttons for CFIUS.[167]

5.4.12 Common Themes in CFIUS Enforcement

The case law discussed above allows us to draw the following implications. The scope of intervention of CFIUS covers a wide variety of sectors, including telecommunications, food, financial, defence industry, and technology. In some of the cases analysed, the US government showed concerns that the Chinese government might have attained security and safety advantages, even if in some of the reviewed transactions a Chinese entity was not directly involved, and even if the involved parties did not operate in the defence sector, did not deal with critical infrastructure or with sensitive data, which are the sectors explicitly identified as important for the national security in the US. Although approval has been given in some of the cases discussed above, it seems that another effective strategy used to effectively prohibit transactions, has been the lengthy timelines, which led to parties withdrawing from their intended transactions after waiting for a decision for considerable periods of time. A recurrent theme is the secrecy

[165] Chase D Kaniecki, William S Dawley, Pete Young, 'CFIUS Threatens to Block Magnachip Deal; Shows Willingness to Interpret its Jurisdiction Broadly', Cleary Gottlieb, 15 December 2021.

[166] Damely Perez, Kimberly Shi, 'Back to the Future: The Committee on Foreign Investment in the United States (CFIUS) Scuppers Another Semiconductor Transaction', Clifford Chance, 11 January 2022.

[167] Jonathan Gafni, 'Thoughts on CFIUS's Review of Wise Road-Magnachip', Linklaters, 14 September 2021.

that surrounds the assessment process and its outcomes, in which it seems that neither the parties nor the public are entitled to information on the process, or the considerations that led to the decision, making CFIUS's review unpredictable at times. Finally, we should also emphasize the impact that a CFIUS investigation can have on the share price of both the acquirer and the target. A CFIUS investigation, even more so a protracted one, is likely to have a downward pressure on the share prices, which can lead to transactions failing because of the knock-on impact.

5.5 The Role of the US Presidency

In addition to the de facto prohibitions of CFIUS, due to harsh mitigation conditions or lengthy reviews, as these were assessed before, POTUS has the authority to prohibit transactions. The chapter will turn now to an analysis of the handful of transactions that POTUS has intervened in and prohibited since 1990.

5.5.1 George HW Bush Administration

In his preface to the March 1990 National Security Strategy of the US, President Bush stated that his turn to lead the country happened in an era where 'the international landscape [was] marked by change that [was] breath-taking in its character, dimension, and pace.'[168] The document emphasized that an 'enduring element' of the US strategy 'has been a commitment to a free and open international economic system'[169] and added that the US should 'never forget the vicious circle of protectionism that helped deepen the Great Depression and indirectly fostered the Second World War'.[170] It further noted that the Administration was committed to work with other countries to 'promote the prosperity of the free market system' and to 'reduce barriers that unfairly inhibit international commerce'.[171] It is in this context that the following case should be read.

5.5.1.1 *China National Aero-Technology Import and Export Corp*

President Bush exercised for the first time the power that was granted to the head of state under the so-called Exon-Florio provision (introduced in 1989) to block the foreign purchase of an American company. The case was brought to public attention when he ordered China National Aero-Technology Import and Export Corp (CATIC) to divest itself of all its interest in MAMCO Manufacturing Co. of Seattle (MAMCO), a company which manufactures metal components for commercial aircraft, because

[168] George HW Bush, 'Preface', in White House, *National Security Strategy of the United States* (March 1990) v https://history.defense.gov/Historical-Sources/National-Security-Strategy/ accessed 15 September 2023.

[169] White House, 'National Security Strategy of the United States' (March 1990) 1 https://history.defense.gov/Historical-Sources/National-Security-Strategy/ accessed 15 September 2023.

[170] ibid.

[171] ibid.

there was credible evidence that led him to believe that, in exercising its control of MAMCO, CATIC might take action that would threaten to impair the national security of the US.[172]

Being the very first instance of a US President blocking a transaction, one would expect a detailed account of the reasoning behind the decision. The ambiguous language used by CFIUS, the President, his spokesman and Administration officials, alongside the secrecy that surrounds the CFIUS decision-making process, did not provide sufficient clarity on the circumstances that comprised such 'impairment to the national security'. What we can surmise is that there was a concern 'that CATIC could use MAMCO as a base for intelligence activities in the US, getting access to Boeing plants' and that CATIC might use the 'purchase as a front to penetrate into other, more promising areas of security.'[173] In addition, it was publicly known by that time that CATIC had violated US export regulations in the past, when it purchased General Electric aircraft engines for the Chinese military.[174] So, it seems that the problem with the approach to national security concerns is, in principle, not the absence of in-depth review by the authorities, but rather the lack of clarity to the wider public about the justification for the approach and decision taken.

5.5.2 Barack Obama Administration

The Obama Administration decided to avoid the winding path of interfering with CFIUS's approach, and let most matters be resolved at the Committee level, even though the number of CFIUS filings increased significantly during both of President Obama's terms.[175] Evidence of such an approach was embodied in Congress's request for the US Government Accountability Office (GAO) to prepare a report regarding the CFIUS process, where it specifically noted that the stance towards Chinese acquirers should be based on 'a strategic rather than overt national security threat'.[176] As a consequence of this attitude, only two deals either were called off by the parties (the takeover of Aixtron, a semiconductor company, by FGC, a Chinese firm) or required divestments by Obama (Chinese SOE Ralls Corp, which was required to divest wind farm assets located near a defence facility).

172 Presidential Order, 1 February 1990, Federal Register Vol 55, No 25, 6 February 1990, *Presidential Documents*, 3935–36.

173 Lawrence R Fullerton and Christopher G Griner, Section of Antitrust Law, Drafting Committee, *Working Papers, Review of Foreign Acquisitions under the Exon-Florio Provision* (American Bar Association Section of Antitrust Law, 1992) 152.

174 ibid.

175 For instance, in the period 2012–14, CFIUS reviewed sixty-eight potential acquisitions involving China, whereas in the three years before the FINSA enactment there were only four. Husisian (n 47) 69.

176 ibid.

5.5.2.1 *Ralls Corporation* (2012)

In the middle of Obama's second term election campaign against Republican Mitt Romney, who was accusing him of being soft on China,[177] Obama blocked a privately owned Chinese company from building wind turbines close to a Navy military site in Oregon, due to national security concerns. According to his Order, there was 'credible evidence' that led him to believe that Ralls Corporation might take action that threatened to impair the national security of the US through the exercise of control over the target assets.[178]

According to the Obama Administration, Ralls Corp had been installing Chinese-originated wind turbine generators by Sany Group, and by the time of the deal[179] had four wind farm projects that were within or in the vicinity of restricted air space at a naval weapons system training facility.[180] The company explained that only one of their four wind farms was in the alleged restricted airspace, and that CFIUS never suggested a remedy to address the specific national security issue, ie only divest interest in the particular wind farm that was at the root of the national security concern.[181] Also, they stated that there were other wind farms in the same area operated by foreigners (from Denmark and Germany),[182] which may incite criticism that the prohibition based on the national security concerns was targeted against Chinese acquirers in particular. In response, the Treasury Department accepting to mitigate these criticisms stressed that the President's decision 'was not a precedent for other investments from China or any other country'.[183]

An interesting development in this case was that Ralls filed a lawsuit against CFIUS for 'ordering it to stop all construction and operations at its projects while the government panel completed its investigation and finalized its recommendation to Obama',[184] comprising the only lawsuit against a CFIUS decision until that time. In 2014, Ralls won its appeal, since the DC Circuit accepted that CFIUS had failed to provide Ralls with 'an opportunity to rebut ... unclassified, non-privileged information',[185] hence 'violating Ralls' due process rights'.[186] The settlement between the US government and Ralls in October 2015 was of the utmost surprise and was due to the concern that despite Ralls'

[177] Rachelle Younglai, 'Obama blocks Chinese wind farms in Oregon over security' (Reuters, 28 September 2012) https://www.reuters.com/article/us-usa-china-turbines/obama-blocks-chinese-wind-farms-in-oregon-over-security-idUSBRE88R19220120928 accessed 15 September 2023.

[178] Presidential Order, 28 September 2012.

[179] 'Ralls opted not to undergo CFIUS review before the international investment, as is usually done by foreign companies, but instead waited until after the transaction had closed to voluntarily file with CFIUS.' See Judy Wang, 'Ralls Corp. v. CFIUS: A New e Foreign Direct Investments to the US' (2016) Columbia Journal of Transnational Law 30, 31.

[180] Younglai (n 182).

[181] ibid.

[182] ibid.

[183] ibid.

[184] ibid.

[185] Stephen Heifetz, 'Ralls and U.S. Government Settle Only CFIUS Suit in History' (*Steptoe International Compliance Blog* 14 October 2015) https://www.steptoeinternationalcomplianceblog.com/2015/10/ralls-and-u-s-government-settle-only-cfius-suit-in-history/ accessed 15 September 2023.

[186] ibid.

winning at first instance, there was a much stronger potential for the US government to win if the litigation went further and the DC Circuit judgment was appealed.[187] The extended litigation could in principle have risked CFIUS's remit to impose mitigation conditions for the approval of transactions.

5.5.2.2 *Aixtron*

Even though there was an unexpected tendency present in CFIUS reviews during the Obama Administration towards a positive stance to Chinese acquirers,[188] this changed in the years 2016–17, and the prospects for deals involving Chinese acquirers to be cleared on national security grounds started to deteriorate.[189]

In 2016, the Department of Commerce issued a report stating that the US government was concerned about how focused Chinese acquirers were on closing the gap relative to the US in their capabilities on semiconductors, and emphasising that the US should be more protective of its technology and manufacturing of semiconductors, since they are essential for US national security. In this context, in 2016 Obama prohibited the acquisition of Aixtron SE, a German semiconductor company with a US subsidiary, by a Chinese SOE in Germany, Grand Chip Investment GmbH.[190] Also, CFIUS called off the sale of Philips NV's Lumileds, a manufacturer of lighting components and LEDs (a form of semiconductor), to a consortium that included several Chinese firms.[191] In another case in the semiconductor sector, Xiamen San'an Integrated Circuit Co, Ltd had to abandon a planned merger with GCS Holdings, which would have brought Global Communications Semiconductors, LLC (GCS Holdings' wholly owned subsidiary in the US) into the San'an Group of companies, and a US-based semiconductor chip manufacturer, Fairchild Semiconductor International, had to reject an acquisition offer from two Chinese firms (China Resources Microelectronics Ltd and Hua Capital Management Co, Ltd) due to CFIUS concerns.[192]

Obama's decision to block the Aixtron deal (Fujian Grand Chip's takeover of the German company and its US subsidiaries[193]) came amidst expectations that his successor, Donald Trump, might adopt an even more hostile attitude towards Chinese investment in the US, with both Democrats and Republicans in Congress calling for a broadening of CFIUS's mandate.[194] Notably, by the time of the Aixtron decision, CFIUS was focused on the scrutiny of (i) investments in the high-tech sector, particularly in the market for semiconductors (especially where the company's technology

[187] 'The US Government's position on the merits ... seemingly was undented. Neither the district court nor the appeals court indicated any interest in second-guessing the Executive Branch's national security views. With a little more give on "process," it appeared the US Government might ultimately prevail in forcing divestment without compensating Ralls.' See Heifetz (n 186).

[188] Husisian (n 47) 69.

[189] Wilson Sonsini Goodrich & Rosati (n 100).

[190] ibid.

[191] ibid.

[192] ibid.

[193] Presidential Order, 2 December 2016.

[194] Schwartz and Mammen (n 37).

has military applications) and (ii) investments involving Chinese acquirers (it is noteworthy that the three presidential actions under CFIUS so far had involved Chinese acquirers).[195]

Alongside the German authorities, the US national security authorities (ie CFIUS) had jurisdiction to review the transaction, because of Aixtron's US subsidiary, Aixtron, Inc. On November 2016, Aixtron stated publicly that CFIUS had informed the parties of their national security concerns regarding the envisaged transaction, and had advised the parties to abandon the deal under the threat of referring the case to President Obama with a recommendation to prohibit the transaction.[196] It is noteworthy that the CFIUS order included any assets of Aixtron not owned by the US business, but that could be within the US, and could also include assets outside the US that are used in the US business's activities.[197]

POTUS adopted the recommendation of CFIUS,[198] to which China's Foreign Ministry commented that there were '"groundless accusations" against Chinese firms by the United States and lamented the "politicization" of what it said was a commercial takeover'.[199] Despite the national security risks being 'groundless' according to China's Foreign Ministry, and the fact that and 'President Obama's Executive Order does not elaborate on specific national security concerns',[200] there was indeed a justification provided for the prohibition. The US Department of the Treasury issued a statement that:

> the national security risk posed by the transaction relates, among other things, to the military applications of the overall technical body of knowledge and experience of Aixtron, a producer and innovator of semiconductor manufacturing equipment and technology, and the contribution of Aixtron's US business to that body of knowledge and experience.[201]

The statement made reference to Aixtron's business as a manufacturer of 'metal-Organic Chemical Vapor Deposition (MOCVD) systems used to build compound semiconductor materials'.[202] Aixtron also manufactures gallium nitride, which has military applications, and was used 'to upgrade US and foreign-owned patriot missile defense systems'.[203] Thus,

[195] Until December 2019.

[196] Michael T Gershberg and Justin A Schenck, 'President Obama Blocks Chinese Acquisition of Semiconductor Manufacturer Aixtron' (Fried Frank International Trade and Investment Alert, 12 August 2016) https://www.friedfrank.com/siteFiles/Publications/FINAL%20-12-8-2016-ITI%20Alert-President%20Obama%20Blocks%20Chinese%20Acquisition%20of%20Semiconductor1.pdf accessed 15 September 2023.

[197] Gershberg and Schenck (n 201) 2.

[198] David McLaughlin, 'Obama Blocks Chinese Takeover of Aixtron as U.S. Security Risk' (Bloomberg, 2016) https://www.bloomberg.com/news/articles/2016-12-02/obama-blocks-chinese-takeover-of-aixtron-as-u-s-security-risk accessed 15 September 2023.

[199] Maria Sheahan, 'China's Fujian drops Aixtron bid after Obama blocks deal' (Reuters, 2016) https://www.reuters.com/article/us-aixtron-m-a-fujian/chinas-fujian-drops-aixtron-bid-after-obama-blocks-deal-idUSKBN13X16H accessed 15 September 2023.

[200] Gershberg and Schenck (n 201) 2.

[201] ibid.

[202] ibid.

[203] Maria Sheahan, 'China's Fujian drops Aixtron bid after Obama blocks deal' (Reuters, 2016)

CFIUS was concerned about the transfer of know-how to China.[204] Furthermore, Obama went beyond the usual approach that US Presidents have taken when prohibiting a transaction, and required the acquirer through its Executive Order to:

> fully and permanently abandon the proposed acquisition of not just the US business [but also] any asset of Aixtron or Aixtron, Inc. used in, or owned for the use in or benefit of, the activities in interstate commerce in the US of Aixtron, Inc., including without limitation any interest in any patents issued by, and any interest in any patent applications pending with, the United States Patent and Trademark Office.[205]

The increasing level of Chinese investment in the US, with particular interest in the US semiconductor industry, keeps raising national security concerns by CFIUS and has led to tougher scrutiny. The trend is for companies to reject offers from Chinese investors, since the results of CFIUS's analyses now are more likely to be averse to such transactions. For instance, this was the case for Fairchild Semiconductor International, a US-based semiconductor chip manufacturer, who rejected an acquisition offer from Chinese investors in 2016[206] 'because of what it said was an "unacceptable level of risk" that CFIUS would reject the deal'.[207]

5.5.3 Donald Trump Administration

During his presidential campaign, President Trump frequently stated that incoming FDIs should be viewed through a national security prism, and he appeared to focus particularly on Chinese investors, who he also accused of taking US employees' jobs.[208] These views were consistent with those of Republicans in Congress, who were looking forward to reinforcing US government review of transactions with a potential national security impact on the US.[209] During his campaign there were 'indications that the new administration will favour an informal "reciprocity" test for foreign investment—i.e. that countries that do not allow a comparable investment in the same sector would not see CFIUS approvals.'[210] These comments have particular importance for China, since it is a country that usually restricts investments from US investors.[211]

204 Gershberg and Schenck (n 201) 2.
205 ibid.
206 Diane Bartz and Liana B Baker, 'Fairchild rejects Chinese offer on U.S. regulatory fears' https://www.reuters.com/article/us-fairchild-semico-m-a/fairchild-rejects-chinese-offer-on-u-s-regulatory-fears-idUSKCN0VP1O8 accessed 15 September 2023.
207 Gershberg and Schenck (n 201) 2.
208 Ana Swanson, 'Trump Blocks China-Backed Bid to Buy U.S. Chip Maker' (The New York Times, 13 September 2017) https://www.nytimes.com/2017/09/13/business/trump-lattice-semiconductor-china.html accessed 15 September 2023.
209 Husisian (n 47) 69.
210 ibid.
211 'Roughly two dozen sectors in China—construction, mining, banking, insurance, and so on—remain effectively off-limits to American investment, because the Chinese government protects its domestic companies through regulations and financial subsidies. Even in sectors that technically allow foreign investment,

The increasing prominence of CFIUS as a potential obstacle that, combined with the US investment climate, was leading to an increased number of CFIUS investigations. Prohibitions of transactions were infrequent (although this started to change slightly for Chinese investments in US technology), and concerns about certain countries' access to bulk data on US citizens were more prevalent.[212] The President on the one hand publicly reaffirmed his support for inward foreign investment, and on the other also expressed support for FIRRMA, which expanded CFIUS's jurisdiction, and expanded the criteria by which CFIUS assesses national security concerns.[213] However, Wolin explains that 'there has been further development of the idea that transactions that originate in certain geographies or that involve certain kinds of technology will be scrutinized very carefully ... those perspectives began during the Obama Administration'.[214] So what Trump proposes 'is not a sea change. It is more of a movement further down that path.'[215]

5.5.3.1 *Lattice Semiconductor*

In a sector where US government has become increasingly wary of US technology firms being acquired by Chinese entities,[216] and in a move that could signal more aggressive scrutiny of China's investors' deal-making ambitions,[217] Trump blocked Chinese private equity firm Canyon Bridge Capital Partners LLC from purchasing Lattice Semiconductor Corp, a US-based company that manufactures programmable logic chips used in communications, computing, as well as industrial and military applications, on grounds of national security.[218]

Regardless of Lattice's efforts to address any outstanding national security concerns, the Administration was not convinced.[219] The White House explained that it prevented the envisaged acquisition on the one hand because the US government relied on the target company's products (the semiconductor industry is a vital one for the US), and on the other given the concerns raised over the acquirer's close ties to China, since the investment group included China Venture Capital Fund Corporation, which was

discriminatory industrial policies tilt the playing field in favor of Chinese firms. Until this changes, Washington would be justified—even obligated—to limit Chinese investment in the U.S. market.' See Jennifer M Harris, 'Writing New Rules for the U.S.-China Investment Relationship' (Council on Foreign Relations, 2017), 1 available at https://www.cfr.org/sites/default/files/report_pdf/Discussion_Paper_Harris_China_OR.pdf accessed 15 September 2023. Also see Covington & Burling LLP, 'CFIUS and Foreign Direct Investment Under President Donald Trump' (2016) https://www.cov.com/-/media/files/corporate/publications/2016/11/cfius_and_foreign_direct_investment_under_president_donald_trump.pdf accessed 15 September 2023.

212 Wilson Sonsini Goodrich & Rosati (n 100).

213 Wolin (n 26).

214 'For example, the Obama Commerce Department put out a report in 2016 saying the US government was quite concerned about the extent to which the Chinese government was focused on closing the gap relative to the US in their basic set of capabilities around semiconductors, essentially saying the US ought to be more protective of its technology and manufacturing advantage in semiconductors, which can be relevant to national security. This line of thinking has to some extent further intensified, in terms of the range of sensitive technologies and capabilities that give the US pause.' (ibid).

215 ibid.

216 Former US President Obama released a report prior to leaving office in January that warned that China's ambitious push to expand its domestic chip production could threaten the semiconductor industry.

217 Swanson (n 213).

218 Presidential Order, 13 September 2017.

219 Swanson (n 213).

owned by state-backed entities.[220] In particular, Mnuchin highlighted four national security concerns of the transaction: (i) the potential transfer of Lattice's intellectual property to Canyon Bridge; (ii) the role of the Chinese government in the transaction; (iii) the importance of the semiconductor supply chain to the US government; and (iv) the US government's use of Lattice products.[221] As shown, this prohibition, the fourth one ever issued by a US President under the Exon-Florio amendment, emphasizes the US government's significant concerns about Chinese investment in the US, especially in technology manufacturers.[222]

5.5.3.2 *Qualcomm*

In a year where the US blocked the $1.2 bn sale of money transfer firm MoneyGram to China's Ant Financial, the digital payments arm of Alibaba,[223] and Trump announced that he would implement tariffs on foreign steel and aluminium companies in order to promote the manufacturing of those commodities in the US,[224] the President blocked a planned takeover of chipmaker Qualcomm by Singapore-based rival Broadcom[225] on grounds of national security.[226]

Despite his Executive Order invoking 'credible evidence' that the proposed $140bn deal threatened to impair the national security of the US,[227] with no further details provided, commentators opined that 'there were concerns the takeover could have led to China pulling ahead in the development of 5G wireless technology [since] [t]he deal would have been the biggest technology sector takeover on record.'[228] Notably, Qualcomm's takeover would have created the world's third-largest maker of microchips, behind Intel and Samsung. Although there were arguments that this was an attempt by President Trump to 'sharpen his nationalist knife',[229] a deal between Qualcomm and Broadcom could have given Huawei the opportunity to solidify its position in the market—a development US politicians wished to prevent, given their

[220] ibid.

[221] Michael Gershberg and Justin Schenck, 'President Trump Blocks Chinese Acquisition of Lattice Semiconductor Corporation' (Harvard Law School Forum on Corporate Governance and Financial Regulation, 2017) https://corpgov.law.harvard.edu/2017/09/24/president-trump-blocks-chinese-acquisition-of-lattice-semiconductor-corporation/ accessed 15 September 2023.

[222] John B Bellinger, Charles A Blanchard III, Ronald D Lee, and others, *New Presidential Order Blocking Chinese Acquisition of Semiconductor Firm Flags a Trend of Heightened CFIUS Review of Chinese Investments* (Arnold & Porter, 2017) https://www.arnoldporter.com/en/perspectives/publications/2017/09/new-presidential-order-blocking accessed 15 September 2023.

[223] CFIUS requested mitigation measures that the parties were unwilling to offer. <https://www.bbc.co.uk/news/business-42549537> accessed 15 September 2023.

[224] Matthew Renda, 'Trump Blocks Tech Company Merger Citing National Security' (Courthouse News Service, 2018) https://www.courthousenews.com/trump-blocks-tech-company-merger-citing-national-security/ accessed 15 September 2023.

[225] Broadcom had grown through acquisitions, but was deemed to be weaker on R&D. BBC, 'Trump blocks Broadcom's bid for Qualcomm on security grounds' (BBC 2018) https://www.bbc.co.uk/news/business-43380893 accessed 15 September 2023.

[226] Presidential Order, 12 March 2018.

[227] BBC (n 226).

[228] ibid.

[229] James Moore, 'Trump blocks $140bn tech mega merger. An example of nasty nationalism or simple pragmatism? It might be both' *Independent* (2018) https://www.independent.co.uk/news/business/comment/donald-trump-qualcomm-broadcom-merger-block-protectionism-regulation-us-a8253306.html.

on-going security concerns around Chinese telecom firms doing business with US carriers.[230] In fact, it was stated by sources close to CFIUS that the US military was concerned that within ten years, Huawei 'would essentially be a dominant player in all of these technologies', which would leave the American carriers with no choice but to buy Huawei equipment.[231] This case arose in a context where 5G is considered a crucial asset[232] for the US economy.[233]

As has been common practice in Executive Orders, the US President did not provide a detailed rationale for his decision. However, a letter from the Treasury Department calling for a review of the transaction explained that the Administration was concerned about Broadcom's relationships with other foreign companies, and 'strongly hinted that those companies of interest are based in China'.[234] The letter also highlighted that Broadcom had reduced spending on R&D in the businesses it acquires, a practice that would most likely make Qualcomm less innovative. This envisaged scenario would in turn be beneficial to Chinese businesses in terms of the development of the technology for the next generation of mobile phones (5G).[235]

In addition to national security concerns, this envisaged takeover raised serious antitrust concerns as well.[236] In addition to the weakening on innovation, the transaction could possibly lead to competition harm as in a more concentrated market firms may have greater incentives to raise prices on existing products as well as reduce product choice or quality.

5.5.3.3 *StayNTouch, Inc*

By executive order of 6 March 2020, President Trump prohibited Beijing Shiji Information Technology Co Ltd (and its wholly owned subsidiary Shiji (Hong Kong) Ltd, 'Beijing Shiji'), a Chinese public company, from acquiring any ownership in StayNTouch, Inc or any of StayNTouch's assets. The latter develops technology platforms used by hotels. On the other hand, Shiji Group is specialized on software for hotels, restaurants, and retail stores.

This Executive Order followed a seven-month review initiated by CFIUS and came more than a year after the acquisition.[237] It suggested that there was credible evidence that the purchaser 'might take action that threatens to impair the national security of

[230] BBC (n 226).

[231] Reuters, 'President Trump halts Broadcom takeover of Qualcomm' (Reuters, 2018) https://www.reuters.com/article/us-qualcomm-m-a-broadcom-merger/president-trump-halts-broadcom-takeover-of-qualcomm-idUSKCN1GO1Q4 accessed 15 September 2023.

[232] According to Mario Morales, vice-president of enabling technologies and semiconductors at global research firm IDC.

[233] BBC (n 226). The US government is dependent on Qualcomm and its role in developing communications systems for the military. The Editorial Board, 'Trump Was Right to Block a Merger' *The New York Times* (2018) https://www.nytimes.com/2018/03/14/opinion/trump-qualcomm-merger.html accessed 15 September 2023.

[234] The Editorial Board (n 234).

[235] ibid.

[236] In fact, according to US research company Gartner, 'if the Broadcom-Qualcomm merger had gone through, just three companies — Samsung, Intel and Broadcom — would have controlled more than 36 per cent of the global market for chips' (ibid).

[237] Olivier J Borgers, 'Foreign Investmen Review, USA', McCarthy Tétrault LLP 2 February 2022.

the United States',[238] without specifying the threat. It ordered the Chinese company to divest itself of StayNTouch and its assets, including customer data, within 120 days.[239]

5.5.3.4 *Infineon*

US national security officials had recommended that President Donald Trump block a proposed $10 bn deal by a German chipmaker, Infineon Technologies AG, to buy Cypress Semiconductor Corp. Indeed, according to officials, this operation might have posed a risk to national security, but no clear explanations were given.[240] However, on 9 March 2020, the two parties announced that CFIUS had cleared the operation.

This case highlights the intensifying concerns about foreign investment in the semiconductor sector. Indeed, Infineon is based in a NATO ally (Germany), but CFIUS had been scrutinizing the transaction for more than eight months.[241] Nevertheless, the Infineon case proves that the United States is still open to foreign investment, even in a very sensitive sector such as semiconductors.

5.5.4 Joe Biden Administration

For the first year since 2016, no Presidential decisions were issued in 2021.[242] However, President Biden went on to sign an Executive Order to ensure robust reviews of evolving national security risks by the Committee on Foreign Investment in the United States. This is the first-ever presidential directive defining national security factors that the CFIUS must consider when reviewing and evaluating transactions.[243]

5.5.5 Common Themes in the Practice of US Presidents

From the abovementioned analysis of cases blocked by US Presidents, four conclusions can be drawn. First, even if the number of occasions where a US President has exercised their right to block a transaction has been limited, US Presidents are increasingly willing to invoke the extraordinary authority granted by Exon-Florio to block or reverse foreign investment for national security reasons.[244] Second, a common theme

[238] Donald Trump, Order Regarding the Acquisition of Stayntouch, Inc. by Beijing Shiji Information Technology Co., Ltd., 6 March 2020.

[239] ibid.

[240] Saleha Mohsin, David McLaughlin, Jenny Leonard, 'Trump Advised to Halt Infineon Deal Amid China Security Risk', Bloomberg UK, 6 March 2020.

[241] Harry Clark, 'President Trump Orders Divestment of U.S. Company; CFIUS Clears Semiconductor Transaction', Orrick, 13 March 2020.

[242] CFIUS, Annual Report CY 2021 (n 55).

[243] Farhad Jalinous, Karalyn Mildorf, Keith Schomig, and others, 'Biden Issues First-Ever Presidential Directive Defining National Security Factors for CFIUS to Consider in Evaluating Transactions', White & Case website, 19 September 2022.

[244] Harry Clark, 'President Trump Orders Divestment of U.S. Company; CFIUS Clears Semiconductor Transaction', Orrick, 13 March 2020.

is the lack of detailed information about the reasons that supported each prohibition. Third, the second term of Obama's Administration signalled an increase in the US government's concern about transactions that have a direct or indirect Chinese government nexus. Fourth, during President Trump's Administration the national security concerns in relation to acquirers representing Chinese interests seem to have become more prevalent.

5.6 National Security Concerns Related to State-Owned Enterprises (SOEs)

One of the recurring national security concerns raised by CFIUS assessments is the threat imposed by 'the growing international presence and investment activity of firms that are owned or controlled by foreign governments'.[245] As opposed to ten years ago, where only one or two SOEs were found 'at the top of the league table',[246] they now 'account for over a fifth of the world's largest enterprises'.[247]

Notably, since China is the world's second-largest economy after the US,[248] particular focus has been placed on Chinese SOEs' activities. If one considers China's holdings of foreign exchange reserves (amounting to $3.061 trillion in March 2020),[249] this 'enable[s] China to expand its foreign investments by acquiring companies and other assets abroad'.[250] China has acquired 'foreign technologies and know-how to advance these objectives as well as to further its national security interests',[251] while exploiting investment opportunities in different countries.

However, from the standpoint of the recipient country of the incoming FDI, China's presence 'may also entail risks [which] may embrace broad national interests, sensitive and newly emergent technologies, and the natural resources of countries receiving China's investments'.[252] Because of such risks, SOEs' activities predictably find resistance in the US, for political, national, security, and economic reasons.[253] Evidence of this is the view of former White House chief strategist Stephen K Bannon, who stated in colloquial language in a prologue to Wolff's book of 2018 that:

[245] Congressional Research Service (n 10) 33. The growth has been such that, by 2010–11, from the Forbes Global 2000 list of the world's largest 2000 public companies, 204 were identified as majority SOEs in that business year, with ownership spread across thirty-seven different countries. China lead the list with seventy SOEs. Przemyslaw Kowalski and others, 'State-Owned Enterprises: Trade Effects and Policy Implications', OECD Trade Policy Paper No 147 (2013) 6.

[246] OECD, *Ownership and Governance of State-Owned Enterprises: A Compendium of National Practices* (2018) 4.

[247] Ibid.

[248] KL Alex Lau, Angus Young, and YN Hong, 'Merger Control in China under the Anti-Monopoly Law: A Competition Regime in Transition' (2016) 37(9) Competition Law 285, 285.

[249] CGTN, 'China's foreign exchange reserves remain stable' (8 July 2019) https://news.cgtn.com/news/2019-07-08/China-s-foreign-exchange-reserves-remain-stable-Ian6GuDliE/index.html accessed 15 September 2023.

[250] Charles Wolf, Jr, and others, *China's Expanding Role in Global Mergers and Acquisitions Markets* (RAND, 2011) xi.

[251] ibid 27.

[252] ibid 2.

[253] ibid 5.

> China's everything. Nothing else matters. We don't get China right; we don't get anything right. This whole thing is very simple. China is where Nazi Germany was in 1929 to 1930. The Chinese, like the Germans, are the most rational people in the world, until they're not. And they're gonna flip like Germany in the thirties. You're going to have a hypernationalist state, and once that happens you can't put the genie back in the bottle.[254]

In the US, Republicans in Congress have demanded that the GAO determines whether CFIUS reviews 'have effectively kept pace with the growing scope of foreign acquisitions in strategically important sectors in the US',[255] while specifically singling out Chinese and Russian SOEs' investments as causes of concern.[256]

We discuss below some important transactions that involve Chinese SOEs in order to assess how CFIUS has approached them.

5.6.1 *Lenovo/IBM*

In 2005, and despite some national security concerns, CFIUS approved the acquisition of IBM's personal computing division by LENOVO, a partially state-controlled company.[257] Moran has asserted that possible threats, such as the leakage of sensitive technology, infiltration, espionage, and disruption were unlikely to arise given the characteristics of the relevant market, which can explain CFIUS's approach.[258]

5.6.2 *CNOOC/Unocal* (2005)

In June 2005, the Chinese Offshore Oil Corp (CNOOC) bid for US oil company Unocal. The latter's total production was less than 1 per cent of domestic oil consumption, and 70 per cent of its assets were gas reserves in Asia.[259] Congress immediately opposed the deal, arguing, inter alia, that China would gain access to 'cavitation' technology—a process where oil is drilled for in deep water—enabling the Chinese state 'to do nuclear tests underground and to mask them so we would not ever be able to detect them'.[260] Such opposition resulted in a non-binding resolution and a call for an instant thorough

254 Michael Wolff, *Fire and Fury* (Little Brown 2018), Prologue.

255 Husisian (n 47) 71.

256 See letter from Robert Pittenger to Hon Gene L Dodaro (15 September 2016) 1.

257 Arik Hesseldahl, 'Lenovo's Global Rise Began With IBM PC Deal a Decade Ago', *Vox* (30 January 2014) <https://www.vox.com/2014/1/30/11622894/lenovos-global-rise-began-with-ibm-pc-deal-a-decade-ago> accessed 15 September 2023.

258 Theodore H Moran, 'Toward a Multilateral Framework for Identifying National Security Threats Posed by Foreign Acquisitions: With Special Reference To Chinese Acquisitions in the United States, Canada, and Australia' (2014) 7(1) China Economic Journal 44.

259 Genevieve Ding, 'The CNOOC Bid for Unocal and US National Security: Was the Political Outcry in Congress Justified?' <https://sites.duke.edu/djepapers/files/2016/10/Ding.pdf> accessed 15 September 2023.

260 House of Representatives Democratic Leader Nancy Pelosi, 30 June 2005, Pelosi Statement on Amendment to Block Chinese Bid to Acquire Unocal <http://www.house.gov/pelosi/press/releases/June05/unocal.html> accessed 7 April 2020.

review of the possible transaction by CFIUS, given that a Chinese state-owned energy company exercising control of critical US energy infrastructure and energy production capacity could threaten US national security.[261] After concerns that the transaction would not receive approval, CNOOC withdrew its bid.[262]

This case represents another example of a transaction that was withdrawn in light of a possible regulatory roadblock by CFIUS. While there is no public evidence to underpin any of the political, economic, or national interest concerns shown by Congress, the reality is that at the time of the proposal, twenty-one countries had oil for export in volumes greater than Unocal's entire production.[263] In addition, there was significant advancement in discovery and production of oil that would have had a positive impact in energy markets (US included) and global energy consumers.[264] In short, it may be the case that Congress overstated the national security threats posed by the takeover, and its position portrayed a protectionist stance towards Chinese SOEs.

5.6.3 *Bain/3Com-Huawei Technologies Co*

In 2007, Bain Capital Partners LLC, an international private investment firm, intended to buy 3Com, a leading US hardware and software network company, for $2.2 bn. At the time, 3Com had already formed a joint venture with Huawei in China—H3C. Huawei would acquire a 16.5 per cent minority shareholding on 3Com as well.[265] In March 2008, Bain abandoned the deal as a result of opposition due to national security concerns. The possible threats consisted of (i) the interest that Huawei would acquire (16.5 per cent), which seemed, however, insufficient to enable the Chinese government to influence how 3Com goods and services were offered; (ii) leakage of sensitive technologies or other capabilities to Chinese users that they would not otherwise have access to, even though many of the products produced by 3Com were already produced in China; and, (iii) potential capability for infiltration, surveillance, or sabotage of US interests.[266]

These transactions involving SOEs reveal the approach of the US government to transactions involving US assets by entities that are owned directly or indirectly by the Chinese government. The US approach has led to the withdrawal of two transactions due to the hostility shown by the US government grounded on national security concerns.

261 US Congress, House 2005, H RES 344 <https://www.congress.gov/bill/109th-congress/house-resolution/344> accessed 15 September 2023.
262 Ding (n 260) 22.
263 Moran (n 259) 45.
264 ibid.
265 ibid 46.
266 ibid 47.

5.7 Conclusion

This chapter examines the assessment of national security in assessing M&A transactions in the US. The chapter focused on the national security concerns, looking at a spectrum of CFIUS's decisions in diverse industries including telecommunications, food, financial, defence industry, and technology. Among the cases, the US government has shown its determination to safeguard US industries from risks to US national security raised by acquisitions of US domestic assets by foreign acquirers. Overall, intervention occurs in a minority of cases, with no surprising trends being identified.

In the assessment of the CFIUS regime, the chapter discussed how the scope of the agency has expanded to the point where now almost any foreign person or entity is potentially within its regulatory reach. In spite of its increased powers, the transparency of the process appears to remain restricted, a shortfall that has been subject to criticism among the parties and scholars. Some M&A transactions have been blocked, while others have been withdrawn by the parties after clear signs of opposition combined with long waiting assessment periods. This chapter has shown that even if the number of transactions that have been blocked remains relatively low, the assessment process would be improved if the parties and the public were provided with more detailed perspective of the CFIUS rationale for its decisions. Finally, the chapter illustrated the role of US Presidents in assessing the national security implications of mergers, and it concluded by focusing on the treatment of deals which involved SOEs, mostly of Chinese origin. More transparency, accountability, and efficiency in the national security assessment process, with the appropriate caveats for confidentiality, would be advisable and welcome.

In an interesting comment published in a widely circulated newspaper in China (*China Daily*) the commentator states that:

> national security and economic security have become the most abused terms since the Donald Trump administration unleashed various protectionist and unilateral trade measures. The Trump administration even called German cars a national security threat to the US, triggering an outcry in Germany.[267]

This denotes the polemic nature of national security assessment amidst a worsening geopolitical environment.

[267] Chen Weihua, 'EU's economic security strategy misguided and self-damaging' *China Daily* (30 June 2023) https://www.chinadaily.com.cn/a/202306/30/WS649e0d79a310bf3a75d6c6a9.html accessed 15 September 2023.

6
National Security and FDI Screening in China

6.1 Introduction

When it comes to merger control under competition law or anti-monopoly law, a competition authority should only take competition elements into account.[1] In terms of statutory merger control rules, there is no significant difference between China and other jurisdictions. In practice, however, it is not uncommon for the Chinese competition authority to diverge from its overseas counterparts when the same transaction is under parallel review. As the Chinese competition regime has raised controversy in the past, including concerns of merger control being influenced by industrial policy, section 6.2 sheds light on whether this controversy is justified.

As merger control does not exist in a competition legal vacuum and, in practice, is also affected by non-competition elements, such as industrial policy and national security, the influence of industrial policy in Chinese merger control is not as widespread as some commentators in academia and/or practice have claimed. The introduction of the fair competition review system (FCRS) in 2016 implies that it would be less likely for the Chinese competition authority to be distracted by industrial policy in its merger review in the future, as will be elaborated in section 6.3, which sets out the legal framework of China's national security review, and looks at the latest developments against the backdrop of the platform economy and an increasingly complicated geopolitical environment.

Section 6.4 explores the national security review. This section discusses how the relationship between the anti-monopoly review and national security review of a transaction evolved from integration to separation in China. Section 6.5 concludes the chapter.

[1] This chapter is co-authored with Yajie Gao, PhD in law, Adviser (Advisory and International Affairs), Hong Kong Competition Commission (HKCC), China; gracegao@compcomm.hk. The opinions expressed in this publication are Yajie Gao's own and do not purport to reflect the views of the HKCC or any of the HKCC's members. Since the Chinese Mainland and Hong Kong Special Administrative Region are two different jurisdictions in competition law, 'China' in this chapter refers to the Chinese Mainland.

6.2 Overview of Merger Control in China

6.2.1 Definition of a 'Merger' and Substantive Competition Analysis in Terms of Statutory Law

In China, a transaction[2] should be notified to the competition authority if a change of control occurs on a lasting basis,[3] which could be a merger, an acquisition, or the establishment of a joint venture.[4] The Chinese competition authority considers similar elements in the substantive competition analysis to those taken into account by other jurisdictions, such as the European Commission, including market share, concentration level, market entry, and expansion (barrier), buyer power, and efficiency.[5] Nevertheless, as of July 2023, the Chinese competition authority has not provided any systematic guidance on which theories of harm (ToHs) could be established for a merger, be it horizontal or non-horizontal.

The State Administration for Market Regulation (SAMR) is entitled to intervene as long as it believes that a merger has or may have competition elimination or restriction effects.[6] Such a substantive merger control mechanism leads to significant uncertainty for stakeholders. The Chinese competition authority's merger control practice occasionally diverges from those of overseas counterparts to the detriment of predictability and transparency. The divergence is reflected not only in applying ToHs and the remedies but also with regard to whether a particular business arrangement constitutes a merger in competition law.

6.2.2 Divergence of China's Practice from Other Jurisdictions—*Maersk/MSC Mediterranean Shipping/CMA CGM* as an Example

The divergence between China and other jurisdictions can be illustrated by referencing a concrete example, namely the Ministry of Commerce (MOFCOM)'s[7] decision in *Maersk/MSC Mediterranean Shipping/CMA CGM*. In June 2014, MOFCOM declared it would block the network centre[8] jointly established by AP Møller-Maersk A/S, MSC Mediterranean Shipping Company SA, and CMA CGM SA,[9] the second prohibited

[2] In this chapter, 'transaction', 'merger', 'acquisition', and 'M&A' are used interchangeably, to all of which merger control rules apply.

[3] Another condition for the merging parties to sustain notification obligations is that the transaction has met the notification threshold.

[4] Standing Committee of the National People's Congress (NPCSC), Anti-Monopoly Law of the PRC (AML), effective as of 1 August 2008 and amended in June 2022, art 25.

[5] AML, art 33. Please note that 'business operator' is the equivalent of 'undertaking' in Chinese anti-monopoly law.

[6] AML, art 34.

[7] MOFCOM was one of the three predecessors of the State Administration for Market Regulation (SAMR), which was in charge of merger control.

[8] The phrase used by MOFCOM is '网络中心'.

[9] *Maersk/MSC Mediterranean Shipping/CMA CGM* MOFCOM Block Notice [2014] No 46 of 17 June 2014 http://fldj.mofcom.gov.cn/article/ztxx/201406/20140600628586.shtml accessed 15 September 2023商务部公

case[10] since the Anti-Monopoly Law of the PRC came into effect in 2008 (2008 AML).[11] MOFCOM observed that the network centre, or the close joint venture,[12] constituted a merger under China's anti-monopoly law. Having acknowledged the rationality of the traditional loose shipping alliance,[13] MOFCOM explained why, in this case, it considered the network centre a merger. MOFCOM differentiated the close joint venture in this case from the traditional shipping alliance based on factors such as cooperation form,[14] operation procedure,[15] expense allocation,[16] sales of unused cargo space,[17] and suspension of shipping service.[18]

MOFCOM was concerned that establishing the network centre would eliminate or restrict competition in the Asia-Europe Route container liner shipping service market.[19] More specifically, MOFCOM observed that the transaction would strengthen the merged entity's controlling power over the market, significantly increase the market concentration level, and further raise entry barriers, to the detriment of rivals, consignors, port operators, and other stakeholders.[20]

Even under international pressure from regulators to block the controversial shipping alliance,[21] the US Federal Maritime Commission (FMC)[22] approved it in March

告2014年第46号商务部关于禁止马士基、地中海航运、达飞设立网络中心经营者集中反垄断审查决定的公告 ('*Maersk/MSC Mediterranean Shipping/CMA CGM*').

[10] The first merger blocked by MOFCOM was *Coca-Cola/Hui Yuan* MOFCOM Block Notice [2009] No 22 of 18 March 2009 http://fldj.mofcom.gov.cn/article/ztxx/200903/20090306108494.shtml accessed 15 September 2023中华人民共和国商务部公告 [2009年] 第22号商务部关于禁止可口可乐公司收购中国汇源公司审查决定的公告.

[11] NPCSC, AML, effective as of 1 August 2008 and amended in June 2022.

[12] The phrase used by MOFCOM is '紧密型联营'.

[13] Typical forms of traditional shipping alliances include but are not limited to ship-sharing and space-swap agreements.

[14] MOFCOM found that by establishing the network centre, the three merging parties maintained technical control over the daily management of all ships on the cooperation routes.

[15] The network centre would be independently in charge of operation management in accordance with the predetermined work procedure.

[16] By prescribing shipping costs, including charter, fuel, port, and cancel fees, the merging parties planned to divide all the routes into different settlement groups, thus uniformly setting and apportioning operation costs.

[17] The network centre would uniformly coordinate unused cargo space instead of any merging party.

[18] *Maersk/MSC Mediterranean Shipping/CMA CGM*, s 4 Substantive Competition Analysis—(1) The Transaction Constitutes a Close Joint Venture, Essentially Different from Traditional Shipping Alliance.

[19] ibid.

[20] ibid s 4 Substantive Competition Analysis—(2)–(5).

[21] Marcus Hand, 'US Federal Maritime Commission approves P3 alliance' *Seatrade Maritime News* (21 March 2014) https://www.seatrade-maritime.com/americas/us-federal-maritime-commission-approves-p3-alliance accessed 15 September 2023.

[22] The FMC's Mission Statement is 'to ensure a competitive and reliable international ocean transportation supply system that supports the US economy and protects the public from unfair and deceptive practices'. It ensures competitive and efficient ocean transportation services by:

> Reviewing and monitoring agreements among ocean common carriers and marine terminal operators (MTOs) serving the U.S. foreign ocean borne trades to ensure that they do not cause substantial increases in transportation costs or decreases in transportation services
>
> Maintaining and reviewing confidentially filed service contracts to guard against detrimental effects to shipping
>
> Providing a forum for exporters, importers, and other members of the shipping public to obtain relief from ocean shipping practices or disputes that impede the flow of commerce
>
> Ensuring common carriers' tariff rates and charges are published in automated tariff systems and electronically available to the public
>
> Monitoring rates, charges, and rules of government-owned or controlled carriers to ensure they are just and reasonable

2014, holding that the agreement would neither reduce competition, unreasonably increase transportation costs nor reduce transportation services under section 6(g) of the Shipping Act. Richard Lidinsky, former chairman of the FMC, issued the sole dissenting opinion, arguing that:

> this agreement is in reality not an alliance or true vessel sharing arrangement. Rather, it is in effect a merger of the top three global liner companies. This agreement will allow the controlling carrier the ability ... to deploy its assets along with those of the other two carriers, to dominate vessel competition and narrow shipper options at U.S. ports.[23]

To address potential concerns, the FMC's only action was to issue alternative reporting requirements to the three parties, in support of its ongoing and close monitoring of the agreement.[24] In June 2014, the European Commission decided not to open an investigation into the proposed alliance.[25] Under European competition law, shipping alliances, such as those discussed in this case, do not qualify as mergers but are subject to Article 101 of the Treaty on the Functioning of the EU. Besides, certain consortium activities benefit from a block exemption.[26]

Some levelled the criticism that MOFCOM's block decision was largely motivated by industrial policy.[27] Competition concerns played an important but not necessarily decisive role in MOFCOM's review process. The China Shipowners' Association proactively lobbied MOFCOM to block the deal.[28] MOFCOM consulted with the Ministry of Transportation and the National Development and Reform Commission (NDRC) before making the final decision. It has been rumoured that the then Director General, Mr Shang Ming, of MOFCOM's Anti-Monopoly Bureau himself specifically paid a visit to the Yangshan deep water port in Shanghai to better understand the industry before blocking the proposed network centre.[29]

> Taking action to address unfavorable conditions caused by foreign governments or business practices in US–foreign shipping trades.

Federal Maritime Commission (FMC), 'About the Federal Maritime Commission' https://www.fmc.gov/about-the-fmc/ accessed 15 September 2023.

[23] FMC, Comments of Commissioner Richard A Lidinsky, Jr on Proposed P3 Vessel Sharing Agreement, 24 March 2014 https://www.fmc.gov/comments-of-commissioner-richard-a-lidinsky-jr-on-proposed-p3-vessel-sharing-agreement/ accessed 15 September 2023.

[24] FMC, 'P3 Agreement Clears FMC Regulatory Review' (20 March 2014) https://www.fmc.gov/p3-agreement-clears-fmc-regulatory-review/ accessed 15 September 2023.

[25] Chris Dupin, No Challenge to P3 in Europe, American Shipper, 4 June 2014 https://www.freightwaves.com/news/no-challenge-to-p3-in-europe accessed 15 September 2023.

[26] Regulation (EC) No 906/2009 on the Application of EU Competition Rules to Certain Agreements, Decisions, and Concerted Practices between Liner Shipping Companies.

[27] Hill Dickinson, 'Proposed P3 Alliance between the Maersk Line, CMA CGM and MSC Mediterranean Shipping has been prohibited' (Lexology, 19 June 2014) https://www.lexology.com/library/detail.aspx?g=6c99651b-0c2f-47bc-845a-8ee96ba3c00b accessed 15 September 2023.

[28] Carlos Tejada, 'China Shows Regulatory Heft by Sinking Shipping Deal' *WSJ* (17 June 2014) https://www.wsj.com/articles/china-shows-regulatory-heft-by-sinking-shipping-deal-1403033524 accessed 15 September 2023.

[29] Frederic Depoortere, Andrew Foster, and Ingrid Vandenborre, 'Navigating Chinese Merger Control: MOFCOM Prohibits P3 Shipping Alliance' (JD Supra, 20 June 2014) https://www.jdsupra.com/legalnews/navigating-chinese-merger-control-mofc-63495/ accessed 15 September 2023.

Section 6.2 briefly shows how merger control-related provisions in China are no different from those of overseas counterparts, for example in the EU. In practice, however, one merger may end up with differentiated review outcomes depending on the jurisdiction concerned, as was the case in *Maersk/MSC Mediterranean Shipping/CMA CGM*.[30]

Taking Germany as an example, in early 2019, the German Federal Ministry for Economic Affairs and Climate Action revealed the National Industrial Strategy 2030.[31] This new industrial strategy would increase the German government's power to potentially block deals in sensitive industries, such as artificial intelligence, robotics, semiconductors, biotech or quantum technology.[32] Even though it was attenuated due to fierce opposition from domestic business groups, for unacceptable state interference in the free market, the National Industrial Strategy 2030 marks Germany's shift towards a more selective and interventionist industrial policy which can have an impact in the outcome of merger enforcement as well.[33]

Interestingly, China, which continues to face international concerns that it allows industrial policy to play a disproportionate role in merger control, has been consistently upgrading the status of competition policy. Section 6.3 below analyses precedents in China, which reflect at least some influence imposed by industrial policy. Through elaborating on the FCRS-related central government documents, legislation, and the Chinese authorities' actions accordingly, section 6.3 predicts that SAMR's review of mergers will be much less affected by industrial policy.

6.3 Industrial Policy

Section 6.2 explores the definition of a 'merger' and the rule on substantive competition analysis in China. It also highlights that anti-monopoly enforcement by the Chinese competition authority may diverge from that of its overseas counterpart(s) in the same business arrangement, be it a 'merger' or an 'agreement'. Section 6.3 is the first part of the main body of this chapter—industrial policy as a non-competition parameter. It

[30] The European Commission informed the P3 partners that it had decided not to open an antitrust investigation into P3 and closed its file; see 'The P3 Network will not be implemented following decision by the Ministry of Commerce (MOFCOM) in China' (CMA CGM, 17 June 2014) https://www.cmacgm-group.com/en/news-medias/the-p3-network-will-not-be-implemented-following-decision-by-the-ministry-of-commerce-mofcom-in-china accessed 15 September 2023.

[31] German Federal Ministry for Economic Affairs and Energy, 'Made in Germany: Industrial Strategy 2030' (February 2019) https://www.bmwi.de/Redaktion/EN/Dossier/industrial-strategy-2030.html accessed 15 September 2023.

[32] Guy Chazan, 'Germany Acts to Stop Sale of Tech Companies to Non-EU Investors' *Financial Times* (30 November 2019 https://www.ft.com/content/d0964cd0-12af-11ea-a7e6-62bf4f9e548a accessed 15 September 2023. 'Competition law must be overhauled to facilitate company mergers in specific situations when a larger company could better compete at a global level' and 'German or European companies should be encouraged to take over key technology companies up for purchase' are among the main points of the National Industry Strategy 2030. DW, Germany Reveals Plan to Stop Foreign Takeovers, 5 February 2019 https://www.dw.com/en/germany-reveals-plan-to-stop-foreign-takeovers/a-47371451 accessed 15 September 2023.

[33] Etienne Schneider, 'Germany's Industrial Strategy 2030, EU Competition Policy and the Crisis of New Constitutionalism. (Geo-)political Economy of a Contested Paradigm Shift' *New Political Economy* (22 June 2022) https://www.tandfonline.com/doi/full/10.1080/13563467.2022.2091535 accessed 15 September 2023.

introduces the history and *status quo* of competition and industrial policy in China, followed by the related case law.

6.3.1 The Fair Competition Review System

In China, industrial policy was introduced by the 1986 Seventh Five-Year Plan on the National Economic and Social Development as a policy tool.[34] Since then, the status of industrial policy has constantly been strengthened by the Chinese authorities.[35] Since the introduction of currency policy by the 1995 People's Bank of China Law, China has gradually established a system to balance the gross social demand and supply based on currency policy, fiscal, and tax policy, and industrial policy.[36]

Nevertheless, an economic policy system circling industrial policy has gradually triggered serious problems. Without the support of competition policy, enterprises are confronted with unfairness in market entry, resource distribution, government preferential policies, and other areas, and this has obstructed industry upgrading and structural optimization. Even though the 2008 AML made 'competition policy' a legal concept,[37] competition policy had not yet become a component of China's long-term economic policy system.[38] Pinpointing the fundamental position of competition policy in the economic policy system is the basic prerequisite and essential guarantee to optimize the environment for the implementation of AML and to improve the effectiveness of anti-monopoly enforcement.[39]

Competition policy has fallen under the purview of China's economic policy system since the State Council approved the NDRC's 2015 Opinions on Key Work of Deepening the Reform of the Economic System, which proposes that '(China) should promote the effective coordination of industrial policy and competition policy and establish and standardize a fair and competitive mechanism for industrial policy'.[40] In October 2015, the Several Opinions of the Central Committee of the Communist Party of China and the State Council on Promoting the Reform of the Price Mechanism specify that '(China should) beef up market price regulation and anti-trust enforcement, and gradually establish the fundamental status of competition policy'.[41] This represents

[34] Suggestions of the Central Committee of the Communist Party of China on Formulating the Seventh Five-Year Plan for National Economic and Social Development (Seventh Five-Year Plan), 23 September 1985 https://www.ndrc.gov.cn/fggz/fzzlgh/gjfzgh/200709/P020191029595672223126.pdf accessed 15 September 2023.

[35] SHI Jianzhong, Comprehensive Interpretation of the AML, 30 June 2022, s 1(2) http://www.zggpjz.com/keji/shuma/9118.html accessed 8 August 2022.

[36] ibid.

[37] AML, art 12, doing research and formulating related competition policy is one of the five duties of the Anti-Monopoly Committee affiliated with the State Council.

[38] ibid.

[39] SHI (n 35).

[40] State Council, 'Opinions of the State Council on Establishing the Fair Competition Review System during the Construction of Market System' (June 2016) http://www.gov.cn/zhengce/content/2016-06/14/content_5082066.htm accessed 15 September 2023.

[41] Xinhua News Agency, 'Several Opinions of the Central Committee of the Communist Party of China and the State Council on Promoting the Reform of the Price Mechanism' (12 October 2015), s 4 <http://www.gov.cn/xinwen/2015-10/15/content_2947548.htm> accessed 8 August 2022.

the first time that the fundamental status of competition policy was recognized by central-level policy.[42]

In June 2016, the Opinions of the State Council on Establishing the Fair Competition Review System during the Construction of Market System (Opinions) officially established China's FCRS.[43] The FCRS is an essential *ex ante* tool to regulate administrative power against elimination or restriction of competition. Before the FCRS, the 2008 AML had been equipped with an *ex post* mechanism to fight against the abuse of administrative power to eliminate or restrict competition.[44]

The Opinions aim to regulate government activities, prevent the formulation of policies that exclude or restrain competition, and gradually clean up and annul provisions and practices that hinder the development of a unified national market and fair competition.[45] In June 2021, SAMR, NDRC, MOFCOM, the Ministry of Finance, together with the Ministry of Justice, released the Detailed Rules for the Implementation of the Fair Competition Review System, explaining and providing more details on the review mechanism and procedure, review standard, exception, third-party evaluation, and assessment, as well as supervision and liabilities, to guarantee the solid implementation of the FCRS.[46]

Taking 2021 as an example, administrative organs and organizations authorized by laws and regulations to manage public affairs at all levels in China reviewed a total of 244,000 newly enacted policies and official documents, cleared 442,000 established policies and official documents, and modified and/or annulled 11,000 policies and measures in breach of the FCRS, thus effectively maintaining a unified national market and fair competition.[47]

The Standing Committee of the National People's Congress (NPCSC) approved the amendment to the 2008 AML on 24 June 2022 (2022 AML),[48] which was the first time the Chinese legislator had amended the 2008 AML since it came into effect around fourteen years earlier.[49] The 2022 AML introduces a new provision, article 5, thus codifying the FCRS within a law, and so placing it at the highest level of the Chinese legal system.

[42] SHI (n 35).

[43] State Council (n 40).

[44] AML, Ch 5—Abuse of Administrative Power to Eliminate or Restrict Competition.

[45] For comments on China's fair competition review system, please see: Huang Yong and Wu Baiding, 'China's Fair Competition Review: Introduction, Imperfections, and Solutions' *CPI Antitrust Chronicle* (March 2017) https://www.competitionpolicyinternational.com/wp-content/uploads/2017/03/CPI-Huang-Wu.pdf accessed 15 September 2023.

[46] SAMR, 'Notice of SAMR and Other Four (Central) Departments on the Detailed Rules for the Implementation of the Fair Competition Review System' (29 June 2021) http://www.gov.cn/zhengce/zhengceku/2021-07/08/content_5623453.htm accessed 15 September 2023.

[47] SAMR, Annual Report of China's Anti-Monopoly Enforcement (2021), p 3 https://www.samr.gov.cn/xw/zj/202206/P020220608430645470953.pdf accessed 20 August 2022.

[48] NPCSC, 'The NPCSC's Decision on Amending the Anti-Monopoly Law of the PRC', 24 June 2022 http://www.npc.gov.cn/npc/c30834/202206/e42c256faf7049449cdfaabf374a3595.shtml accessed 20 August 2022.

[49] For comments on the 2022 AML, please see: Wei HAN and Liang LI, 'The New Anti-Monopoly Law of the People's Republic of China: Changes and Remaining Issues' *CPI* (7 August 2022) https://www.competitionpolicyinternational.com/the-new-anti-monopoly-law-of-the-peoples-republic-of-china-changes-and-remaining-issues/ accessed 15 September 2023.

Article 5 of the 2022 AML prescribes that 'The State establishes and perfects the fair competition review system. Administrative organs and organizations authorized by laws and regulations to manage public affairs should go through the fair competition review procedure before formulating rules concerning economic activities of market players.' We can wait to see whether the Chinese competition authorities will be less distracted by industrial policy in their anti-monopoly enforcement.

6.3.2 Precedents Showing the Impact of Industrial Policy on M&A Assessment

6.3.2.1 *Seagate/Samsung* and *Western Digital/Hitachi*

Seagate/Samsung and *Western Digital/Hitachi* are two typical examples in the hard disk drive (HDD) market, which embody not only the peculiarities of Chinese competition authority's merger control enforcement but also the role played by industrial policy in China. Neither the European Commission[50] nor the US competition authority[51] challenged *Seagate/Samsung*. Again, MOFCOM's practice demonstrates how China's merger control regime has become increasingly relevant to global transactions, which have had to deal with greater uncertainty as a result.

In 2011, the MOFOCM conditionally cleared Seagate's acquisition of Samsung's HDD businesses.[52] Besides potential harm to HDD manufacturers' innovation incentive and speed,[53] MOFCOM was concerned that the acquisition would increase the possibility for the merged entity and three rivals to coordinate,[54] thus eliminating or restricting competition in the HDD market.[55] Consumer welfare would suffer in the form of higher prices.[56]

To alleviate relevant competition concerns, MOFCOM imposed a stand-alone hold-separate order[57] and a series of behavioural remedies.[58] Through the stand-alone

[50] European Commission, 'Mergers: Commission Clears Proposed Acquisition of Samsung's Hard Disk Drive Business by Seagate Technology', 19 October 2011 https://ec.europa.eu/commission/presscorner/detail/en/IP_11_1213 accessed 15 September 2023.

[51] US Federal Trade Commission (FTC), 'Seagate Technology PLC's Proposed Acquisition of the Hard Disk Drive Business of Samsung Electronics Co, Ltd', 7 December 2011 https://www.ftc.gov/legal-library/browse/cases-proceedings/closing-letters/seagate-technology-plcs-proposed-acquisition-hard-disk-drive-business-samsung-electronics-co-ltd accessed 15 September 2023.

[52] *Seagate Technology/Hard Disk Drive Business of Samsung* MOFCOM Conditional Clearance Notice [2011] No 90 of 12/12/2011 http://fldj.mofcom.gov.cn/article/ztxx/201112/20111207874274.shtml accessed 15 September 2023 商务部公告2011年第90号关于附条件批准希捷科技公司收购三星电子有限公司硬盘驱动器业务反垄断审查决定的公告 (*Seagate/Samsung*).

[53] *Seagate/Samsung*, s 2 Competition Analysis—(5).

[54] In 2010, or before the acquisition, there were five players in the global HDD market: Seagate, Western Digital, Hitachi, Toshiba and Samsung, with market shares of 33 per cent, 29 per cent, 18 per cent, 10 per cent and 10 per cent respectively. For more details, please see *Seagate/Samsung*, s 2 Competition Analysis—(2).

[55] MOFCOM counted on market status, procurement model, capacity utilization, and other elements to establish the coordinated theory of harm. For more details, please see *Seagate/Samsung*, s 2 Competition Analysis.

[56] *Seagate/Samsung*, s 2 Competition Analysis—(6).

[57] Wei Han, Ranran Yin, and Zeng Xiong, 'Standalone Hold Separate Orders as Remedies in Chinese Merger Control', in Adrian Emch and Wendy Ng (eds), *Wang Xiaoye: The Pioneer of Competition Law in China—Liber Amicorum* (Concurrences 2019).

[58] *Seagate/Samsung*, s 4 Review Decision.

hold-separate remedy, MOFCOM required the merged entity to sustain Samsung's HDD businesses as an independent competitor in the relevant market.[59] MOFCOM revoked the stand-alone hold-separate remedy, considering that it would save Seagate manufacture and R&D costs without substantively imposing side effects on competition.[60]

In 2012, MOFCOM conditionally cleared Western Digital's acquisition of Hitachi.[61] More specifically, Western Digital would acquire all the shareholdings in Viviti Technologies Ltd (Viviti). Viviti indirectly controlled Hitachi Global Storage Technologies Singapore Pte Ltd through Hitachi Global Storage Technologies Netherlands BV to engage in HDD businesses.[62]

Similar to the substantive competition analysis in *Seagate/Samsung*, MOFCOM found that the acquisition would further increase the possibility for the remaining market players, Seagate, Western Digital, Hitachi, Toshiba, and Samsung, to coordinate, thus eliminating or restricting competition in the HDD market.[63] Besides, MOFCOM was concerned that the pace of innovation would slow down post-acquisition, in the form of postponing the introduction of innovative products and prolonging the lifecycle of the incumbent products, for example.[64] Considering China was among the countries and regions that consumed the most personal computers, Chinese consumers would suffer, as observed by MOFCOM.[65]

To have the acquisition cleared, Western Digital proposed to maintain Viviti as an independent competitor in the HDD market, or the stand-alone hold-separate remedy, among other structural and behavioural remedies.[66] In 2015, MOFCOM partially revoked the remedies above.[67] MOFCOM observed that neither Western Digital nor Hitachi was able to provide all types of HDDs. The separation of both parties' manufacture and R&D increased costs to the detriment of R&D, their competitive power, and customers. Accordingly, MOFCOM revoked both parties' obligations to keep their manufacturing and R&D activities separate but maintained their obligation to keep brands and sales independent.[68]

[59] ibid.

[60] *Seagate Technology/Hard Disk Drive Business of Samsung* MOFCOM Notice on Revising the Restrictive Conditions [2015] No 43 of 22 October 2015 http://fldj.mofcom.gov.cn/article/ztxx/201510/20151001144105.shtml accessed 15 September 2023 商务部公告2015年第43号 关于变更希捷科技公司收购三星电子有限公司硬盘驱动器业务经营者集中限制性条件的公告 (*Seagate/Samsung—Remedy Revised Decision*), s 3 Competition Analysis—(2).

[61] *Western Digital/Hitachi* MOFCOM Conditional Clearance Notice [2012] No 9 of 2 March 2012 http://fldj.mofcom.gov.cn/article/ztxx/201203/20120307993758.shtml accessed 15 September 2023 商务部公告2012年第9号 关于附加限制性条件批准西部数据收购日立存储经营者集中反垄断审查决定的公告 (*Western Digital/Hitachi*).

[62] ibid s 2 Competition Analysis—(1).

[63] ibid s 2 Competition Analysis—(8).

[64] ibid s 2 Competition Analysis—(5).

[65] ibid s 2 Competition Analysis—(8).

[66] ibid s 4 Review Decision.

[67] *Western Digital/Hitachi* MOFCOM Notice on Revising the Restrictive Conditions [2015] No 41 of 19 October 2015 http://fldj.mofcom.gov.cn/article/ztxx/201510/20151001139040.shtml accessed 15 September 2023 商务部公告2015年第41号关于变更西部数据收购日立存储经营者集中限制性条件的公告 (*Western Digital/Hitachi—Remedy Revised Decision*).

[68] ibid s 3 Competition Analysis—(2), s 4—Negotiation and Review Decision.

MOFCOM has been criticized for its review of *Seagate/Samsung* and *Western Digital/Hitachi* for at least two reasons: (a) industrial policy and (b) the over-burdensome remedies, neither of which are sufficiently solid, however.

(a) Industrial policy. Some comment that MOFCOM's conditional clearance of the two cases aimed to protect large numbers of downstream manufacturers of desktops and notebook computers, considering China has one of the highest levels of personal computer consumption. MOFCOM may have considered China particularly vulnerable to a more concentrated HDD industry.[69] Others share similar opinions—MOFCOM imposed remedies in both cases, not limited to *Western Digital/Hitachi*, to guarantee that Chinese downstream market players, including computer manufacturers, could have continuous access to important input.[70]

Even when defining a globally relevant market, MOFCOM does not avoid focusing on the domestic market. MOFCOM is bound by the legislative purposes of the AML, such as national economic development.[71] It does not necessarily go against competition policy.

If MOFCOM found a lack of countervailing buyer power that would harm domestic consumers' welfare and lead to higher prices and less innovative products more specifically, then it had every reason to challenge the transaction. The protection of domestic personal computer manufacturers is not necessarily driven by industrial policy: it could rather aim primarily to maintain competition in the HDD market, thus benefiting end consumers.

(b) Peculiarity of the stand-alone hold-separate remedy. Even though MOFCOM cleared *Seagate/Samsung* and *Western Digital/Hitachi*, it prohibited merging parties from integrating their respective HDD R&D, manufacturing and sales businesses. MOFCOM required the relevant businesses to operate separately for a period as if the acquisitions had not happened. It was the first time that the Chinese competition authority had imposed the stand-alone hold-separate remedy.[72] Practitioners claim that this third-type remedy, alongside structural and behavioural remedies, causes huge monitoring and implementation costs.[73] In comparison, structural remedy divestment, for example, is a more common option to eliminate competition concerns in horizontal mergers, as shown by relevant practices in the EU and the US.[74]

[69] Arthur Burke, Joel Cohen, Arthur Golden et al, 'Chinese Antitrust Authorities Approve *Western Digital/Hitachi GST Deal* with Significant Conditions', Davis Polk Client Memorandum, 9 March 2012 https://www.davispolk.com/sites/default/files/files/Publication/02ebb877-46da-4ecd-bdaf-15b4120c8c2d/Preview/PublicationAttachment/f7c56be9-b90c-48c0-bb6c-17b6e5e4302a/030912_PRCUpdate.pdf accessed 15 September 2023.

[70] Peter J Wang, 'Lessons from Four Years of Antitrust Enforcement in China' (Jones Day, September 2012) https://www.jonesday.com/en/insights/2012/09/lessons-from-four-years-of-antitrust-enforcement-in-china accessed 15 September 2023.

[71] AML, art 1.

[72] Lisha Zhou, 'MOFCOM Western Digital and Seagate Hold Separates Evaluated by Economist', PaRR, 4 March 2015 https://app.parr-global.com/intelligence/view/prime-1976353 accessed 20 August 2022.

[73] ibid.

[74] Conor A Reidy, 'DOJ's Merger Remedies Manual Reaffirms the Agency's Preference for Structural Remedies', Winston and Strawn, 10 September 2020 https://www.winston.com/en/competition-corner/dojs-merger-remed

Western Digital/Hitachi was also conditionally cleared by the European Commission[75] and the US Federal Trade Commission,[76] requiring Western Digital to divest the 3.5-inch HDD-related assets. MOFCOM's imposition of the stand-alone hold-separate remedy in *Seagate/Samsung* could plug a potential enforcement gap in the European competition legal system, the so-called 'first come, first served' or priority rule. In *TUI/First Choice*[77] and *KarstadtQuelle/Thomas Cook*,[78] the European Commission showed its support of the priority rule when two transactions are notified in close proximity.[79]

In accordance with the priority rule, the European Commission reviews the first notified merger as if the second notified merger does not exist. Subsequently, the European Commission reviews the second notified merger as if the first notified merger has already been implemented. Accordingly, the firstly notified merger resulting in a four-to-three situation is less likely to trigger competition concerns than the second notified merger resulting in a three-to-two scenario,[80] as demonstrated by the EC's practice in *Seagate/Samsung*[81] and *Western Digital/Hitachi*.[82] *Seagate/Samsung* benefited from being notified to the EC one day earlier than *Western Digital/Hitachi*.[83]

Procedurally and substantively, *Western Digital/Hitachi* suffered unfair treatment, considering it was the first of the two HDD transactions to initiate the pre-notification

ies-manual-reaffirms-the-agencys-preference-for-structural-remedies.html accessed 15 September 2023. Simon Vande Walle, 'Remedies in EU Merger Control— An Essential Guide' (2021), s 4.2.1—The Commission's Preference for Divestment https://ssrn.com/abstract=3782333 accessed 15 September 2023.

75 European Commission, 'Mergers: Commission Clears Western Digital's Acquisition of Hitachi's Hard Disk Drive Business subject to Conditions', 23 November 2011 https://ec.europa.eu/commission/presscorner/detail/en/IP_11_1395 accessed 15 September 2023.

76 US FTC, 'FTC Issues Modified Final Order Settling Charges that Western Digital's Acquisition of Hitachi Global Storage Technologies Was Anticompetitive in Market for Desktop Hard Disk Drives', 9 May 2013 https://www.ftc.gov/news-events/news/press-releases/2013/05/ftc-issues-modified-final-order-settling-charges-western-digitals-acquisition-hitachi-global-storage accessed 15 September 2023.

77 *TUI/First Choice* (Case COMP/M. 4600) Commission Decision of 4 June 2004.

78 *KarstadtQuelle/Thomas Cook* (Case COMP/M. 4584) Commission Decision of 26 March 2007.

79 Kyriakos Fountoukakos, Craig Pouncey, James Robinson, et al, '"First Come First Served": The European Commission's Priority Rule in *Seagate/Samsung* and *Western Digital/Hitachi* and Practical Implications', 20 February 2012, Herbert Smith Freehills LLP https://www.lexology.com/library/detail.aspx?g=5f310bd9-e0bf-4857-ac0d-52858d4034d1 accessed 15 September 2023.

80 In the markets for 3.5-inch Desktop HDD and Consumer Electronics HDD, only the merged *Seagate/Samsung* imposed effective competitive constraints on the merged Western Digital. It was problematic since, for security of supply reasons, most customers multi-source HDD. Toshiba just entered the 3.5-inch business critical HDD, while the European Commission was not sure whether Toshiba could replace the competitive constraint imposed by the acquiree. For more details, please see *Western Digital Ireland/Viviti Technologies* (Case COMP/M. 6203) Commission Decision of 23/11/2011, ss 5.4.3., 5.4.4., and 5.4.5.

81 European Commission, 'Mergers: Commission Clears Proposed Acquisition of Samsung's Hard Disk Drive Business by Seagate Technology', 19 October 2011: 'The Seagate/Samsung deal was assessed independently of Western Digital's proposed acquisition of the HDD and Solid State Drives (SSDs) businesses of Hitachi Global Storage Technologies which was notified one day later and is still pending' https://ec.europa.eu/commission/presscorner/detail/en/IP_11_1213 accessed 15 September 2023.

82 European Commission, 'Mergers: Commission Clears Western Digital's Acquisition of Hitachi's Hard Disk Drive Business Subject to Conditions', 23 November 2011: 'Western Digital notified its proposed acquisition of HGST to the Commission on 20 April 2011. Pursuant to a priority rule ("first come, first served") based on the date of notification, the present merger is assessed taking into account the *Seagate/Samsung* merger in the same sector that was notified one day earlier and approved by the Commission on 19 October (see IP/11/1213)' https://ec.europa.eu/commission/presscorner/detail/en/IP_11_1395 accessed 15 September 2023.

83 Kyriakos Fountoukakos et al, '"First Come First Served": the European Commission's Priority Rule in *Seagate/Samsung* and *Western Digital/Hitachi* and Practical Implications', 20 February 2012, Herbert Smith Freehills LLP https://www.lexology.com/library/detail.aspx?g=5f310bd9-e0bf-4857-ac0d-52858d4034d1 accessed 15 September 2023.

discussion with the European Commission.[84] The EU Merger Control Regulation[85] is silent with regard to the appropriate date for allocating the priority. Western Digital lodged an appeal with the General Court, seeking to annul the European Commission's decision for lack of legal basis for the priority and adherence to the general principles of fairness and good administration. Later, Western Digital withdrew the appeal.[86]

In comparison, MOFCOM imposed the stand-alone hold-separate remedy in *Seagate/Samsung*, requiring Seagate and Samsung to operate separately in the HDD market for one year. MOFCOM reviewed each of the two transactions as if the other had not happened and adopted a more holistic approach. More specifically, MOFCOM's reviews of *Seagate/Samsung* and *Western Digital/Hitachi* did not interfere with each other.

As of July 2023, the Chinese competition authority has imposed the stand-alone hold-separate remedy in around ten mergers. The Chinese competition authority imposes stand-alone hold-separate remedies when structural remedies are not possible and behavioural remedies cannot fully resolve the competition concerns.[87] Even if this overburdens and creates uncertainty for stakeholders, the stand-alone hold-separate remedy also gives the Chinese competition authority leeway to retrospectively review the same case four years later.

6.3.2.2 *Walmart/Newheight*

On 16 December 2011, Walmart notified MOFCOM of its increasing shareholdings in Newheight Holdings from 17.7 per cent to 51.3 per cent. Newheight Holdings controlled the direct online sales business of Yi Shi Duo No 1 Shop (Yi Hao Dian) through its wholly owned subsidiary—Xin Gang Ling Hong Kong and Newheight Shanghai (*Walmart/Newheight*).[88] Through the acquisition, Walmart obtained control of Yi Hao Dian's direct online sales businesses.[89] The MOFCOM was concerned that the acquisition would eliminate or restrict competition in China's B2C online retail market.[90]

More specifically, Walmart was the main (and important) competitor in China's offline retail market,[91] having competitive advantages in terms of purchase, storage, product line, offline shop network, services, and brand reputation. Yi Hao Dian was the biggest online retailer in China. MOFCOM found that logistics and services were the key to online retail development. In China's offline retail market, Walmart had established advanced storage and delivery systems, obtained extensive supply channels,

[84] ibid.

[85] Council Regulation (EC) No 139/2004 of 20 January 2004 on the Control of Concentrations between Undertakings (the EU Merger Regulation) (Text with EEA relevance) [2004] OJ L 24/1–22.

[86] Case T-452/11: Order of the General Court of 20 September 2012—*Western Digital and Western Digital Ireland v Commission.*

[87] Jiang, 'Chinese, and Foreign Experts Offer Advice and Suggestions on Implementation of the Anti-monopoly Law' *Legal Daily* (28 May 2014).

[88] *Walmart/Another 33.6 per cent Shares in Newheight Holdings* MOFCOM Conditional Clearance Notice [2012] No 49 of 14 August 2012 http://fldj.mofcom.gov.cn/article/ztxx/201303/20130300058730.shtml accessed 15 September 2023 商务部公告2012年第49号关于附加限制性条件批准沃尔玛公司收购纽海控股33.6%股权经营者集中反垄断审查决定的公告 ('*Walmart/Newheight*').

[89] ibid s 2 Competition Analysis.

[90] ibid s 1 Case Filing and Review Procedure.

[91] The phrase used by MOFCOM is '实体超市'.

and built its brand reputation. MOFCOM observed that Walmart could leverage its competitive advantage in the offline retail market to that of the online retail market, in which Yi Hao Dian was active.[92]

In essence, MOFCOM was concerned that Yi Hao Dian's dominant position in China's online retail market would be strengthened. To eliminate MOFCOM's competition concern, Walmart proposed that Newheight Shanghai would only use its online platform to engage in retail business directly.[93] This commitment was lifted by MOFCOM four years later in June 2016 for the following reasons: (a) during 2012–16, China's online retail experienced rapid growth, and (b) Yi Hao Dian gradually lost its competitive advantage during this period.[94]

Nevertheless, with respect to China's value-added telecommunications services (VATS) market, it seemed that MOFCOM's substantive competition analysis was implicitly led by industrial policy. It was possible for the merged entity to enter China's VATS market through Yi Hao Dian. MOFCOM held that the merged entity would obtain a competitive advantage in China's VATS market by using comprehensive competitive advantages in the offline and online retail markets, thus rapidly expanding relevant businesses. The merged entity's right to determine price vis-à-vis online platform users would be substantially enhanced, thus eliminating or restricting competition in China's VATS market.[95]

To remove MOFCOM's concerns above, Walmart committed that (a) Newheight Shanghai would not make use of its online platform to provide online services to Walmart before obtaining the VATS licence, and (b) post-acquisition Walmart would not engage in Yi Hao Dian's VATS through the variable interest entity.[96] The remedies were abolished because the entry barrier to China's VATS market had been removed. In June 2015, restrictions on the percentage of foreign capital in China's online data processing and transaction processing businesses (operational e-commerce) were cancelled.[97]

Even though MOFCOM did not impose VATS-related remedies, in practice, the merged entity should legally not engage in China's VATS. MOFCOM, as a competition agency, did the work that a sectoral regulator should have done. In China, it is the Ministry of Industry and Information Technology (MIIT) that determines which entity can enter the VATS market.[98] The specific operator of VATS can only be changed upon approval of the MIIT or its provincial branches.[99] In this case, before the acquisition, it was Newheight Shanghai that was qualified to run VATS, online data processing and

[92] *Walmart/Newheight*, s 2 Competition Analysis.

[93] ibid s 4 Review Decision—(1).

[94] MOFCOM Notice [2016] No 23 of 08 June 2016 about Relieving Remedies Imposed on the *Walmart/Another 33.6 per cent Shares in Newheight Holdings* http://fldj.mofcom.gov.cn/article/ztxx/201606/20160601335200.shtml accessed 15 September 2023 商务部公告2016年第23号关于解除沃尔玛收购纽海控股33.6%股权经营者集中限制性条件的公告 (*'Walmart/Newheight—Relieve of Restrictive Conditions'*).

[95] *Walmart/Newheight*, s 2 Competition Analysis.

[96] ibid s 4 Review Decision—(2)(3).

[97] *Walmart/Newheight*—Relieve of Restrictive Conditions, s 3 Competition Analysis.

[98] State Council of the PRC, Telecommunications Regulation of the PRC (2016 Revision) (Telecommunications Regulation), arts 7, 14.

[99] Telecommunications Regulation, art 15.

transaction processing business (operational e-commerce) more specifically, in China. If Walmart determined to run Newheight's VATS after the acquisition, be it directly or indirectly, it had to obtain approval from the MIIT.

6.3.3 The Blurring Boundary Between Industrial Policy and National Security

In recent years, a large percentage of conditionally cleared mergers and acquisitions (M&As) have occurred in industries that are of strategic importance to China, such as life science,[100] semiconductor,[101] and the general IT and technology area,[102] which feature in China's Thirteenth Five-Year Plan released in March 2016.[103]

This does not mean that if a transaction concerns certain industries or sectors of strategic significance to China, it is likely to be challenged by SAMR. Instead, it means that China would strengthen the coordination of competition and industrial policy in such cases and promote the transformation of industrial policy to be inclusive and functional to ensure that industrial policy represents fair competition principles. Accordingly, industrial and competition policy form a policy synergy to jointly stimulate the innovative development of the economy.[104]

[100] Eg, *Danaher/Medical Life Science Biopharmaceutical Business of GE* SAMR Conditional Clearance Notice of 28 February 2020 http://www.samr.gov.cn/fldj/tzgg/ftjpz/202002/t20200228_312297.html accessed 24 August 2022 市场监管总局关于附加限制性条件批准丹纳赫公司收购通用电气医疗生命科学生物制药业务案反垄断审查决定的公告.

[101] Such as *Infineon Technologies/Cypress Semiconductor* SAMR Conditional Clearance Notice of 08 April 2020 http://www.samr.gov.cn/fldj/tzgg/ftjpz/202004/t20200408_313950 html accessed 24 August 2022 市场监管总局关于附加限制性条件批准英飞凌科技公司收购赛普拉斯半导体公司股权案反垄断审查决定的公告.

In July 2018, Qualcomm gave up the acquisition of NXP Semiconductors, the largest-ever deal in the semiconductor industry. In response, SAMR expressed serious concerns about the profound (side/negative) influence the transaction might have on the global semiconductor industry. SAMR stated it had negotiated with Qualcomm about how to eliminate competition concerns but was not satisfied with the latest round of commitments made by Qualcomm. SAMR praised Qualcomm's active cooperation and expressed regret at Qualcomm's giving up the deal when it was still within the legal review period. For more details, please see Tech.china.com.cn, 'Qualcomm Gives up the Acquisition of NXP, SAMR Respects Both Parties' Choice' (27 July 2018) http://tech.china.com.cn/it/20180727/344234.shtml accessed 15 September 2023.

As for *Broadcom/Qualcomm*, which failed CFIUS's review in the US, China's MOFCOM only commented that it had noticed the relevant reports without providing any detailed opinions on this transaction. For more details, please see MOFCOM—Press Conference Homepage, 'We have noted the potential mega-merger of Qualcomm and Broadcom. Will MOFCOM conduct a strict and lengthy review? Now that the semiconductor industry is a vital strategic industry in China, will MOFCOM focus more on protecting the interests of Chinese enterprises during the scrutiny? Thank you.' (9 November 2017), 20 November 2017 http://english.mofcom.gov.cn/article/pressconferencehomepage/foreigninvestment/201711/20171102676177.shtml accessed 15 September 2023.

[102] *Nvidia/Mellanox* SAMR Conditional Clearance Notice of 16 April 2020 http://www.samr.gov.cn/fldj/tzgg/ftjpz/202004/t20200416_314327.html accessed 23 August 2022 市场监管总局关于附加限制性条件批准英伟达公司收购迈络思科技有限公司股权案反垄断审查决定的公告.

[103] China planned to vigorously promote the innovation and industrialization of emerging industries, including but not limited to advanced semiconductors, robotics, additive manufacturing, intelligent systems, new-generation aviation equipment, space technology integrated service systems, intelligent transportation, precision medicine, efficient energy storage, and distributed energy systems, intelligent materials, high-efficiency energy conservation, and environmental protection, virtual reality, interactive film and television. For more details, please see Xinhua News Agency, 'Outline of the Thirteenth Five-Year Plan for National Economic and Social Development of the People's Republic of China' (17 March 2016), s 1, ch 23 http://www.gov.cn/xinwen/2016-03/17/content_5054992.htm accessed 15 September 2023.

[104] WU Zhenguo (Director General, Department I of Anti-Monopoly Enforcement, SAMR), 'China's Approach of Anti-Monopoly Regulation—Historical Review and Outlook' (2022) 16 Tsinghua University Law Journal 4.

During President XI Jinping's visit to Wuhan, Hubei, in June 2022, he pointed out that science and technology (S&T), self-reliance, and self-improvement are the foundation of China's prosperity and security. President XI emphasized how essential it was to harness the lifeblood of S&T and consistently upgrade the independence, autonomy, and security of China's development. Under this guidance, more new technologies and industries would be cultivated, while new fields and paths for economic development would be opened. China would obtain new advantages in international competition.[105]

Against the backdrop of the increasingly complicated international environment, the analysis of industrial policy could not be separated from that of national security. Taking the US as an example, President Joe Biden signed the bipartisan CHIPS and Science Act (H.R.4346) in August 2022. The act aims to keep the US as world-leader in the nanotechnology, clean energy, quantum computing, and artificial intelligence industries by strengthening American national security, investment in R&D, S&T, and the workforce of the future, among other aspects.[106]

The act provides $52.7 billion for American semiconductor R&D, manufacturing, and workforce development.[107] For ten years following their obtaining of the award, covered entities 'may not engage in any significant transaction, as defined in the agreement, involving the material expansion of semiconductor manufacturing capacity in the People's Republic of China or any other foreign country of concern'.[108] The act requires recipients of CHIPS funding, or covered entities, to go through a mandatory notification process for planned transactions in China, which is similar to the CFIUS process.[109]

Section 6.3 elaborates on the role played by industrial policy in China's merger control practice. Chinese authorities used to place greater value on industrial policy. Without the support of competition policy, the development of China's economy has faced various problems. With the establishment of the FCRS in 2016 and the codification of the FCRS by the 2022 AML, it is predicted that SAMR's review of mergers will be less likely to be influenced by industrial policy.

Via analysis of several precedents, section 6.3 has shown that the Chinese competition authority has not been as influenced by industrial policy in its merger review as some have claimed. It is common practice to protect the domestic market, even if a competition authority defines a globally relevant geographic market. The peculiar

105 Xinhua News Agency, 'During His Inspection in Wuhan, Hubei, (President) XI Jinping Emphasizes: Firmly Grasp the Lifeblood of Science and Technology in China's Own Hands, and Continuously Improve the Independence, Autonomy, and Security of China's Development' (29 June 2022) https://www.miit.gov.cn/xwdt/szyw/art/2022/art_6b906abb44da45b9b9d171416edb2264.html accessed 15 September 2023.

106 White House, 'CHIPS and Science Act Will Lower Costs, Create Jobs, Strengthen Supply Chains, and Counter China' (Fact Sheet, 9 August 2022) https://www.whitehouse.gov/briefing-room/statements-releases/2022/08/09/fact-sheet-chips-and-science-act-will-lower-costs-create-jobs-strengthen-supply-chains-and-counter-china/ accessed 15 September 2023.

107 ibid.

108 CHIPS and Science Act (H.R.4346), s 103—Semiconductor Incentives.

109 Winston and Strawn, 'The CHIPS Act Creates a New, CFIUS-Like, Outbound Investment Review Process for the Semiconductor Industry' (22 August 2022) https://www.winston.com/en/global-trade-and-foreign-policy-insights/the-chips-act-creates-a-new-cfius-like-outbound-investment-review-process-for-the-semiconductor-industry.html accessed 15 September 2023.

remedy category in China, stand-alone hold-separate, comes with implementation and supervision risks. Nevertheless, it also saves MOFCOM from the dilemma its European counterpart has been dragged into by the priority principle, as shown in *Seagate/Samsung* and *Western Digital/Hitachi*. Sometimes, the seemingly industrial-policy-driven remedy makes no significant difference to the merged entity's businesses, whether imposed by the Chinese competition authority or not, as exhibited by *Walmart/Newheight*.

A high percentage of the M&As challenged by SAMR in recent years circle around high S&T-related industries, and as such, they concern China's development, including national security. With evolving globalization,[110] when it comes to certain industries, such as semiconductors, artificial intelligence, quantum computing, and life science, non-competition interests that might affect SAMR's merger control in practice are no longer limited to industrial policy but are also intertwined with national security, as will be shown in section 6.4 below.

6.4 National Security

In China, the National Security Law of the PRC (National Security Law) was passed as early as 1993 and amended in 2009 and 2015, respectively.[111] Article 2 of the National Security Law defines 'national security' as 'a status in which the state political power, sovereignty, unity, territorial integrity, welfare of the people, sustainable economic and social development, and other major interests of the state interests of the state are at relatively little risk and are not threatened internally or externally, so a sustained security status can be maintained'.

The National Security Law regards the security review of 'foreign investment' as an essential component of the national security review, covering both traditional and non-traditional notions of security. The National Security Law puts forward specific requirements for the tasks of maintaining national security in the economy, finance, food, culture, independent innovation capability, networks, and information.[112] For the first time, the National Security Law provides a direct basis for the national security review of foreign investment at the level of law.

The first legal document based on which the Chinese authorities undertook a national security review of foreign capital investment in domestic enterprises was the 2003 Interim Provisions on Mergers and Acquisitions of Domestic Enterprises by Foreign Investors.[113] If there are major factors that seriously impact market competition, the

[110] White and Case, 'Policy Shifts May Signal A New Chapter in the Story of Globalization', in '2021 Annual Review' https://www.whitecase.com/insight-our-thinking/policy-shifts-may-signal-new-chapter-story-globalization accessed 15 September 2023.

[111] NPCSC, National Security Law of the PRC (National Security Law), enacted in 1993 and revised in 2009 and 2015, with the 2015 revision effective as of 1 July 2015.

[112] ibid art 59.

[113] The Ministry of Foreign Trade and Economic Cooperation, the State Taxation Administration (STA), the State Administration for Industry and Commerce (SAIC), and the State Administration of Foreign Exchange

national economy, people's livelihoods, or state economic security, foreign investors should report these to the Ministry of Foreign Trade and Economic Cooperation and the State Administration for Industry and Commerce.[114]

6.4.1 Cohesion of the Anti-Monopoly Review and the National Security Review of M&As

The 2003 Interim Provisions on Mergers and Acquisitions of Domestic Enterprises by Foreign Investors were replaced by the Provisions on Mergers and Acquisitions of Domestic Enterprises by Foreign Investors in 2006 (Provisions on M&As of Domestic Enterprises by Foreign Investors).[115] The Provisions on M&A of Domestic Enterprises by Foreign Investors have a specific chapter, Chapter 5, focusing on anti-monopoly review.

The 2008 AML systematically established the merger control system in China through Chapter 4—Concentration of Business Operators—along with rules against other monopolistic conducts. The 2008 AML officially separated the 'anti-monopoly review' from the 'national security review' and recognized the necessity of a national security review. More specifically, besides the anti-monopoly review, a foreign investor should also go through the national security review procedure when it plans to participate in the concentration of business operators by merging or acquiring a domestic enterprise or by any other means where national security is involved.[116]

The 2009 Provisions of the Ministry of Commerce on Mergers and Acquisitions of Domestic Enterprises by Foreign Investors (MOFCOM Provisions on M&As of Domestic Enterprises by Foreign Investors)[117] revised the Provisions on M&A of Domestic Enterprises by Foreign Investors. MOFCOM Provisions on M&A of Domestic Enterprises by Foreign Investors delete Chapter 5 (Anti-Monopoly Review), thus confirming the separation of the anti-monopoly review of relevant M&As[118] from the review and approval by other Chinese authorities of other aspects of the transactions.[119] When engaging M&As concerning Chinese enterprises, foreign investors should neither disturb the social economic order, harm the public interest, nor take action that would lead to the loss of state-owned assets, among other principles.[120]

(SAFE), Interim Provisions on Mergers and Acquisitions of Domestic Enterprises by Foreign Investors, enacted in January 2003, effective as of April 2003, and now expired.

114 ibid art 19.

115 MOFCOM, the State-Owned Asset Supervision and Administration Commission of the State Council, the STA, the SAIC, China Securities Regulatory Commission, the SAFE, Provisions on Mergers and Acquisitions of Domestic Enterprises by Foreign Investors, enacted in August 2006, effective as of September 2006 and now revised.

116 AML, art 38.

117 MOFCOM, Provisions of MOFCOM on Mergers and Acquisitions of Domestic Enterprises by Foreign Investors (MOFCOM Provisions on M&As of Domestic Enterprises by Foreign Investors), enacted and effective as of 22 June 2009.

118 ibid art 51.

119 Other relevant Chinese authorities include but are not limited to the SAIC and the SAFE.

120 MOFCOM Provisions on M&As of Domestic Enterprises by Foreign Investors, art 3.

Article 12 of MOFCOM Provisions on M&As of Domestic Enterprises by Foreign Investors requires that the foreign investor notify MOFCOM of an acquisition if two conditions are met: (a) the foreign investor obtains actual control of a Chinese enterprise; (b) the acquisition concerns a critical industry, affects, or may affect, the security of the national economy, or causes transference of actual control over the domestic enterprise with a well-established Chinese brand.[121] MOFCOM, together with other competent government departments, may request the merging parties to terminate the acquisition, assign relevant equities or assets, or take any other effective actions, if the acquisition materially affects or may materially affect the security of the national economy and the foreign investor fails to notify the acquisition.[122] To some extent, Article 12 could explain MOFCOM's blocking of Coca-Cola's acquisition of Hui Yuan due to the importance of the latter's brand.

The 2022 AML introduces the classification and grade mechanism through article 37.[123] 'Classification and grade mechanism' was first mentioned by the Opinions of the Central Committee of the Communist Party of China and the State Council on Accelerating the Construction of a National Unified Market, released in April 2022. The Opinions raise the requirement to 'intensify the review of mergers in finance, media, science & technology, people's livelihoods and other sectors and industries, as well as those involving start-up, new business model and labour-intensive industries, improve review quality and efficiency, and beef up the detection, alert and prevention of monopoly risks'.[124] It is predicted that SAMR will intensify its review of M&As in the industries above, directly or indirectly connected with national security.

6.4.2 Case Law

6.4.2.1 *Coca-Cola/Hui Yuan*

Coca-Cola/Hui Yuan[125] was the first transaction prohibited by the Chinese competition authority since the 2008 AML came into effect. After consulting relevant stakeholders,[126] MOFCOM expressed its concerns from three perspectives: (a) The merged Coca-Cola would have the ability to leverage its dominant position in the carbonated soft drink market to the fruit juice market, thus eliminating or restricting competition in the fruit juice market and further harming consumers' legitimate rights and interests.

[121] ibid art 12.

[122] ibid.

[123] For a discussion of the classification and grade mechanism, please see Wei Han, Yajie Gao, 'The Chinese National People's Congress Amends the National Competition Law Act, in the First Update in Fifteen Years and Includes a New Grading System for Merger Control', 24 June 2022, e-Competitions, art No 107267.

[124] Xinhua News Agency, 'Opinions of the Central Committee of the Communist Party of China and the State Council on Accelerating the Construction of a National Unified Market, s 7—Further Regulate Unfair-Competition-Related and (Improper) Market-Intervention-Related Conducts', 10 April 2022 http://www.gov.cn/zhengce/2022-04/10/content_5684385.htm accessed 15 September 2023.

[125] *Coca-Cola/Hui Yuan* MOFCOM Block Notice [2009] No 22 of 18 March 2009 http://fldj.mofcom.gov.cn/article/ztxx/200903/20090306108494.shtml accessed 15 September 2023 中华人民共和国商务部公告 [2009年] 第22号商务部关于禁止可口可乐公司收购中国汇源公司审查决定的公告.

[126] ibid s 3—Review Work.

(b) Brand was a key (input) for effective competition in the fruit juice market. The merged Coca-Cola would control two well-known brands, 'Mei Zhi Yuan' and 'Hui Yuan'. Accordingly, the merged Coca-Cola's controlling power over the fruit juice market would be strengthened. The MOFOCM applied the leveraging ToH, considering that Coca-Cola already had a dominant position in the carbonated soft drink market. MOFCOM was concerned that the acquisition would significantly increase entry barriers to the fruit juice market.

(c) MOFCOM estimated that the acquisition would foreclose small fruit juice competitors and constrain the ability of other fruit juice market players to participate in competition and innovation, thus damaging the effective competition in and development of China's fruit juice market.[127]

The notified acquisition provoked public opposition for the reason of industrial security, and in particular, national security. Some hold that 'Hui Yuan' is not only a famous trademark but also a 'national brand', which is, however, not a legal term. Opponents were concerned that it would become more difficult to establish famous and successful Chinese brands if famous domestic brands still at the development stage were so easily and arbitrarily sold to foreign investors.[128] An academic from the research institute affiliated with MOFCOM denied the role played by the concern over national security in MOFCOM's review of *Coca-Cola/Hui Yuan*.[129]

6.4.2.2 Carlyle *Group/XCMG*

In October 2005, Carlyle Group entered into an agreement with Xuzhou Construction Machinery Group (XCMG) to acquire 85 per cent of Xugong Group Construction Machinery Co Ltd (XCMC) for $375 million. Before the planned acquisition, XCMC was wholly controlled by XCMG, wholly owned by the Xuzhou State-owned Assets Supervision and Administration Commission.[130] XCMC was the largest construction machinery manufacturer and distributor in China.

At that time, China's AML had not yet been enacted. The merging parties submitted an anti-monopoly report to prove that Carlyle Group's acquisition of China's largest machinery manufacturer would not obstruct domestic competition. The transaction had to obtain approval from NDRC and MOFCOM, given that it was a foreign investment project worth more than $100 million.

While the merging parties awaited MOFCOM's approval, a domestic private competitor, SANY Group, proposed to acquire XCMC for $400 million. The then CEO of SANY Group listed reasons why XCMC should not be sold to a foreign investor,

[127] ibid s 4—Competition Issues.

[128] Eg, Xufeng Zhang, 'Analysis of Coca-Cola's Acquisition of Hui Yuan', Golden Education, 22 December 2014 https://m.gaodun.com/guoshui/647299.html accessed 15 September 2023.

[129] news.ifeng.com, Expert from MOFCOM: Coca-Cola/Hui Yuan Does Not Concern National Security, 5 September 2008 https://news.ifeng.com/c/7fYQRH63PWq accessed 28 August 2022.

[130] Carlyle, 'The Carlyle Group Agrees to Acquire an 85% Stake in Xugong Group Construction Machinery Co Ltd for US$ 375 million (CNY 3 billion)', 24 October 2005 https://www.carlyle.com/media-room/news-release-archive/carlyle-group-agrees-acquire-85-stake-xugong-group-construction accessed 11 September 2022.

including (a) XCMC engaged in industries of strategic importance to the state and (b) XCMC was under-valued, which would lead to the loss of state-owned assets.[131]

In October 2006, Carlyle Group modified relevant provisions, proposing to decrease the acquisition of shareholding in XCMC from 85 per cent to 50 per cent. In early 2007, Xinhua News Agency submitted three reports to the central government, challenging the transaction from several perspectives, leading to MOFCOM's prohibition.[132]

While stakeholders were waiting for MOFCOM's approval, the *Several* Opinions of the State Council on Accelerating the Revitalization of the Equipment Manufacturing Industry[133] were released in February 2006. More specifically, Article 7 of Section III prescribes that 'For key equipment manufacturing enterprises that play a key role in the field of major technical equipment manufacturing, on the basis of ensuring the state's controlling power and leadership, they should be supported to carry out cross-industry, cross-regional, and cross-ownership reorganization. The opinions of the relevant departments of the State Council shall be sought when the controlling rights of large key equipment manufacturing enterprises are transferred to foreign capital.'[134] The opinions represent the Chinese authorities' position with regard to the protection of key industries concerning national security.

6.4.2.3 *Yonghui/Zhongbai*

On 15 August 2019, Yonghui Superstores (Yonghui) obtained SAMR's unconditional clearance of its increased shareholdings in Zhongbai Holdings Group Co Ltd. (Zhongbai) from 29.86 per cent to 40 per cent, to become the latter's biggest shareholder.[135] Just a few days later, on 21 August 2019, both merging parties declared that they had received NDRC's notice to file for the security review of the transaction.[136] On 8 November 2019, the security review entered the special review stage.[137] On 16 December 2019, Yonghui declared it was cancelling the tender offer, maintaining its shareholdings of 28.96 per cent in Zhongbai and supporting Wuhan State-Owned Assets Marketing Company's position as actual controller of Zhongbai.[138]

[131] News.sohu.com, 'Carlyle Group Failed to Invest in XCMC, while State-Owned Assets were on the Verge of a Fire Sale', 24 July 2008 http://news.sohu.com/20080724/n258337881.shtml accessed 15 September 2023.

[132] Cj.sina.com, 'Why Carlyle Fails in China', 18 November 2017 https://cj.sina.com.cn/article/detail/6390473642/487314?cid=76568 accessed 15 September 2023.

[133] Guo Fa [2015] No 68.

[134] State Council, 'Several Opinions of the State Council on Accelerating the Revitalization of the Equipment Manufacturing Industry' (Summary), Guo Fa [2006] No 8, released on 28 March 2008 http://www.gov.cn/zhengce/content/2008-03/28/content_3083.htm accessed 15 September 2023.

[135] SAMR, Unconditional Clearance Case List during 12–18 August 2019 https://www.samr.gov.cn/fldes/ajgs/wtjjz/202204/t20220424_343731.html accessed 11 September 2022.

[136] Yonghui Superstores, 'Announcement on Receiving the Notice of the National Development and Reform Commission on the Security Review of Foreign Investment', 23 August 2019 http://static.cninfo.com.cn/finalpage/2019-08-23/1206554780.PDF accessed 15 September 2023.

[137] Finance.china.com.cn, 'Yonghui's Tender Offer to Zhongbai is Facing the National Development and Reform Commission's Special (Security) Review' (14 November 2019) http://finance.china.com.cn/stock/20191114/5122495.shtml accessed 15 September 2023.

[138] Xueqiu.com, 'Tender Offer Cancelled! Why Yonghui Superstores Gives up the Position of Controlling Shareholder of Zhongbai Holdings Group?' (17 December 2019) https://xueqiu.com/1333325987/137528597 accessed 15 September 2023.

This was the first case involving a national security review since NDRC took over MOFCOM's responsibilities for security reviews of foreign investments.[139] At least two reasons can shed some light on the national security review: (a) Yonghui was recognized as a foreign investor, even though its biggest shareholder was the Dairy Farm Company Group Ltd, a Hong Kong-registered private equity group; and (b) even if the main business scope of both merging parties was retailing, which might not fall within the scope of the security review prescribed by the Measures for Security Review of Foreign Investment to be discussed later, retailing has nevertheless attracted NDRC's attention.

In recent years, foreign capital investment in the supermarket sector has rarely triggered a national security review. Some criticize that the national security review has become a tool to gain controlling power over listed companies.[140] *Yonghui/Zhongbai* further muddies the waters in terms of a lack of predictability and transparency of national security reviews in China. Still, obtaining basic knowledge of China's national security review legal regime helps stakeholders analyse and predict accordingly.

6.4.3 Legal Framework of National Security Review

In 2011, with continuing economic globalization and the further expansion of China's opening up to the outside world, investments made by foreign investors through M&As significantly increased. To guide the orderly development of M&As of domestic enterprises by foreign investors and safeguard national security, the State Council established the security review system through the Notice of the General Office of the State Council on the Establishment of the Security Review System for Mergers and Acquisitions of Domestic Enterprises by Foreign Investors (State Council Notice on Security Review).[141]

It is China's first systematic legal framework for the national security review of foreign investment. The State Council Notice on Security Review covers industries under the security review mechanism, the content of security reviews, relevant working mechanisms, and review procedures. In the same year, 2011, the Interim Provisions of the Ministry of Commerce on Issues Related to the Implementation of the Security Review System for Mergers and Acquisitions of Domestic Enterprises by Foreign Investors[142] and the Provisions of the Ministry of Commerce on the Implementation

[139] Xingang Yu et al, 'Is the Era 2.0 of Security Review of Foreign Investment Coming?' (4 September 2019) https://mp.weixin.qq.com/s?__biz=MjM5ODI5MzI0NA==&mid=2651309683&idx=1&sn=69c57ff9993ce2be8f16de2510a1cbdf accessed 15 September 2023.

[140] Huang Kai, 'Why Yonghui's Acquisition of Zhongbai Fails (Mainly) Because of National Security Review?' (20 December 2019) https://xueqiu.com/7289558063/137704797 accessed 15 September 2023.

[141] General Office of the State Council, Notice of the General Office of the State Council on the Establishment of the Security Review System for Mergers and Acquisitions of Domestic Enterprises by Foreign Investors (State Council Notice on Security Review), enacted in February 2011 and effective as of March 2011.

[142] MOFCOM, Interim Provisions of the Ministry of Commerce on Issues Related to the Implementation of the Security Review System for Mergers and Acquisitions of Domestic Enterprises by Foreign Investors, effective between 5 March 2011 and 31 August 2011.

of the Security Review System for Mergers and Acquisitions of Domestic Enterprises by Foreign Investors[143] were released, providing more detailed guidance on procedure-related issues regarding security reviews of foreign M&As.

6.4.3.1 Scope of Security Review

The State Council Notice on Security Review applies when (a) foreign investors engage in M&As of domestic military industrial enterprises and supporting military-industrial enterprises, enterprises surrounding major and sensitive military facilities, and other entities relating to national defence security; or (b) foreign investors engage in M&As of domestic enterprises relating to important agricultural products, energies and resources, infrastructural facilities, and transportation services, as well as key technologies, manufacturing of major equipment, and other industries relating to national security, and where they would obtain actual controlling power over domestic enterprises.[144]

In 2015, the Notice of the General Office of the State Council on Printing and Distributing the Trial Measures for the National Security Review of Foreign Investment in Pilot Free Trade Zones (State Council Notice on Security Review in Pilot Free Trade Zones)[145] expanded the scope of the security review to include 'important culture, important information technology products and services'.[146] This change echoes the enactment of the National Security Law in the same year and the Cybersecurity Law of the PRC (Cybersecurity Law) under deliberation then, representing the urgency of protecting cultural security and cybersecurity in the new era.

There is an unofficial list of industries under the purview of China's national security review.[147] The list is only for preliminary reference and does not constitute a legally binding list for stakeholders. For more details about the list, please find the appendix to this chapter.

6.4.3.2 Content of Security Review

During the security process, competent authorities focus on a transaction's influence over (a) the production ability of domestic products, the provision ability of domestic services and relevant equipment required by national defence; (b) the stable operation of the national economy; (c) the maintenance of good public order; and (d) the key-technologies-related R&D ability in relation to national security.[148]

[143] MOFCOM, Provisions of the Ministry of Commerce on the Implementation of the Security Review System for Mergers and Acquisitions of Domestic Enterprises by Foreign Investors, enacted on 25 August 2011 and effective as of 1 September 2011.

[144] State Council Notice on Security Review, art 1(1). Please note that art 1(2) also defines what a 'merger or acquisition of a domestic enterprise by a foreign investor' is, the scope of which is much wider than in the anti-monopoly review of mergers in China.

[145] General Office of the State Council, Notice of the General Office of the State Council on Printing and Distributing the Trial Measures for the National Security Review of Foreign Investment in Pilot Free Trade Zones, enacted in April 2015 and effective as of May 2015.

[146] ibid art 1(1).

[147] Ping Xu and Lijuan Yao, 'Epoch-Making Changes in China's Foreign Investment Legislation' *China Law Insight* (20 January 2015) https://shorturl.at/bgpY3 accessed 15 September 2023.

[148] State Council Notice on Security Review, art 2.

6.4.3.3 Relevant Working Mechanism

In practice, the joint ministerial meeting for the security review of M&As of domestic enterprises by foreign investors (Joint Meeting) assumes the security review work in specific cases. The Joint Meeting is guided by the State Council and led by NDRC and MOFCOM. In accordance with the industry and/or the sector touched upon by the transaction, the relevant sectoral regulator joins NDRC and MOFCOM to carry out the security review work.[149]

The Joint Meeting's major duties include (a) analysing the influence of M&As of domestic enterprises by foreign investors on national security, (b) studying and coordinating the major issues arising from the security review of M&As of domestic enterprises by foreign investors, and (c) conducting the security review of the M&As of domestic enterprises by foreign investors and making decisions where necessary.[150]

To adapt to the needs of promoting the formation of a new pattern for comprehensive opening-up and to effectively guard against and resolve national security risks while actively promoting foreign investment,[151] pursuant to the Foreign Investment Law of the PRC, the National Security Law, and other laws and regulations, NDRC and MOFCOM enacted the Measures for Security Review of Foreign Investment in 2020, which came into effect on 18 January 2021. Since then, national security reviews have not been limited to foreign investors' M&As of domestic enterprises but have extended to greenfield investment and other forms of investment.[152]

The Measures for Security Review of Foreign Investment generally copy and paste the State Council Notice on Security Review and the State Council Notice on Security Review in Pilot Free Trade Zones in terms of the basic structure, except for the review working mechanism and the design of review organizations. The Measures for Security Review of Foreign Investment express that the state shall establish a foreign investment security review work mechanism (Work Mechanism) to be responsible for organizing, coordinating, and guiding the security review of foreign investment. The Work Mechanism's General Office is set within NDRC, led by NDRC and MOFCOM, and responsible for the daily security review of foreign investment.[153]

6.4.3.4 Review Procedure

Generally, the security review comprises two steps. First, the foreign investor files an application to MOFCOM. If MOFCOM opines that the transaction falls under the scope of the security review, it requests the Joint Meeting to initiate the security review procedure within five working days.[154] Where relevant department(s) of the State Council, national industrial association(s), competitor(s), or enterprise(s) from upstream or downstream market(s) deem it necessary to conduct a security review,

[149] ibid art 3.
[150] ibid.
[151] NDRC, MOFCOM, Measures for Security Review of Foreign Investment, enacted in December 2020 and effective as of January 2021, art 1.
[152] ibid art 2(2).
[153] ibid art 3.
[154] State Council Notice on Security Review, art 4.

it/they may put forward proposals to MOFCOM accordingly. The Joint Meeting may then decide to conduct a security review if it deems this necessary.[155]

Second, the Joint Meeting conducts a general review of the transaction as requested by MOFCOM. If a transaction fails the general review, it enters the stage of special review. Merging parties should cooperate with the Joint Meeting in the security review process, provide required materials and information, and attend relevant inquiries.[156]

The general review is conducted by a Joint Meeting by consulting stakeholders in writing. Upon application from MOFCOM for the security review, the Joint Meeting should consult the opinions of the relevant department(s) in writing within five working days. Relevant department(s) should provide their opinions in writing within twenty working days of receiving the consultation request from the Joint Meeting. If the relevant department(s) hold that the transaction will not negatively effect on national security, then there is no need to move on to the special review stage. The Joint Meeting should produce review opinions within five working days of receiving the opinions of all the stakeholders in writing and delivering a written notice to MOFCOM accordingly.[157]

The Joint Meeting should initiate the special review within five working days of receiving written opinions if relevant department(s) hold(s) that the transaction would negatively influence national security. If different departments within the Joint Meeting reach a general consensus, the Joint Meeting provides its review opinions accordingly. If there are major disagreements, the Joint Meeting reports the transaction to the State Council. The Joint Meeting should complete the special review or report the transaction to the State Council within sixty working days of initiating the special review. Upon completion of the special review, the Joint Meeting delivers a written notice to MOFCOM.[158]

During the security review process, merging parties can file an application to MOFCOM to revise or withdraw the transaction.[159] The written opinions on the security review should be delivered by MOFCOM to the notifying parties.[160] If a transaction has caused or may cause significant damage to national security, the Joint Meeting requires MOFCOM and other relevant departments to terminate the transaction, requires the merging parties to transfer relevant shareholdings, assets, or takes other measures to eliminate the potential damage to national security.[161]

Under the 2021 Measures for Security Review of Foreign Investment, if one of the two conditions below is met, the foreign investor or relevant domestic party (Party Concerned) shall notify the Work Mechanism's General Office of the investment before

[155] ibid.
[156] ibid.
[157] ibid.
[158] ibid.
[159] State Council Notice on Security Review, art 4(4). A similar arrangement can be found in the Measures for Security Review of Foreign Investment, art 11.
[160] ibid art 4(5).
[161] ibid art 4(6). A similar arrangement can be found in the Measures for Security Review of Foreign Investment, art 12.

implementation: (a) investment in military industry, military industry supporting facilities or other fields concerning national defence security, as well as investment in the surrounding areas of military facilities and military industry facilities; or (b) investment in important agricultural products, energy and resources, equipment manufacturing, infrastructure, transportation services, important cultural products and services, information technology and Internet products and services, important financial services, key technologies and other essential fields concerning national security, or where there is a concern over obtaining actual control of the domestic enterprise.[162] Article 4 of the Measures for Security Review of Foreign Investment defines what 'actual control' is, which is similar to the 'change of control' under the anti-monopoly review of mergers.

Contingent on the working needs, the Work Mechanism's General Office can entrust relevant departments of the people's governments at provincial, autonomous regional and municipal levels to collect and transfer materials submitted by the Party Concerned in relation to the notification.[163] The Party Concerned should not implement the investment before the Work Mechanism's General Office has made its final decision. Within fifteen working days of receipt of the relevant materials, the Work Mechanism's General Office should decide on whether the foreign investment notified shall be subject to a security review and notify the Party Concerned of the decision in writing.[164]

The national security review of foreign investment consists of general and special reviews. If the Work Mechanism's General Office decides to conduct a security review of the foreign investment notified, it completes the general review within thirty working days.[165] After the general review, the Work Mechanism's General Office will clear the investment if it is of the opinion that the foreign investment does not affect national security. Conversely, if it believes opinion that the foreign investment affects or may affect national security, the Work Mechanism's General Office will decide to initiate the special review.[166]

The special review of the Work Mechanism's General Office ends with one of the three following decisions: (a) a clearance decision where the foreign investment notified does not affect national security; (b) a block decision where the foreign investment notified affects national security; or (c) a conditional clearance decision where imposing additional conditions on the foreign investment notified serves to eliminate its impact on national security, and the Party Concerned accepts the additional conditions in writing. The special review shall be completed within sixty working days and may be extended under special circumstances. The Party Concerned shall be notified in writing of the extension of the review period.[167]

162 Measures for Security Review of Foreign Investment, art 4.
163 ibid art 6.
164 ibid art 7.
165 ibid art 8(1).
166 ibid art 8(2).
167 ibid art 9.

The Measures for Security Review of Foreign Investment introduce unfavourable credit records in the relevant national credit information system if the Party Concerned (a) does not notify the Work Mechanism's General Office of the foreign investment as legally required; (b) implements the foreign investment before obtaining the final decision of the Work Mechanism's General Office; (c) provides false or misleading information; or (d) fails to implement the investment in accordance with the relevant conditions.[168]

The 2011 State Council Notice on Security Review and the 2015 State Council Notice on Security Review in Pilot Free Trade Zones are still valid. As such, uncertainties remain as to whether these two Notices or the 2021 Measures for Security Review of Foreign Investment prevail. The State Council needs to provide clear guidance in this regard.

6.4.3.5 Anti-Circumvention Mechanism

MOFCOM, or the Joint Meeting, should judge whether to conduct a security review based on the substantive content and actual impact of a transaction. Foreign investors should not circumvent the security review by any means, be it by holding shares on behalf of others, via trusts, multi-level reinvestment, leasing, loans, agreement-based control, or overseas transactions.[169]

6.4.3.6 What if There Are Changes to the Transaction?

If previously a transaction was not submitted to the Joint Meeting for a security review or the Joint Meeting held that the transaction did not adversely affect national security, the merging parties might subsequently modify the transaction, revise relevant documents, change business activities, or make other changes. If the modification, revision, or change makes the transaction fall under the purview of the national security review, then the merging parties should suspend relevant activities, and the foreign investor should notify MOFCOM or the Work Mechanism's General Office.[170]

Section 6.4.3 elaborates on the scope, content, relevant working mechanism, procedure, anti-circumvention mechanism, and legal response to a transaction of the national security review, should any changes occur. The concept of 'national security' is not set in stone. The state develops and continues to improve the national security strategy through comprehensively assessing international and domestic security situations, specifying the guidelines for medium- and long-term objectives of national security strategies and national security policies, tasks, and measures in key fields.[171]

[168] ibid arts 16–19.

[169] MOFCOM, Provisions of the Ministry of Commerce on the Implementation of the Security Review System for Mergers and Acquisitions of Domestic Enterprises by Foreign Investors, effective as of September 2011, art 9.

[170] ibid art 10. A similar arrangement can be found in the Measures for Security Review of Foreign Investment, art 14.

[171] National Security Law, art 6.

Besides the more traditional areas that fall within the scope of national security, such as the state's territorial sovereignty and maritime rights and interests, the basic economic system and socialist market economic order, the macro-financial system, natural resources, and energy, food, the advanced socialist culture, the regional ethnicity autonomy system, conservation of the ecosystem, and the peaceful utilization of nuclear energy and nuclear technology,[172] the Chinese authorities are also paying increased attention to more cutting-edge areas, such as cyber and information security,[173] to be discussed in section 6.4.4.

6.4.4 Cyber and Information Security

Since the Cybersecurity Law was enacted in November 2016,[174] China has gradually built up the cybersecurity legal system by following it with the Regulation on the Protection of the Security of Critical Information Infrastructure (Regulation on the Protection of CII),[175] the Data Security Law of the PRC (Data Security Law),[176] the Personal Information Protection Law of the PRC (Personal Information Protection Law),[177] the Measures for Cybersecurity Review,[178] and others. The relevant authority is the Cybersecurity Administration of China (CAC), which has stated that this review aims to examine data processing activities that may impact national security as well as preserve the supply chain security for critical information infrastructure so as to mitigate hidden risks and safeguard national security.[179]

6.4.4.1 *Didi Chuxing/Uber China*

Didi Chuxing's acquisition of Uber China (*Didi Chuxing/Uber China*) is among the most discussed transactions that should have been comprehensively reviewed by the Chinese competition authority. Besides controversies around the notion of variable

[172] ibid arts 17–31.

[173] ibid art 25.

[174] NPCSC, Cybersecurity Law of the PRC (Cybersecurity Law), enacted in November 2016 and effective as of June 2017. The Cyberspace Administration of China solicited public opinions on the amendment to the Cybersecurity Law during 12 September and 29 September 2022. For more details, see Cyberspace Administration Website, 'Notice on Publicly Soliciting Opinions on the Decision on Amending the Cybersecurity Law of the PRC' http://www.gov.cn/xinwen/2022-09/14/content_5709805.htm accessed 16 August 2023.

[175] State Council, Regulation on the Protection of the Security of Critical Information Infrastructure (Regulation on the Protection of CII), enacted in April 2021 and effective as of September 2021.

[176] NPCSC, Data Security Law of the PRC (Data Security Law), enacted in June 2021 and effective as of September 2021.

[177] NPCSC, Personal Information Protection Law of the PRC (Personal Information Protection Law), enacted in August 2021 and effective November 2021.

[178] The Cyberspace Administration of China, NDRC, the Ministry of Industry and Information Technology, the Ministry of Public Security, the Ministry of State Security, the Ministry of Finance, MOFCOM, the People's Bank of China, SAMR, the National Radio and Television Administration, the National Administration of State Secrets Protection, and the State Cryptography Administration, Measures for Cybersecurity Review, enacted in November 2021 and effective as of February 2022.

[179] John Jiang et al, 'China's Cybersecurity Review Regime: Framework and Latest Trends' (Lexology, 6 April 2023) https://www.lexology.com/library/detail.aspx?g=dd7d2c5a-b301-4f0c-a72b-226423ec9a74 accessed 15 September 2023.

interest entity[180] and the turnover-based notification threshold,[181] the *Didi Chuxing/ Uber China* has attracted widespread attention. Didi Chuxing debuted as a publicly traded company on the New York Stock Exchange on 30 June 2021[182]. Didi kept the acquisition low-profile on purpose; it was clearly aware of the corresponding risks arising from the laws on cybersecurity, but it still chose to go public without properly communicating with the competent Chinese authorities.[183]

Just three days after Didi's IPO, the CAC released the Notice on the Initiation of Cybersecurity Review of 'Didi Chuxing' on 2 July 2021. During the cybersecurity review, Didi Chuxing suspended the function of registering new accounts[184] and delisted the 'Didi Chuxing' app from app stores.[185] On 16 July 2021, the CAC, together with the Ministry of Public Security, the Ministry of National Security, the Ministry of Natural Resources, the Ministry of Transport, the State Administration of Taxation, and SAMR, sent investigation staff to the premises of Didi Chuxing to start a cybersecurity review.[186]

After about one year of investigation, on 21 July 2022, in accordance with the Cybersecurity Law, the Data Security Law, the Personal Information Protection

[180] The variable interest entity (VIE) structure is an 'agreement control' arrangement. The controller controls both the operation and balance sheet of the operating company in China through a series of agreements instead of shareholdings. With the VIE structure, the controlling non-operating company is registered overseas for finance and tax reasons and signs a series of agreements with a Chinese natural or legal person. The Chinese natural or legal person usually holds assets or runs businesses in industries that are not totally open to foreign capital. For more details, please see Ping Xu, 'Variable Interest Entity (VIE) Structure for Foreign Investment in the PRC May Face Challenge' (King and Wood, 20 October 2011) https://www.chinalawinsight.com/2011/10/articles/foreign-investment/variable-interest-entity-vie-structure-for-foreign-investment-in-the-prc-may-face-challenge/ accessed 15 September 2023.VIE is a grey area in China and used to be the excuse of most digital companies to circumvent the notification obligation of M&As they undertook. By punishing Alibaba, Tencent, and SF for not performing their notification obligations with CNY 500,000, MOFCOM made it clear that VIE is no longer an excuse for digital companies to circumvent notification obligations. For more details, please see SAMR, 'Person in Charge from SAMR Answers Questions Raised by Journalists in Relation to Alibaba's Acquisition of Intime Retail, Tencent's Acquisition of New Classics Media, and SF's Acquisition of Zhongyou Zhidi That Should Have Been Notified' (14 December 2020) http://www.samr.gov.cn/xw/zj/202012/t20201214_324336.html accessed 16 August 2023.

[181] Regarding whether turnovers of Didi and Uber China had met the notification threshold, stakeholders diverged. The spokesperson for MOFCOM, Danyang SHEN, commented that the transaction should be suspended unless notified. In comparison, Didi's representative argued that neither Didi nor Uber China had made any profit by August 2016. Besides, Uber China's turnover did not surpass the notification threshold. For more details, please see Bin PENG, 'Merger Between Didi and Uber China Trapped in the "Rashomon" of Anti-Monopoly Notification, Expert Advised MOFCOM to Proactively Intervene' (*Southcn*, 3 August 2016) http://news.southcn.com/china/content/2016-08/03/content_152924090.htm accessed 16 August 2023.

[182] Rey Mashakethi, 'Everything You Need to Know about Chinese Ride-Sharing Giant Didi's IPO' *Fortune* (30 June 2021) https://fortune.com/2021/06/29/didi-ipo-china-ride-sharing-everything-to-know/ accessed 15 September 2023.

[183] 'How Serious It is for Didi to Go Public on New York Stock Exchange', 7 July 2021 https://zhuanlan.zhihu.com/p/387451538 accessed 15 September 2023.

[184] CCTV, 'The Cybersecurity Administration of China Initiates Cybersecurity Review of Didi Chuxing' (3 July 2021) https://news.cctv.com/2021/07/03/ARTIHdpWJ8yBxQoP1K2IgdYs210703.shtml accessed 15 September 2023.

[185] Cybersecurity Administration of China (CAC), Notice on Delisting 'Didi Chuxing', 4 July 2021 http://www.cac.gov.cn/2021-07/04/c_1627016782176163.htm accessed 15 September 2023.

[186] CAC, 'The CAC, and Other Six Central Government Departments Send Investigation Staff to the Premises of Didi Chuxing S&T Co, Ltd to Initiate Cybersecurity Review', 16 July 2021 http://www.cac.gov.cn/2021-07/16/c_1628023601191804.htm accessed 15 September 2023.

Law, the Administrative Punishment Law of the PRC,[187] and others, the CAC imposed fines of CNY 8.026 billion on Didi Chuxing, and CNY 1 million on CHENG Wei (chairman of the board and CEO) and LIU Qing (president) respectively.[188]

As outlined by a representative from the CAC, Didi Chuxing had engaged in eight general types of illegal conduct: (a) illegal collection of screenshot information from users' mobile phone albums; (b) excessive collection of user clipboard information and application list information; (c) over-collection of passenger facial recognition information; (d) excessive collection of precise location (longitude and latitude) information when passengers evaluate the chauffeur service, the app is running in the background, and the mobile phone is connected to the orange video recorder device; (e) excessive collection of driver education information and storing personal ID information of registered drivers; (f) without informing passengers, analysing passenger travel intention information, resident city information, and trans-city business/travel information; (g) frequently requesting irrelevant 'phone permissions' when passengers use ride-sharing services; and (h) not accurately and clearly explaining the purposes of information processing.[189]

In May 2022, Didi Chuxing declared it was delisting its American Depositary Shares from the New York Stock Exchange.[190] To fill the gaps triggered by the Didi Chuxing incident, the Chinese legislator has enacted or revised cybersecurity-related rules, such as the Measures for Cybersecurity Review. It establishes a cybersecurity review mechanism for network products and services that may put China's national security at risk.[191] Online platform operators that control the personal information of more than one million users must now file a report to the CAC for cybersecurity review before going public abroad.[192] Accordingly, if a Chinese company invests in an overseas public-listed company, thus becoming indirectly listed in an overseas stock market, it may also have to go through the cybersecurity review procedure. The Measures for the Cybersecurity Review also provide a list of elements for the CAC's reference when conducting a cybersecurity review procedure and guidance on the review procedure.[193]

[187] NPCSC, Administrative Punishment Law of the PRC, enacted in March 1996, and revised in 2009, 2017, and 2021.

[188] CAC, Decision of the CAC on the Administrative Punishment of Didi Global Co, Ltd over the Concern of Cybersecurity, 21 July 2022 http://www.cac.gov.cn/2022-07/21/c_1660021534306352.htm accessed 15 September 2023.

[189] CAC, 'Representative from the CAC Answers Questions Raised by Journalists Concerning the Cybersecurity-Related Administrative Punishment Decision Against Didi Chuxing Global Co, Ltd', 21 July 2022 http://www.cac.gov.cn/2022-07/21/c_1660021534364976.htm accessed 15 September 2023.

[190] DiDi, 'DiDi Provides Notification to Delist its ADSs from NYSE' (23 May 2022) https://ir.didiglobal.com/news-and-events/news/news-details/2022/DiDi-Provides-Notification-to-Delist-its-ADSs-from-NYSE/default.aspx accessed 15 September 2023.

[191] Trade Commissioner Service (Canada), 'China's cybersecurity regime' (12 October 2022) https://www.tradecommissioner.gc.ca/china-chine/cyber-security_cyber-securite_china-chine.aspx?lang=eng accessed 15 September 2023.

[192] Measures for Cybersecurity Review, art 7.

[193] ibid art 10.

6.4.4.2 Special Attention Should be Paid by Merging Parties Regarding Cybersecurity, Especially Data Security

If at least one merging party is an operator of critical information infrastructure (CII),[194] the merged entity should store personal information and important data generated during its domestic operation in China. If it is indeed necessary to transfer such data overseas, a security assessment must be conducted in accordance with the measures developed by the national cyberspace administration in conjunction with relevant departments of the State Council.[195]

In July 2022, the CAC published the Measures for the Security Assessment of Data Export,[196] providing guidance for data processors who transfer important data and personal information overseas in their daily activities. The Measures provide an *ex ante* evaluation and constant supervision mechanism.[197] Data processors meeting certain conditions[198] should self-assess, such as the legality, appropriateness, and necessity of overseas recipient's data processing purpose and scope,[199] before submitting the application to the CAC through provincial branches.[200] Domestic data processors should explicitly list data protection obligations to be borne by overseas data recipient(s).[201] The security assessment focuses on data export's influence over national security, public interest, and individual or organization's legitimate rights and interests.[202]

Together with other central department(s), provincial branch(es) and professional organizations,[203] the CAC should finish the data security assessment within forty-five working days, which could be properly postponed when necessary.[204] The CAC's data security assessment result is effective for two years.[205] Within that period, the CAC could require data processors to suspend data export if finding risks, until rectification meets the requirement. Then, domestic data processors should initiate a new round of data security assessment process.[206] Besides notification to SAMR, it is foreseeable that merging parties may also have to go through the data security assessment process.

A low pass rate for security review of cross-border data transfers presents challenges triggered by self-assessment. In early July 2023, the Shanghai branch of the

194 CII refers to any network facilities and information systems in important industries and fields—such as public communication and information services, energy, transportation, water conservancy, finance, public services, e-government, and science, technology, and industry for national defence—that may seriously endanger national security, the national economy or people's livelihoods, or harm the public interest if they are damaged, lose their functions, or their data are leaked—regulation on the Protection of CII, art 2.

195 Cybersecurity Law, art 37.

196 CAC, Measures for the Security Assessment of Data Export, enacted in July 2022 and effective as of September 2022.

197 ibid art 3.

198 ibid art 4.

199 ibid art 5.

200 ibid art 7.

201 ibid art 9.

202 ibid art 8.

203 ibid art 10.

204 ibid art 12.

205 ibid art 14.

206 ibid art 17.

CAC revealed that it had received applications for security review of cross-border data transfers from 542 data processors, while only three passed the security review and ten failed.[207] Accordingly when conducting the self-assessment for cross-border data transfers, the merged entity should guarantee that the purpose, scope, and method of overseas data recipient's data processing meet the legality, appropriateness, and necessity principles.[208]At the macro level, Chinese authorities equally emphasize the economic value of big data and accompanying risks. The Central Committee of the Communist Party of China and the State Council's Opinions on Building a Data-Based System to Batter Play the Role of Data Element were released in December 2022.[209] Having recognized the roles played by big data in productivity, distribution, circulation, consumption, and social services, the Opinions point out that the establishment of a data-based system is essential for national development and security. During the latest round of central government institutional reform,[210] the State Data Bureau was established. The State Data Bureau is responsible for coordinating and promoting the construction of data infrastructure, coordinating the integration, sharing, development, and utilization of data resources, and coordinating the promotion of digital China, digital economy, digital society planning, and construction, etc.[211]

Section 6.4 has introduced the cohesion of the anti-monopoly review and the national security review of M&As. Taking *Coca-Cola/Hui Yuan*, *Carlyle Group/XCMG*, and *Yonghui/Zhongbai* as typical examples, this section has shown how national security may make a difference to the competition authority's anti-monopoly review of mergers. The section then introduces the legal framework of the national security review in China. It ends with the latest development of national security—cyber and information security, with a discussion of the Didi Chuxing incident and by presenting the new security risks that merging parties have faced.

6.5 Conclusion

This chapter elaborates on non-competition interests in China's merger control. It starts with the general rules and alerts the reader to the peculiarities of the Chinese competition authority's enforcement in section 6.2. Section 6.3 discusses industrial policy. The Chinese competition authority's focus on its domestic market is mirrored worldwide.

207 Wang Juan, 'Low Pass Rate for Security Reviews of Outbound Data Transfers in China's Shanghai Highlights Self-Assessment Challenges' *MLex* (6 July 2023) https://content.mlex.com/#/content/1483033/low-pass-rate-for-security-reviews-of-outbound-data-transfers-in-china-s-shanghai-highlights-self-assessment-challenges accessed 15 September 2023.

208 ibid.

209 Xinhua News Agency, 'Central Committee of the Communist Party of China and the State Council's Opinions on Building a Data-Based System to Batter the Role of Data Element' (19 December 2022) http://www.gov.cn/zhengce/2022-12/19/content_5732695.htm accessed 15 September 2023.

210 Xinhua News Agency, 'Central Committee of the Communist Party of China and the State Council Issue the "Party and State Institutional Reform Plan' (16 March 2023) http://www.gov.cn/zhengce/2023-03/16/content_5747072.htm accessed 15 September 2023.

211 ibid s 3(14).

Even if MOFCOM has been criticized for being affected by industrial policy, it is expected that with the codification of the FCRS, it is predicted that SAMR's merger control will be less likely to be influenced by industrial policy in the future.

Today, there is no clear boundary between industrial policy and national security, as explored in section 6.4, which illustrates both substantive and procedural aspects of national security review in China. Perhaps it is not always clear whether a specific industry or sector falls under the scope of the national security review. What is clear, however, is that we should expect more national security reviews, including by CAC by competent Chinese authorities, in the future, considering the massive data generated by the business operators in their daily activities.

Appendix: 'Unofficial' List of Industries Potentially Falling under the Purview of China's National Security Review

- planting of cereals and other crops
- livestock breeding
- pig breeding
- poultry breeding
- natural crude oil and natural gas exploration
- service activities related to oil and natural gas exploration
- ferrous metal mining and dressing industry
- non-metallic mining and dressing industry
- edible vegetable oil processing
- manufacture of starch and starch products
- petroleum processing
- coking and nuclear fuel processing industry
- organic chemical raw material manufacturing
- ferrous metal smelting and rolling processing industry
- non-ferrous metal smelting and rolling processing industry
- mining and quarrying equipment manufacturing
- oil drilling, special equipment manufacturing
- metallurgical special equipment manufacturing
- special equipment manufacturing for refining and chemical production
- textile special equipment manufacturing
- tractor manufacturing
- mechanized agricultural and gardening machinery manufacturing
- medical instrument, equipment, and machinery manufacturing
- environmental protection
- social public safety and other special equipment manufacturing
- metal shipbuilding
- aerospace vehicle manufacturing
- motor manufacturing
- transmission, distribution, and control equipment manufacturing
- industrial automatic control system device manufacturing
- electrical instrument and meter manufacturing
- drawing, calculation, and measuring instrument manufacturing
- hydroelectric power
- nuclear power generation
- other energy generation
- electricity supply

- thermal production and supply
- gas production and supply
- production and supply of tap water
- sewage treatment and its recycling
- freight train station
- other road transport support activities
- rail transport
- freight port
- other water transport auxiliary activities
- air transport auxiliary activities
- airport
- pipeline transportation industry
- loading and unloading
- other warehousing
- national post
- other delivery services
- telecommunications and other information transmission services
- wholesale industry
- retail industry
- marine service
- energy mineral geological exploration
- solid mineral geological exploration
- basic geological exploration

7

National Security and FDI Screening in Russia, Japan, India, and South Africa

7.1 Introduction

As we have seen in this book, the world has experienced the effects of economic globalization, a trend once seen as irreversible.[1] Most recently, the debate about the virtues of globalization has been refuelled by developed economies. As an illustration, Donald Trump, during his election campaign, pledged that he would raise trade barriers, withdraw from some trade agreements, and limit imports, among other measures, arguing that globalization helped 'the financial elite' while leaving 'millions of our workers with nothing but poverty and heartache'.[2] In the United Kingdom (UK), Brexit was a clear sign that globalization was no longer perceived as a panacea[3] and, having left the European Union (EU), the UK sought to protect its companies from unattractive foreign investors by widening the national security rules.[4] Similar concerns arose in countries such as Russia, South Africa, India, and Japan.

The aim of the chapter is not to detail each of these regimes but rather to discuss their main features, the historical background that led to the specific protectionist stance of each regime, and the challenges they entail for the legal and investment communities.

More recently, the pandemic caused a severe shock to international flows, including trade, foreign investments, and international travel.[5] It also highlighted the vulnerability of global supply chains. Indeed, the Covid-19 pandemic has reinvigorated the debate about the need to reassess the global trade model. The outbreak made governments reflect on the merits of globalized supply chains and the security of supply.[6] In

[1] Gao Shangquan, 'Economic Globalization: Trends, Risks, and Risk Prevention' (2000) CDP Background Paper No 1 ST/ESA/2000/CDP/1 https://www.un.org/development/desa/dpad/wp-content/uploads/sites/45/publication/CDP-bp-2000-1.pdf accessed 15 September 2023.

[2] Nick Corasaniti, Alexander Burns, and Binyamin Appelbaum, 'Donald Trump Vows to Rip Up Trade Deals and Confront China' *New York Times* (28 June 2016) https://www.nytimes.com/2016/06/29/us/politics/donald-trump-trade-speech.html accessed 15 September 2023.

[3] For a good discussion about why most British people voted for Brexit, see Harold D Clarke, Matthew Goodwin, and Paul Whiteley, *Brexit: Why Britain Voted to Leave the European Union* (CUP 2017).

[4] Liz Alderman, 'Its Eye on China, Britain Pushes Back on Foreign Takeovers' *New York Times* (24 July 2018) https://www.nytimes.com/2018/07/24/business/uk-china-takeovers-national-security.html accessed 15 September 2023. For a comprehensive overview of the legal framework adopted to tighten the FDI rules in the UK, see ch 4 of this book, 'National Security and FDI Screening in the UK' and Ioannis Kokkoris, 'National Security as a Public Interest Consideration in UK Merger Control' (2021) Journal of Strategic Security 14(2) 47.

[5] S A Altman, 'Will Covid-19 Have a Lasting Impact on Globalization' *Harvard Business Review* (20 May 2020).

[6] Philip Lowe, Adam Kidane, and Alec Burnside, 'Industrial Policy and EU Merger Control: Finding the Right Tools' in Ioannis Kokkoris and Nicholas Levy (eds), *Research Handbook on Global Merger Control* (Edward Elgar 2023) 273; Ioannis Kokkoris, 'EU Merger Control and National Security Assessment: A Moving Target', in Ioannis

response to the pandemic, several jurisdictions seeking to protect their economic sovereignty either introduced or updated screening regimes for foreign investment on national security grounds.

But also, the Covid crisis has shown that as developing countries' productive and investment footprints are less diversified, they are more likely to be exposed to systemic risks.

According to the United Nations Conference on Trade and Development (UNCTAD)'s 2022 *World Investment Report*, the global environment for international business and cross-border investment changed dramatically in 2022 because of the war in Ukraine, causing a triple food, fuel, and finance crisis in many countries worldwide.

Indeed, UNCTAD's 2021 *World Investment Report* indicated that in 2020, sixty-seven countries adopted policy measures related to foreign investment, most of which took place in developed economies, largely as a response to the pandemic and mainly restrictive.[7] The report noted that the number of restrictive policy measures in reaction to the pandemic superseded those adopted during the financial crisis 2007–09.[8] It also outlined that even if the vast majority of foreign direct investment (FDI) measures have been generally adopted by developed economies (81 per cent), an important number of developing and emerging economies are mirroring the movement.[9] The types of measures vary from country to country: some are temporary and others are permanent, some have lowered the thresholds that trigger intervention, some have expanded the prior approval requirements for FDI, and others have established strategic sectors where the special power regime is applied strictly.[10]

In its 2022 report,[11] UNCTAD indicated that in 2021, 53 economies introduced 109 policy measures related to foreign investment—a decrease of approximately 28 per cent compared with 2020.

On the one hand, developed countries expanded protection from foreign traders. More particularly, two-thirds of the policy measures less favourable to investment adopted in 2021 concerned the introduction or tightening of national security concerns, and nearly all of them were adopted by developed economies.[12] On the other hand, developing countries continued to liberalize and promote investments. For instance, at least thirty developing countries implemented various promotion and facilitation measures.[13] The number of measures more favourable to investment (fifty-five) declined but remained the majority.

Kokkoris and Nicholas Levy (eds), *Research Handbook on Global Merger Control* (Edward Elgar 2023) 328; K Fountoukakos, V Roberts, and R Allen, 'Addressing National Security Concerns in the Merger Context', in Ioannis Kokkoris and Claudia Lemus (eds), *Research Handbook on the Law and Economics of Competition Enforcement* (Edward Elgar 2022) 217.

[7] UNCTAD, *World Investment Report 2021: Investing in Sustainable Recovery* 109 https://unctad.org/system/files/official-document/wir2021_en.pdf accessed 15 September 2023.

[8] ibid.

[9] ibid 109, 111.

[10] See the summary of the measures, ibid 111–13.

[11] UNCTAD, *World Investment Report 2022: International Tax Reforms and Sustainable Investment*, 56 https://unctad.org/system/files/official-document/wir2022en.pdf accessed 15 September 2023.

[12] ibid 58.

[13] ibid 60.

This chapter focuses on the measures adopted in Russia, Japan, India, and South Africa. These jurisdictions are pertinent case studies as their unique characteristics offer us the opportunity to provide some reflections. For instance, the collapse of the Soviet Union was a watershed moment for liberal thinkers who have sought to keep governments separated from business. Despite the expectations, the Russian regime has seen the FDI rules as the right tool to advance geopolitical priorities (section 7.2). Like other countries, Japan has expanded the scope of review by lowering the thresholds from 10 per cent to 1 per cent and by including more than 500 companies in 12 industries relevant to national security. Unlike most jurisdictions, Japan has incorporated some foreign investment screening exemptions (section 7.3). India has crafted its national security measures grounded on land borders. This tactic was to protect its companies from opportunistic takeovers during the pandemic (section 7.4). In South Africa, a screening mechanism of foreign investments was introduced in 2018 but is not yet in force (section 7.5). In this context, this chapter suggests that for the business community, it is difficult to navigate all these distinctive rules, that foreign investment rules have proven to be reciprocal tools, and if applied without sufficient caution, governments are putting the benefits of free markets in peril.

7.2 National Security and FDI Screening in Russia

In 1991, the Soviet Union was dissolved. The collapse of the Soviet Union unveiled the challenges of having a state-run economy: lack of innovation, slow growth, high concentration, and strong dependence on its natural resources.[14] Prior to the dissolution, from the second half of the 1980s and under the influence of Mikhail Gorbachev, an economic and political restructuring began. Among the most significant reforms, in 1987, international joint ventures were permitted. In 1988, after several decades, private ownership was again declared legal.[15] Later in 1990, thanks to the special economic powers granted to Gorbachev, including those orientated to the privatization of state assets, unlimited foreign participation was authorized.[16] In 1993, special economic zones were created to expand exports, generate jobs, and boost innovation.[17]

[14] Andrey Popovich, 'Investing in Emerging Markets: Finding out How Political Risk Influences FDI in Russia', (20 April 2007). Available at SSRN: https://ssrn.com/abstract=996414 accessed 15 September 2023.

[15] Known as the 'Law on Cooperatives', USSR Supreme Soviet, 26 May 1988. English version available at https://soviethistory.msu.edu/1985-2/cooperatives/cooperatives-texts/law-on-cooperatives/ accessed 15 September 2023.

[16] Popovich (n 14) 42. For a comprehensive description and evaluation of the progress of Russia privatization, see Maxim Boycko, Andrei Shleifer, and Robert W Vishny, 'Privatizing Russia', Brookings Papers on Economic Activity, 2: 1993, available at https://scholar.harvard.edu/files/shleifer/files/privatizingrussia.pdf accessed 15 September 2023.

[17] For an explanation of the implementation process of industrial cluster policies in Russian regions with special economic zones, see Sergey Sosnovskikh, 'Industrial Clusters in Russia: The Developments of Special Economic Zones and Industrial Parks' (2017) 3 Russian Journal of Economics 174–99.

In 2002, Russian citizens were allowed to buy and sell farmland for the first time since the Bolshevik Revolution of 1917.[18]

Accession to the World Trade Organization (WTO) was also a milestone in Russia's liberalization process. Having applied for a membership in June 1993, it took almost twenty years to be admitted. As part of the accession process, Russia had to pass significant packages of legislation to conform with the requirements of the WTO in conjunction with an array of other commitments.[19] Finally, on 22 August 2012, the Russian Federation became the 156th WTO member.[20] In terms of inwards foreign investments, Russia initiated the liberalization process amidst a lack of interest on the part of foreign investors. Various reasons led to this unwillingness: political instability, poor business climate, inadequate tax law, property and creditor rights issues, a weak banking sector, and corruption.[21] The statistics will provide us with a better understanding of the FDI inflow in Russia.

Until 1998, FDI inflows did not exceed $1.4 bn per year.[22] This data becomes relevant once we look at the FDI net inflows reported in billions of dollars in subsequent years: 2.7 in 2000, 2.7 in 2001, 3.4 in 2002, 7.9 in 2003, 15.4 in 2004, 12.8 in 2005, 29.7 in 2006, 55.1 in 2007, and 72.8 in 2008.[23] The financial crisis impacted this growth trajectory but years later it was gradually resumed.[24] UNCTAD's 2022 *World Investment Report*[25] considered Russia to be the ninth top host economy in the world.

Among the most restricted sectors for foreigners, the legal sector, financial services and insurance, transport and storage, and extractive industries have been overly protected by the government.[26] Indeed, the most attractive industries in Russia, including oil, gas, and energy, are considered strategic, and subsequently the government substantively restricts FDI inflow in these sectors.[27] Regarding the financial sector, it has gradually been opened to foreigners, albeit the government dictates the volume of foreign capital participation.[28] Additionally, those investors willing to access Russian financial services need to overcome two important hurdles: first, domestic banks do not

[18] See Sharon LaFraniere, 'Russian Lawmakers Grant Right to Sell Farmland' *The Washington Post* (27 June 2002), available at https://www.washingtonpost.com/archive/politics/2002/06/27/russian-lawmakers-grant-right-to-sell-farmland/65dcfc80-7930-451d-82b3-c386be3326f4/ accessed 15 September 2023.

[19] It has been reported that during the first administration of President Vladimir Putin, Russia passed about forty-two packages of legislation to adhere to WTO requirements. See David Tarr and Natalya Volchkova, 'Russian Trade and Foreign Direct Investment Policy at the Crossroads', The World Bank, Policy Research Working Paper 5255, p 2 (March 2010).

[20] WTO, Accessions: Russian Federation, available at https://www.wto.org/english/thewtoe/acce/a1russiee.htm accessed 15 September 2023.

[21] See Rudiger Ahrend, 'Foreign Direct Investment into Russia—Pain Without Gain? A Survey of Foreign Investors', (May 2000). Available at SSRN: https://ssrn.com/abstract=620122 accessed 15 September 2023.

[22] See Yuriy Zaytsev, 'Diagnostics of FDI Inflow in Russia: Theoretical and Practical Issues' (28 January 2015). Available at https://ssrn.com/abstract=2591399 accessed 15 September 2023.

[23] See World Bank, *World Development Indicators* (2009), available at https://databank.worldbank.org/source/world-development-indicators accessed 15 September 2023.

[24] See UNCTAD, 'Global investment trends monitor' (28 January 2014, no 15) https://unctad.org/system/files/official-document/webdiaeia2014d1en.pdf accessed 15 September 2023.

[25] UNCTAD (n 11) 9.

[26] Zaytsev (n 22) 4.

[27] ibid 6.

[28] See Russian Federal Law No 395-1, 2 December 1990, 'On Banks and Banking Activity'.

follow international standards when publishing their reports, and second, creditors and owners are not sufficiently protected by the law.[29]

So far, we have seen that from the early 2000s, the Russian economy has become more liberal towards FDI; however, this new approach has been adopted in tandem with conflicting policies that have prevented higher levels of foreign investment. In particular, it has been reported that inconsistencies have resulted from the numerous restrictive laws and other policies in the form of presidential decrees, internal directives of the government and ministries, and federal and local procedures.[30]

Also, more recently, sanctions and countersanctions, mainly taken in response to the war in Ukraine, are drastically affecting FDI to and from Russia. Indeed, they mostly lead to the halting of existing investment projects and the cancellation of announced projects. On 6 April 2022, the European Commission issued guidance on how to screen FDI from Russia. It notably calls for vigilance against Russian FDI into the EU in a sense that these investments 'may pose a threat to security or public order in Member States'.[31] This position was also joined by the Biden Administration. The latter adopted on 6 April 2022 an Executive Order 'prohibiting new investment in and certain services to the Russian Federation in response to continued Russian Federation aggression'.[32]

The next section traces the most significant FDI regulations in Russia and examines its most recent developments.

7.2.1 The Regulatory Framework

Aiming to protect the rights of foreign investors, in 1991, an Investment Code was enacted and enhanced later in 1999 by the Law on Foreign Investment No 160-FZ.[33] The Law on Foreign Investment, among other things, defined the status of a foreign investor, the legal regimes for foreign investments, and the guarantees and benefits provided to foreign investors active in Russia.[34] Despite their existence, these laws were not applied in practice and instead there was a default position in which the influence of the Russian government over the economy was significant. This posture was officially formalized in 2008 with the adoption of the first foreign investment regime, whose main purpose

[29] Zaytsev (n 22) 6.

[30] Joel Bergsman, Harry G Broadman, and Vladimir Drebenstov, 'Improving Russia's Foreign Direct Investment Policy Regime' (2001) https://ssrn.com/abstract=288774 accessed 15 September 2023.

[31] Communication from the Commission, Guidance to the Member States concerning foreign direct investment from Russia and Belarus in view of the military aggression against Ukraine and the restrictive measures laid down in recent Council Regulations on sanctions (Council Regulation (EU) No 833/2014 concerning restrictive measures in view of Russia's actions destabilizing the situation in Ukraine ([2014] OJ L 229/1) and its amendments and Council Regulation (EC) No 765/2006 of 18 May 2006 concerning restrictive measures given the situation in Belarus ([2006] OJ L 134/1) and its amendments) [2022] OJ C 151 I/01.

[32] Herbert Smith Freehills, 'Commission issues Guidance on FDI from Russia and Belarus and calls for greater scrutiny due to increased risk of harm to security or public order', 12 April 2022.

[33] US Department of State, 'Investment Climate Statements for 2016: Russia' https://www.ecoi.net/de/dokument/1036685.html accessed 15 September 2023. The English version of the Law on Foreign Investments, Law No N 160-FZ, 9 July 1999 is available at https://investmentpolicy.unctad.org/investment-laws/laws/87/russian-federation-foreign-investment-law accessed 15 September 2023.

[34] Law No N 160-FZ, 9 July 1999.

was to protect the Russian national security, an endeavour previously achieved using merger control rules.[35] The regime was regulated by the Federal Law No 57-FZ 'On the Procedure of Making Foreign Investments in Companies of Strategic Importance for National Defence and State Security' (also known as the 'Strategic Investment Law'), which came into force on 7 May 2008.[36]

Adopting the Strategic Investment Law was pursued to ensure the entire government's control over the natural resources in the country, especially oil and gas. It has been said that the Yukos affair paved the way for the enactment of this regulation. In 2003, the government tried to gain control of the most profitable private oil company in Russia at that time, Yukos. The senior managers of the company were prosecuted under allegations of tax evasion and embezzlement, and the government sought to freeze their assets.[37]

As a consequence of the events related to Yukos, the Strategic Investment Law was enacted with the aim to apply stricter control to investments in strategically important sectors of the economy.[38] To this end, the Government Commission on Monitoring Foreign Investment (the Government Commission, hereafter) was created and bestowed with control over foreign investment, headed by the Chairman of the Russian government and composed of the head of certain ministries and other government bodies.[39] Article 6 of the law defined the conditions under which foreign investment will operate in forty-five strategic sectors that can be divided into four categories: natural resources, defence, media, and monopolies.[40] Among the strategic sectors: nuclear

[35] Organisation for Economic Cooperation and Development (OECD) Investment Policy Review: Russian Federation https://www.oecd.org/daf/inv/investment-policy/41065076.pdf (last visited 12 October 2023).

[36] Federal Law No 57-FZ 'On the Procedure of Making Foreign Investments in Companies of Strategic Importance for National Defence and State Security'.

[37] RG Gidadhubli, 'Yukos Affair: Putin Attacks Russia's Oil Barons' (2003) 38 Economic and Political Weekly 4949.

[38] Foreign public investors are prohibited from obtaining control over strategic entities or acquiring more than 25 per cent of a strategic entity's property and must obtain the consent of the Government Commission for acquisitions of the reduced stakes in strategic entities or acquisition of blocking rights concerning such entities. Igor Ostapets, 'Foreign Direct Investment Reviews 2021: Russian Federation', White and Case, https://www.whitecase.com/insight-our-thinking/foreign-direct-investment-reviews-2021-russian-federation accessed 15 September 2023.

[39] See US Department of State (n 33).

[40] Clifford Chance, 'A Legal Overview of Foreign Investment in Russia's Strategic Sectors', May 2014, available at https://www.cliffordchance.com/content/dam/cliffordchance/briefings/2014/05/a-legal-overview-of-foreign-investment-in-russias-strategic-sectors.pdf accessed 15 September 2023.

The Strategic Investments Law provides an exhaustive list of activities of strategic importance and forty-eight types of business activities, grouped in the following categories:

- nuclear and radioactive materials;
- military equipment;
- aviation and space;
- oil and gas;
- natural resources;
- mining exploration and production;
- mass media and telecoms;
- harvesting (catching) of aquatic biological resources; ('aquatic biological resources' is replaced with fishing in October 2022);
- coding and cryptographic equipment;
- printing and publishing;
- use of agents of infectious diseases (except for companies engaged in food production);
- services in seaports and river ports; and
- services provided by natural monopolies such as:

  oil and gas pipeline transport;
  railroad transport;

and radioactive materials, devices and waste, aviation and space, natural resources, exploration, and production of minerals on subsoil plots of federal value, use of subsoil plots of federal value (oil and gas), coding and cryptographic equipment, mass media and telecommunications, and use of agents of infectious diseases (except food production).[41] The statute introduced the obligation for foreign investors intending to control any business operating in these strategic sectors to request prior authorization from the Government Commission.[42]

In 2008 and 2009, two decrees of the government of the Russian Federation were adopted, providing some rules for the preliminary approval and submission of information where transactions of strategic importance for national security and defence are involved.[43]

This considerable expansion of the strategic status of specific sectors, some of which do not seem to be strategic in many economies, has been the object of continuous criticism, along with the length of the procedures, which can last between four to seven months.[44] Furthermore, the Strategic Investment Law amended the Law on Foreign Investment No 160-FZ of 1999, according to which any foreign investor acquiring 25 per cent or more of a strategic or non-strategic Russian entity must obtain prior approval.[45] In other words, foreign investors need to observe two distinct pieces of legislation, both of which can trigger screening reviews. Likewise, even if the list of strategic sectors contained in the Strategic Investment Law is exhaustive, further amendments gave the right to the chair of the Government Commission to present for consideration the Commission transactions conducted by foreign investors involving almost any Russian business entity, not just strategic ones.[46]

Since the enactment of the regime, a number of updates have been made, which will be briefly presented below.

On 1 July 2017, a legal provision came into force limiting the range of entities that have the right to establish control over strategic companies.[47] On 30 July 2017, an amendment took place expanding the list of transactions requiring strategic investment clearance and changing the powers of the Government Commission. Now, for instance, the operation of an electronic trading platform is considered a new strategic activity.[48] On 12 June 2018, an amendment entered into force introducing the

services in airports;
water supply, and so on.

R Verdenikov and D Domnin, 'FDI Guide Russia', https://www.ibanet.org/document?id=FDI-Guide-Russia-2022 accessed 15 September 2023.

[41] The Federal Law 'On procedures for foreign investments in companies having strategic importance for the national security and defence' No 57-FZ, 29 April 2008.
[42] Tarr and Volchkova (n 19).
[43] Decrees of the government of the Russian Federation No 795, 27 October 2008, and No 838, 17 October 2009.
[44] Clifford Chance (n 40); Tarr and Volchkova (n 19); Bergsman, Broadman, and Drebenstov (n 30).
[45] Clifford Chance (n 40).
[46] Ostapets (n 38).
[47] Federal Law No 155-FZ, 1 July 2017, known as the Russian Strategic Enterprises Law.
[48] Federal Law No 165-FZ, 18 July 2017.

concept of non-disclosing companies and clarifying the strategic clearance process.[49] In December 2018, a decree was issued detailing the scope of the information to be disclosed, together with the procedure for the provision and registration of the data.[50] In December 2019, the Ministry of Justice approved Federal Antimonopoly Service (FAS) administrative regulations regarding foreign company information on beneficiaries, beneficial owners, and controlling persons.[51] On 8 July 2020, a draft of a legal provision prepared by FAS was approved by the State Duma clarifying the scope of corporate rights. Thus, voting rights temporarily transferred through any agreement or transaction can trigger clearance under the Strategic Investments Law.[52] In 2021, the foreign investment rules were intensified in two specific industries: mass media and fishing.[53]

As it currently stands, the list of activities of 'strategic importance' comprises forty-seven activities.[54] These strategic sectors of the economy notably include military technology, nuclear power, aircraft and the space industry, the development of subsoil fields of federal significance (strategic fields), natural monopolies (eg, oil and gas pipeline transportation, railroads, transportation terminals, and airports), certain marine port operations as well major telecommunications and print media.[55]

7.2.2 Main Authorities and Procedures

In a nutshell, in Russia, FDI screening for national security is conducted through (a) mandatory filing of the proposed investments in strategic sectors for which prior consent should be obtained in order to proceed with the investment; (b) *post facto* notification when, due to the change in voting rights distribution, the foreign investor gains control over the enterprise in the sectors of concern; (c) pre-authorization procedure for cases when the establishment of a foreign investor control is not clearance.[56]

The FAS—the Russian Competition Authority—is responsible for monitoring FDIs.[57] FDI filing is submitted to the FAS, but also, during a merger control review, the FAS can request disclosure of information to assess the need for clearance subject to the Foreign Investments Law and the Strategic Investments Law. Based on the information provided by the interested parties, FAS checks if the acquirer is a foreign investor, if the

[49] Federal Law No 122-FZ.

[50] Decree No 1456 of the Government of the Russian Federation.

[51] Decree No 1691/19 of FAS Russia.

[52] Draft Federal Law No 946057-7.

[53] Evgeniya Rakhmanina, 'Russian Foreign Investment Regime: Some Rules Tightened, Others Relaxed', Linklaters (25 November 2021), available at https://www.linklaters.com/en/insights/blogs/foreigninvestmentlinks/2021/november/russian-foreign-investment-regime-some-rules-tightened-others-relaxed accessed 15 September 2023.

[54] Ostapets (n 38).

[55] Herbert Smith Freehills, 'Legal Guide for Foreign Investors in Russia' (February 2019) https://www.herbertsmithfreehills.com/file/33191/download?token=mirSmy_z accessed 15 September 2023.

[56] UNCTAD, 'The Evolution of FDI Screening Mechanisms: Key Trends and Features' (2023) Investment Policy Monitor No 25 https://unctad.org/publication/evolution-fdi-screening-mechanisms-key-trends-and-features accessed 15 September 2023.

[57] Decree of the Government of the Russian Federation No 510, 6 July 2008.

Russian asset(s) is part of a strategic sector and if the transaction is subject to the relevant tests for approval.[58] The FAS can consult with the Ministry of Defence, the Federal Security Service, and other governmental institutions if the transaction should be referred to the Chairman for his decision. The FAS will send the file to the Chairman if at least one positive response is given.[59] In the natural monopolies sector, acquisitions of more than 10 per cent of fixed assets require approval from the FAS.[60]

The Government Commission reviews submitted notifications where the target is a strategic company and under the Strategic Investments Law decides *ex ante* whether there is a threat to national security and defence. Notoriously, the provision does not indicate the criteria or the scope of the review.[61] Preliminary proceedings are held by the FAS, where applications are submitted. Applicants cannot approach the Government Commission directly, and for this reason, the FAS acts as a 'secretary' by checking all documents, coordinating agencies, and preparing a draft of the decision to the Government Commission. Once the application is submitted, the procedure might take from four to seven months.[62] Since 2 February 2016, the Chairman of the Government Commission has the right to decide whether the final decision can be made in the absence of Government Commission members (absentee voting).[63] Moreover, the Government Commission is not obliged to disclose the reasons why a transaction has been rejected.[64] Although in theory, the Government Commission's decisions can be challenged before the Russian Federation Supreme Court, in practice no decision has yet been challenged.[65] In the banking sector, the Central Bank of Russia approves foreign investment transactions.[66] Also, amendments introduced in 2017 gave the Chairman of the Government Commission the right to decide that prior approval is required for any transaction by any foreign investor if this is needed to ensure national defence and state security.[67]

Transactions executed in breach of the Strategic Investments Law are null and void.[68] If it is not possible to apply the consequences of invalidity on a void transaction, the FAS can bring a lawsuit before the Russian courts seeking to remove the foreign investor of

[58] Alexander Viktorov and Olga Kovtunova, 'The Foreign Investment Regulation Review: Russia', The Law Reviews (17 October 2021), available at https://thelawreviews.co.uk/title/the-foreign-investment-regulation-review/russia (Last visited 12 April 2022).

[59] Ostapets (n 38).

[60] The Federal Law 'On natural monopolies' No 147-FZ, 17 August 1995.

[61] Ostapets (n 38).

[62] Alexander Viktorov and Olga Kovtunova, 'The Foreign Investment Regulation Review: Russia', The Law Reviews (17 October 2021), available at https://thelawreviews.co.uk/title/the-foreign-investment-regulation-review/russia (Last visited 12 April 2022).

[63] Decree of the Government of the Russian Federation No 46, 30 January 2016.

[64] Torsten Syrbe and Any Tangyan, 'Russia', in Veronica Roberts (ed), *Foreign Direct Investment Regulation Guide* (Global Competition Review 2021) https://www.cliffordchance.com/content/dam/cliffordchance/briefings/2021/12/article_russia_fdi.pdf accessed 15 September 2023.

[65] ibid; Léon Korsten and others, 'Multi-Jurisdiction Guide for Screening Foreign Investments' (DLA Piper, May 2021) 128–30 https://www.dlapiper.com/en/chile/insights/publications/2021/05/multi-jurisdiction-guide-for-screening-foreign-investments/ accessed 15 September 2023.

[66] The Federal Law 'On banks and banking activities' No 395-I, 2 December 1990 and the Law of the Russian Federation 'On the organisation of insurance business in the Russian Federation' No 4015-I, 27 November 1992.

[67] Ostapets (n 38).

[68] Ostapets (n 38).

its rights to vote at the shareholders' meeting of the strategic company or to invalidate those decisions adopted after the violation of the law.[69] Undertakings can be subject to fines of up to one million roubles for failure to notify or obtain prior approval.[70] Parties can provide documents, discuss the transaction, and potential remedies with the FAS before filing under the Strategic Investments Law.[71] The FAS will deny approval under the Competition Law if the same transaction is not approved by the Government Commission under the Strategic Investments Law.[72] The Government Commission is also entitled to conduct an assessment of submitted data. Additionally, operational units of the Federal Security Service agencies are entitled to undertake operational search measures to establish whether foreign investors or third parties have real intentions to take control of a company of strategic importance.[73] Likewise, Law FZ-242 requires that since 1 September 2015, personal data of Russian citizens be handled and stored on local servers to increase state security. Given the scope of the provision, all Russian and foreign companies need to observe the rules contained in the provision, albeit proper guidance about how to implement them is scant.[74]

The analysis presented herein has evidenced that applying national security concerns has facilitated tightened control over foreign investments in a wide range of sectors seen by the Russian government as strategic, even if the same sectors do not fall into the same category in other jurisdictions. Sectors that fall within the scope of the screening include not only those directly related to the state defence and security (eg, operations with nuclear materials, production of weapons, and military machines) but also indirectly related sectors (eg, TV and radio broadcasting over certain territories, extraction of water bioresources, and publishing activities).[75]

The next part will refer to the most recent developments triggered by Russia's invasion to Ukraine. The foregoing analysis aims to show how foreign investment rules represent effective tools to counteract geopolitical tensions. It also suggests that there are two closely intertwined realities. The first is that cross-border transactions involve a state-power interaction. The second is that national security concerns in times of turmoil can be used as a non-military response, leaving the outcome of the markets and market players at the discretion of the governments.[76]

As part of the coordinated response to the invasion of Ukraine, several governments and private companies across the world imposed a range of economic restrictions on the Russian economy. As an illustration, some countries banned the sale of

[69] Clifford Chance (n 40).
[70] ibid.
[71] Syrbe and Tangyan (n 64).
[72] Clifford Chance (n 40).
[73] For a brief overview of Russia's System of Operative Search Measures (SORM), see National Protective Security Authority, 'Geography and Ownership Risks for Users' (17 February 2022) https://www.npsa.gov.uk/geography-and-ownership-risks-users accessed 15 September 2023.
[74] See US Department of State (n 33).
[75] Ostapets (n 38).
[76] For a great analysis of the interventions in foreign takeovers on national security grounds to preserve state power, see Ashley Thomas Lenihan, *Balancing Power Without Weapons: State Intervention into Cross-Border Mergers and Acquisitions* (CUP 2018).

certain goods to Russia, the Russian international reserves were frozen by some central banks, foreign firms left the country or cut supplies,[77] and United States (US) imposed an embargo on Russian oil and gas.[78] The Russian government was not insusceptible to such economic sanctions and on 1 March 2022, imposed further foreign investment restrictions. Decree 81, 'On Additional Temporary Economic Measures to Ensure the Financial Stability of the Russian Federation', established a unique procedure for Russian residents that engage in transactions involving non-residents.[79]

Decree 81 targets investors based in countries that have imposed economic restrictions on the Russian economy. Hence, the special procedure applies to transactions that involve the provision of credits and loans, transfer of title to securities, and transfer of title to real state. According to Decree 81, the Government Commission will review and decide on those transactions. This approval mechanism added difficulties for foreign investors to divest from their business.

In addition, Decree 81 has prohibited Russian joint-stock companies from paying dividends to foreign shareholders and has suspended the transfer of money from accounts of non-resident undertakings from countries that have imposed economic sanctions.[80] Likewise, on 4 March 2022, the Russian government blocked Facebook alleging that Meta was spreading fake news about the war.[81]

Putin also signed another Presidential Decree No 95 on 'Temporary Order of Settlement of Obligations to Certain Foreign Lenders' which sets out a procedure for the performance by debtors, who are Russian residents, the Russian Federation, the constituent entities of the Russian Federation or municipalities, of their obligations (i) under credits and loans, as well as (ii) financial instruments (ie, including securities and derivatives) to Specific Foreign Persons.[82]

Also, in March 2022, Decree No 295 was issued by the Russian government. This Decree established the procedure for the issuance of governmental authorizations as far as controlled operations are concerned.

On 2 May 2022, Russia adopted Decree No 254 'On interim procedures for the fulfilment of corporate finance obligations toward certain foreign creditors'. The Decree mainly established new restrictions on the distribution of profits by limited liability companies: payment of distributed profit must be made only within certain limits, namely through S-type bank accounts, and payment made in rubles. The Decree also clarified the application of the previously introduced restrictions (specifically, set out in

[77] 'Russia's economy—Wounded bear' *The Economist* (2 April 2022).

[78] 'Briefing—The War in Ukraine, Confidence from the bunker' *The Economist* (2 April 2022). For deep analysis, visit https://www.economist.com/ukraine-crisis accessed 15 September 2023; See also 'The economic weapon—Western sanctions on Russia are like none the world has seen' *The Economist* (5 March 2022).

[79] Konstantin Baranov and Artashes Oganov, 'Russia Imposes Additional Restrictions on Transactions with Foreign Investors', (CMS Law-Now, 7 March 2022) https://www.cms-lawnow.com/ealerts/2022/03/russia-imposes-additional-restrictions-on-transactions-with-foreign-investors accessed 15 September 2023.

[80] ibid.

[81] 'Amid Russia's war, America Inc reckons with the promise and peril of foreign markets' *The Economist* (12 March 2022).

[82] Natalia Nikitina and Dmitry Lapshin, 'Special Economic Measures Have Been Adopted', 11 March 2022, https://www.jdsupra.com/legalnews/special-economic-measures-have-been-8703334/.

Presidential Decree dated 1 March 2022 No 81 and Presidential Decree dated 5 March 2022 No 95).[83]

On 5 August 2022, Russia set out new restrictions in financial, fuel, and energy sectors for certain foreign investors. Thus, a Presidential Decree No 520 established a ban to conduct any transaction resulting directly or indirectly in acquisition, modification, termination, or creation of any encumbrance over the rights to own, use, or dispose of securities, participatory interests in the share capitals or in certain Russian legal entities absent a specific permission by the Russian government.[84] This new ban will restrict the ability of investors to exit from their Russian investments or to restructure their Russian holdings without specific permission from the President.[85] This Decree is currently only applicable to shares and interests in specific companies and projects, as well those from the energy and banking sectors.[86] It is said that this new restriction prevented a foreign energy company involved in the Sakhalin-1 project (a consortium for production of oil and gas) from divesting its shares by selling them to another investor before they were forcibly transferred to the new operating company.[87]

A few weeks later, in September, Russia decided to extend the mechanism established in March 2022 by restricting certain FDI transactions in Russian limited liability companies. A Presidential Decree No 618 states that 'the government's prior approval will be required for transactions that result directly or indirectly in creating, modifying, or terminating (i) rights to own, use, or divest of any participatory interest in any LLC; (ii) other rights allowing the determination of the terms and conditions of management of any LLC; or (iii) other rights allowing the determination of the terms and conditions of entrepreneurial activity of any LLC'.[88] This new Decree will principally affect participatory interests in Russian limited liability companies. It appears that the broad terms used create the possibility that the restrictions could extend to pledge or option agreements, management or even shareholder agreements and articles of association, in which case they would provide a targeted person or entity controlling or extensive rights. The Decree could also extend to indirect transactions occurring outside of Russia.[89] From now on, any investor planning to restructure or sell their businesses will be required to get approval from the Sub-commission of the Government Commission

[83] Alexander Bychkov and Vladimir Efremov, 'New Russian Presidential Decree imposes new restrictions on distribution of profits and introduces certain clarifications to the existing limitations', 5 May 2022, https://sanctionsnews.bakermckenzie.com/new-russian-presidential-decree-imposes-new-restrictions-on-distribution-of-profits-and-introduces-certain-clarifications-to-the-existing-limitations/.

[84] UNCTAD, Investment Policy Hub, 'Russian Federation sets out new restrictions in financial, fuel and energy sectors for certain foreign investors', 5 August 2022

[85] Andrey Ignatenko and others, 'Update: Russia Introduces Ban Restricting Ability of Investors to Exit from Russian Investments in Certain Industries' (JDSUPRA, 11 August 2022).

[86] Georg Scherpf, 'Update on Measures Faced by Foreign Investors in Russia' (Clyde and Co, 16 January 2023) https://www.clydeco.com/en/insights/2023/01/update-on-measures-faced-by-foreign-investors-in-r accessed 15 September 2023.

[87] Jennifer A Josefson and others, 'Update: Russia Introduces Ban Restricting Ability of Investors to Exit from Russian Investments in Certain Industries', 10 August 2022.

[88] UNCTAD, Investment Policy hub, 'Russian Federation Restricts Certain FDI Transactions in Russian Limited Liability Companies', 8 September 2022.

[89] Scherpf (n 86).

for Foreign Investment Control.[90] Thus, Decree No 618 creates legal uncertainty in a sense that Russia seeks to reserve the right to decide who would be allowed to leave the Russia market and under what conditions.[91]

On 19 September 2022, the Russian government introduced amendments establishing a procedure for approval of transactions involving shares in Russian limited liability companies. The procedure is the same as that for adopting other controlled operations. In other words, the Government Commission ('sub-commission' under the terms of the decree) can decide to approve the operation without reservation, approve it under certain conditions or reject it. If the commission approves the operation, it must define the period of validity of its authorization. It is important to note that no deadline for examining applications has been defined by the Decree.[92]

The Russian administration also made the transfer of shares in Russian stock corporations by 'unfriendly persons' subject to the consent of the Government Commission for Control of Foreign Investment with Decree No 737 in October 2022.

At the end of December 2022, the Russian finance ministry announced that investors from 'unfriendly' countries selling stakes in Russian assets may have to do so at half-price or less. It added that Moscow could potentially take a 10 per cent cut of any transaction.[93] Two more new types of 'strategic' activities were introduced, ensuring the protection of fuel and energy facilities from unlawful interference at such facilities.

We should note that during 2023, there has been a flurry of new rules and clearance requirements for investors. The key clearances at the moment of writing are, on the one hand, from the Sub-commission for transactions in respect of Russian entities (all Russian LLCs and certain Russian JSCs) and where one of the parties to the transaction (or in some cases, specifically the seller) is—or is controlled by—a hostile foreign nation person (defined broadly to include any legal entity registered in, carries out its activities mostly in or derives most of its profit from a hostile foreign nation or is a citizen of a hostile foreign nation) and, on the other hand, the one from the President of Russia for entities active in the fuel and energy sector or engaged in activities involving specific subsoil resources or on land plots containing such, credit institutions (and included in relevant list[94]) as well as strategic enterprises (as listed in pre-existing Decree 1009), where the sellers are (or are controlled by) hostile foreign nation persons.[95]

[90] Andrey Ignatenko and others, 'Update: Russia Introduces Restrictions on Investors' Ability to Restructure Holdings in or Exit Russian LLCs', JDSUPRA, 19 September 2022.

[91] Björn Paulsen and Ilya Hatskevich, 'Russian Government Commission Regarding Transactions and Dividend Payments' *Noerr* (9 January 2023).

[92] David Lasfargue, 'Russian Counter Measures—Recent Developments', 29 September 2022, https://www.jeantet.fr/en/2023/09/russian-counter-measures-recent-developments-2/.

[93] Reuters, 'Russia Outlines Plan for 'Unfriendly' Investors to Sell Up at Half-Price', 30 December 2022.

[94] For the fuel and energy sector: Decree of the President of the Russian Federation dated 9 November 2022 No 372-rp, 9 November 2022; For the activities involving specific subsoil resources or land plots containing such: Decree of the President of the Russian Federation dated 26 October 2022 No 357-rp.

[95] Evgeniya Rakhmanina, 'Leaving Russia: the Price of Exit and Other Regulatory Hurdles' (Linklaters, 16 January 2023) https://www.linklaters.com/en/insights/blogs/foreigninvestmentlinks/2023/january/leaving-russia-the-price-of-exit-and-other-regulatory-hurdles accessed 15 September 2023.

7.2.3 The Case Law

In 2020, the FAS considered forty-five applications by foreign investors and sent eleven for review, ten of which were approved and one rejected.[96] Before concluding our review of the Russian FDI regime, we discuss below two indicative transactions in which FDI rules have been applied in Russia.

7.2.3.1 *Nabors/Tesco*

In 2017, Nabors Industries Ltd (Nabors), an American company provider of drilling equipment and services, among others, and Tesco Corporation (Tesco), a global leader in the provision of technology-based solutions for the upstream energy industry, announced the acquisition of Tesco by Nabors.[97] While the transaction was approved by the US Department of Justice and the Canada Competition Bureau, the Russian authority dissented.[98] In this case, the concept of 'related business activities' included in the list of activities considered to be strategic was applied in a broad manner. According to the FAS, the activity performed by the acquired company, 'running casing services for drilling', is a strategic activity that is an integral part of a technological process for the geological study of subsurface resources or exploration and mining of mineral resources in subsoil areas of federal significance.[99]

Hence, the FAS determined that the acquired company had strategic significance, so its approval was subject to the Strategic Investments Law procedure. However, as the parties failed to obtain prior approval, the acquired entity was fined, and the court deprived the foreign investor of its voting rights in the Russian strategic company. Subsequently, the Constitutional Court declared that organizations providing oilfield services in subsoil areas of federal value are business entities of strategic importance in ensuring the country's defence and state security.[100]

This judicial decision confirmed the broad interpretation of the concept of related business activities applied by the FAS.

7.2.3.2 *Otkritie Industrial Investments LLC/AGD Diamonds JSC*

Otkritie Industrial Investments LLC (Otkritie), a subsidiary of the Otkritie group, acquired 100 per cent of the shares of AGD Diamonds JSC (AGD). Three years after the transaction was concluded, the FAS filed a lawsuit before the court seeking to invalidate it and impose injunctive remedies.[101] The FAS substantiated its claim by indicating that

[96] Ostapets (n 38).

[97] 'Nabors and TESCO Announce Transaction Status Update', (7 November 2017), available at https://electricenergyonline.com/article/energy/category/oil-gas/89/665416/nabors-and-tesco-announce-transaction-status-update.html accessed 15 September 2023.

[98] ibid.

[99] Clifford Chance (n 40).

[100] ibid.

[101] Alrud, 'Spotlight: Foreign Investment Review Procedure in Russia' (Lexology, 21 October 2020) https://www.lexology.com/library/detail.aspx?g=bd881259-5642-4a9c-bb97-c9e1b59bfd64 accessed 15 September 2023.

Otkritie omitted to provide information to the FAS and the Government Commission about the foreign citizenship of certain beneficiaries.

On 29 May 2020, the court upheld the FAS decision and, therefore, imposed the following prohibitions as injunctive remedies on Otkritie: to implement any transaction in respect of AGD, to change its charter and other internal acts, to increase or decrease its charter capital, to initiate reorganization or liquidation processes, and to change the rules of its current licences and other permits.[102]

The above analysis has demonstrated a shift in foreign investment policy in Russia. Countries have departed from the notion that open markets and trade liberalization attract investors by easing cross-border transactions, which bring countries closer forcing them to leave their differences behind.

The new approach sees economic sanctions, particularly foreign restrictions, as necessary tools that allow countries to defend themselves from competitors, enemies, invaders, and opportunistic investors. This new approach raises some concerns though. First, the legitimacy of this state intervention is controversial. Second, markets and market players need to learn and adapt to high levels of uncertainty. Third, as the imposition of economic sanctions from one side triggers retaliation from the other, the global economy might face high levels of volatility. Fourth, unrestricted foreign investment rules could undermine the benefits of a globalized world, therefore the adoption and application of appropriate restrictions deserve more scrutiny.

7.3 National Security and FDI Screening in Japan

Japan's attitude towards inwards FDI has been reserved mainly because foreign investment represents a menace to national ambitions. The statistics show how this view has been embedded. By the end of the 1990s, there was virtually no mergers and acquisitions activity in Japan, and while in 2003, the percentage of inwards foreign investment in some European countries ranged from 20 to 40 per cent and in the US, around 14 per cent, in Japan, it reached over 2 per cent.[103] Although Japan has adopted some liberalization measures and has tried to encourage foreign investments, a rooted protectionist culture has made the integration of foreign companies into the Japanese economy difficult. A summary of some key features might facilitate our understanding of the FDI developments in Japan, as seen next.

It has been reported that the first foreign investment activity in Japan took place in the early 1600s, with some Dutch and British investors entering the market.[104] The trade activity was also accompanied by missionaries who converted a significant amount of Japanese to Christianity. This conversion provoked the imposition of severe rules from

[102] ibid.

[103] See UNCTAD, *World Investment Report 2004: The Shift Towards Services* https://unctad.org/system/files/official-document/wir2004en.pdf accessed 15 September 2023.

[104] Ralph Paprzycki and Kyoji Fukao, 'The Extent and History of Foreign Direct Investment in Japan' (2006) Hi-Stat Discussion Paper No 84, 11 https://ssrn.com/abstract=886000 accessed 15 September 2023.

the Japanese government aimed at obstructing the conversion process, which resulted in the emergence of a view whereby foreigners were unpopular and their investments proscribed.[105] Then, the Meiji Era (1868–1945) brought a different approach in which foreign investment was revamped after the commercial law was revised in 1899 allowing American and European countries to enter the Japanese market.[106] This era of foreign investment reinvigoration came to an end in the 1930s with the adoption of a nationalism policy translated into the expropriation and immobilization of US assets in 1941.[107] Later, the expropriation decisions were reversed and those countries that operated in Japan before the war were welcomed again, with some limitations.[108]

As seen in more detail, in 1949 and 1950, two main pieces of law were enacted, setting out the rules for screening foreign proposals. These legislative initiatives were followed by a liberalization process required to join the Organisation for Economic Cooperation and Development (OECD) in 1964.[109] Yet many sectors were deemed to be of utmost importance and not accessible to foreign investors due to structural hurdles such as the shareholding percentage they could acquire.[110]

During the 1970s and 1980s, the liberalization process was gradually broadened and significantly expanded after Japan was afflicted by an economic recession in the early 1990s, forcing the adoption of a more flexible approach towards FDI.[111] As part of the measures, some tax incentives and support services for foreign investors were introduced; the Investment Council was created; the retail, finance, insurance, and telecommunications sectors were deregulated, and the Ministry of Economy, Trade, and Industry (METI, previously the Ministry of International Trade and Industry—MITI) was portrayed as an advocator of FDI instead of an opponent, as it was regarded until then.[112] Yet the measures did not alter the foreign ownership limits on national security grounds in sectors such as agriculture, mining, air and maritime transportation.[113] Before becoming one of the most ambitious policies to attract FDI, known as the Abenomics policy, it is important to refer to some practical barriers that hindered the effectiveness of the FDI policies adopted by the Japanese government for many decades.

One barrier refers to the *Keiretsu*, a phenomenon in which Japanese companies increased their cross-shareholdings. This was accompanied by a policy according to which foreigners could acquire Japanese companies. However, when seeking to acquire

[105] ibid 11–12.

[106] Mark Mason, *American Multinationals and Japan: The Political Economy of Japanese Capital Controls, 1899-1980* (Brill 1992).

[107] Paprzycki and Fukao (n 104) 13.

[108] Mason (n 106) 146–47.

[109] OECD, 'Japan: Half a Century of OECD Membership', available at https://www.oecd.org/japan/japan-half-a-century-of-oecd-membership.htm accessed 15 September 2023.

[110] Mason (n 106) 204; see also Ralph Paprzycki, 'What Caused the Recent Surge of FDI into Japan?' (2004) Hi-Stat Discussion Paper No 31, 2 https://ssrn.com/abstract=885983 accessed 15 September 2023.

[111] Paprzycki (n 110) 4.

[112] Paprzycki and Fukao (n 104) 17–18. To illustrate how Japan's trade ministry used to shield the domestic market from foreigners, see 'Japan's Basic Industries Under Pressure' *The Economist* (7 September 2006), in which it was reported that steelmakers were advised by the Ministry 'to adopt poison pills to protect themselves from foreign takeovers'.

[113] Paprzycki and Fukao (n 104) 17–18.

these local companies, the consent of the target company was required. Thus, given the increased participation of Japanese shareholders in most local companies, it was almost impossible for foreigners to obtain consent and, therefore, to acquire them. This tactic was complemented by a preference to do business with firms that were part of the same group.[114]

Another barrier is concerned with the *sarariman* or 'corporate warrior' figure. Companies use this figure to incentivize employees to remain with the same company for many years as at the end of their careers, they are prized with good salaries.[115] This incentive has made it difficult for outsiders to attract workers, who are reluctant to change their jobs. Nonetheless, the unemployment created by the economic crisis in the 1990s facilitated the attraction of FDI, together with the reforms introduced by the Abenomics policy described next.

In June 2013, the Prime Minister of Japan, Shinzo Abe and his administration published an inward FDI strategy according to which a target of inward FDI was set at thirty-five trillion yen by 2020.[116] Aiming to achieve the target, the Japanese government has frequently explored different policies. These policies have been crafted by a group of experts on FDI, namely the Expert Group on Foreign Investment in Japan, who, in 2014, published a report in which three areas were recognized as relevant for promoting inward FDI.[117] A first area deals with the main economic divergences between the Japanese and the global system in terms of taxes, employment, corporate governance, mergers, and regulations as well as procedures. A second area covers intergovernmental agreements, and a third area covers reforms orientated to improve the living conditions of foreigners in Japan.[118] In response to the recommendations included in the third area, the Japanese government in March 2015 published the 'Five Promises for Attracting Foreign Business to Japan'.

Among the promises, the government committed to 'make it easier to live in Japan without Japanese language skills' and to establish 'Investment Advisor Assignment System' whose main task is to facilitate direct interaction between state ministers of Japan and foreign investors.[119] Also, as part of the first area, a dedicated working group for Revising Regulations and Administrative Procedures was created in 2016, whose report in April 2017 suggested some reforms to alleviate the challenges that foreign businesses face in incorporating and registering companies, legalizing residency, dealing with multiple authorities, and unnecessary procedures for imports.[120] Overall, according to a study conducted by Hoshi and Kiyota, if Japan is capable of removing the

[114] ibid 15–16; Paprzycki (n 110) 5–6.

[115] Paprzycki (n 110) 11.

[116] See US Department of State, '2021 Investment Climate Statements: Japan' https://www.state.gov/reports/2021-investment-climate-statements/japan/ accessed 15 September 2023.

[117] Takeo Hoshi and Kozo Kiyota, 'Potential for Inward Foreign Direct Investment in Japan' (2019) NBER Working Paper No w25680, 3–4 https://www.nber.org/papers/w25680 accessed 15 September 2023.

[118] ibid.

[119] ibid 4.

[120] See Council for Promotion of Foreign Direct Investment in Japan—Working Group for Revising Regulations and Administrative Procedures—Final Report, (24 April 2017), available at http://www.invest-japan.go.jp/policy/simplifyregulationsandprocedures/compilationreporten.pdf accessed 15 September 2023.

barriers that have impeded high levels of inward FDI, it is likely that the results will exceed the initial target set out by the Abenomics.[121]

The analysis presented herein has shown to what extent ideological and cultural factors have shaped the inward FDI performance in Japan and how the government has, at times, tried to embed or rescind them. The next part explores the FDI rules that apply in Japan in more detail.

7.3.1 The Regulatory Framework

Today, the FDI regime applies to inward direct investment (ie, certain transactions or acts conducted by foreign investors concerning certain designated businesses) and Specified Acquisitions (ie, acquisition by a foreign investor of shares or other equity interests in a domestically unlisted company by transfer from another foreign investor but which is engaged in any of the prescribed types of 'restricted businesses').[122] If the investment target company is not engaged in a business in a designated business sector, the foreign investor will only need to submit a post-investment report after the investment has been made.[123]

In 1949, the Foreign Exchange Control Law (the FX Law) was enacted and one year later the Foreign Investment Law.[124] For two decades, these two legal provisions were used to screen foreign investment proposals and to repeal them effectively. Article 1 of the Foreign Investment Law established that foreign investment was only accepted if it 'contributed (1) to the attainment of self-sufficiency and the sound development of the Japanese economy and (2) to the improvement of Japan's balance of payments'.[125]

During the liberalization process during the 1960s, a reform was introduced permitting those investments that did not '(1) unduly oppress small-size enterprises, (2) seriously disturb industrial order, and (3) seriously impede the domestic development of industrial techniques.'[126] This reform did not represent a significant change as the factors were interpreted in a very discretionary manner. Thus, in 1980, the Foreign Investment Law was completely abolished, imposing the duty to notify the foreign investment instead of seeking prior approval that was modified later in 1992 by imposing the obligation to report *ex post*.[127] A new reform took place in 2007 according to which investors were obliged to notify the Minister of Finance

[121] Hoshi and Kiyota (n 117) 15.

[122] Hogan Lovells, 'APAC Foreign Direct Investment Legal Guide— Japan' (November 2022), https://www.engage.hoganlovells.com/knowledgeservices/apac-foreign-direct-investment-fdi-legal-guide/japan accessed 15 September 2023.

[123] Masaki Mizukoshi, Yuka Hirano, and Kei Sukada, 'Japan: Foreign Direct Investment Regulations' *Global Competition Review* (6 December 2022) https://globalcompetitionreview.com/guide/foreign-direct-investment-regulation-guide/second-edition/article/japan accessed 15 September 2023.

[124] For a translation of Japan's 1949 Foreign Exchange Control Law, see http://www.steptoe.com/assets/attachments/4066.pdf accessed 15 September 2023.

[125] Paprzycki and Fukao (n 104) 14.

[126] ibid.

[127] ibid.

of transactions involving designated industries, including those that produce arms, nuclear reactors, and dual-use of products, to 'prevent the proliferation of weapons of mass destruction and damage to ... defence production and technology infrastructure'.[128]

In June 2020, an amendment to the FX Law known as the 'Foreign Exchange and Foreign Trade Act' (FEFTA) came into effect.[129] The main purpose of the reform was to ensure an appropriate review of the FDI that could potentially undermine national security. The FEFTA expanded the scope of persons who must obtain approval for an inbound investment[130] and introduced approval for a foreign investor to exercise the following shareholder rights in a designated company (known as the FDI Shareholder Rights Amendments): (i) when the foreign investor or a closely related person wants to serve as a director or corporate auditor of a designated company, (ii) if the nomination is made by the foreign investor or a third party, and (iii) if the foreign investor proposes the transfer or cessation of a designated business sector by way of business transfer, merger, demerger or share transfer.[131]

FEFTA also lowered the threshold for pre-transaction approval from 10 per cent to 1 per cent for the acquisition of shares of publicly traded companies operating in designated business sectors (with some exemptions).[132] The designated business sectors are divided into core business sectors and non-core business sectors according to how they affect national security;[133] some sectors can fall under one or more category depending on the specific activity (eg, software is generally considered non-core, but cybersecurity services are classed as core designated sectors). The original list contained 155 of the almost 1,500 sectors that make up Japan's Standard Industrial Classification and is periodically updated. Several new sectors were included among the core sectors in 2023. Table 7.1 summarizes the current regime.

[128] UNCTAD, *World Investment Report 2016: Investor Nationality—Policy Challenges* 96 https://unctad.org/system/files/official-document/wir2016_en.pdf accessed 15 September 2023.

[129] 'Foreign Exchange and Foreign Trade Act' (FEFTA), Japanese version available at https://elaws.e-gov.go.jp/document?lawid=324AC0000000228 accessed 15 September 2023.

[130] Individuals who do not reside in Japan (non-residents); entities or other groups established under laws or regulations of or having their principal offices in foreign countries; entities in which an individual or entity described above holds 50 per cent or more of the total voting rights; partnerships operating in the investment business of which 50 per cent or more of the total capital has been contributed by foreign entities, foreign groups or non-residents, or most general partners are non-residents; and entities in which the majority of directors or representative directors are non-residents. See Jun Usami and others, 'Foreign Direct Investment Reviews 2021: Japan' (White and Case, 20 December 2021) https://www.whitecase.com/publications/insight/foreign-direct-investment-reviews-2021-japan accessed 15 September 2023.

[131] Approval is not always required for each proposal; such an obligation depends on the foreign investor's ownership level in the designated company, the public/private ownership status of the designated company, and the proposal being voted upon. The filing procedure is like the acquisition of shares or voting rights; there are no filing fees, and the sanctions for non-compliance are imprisonment for up to three years and monetary penalties of up to JPY 1,000,000) that can be increased to up to three times the amount of the transaction value (difficult to calculate) (ibid).

[132] Haruka Murata and Megumi Oide, 'Foreign Direct Investment in Japan' (Pinsent Masons, 1 March 2022) https://www.pinsentmasons.com/out-law/guides/foreign-direct-investment-in-japan accessed 15 September 2023.

[133] Mizukoshi (n 123).

Table 7.1 Core and Non-Core Designated Business Sectors (2023)

Core	Partly core	Non-core
Weapons	Electricity	Heat supply
Aircrafts	Gas	Broadcasting
Nuclear facilities	Telecommunications	Public transportation
Space	Water supply	Biological chemicals
Dual-use technologies	Railways	Security services
Pharmaceutical, medical devices	Oil	Agriculture, forestry, fisheries
Cybersecurity	Construction	Leather manufacture
Fertilizers		Air transportation
Permanent magnets		Maritime transportation
Machine tools, industrial robots		Other software
Semiconductors		
Storage batteries		
Natural gas wholesaling		
Metal mining and refining		
Marine equipment		
Metal 3D printers		

Based on Japan Ministry of Finance, 'Rules and Regulations of the Foreign Exchange and Foreign Trade Act' (24 April 2020) https://www.mof.go.jp/english/policy/international_policy/fdi/kanrenshiryou01_20200424.pdf; 'Addition to the Core Business Sectors of the FEFTA to Secure Stable Supply Chains' (24 April 2023) https://www.mof.go.jp/english/policy/international_policy/fdi/relateddocument_20230424.pdf.

Core designated business sectors require mandatory prior notification unless exempted. The website of the Japanese Ministry of Finance lists companies conducting business activities in (i) non-designated business sectors (subject to post-investment report only), (ii) only in non-core designated business sectors, and (iii) in core designated sectors.

On 9 March 2023, the government launched a public consultation on the draft amendments to the regulatory notices adding the core business sectors of the FEFTA. Following the consultation, the following business sectors have been added to the core business sectors to secure stable supply chains and address the risk of technology leakage and diversion of commercial technologies into military use: fertilizers (potassium chloride, etc and importing), permanent magnets (manufacturing/material manufacturing), machine tools/industrial robots (manufacturing, etc), semiconductors (manufacturing of manufacturing equipment, etc), storage batteries (manufacturing/material manufacturing), natural gas (wholesaling), metals and mineral products (refining), marine equipment (engine manufacturing, etc), and metal 3d printers (manufacturing/metal powder manufacturing).[134]

It is compulsory to notify the investment involving listed companies when 1 per cent or more of the shares or voting rights are involved in a listed Japanese company.[135] Now,

[134] Ministry of Finance, 'Publication of the Amendment to the Public Notices Adding the Core Business Sectors of the Foreign Exchange and Foreign Trade Act to Secure Stable Supply Chains' (24 April 2023) https://www.mof.go.jp/english/policy/international_policy/fdi/20230424.html accessed 15 September 2023.

[135] Usami (n 130).

it is also mandatory to notify operations leading to the appointment of a director of a target company and the transfer or discontinuance of a target company's business operations in a designated business sector.[136]

Due to the amendment, the number of prior notifications increased sharply in 2019 and this trend continued in 2020 and 2021. According to statistical data released by the Ministry of Finance (MOF) in June 2022, there were 2,859 prior notifications in 2021, significantly more than the 2,171 prior notifications in 2020.[137] Figure 7.1 shows the evolution of the number of prior notifications between 2015 and 2022. The graph shows a significant increase since 2019.[138]

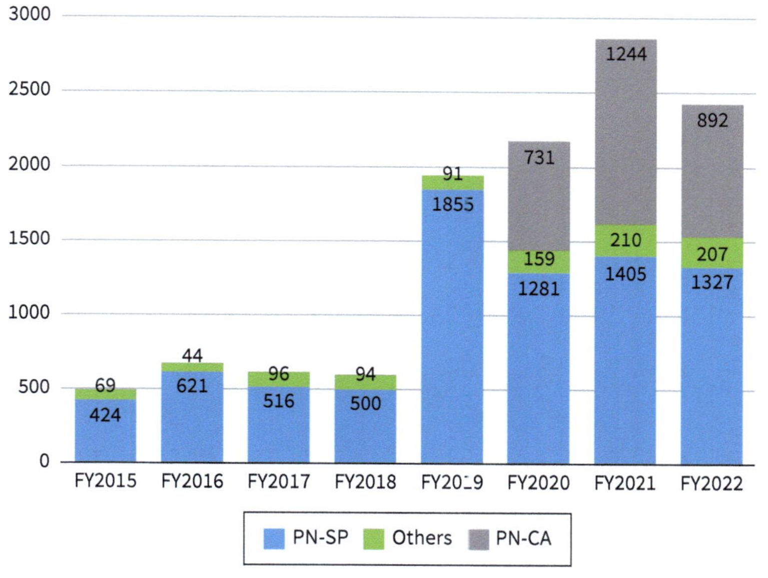

Figure 7.1 Number of Prior Notifications (FY2015–FY2022)

Based on data from Ministry of Finance, 'Number of Prior-Notification under Foreign Exchange and Foreign Trade Act (FY 2021)' https://www.mof.go.jp/english/policy/international_policy/fdi/20220610.html, and Number of the Prior-notification under the Foreign Exchange and Foreign Trade Act (FY 2022) *https://www.mof.go.jp/english/policy/international_policy/fdi/Data/20230623.html*

Notes: stock purchases (SP), certain actions (CA); the number for 2020 is not comparable with another year due to the full implementation of the Foreign Exchange and Foreign Trade Act in June 2020; others include prior notifications for change of business purposes, making loans, bond acquisition, transfer of shares, the establishment of a branch office, acquisitions of business and joint exercise of voting rights, etc.

Table 7.2 shows the number of prior notifications by business sector between 2015 and 2022.[139]

[136] Mizukoshi (n 123).

[137] ibid.

[138] (i) Voting at the shareholder's meeting for nomination of the foreign investor itself or its closely related person as a board member of the investee company, and (ii) voting at the shareholder's meeting for a proposal made by those foreign investors, to transfer or dispose of the investee company's business activities in the designated business sectors.

[139] Ministry of Finance, 'Number of Prior-Notification under Foreign Exchange and Foreign Trade Act (FY 2021)' https://www.mof.go.jp/english/policy/international_policy/fdi/20220610.html accessed 15 September 2023.

Table 7.2 Number of Prior Notifications by Sector (FY2015–FY2022)

							FY2021				FY2022			
	FY2015	FY2016	FY2017	FY2018	FY2019	FY2020	PN-SP	Others	PN-CA	Total	PN-CA	Others	PN-SP	Total
Weapons, etc.	127	149	171	233	188	165	196	10	134	340	103	9	121	233
Aircrafts	0	6	2	19	23	22	11	2	10	23	18	2	17	37
Nuclear facilities	0	0	2	12	10	4	2	1	3	6	7	0	10	17
Space	0	2	3	15	16	16	25	1	9	35	10	0	17	27
Cybersecurity	-	-	-	-	1,457	1,599	994	105	863	1,962	696	104	984	1,784
Metal mining etc. of critical minerals	-	-	-	-	-	-	4	0	0	4	0	0	4	4
Construction service business etc. which improves or maintains port facilities on Designated Remote Islands	-	-	-	-	-	-	4	0	0	4	0	6	8	14
Electricity/Gas, etc.	285	437	395	318	235	386	328	96	83	507	77	72	225	374
Telecommunications	29	17	18	14	-	-	-	-	-	-	-	-	-	-
Broadcasting	0	0	2	7	2	11	14	0	16	30	0	1	3	4
Water supply	2	2	5	3	6	3	2	0	0	2	2	0	3	5
Railway	3	1	1	3	2	1	3	1	4	8	1	9	26	36
Public transportation	6	23	9	0	0	0	0	0	0	0	0	0	2	2
Biological chemicals/ Pharmaceutical manufacturing, etc.	20	28	14	19	34	76	69	3	72	144	80	5	24	109

Security services	47	57	44	40	77	21	57	1	27	85	18	1	27	46
Agriculture, Forestry and Fisheries	31	64	76	94	96	53	69	0	62	131	44	5	47	96
Oil	56	61	53	49	46	38	75	2	54	131	47	3	28	78
Leather manufacture	19	35	31	10	29	2	0	0	4	4	5	0	5	10
Air transportation	20	24	33	31	11	7	2	1	4	7	0	3	3	6
Maritime transportation	21	39	33	36	31	11	49	1	162	212	23	0	3	26
Total number of PN	493	665	612	594	1,946	2,171	1,405	210	1,244	2,859	892	207	1,327	2,426
Sum of the PN by sectors	666	945	892	903	2,263	2,415	1,904	224	1,507	3,635	1,131	220	1,557	2,908

Based on data from Ministry of Finance, 'Number of Prior Notifications under Foreign Exchange and Foreign Trade Act (FY 2021)' https://www.mof.go.jp/english/policy/international_policy/fdi/20220610.html, and 'Number of the Prior Notifications under the Foreign Exchange and Foreign Trade Act (FY 2022)' https://www.mof.go.jp/english/policy/international_policy/fdi/Data/20230623.html.

Notes The PN for companies that conduct business in multiple business sectors are counted in each sector. For FY2020 and beyond, the number of 'PN-SP' is Prior Notification for Stock Purchases. 'Others' is a change of business purpose, making of loan, bond acquisition, transfers of shares, the establishment of the branch office, acquisition of the business and joint exercise of voting rights, etc. 'PN-CA' is a Prior Notification for Certain Actions.

Table 7.2 shows that the three top sectors are cybersecurity, with a total of 1,784 prior notifications in 2022 (down from 1,962 in 2021); electricity and gas, with 374 prior notifications (507 in 2021), and weapons, with 233 prior notifications (340 in 2022). The focus of the Russian regime, as this data portrays, is not at odds with other major national security regimes such as the US, the UK, and China.

In addition, approval post-acquisition is contemplated: (i) to appoint directors and statutory auditors to the listed Japanese company, or (ii) propose to transfer or dispose of a designated business sector. Foreign investors are divided into three groups under the exemption rules: (i) foreign financial institutions, (ii) general investors, and (iii) non-qualified foreign investors.

As far as exemption from prior notification is concerned and regarding inward investment to designated but non-core business sectors, the three following conditions need to be observed: (i) the foreign investor and its closely related persons will not serve on the board of the target company as directors or audit and supervisory board members, (ii) the foreign investor will not make proposals at shareholders' meetings, whether directly or through third parties, to dispose of material businesses in designated industries, (iii) the foreign investor will not access sensitive confidential technologies related to the target company's business in designated industries.[140] Regarding inward direct investment to designated and core business sector, the following conditions need to be met: (i) investors will not attend the investee companies executive board or committees that make important decisions in these activities, (ii) investors will not make proposals, in a written form, to the executive board of the investee companies or board members requiring their responses and/or actions by certain deadlines.[141]

In October 2021, two new categories within the mining sector were added to the core sectors under the FEFTA.[142] Also, in June 2021, the Act on Review and Regulation of Real Estate Usage was enacted to control the transfer and use of real estate properties located near or in places of significant importance from a national security point of view.[143] This real state property regulation applies regardless of nationality, but foreign investors need to be aware.

Table 7.3 shows the scope of the notification exemption depending on the type of foreign investor.[144]

140 Usami (n 130).

141 Funds Axis, 'Japan's FEFTA Pre-Notification Requirements FAQs', 3 September 2021

142 Michihiro Nishi and others, 'Japan', in Veronica Roberts (ed), *Foreign Direct Investment Regulation Guide* (Global Competition Review 2021).

143 ibid.

144 Baker McKenzie, 'Japan: Strengthened Restrictions Under New Foreign Direct Investment Rules' (26 May 2020) https://insightplus.bakermckenzie.com/bm/antitrust-competition_1/japan-strengthened-restrictions-under-new-foreign-direct-investment-rules accessed 15 September 2023.

Table 7.3 Exemption Mechanisms: Investor Type, Scope, and Requirements

	Investor type	Scope	Requirements
Blanket exemption	Foreign financial institutions	Core, non-core sectors	PN exempted if all three conditions are met; post-investment report required for >10% acquisition
Regular exemption	General investors (including sovereign wealth funds and public pension funds, if accredited)	Non-core sectors	PN exempted if all three conditions are met; post-investment report required for >1% acquisition
		Core sectors	PN exempted if <10% acquisition and all three conditions are met; post-investment report required for >1% acquisition
No exemption	Investors previously sanctioned for FEFTA violation, SOEs (if not accredited)	Core, non-core sectors	No exemption applicable

Based on Japan Ministry of Finance, 'Rules and Regulations of the Foreign Exchange and Foreign Trade Act' (24 April 2020) https://www.mof.go.jp/english/policy/international_policy/fdi/kanrenshiryou01_20200424.pdf.

7.3.2 Main Authorities and Procedures

As mentioned above, in Japan, a foreign investor carrying out an inward direct investment as defined in the law will be required to file either (a) a prior notification when a foreign investor intends to engage in businesses that are likely to cause a situation that impairs national security; or (b) a post facto report, when the investment does not fall under the previous category. Failure to file a prior notification or post facto report can result in criminal and administrative penalties.[145]

Under the Japanese regime, 'foreign investors are asked to submit a prior notification'. The notion of 'foreign investor' designates (i) individuals who do not reside in Japan ('non-resident'), (ii) entities established under laws or regulations of, or having their principal offices in, foreign countries, (iii) entities in which an individual or entity described above holds 50 per cent or more of the total voting rights, (iv) partnerships operating in the investment business of which 50 per cent or more of the total capital has been contributed by foreign entities, foreign groups or non-residents, or the majority of general partners are non-residents, and (v) entities in which the majority of directors or representative directors are non-residents.[146]

Japan's MOF and its ministries with jurisdiction over the target entity's business review FDIs under FEFTA.[147] Before 1 October 2017, only inward direct investment

[145] UNCTAD (n 56).
[146] Usami (n 130).
[147] ibid.

transactions were reviewed. Now, under the FEFTA, because of the increasing complexity of foreign investment, two types of transactions are reviewed: (i) designated acquisition: this is a transaction where a foreign investor acquires shares of a non-listed company from another foreign investor, and (ii) inward direct investment: it includes a wide range of transactions where a foreign investor is involved.[148] Furthermore, in October 2017, the FEFTA also introduced enforcement measures for the breach of those restrictions.

The filing takes place through the Bank of Japan, where some inward direct investment filings need to take place six months in advance.[149] Transactions subject to a prior notification filing cannot be closed until the expiration of a thirty calendar day waiting period from the date prior to when the notification was filed. The waiting period can be reduced to two weeks or extended up to four months.[150] If the MOF and the ministry with jurisdiction over the transaction find it problematic in terms of national security, they can recommend that the foreign investor change its content or withdraw the transaction.[151] This recommendation is likely to take place if the investment: (i) impairs national security, (ii) impedes public order, (iii) impedes the protection of public safety, or (iv) has a significant adverse effect on the smooth management of the Japanese economy.[152]

Within ten days after receiving the recommendation, the foreign investor should notify the MOF and the ministry as to whether it will accept it. If the foreign investor does not respond or refuses to accept the recommendation, the MOF and the relevant ministries may order a modification of the content of the transaction or its termination before the waiting period is over.[153] Once approval is obtained, certain inward direct investments require a post-transaction filing within forty-five days of the completion of the transaction or the act.[154] An objection decision can be appealed before the relevant ministry, whose resolution can be reviewed by the court.[155]

[148] Where a foreign investor acquires shares or voting rights of a listed target entity; acquires shares of an unlisted target entity; consents to material changes to the business purposes of an unlisted target company at any beneficial ownership level (or a listed target company where the foreign investor's beneficial ownership accounts for one-third or more of the target company's total voting rights); consents to shareholder meeting proposals that are defined to have a material impact on the target Japanese company's business; obtains proxy voting authority where the target company is publicly listed and the aggregate voting rights beneficially owned by the foreign investor after obtaining such proxies equals or exceeds 10 per cent of the total voting rights, or the target company is not publicly listed; agrees with other foreign investors to jointly exercise their respective beneficially owned voting rights of a publicly listed company, where the aggregate beneficially owned voting rights across all relevant investors account for 10 per cent or more of the total voting rights of the publicly listed company; lends to a Japanese company where both the amount owed to the foreign investor exceeds JPY 100 million and the aggregate amounts owed including corporate bonds by the foreign investor exceeds 50 per cent of the target company's debt; purchases corporate bonds that are issued to the specific foreign investor, the redemption date is more than one year, the balance exceeds JPY 100 million and the aggregate balance due on the bonds and under other loans made by the foreign investor account for more than 50 per cent of the target company's debt.

[149] Murata and Oide (n 132).

[150] ibid; Korsten and others (n 65).

[151] The Council on Customs, Tariff, Foreign Exchange, and Other Transactions provides opinion.

[152] Korsten and others (n 65) 128.

[153] Usami (n 130).

[154] Voting in favour of proposals at shareholders' meetings does not require a post-transaction filing.

[155] Korsten and others (n 65) 131.

In order to increase the legal certainty and predictability of the screening process for investors, the MOF, in May 2020, published factors to be considered in authorities' screening of foreign inward direct investment and specified transactions under the Forex Act.[156] These include the degree of impact of the investment on terms and condition of supply, the effect on the protection of national security, the maintenance of public order, safeguarding of public safety, or smooth functioning of the Japanese economy, the possibility of the degree of impact on the protection of national security and other domains.[157]

In May 2022, Japan approved an 'Act on the promotion of national security through integrated economic measures'. The Act mainly establishes several support measures to ensure stable supplies of materials that significantly affect the existence, ordinary lives, and economic activities of the Japanese public.[158] It states four policies in order: (1) strengthen supply chains for essential resources (eg, semiconductors and pharmaceuticals), (2) ensure the reliability of critical infrastructure, (3) promote the development of critical advanced technology, and (4) establish a non-public patent system for certain patents.[159]

More recently, Japan published a new National Security Strategy (NSS). In the 'Promoting Economic Security Policies to Achieve Autonomous Economic Prosperity' section, the Japanese administration states that it will take 'additional measures to enhance investment screening and export control as well as response to forced technology transfer'.[160] The main elements of the NSS relates to diplomatic capabilities, defence, economic, technological, and intelligence capabilities.[161]

Finally, in April 2023, the Japanese government approved some amendments to the FEFTA, widening its scope to nine further industries: semiconductors, storage batteries, natural gas, manufacturing and industrial robots, metal and mineral products, metal 3D printers, permanent magnets, fertilizers, and marine equipment. It also clarified that drones fall under the aircraft sector, which was already covered by the act.[162]

156 Mizukoshi (n 123).

157 Ministry of Finance, 'Factors to be Considered in Authorities' Screening of Prior Notification for Inward Direct Investment and Specified Acquisition Under the Foreign Exchange and Foreign Trade Act' (Press Release, 8 May 2020) https://www.mof.go.jp/english/policy/international_policy/fdi/gaitamehou_20200508.htm accessed 15 September 2023.

158 Kana Itabashi and others, 'Japan: New Act on the Promotion of Japan's Economic Security Enacted', Baker McKenzie, 10 July 2022.

159 Masaki Mizukoshi, Yuka Hirano, and Kei Sukada, *Japan: Foreign Direct Investment Regulations*, *Global Competition Review* (6 December 2022).

160 Japanese Government, 'National Security Strategy of Japan' (December 2022) 31 https://www.cas.go.jp/jp/siryou/221216anzenhoshou/nss-e.pdf accessed 15 September 2023.

161 ibid 31.

162 Ministry of Finance, 'Publication of the Amendment to the Public Notices Adding the Core Business Sectors of the Foreign Exchange and Foreign Trade Act to Secure Stable Supply Chains' (24 April 2023) https://www.mof.go.jp/english/policy/international_policy/fdi/20230424.html accessed 15 September 2023.

7.3.3 The Case Law

For example, we present below the assessment of a transaction in the FDI rules applied in Japan.

7.3.3.1 *Children's Investment Fund/J-Power*

In January 2008, the Children's Investment Master Fund (a British hedge fund, the Children's Fund) proposed to increase its holdings in J-Power (a Japanese electric wholesale company) from 9.9 per cent to more than 20 per cent.[163] In April 2008, the government recommended that the Children's Fund to stop the acquisition of the announced shares, as it could impair J-Power's plan to build a nuclear plant. In May 2008, after the Children's Fund ignored the recommendation, Japan's METI objected to the deal based on the argument that the purpose of the Children's Fund was to maximize profits, an aim that was incompatible with J-Power's function as an energy provider and insisted that such a transaction would impair J-Power's ability to crystalize the plan to construct a nuclear plant.[164]

This case, albeit not a representative sample, illustrates that the most significant barrier to inward FDI in Japan has been the attitude against foreign investors. This mentality has been translated into effective barriers by the Japanese business community that have sometimes resonated with the policies and law reforms adopted by the government. Indeed, the posture of the Japanese government towards inwards foreign investment has been sometimes strict and sometimes lenient. Yet even if great efforts have been made to facilitate the entry of foreign investors, as the measures adopted under the Abenomics policy, the most recent reform (FEFTA) has broadened the scope of FDI review and incorporated a large number of sectors as restricted.

Arguably, the relevant question is how to interpret the concepts of national security, public order or, even more challenging, the smooth management of the Japanese economy. The insufficient elaboration of the meaning of these concepts adds to the difficulty for a foreign investor considering investments in Japan.

7.4 National Security and FDI Screening in India

In India, the control of foreign investment has been shaped by some significant historical events. Before attaining its independence from British rule on 15 August 1947, the Indian economy witnessed an approach that sought to assist British businesses, whereas

[163] See Souichirou Kozuka, 'Foreign Direct Investment, Public Interest and Corporate Governance: Japan's Recent Experience' (2010) https://ssrn.com/abstract=1731425 accessed 15 September 2023.

[164] ibid.

Indian businesses were ignored.[165] This trend has been branded as the 'drain of wealth' from India to Britain.[166] A growing sense of discrimination and resentment from locals was nurtured who had seen the control of the economy in the hands of foreigners. Once independence was attained, the Indian government did not embrace the protectionist view proposed by the domestic industry and instead promulgated the Industrial Policy Resolution of 1948 in which a cautious welcome to foreign investors was announced.[167]

India was confronted with economic turbulence from 1965 to 1981, resulting in the adoption of the earlier advocated protectionist measures. Among them: (i) the creation of the Foreign Investment Board in 1968 to strictly scrutinize investment proposals from foreigners,[168] (ii) the adoption of the Monopolies and Restrictive Trade Practices Act (MRTP) in 1969 to avoid concentration and control monopoly,[169] (iii) the announcement of an Industrial Policy Statement in 1963, introducing compulsory licensing according to the size of the firms,[170] and, (iv) the enactment of the Foreign Exchange Regulatory Act (FERA) in 1973, listing some sectors in which foreigners could participate albeit most of them were unattractive, and imposing the obligation to have a domestic collaborator in case they decided to participate.[171] Contrary to what it was expected, the application of these protectionist measures did not alleviate the economic difficulties, so gradually in the mid-1980s, a renewed resistance towards inward flows started to take place.[172]

But it was the balance of payments crisis in 1990–91 that forced India to radically replace its protectionist policies with a more lenient approach.[173] Thus, some sectors were opened to foreign investors,[174] the Foreign Investment Promotion Board was created with the purpose to negotiate with multinationals and facilitate their entry,[175] some

[165] Aniruddha Rajput, 'Protection of Foreign Investment in India and International Rule of Law: Rise or Decline?' (2017) KFG Working Paper Series No 10, Berlin Potsdam Research Group 'The International Rule of Law—Rise or Decline?' https://ssrn.com/abstract=3135261 accessed 15 September 2023; Michael Kidron, *Foreign Investment in India* (OUP 1965) 9.

[166] David Malone, C Raja Mohan, and Srinath Raghavan, *The Oxford Handbook of Indian Foreign Policy* (OUP 2015) 291.

[167] Ministry of Micro Small and Medium Enterprises, Industrial Policy Resolution (IPR), 1948 https://web.archive.org/web/20190916020659/http://laghu-udyog.gov.in/policies/iip.htm accessed 15 September 2023.

[168] Nagesh Kumar, 'Liberalisation and Changing Patterns of Foreign Direct Investments' (1998) 33(22) Economic and Political Weekly 1321.

[169] Jatinder Singh, 'Economic Reforms and Foreign Direct Investment in India: Policy, Trends and Patterns' (2010) 8(4) IUP Journal of Financial Economics 61.

[170] ibid.

[171] ibid; Rajput (n 165) 11. FERA imposed the 40 per cent rule, according to which a 40 per cent cap on domestic ownership was imposed.

[172] Rajiv Kumar, 'Nationalisation by Default: The Case of Coal in India' (1981) 16(18) Economic and Political Weekly 824. As an illustration of this new posture, the 40 per cent rule was removed. See also Ram Mohan R Yallapragada and Madhu R Paruchuri, 'Foreign Direct Investment in India: A Lost Opportunity' (2003) 30 Southwestern Economic Review 27 http://www.ser.tcu.edu/2003-Pro/SEP2003%20Yallapragada%20Paruchuri%2027-34.pdf accessed 15 September 2023.

[173] Arvind Panagariya, *India: The Emerging Giant* (OUP 2013) 103–05.

[174] From 1997 to 1998, foreigners were allowed 100 per cent participation in the civil aviation sector, up to 51 per cent in land transport and up to 74 per cent in the construction and maintenance of roads and bridges. See Kulwindar Singh, 'Foreign Direct Investment in India: A Critical Analysis of FDI from 1991–2005' (2005) 13 https://ssrn.com/abstract=822584 accessed 15 September 2023.

[175] ibid 10.

licensing obligations were eliminated,[176] and FERA was abolished and substituted with the Foreign Exchange Management Act (FEMA), whose main objective was to encourage inward flows.[177] This set of measures were announced by the government as the 'Open door Policy'.[178] It has been reported that this open approach towards foreign investment has had a positive impact on the Indian economy.[179] Figure 7.2 illustrates this positive evolution.[180]

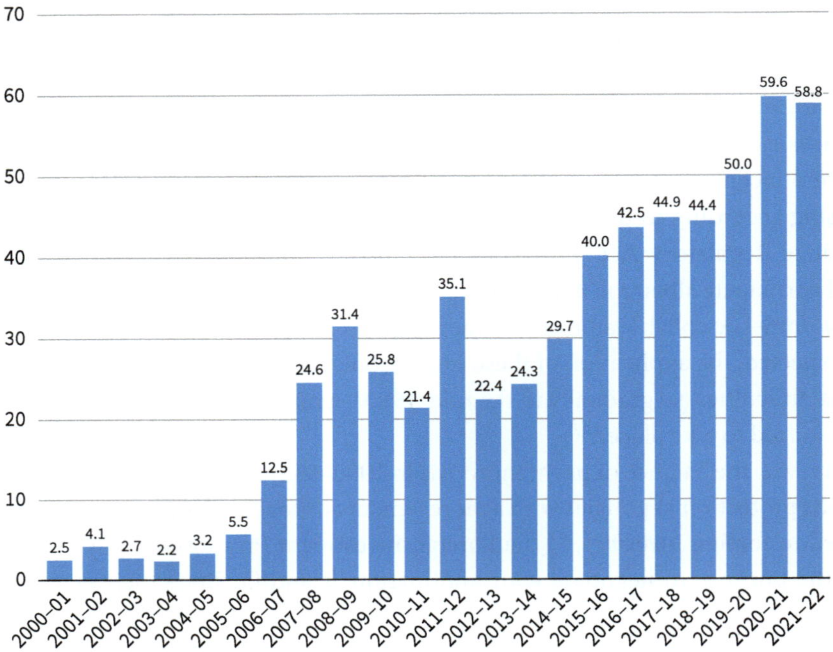

Figure 7.2 FDI equity inflow by financial year (FY 2000–01/FY 2021–22)

Based on Ministry of Commerce and Industry—Department for Promotion of Industry and Internal Trade, 'Quarterly Fact Sheet on Foreign Direct Investment (FDI)' (June 2022) <https://dpiit.gov.in/sites/default/files/FDI_Factsheet_March_2022_23May2022.pdf> accessed 15 September 2023

Section 7.4.1 explores in more detail the regulation of FDI in India.

7.4.1 FDI: Regulatory Framework in India

As indicated above, during the 1970s, the control of FDI was strongly promoted. In particular, the FERA of 1973 played a significant role by giving the Reserve Bank of India jurisdiction to regulate and control investment activities carried out by foreigners, such as exchange payments, acquisition of immovable property, and transfer of securities.[181]

[176] Economic Department—Ministry of Finance and Company Affairs, Survey 1992–1993 (1993) 123.

[177] Rajput (n 165).

[178] Singh (n 169).

[179] Ameya Patil, 'Impact of FDI on Indian Economy', (January 30, 2015). National Conference on Impact of FDI on Indian Economy, 2017, available at SSRN: https://ssrn.com/abstract=3000756.

[180] Department for Promotion of Industry and Internal Trade, FDI GRAPHS, 2022, < https://dpiit.gov.in/publications/fdi-statistics>

[181] George SK and Sandeep Babu, 'A Guide to Foreign Direct Investment in India', 7 CT UNCOURT 20 (2020).

It also restricted foreign companies entailing the reduction of their shareholdings in Indian companies to a maximum of 40 per cent.[182] Then, the 'Open door Policy' introduced in 1991 made the application of FERA incompatible with the aim of attracting foreign investments. As a result, in 1999, the FEMA was enacted, reducing the restraints on FDI and in 2000, some regulations were adopted to facilitate the application of FEMA.[183] FEMA and its regulations provide sector-specific investment caps (that routinely, usually every six months or every year, are updated), requirements for investment, and designation of sectors in which FDI is prohibited.[184] The Department for Promotion of Industry and Internal Trade (DPIIT) is responsible for issuing the FDI policy.[185]

According to the regulations, FDI is permitted in many sectors, and investors need to follow two routes: (i) the Automatic Route, where prior approval from the government is not required; it is only necessary to inform the Reserve Bank of India of the investment and (ii) the Government Route, where prior approval is required based on the prescribed sectoral thresholds.[186] FDI in specific sectors is permitted under the Automatic Route up to a certain threshold. Once the threshold is met, the investment may need government approval or not be permitted at all. FDI in sectors not covered by the FDI policy and therefore not specifically prohibited is permitted up to 100 per cent through the Automatic Route, subject to applicable laws, security, and other conditions.[187] Any kind of private investment in strategic sectors such as lottery business, gambling, atomic energy, and railway operations (except certain exempted activities in railway infrastructure which is subject to specified conditions) is prohibited.[188] In cases where the inflow is covered under the Government Route and is more than INR 50 bn, in addition to the approval of the Administrative Ministry/Department/Competent Authority, prior approval of the Cabinet Committee of Economic Affairs, a special committee formed to oversee the economic policy framework of the Government of India (GoI), is also required.[189]

[182] ibid.

[183] ibid.

[184] Rudra Kumar Pandey, Sanyukta Sowani, and Akash Deep Singh, 'The Foreign Investment Regulation Review in India' *The Law Reviews* (17 October 2021) https://thelawreviews.co.uk/title/the-foreign-investment-regulation-review/india accessed 15 September 2023.

[185] Sayak Maity, 'Foreign Direct Investment Reviews 2021: India' (White and Case, 20 December 2021) https://www.whitecase.com/publications/insight/foreign-direct-investment-reviews-2021-india accessed 15 September 2023.

[186] George SK and Sandeep Babu, 'A Guide to Foreign Direct Investment in India', 7 CT UNCOURT 20 (2020); Pandey and others (n 184). The Secretariat for Industrial Assistance (SIA) or the Foreign Investment Promotion Board (FIPB) oversee the Government Route, see Shamsher Singh and Neelam Turan, 'Classified Routes of Foreign Direct Investment in India' (2013) 4(4) International Journal of Research in Commerce and Management 55. Approval is given by the ministry of the involved sector with the agreement of DPIIT. See US Department of State, '2020 Investment Climate Statements: India' https://www.state.gov/reports/2020-investment-climate-statements/india/ accessed 15 September 2023.

[187] Pandey and others (n 184).

[188] ibid.

[189] Ministry of Commerce and Industry—Department for Promotion of Industry and Internal Trade, 'Consolidated FDI Policy 2020' para 4.15 https://dpiit.gov.in/sites/default/files/FDI-PolicyCircular-2020-29October2020.pdf accessed 15 September 2023.

Every sector has distinctive FDI rules. For instance, the 2015 Insurance Act increased the FDI threshold from 26 per cent to 49 per cent, providing that insurance companies must preserve 'Indian management and control'.[190] In relation to renewable energy, foreign investors are allowed 100 per cent participation through the Automatic Route as long as they comply with the sector regulations.[191] India also shifted to allow 100 per cent foreign participation in the telecommunication service industry, including all services and infrastructure providers, through the Automatic Route.[192]

Table 7.4 illustrates the FDI cap for the main sectors and the threshold where FDI approval is required from the relevant ministry/department, according to the specific sector.[193]

Table 7.4 FDI cap and entry route by sector

Sector/Activity	% of Equity / FDI cap	Entry route (thresholds where approval is required)
Mining—titanium	100%per cent	Up to 100% (government route only for mining and mineral separation of titanium-bearing minerals and ores, its value addition and integrated activities)
Defence	100%	Beyond 74%, government route wherever it is likely to result in access to modern technology or for other reasons to be recorded
Satellites	100%	Government route
Broadcasting content services	49%	Government route
	26% for uploading/streaming of News & Current Affairs through Digital Media.	Government route
	100% for up-linking of Non-'News & Current Affairs' TV Channels/ Down-linking of TV Channels	Automatic route
Print media (newspapers and current affairs)	26%	Government route
Civil aviation (air transport services)	100%	Automatic up to 49% (Automatic up to 100% for NRIs) and government route beyond 49%
Private security agencies	74%	Automatic route up to 49% and government route beyond 49% and up to 74%

190 Insurance Regulatory and Development Authority Act, 1999.

191 Electricity Act, 2003.

192 UNCTAD (n 11) 62.

193 Ministry of Commerce and Industry—Department for Promotion of Industry and Internal Trade (n 189).

Table 7.4 Continued

Sector/Activity	% of Equity / FDI cap	Entry route (thresholds where approval is required)
Telecom services	100%	Automatic up to 49% and government route beyond 49%
Trading		
	100%	Automatic route
	51% for *multi-brand* retail trading	Government route
Banking sector	74% for private sector	Automatic up to 49% and government route beyond 49% and up to 74%
	20% for public sector	Government route
Insurance	49% (insurance company)	Automatic route
	100% (intermediaries or insurance intermediaries)	Automatic route
Pharmaceuticals	100%	Automatic up to 74% and government route beyond 74%

Based on Ministry of Commerce and Industry—Department for Promotion of Industry and Internal Trade, 'Consolidated FDI Policy 2020' https://dpiit.gov.in/sites/default/files/FDI-PolicyCircular-2020-29October2020.pdf accessed 15 September 2023.

Also, in April 2022, pursuant to an amendment to the non-debt instruments (NDI) Rules, a new paragraph was inserted for the Life Insurance Corporation of India (LIC): from now FDI up to 20 per cent is now allowed in LIC under the Automatic Route, subject to certain conditions such as compliance with the Life Insurance Corporation Act, 1956 and the Insurance Act, as applicable.[194]

In addition, in certain cases, security clearance from the Ministry of Home Affairs (MHA) is necessary. According to the government, FDI in the following sectors will require approval by MHA: broadcasting, telecommunication, satellites—establishment and operation, private security agencies, defence, civil aviation and mining and mineral separation of titanium-bearing minerals and ores, its value addition and FDI from an entity of a country which shares a land border with India or where the beneficial owner of investment into India is situated in or is a citizen of any such country and/or transfer of ownership of any existing or future FDI in an entity in India, directly or indirectly, resulting in the beneficial ownership falling within the restriction/purview of paragraph 3.1.1(a) of the FDI Policy.[195]

For instance, as far as the defence sector is concerned, several conditions have been prescribed: the application for grant of a licence to be reviewed by DPIIT, the Ministry of Commerce and Industry in consultation with the Ministry of Defence and the Ministry of External Affairs (MEA); investments in this sector are subject to security

[194] GoI, Press Release Note No 1 (2022 Series), 'Review of FDI Policy for permitting foreign investment in Life Insurance Corporation of India (LIC) and other modifications for further clarity of the existing FDI Policy', 14 March 2022.

[195] GoI, Ministry of Commerce and Industry, Department for Promotion of Industry and Internal Trade, No 1/8/2016-FDI Policy, 9 November 2020.

clearance by the MHA; and the investee company receiving the FDI is to be structured to be self-reliant in terms of designing and development of the products. The time limit for submission of comments by MHA for operations requiring security clearance is six weeks.[196] Also, the investee company or the joint venture, as the case may be, is also to provide for the maintenance and life-cycle support facility for the products manufactured or developed by it in India.[197]

In 2002, the Competition Act was enacted to regulate antitrust issues relating to FDI transactions. Acquisitions of shares, voting rights or control in a company need to meet the requirements of the Competition Commission of India (CCI).[198] The central government, through various committees and ministries, has extensive power to override the Competition Commission on public interest grounds. Likewise, on national grounds, through a notification, the central government can exempt the application of the Competition Act indefinitely.[199] The FDI approval procedure under FEMA is separate from the merger control procedure before the CCI.

In April 2018, the Reserve Bank of India (RBI) announced that all payment system providers must store their Indian transaction data in India, a mandate that in October 2018 was extended to the banking industry.[200] Later, in December 2018, the Indian government announced a set of limitations on the operation of e-commerce by foreigners.[201]

In 2019, two amendments introduced rules to debt instruments (DI rules) and NDI rules).[202] Debt instruments include government/corporate bonds and loans, among others. The RBI governs and monitors them.[203] Non-debt instruments include all investments in equity instruments in incorporated public or private entities and all instruments of investment recognized in the FDI policy, among others. The NDI rules define a foreign investment as 'any investment made by a person resident outside India on a repatriable basis in equity instruments of an Indian company or to the capital of a LLP'.[204] The Ministry of Commerce and Industry, GoI regulate non-debt instruments. The main contribution of the DI and NDI rules has been the clarification of the

[196] ibid.

[197] Radhika Gaggar and others, 'India: Foreign Direct Investment Regulations' *Global Competition Review* (6 December 2022) https://globalcompetitionreview.com/guide/foreign-direct-investment-regulation-guide/second-edition/article/india accessed 15 September 2023.

[198] The FDI procedure is separate from the merger control procedure before the CCI.

[199] Competition Act 2002, s 54.

[200] US Department of State (n 186).

[201] ibid.

[202] 'Foreign Exchange Management (Non-debt Instruments) Rules' (2019) https://thc.nic.in/Central%20Governmental%20Rules/Foreign%20Exchange%20Management%20(Non-debt%20Instruments)%20Rules,%202019.pdf accessed 15 September 2023.

[203] The NDI and DI norms replace the Foreign Exchange Management (Transfer of Issue of Security by a Person Resident Outside India) Regulations, 2017 (TISPRO), and the Foreign Exchange Management (Acquisition and Transfer of Immovable Property in India) Regulations, 2018 (ATIP). See PDS Legal, 'Foreign Exchange Management (Non-debt Instruments) Rules, 2019: Key changes' *Lexology* (29 November 2019) https://www.lexology.com/library/detail.aspx?g=af6d48e1-f1e6-485c-b4ad-de3c012cca29 accessed 15 September 2023.

[204] 'Foreign Exchange Management Rules' (n 208) Ch I, art 2, letter (s) https://thc.nic.in/Central%20Governmental%20Rules/Foreign%20Exchange%20Management%20(Non-debt%20Instruments)%20Rules,%202019.pdf accessed 15 September 2023.

authority responsible for overseeing each type of instrument.[205] NDI rules prohibit investment by a person resident outside India in the following sectors:[206]

i. Lottery business, including government/private lotteries, online lotteries, etc, (including foreign technology collaboration in any form).
ii. Gambling and betting, including casinos.
iii. Chit funds (a type of rotating savings and credit association system practised in Pakistan, India, Bangladesh, Sri Lanka, and other Asian countries).
iv. Nidhi companies (a type of non-banking financial company recognized under the Companies Act, 2013).
v. Trading in Transferable Development Rights.
vi. Real estate business (it does not include development of townships, construction of residential/commercial premises, roads or bridges, and Real Estate Investment Trusts) or construction of farmhouses.
vii. Manufacturing cigars, cheroots, cigarillos, and cigarettes, tobacco or tobacco substitutes.

In 2020, due to the Covid-19 pandemic, the GoI upon concerns of opportunistic acquisitions, introduced specific prohibitions on FDI from countries sharing a land border with India (bordering countries).[207] These included Afghanistan, Bangladesh, Bhutan, China, Myanmar, Nepal, and Pakistan, among others. FDI proposals from investors in these countries are permitted only through the Government Route.[208] Similarly, any transfer of ownership of any existing or future FDI in an Indian entity, directly or indirectly by having beneficial owners, which may result in the change of beneficial ownership to an entity from a Bordering Country, shall also go through the Government Route regardless of the size of the transaction. Further, the reform determined that countries of concern, including Afghanistan, Bangladesh, Bhutan, China, Democratic People's Republic of Korea, Hong Kong, Iran, Macau, Nepal, Pakistan, and Sri Lanka, require prior approval from RBI to acquire immovable property, except on leases for less than five years.[209]

Two years later, one may note that the approvals granted have been low. Indeed, the Ministry of Commerce and Industry published a press release saying that out of 347 FDI proposals, '66 proposals have so far been granted approval by the Government. 193 cases have been rejected or closed or withdrawn'.[210]

[205] PDS Legal (n 203).
[206] See UK India Business Council, 'Indian FDI Restrictions' https://www.ukibc.com/india-guide/how-india/fdi-restrictions/ accessed 15 September 2023.
[207] Neha Sinha and Radhika Malpani, 'Foreign Direct Investment Regimes: India 2023' (ICLG, 30 November 2022) https://iclg.com/practice-areas/foreign-direct-investment-regimes-laws-and-regulations/india accessed 15 September 2023.
[208] Press Note No 3 (2020 Series), DPIIT File No 5(5)/2020-FDI Policy, 17 April 2020.
[209] ibid.
[210] Ministry of Commerce and Industry, 'FDI From Neighbouring Countries' (16 March 2022) https://pib.gov.in/PressReleasePage.aspx?PRID=1806626 accessed 15 September 2023.

In addition, on the grounds of national security, the GoI requires (i) FDI proposals from Pakistan/Bangladesh and (ii) FDI proposals in broadcastings, telecommunication, satellites (establishment and operation), private security agencies, defence, civil aviation, and mineral separation of titanium-bearing minerals and ores, its value addition and integrated activities, to go through security clearance from the MHA in addition to the approval of the concerned Administrative Ministries/Departments.[211] In the defence and private security sectors, besides the approval of the GoI and MHA, compliance with specific provisions is also mandatory.[212] Currently, the criteria used to review the investments and the meaning of beneficial owners remain absent, and the number of approvals under this 2020 reform restricted.[213]

Figure 7.3 shows the distribution of FDI with respect to the various sectors of the economy.[214] As in other countries, computers and IT are the sectors of most focus for the Indian regime.

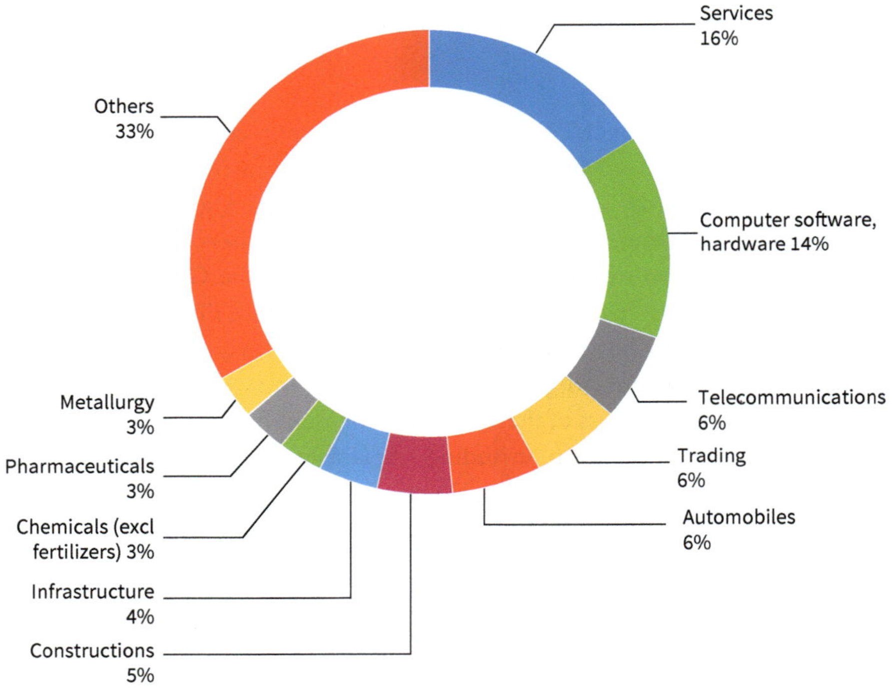

Figure 7.3 FDI equity inflow by sector (FY 2021–22)

Based on Ministry of Commerce and Industry—Department for Promotion of Industry and Internal Trade, 'Quarterly Fact Sheet on Foreign Direct Investment (FDI)' (June 2022) <https://dpiit.gov.in/sites/default/files/FDI_Factsheet_March_2022_23May2022.pdf> accessed 15 September 2023

[211] Press Note No 3 (2020 Series), DPIIT File No 5(5)/2020-FDI Policy, 17 July 2020; See also Pandey (n 187).
[212] Press Note No 3 (2020 Series), DPIIT File No 5(5)/2020-FDI Policy, 17 July 2020.
[213] Maity (n 185).
[214] Department for Promotion of Industry and Internal Trade, FDI GRAPHS, 2022, https://dpiit.gov.in/sites/default/files/Fdigraphs12.pdf

In 2021, India launched the National Single-Window System to promote and facilitate investment by establishing a one-stop shop for approvals and clearances needed by investors, entrepreneurs, and businesses. This new system is meant to guide and help the applicants in a very simple manner.[215] Similarly, as part of its process of liberalization, the administration pushed many higher thresholds. Indeed, for instance, in the insurance and defence sectors, the ceiling for FDI under the Automatic Route for both these sectors has been increased from 49 per cent to 74 per cent. Also, the government has permitted 100 per cent investment in telecom companies through its Automatic Route. Previously, 49 per cent of FDI was permitted in telecoms through the Automatic Route, with any larger FDI requiring prior government approval[216] (see Table 7.4).

Because of the liberalization, the government reported in August 2021 that FDI equity inflow to India had increased by 168 per cent during the financial year 2021–22.[217] However, in 2022, the government stated that FDI equity inflow had decreased by 6 per cent over the last year.[218]

Regarding recent legal developments, the government has received complaints from trader and industry associations against marketplace e-commerce entities alleging violations of the FDI Policy in the e-commerce sector.[219]

7.4.2 Main Authorities and Procedures

In 2017,[220] the jurisdiction to review proposals under the Government Route was removed from the Foreign Investment Promotion Board (an inter-ministerial body set up for reviewing and processing FDI proposals) and transferred to the relevant Administrative Ministries/Departments/Competent Authority responsible for the same along with the MHA and the DPIIT.[221] The DPIIT has the power to consider proposals in case of rejection by the concerned Administrative Ministry/Department. The GoI has set up an online single-point interface, 'The Foreign Investment Facilitation Portal' (FIFP), to facilitate the submission of FDI proposals.[222] Any FDI under the Automatic Route or Government Route needs to be reported to the RBI in a prearranged format known as the Standard Operating Procedure (SOP).[223] All FDI proposals under

[215] Ministry of Commerce and Industry, 'National Single Window System for Investors and Businesses Launched by Shri Piyush Goyal' (22 September 2021) https://pib.gov.in/PressReleasePage.aspx?PRID=1756966 accessed 15 September 2023.

[216] Pinsent Masons, 'Foreign Direct Investment in India' (7 June 2023) https://www.pinsentmasons.com/out-law/guides/foreign-direct-investment-india accessed 15 September 2023.

[217] Indian Government, Quarterly Fact Sheet on Foreign Direct Investment from April 2000 to June 2021, https://dpiit.gov.in/sites/default/files/FDIFactsheetJune2021.pdf

[218] Indian Government, Quarterly Fact Sheet on Foreign Direct Investment from April 2000 to June 2022, https://www.hcilondon.gov.in/docs/1662177488FDI%20Factsheet%20April%20-June%202022.pdf

[219] Hogan Lovells (n 122).

[220] OM No 01/01/FC12017, 5 June 2017.

[221] US Department of State (n 186).

[222] See Ministry of Commerce and Industry, Department for Promotion of Industry and Internal Trade, 'Foreign Investment Facilitation Portal', https://fifp.gov.in accessed 15 September 2023.

[223] GK Kedia and Co, 'How to Apply for Foreign Direct Investment Proposals Through Foreign Investment Facilitation Portal (FIFP)' (2 February 2021) https://gkkediaandco.com/how-to-apply-for-foreign-direct-investment-proposals-through-foreign-investment-facilitation-portal-fifp/ accessed 15 September 2023.

the Government Route need to be filed on the FIFP for approval from the GoI prior to completion of the transaction. Once the proposal has been filed, the DPIIT identifies and assigns the concerned administrative ministries/departments, in accordance with the relevant sector in which the transaction is involved, for their assessment and final decision.[224] If the proposed transaction involves two ministries/departments, the DPIIT may seek the approval of both. Foreign investors can engage in advance consultations with the authorities, by which a prescribed form needs to be submitted to the DPIIT for its comments.

In terms of procedure, once the proposal has been filed on the FIFP, the same is circulated by DPIIT within two days to the RBI for its comments.[225] Proposals which require additional security clearance from MHA are referred to it, such as a proposal for investment in the broadcasting, private security agencies and defence sectors, among others.[226] All proposals are also forwarded to the MEA and Department of Revenue (DoR) for information and comments. Within four weeks of filing the proposal, the concerned ministry/Department is required to upload their comments on the portal.[227] Comments on the proposal are provided directly to the Competent Authority within six weeks from the date of filing (part 1).[228] Once part 1 is over, the Competent Authority may, within one week, request clarifications that the applicant needs to respond to within one week. If the Competent Authority intends to reject the proposal, a period of two weeks is provided to DPIIT for additional consideration and to make a final decision.[229] On average, an approval or rejection decision of the proposal takes between eight to ten weeks. In case the approval of the Competent Authority is pending clearance, the transaction cannot be closed. No third parties, including parties to the proposal, are involved in the review procedure.

In addition, the applicant does not have the opportunity to defend his case in case of rejection. The review process of proposals for foreign investments is an internal procedure of the government in which it has complete discretion for approving or rejecting them. Thus, aspects such as how national security or interest aspects are considered remain unclear.[230] Also, the government is not obligated to provide any reason or justification to the parties for rejecting the proposal. The final decision in relation to a proposal may be published as a notification on the FIFP website. The applicant may seek a reconsideration of the proposal by requesting the Competent Authority or DPIIT, an administrative procedure. Remedies are not contemplated as such. Nonetheless, at the discretion of the concerned administrative ministry/department and post consultation with DPIIT, remedies offered by the applicants may be considered.

[224] ibid.
[225] Pandey and others (n 187).
[226] ibid.
[227] GK Kedia and Co (n 223).
[228] ibid.
[229] ibid.
[230] Maity (n 185).

The Indian regime incorporates sanctions for non-compliance.[231] Any violation of the FEMA or any rule, regulation, or any condition subject to which an authorization is issued by RBI, upon adjudication by the relevant authorities, renders parties liable for a penalty of three times the sum involved, where the amount can be quantified. If the amount is not quantifiable, a penalty of up to INR 2 million applies. In case of successive violations, a further daily penalty of up to INR 5,000 (for every day of violation) is imposed. If the penalty is not paid, the defaulting individual(s) shall be liable to imprisonment for up to three years. The adjudicating authority has the power to order the confiscation of any currency, security or any other money or property in relation to the contravention.

7.4.3 The Case Law

Before concluding our analysis, we discuss below the assessment of a transaction in which the FDI rules have been applied in India.

7.4.3.1 *Bycell Telecommunications India P Ltd (Bycell) v Union of India and Ors*

In this case, after the FIPB had approved Bycell to operate in the telecommunications sector in India on 17 January 2006, it decided to revoke it on 11 May 2009.[232] This cancellation took place after the MHA withdrew the security clearance of Bycell on 1 May 2009 based on some concerns about the credentials of the investor.[233] The FIPB stated that even if the petitioner had complied with requirements under the laws relating to foreign investment, lack of a security clearance was a valid ground to revoke an application.[234]

This case illustrates the retroactive powers the authorities enjoy reviewing, challenging, or unwinding approved transactions, a practice used more frequently before the FIPB was terminated.

7.4.3.2 *Shanghai Fosun Pharmaceutical Group/Gland Pharma Ltd*

In 2017, Shanghai Fosun Pharmaceutical Group Co (Fosun), a Chinese firm, and Gland Pharma Ltd (Gland), an Indian producer of export-quality medicines such as anti-coagulants, anaesthetics, and a variety of injectables, announced the intention of Fosun to acquire 86 per cent of Gland for more than $1 bn.[235] The announcement raised national security concerns in the Cabinet Committee on Economic Affairs, the

[231] CS Vanaja and Monica Thakur, 'Consequences of Non-Compliance Under FEMA ACT, 1999', R&A Associates, 18 May 2020, available at https://www.rna-cs.com/consequences-of-non-compliance-under-fema-act-1999/ accessed 15 September 2023.

[232] Delhi High Court, *Bycell Telecommunications India vs Union of India & Ors*, 16 April 2010, available at https://indiankanoon.org/doc/150083441/ accessed 15 September 2023</IBT/>.

[233] ibid.

[234] ibid.

[235] Amy Kazmin and Jyotsna Singh, 'India Raises Concerns at Fosun's $1.1bn Deal to Buy Gland Pharma' *Financial Times* (2 August 2017) https://www.ft.com/content/7b18f8a4-7750-11e7-a3e8-60495fe6ca71 accessed 15 September 2023.

institution responsible for making the final decision, according to which there was a possibility of 'India losing its edge on a particular drug where it has a significant presence internationally, as well as its access to our own market'.[236]

Despite having received clearance from the CCI and the Foreign Investment Promotion Board, Fosun decided to decrease its acquisition of Gland. By reducing the size of the transaction by up to 74 per cent, Fosun was able to use the Automatic Route, evading the national concerns expressed by the Cabinet Committee on Economic Affairs.[237]

This case shows the discrepancies among different decision-makers over the same transaction, the power that the Indian government enjoys by forcing the reduction of intended foreign ownership share, and how firms can find ways to accommodate their needs without exposing their deals to strict scrutiny.

7.4.3.3 *Flipkart (a Walmart-owned e-commerce group)*

In 2014, India's Enforcement Directorate, an agency that investigates financial crimes, launched a probe into Flipkart, a start-up founded in 2007 by two former Amazon employees and sold to Walmart in 2018, to determine whether the firm violated a ban on FDI in the retail sector between 2009 and 2015.[238]

According to the Enforcement Directorate, the alleged FDI violation took place because the firm raised money from foreign investors early on to grow its platform, ignoring foreign investment laws that at the time strictly regulated multi-brand retail and restricted such companies to operating a marketplace for sellers.[239]

In July 2021, the Enforcement Directorate issued a 'show cause notice' in which it asked the two founders and the current investor to explain why they should not face a fine of $1.35 bn 'for the lapses'. The parties had ninety days to respond to the notice. The case is still ongoing and illustrates how those investigations for potential breaches of FDI regulation can take years, that potential infringers might face significant fines and that investigations are not precluded even when the possible wrongdoing took place many years ago.

The study of the FDI control in India has portrayed a country that has transitioned from a stringent view of FDI to a more open approach. Although this openness posture has signified an apparent welcome environment for outsiders, the reality is far from optimal. There are still limitations in a few sectors. The reasons why foreign investment is banned or limited in certain sectors while quite extensive in others are still unclear. Likewise, the FDI regime is complex, albeit the reforms introduced by the

[236] ibid.

[237] Aneesh Phadnis, 'Fosun Pharma to buy 74% stake in Gland for $1.09 billion' *Business Standard* (18 September 2017), available at https://www.business-standard.com/article/companies/fosun-pharma-to-buy-smaller-stake-in-gland-for-1-09-bn-117091700619l.html accessed 15 September 2023.

[238] CNBC, 'India's Enforcement Agency Threatens Flipkart and Founders with $1.35 Billion Fine', 4 August 2021, available at https://www.cnbc.com/2021/08/05/india-enforcement-agency-threatens-flipkart-and-founders-with-fine.html accessed 15 September 2023.

[239] Vandana Nampoot, 'ED Issues Show Cause Notice to Flipkart Over Alleged Forex Violations' *UpTurn Business* (5 August 2021) https://www.businessupturn.com/companies/ed-issues-show-cause-notice-to-flipkart-over-alleged-forex-violations/ accessed 15 September 2023.

Indian government have provided some clarity in relation to the authority responsible for overseeing the investment. The existence of concurrent jurisdiction by multiple authorities to screen inward flows, accompanied by a range of rules and sector-specific regulations, imposes a heavy burden on businesses. If one considers that the FDI in India is intrinsically complex, adopting more rules related to bordering countries in 2020, in which national security concerns can be used to impair investment from investors from these countries, the review process becomes more controversial. A more simplified procedure, perhaps a unique authority with jurisdiction over FDI, less discretion and more clarity about the criteria that the government should apply when dealing with FDI applications, more opportunities from foreign investors to participate in the review process and substantiated decisions would offer more confidence to the business community.

7.5 National Security and FDI Screening in South Africa

Unlike Russia, Japan, and India, South Africa does not illustrate strong resistance against foreign investments. The Trade and Investment South Africa is a division of the Department of Trade and Investment (DTI). Its purpose is to support incoming FDI. The perception of a country's investment climate is crucial, as it affects the flow of FDI into the country. The Trade in Services Agreement (TISA) is tasked with changing the perceptions of foreign investors of the South African investment climate.[240]

Despite this open attitude, the country has been incapable of attracting sufficient FDI flows. A range of circumstances has provoked these low rates of FDI, which this section explores, aimed at understanding the investment landscape in South Africa and the reasons why, although a screening mechanism for foreign investments was introduced in 2018, it has not yet come into force. Foreign firms have been present in South Africa since the nineteenth century when the discovery of precious metals attracted them.[241] The extraction of minerals by foreign companies promoted South African economic growth until 1933, when the gold standard policy adopted post World War I failed.[242] This was further aggravated by the devastating economic effects left by World War II.

In response, as observed in many other developing economies, in 1948, South Africa incorporated import substitution policies to replace formerly imported goods with domestically produced goods.[243] This policy prevailed until the 1960s. The adoption of

[240] Ephraim Monde Faku, 'The Regulatory and Policy Variables Influencing FDI in South Africa' (2022) 22 Journal of Public Affairs e2689.

[241] John Mayer, 'South Africa's Reformed Investment Regime as a Model for Developing Countries' (2022) 25(4) Lewis and Clark Review 1247, 1256; Stephen Gelb and Anthony Black, 'Foreign Direct Investment in South Africa' in Saul Estrin and Klaus E Meyer (eds), *Investment Strategies in Emerging Markets* (Edward Elgar 2004) 177.

[242] For a good explanation of the gold standard policy, see Chrisie Swanepoel and Philip T Fliers, 'The Fuel of Unparalleled Recovery: Monetary Policy in South Africa Between 1925 and 1936' (2021) 36(2) Economic History of Developing Regions 213.

[243] Gelb and Black (n 241). For an interesting background and discussions about import substitution, see Werner Baer, 'Import Substitution and Industrialization in Latin America: Experiences and Interpretations' (1972) 7(1) Latin American Research Review 95–122; Albert O Hirschman, 'The Political Economy of Import-Substituting Industrialization in Latin America' (1968) 82(1) The Quarterly Journal of Economics 1–32; David

these protectionist measures was also fuelled by the economic sanctions and isolation imposed by the international community in opposition to the apartheid system then in place.[244] Then, in 1961, a massacre in Sharpeville accelerated a balance of payments crisis that resulted in the adoption of a dual currency.[245] The massacre also added more criticism from the international community, more domestic political instability, more government intrusion, and scepticism from foreign investors.[246] As South Africa continued witnessing great levels of violence and instability provoked by the apartheid system, in the 1980s the country was subject to further severe international financial sanctions.[247] As a result, between 1984 and 1988, more than 200 US firms and 20 per cent of the UK-based firms exited the country.[248] Finally, in the early 1990s, negotiations between the government and the African National Congress (ANC) and other parties led to the end of apartheid.[249]

In April 1994, South Africa successfully transitioned to democratic governance.[250] The ANC was elected and tasked with the challenges inherited by the apartheid system, such as unskilled labour, great levels of poverty, and deprived access to health care and other basic needs.[251] The core objectives of the ANC were deregulation, privatization, and attraction of new foreign investments.[252] Thus, new regulations promoting FDI were enacted, including the reduction of tax rates and import tariffs.[253] In addition, the ANC aimed at the de-racialization of the economy,[254] a goal that was positively incorporated in the Black Economic Empowerment Act (BEE) of 1994 that sought to transfer ownership, management, and control of South African firms.[255] It was also included in the Constitution 1996, whose Article 25, for example, allows expropriation subject to compensation in order to alleviate inequality.[256] Likewise, in 1996, the ANC

Felix, 'Import Substitution and Late Industrialization: Latin America and Asia Compared' (1989) 17 World Development 1455–469.

244 Amy Bogran and Hunter R Clark, 'Foreign Direct Investment in South Africa' (1999) 27 Denver Journal of International Law and Policy 337.

245 ibid; Gary S. Eisenberg, 'The Policy and Law of Foreign Direct Investment in the New South Africa' (1994) 28 Journal of World Trade 5, 16–17; Bruce Kidd, 'The Campaign Against Sport in South Africa' (1988) 43(4) International Journal 643–64 (Autumn,; Richard J Payne, 'Japan's South Africa Policy: Political Rhetoric and Economic Realities' (1987) 86(343) African Affairs 167–78;

246 Gelb and Black (n 241).

247 Athanasios Arvanitis, 'Foreign Direct Investment in South Africa: Why Has it Been So Low' in Michael Nowak and Luca Antonio Ricci (eds), *Post-Apartheid South Africa: The First Ten Years* (International Monetary Fund 2005) 65.

248 Gelb and Black (n 241) 178. Anthony Black, 'The Evolution and Impact of Foreign Direct Investment into South Africa Since 1994' in Haroon Bhorat and others (eds), *The Oxford Companion to the Economics of South Africa* (OUP 2014).

249 Mayer (n 241) 1257.

250 Black (n 248). Michael Kransdorff, 'Tax Incentives and Foreign Direct Investment in South Africa' (2010) 3(1) Consilience 68.

251 Mayer (n 241) 1257.

252 Gelb and Black (n 241) 178; Black (n 248).

253 Bogran and Clark (n 244).

254 David Schneiderman, 'Promoting Equality, Black Economic Empowerment, and the Future of Investment of Rules' (2009) 25(2) South African Journal of Human Rights 246, 251.

255 Anagaw Derseh Mebratie and Arjun S Bedi, 'Foreign Direct Investment, Black Economic Empowerment and Labour Productivity in South Africa' IZA Discussion Paper No 6048 (October 2011) 7 https://d-nb.info/1016697910/34 accessed 15 September 2023.

256 South African Constitution, 1996, ch 2, s 25 provides that: 'The state must take reasonable legislative and other measures . . . to foster conditions which enable citizens to gain access to land on an equitable basis.'

government announced a macro-economic policy known as the Growth, Employment and Redistribution (GEAR) strategy, pursuing fiscal discipline, investor confidence, and macro-economic stability through (i) a rapid expansion of non-traditional exports and (ii) an increase in private sector investment.[257]

In 1999, the International Investment Council was created to facilitate FDI by easing the existing administrative burdens.[258] Additionally, the DTI introduced a Foreign Investment Grant (FIG) programme consisting of cash incentives to foreigners willing to invest in specific sectors.[259]

After the introduction of the policies and reforms indicated above, by 2002, the FDI in South Africa represented just 1.4 per cent of South African GDP.[260] This proportion contrasts with the percentage seen in some other developing economies in the same period of 3.5 per cent.[261] In an attempt to improve the low levels of FDI, the BEE was reviewed and amended in 2001.[262] Hence, for instance, in the mining charter the target of ownership by historically disadvantaged South African was reduced from 51 to 25 per cent. Nonetheless, it has been reported that between 2003 and 2011, FDI in South Africa represented less than 1.5 per cent.[263]

Some recent statistics show that FDI remains in decline in South Africa. Thus, in terms of billions of dollars, the country received 5.4 in 2018, 4.6 in 2019 and 3.1 in 2020.[264] In spite of the lack of significant FDI restrictions in South Africa and the initiatives to attract FDI, the rates are low. Some commentators have tried to explain the reasons why South Africa is not attracting FDI, having noted that the following factors negatively impact the decisions of potential investors: high levels of crime, unskilled labour, low levels of privatization, high levels of inequality, difficulty in meeting the BEE criteria and its lack of clarity and consistency, and the ecological deficit provoked by the unreserved exploitation of natural resources, among others.[265]

Among the top thirty African destinations for FDI, the countries with the largest average annual FDI stock values are Mauritius, South Africa, Nigeria, and Egypt, which account for nearly 65 per cent of the average annual FDI stock on the continent in

[257] Brendan Vickers, 'An Overview of South Africa's Investment Regime and Performance'; UNCTAD, *World Investment Report 2001: Promoting Linkages* https://unctad.org/system/files/official-document/wir2001_en.pdf accessed 15 September 2023

[258] IGD (2005) Investment Policy in South Africa: An Agenda for Action. CUTS Centre for Competition.

[259] Mebratie and Bedi (n 255).

[260] Black (n 248).

[261] ibid.

[262] Schneiderman (n 254) 252–54. On 9 January 2004, the Broad-based Black Economic Empowerment Act was signed into law.

[263] Black (n 248).

[264] Magdalene Williams, Ahmad Abu Alrub, and Mehmet Aga, 'Ecological Footprint, Economic Uncertainty and Foreign Direct Investment in South Africa: Evidence from Asymmetric Cointegration and Dynamic Multipliers in a Nonlinear ARDL Approach' (2022) 12(2) SAGE Open, https://doi.org/10.1177/21582440221094607.

[265] Schneiderman (n 254) 273; Williams, Alrub, and Aga (n 264) 1–2; UNCTAD, *World Investment Report 2001: Promoting Linkages* https://unctad.org/system/files/official-document/wir2001_en.pdf accessed 15 September 2023; Faku (n 240).

2014–18. South Africa's average annual inward FDI stock was $56 bn in 2004–08 rising to $114 bn in 2014–18.[266]

The next section explores the FDI rules in the South African legal system in more detail.

7.5.1 The Regulatory Framework

There are a number of laws that affect FDI in South Africa, not all of which relate to national security. The major laws in relation to FDI include:[267]

1. The Companies Act governs the registration and operation of companies in South Africa.
2. The Protection of Investment Act provides for the protection of investors and their investments.
3. The Labor Relations Act provides protection for employees against unfair dismissal and unfair labour practices.
4. The Customs and Excise Act provides general incentives to investors in various sectors.
5. The Competition Act is responsible for investigating, controlling, and evaluating of restrictive practices, abuse of dominant positions, and mergers.
6. The Special Economic Zones Act provides national economic growth and exports by using support measures to attract foreign and domestic investments and technology.

In 1961, the Exchange Control Regulations, known as the EXCON Regulations or the Regulations, in conjunction with the Currency and Exchanges Manual for Authorised Dealers (AD Manual), were adopted.[268] Under the Regulations, when a foreign investor acquires shares in a South African company those shares need to be endorsed 'non-resident' by a South African bank, or authorized dealer, subject to the provision of supporting documentation and information.[269] Also, if a foreign company seeks to acquire more than 15 per cent of a bank-issued capital, such a transaction requires approval from the South African Reserve Bank (SARB).[270]

[266] Stephen Morgan, Farris Jarrad, and Michael E Johnson, 'Foreign Direct Investment in Africa: Recent Trends Leading up to the African Continental Free Trade Area (AfCFTA), Number EIB-242 (October 2022), US Department of Agriculture, Economic Research Service.

[267] US Department of State, '2022 Investment Climate Statements: South Africa' https://www.state.gov/reports/2022-investment-climate-statements/south-africa/ accessed 15 September 2023.

[268] Exchange Control Regulations 1961, available at http://www.saflii.org/za/legis/consolreg/ecr1961279/ accessed 15 September 2023.

[269] South African Reserve Bank, 'Currency and Exchanges Guidelines for Business Entities', 10 July 2019, available at https://www.resbank.co.za/content/dam/sarb/what-we-do/financial-surveillance/general-public/Currency%20and%20Exchanges%20Guidelines%20for%20Business%20Entities.pdf accessed 15 September 2023.

[270] The Banks Act 94 of 1990. See also OECD, 'Regulatory Environment for Foreign Direct Investment', (May 2005) https://www.oecd.org/investment/investmentfordevelopment/34783838.pdf accessed 15 September 2023.

In 1998, the Competition Act was enacted.[271] Later, in 2003, the Broad-Based Black Economic Empowerment (B-BBEE) framework imposed certain sector-specific restrictions. For instance, in the mining sector, South Africans must own at least 25 per cent of any mining company.[272] Also, a foreign investor may be required to enter into agreements with historically disadvantaged people regarding, among other things, ownership and management of its potential acquired entity.[273] In 2008, the Companies Act was enacted,[274] which provides for the incorporation, registration, organization, and management of companies, the capitalization of profit companies and the registration of offices of foreign companies carrying on business in South Africa.[275] According to the Companies Act, the Take Over Regulation Panel (TRP) was established to regulate the transactions of regulated companies. It should be noted that only certain companies qualify as regulated companies.[276] In 2013, the Domestic Treasury Management Companies (DTMC) regime came into effect, allowing South African companies, including those majority-owned by foreign investors, to establish one subsidiary as a holding company to hold African and offshore operations, without being subject to exchange control restrictions.[277] On 13 December 2019, the SARB expanded the scope of the DTMC regime, including specific financial services sectors, and clarified some aspects.[278]

In 2015, the Protection of Investment Act (the Investment Act) was enacted, providing a degree of protection to investors in relation to their investments while reinforcing transparency and aiming to achieve a balance of rights and obligations that apply to all investors.[279]

The Investment Act defines investment within the context of FDI as: (i) any lawful enterprise established, acquired, or expanded by an investor in accordance with the laws of the Republic of South Africa, committing resources of economic value over a reasonable period in anticipation of profit; (ii) the holding or acquisition of shares, debentures, or other ownership instruments of such an enterprise; and (iii) the holding, acquisition, or merger by such an enterprise with another enterprise outside the Republic to the extent that the holding, acquisition, or merger with another enterprise outside the Republic influences an investment contemplated by and in the Republic.[280]

[271] Competition Act 89 of 1998. Available at https://www.gov.za/documents/competition-act accessed 15 September 2023.

[272] The Mineral and Petroleum Resource Development Act of 2002.

[273] B-BBEE, available at http://www.thedtic.gov.za/financial-and-non-financial-support/b-bbee/broad-based-black-economic-empowerment/ accessed 15 September 2023.

[274] Companies Act 71 of 2008, available at https://www.gov.za/documents/companies-act accessed 15 September 2023.

[275] ibid.

[276] ibid.

[277] Peter Dachs, 'South Africa: Exchange Control and Tax Dispensation for Domestic Treasury Management Companies', ITR, (28 January 2014) https://www.internationaltaxreview.com/article/b1f9jz21lvscc6/south-africa-exchange-control-and-tax-dispensation-for-domestic-treasury-management-companies accessed 15 September 2023.

[278] Cliffe Dekker Hofmeyr, 'Tax and Exchange Control Alert', (14 February 2020) https://www.cliffedekkerhofmeyr.com/export/sites/cdh/en/news/publications/2020/tax/Downloads/Tax-and-Exchange-Control-Alert-14-February-2020.pdf accessed 15 September 2023.

[279] Protection of Investment Act 22 of 2015, which came into operation on 13 July 2018.

[280] ibid.

The Investment Act does not impose a review of inbound foreign investment. Instead, the Investment Act provides that investors will receive fair administrative, legislative, and judicial processes, as well as substantiated written decisions related to their investment proposals, and those foreign investors and their investments will be treated without any discrimination.[281] Yet the Investment Act clearly stipulates that the government has the right to regulate when aspects such as 'redressing historical, social and economic inequalities and injustices' are involved.[282]

In 2018, the Competition Amendment Act[283] reformed the Competition Act of 1998 by (i) introducing the screening mechanism of foreign investments in South Africa; (ii) establishing the creation of a foreign investment committee (FIC) responsible for reviewing and approving or rejecting transactions that: constitute a merger as defined in the Competition Act, involve a foreign acquiring firm and the implementation of which may have an adverse effect on the national security interests of South Africa; (iii) requiring that the President of South Africa has the duty to constitute the FIC—comprised of twenty-eight ministers and officials chosen by the President; (iv) defining a foreign acquiring firm as an acquiring firm incorporated, established, or formed under the laws of a country other than South Africa or whose place of effective management is outside South Africa; (v) determining that the President of South Africa needs to identify and publish in the Gazette a list of national security interests, including the markets, industries, goods or services, sectors, or regions in which the merger involving a foreign acquiring firm must be notified to the South African government; (vi) suggesting that the President should consider a merger's impact on the economic and social stability of South Africa, including the potential impact of a merger transaction, as stated by the Competition Act:

- (i) On the country's defence capabilities and interests.
- (ii) On the use or transfers of sensitive technology or know-how outside the Republic of South Africa.
- (iii) On the security of infrastructure, including processes, systems, facilities, technologies, networks, assets, and services essential to the health, safety, security or economic well-being of citizens and the effective functioning of governments.
- (iv) On the supply of critical goods or services to citizens or the supply of goods or services to government.
- (v) To enable foreign surveillance or espionage or hinder current or future intelligence or law enforcement operations.
- (vi) On the Republic's international interests, including foreign relationships.
- (vii) To enable or facilitate the activities of illicit actors, such as terrorists, terrorist organizations or organized crime, and
- (viii) On the economic and social stability of the Republic.

[281] ibid §6(1), §6(2)-(4), §8(1).

[282] Protection of Investment Act 22 of 2015 §12(1)(a).

[283] Competition Amendment Act of 2018, published on 14 February 2019, but the sectors introducing FDI screening are not yet in force.

Thus, the new FDI Screening Rules under section 18A will apply only to 'notifiable mergers',[284] involving a 'foreign acquiring firm',[285] and affecting 'national security interests'.[286]

At the time of writing, the President had not established the committee or published the list of national security interests. Therefore, a wide range of sectors are currently open to foreign investment, except for the energy, mining, banking, insurance, defence, and commercial broadcasting services, where government approval for foreign participation is required. In 2022, The types of business activities that the Minister of Home Affairs considers to be within the national interests included:[287]

a. agro-processing;
b. business process outsourcing and information technology-enabled services;
c. capital and transport equipment, metals, electrical machinery and apparatus;
d. textiles, clothing, and leather;
e. electrotechnical (this includes, eg, advanced telecommunications, software development and smart metering);
f. green economy industries (including power generation and renewable energy);
g. oil and gas; and
h. mineral benefaction and infrastructure development.

For instance, as far as the banking sector is concerned, The Banks Acts provides that no person other than the controlling entity of the bank—a local or foreign entity—may acquire more than 15 per cent of the total nominal value or the total voting rights in respect of the issued shares of a bank without the prior approval of the Prudential Authority or the Minister of Finance, depending on the number of shares or voting

[284] The Competition Commission must be notified of all intermediate mergers and acquisitions if the value of the proposed merger equals or exceeds ZAR 600 million (calculated by either combining the annual turnover of both firms or their assets) and the annual turnover or asset value of the transferred/target firm is at least ZAR 100 million.

If the combined annual turnover or assets of both the acquiring and transferred/target firms are valued at or above ZAR 6.6 bn, and the annual turnover or asset value of the transferred/target firm is at least ZAR 190 million, the merger must be notified to the Competition Commission as a large merger.

A merger, as contemplated in s 12 of the Competition Act, is said to occur when one or more firms directly or indirectly acquire or establish direct or indirect control over the whole or part of the business of another firm. Control, in turn, may be established in a number of ways, including, for example, via:

- the beneficial ownership of more than 50 per cent of the issued shares in a firm;
- the entitlement to vote for the majority of the votes that may be cast at an annual general meeting;
- the ability to appoint or remove the majority of the directors of a firm; or
- the ability to materially influence the strategic business policy of a firm in a manner comparable to control.

FDI Guide, South Africa, https://www.compcom.co.za/merger-thresholds/ accessed 15 September 2023.

[285] Foreign acquiring firm is also defined in the Competition Act, and refers to an acquiring firm that was incorporated, established or formed under the laws of a country other than the Republic of South Africa or whose place of effective management is outside the Republic.

[286] In terms of the Competition Act, the President must identify and publish a list of 'national security interests' that include the markets, industries, goods or services, sectors or regions.

[287] Deon Govender Sibusiso Ngwila, 'The Foreign Investment Regulation Review: South Africa' *The Law Reviews* (21 October 2022) https://thelawreviews.co.uk/title/the-foreign-investment-regulation-review/south-africa accessed 15 September 2023.

rights to be acquired. For the insurance sector, the Insurance Act prohibits investors from concluding insurance business in South Africa absent an appropriate licence granted by the Prudential Authority.[288] Regarding the broadcasting and telecommunication sectors, the Electronic Communication Act 2005 prohibits foreigners from directly or indirectly exercising control over a commercial broadcasting licence or having a financial interest in the voting shares or paid-up capital exceeding 20 per cent in a commercial broadcasting licensee unless exempted by the Independent Communications Authority of South Africa. Sector-specific advice should be obtained prior to an investment.[289]

The literature notes that the content of the national security provision and its application is still not clear and will therefore depend on criteria published by the President at a later time.[290]

In September 2022, the FSCA (South African Financial Sector Conduct Authority) introduced amendments to Regulation 28 to encourage pension funds to invest in green and other ESG (Environmental, Social, and Governmental) investments. The main aim of the administration is to facilitate the achievement of ESG-related goals.[291]

7.5.2 Main Authorities and Procedures

The Competition Commission (CC), a statutory body that was established by the Competition Act 89 of 1998, is the investigation and enforcement agency.[292] The Competition Tribunal (CT), established under the Competition Act, acts as the adjudicative body.[293] The FIC will review an investment by a foreign acquiring firm if it constitutes a notifiable merger in terms of the Competition Act, according to prescribed financial thresholds and relates to a list of national security interests identified by the President of South Africa.[294] The SARB enforces compliance with South Africa's exchange control regulations through authorized dealers, usually banks, to ensure that the exchange control rules when sending and receiving funds across South African borders are observed.[295] The TRP is responsible for the transactions of regulated

[288] ibid.

[289] Erza Davids, 'FDI Guide: South-Africa' (2022) https://www.ibanet.org/document?id=FDI-Guide-South-Africa-2022 accessed 15 September 2023.

[290] Joyce Karanja and others, 'Foreign Direct Investment: An Overview of Policy and Regulatory Developments in East and Southern Africa' (ICLG, 30 November 2022) https://iclg.com/practice-areas/foreign-direct-investment-regimes-laws-and-regulations/2-an-overview-of-policy-and-regulatory-developments-in-east-and-southern-africa accessed 15 September 2023.

[291] Dawid de Villiers, 'Regulators take steps to encourage ESG in the financial services industry', 13 September 2022, https://www.fanews.co.za/article/compliance-regulatory/2/general/1082/regulators-take-steps-to-encourage-esg-in-the-financial-services-industry/35439.

[292] Competition Act 89 of 1998. Available at https://www.gov.za/documents/competition-act accessed 15 September 2023.

[293] ibid.

[294] Competition Amendment Act of 2018, published on 14 February 2019.

[295] South African Reserve Bank, 'Currency and Exchanges Guidelines for Business Entities', 10 July 2019, available at https://www.resbank.co.za/content/dam/sarb/what-we-do/financial-surveillance/general-public/Currency%20and%20Exchanges%20Guidelines%20for%20Business%20Entities.pdf accessed 15 September 2023.

companies.[296] The Prudential Authority, operating within the Administration of the SARB, approves the establishment of a representative office or a local branch of foreign banks in South Africa and grants licences to conduct insurance business in the country.[297] The Independent Communications Authority has jurisdiction to oversee the limitations of foreign control over commercial broadcasting services.[298]

Currently, there is no uniform oversight and assessment of foreign investments in South Africa. However, on 28 September 2021, South Africa introduced a new requirement under which private security companies must be at least 51 per cent owned and controlled by South African citizens.[299] This new amendment gives the minister some discretion and allows the minister to prescribe a different percentage ownership and control in respect of different categories of security business such as guarding, response security, assets in transit, importers and distributors of monitoring devices, and security advisors.[300] Likewise, apart from the national security considerations introduced by the Competition Amendment Act of 2018, no other rules govern FDI.

FDI limitations in some sectors have been introduced by sectoral regulation. According to the Competition Amendment Act, the FIC assesses whether a merger involving a foreign acquiring firm may adversely affect the national security interest of the Republic.[301] The review procedure has a number of steps. The foreign acquiring firm must notify the CC of the intended merger and, at the same time, must file a notice to the FIC if the merger relates to the list of national security interests. Prior approval is required, and notification is mandatory. Within sixty days of receipt by the FIC, or a longer period agreed by the President, the FIC must decide[302] whether the merger may have an adverse effect on the national security interests of the Republic. During its consideration, the FIC may consult and seek the advice of the CC or any other relevant regulatory authority or public institution. The opinion of FIC is then transmitted to the Minister of Trade and Industry, who, within thirty days: (i) publishes a notice in the Gazette of the decision to approve, conditionally approve or prohibit the implementation of a merger, and (ii) informs the National Assembly, in appropriate detail, of the decision.[303]

[296] Companies Act 71 of 2008, available at https://www.gov.za/documents/companies-act accessed 15 September 2023.

[297] The Insurance Act of 2017 prohibits persons from conducting insurance business in South Africa without a licence issued by the Prudential Authority.

[298] The Electronic Communications Act of 2005 provides that a foreign investor may not, whether directly or indirectly, (i) exercise control over a commercial broadcasting licensee or (ii) have a financial interest or an interest in voting shares or paid-up capital in commercial broadcasting licensee exceeding 20 per cent. Also, the Independent Communications Authority may refuse to transfer a licence where the transferee's ownership and control by historically disadvantaged persons is less than 30 per cent.

[299] Private Security Industry Regulation Amendment Act No 18 of 2014.

[300] Rian Geldenhuys, Trade Law Chambers, 'Foreign Ownership of Private Security Industry At Risk', 2021, https://www.tradelawchambers.com/raxo-what-s-on/66-foreign-ownership-of-private-security-industry-at-risk.html.

[301] CMS Law-Now, 'Foreign Direct Investment in South Africa' (30 November 2020) https://www.cms-lawnow.com/ealerts/2020/11/foreign-direct-investment-in-south-africa accessed 15 September 2023.

[302] There is no set time for decision-making.

[303] Competition Amendment Act of 2018, published on 14 February 2019.

The CC and the CT may not consider a merger under their jurisdiction if the foreign firm fails to notify the FIC. The CC and the CT do not need to issue a decision in transactions where the minister has published a notice in the Gazette prohibiting the implementation of the merger on national security grounds. The FIC may revoke its approval if: (i) it was based on incorrect information for which a party to the merger is responsible, (ii) the approval was obtained by deceit, or (iii) a firm concerned has breached an obligation to the approval. If the FIC revokes its permission, the CC or CT's approval or conditional approval of the merger is deemed to be revoked. Unless the FIC determines otherwise, the CC's or CT's approval or conditional approval of a merger involving a foreign firm is revoked if the foreign acquirer fails to notify the FIC.[304]

These are the sanctions for non-compliance: the CT may impose an appropriate penalty after considering different factors such as the nature, gravity, and extent of the contravention, the behaviour of the respondent, the market circumstances in which the contravention took place, the level of profit derived from the contravention, the degree of cooperation shown by the respondent, and whether the respondent has previously contravened the Act.[305] Judicial review has not specifically provided for in the Competition Amendment Act. Likewise, recent amendments to the Competition Act provide that neither the CT nor the Competition Appeal Court has jurisdiction over matters relating to the foreign acquiring provision (other than in relation to imposing penalties for non-compliance) and merging parties' recourse in respect of decisions of the Committee is expected, therefore, to lie outside the jurisdiction of the competition authorities.[306]

Presently, the scrutiny of mergers and acquisitions in which foreign investors are involved takes into consideration its impact on jobs, local industry, and the ability of small businesses or firms controlled or owned by historically disadvantaged persons to become competitive and retain South African ownership of key sectors (known as 'public interest priorities/considerations').[307] The CC and CT have the authority to approve or prohibit a merger solely based on its effects on public interest, and as part of the assessment they will generally: (ii) determine whether any such effect is merger specific; (ii) determine whether any such effect is substantial; (iii) determine whether any positive effects would outweigh the likely negative effects; (iv) consider possible remedies to address any substantial negative public interest effect.[308]

There are no relevant cases of application of FDI rules in South Africa as the Competition Amendment Act is not yet in force. However, in the second half of 2021, Prosus, a global investment group that operates worldwide, bought 45 per cent of

[304] ibid.

[305] ibid.

[306] Karanja (n 290).

[307] Tembinkosi Bonakele, 'South Africa: Jurisdictional, Substantive, and Policy Issues Including a Focus on Digital Markets', in Ioannis Kokkoris and Nicholas Levy (eds), *Research Handbook on Global Merger Control* (Edward Elgar 2023) 563.

[308] On 8 June 2016, the CC published guidelines indicating how public interest factors would be assessed in reviewing mergers. See Guidelines for the Assessment of Public Interest Provisions in Mergers, available at https://www.compcom.co.za/guidelines-for-the-assessment-of-public-interest-provisions-in-mergers/ accessed 15 September 2023.

Naspers shares, a global consumer internet group based in South Africa. The transaction was declared unconditionally. The latter considerably increased the amount of financial transactions in South Africa and more broadly in Africa in 2021.[309]

The examination of the South African case gives us the opportunity to offer the following reflections. Despite the many attempts to make the country attractive to foreign investors, South Africa has failed to do so. Even if, at least in theory, many sectors are open to foreigners, in reality, the country is still dealing with the stigma of social and political instability created by the damaging history of apartheid. This heinous legacy indicates that foreign investors fear that potential civil unrest can occur anytime deteriorating the conditions of their investments. More worrisome is the possibility that the government can make intrusive decisions underpinned by the constitutional and legal mandate to protect inequality. This mandate overrides the protection that the Investment Act offers to foreign investors.

In addition, the burden of meeting the rules imposed by the BBE is perhaps one of the main obstacles, as foreign investors must make great efforts to comply with them. Overall, it seems virtually impossible to reconcile two contradictory policies: to offer fair treatment to outsiders while at the same time ensuring special protection to locals. Also, adopting FDI rules based on national security concerns contradicts the goal of attracting new foreign investments. Hence, it is no surprise the envisaged FDI screening mechanism adopted in South Africa in 2018 is not yet in force. It could be assumed, that although the country followed the common path of tightening the participation of foreigners in domestic markets, as observed elsewhere, the economic realities of the country demand other responses. Indeed, if before the Covid-19 pandemic, the country was facing its second recession in two years; now that the economic effects of the pandemic have left the country in a more calamitous situation,[310] the imposition of explicit restrictions on entry appear to be less desirable.

7.6 Concluding Remarks

As this chapter shows, the adoption of unrestricted FDI rules in Russia has been crucial to protect not just its commanding position in the strategic natural resources industry, Russia's main source of hard currency, and expand to a vast array of sectors. The economic sanctions imposed on Russia after its invasion of Ukraine have elicited the adoption of stricter FDI rules targeting those countries who have deployed them. Hence, the adoption of specific FDI restrictions based on national security has become a tool used to respond to foreign measures on the Russian economy.

Like Russia, India has also developed new national security rules for FDI screening to target specific land border countries. The threat posed by opportunistic takeovers during the Covid-19 pandemic induced the adoption of some measures to protect

[309] UNCTAD (n 11) 13.

[310] 'Covid-19 has Throttled South Africa's Economy' *The Economist* (18 July 2020).

domestic industries from the intervention of geopolitical rivals, including China. Unlike Russia, since India adopted its 'Open Door Policy' in 1991, foreign participation has been welcomed, and the government is portrayed as welcoming globalization, at least in theory. In practice, this notion is overshadowed by a sense of discouragement since firms need to navigate a set of complex specific-sector restrictions and multiple authorities with shared jurisdiction. In its efforts to encourage foreign investments, the Indian government has created a screening mechanism. Under the new screening mechanism, the government enjoys full discretion to decide on national security issues in relation to FDI; it applies at times unclear national security or national interest considerations, applicants are not involved in the review process, and, if a proposal is rejected, the Indian government will not inform of the reasons for rejection.

Japan has also established a screening regime and recently adopted FDI measures to counteract the Covid-19 blow. It lowered the threshold for pre-transaction approval from 10 per cent to 1 per cent, designated business sectors as core (eg, weapons) or non-core (eg, electricity) according to the degree they affect national security and exempted some from mandatory notification. Although the business community welcomes such an exemption, some concerns persist. Investors need to keep in mind strict filing times and be ready to accept a wide array of recommendations aimed at addressing national security, public order, public safety, or smooth management of the Japanese economy issues raised by their proposals or abandon them. The meaning of these issues is uncertain, as is the whole review process. More worryingly, the adoption of unclear national security concerns without proper oversight can reinforce the resistance that, for decades, Japan has shown towards foreign investors. In this context, the strategy introduced by the Prime Minister of Japan, Shinzo Abe, in 2013, and the subsequent reforms seeking to remove the barriers impeding high levels of inward FDI have been tested.

The strengthening of FDI rules has echoed across South Africa. This decision is at odds with the South Africa's efforts for decades to attract investors. Contrary to what we have seen in Russia, India, and Japan, whose interventions in foreign takeovers have been crafted to protect their national security, in South Africa, traditionally, high levels of crime have deterred foreign investors. Now that the pandemic seems to have receded, South Africa faces a precarious economic situation with pressing social problems rising. Therefore, it is no surprise that the South African government has not yet implemented the reform sought to intervene in foreign takeovers on national security grounds since 2018. The real question for the government now is not whether they can control inward FDI but at what price for the economy and the country. A further question is how to reconcile two policies that clash: on the one hand, the protection of the legal rights of foreign investors and, on the other, the broader social priorities of the South African economy. A particularly complex relationship indeed.

8

Merger Control as Industrial Policy

National Security and Public Interest Considerations

8.1 The Rise of Economic Nationalism and Protectionism

8.1.1 Economic Nationalism and Protectionism in the European Union

In the European Union (EU), advocates highlighting the need for competition law enforcement to protect national economies and other non-competition goals have been fairly vocal. In Germany, a country with an ordoliberal tradition—the anathema to economic nationalism—whereby the level of government intervention was strictly limited to enforcing the competition rules and preventing concentrations of economic power, as economic analysis was deemed enough to deal with antitrust issues and thus any political interference was unconceivable.[1] The Economy Minister Peter Altmaier in February 2019 presented the National Industrial Strategy 2030, a proposal that encourages the adoption of a forceful nationalist industrial policy.[2] The initiative, which attempts to contain the technological dominance of China, advocates for the increase of manufacturing share in gross domestic product (GDP) both in Germany and the EU, closing EU value chains to imports from outside the EU, designating specific German firms as 'national champions', modifying EU competition law to facilitate the creation of EU champions, allowing the German government to buy shares of companies to prevent foreign acquisitions, and increasing to a greater extent the state support of industrial sectors of 'great economic significance'.[3] A number of these recommendations would be inconceivable in the past pursuant to the standard approach to merger control enforcement. In Altmaier's view, size matters and currently, the EU competition law averts the creation of big firms that are required to undertake giant projects or that will bring efficiency gains.[4] It has been explained that after many years of increasing trade with China, Germany suddenly realized that China was not a mere significant

[1] David J Gerber, *Law and Competition in Twentieth-Century Europe: Protecting Prometheus* (OUP 2010) 232; Nicolas Petit, 'Competition Cases Involving Platforms: Lessons from Europe' (17 October 2018) 2 https://ssrn.com/abstract=3285277 accessed 15 September 2023.

[2] See German Federal Ministry for Economic Affairs and Energy, 'Made in Germany: Industrial Strategy 2030' (February 2019) https://www.bmwi.de/Redaktion/EN/Dossier/industrial-strategy-2030.html accessed 15 September 2023.

[3] ibid.

[4] ibid.

new market to be explored but rather a systematic competitor whose rules favour its domestic firms, a realization that forced a rethinking of Germany's policies.[5]

The concerns shown by Germany in relation to Chinese technological advancement have been growing and shared by some other Member States. Soon after the Commission denied the merger between Siemens and Alstom,[6] two leading firms in the railway industry, there was a storm of criticism based on the idea that it was necessary to create a European champion capable of stopping Chinese dominance in this sector by CRRC, China's national rail company. The German and French governments, who had lobbied for the merger, claimed that the Commission ignored that the Chinese train industry is highly subsidized and announced initiatives aimed at including industrial policy considerations as part of the EU merger regulation.[7] Later, a joint initiative signed by the French, German, and Polish governments sought that the Commission's merger strategy was guided by the Competitiveness Council, under the assumption that it was necessary to recognize 'the competitiveness of EU industrial sectors in order to provide input into the European Commission's strategy and policy'.[8] This active pressure to reintroduce protectionism policies seem to contradict the severe concerns expressed by France against industrial policy in the past.[9] However, one cannot forget that between 1958 and 1974 the French industrial policy successfully achieved a strong national industry, and that recently President Macron tried to revive French industry by reducing corporate taxes, increasing innovation incentives, and improving vocational training.[10]

Even if it may look like that the claims to reinvigorate an EU industrial policy come just from the Member States, the truth is that the European Commission is also fuelling a nationalist mindset through what has been named the 'European Industrial Renaissance'.[11] This initiative announced in 2014 seeks to recuperate the manufacturing capacity that has been transferred to China and to recover the EU economy that has

[5] 'Germany's fear of China. How China has Pushed Germany to Rethink Industrial Policy' *The Economist* (21 February 2019). In January 2019, the Federation of German Industries (BDI) demanded from the German Federal Government and the European Commission a new policy to respond to the growing challenges posed by China, whereby fifty-four recommendations were included in a paper titled 'Partner and Systemic Competitor: How to Deal with China's State-Controlled Economy?' https://issuu.com/bdi-berlin/docs/201901_policy_paper_bdi_china accessed 15 September 2023.

[6] Case M.8677 *Siemens/Alstom*.

[7] Massimo Motta and Martin Peitz, 'Competition Policy and European Firms' Competitiveness' (20 February 2019) https://cepr.org/voxeu/blogs-and-reviews/competition-policy-and-european-firms-competitiveness accessed 15 September 2023; see also German Federal Ministry for Economic Affairs and Energy and French Ministry of Economy and Finance, 'Franco-German Manifesto for a European Industrial Policy Adapted to the 21st Century', https://www.bmwk.de/Redaktion/DE/Downloads/F/franco-german-manifesto-for-a-european-industrial-policy.pdf accessed 15 September 2023.

[8] See German Federal Ministry for Economic Affairs and Energy, French Ministry of Economy and Finance and Polish Ministry of Entrepreneurship and Technology, 'Modernising EU Competition Policy' (4 July 2019) https://www.bmwi.de/Redaktion/DE/Downloads/M-O/modernising-eu-competition-policy.pdf?__blob=publicationFile&v=4 accessed 15 September 2023.

[9] Karl Aiginger and Dani Rodrik, 'Rebirth of Industrial Policy and Agenda for the Twenty-First Century' (2020) 20 Journal of Industry, Competition and Trade 189, 195.

[10] Arguably, efforts are needed to address problematic issues that businesses must confront in France, such as the process of establishing a company (ibid). The French President Emmanuel Macron has also advocated for a 'Buy European Act', see 'Macroeconomics: French Front-Runner Seeks to Reinvent EU Trade' *Politico* (5 March 2017) https://www.politico.eu/article/macronomics-french-front-runner-seeks-to-reinvent-eu-trade/ accessed 15 September 2023.

[11] European Commission, Communication 'For a European Industrial Renaissance' COM (2014) 014 final.

been stagnated since 2008, partly due to the imposition of austerity measures, lack of public investment, and a reduction of private investments.[12] This initiative has been accompanied by different programmes such as 'Better Regulation', 'Regulatory Fitness and Performance Programme' (REFIT), or 'Competitiveness Proofing, whose main goal is to eradicate existing legislation that makes business expensive or have far-reaching competitive effects for particular EU sectors.[13] Competition law is amidst the legislation that might be circumvented, which according to Wigger was a common tactic soon after the European integration took place. She outlines that during that period, described by the neoliberals as 'Eurosclerosis', the Commission showed a lenient approach by permitting generous state aids and tax reductions, facilitating the consolidation of European champions through mergers and acquisitions, and tolerating crisis cartels that fixed prices or limited outputs.[14] Such a flexible approach towards concentration continued after the European merger regulation was adopted, an approach illustrated by the number of prohibited mergers between 21 September 1990 and 31 May 2023, which accounted for just 32 out of 8,862 notified mergers (0.36 per cent).[15]

8.1.2 Economic Nationalism and Protectionism in the United States

Moving to the other side of the Atlantic, the United States (US), a country that has tried to depict itself as one of the most market-oriented economies in the world with little inclination towards industrial intervention, is rather an interesting case in the context of protectionist measures. During the 1950s and 1960s, the US was the global dominant foreign investor, a pattern that changed dramatically during the 1970s; as an illustration, by the end of 1988, US investments abroad represented $1.25 trillion compared to $1.79 trillion foreign investments in the US.[16] In terms of foreign direct investment, the increase was from $14 bn in 1971, to $83 bn in 1980, and to $329 bn by the end of 1988.[17] This shift in foreign market participation alarmed the US regime which was concerned that '[o]nce they own your assets, they own you', and forced the adoption of measures to contain the uncontrolled flow of foreign investment.[18] In particular, the acquisition of assets in the defence industry represented a major threat for which in 1976, President Gerald Ford established the Committee on Foreign Investment in the United States (CFIUS) to oversee this type of transactions and try to assess the potential risks

[12] Francesca Barbiero and Zolt Darvas, 'In Sickness and Health: Protecting and Supporting Public Investment in Europe' (2014) Bruegel Policy Contribution No 2/2014.

[13] Angela Wigger, 'The New EU Industrial Policy: Authoritarian Neoliberal Structural Adjustment and the Case for Alternatives' (2019) 16(3) Globalizations 353, 356. For other reforms, see European Commission, Communication 'Investing in a Smart, Innovative and Sustainable Industry: A Renewed EU Industrial Policy Strategy' COM (2017) 479 final.

[14] Wigger (n 13) 358–59.

[15] See European Commission, 'Statistics on Mergers Cases' (5 March 2021) https://ec.europa.eu/competition-policy/mergers/statistics_en accessed 15 September 2023.

[16] Thomas Omestad, 'Selling Off America' (1989) 76 Foreign Policy 119, 121–23.

[17] ibid 124.

[18] ibid 125.

they entail for the economy and the country.[19] The establishment of this Committee did not show the effectiveness expected and in 1988, a bill presented by Senator James Exon and Representative James Florio, the Exon-Florio Act, gave power to the President of the US to prohibit foreign acquisitions that threaten the 'national security, essential commerce and economic welfare'.[20] The Exon-Florio Act was a response to the Japanese investors who, in 1987, acquired a significant number of US high-tech firms. In the same year, there was a staggering number of megadeals through cross-border mergers and acquisitions involving real estate, electronics, electrical equipment, or chemicals.[21] As part of the government response, in December 1988, President Reagan equated CFIUS to cabinet-level, made it responsible for enforcing the Exon-Florio Act, and authorized the Chairman of CFIUS, the Secretary of the Treasury, to implement further regulations.[22] Likewise, there were attempts to modify the US merger rules seeking to transform them into industrial policy instruments capable of repealing the uncontainable foreign trade.[23] One bill, for instance, intended to introduce a probable lessening of competition standards instead of a possible,[24] and another sought to give powers to the President to safeguard mergers in industries that, according to the International Trade Commission, were susceptible to foreign competition harm.[25] The bills did not receive support, especially from the pro-antitrust Democrats in Congress.

Similar to Europe, the US is currently concerned about the significant increase of inbound investment in the American economy.[26] In particular, there are concerns in the US that certain foreign countries will take over the leadership in the technological sector enjoyed by the American firms, using illegal tactics such as 'large-scale subsidies, forced technological transfers, closed market access to foreign companies,[27] and intellectual property expropriation'.[28] We do not accept these comments at face value, we

[19] Executive Order 11858 (7 May 71975). Among the US government reports of foreign acquisitions of defence industrial base, see Secretary of Defense Dick Cheney, Defense Management: Report to the President, July 1989; US Department of Defense, Defense Policy Advisory Committee on Trade, US Government Policy Options Affecting Defense Trade, and the US Industrial Base, November 1988.

[20] PL 100-418, 102 Stat 1107 (to be codified as §721 of the Defense Production Act of 1950, 50 USC App §2061 et seq). The Senate-House conference in 1988 reported that the new legislation 'in no way intend[ed] to impose barriers to foreign investment', that the national security standard of review was 'intended to be interpreted broadly and without limitation to particular industries', given the President 'the flexibility to deal with any foreign control attempt which the President deems to pose a threat to national security'. See HR Rep No 576, 100th Congress, Second Session, 926–27 (1988).

[21] US Department of Commerce, Foreign Direct Investment in the United States: 1987 Transactions, 1988, 3, 10.

[22] Executive Order 12661, 27 December 1988; 54 Fed Reg 29744 (to be codified at 31 CFR pt 800).

[23] Joel Davidow and Paul Schott Stevens, 'Antitrust Merger Control and National Security Review of Foreign Acquisitions in the United States' (1990) 24 Journal of World Trade 39, 49.

[24] Merger Modernization Act of 1986, s 2160, and HR Rep No 4247, 99th Congress, Second Session, 1986.

[25] Promoting Competition in Distressed Industries Act, s 2161, and HR Rep No 4251, 99th Congress, Second Session, 1986.

[26] It has been reported that between 2003 and 2015, Chinese FDI into the US focused on electronics, industrial machinery, software and information technology services, and communications. The statistics also show that from 2014 to 2016 Chinese companies invested $14.2 bn in Information and Communications technology, with more than 95 per cent going to acquisitions. See Rhodium Group, 'The US-China Investment Hub', https://www.us-china-investment.org/fdi-data accessed 15 September 2023.

[27] 'Made in China 2025 and the Future of American Industry', Hearing Before the Committee on Small Business and Entrepreneurship United States Senate 116th Congress, First Session, 27 February 2019, https://www.govinfo.gov/content/pkg/CHRG-116shrg35699/pdf/CHRG-116shrg35699.pdf accessed 15 September 2023.

[28] In 2018, the National Counterintelligence and Security Centre reported that cyber espionage is a persisting tactic used by certain countries to steal US intellectual property, trade secrets, technology, and proprietary information. Specifically, it outlined that: 'China has expansive efforts in place to acquire U.S. technology to include

present them to set the context of why we see proliferation of national security regimes. An array of industrial policy proposals have emerged aimed at appeasing these concerns, such as stronger actions to support US advanced industries, tax reforms, a deeper North American supply chain, stronger screening of inward investments, and even 'to block the sales of U.S company equipment, block access to all banking and security systems'.[29] Yet some of the industrial policy initiatives to support the US economy are not new. Since the 1970s, collaborative innovation among universities, businesses, and laboratories has been encouraged by the government.[30] Likewise, it has been indicated that the rapid growth of Silicon Valley was facilitated by the contracts signed with the US Department of Defense. In addition, support to the energy industry has been provided by the US Department of Energy in the form of loans and grants to private firms, which by 2009 amounted to more than $40 billion.[31] More recently, President Joe Biden has unveiled an expansive spending bill directed at social needs, infrastructure, domestic chains, and recovery of manufacturing jobs joined by an increase in corporate taxes.[32] All these actions have been described as a clear indication that the US continues having a profound inclination towards protectionism and industrial policy.[33]

8.1.3 Economic Nationalism and Protectionism in China and Japan

In addition to the EU and the US, there are several other jurisdictions where industrial policies have supported significant growth of national sectors or companies. For example, during the 1950s and 1970s, Japan's industrial tactics led to the growth of their national companies into globally powerful firms. By the 1980s, twenty of the 100 largest

sensitive trade secrets and proprietary information. It continues to use cyber espionage to support its strategic development goals, science and technology advancement, military modernization, and economic policy objectives. China's cyberspace operations are part of a complex, multipronged technology development that uses licit and illicit methods to achieve its goals.' The report also indicates that in 2017, China introduced a cyber security law in which the government will access data owned by foreign companies for national security reviews. The US government is concerned that the data may be misappropriated or misused. See National Counterintelligence and Security Centre, 'NCSC Releases 2018 Foreign Economic Espionage in Cyberspace Report' (26 July 2018) https://www.dni.gov/files/NCSC/documents/news/20180724-ncsc-press-release-foreign-econ-esp-cyber.pdf accessed 15 September 2023.

[29] 'Made in China 2025 and the Future of American Industry' pp 29, 31, and 66; See also White House, 'Building Resilient Supply Chains, Revitalizing American Manufacturing and Fostering Broad-Based Growth: 100-Day Reviews under Executive Order 14017' (June 2021), https://www.whitehouse.gov/wp-content/uploads/2021/06/100-day-supply-chain-review-report.pdf accessed 15 September 2023.

[30] Known as Advanced Manufacturing Institutes. Aiginger and Rodrik (n 9) 194.

[31] Dani Rodrik, 'The Return of Industrial Policy' (Project Syndicate, 12 April 2010) https://serviciosenlinea.comfama.com/contenidos/servicios/Gerenciasocial/html/Cursos/Harvard/lecturas/6-The_Return_of_Industrial_Policy-Rodrik.pdf accessed 15 September 2023.

[32] Dani Rodrik, 'Beware Economist Bearing Policy Paradigms' (Project Syndicate, 11 May 2021), https://www.project-syndicate.org/commentary/economic-policy-must-abandon-universal-paradigms-by-dani-rodrik-2021-05 accessed 15 September 2023. For an interesting discussion about what policies the US should adopt to counteract China's dominance see Robert D Atkinson, 'US Trade Policy at a Turning Point' [2021] The International Economy 16.

[33] 'The New Geopolitics of Global Business' *The Economist* (5 June 2021) https://www.economist.com/leaders/2021/06/05/the-new-geopolitics-of-global-business accessed 15 September 2023.

firms on the Fortune 500 list were Japanese.[34] But perhaps more importantly, it has been observed that industrial policies are tools commonly used to repeal the expansion of foreign companies at the expense of the domestic ones. The core of China's industrial policy is the development of globally strong companies, a strategy consistently pursued. Early in the 1990s, the Chinese government had expressed 'Our nation's position in the international economic order will be to a large extent determined by the position of our nation's large enterprises and groups.'[35] This goal was accompanied by measures such, inter alia, non-tariff barriers, obstructions to enter local markets or conditions such as the transfer of technology in exchange for market access, government procurement, and privileged loans from state banks.[36] Similarly, as some authors have noted, China focused on three pillars: (i) technical and managerial knowledge, (ii) support to innovative entrepreneurship, and (iii) guaranteed access to natural resources to private and public undertakings.[37] At the same time, China recognized the importance of supporting key enterprises, having selected during 1991 and 1996, 120 large companies that received support from the government, while other companies were subject to a mass privatization process under the motto 'grasp the large, let go of the small'.[38] Also, China did not hesitate shutting down state-owned enterprises (SOEs) that were inefficient and as a result between 1990 and 2000 many of them were terminated.[39] Hence, China's strategy has resulted in presence in the global market that by 2021 accounts for 18 per cent of global GDP, and 20 per cent of business activity.[40]

8.2 Merger Control as Industrial Policy

Against this backdrop, this section examines to what extent governments should reserve for themselves the right to intervene in the markets through the adoption of industrial policies and whether competition policy might be the proper tool to do so. This question comes with the recognition that economic nationalism should not be regarded as a short-term phenomenon.[41] Yet, even if in protecting our national economies, we respond with an urge to intervene, some commentators have expressed their concerns about the proliferation of industrial policies and provided some principles that need to be observed to prevent undesirable consequences. It has also been noted that industrial policies need to be designed taking into consideration other policies, in a complementary fashion, rather than as an isolated and potentially contradictory interaction.[42]

[34] Peter Nolan, 'China and the Global Business Revolution' (2002) 26(1) Cambridge Journal of Economics 119, 120.
[35] ibid 121.
[36] ibid.
[37] Albert Schweinberger, 'State Capitalism, Entrepreneurship, and Networks: China's Rise to a Superpower' (2014) 48(1) Journal of Economic Issues 169, 173.
[38] ibid.
[39] ibid.
[40] *The Economist* (n 33).
[41] Sam Pryke, 'Economic Nationalism: Theory, History, and Prospects' (2012) 3(3) Global Policy 281, 282.
[42] Aiginger and Rodrik (n 9) 200.

Likewise, it has been said that policies on economic growth should be guided by clear goals, strategies, and resources.[43] For example, the literature has identified government support to certain technologies, such as artificial intelligence, or certain sectors and products, as beneficial. By contrast, granting subsidies to encourage the emergence of national champions, enacting import protection measures or encouraging the development of products that involved low standards has been described as harmful.[44]

In relation to the use of merger control as an instrument to implement industrial policies, it is evident that governments acknowledge that by weakening their enforcement in specific sectors or concerning companies they can influence the development of markets and address market failures. However, using competition law as an industrial policy tool is risky and requires careful consideration. One of the most worrisome risks is regulatory capture,[45] that appears to be more prevalent when competition law is envisaged to protect other interests beyond just competition, an aspect that is aggravated if the decision-makers are not accountable and independent.[46] This concern was expressed in a letter signed by a number of European industrial economists in response to the initiative to relax competition rules endorsed by the French and German governments soon after the Siemens and Alstom merger was blocked by the European Commission, which described such a proposal as a way to facilitate 'political opportunism'.[47] To mitigate the risk of regulatory capture, it has been suggested that subject matter experts, rather than politicians, should be responsible for the decision-making process.[48] It has also been outlined that if competition authorities restrict their enforcement activities to only competition considerations, it would impede the interference of groups of interests in the decision-making process improving transparency and accountability. Put differently, if competition enforcement includes non-economic

[43] ibid.

[44] ibid 201.

[45] The notion of regulatory capture can be traced back to Stigler's pathbreaking contribution in the area—George J Stigler, 'The Theory of Economic Regulation' (1971) 2(1) Bell Journal of Economics and Management Science 31—and it can be understood broadly as the influence that special interest groups can exert on government action, or more narrowly the influence that regulated firms can exert on regulating agencies. See Ernesto Dal Bò, 'Regulatory Capture: A Review' (2006) 22(2) Oxford Review of Economic Policy 203.

[46] Mario Mariniello, Damien Neven, and Jorge Padilla, 'Antitrust, Regulatory Capture, and Economic Integration' (July 2015) Bruegel Policy Contribution 2015/11 https://www.bruegel.org/sites/default/files/wp_attachments/pc_2015_11_.pdf accessed 15 September 2023. For further insights about private interests and their influence on the political process, see also Bob Jessop, 'The Crisis of the National Spatio-Temporal Fix and the Tendential Ecological Dominance of Globalizing Capitalism' (2000) 24(2) International Journal of Urban and Regional Research 323, 330; Cass R Sunstein, 'Interest Groups in American Public Law' (1985) 38 Stanford Law Review 29.

[47] Massimo Motta and others, 'Open Letter by European Industrial Economists: More, not Less, Competition is Needed in Europe' (9 February 2019) https://www.linkedin.com/pulse/open-letter-european-industrial-economists-more-less-needed-motta accessed 15 September 2023.

[48] Jeromin Zettelmeyer, 'The Return of Economic Nationalism in Germany' (March 2019) Peterson Institute for International Economics Policy Briefs 19–24, 11 https://www.piie.com/publications/policy-briefs/return-economic-nationalism-germany accessed 15 September 2023. Paul Seabright, 'National and European Champions—Burden or Blessing?' (2005) 6(2) CESifo Forum 52, has added that politicians are ill-prepared to identify and stop unsuccessful projects. For further discussion and implications, see Wim Naudé, 'Industrial Policy: Old and New Issues' (September 2010) WIDER Working Paper 2010/106 https://www.wider.unu.edu/publication/industrial-policy accessed 15 September 2023.

considerations, that would attract politicians whose intervention could undermine the independence of the competition authorities.[49]

Another adverse consequence of weakening merger control rules to attain a wider range of non-competition related goals is the resulting weakening of competitive pressure in the market. In the short-term, consumers might face higher prices with less choice and, in the long-term, undertakings will have fewer incentives to innovate, invest or improve the quality of their products or services.[50] In this sense, it has been recommended to adopt industrial policy considerations in competition law enforcement only on an exceptional basis, and in a proportionate manner in relation to mergers, and to apply the rules in a flexible way only when concerns with regard to the security of supply, military or other strategic sectors are introduced.[51] It has also been indicated that initiatives seeking a less strict application of the merger rules as a way to consolidate national champions may lead firms to use national security concerns on foreign direct investment (FDI) as a back door industrial policy mechanism. It has also been suggested that the adoption of less intrusive measures oriented to foster a culture of innovation and a low-cost business environment would be preferable as those would make the markets more competitive.[52]

The analysis has so far focused on adopting industrial policies to strengthening industries and pre-empting FDI that is adverse to the industrial strategies of the EU, the US, China, and Japan. The chapter also discusses the potential relaxation of merger control to advance industrial policy considerations. The next part looks at the debate around the issues that competition policy and enforcement should aim to address. In most jurisdictions, the consumer welfare approach has been accepted as the primary goal of competition regimes,[53] which focuses on ensuring output growth and low prices.[54] Lately, concerns have grown alleging that this narrow view that looks at volumes and prices ignores and keeps unresolved other issues generated by market power affecting workers, suppliers, and independent entrepreneurs.[55] Yet, this is not a recent concern: as early as in 1897, the US Supreme Court in assessing a price cartel

[49] Stefan Thomas, 'Normative Goals in Merger Control—Why Merger Control Should Not Attempt to Achieve "Better" Outcomes than Competition', in Ioannis Kokkoris and Claudia Lemus (eds), *Research Handbook on the Law and Economics of Competition Enforcement* (Edward Elgar 2022) 143. Mariniello, Neven, and Padilla (n 46) 7 consider that all non-competition goals should be abandoned.

[50] Motta and Peitz (n 7).

[51] ibid.

[52] ibid.

[53] OECD, Public Interest Considerations in Merger Control—Background Note (2016), DAF/COMP/WP3(2016)3, 5 https://one.oecd.org/document/DAF/COMP/WP3(2016)3/En/pdf accessed 15 September 2023. Consumer welfare is understood as consumer surplus referring to the 'excess of social valuation of a product over the price actually paid'. See Maurice E Stucke, 'Reconsidering Antitrust's Goals' (2012) 53 Boston College Law Review 551, 575.

[54] The argument, according to this approach, is that 'if consumers lose from a practice, then it is counted as anticompetitive, even if the consumer losses are completely offset by producer gains', see Herbert Hovenkamp, 'Is Antitrust's Consumer Welfare Principle Imperiled?' (2009) 45(1) Journal of Corporation Law 65.

[55] Lina M Khan, 'The New Brandeis Movement: America's Antimonopoly Debate' (2018) 9 Journal of European Competition Law and Practice 131–32. Vaheesan argues that 'the consumer welfare model represents an impoverished understanding of corporate power. It focuses principally on one aspect of business power—power over consumers—and ignores other critical manifestations'. See Sandeep Vaheesan, 'The Twilight of the Technocrats' Monopoly on Antitrust?' (2018) 127 Yale Law Journal Forum 980, 990.

case devoted some attention to the conditions of the workers who could lose their jobs because of the anti-competitive conduct.[56] However, as a more-economic-based approach in competition enforcement permeated many jurisdictions, the assessment of the wider impact of mergers and acquisitions and anti-competitive conducts on non-competition issues seems to have been attenuated.[57] Some commentators illustrate this shift by looking at the EU, where the first merger regulation proposal contemplated the possibility of bypassing its application 'in the common interest of the Community', an option that at a later stage disappeared from the wording of the final text of the adopted regulation.[58] Although this static economic approach was embraced for a while where the introduction of industrial policy considerations were resisted,[59] it appears that progressively the calls for questioning whether wider factors, such as wealth and income inequality, should be a competition law concern, started to resonate.[60] Simultaneously, some fear that this flexible approach would adversely impact administrability, credibility, and predictability,[61] and that the integration of broader goals would be problematic for competition enforcement, particularly for mergers, which is the focus of this book.

This chapter has so far provided an overview of the nature of economic nationalism. This inherent inclination to support domestic industries and/or repeal foreign investment has been evident for some time and will likely continue to be relevant across jurisdictions. Merger control has not been immune to this preference where, for instance, merger control has been used to introduce or complement wider industrial policy or

[56] *United States v Trans-Missouri Freight Association* US Supreme Court 166, 290 (1897), in which it was stated that: 'Trade or commerce under those circumstances may nevertheless be badly and unfortunately restrained by driving out of business the small dealers and worthy men whose lives have been spent therein, and who might be unable to readjust themselves to their altered surroundings.'

[57] Ioannis Kokkoris and Athanassios Skourtis, 'Is Consumer Welfare Still Fit for Purpose in the EU Competition Regime?', in Ioannis Kokkoris and Claudia Lemus (eds), *Research Handbook on the Law and Economics of Competition Enforcement* (Edward Elgar 2022) 410.

[58] European Commission, Proposal for a Regulation (EEC) of the Council on the control of concentrations between undertakings, COM (73) 1210 final, art 1(3); Council Regulation (EEC) No 4064/89 of 21 December 1989 on the control of concentrations between undertakings.

[59] Lord Brittan asserted that: 'we had to resist the pressures that were bound to be applied, and which were applied, by those seeking to use the Merger Regulation as an instrument of industrial policy, notwithstanding the clear tenor of the Regulation itself. I was determined to resist this, not because I was against any form of industrial policy, but because I thought that the best industrial policy was to ensure that competition prevailed in the EU'. See Lord Brittan, 'The Early Days of EC Merger Control' in International Bar Association, *EC Merger Control: Ten Years On* (2000) 3; see also Neelie Kroes, 'European Competition Policy—Delivering Better Markets and Better Choices' (European Consumer and Competition Day, London, 15 September 2005) https://ec.europa.eu/commission/presscorner/detail/en/SPEECH_05_512 accessed 15 September 2023, according to which 'Consumer welfare is now well established as the standard the Commission applies when assessing mergers'; and Sir Phillip Lowe, 'Consumer Welfare and Efficiency—New Guiding Principles of Competition Policy?' (Thirteenth International Conference on Competition and Fourteenth European Competition Day, Munich, 27 March 2007) https://ec.europa.eu/competition/speeches/text/sp2007_02_en.pdf accessed 15 September 2023: 'Ladies and Gentlemen, my overall message is short and simple. Yes, consumer welfare and efficiency are the new guiding principles of EU competition policy. Whilst the competitive process is important as an instrument, and whilst in many instances the distortion of this process leads to consumer harm, its protection is not an aim in itself. The ultimate aim is the protection of consumer welfare, as an outcome of the competitive process'.

[60] Margrethe Vestager has expressed in the GCLC Annual Conference that: 'Like any of the other rules that govern our world, we have competition rules because we believe they make our society a better place to live. That they make our markets work more fairly for consumers.' See 'Fairness and competition' (GCLC Annual Conference, Brussels, 25 January 2018) https://content.next.westlaw.com/practical-law/document/Ib16557c101b011e89bf099c0ee06c731/Speech-by-Margrethe-Vestager-on-fairness-and-competition accessed 15 September 2023.

[61] See Kokkoris and Skourtis (n 57) to understand these concepts.

other priorities unrelated to competition law and merger control. When merger control is used to accomplish a wider number of goals, it is more likely that politicians, who are more prone to regulatory capture, will be involved risking the independence of the competition authorities, and this makes competition enforcement less credible, less predictable, and less easy to administer. Governments should intervene only in exceptional cases, considering the potential adverse impact on competition enforcement. The adoption of an industrial strategy should be transparent and well justified in order to prevent adverse consequences on FDI and the broader prosperity of the economy and the country. Following this overview of the impact of industrial policy on merger control, the next section of the chapter focuses on the public interest considerations (national security being one of the most important public interest considerations) contemplated across different merger control regimes aimed at examining to what extent different jurisdictions have chosen to take them into consideration and whether they exert a prevalent influence in the merger assessment.

8.3 Public Interest Considerations in Merger Control

The application of merger rules is usually based solely on competition objectives, whereby the assessment of a transaction focuses only on its pro-competitive or anti-competitive effects from an allocative efficiency and consumer welfare point of view without considering other public interest considerations. Although less frequently applied, most jurisdictions also integrate a form of public interest consideration in their merger review analysis.[62] We should note that there is no exact definition of public interest, and the concept varies from one jurisdiction to another and seems to be framed according to the social, cultural, and political context within which it is considered.[63] These public interest considerations can be included as a principle in the preamble of the competition law, as a clause in which the objectives of the competition regime are stated, or as a precise article or section of the competition regime that provides that public interest considerations should be integrated as part of the merger assessment process.[64] It is also possible that even if the public considerations are not explicitly framed in any piece of law they unofficially inform the outcome of a merger

[62] David Reader has indicated that approximately 88 per cent of the domestic merger regimes worldwide have incorporated some form of public interest criteria within their merger control laws. See David Reader, 'Accommodating Public Interest Considerations in Domestic Merger Control: Empirical Insights', University of East Anglia and Centre for Competition Policy, CCP Working Paper 16-3 (February 2016): 58.

[63] Organisation for Economic Cooperation and Development (OECD), Public Interest Considerations in Merger—Executive Summary of the Roundtable (2017) DAF/COMP/WP3/M(2016)1/ANN5/FINAL https://one.oecd.org/document/DAF/COMP/WP3/M(2016)1/ANN5/FINAL/en/pdf accessed 15 September 2023; Oliver Budzinski and Annika Stohr, 'Public Interest Considerations in European Merger Control Regimes', in D Bosco and MS Gal (eds), *Challenges to Assumptions in Competition Law* (Edward Elgar 2021) 184, 187.

[64] OECD (n 63) 2; By 2016, twelve Member States in the EU reported that public interest considerations are part of their merger control reviews or are incorporated within the decision-making process, See European Competition Network, 'Public Interest Regimes in the European Union—Differences and Similarities in Approach: Final Report of the EU Merger Working Group' (10 March 2016), https://ec.europa.eu/competition/ecn/mwg_public_interest_regimes_en.pdf accessed 15 September 2023.

review.[65] In general terms, based on public interest considerations a merger that can cause competitive harm can be approved, while a merger that does not induce any competitive concern can be blocked.

The accommodation of public interest criteria in a merger regime seems to respond to socio-economic variables. A study by Reader looked at different jurisdictions whose merger frameworks included some public interest considerations.[66] His study suggested that jurisdictions in the same region tend to converge around what social considerations are of potential interest to merger control. The author observed that this confluence might be elicited by the commonality of issues afflicting the region.[67] Also, the type of legal system appears to influence the scope of public interest considerations as, for instance, civil law jurisdictions have shown a preference for the adoption of a more restrictive approach by limiting the opportunities in which discretionary decisions can take place.[68] It has also been observed that those countries that are distinguished by the degree of how open their regime towards foreign investment tend to limit the use of public considerations or, in other words, that countries that do not welcome foreign investment are more inclined to accommodate them.[69] Hence, the list of factors that can be considered as a public interest can be narrow or broad, can respond to the protection of specific sectors such as energy, media, and defence, can refer to economic issues such as small and medium enterprises or economic development, and to a wide variety of aims such as environment, employment, and public health.[70] Given the vagueness of the public interest concept coupled with the possibility of including multiple factors as part of it, it could be challenging for competition authorities to identify with precision where the public interest lies or clearly determine if the effects of a transaction are competition related, making the review process inconsistent and unpredictable.[71] It also carries the risk that private interests could be concealed under the appearance of public interests, permitting the use of competition law to gain added wealth at the expense of society, which could undermine confidence. At the same time, the accommodation of broad public interest considerations creates an inability to oppose similar measures in other jurisdictions, resulting in fewer opportunities for domestic firms to expand overseas.[72] In consequence, policymakers should reflect carefully on the implications of widening the scope of public interest intervention in merger control. It can be argued that it would be appropriate to exceptionally

[65] ibid 3.

[66] David Reader, 'Accommodating Public Interest Considerations in Domestic Merger Control: Empirical Insights', CCP Working Paper 16-3 https://papers.ssrn.com/sol3/papers.cfm?abstract_id=2736917 26.

[67] ibid 30–32.

[68] ibid 40–43.

[69] ibid 54–55.

[70] OECD (n 63) 3.

[71] ICN Merger Working Group: Analytical Framework Sub-group, 'The Analytical Framework for Merger Control', Final Paper for ICN Annual Conference Office of Fair Trading, London, 7, 14 (2002) https://centrocedec.files.wordpress.com/2015/07/analytical-framework-for-merger-control-2002.pdf accessed 11 June 2021. This report established that businesses cannot easily identify the non-competition interests that a concentration might harm as the merger rules do not often specify them.

[72] Competition and Markets Authority, 'Alex Chisholm Speaks About Public Interest and Competition-based Merger Control', Speech (11 September 2014), https://www.gov.uk/government/speeches/alex-chisholm-speaks-about-public-interest-and-competition-based-merger-control accessed 10 June 2021.

endure such repercussions in cases where the attainment of a specific public interest exceeds the benefit of having competitive markets or where by allowing an anticompetitive merger, a prevalent public interest is accomplished, following an objective criterion that should be applied in a non-discriminatory manner.[73] With this in mind, the next part examines in some detail the assessment of the public interest considerations in different merger control regimes.

8.3.1 Public Interest Considerations: Assessment

As stated above, some jurisdictions explicitly accommodate the examination of public interest considerations as part of their merger assessment process, not as an exception but rather integrated within an economic-based approach towards the assessment of a transaction. For instance, the standard for merger review in South Africa provides for a comprehensive analysis of competition effects, potential efficiency or pro-competitive gains, as well as public interest considerations, whereby the South African competition authority (the Competition Commission South Africa or the CCSA) is entrusted with the task of striking a balance between all of these considerations.[74] Thus, section 12A(3) of the Competition Act provides that: 'When determining whether a merger can be justified on public interest grounds, the Competition Commission or the Competition Tribunal must consider the effect that the merger will have on a) particular industrial sector or region; b) employment; c) the ability of small businesses, or firms controlled or owned by historically disadvantaged persons, to become competitive; and d) the ability of national industries to compete in international markets.'[75] For the application of the standard of review, guidelines have been produced aimed at facilitating merger assessment by following a five-step analysis: 1) the determination of the likely impact of the transaction on the public interest; 2) the determination of whether the alleged impact on a specific public interest is a result of that merger (merger-specific); (3) the determination of whether this impact is substantial; (4) the consideration of whether the merger parties can show a positive effect on the particular public interest; and (5) the consideration of possible remedies to address any likely negative effects on public interest.[76] It has been reported that from 2002–16, an average number of 4,500 transactions were reviewed, of which 247 were conditionally approved, and 184 of those remedies sought to overcome public interest issues.[77]

[73] Budzinski and Stohr (n 63) 5.

[74] OECD, Public Interest Considerations in Merger Control – Note by South Africa (2016) DAF/COMP/WP3/WD(2016)13 https://one.oecd.org/document/DAF/COMP/WP3/WD(2016)13/en/pdf accessed 15 September 2023.

[75] S 12A(3) of South Africa's Competition Act, No 89/1998, as amended by Competition Amendment Act, No 35 of 1999, Competition Amendment Act, No 15 of 2000, Competition Second Amendment Act, No 39 of 2000.

[76] See Competition Commission South Africa, 'Guidelines for the Assessment of Public Interest Provision in Mergers' https://www.compcom.co.za/wp-content/uploads/2017/11/Gov-Gazette-Public-Interest-Guidlines.pdf accessed 15 September 2023. The guidelines seek to provide clarity about how to approach each public interest factor included in the Competition Act.

[77] OECD (n 63) 9.

A good case that serves to illustrate the intersection between competition and public interest considerations and how the CCSA balances them is the ECP Africa Fund, Burger King South Africa (BKSA), and Grand Foods merger, which was the first case to be prohibited on public interest grounds in June 2021.[78] The transaction consisted of ECP Africa, a private equity fund, acquiring BKSA, which operates more than ninety fast food restaurants in South Africa, and Grand Foods Meat Plant Ltd (Grand Foods), whose main activity is the supply of burger patties to BKSA.[79] The Commission found that the transaction did not have the potential to substantially prevent or lessen competition in any of the relevant markets but was concerned that it might negatively affect public interest. In particular, CCSA established that more than 68 per cent of the acquired firms were owned by historically disadvantaged persons (HDPs) and that the acquiring firm was not owned by any HDPs, which led CCSA to conclude that after the merger, the ownership by HDPs will disappear. According to section 12A(3)(e) of the Competition Act 1998, a merger case needs to promote the levels of ownership of HDPs. As a result, CCSA prohibited the transaction because it could not be justified on substantial public interest grounds.[80]

The South African Competition Tribunal on appeal clarified that in the interplay between competition analysis and public interest considerations, it is necessary to consider other non-competition goals, especially if competition is not harmed because of the transaction.[81] The South African Competition Tribunal has also clarified that: 'section 12 A makes use of the term "justified" in conjunction with the public interest inquiry. It is not used in the sense that the merger must be justified independently on public interest grounds. Rather it means that public interest conclusions are justified in relation to prior competition conclusions'.[82] The protection of public interests was also evident in the *Walmart/Massmart* case, whose approval was conditioned to some measures aimed at redressing the loss of employment and sales by local suppliers, particularly Small, Medium and Micro Enterprises (SMMEs).[83] Also, in the *Kansai/Freeworld* case, where measures to increase South Africa's manufacturing capacity and to safeguard Black people, such as the prohibition of retrenchments for three years after the merger, the obligation to continue manufacturing in South Africa for ten years, to invest in research and development and to implement a Black Economic Empowerment (BEE), were imposed.[84] Specifically, the BEE, that is governed by the Black Economic[85] Empowerment Act, 2003, is a policy oriented to enhance the participation of Black

[78] Competition Commission South Africa, 'Commission Prohibits Acquisition Between ECP Africa Fund, Burger King South Africa and Grand Foods' (Press Release, 1 June 2021) https://www.compcom.co.za/wp-content/uploads/2021/06/COMMISSION-PROHIBITS-ACQUISITION-BETWEEN-ECP-AFRICA-FUND-BURGER-KING-SOUTH-AFRICA-AND-GRAND-FOODS-.pdf accessed 15 September 2023.

[79] ibid.

[80] ibid.

[81] *Shell South Africa Proprietary Limited and Tepco Petroleum Proprietary Limited*, case no 66/LM/Oct 01.

[82] *Harmony Gold Mining Company Limited and Gold Fields Limited*, Tribunal case no 93/LM/Nov04, para 56.

[83] Competition Commission of South Africa, Case No 2010Nov5445; Tribunal case no 73/LM/Nov10 of 29 June 2011.

[84] Competition Commission South Africa, 'Kansai's Acquisition of Freeworld Approved With Conditions' (Press Release, 19 April 2011), http://www.compcom.co.za/wp-content/uploads/2014/09/Press-release-Acquisition-of-Freeworld-by-Kansai.pdf accessed 15 September 2023.

[85] South African Government, 'Department of Trade and Industry Opposes the Hostile Takeover Bid by Kansai Paint Company Ltd of Freeworld Coatings Pty Ltd, at the Competition Commission' (Press release, 31 March 2011)

people in the South African economy. The BEE is used as proxies to measure the observance of the strategy, the levels of ownership, management control, skills development, enterprise/supplier and socio-economic development. Thus, the imposition of the above measures alleviated the public interest concerns arising from the transaction.[86]

In New Zealand, according to the Commerce Act 1986, the New Zealand Commerce Commission is obliged to apply the public interest benefit test if the merger would substantially lessen competition. The Commerce Commission will assess whether the benefit to the public would outweigh any anti-competitive effects.[87] In other words, the first step of merger assessment is the determination of whether it is possible that the transaction would substantially lessen competition, and the second step, in case the answer to the first question is positive, is to determine whether to authorize the merger based on the benefits brought by it. In assessing the potential benefits vs the harm, the Commission might consider productive efficiency (eg, economies of scales or scope), dynamic efficiency (eg, ability or incentive to innovate), and other benefits such as environmental developments.[88] Most recently, in December 2020, the Commission published updated merger guidelines in which it was indicated that aspects such as the environment, health, media or social welfare are public benefits relevant for the assessment of the Commission.[89] Similarly, in Australia after a recent reform in 2017, the Australian Competition and Consumer Commission (ACCC) is entitled to decide whether any detriment from the substantial lessening of competition would be outweighed by the public interest benefits offered by a merger and therefore approval can be granted.[90] It is worth mentioning that before the reform, the Australian Competition Tribunal (one of the three decision-making bodies that review transactions in Australia) was responsible for assessing transactions where public considerations were involved.[91]

Unlike South Africa, New Zealand, and Australia, in the EU, the assessment of public interest considerations is not integrated within the economic-based analysis but operates as an exception. Hungary is one of the countries that contemplates public interest considerations in merger control by clearly stating in article 24/A of the Competition Act that those transactions that support the preservation of jobs or the guarantee

https://www.gov.za/department-trade-and-industry-opposes-hostile-takeover-bid-kansai-paint-company-ltd-freeworld accessed 15 September 2023.

[86] See Amber Kardamilakis, 'Broad-based Black Economic Empowerment—Basic Principles', Norton Rose Fulbright (July 2018), https://www.nortonrosefulbright.com/en/knowledge/publications/fe87cd48/broad-based-black-economic-empowerment---basic-principles accessed 15 September 2023.

[87] Commerce Act 1986, s 67.

[88] OECD, Public Interest Considerations in Merger Control—Note by New Zealand (2016) DAF/COMP/WP3/WD(2016)7 https://one.oecd.org/document/DAF/COMP/WP3(2016)7/en/pdf accessed 15 September 2023.

[89] New Zealand Commerce Commission, Authorisation Guidelines Updated December 2020, para 37, https://web.archive.org/web/20210127090604/https://comcom.govt.nz/__data/assets/pdf_file/0012/91011/Authorisation-Guidelines-December-2020.pdf accessed 15 September 2023.

[90] Australian Competition and Consumer Commission, Merger Guidelines, https://www.accc.gov.au/system/files/Merger%20guidelines%20-%20Final.PDF accessed 15 September 2023.

[91] Public Interest Considerations in Merger Control—Note by Australia—Working Party No 3 on Co-operation and Enforcement, DAF/COMP/WP3/WD(2016)1 (20 May 2016): 2, https://www.oecd.org/officialdocuments/publicdisplaydocumentpdf/?cote=DAF/COMP/WP3/WD(2016)1&docLanguage=En accessed 15 June 2021.

of supply can be considered of strategic importance at the national level, and therefore they are not subject to the obligation to notify.[92] In Italy, the Italian Competition Authority (AGCM) under exceptional circumstances, can either approve or prohibit a merger if relevant national economic interests are involved, and, particularly in the banking sector, AGCM has the power to clear a merger to protect the economic stability of one or more of the merging parties.[93] France provides that the Minister for Economic Affairs can accommodate non-competition considerations such as employment, industrial development, and competitive conditions of local firms.[94]

Similarly, the Competition and Consumer Protection Act of Poland states that it is possible for the President of the Office of Competition and Consumer Protection (OCCP) to authorize an anti-competitive merger that is expected to contribute to economic development or technical progress, or positively impact the national economy.[95] A country that offers a considerable list of public interest factors that can lead to a prohibition of a pro-competitive transaction is Spain, where the Council of Ministers can look at protection of public security or public health, free movement of goods and services within the national territory, environment protection, promotion of technological research and development, and the guarantee of adequate maintenance of the objectives of sectoral regulation issues.[96] In Portugal, the Council of Ministers can intervene if strategic interests of the national economy may be compromised.[97] In Germany, it is the Minister of Economic Affairs who has the power to assess mergers initially blocked by the competition authority (the *Bundeskartellamt*) as a result of the impact on competition. The Minister can consider other non-competition aspects related to macroeconomic benefits, competitiveness of undertakings relative to international competition, or outstanding interests of the public.[98]

In most Member States where public considerations are clearly indicated as part of merger assessment, national security and plurality of media are listed as part of these considerations.[99] Another interesting feature is when a Member State acknowledges in its competition regime the importance of public interests but does not provide a precise list of factors. Such is the case in the Netherlands, where the Minister of Economic Affairs can decide a merger grounded on unspecified public considerations,[100] or in

[92] Art 24/A, Act LVII of 1996 on the Prohibition of Unfair and Restrictive Market Practices (also known as the Hungarian Competition Act), https://www.gvh.hu/pfile/file?path=/en/legal_background/rules_for_the_hungarian_market/competition_act/competition-act-documents/jogihatter_tpvt_hataly_20190101_a&inline=true accessed 15 September 2023.

[93] Law No 287/90, arts 25(2) and 25(5-bis).

[94] Code of Commerce, art L. 430—7 -1.

[95] Act of 16 February 2007 on Competition and Consumer Protection, art 20 2(1)(2). The Court of Competition and Consumer Protection of Poland has stressed the importance of examining public interest considerations in merger review: 'The protection of competition is not the sole goal of the Competition Act [but rather] achieving certain benefits in a general socio-economic interest. If such benefits can also be achieved by restricting competition, activities leading to such restraints are not seen as prohibited by the Act'. See *Orzeł Biały*, SOKiK's judgment of 13 April 2011, XVII Ama 78/09.

[96] Competition Act 15/2007, art 10.

[97] Art 41 of the 2014 PCA's by-laws.

[98] §42 GWB.

[99] European Competition Network (n 64) 3.

[100] Dutch Competition Act, art 47. The Minister of Economic Affairs approves the merger if it finds that certain public interests, which are not specified, outweigh the impediment to competition.

Austria, where the Federal Cartel Prosecutor can defend unregistered public interests in important cases or industries.[101] By looking at EU merger control regimes where public interest considerations are explicitly recognized, it is noticeable that they are diverse. It is also evident that several Member States prefer to frame the public interest considerations in a detailed and confining way, while a small number of them, even if expressly recognized the incorporation of public interest in merger control assessment, do not specify what can be considered a public interest. Another interesting feature is that when the public interest is applied, in most cases, the decision power is transferred to a governmental body that is different from the competition authority, as the next case shows.

The *Agripole/Cofigeo* merger in France is illustrative for various reasons.[102] For the first time since the introduction of non-competition considerations in the merger review control that took place in 2008, the Minister for Economic Affairs in 2018 overturned the decision of the French Competition Authority, as his priority was to maintain employment regardless of the negative effects on competition.[103] In this case, the market involved was the canned ready meals, in which after the merger the new entity would become the leader by having 80 per cent of market shares for Italian ready meals and 70 per cent for Asian ready meals. The high market shares concerned the competition authority which ordered the divestiture of some assets to protect consumers from a potential price increase. Nevertheless, the Minister found that the obligation to sell some assets was detrimental from an industrial strategy point of view and that the merger was needed to reinvigorate the sector. As a result, the Minister cleared the transaction after Cofigeo committed to maintain employment for at least two years. Thus, this case shows that when competition concerns conflict with other political priorities, the former can be effectively overshadowed by the latter.

There are a few jurisdictions where the public interest considerations are not unequivocally framed in the legislation but informally influence the outcome of a merger review. For instance, in the Slovak Republic, the Antimonopoly Office can prohibit those transactions that create or strengthen a dominant position pursuant to the Slovak Act on Protection of Competition 2009.[104] While the Antimonopoly Office has often informed its merger reviews focusing on market concentration levels, non-competition considerations have sometimes played a role.[105] This was the case in a transaction that took place in the market of electric motors for washing machines, where despite high

[101] §75 KartG.

[102] Autorité de la Concurrence, Decision 18-DCG-95 14 January 2018, https://www.autoritedelaconcurrence.fr/en/communiques-de-presse/14-june-2018-acquisition-william-saurin accessed 15 September 2023.

[103] Emmanuelle Van Den Broucke, 'The Minister of Economy Intervenes to Authorize the Takeover of William Saurin by Cofigeo Without Divestment of Assets' (Dentons Competition Newsletter, August 2018) https://www.dentons.com/en/insights/newsletters/2018/august/27/paris-competition-newsletter/competition-newsletter-august-2018 accessed 15 September 2023.

[104] Art 12(6) of the Slovak Act on Protection of Competition of 2009 provides that the Antimonopoly Office shall prohibit a concentration 'which would significantly distort competition on the relevant market mainly due to the creation or strengthening of dominant position'.

[105] Jurgita Malinauskaite, 'Development of Merger Control in Slovakia and Slovenia' (2012) 23(3) European Business Law Review 375, 401.

concentration levels, the merger between MEZ a.s. and Siemens AG was approved.[106] The Antimonopoly Office concluded that despite the anti-competitive effects, the benefits offered by the transaction, such as a more competitive market abroad and a highly qualified production by Slovak employees, justified the approval of the transaction.[107]

In some other jurisdictions, merger control regimes do not include factors relevant to the public interest as part of the assessment. Japan is a country that illustrates this approach, where the Japanese Antimonopoly Act restricts the analysis only to the restriction of competition,[108] and the Japan Fair Trade Commission (JFTC) does not need to consult its merger decisions with any other governmental bodies, and its merger decisions cannot be reversed by any ministerial body.[109] Equally, in Mexico, the merger review focuses only on competition factors and the Federal Economic Competition Law (LFCE) does not include the examination of public interest considerations.[110] The US is a particular case in which the antitrust agencies, the Department of Justice (DOJ), and the Federal Trade Commission (FTC) review mergers based solely on an economic grounds.[111] However, this very strict approach contrasts with the mergers taking place in some regulated sectors where the analysis of public interest considerations is frequent and broad.[112] The accommodation of public interest factors within the merger control review can also be assessed from the perspective of the competition authority in charge of the assessment, which is the focus of the next section.

8.3.2 Public Interest Considerations: Institutional Design

Two main types of institutional design have been identified among the different jurisdictions for assessing public interest considerations: (i) a single authority model and (ii) a dual authority model. As stated earlier, South Africa has adopted the single authority model, as the Competition Commission of South Africa has the power to evaluate the competition and non-competition considerations, strike a balance between them and make a final decision.[113] In relation to the dual authority model, it has been noted that

[106] *MEZ a.s. Michalovce/Siemens AG* (1994).

[107] Alena Cernejova, 'Case Comment. Slovakia: Joint Venture with Foreign Partner' (1994) 15(4) European Competition Law Review, 125.

[108] Antimonopoly Act, Ch 4, art 10(1) that provides: No company may acquire or hold shares of any other companies if its acquisitions of shares substantially restrain competition in any particular field of trade, nor may any company use unfair practices to acquire or hold shares in another company.

[109] OECD, Public Interest Considerations in Merger Control—Note by Japan (2016) DAF/COMP/WP3/WD(2016)4 https://www.oecd.org/officialdocuments/publicdisplaydocumentpdf/?cote=DAF/COMP/WP3/WD(2016)4&docLanguage=En accessed 15 September 2023.

[110] Available in English at https://www.cofece.mx/wp-content/uploads/2018/03/Federal_Economic_Competition_Law.pdf accessed 15 September 2023.

[111] S 7 of the Clayton Act indicates that those transactions 'where in any line of commerce or in any activity affecting commerce in any section of the country, the effect of such acquisition may be substantially to lessen competition, or to tend to create a monopoly, are prohibited'. See 15 USC § 18.

[112] See Ioannis Kokkoris, *US Merger Control: Public Interest Considerations in US Merger Control* (OUP 2024).

[113] OECD, Public Interest Considerations in Merger Control—Background Note (2016), DAF/COMP/WP3(2016)3 https://one.oecd.org/document/DAF/COMP/WP3(2016)3/En/pdf accessed 15 September 2023. In the EU, Poland has chosen the single model where the NCA assesses the public interest considerations of the merger without ministerial intervention, see European Competition Network (n 64).

the body in charge of the public interest review (a sector regulator or a government department) enjoys broad discretion and the power to overturn the recommendation or decision of the competition authority. Germany, like most of the OECD members, has adopted this dual setting model,[114] where the *Bundeskartellamt* is entrusted with the analysis of competition concerns and the Minister for Economic Affairs and Energy reviews the merger on public interest grounds.[115] Thus, if a merger is prohibited because it would significantly impede effective competition, the parties can still seek ministerial approval. In the *EDEKA/Tengelmann*[116] case where EDEKA intended to acquire 451 Tengelmann's outlets, for instance, the Minister of Economic Affairs and Energy approved the merger based on job protection considerations, despite the opposition from the *Bundeskartellamt*[117] and the recommendation given by its own advisory committee that the alleged benefits would be uncertain and will not outweigh the competitive harm.[118] At the end, the merger was cleared, and the President of the Monopolies Commission resigned.[119] A study has shown that between 1974 and 2016, the Minister has approved a total of nine mergers (*EDEKA/Tengelman* included), with the most prevalent consideration being job protection, followed by securing energy supply.[120]

Looking more widely, another study that took seventy-five countries as a sample concluded that: (i) when the public interest factor responds to a particular sector, there is an inclination to appoint a regulator as decision-maker, (ii) if the public interest factor is integrated with the economic-based analysis, then it is more likely that the national competition authority will be designated, as decision-maker, and (iii) when the public interest factor has been 'reduced' to an exception, then it is expected that a politician will be the decision-maker.[121] In terms of who is more suitable for deciding public interest considerations, it has been argued that in relation to sectoral issues the expertise of the regulator should be preferred. It has also been said that, regardless of sector concerns, in choosing the decision-maker two aspects are relevant: first, it should not be ignored that competition authorities are experts and independent, and second, that politicians have been elected by the citizens and therefore they have the legal authority to solve

[114] OECD (n 63) 3.

[115] §36 (1) GWB. Before the Minister decides, an opinion is required from the Monopolies Commission, an independent advisory body that provides statutory and specialized opinions.

[116] *Bundeskartellamt, Prohibition of Acquisition of Kaiser's Tengelmann outlets by Edeka* Case Summary, B2-96/14, 31 March 2015, https://www.bundeskartellamt.de/SharedDocs/Entscheidung/EN/Fallberichte/Fusionskontrolle/2015/B2-96-14.pdf?__blob=publicationFile&v=2 accessed 15 September 2023.

[117] The *Bundeskartellamt* was concerned about the elimination of an essential competitor in an already highly concentrated food retail regional markets and municipal districts, worsened by important barriers to entry, that would result in a significantly reduced consumer choice. ibid.

[118] See *Monopolkommission* special opinion No 70 *Edeka/Tengelmann*, https://www.monopolkommission.de/de/gutachten/sondergutachten/sondergutachten-ministererlaubnis/119-sondergutachten-70.html accessed 15 September 2023.

[119] A distinction should be made between the German Monopolies Commission and the *Bundeskartellamt*. The former is a permanent, independent expert committee which advises the government, including the Minister of Economic Affairs and Energy, in the areas of competition policymaking, competition law, and regulation (see https://www.monopolkommission.de/en/monopolies-commission/mission.html accessed 15 September 2023). The latter is the German competition authority (see https://www.bmwi.de/Redaktion/EN/Artikel/Ministry/bundeskartellamt-bkarta.html accessed 15 September 2023.)

[120] Budzinski and Stohr (n 63) 199.

[121] David Reader, 'Accommodating Public Interest Considerations in Domestic Merger Control: Empirical Insights', 21–22.

elemental societal matters. The implication of the last consideration is that as competition authorities do not have such legal authority, then they should not be dealing with aspects that are fundamental to society.[122] As indicated earlier, given the vagueness of the public interest concept and the risk that private interests can permeate decision-making, it seems that the expertise and independence of national competition authorities is preferable. Yet, the debate remains unsettled and reaching a consensus appears unlikely.

8.3.3 Public Interest Considerations: Procedural Aspects

In procedural terms, a variety of features respond to the diverse assessment approaches and institutional designs that various jurisdictions have chosen to assess public interest. For instance, in those countries where the public interest test is embedded in the general review process, like South Africa, there is no separate or specific set of rules administering the analysis of non-competition factors.[123] In jurisdictions where the dual agency setting is adopted, there is a range of different procedural options. In France, for instance, the Minister of Economic Affairs have the option to request the initiation of an in-depth investigation by referring the case to Phase II and the option to, once Phase II has been terminated and decided by the French competition authority, to overrule the decision of the latter.[124] In Germany, after a merger has been prohibited, the parties have the right to request ministerial intervention. Once the Minister is involved, an assessment is provided by a group of experts (*Monopolkommission*), and the parties can then express their opinion through a public hearing, and finally, the Minister offers its assessment.[125] Other jurisdictions have a more complex assessment process as is the case of Canada, where if a merger relates to specific regulated sectors, the parties need to observe specific rules. In the finance sector, the parties need to notify concurrently the Competition Bureau (the Bureau) and the Office of the Superintendent of Financial Institutions; the former assesses the competition issues and the latter the prudential considerations relevant to the transaction.[126] In the transport sector, according to the Canada Transportation Act (CTA) the merging parties need to notify the transaction to the Minister of Transport, who has forty-two days to make their view public concerning the transaction, and if some issues affecting the public interest are found, then the parties need to wait until the Governor in Council makes a final decision.[127]

[122] ibid 59.

[123] European Competition Network, 'Public Interest Regimes in the European Union—Differences and Similarities in Approach', Final Report of the EU Merger Working Group (10 March 2016): 5.

[124] Budzinski and Stohr (n 63) 192.

[125] European Competition Network, 'Public Interest Regimes in the European Union—Differences and Similarities in Approach', Final Report of the EU Merger Working Group (10 March 2016): 5.

[126] OECD, Public Interest Considerations in Merger Control—Note by Canada (2016) DAF/COMP/WP3/WD(2016)2 https://www.oecd.org/officialdocuments/publicdisplaydocumentpdf/?cote=DAF/COMP/WP3/WD(2016)2&docLanguage=En accessed 15 September 2023.

[127] Canada Transportation Act, paras 53.1(5) and 53.2(1).

A final case study is the US, where the examination of public interest considerations in some regulated sectors in merger reviews is even more complicated. As an illustration, in the banking sector, three different regulators, the Office of the Comptroller General, the Federal Deposit Insurance Corporation, and the Board of Governors of the Federal Reserve System have jurisdiction to assess certain transactions according to the financial institution involved in the transaction, and together with the DOJ review the competitive effects of the respective deals. Additionally, the regulators also apply a public interest test, whereby there is a different procedure before each regulator, and if the regulator considers that the public benefits offered by the transaction outweigh the anti-competitive effects it has the power to approve it. If the DOJ finds that the merger would have negative effects on competition, then it needs to challenge the transaction before the courts.[128]

There are a number of reflections that we can draw from the above analysis. First, any attempt to isolate merger review from political attention would be in vain, as the implications of a merger decision can impact a few areas where governments might feel inclined, or even compelled, to intervene. Second, it seems prudent to abandon the notion and the quest that competition law, particularly merger control, has the potential to solve all societal issues separately from the impact on competition. Recognizing some boundaries and limitations in merger enforcement would make it more effective and realistic. Third, identifying clear goals would also facilitate the interaction between stakeholders, competition authorities, governmental bodies, courts, and the business community. A common understanding of what represents a concrete public interest might reduce conflicting decisions between competition and public interest considerations. Fourth, transparent and clear procedures are critical for the decision-making of authorities responsible for assessing public interest considerations of transactions. If one considers that a merger control process is intrinsically complex, then it is crucial to evade concurrent enforcement systems where merging parties additionally need to deal with the presence of multiple reviewers, standards, rules, and aims of enforcement. Lastly, policymakers should examine if other legislative and enforcement instruments would be more effective in achieving public interest goals to keep political intervention limited to a minimum in the merger assessment process, an approach that could contribute to business and consumer confidence. The next section will examine the assessment of national security concerns, considering that this factor is recognized in many jurisdictions and has been the subject of increasing reforms.

8.4 National Security as a Public Interest Consideration

The adoption of national security concerns in the context of merger control review has been a common strategy used by some nations to safeguard their essential interests, whereby many jurisdictions deal with national security concerns through separate FDI

[128] For an analysis, see Kokkoris (n 112).

regimes instead of reviewing them as part of the competition-focused merger control regime. More recently, the adoption or strengthening of national security controls has become more prominent in response to the remarkable increase of foreign acquirers, particularly but not exclusively by Chinese investors, and as a measure to protect certain businesses negatively affected by the Covid-19 pandemic from opportunistic foreign acquirers.[129] As an illustration of the latter, in April 2020, France lowered the thresholds to review acquisitions involving foreign investors. In the same month, Italy extended FDI jurisdiction to new sectors such as food, health, finance, and insurance. Also, in April 2020, India tightened the rules of FDI to restrain 'opportunistic takeovers/acquisitions of Indian companies due to the current Covid-19 pandemic'.[130] Earlier in March 2020, Australia announced that during the pandemic, the thresholds to review foreign acquisitions would be lowered 'to safeguard the national interest as the coronavirus outbreak puts intense pressure on the Australian economy and businesses'.[131] In July 2020, Canada also announced that it would apply more strictly the Investment Canada Act (ICA) to protect business related to public health or supply of critical goods and services to Canadians from opportunistic behaviour by state-owned enterprises and entities linked to foreign governments.[132] Even if the merger reforms introduced by the pandemic seem temporary, the underlying outcome is that countries have realized that such amendments can be an immediate response to offset the threats faced in times of crisis. As the next part shows, this has occurred in an increasing number of jurisdictions.

A relevant aspect being highlighted is that although the examination of national security concerns as part of the merger review has expanded across many jurisdictions, a precise definition of national security remains absent in most of them.[133] Another distinctive feature is that some regimes have tailored their regulations to address concerns that arose from specific countries, as is the case with the US, whose latest legislative processes have openly discussed the increase in foreign investment activity by Chinese state-owned companies, the notion that such investments are part of a government-coordinated approach, and the concern that the unlimited governmental support that Chinese companies receive makes it probable that other private investors cannot compete on fair conditions.[134] Interestingly, some other jurisdictions which have usually

[129] Herbert Smith Freehills, 'Covid-19: Pressure Points: Foreign Direct Investment Regulation—Drawbridges Continue to Rise in Response to the Pandemic (Global)', 21 May 2020, https://www.herbertsmithfreehills.com/latest-thinking/Covid-19-pressure-points-foreign-direct-investment-regulation---drawbridges-continue accessed 28 June 2021.

[130] ibid.

[131] ibid.

[132] Michael Laskey, Peter Flynn, and Kirsten Cirella, 'Foreign Direct Investment Regimes: Canada 2021' (ICGL, 30 November 2022) https://iclg.com/practice-areas/foreign-direct-investment-regimes-laws-and-regulations/canada accessed 15 September 2023.

[133] Joel Davidow and Paul Schott Stevens, 'Antitrust Merger Control and National Security Review of Foreign Acquisitions in the United States' (1990) 24 Journal of World Trade 39, 52; 'Addressing National Security Concerns in the Merger Context', in Kokkoris I and Lemus C (eds), *Research Handbook on the Law and Economics of Competition Enforcement* (Edward Elgar 2022) 217. It should be noted that in the US, FINSA tried to fill the gap by including threats to homeland security and critical infrastructure as part of the definition of national security. 50 USC §4565(a)(5).

[134] James K Jackson, 'The Committee on Foreign Investment in the United States (CFIUS)' (Congressional Research Service, 3 July 2018) RL33388, 41.

been more reserved towards certain foreign investors, are now becoming more uninhibited. As an illustration, in January 2021, Australia blocked an intended transaction in which a Chinese state-owned company bid for a local building contract, on national security grounds. The decision raised concerns that the Australian government was sending clear signals to Chinese investors that their transactions would face 'tougher scrutiny'.[135] Likewise, in 2016, Germany referred to China as a potential strategic threat when deciding the acquisition of Aixtron by the Fujian Grand Chip Investment Fund,[136] and in 2018, the French Minister of the Economy reported that many Chinese deals were blocked by him, without providing further details.[137]

In relation to the scope of national security assessment, the tendency is that the number of factors that can be considered as national security concerns increases progressively. The US is a good example, where gradually, more factors are included as part of the national security list. Initially, they included factors relevant to national defence (human resources, products, technology, materials, energy supplies, and other critical resources),[138] and then enhanced by risks to national security such as the potential disclosure of substantial pools of personal information, the potential loss of one of only a few US suppliers in certain sectors, and the potential loss of US technological advantages,[139] and more recently amplified by accommodating concerns arising from certain foreign non-controlling investments involved in critical technology, critical infrastructure, or sensitive personal data, and real estate transactions that previously fell outside CFIUS's jurisdiction.[140] In 2021, the Senate Foreign Relations Committee approved with a bipartisan vote the Strategic Competition Act bill, which included—among other provisions mostly addressed at curtailing Chinese influence—rules aimed at extending the scope of CFIUS review to certain gifts and contracts arranged between foreign persons and US higher education institutions.[141] The bill was then consolidated into the United States Innovation and Competition Act of 2021, but was ultimately left

[135] Jamie Smyth, 'Australia Cites National Security to Block China Buying Local Builder' *Financial Times* (12 January 2021) https://www.ft.com/content/3b233463-9eeb-4781-ab0c-50c3861d142d accessed 15 September 2023.

[136] Although, in this case, the government had initially approved the transaction, the Economy Ministry revoked the decision based on 'previously unknown security-related information'. See Maria Sheahan and Caroline Copley, 'Germany Stalls Chinese Takeover of Aixtron, Citing Security Worries' (Reuters, 24 October 2016) https://www.reuters.com/article/us-aixtron-m-a-fujian-germany-idUSKCN12O13G accessed 15 September 2023.

[137] Herbert Smith Freehills, 'Foreign Investment: Rising Tides of Politics in Regulation' (17 December 2020) 5 https://www.herbertsmithfreehills.com/latest-thinking/foreign-investment-rising-tides-of-politics-in-regulation-updated-report accessed 15 September 2023.

[138] S 721(f) of the Defense Production Act 1950.

[139] CFIUS, Annual Report to Congress CY 2015 https://home.treasury.gov/system/files/206/Unclassified-CFIUS-Annual-Report-report-period-CY-2015.pdf accessed 15 September 2023.

[140] US Department of Treasury, 'Summary of the Foreign Investment Risk Review Modernization Act of 2018' https://home.treasury.gov/system/files/206/Summary-of-FIRRMA.pdf accessed 15 September 2023.

[141] US Senate, Committee on Foreign Relations, 'Strategic Competition Act of 2021' (15 April 2021) https://www.congress.gov/117/bills/s1169/BILLS-117s1169is.pdf accessed 15 September 2023. The bill responded to concerns that China is exploiting the open research and development of US higher education institutions; see the US Senate, Permanent Subcommittee on Investigations, 'China's Impact on the U.S. Education System' (22 February 2019) https://www.hsgac.senate.gov/wp-content/uploads/imo/media/doc/PSI%20Report%20China%27s%20Impact%20on%20the%20US%20Education%20System.pdf accessed 15 September 2023.

out of the final version which became law as the CHIPS and Science Act in 2022; it has been reported that a new effort to revive the bill might be in the works.[142]

In the UK, a new regime for the review of transactions and investments on national security grounds, the National Security and Investment Act 2021 (NSIA),[143] was introduced, to replace the current merger control regime set out in the Enterprise Act 2002 (EA02). The reform broadens the scope of foreign investment screening by making notification mandatory in seventeen sensitive sectors that cover energy, defence, transport, AI, quantum technologies, advanced robotics, data infrastructure, and cryptographic authentication, among others.[144] Moreover, the new regime has omitted a clear definition of national security to facilitate a wider interpretation and, therefore, easy application.[145] In addition, the NSIA imposes indefinite periods where the Secretary of State can review past transactions that were not notified and five years to review those that are not notifiable but pose a suspected national risk. In both cases, the time shortens to six months once the Secretary of State becomes aware of the transaction. Contrary to what the EA02 provided, the new NSIA does not establish thresholds for certain transactions, which signifies that even small operations will be subject to scrutiny.[146] Notably, the NSIA does not target only overseas entities, but may apply to national entities involved with such national security risks.

Similarly, the EU enacted Regulation (EU) 2019/452 of the European Parliament and of the Council of March 2019 (the Regulation) that established a framework for screening foreign direct investments into the EU, that came into force from October 2020.[147] The Regulation includes five factors that Member States may consider likely to trigger security or public order concerns if acquired by foreign investors: 1) critical infrastructure, including energy, transport, water, health, communications, media, data processing or storage, aerospace, defence, electoral or financial infrastructure, and sensitive facilities, as well as land and real estate crucial for the use of such infrastructure; 2) critical technologies and dual use items, including artificial intelligence, robotics, semiconductors, cybersecurity, aerospace, defence, energy storage, quantum

[142] Morgan Chalfant, 'Senators are Talking About Another Big China Bill', *Semafor* (10 February 2023), https://www.semafor.com/article/02/10/2023/senators-are-talking-about-another-big-china-bill accessed 15 September 2023.

[143] On 29 April 2021, the National Security and Investment Bill was granted Royal Assent, see Department for Business, Energy and Industrial Strategy, 'National Security Bolstered as Bill to Protect Against Malicious Investment Granted Royal Assent', Press Release (29 April 2021), https://www.gov.uk/government/news/national-security-bolstered-as-bill-to-protect-against-malicious-investment-granted-royal-assent accessed 15 September 2023.

[144] The UK government has refined the definition of the seventeen sectors to assist merging parties in self-assessing whether they need to notify their transactions according to the rules contained in the NSA. See Department for Business, Energy and Industrial Strategy, 'National Security and Investment: Sectors in Scope of the Mandatory Regime—Government Response to the Consultation on Mandatory Notification in Specific Sectors Under the National Security and Investment Bill' (March 2021), https://assets.publishing.service.gov.uk/government/uploads/system/uploads/attachment_data/file/965784/nsi-scope-of-mandatory-regime-gov-response.pdf accessed 15 September 2023.

[145] Mark Jones and others, 'UK National Security and Investment— Now is the Time to Act' (Hogan Lovells, 30 April 2021) https://www.engage.hoganlovells.com/knowledgeservices/news/uk-national-security-and-investment-now-is-the-time-to-act accessed 15 September 2023.

[146] ibid.

[147] [2019] OJ L 79/I 1.

and nuclear technologies as well as nanotechnologies and biotechnologies; 3) supply of critical inputs, comprising energy or raw materials, as well as food security; 4) access to sensitive information, including personal data, or the ability to control such information; and 5) the freedom and pluralism of media.[148] Like the US and the UK, the EU regulation on FDI does not define security and public order.[149]

The German Investment control has also been constantly revamped. The last change took place in May 2021 when the Seventeenth Amendment Ordinance to the AWV entered into force, completing the adaptation to the amendment made to the AWG (Foreign Trade and Payments Act), which impressively increases the list of critical sectors and technologies that require investment screening.[150] The reform includes the following sectors as part of the investment control law: artificial intelligence, robotics, nanotechnology, quantum technology, semiconductors, 3D printing, and autonomous driving/flying, as well as security-relevant companies in food safety, aviation or the raw materials industry.[151] Before this amendment, in June 2020, another reform introduced a mandatory FDI filing for investments above 10 per cent voting rights in German firms active in critical infrastructures and technologies by non-EU investors covering personal protective equipment, numerous pharmaceuticals, and medicinal products, and devices for in-vitro diagnostics.[152] In France, the list of sectors that initially required prior authorization from the French Ministry of Economy as they raise public safety or national defence concerns (research, production or trading of weapons, munitions or explosive powders or substances) has been enlarged and modernized with the inclusion of activities involving artificial intelligence and robotics sectors.[153]

In China, new measures for security review of foreign investments came into force on 18 January 2021.[154] According to the new provision issued by the National Development and Reform Commission and the Ministry of Commerce, foreign investment refers to investments made in the People's Republic of China (PRC) by foreign investors, directly or indirectly, in newly constructed projects or the establishment of enterprises in the PRC, acquisitions of equity rights or assets through merger,

148 Reg (EU) 2019/452, art 4(1).

149 Kyriakos Fountoukakos, Veronica Roberts, and Ruth Allen, 'Addressing National Security Concerns in the Merger Context', in Ioannis Kokkoris and Claudia Lemus (eds), *Research Handbook on the Law and Economics of Competition Enforcement* (Edward Elgar 2022).

150 17th Amendment Ordinance to the AMW (Foreign Trade and Payments Act), available in German at https://www.bmwi.de/Redaktion/DE/Downloads/P-R/referentenentwurf-siebzehnte-verordnung-zur-aenderung-der-aussenwirtschaftsverordnung.pdf?__blob=publicationFile&v=10 accessed 15 September 2023.

151 Roland M Stein and Leonard Von Rummel, 'The Draft Bill of the 17th Amendment Ordinance of the AWV (Foreign Trade and Payments Ordinance)—A First Analysis' *Lexology* (9 February 2021), https://www.lexology.com/library/detail.aspx?g=7a5eff24-834c-4667-9a28-7eaae301c853 accessed 15 September 2023.

152 Harmut Krause, Alexander Wupper, and Udo Herbert Olgemoller, 'Foreign Direct Investment Screening in Germany—Most Recent Developments—What Foreign Investors Need to Consider', Allen and Overy (19 June 2020). It has been reported that these changes responded to rumours that President Donald Trump intended to buy CureVac, a German pharmaceutical company, to ensure Covid-19 vaccine production for the US. See Veronica Roberts, Kyriakos Fountoukakos, Marius Boewe, and Charlie Roberts, 'Covid-19 and Foreign Direct Investment Regulation—Drawbridges Continue to Rise in Response to the Pandemic' *Lexology* (21 May 2020) https://www.lexology.com/library/detail.aspx?g=725393e0-08bf-4c39-8aad-b7932192e78a accessed 15 September 2023.

153 Decree No 2018-1057 dated 29 November 2018, Official Gazette on 1 December 2018.

154 Measures for Security Review of Foreign Investments, English translation available at https://www.bakermckenzie.com/-/media/files/insight/publications/2021/01/foreign_investment_security_review_measures.pdf?la=en accessed 15 September 2023.

acquisitions or other means.[155] The new rules cover the military industry and other important sectors: agricultural products, energy sources, resources, major equipment, infrastructure facilities, transportation services, cultural products and services, technology, and Internet products and services, financial services, and key technologies, and other important sectors.[156] Notably, the list is non-exhaustive so it could be expected that a great number of operations involving a variety of sectors falling within the scope, as indeed categories such as 'cultural products' or 'other important sectors' leave room for ample interpretation and discretion to the authority. Also, it comes as no surprise that this reform tightens the rules for foreign acquisitions since merger control rules in China have focused on targeting foreign companies, an aspect that has not changed despite the introduction of article 2 of the Anti-Monopoly Law (AML), which stretched merger review to 'monopoly conduct in economic activities within People's Republic of China'.[157] As Zheng has reported, although the initiative to screen operations involving Chinese companies appeared more intrusive than most other jurisdictions, there has been no strengthening of the intervention in transactions involving domestic companies and the focus remains on foreign companies rather than domestic ones.[158] Remarkably, in July 2021, for the first time ever a merger between domestic companies was blocked on antitrust grounds, a decision that represents an important precedent and eventually an indication that the Chinese competition authority will assess domestic deals as cautiously as the ones involving foreign acquirers.[159]

Each regime has devised significant sanctions for non-compliance. Significant fines are commonplace to ensure the enforcement of the expanded intervention authority. For example, in the UK, they consist of (a) up to 5 per cent of the worldwide turnover of the business in question or (b) £10 million,[160] and in France, fines amount to the greater of: (i) twice the amount of the noncomplying investment, (ii) 10 per cent of the annual turnover of the company subject to the investment, and (iii) €5 million for companies and €1 million for natural persons.[161] Remarkably, the amendment to the German FDI adopted in June 2020 provides that is a criminal offence to share information before an FDI transaction has been approved and carries an imprisonment sentence of up to five years for breaching this rule.[162] A similar position was also adopted in the UK where

[155] Measures for Security Review of Foreign Investments, art 2.

[156] ibid art 4.

[157] Anti-Monopoly Law of the People's Republic of China (2008), art 2.

[158] Wentong Zheng, 'State Capitalism and the Regulation of Competition in China' in Michael W. Dowdle, John Gillespie, and Imelda Maher (eds), *Asian Capitalism and the Regulation of Competition* (CUP 2013) 144, 160.

[159] Pei Li and Yingzhi Yang, 'Chinese Antitrust Regulator to Block Tencent's Videogaming Merger—Sources' (Reuters, 5 July 2021) https://www.reuters.com/world/china/chinese-antitrust-regulator-block-tencents-videogaming-merger-sources-2021-07-05/ accessed 15 September 2023; Robin Mak, 'Tencent E-sports Defeat Exposes Tech M&A Weakness' (Reuters, 12 July 2021), https://www.reuters.com/breakingviews/tencent-e-sports-defeat-exposes-tech-ma-weakness-2021-07-12/ accessed 15 September 2023.

[160] National Security and Investment Act 2021.

[161] Plan d'Action pour la Croissance et la Transformation des Entreprises, also known as the Loi Pacte (the 'Pacte Law'), French version available at https://www.legifrance.gouv.fr/loda/id/JORFTEXT000038496102/ accessed 15 September 2023.

[162] Harmut Krause, Alexander Wupper, and Udo Herbert Olgemoller, 'Foreign Direct Investment Screening in Germany—Most Recent Developments—What Foreign Investors Need to Consider', Allen and Overy (19 June 2020).

non-compliance can mean imprisonment sentences of up to five years.[163] China's new FDI reform considers that if false information has been provided to obtain approval or if the entities do not observe the conditions imposed for approval, the operation would be voided, which will be accompanied by further penalties according to the relevant national regulations.[164] Interestingly, France has introduced some interim sanctions consisting of the suspension of investor's voting rights, the preclusion or limitation of the distribution of dividends to such investors, the suspension of any disposal of assets, and the appointment of a government representative within the French company.[165]

The above analysis of the approach to national security assessing of FDI that the EU, the US, China, and Japan follow illustrates a further expansion of the sectors likely to raise national security concerns and a general strengthening of the national security assessment regime. While the number of factors that could fall within the screening review is broader, the definition of national security remains narrow. This facilitates the enforcement of the new rules but is detrimental to the principles of transparency, predictability, and certainty that should inform these interventions. Another important aspect is that technology has been recognized as a critical asset and deserves the utmost protection in an increasing number of jurisdictions. Such protection does not relate just to corporate undertakings and assets (including land) but also to higher education institutions, as the last legislative proposals in the US have shown. Lastly, it is important to bear in mind that the expansion of screening powers in assessing transactions implies a higher number of reviews and, along with that, a significant workload increase; in consequence, more resources need to be allocated to avoid bottlenecks in the assessment of transactions, a burden that merging parties should not endure. After exploring some of the most relevant aspects of the rules on assessing transactions on national security grounds among different jurisdictions, the next part discusses some seminal decisions to assess how these rules apply in more detail.

In 2019, the National Development and Reform Commission (NDRC), the authority in charge of carrying out the national security review in case of foreign investment in China, requested the parties of a merger to file a national security review application resulting in the termination of the deal.[166] In April 2019, Yonghui Superstores Co Ltd announced its intention to increase its stake in Zhongbai from 29.86 per cent to up to 40 per cent, with both entities significantly participating in the chain supermarket sector.[167] In August 2019, soon after the competition authority—SAMR approved the operation, the NDRC ordered the parties to file a national security review application due to concerns related to the military sector, and later in December 2019, the parties withdrew the deal as apparently they were unable to address them.[168] Considering

[163] National Security and Investment Act 2021.

[164] Measures for Security Review of Foreign Investments, arts 16, 17, 18, and 19.

[165] The Action Plan for Business Growth and Transformation Act of 23 May 2019 (the Pacte Law).

[166] Xu Ping and Wood Mallesons, 'Public Mergers and Acquisitions in China: Market Analysis Overview' (Thomson Reuters Practical Law, 1 September 2020) https://uk.practicallaw.thomsonreuters.com/w-027-8552 accessed 15 September 2023.

[167] ibid.

[168] ibid.

that NDRC did not publish any details about its assessment of the safety issues that the transaction entailed, it is difficult to elaborate further on its analysis. Nonetheless, merging parties must be aware that the NDRC might request a national security review filing and that obtaining approval from SAMR does not guarantee that the transaction will proceed. Perhaps what is very important but also worrying at the same time, is the lack of information about the reasons that led to infer a national security concern, an omission that certainly erodes the confidence of stakeholders in the national security review regime.

In the US, CFIUS ordered the termination of an American company in a joint venture created in 2019 with Chinese partners. Ekso Bionics Holdings, Inc (Ekso) a manufacturer of robotic mechanical suits, 'exoskeletons',[169] partnered with Zhejiang Youchuang Venture Capital and Shaoxing City Keqiao District Paradise Silicon Intelligent Robot Industrial Investment Partnership to extend the exoskeletons market in China and the Asian markets.[170] According to the terms of the deal, Ekso would license its manufacturing technology in return for a 20 per cent ownership position, and the Chinese partners would contribute about $90 million in cash.[171] The Department of Defence and the Treasury Department made some inquiries about the joint venture, resulting in a voluntary notice to CFIUS in December 2019, although the products involved did not fall within the national security regulations. In May 2020, after imposing some interim measures, CFIUS announced that the security concerns were insurmountable and, as a result, requested the termination of Ekso's role in the joint venture.[172] It has been reported that Ekso's claims that CFIUS did not have jurisdiction to review the transaction considering that it did not involve a foreign investment in a US business, Ekso did not transfer any rights or control, and its role in the joint venture consisted of know-how and a non-exclusive licence to manufacture its technology, were not enough to prevent the termination order from CFIUS.[173]

Some commentators seem to support Ekso's claims by indicating that the application of the US export control laws would have been more appropriate in this case than CFIUS' intervention.[174] It has also been indicated that according to Ekso, the joint venture did not have the power to appoint members of Ekso's board and that according to CFIUS regulation a transaction solely involving the licence of intellectual property to

[169] Exoskeletons can be used to help people with mobility issues and can be used to help soldiers carry heavier weapons while moving quickly. See David Wang, Shaun Wu, Scott Flicker, and Quinn Dang, 'CFIUS Extends its Reach to Order the Termination of Ekso Bionic's Role in Joint Venture in China', Paul Hastings (10 June 2020) https://www.paulhastings.com/insights/client-alerts/cfius-extends-its-reach-to-order-the-termination-of-ekso-bionics-role-in-joint-venture-in-china accessed 15 September 2023.

[170] Press Release, 'Ekso Bionics Announces CFIUS Determination Regarding China Joint Venture' (20 May 2020), https://www.globenewswire.com/news-release/2020/05/20/2036681/0/en/Ekso-Bionics-Announces-CFIUS-Determination-Regarding-China-Joint-Venture.html accessed 15 September 2023.

[171] ibid.

[172] ibid.

[173] David Wang and others, 'CFIUS Extends its Reach to Order the Termination of Ekso Bionic's Role in Joint Venture in China' (Paul Hastings, 10 June 2020).

[174] Paul Marquardt, Chase D Kaniecki, and Nathanael Kurcab, 'CFIUS Blocks Joint Venture Outside the United States, Releases 2018–2019 Data, and Goes Electronic', Cleary Gottlieb (June 3, 2020), https://www.clearytradewatch.com/2020/06/cfius-blocks-joint-venture-outside-the-united-states-releases-2018-2019-data-and-goes-electronic/ accessed 15 September 2023.

a foreign entity is not considered an acquisition of control.[175] This case illustrates that the power to review suspicious transactions is not confined to types of assets, control, market shares or acquisition of US companies, and it could simply rest on the possibility of disclosure of information. This approach reveals that the scope of reviewing the national security implications of foreign investments in the US is wide, covering various types of business models and structures of transactions/FDI, and can be targeted to foreign acquirers from specific jurisdictions. CFIUS' extensive jurisdiction and intense scrutiny could be an effective tool to respond to economic and (geo)political tensions.

In Canada, on 26 October 2017, China Communications Constructions Company International Holding Limited (CCCI) announced its intention to acquire the Canadian construction firm Aecon Group Inc, that participates in the construction of nuclear power stations, military facilities, and communications infrastructure.[176] Under the Investment Canada Act, the security and intelligence agencies and the Department of Public Safety conducted a national security review, in which factors such as the implications of the transaction in terms of Canada's critical infrastructure, the prospective transfer of technology involving military applications, and the risk of foreign surveillance or espionage, are assessed.[177] In May 2018, the Canadian federal government decided to block the deal on the grounds that it would have been instrumental to Canada's national security, according to the advice received from the national security agencies, although the official announcement did not incorporate any specific reasons for the prohibition.[178] In an official statement, the Canadian Minister of Innovation Science and Economic Development, Navdeep Bains, briefly noted that 'Our government is open to international investment that creates jobs and increases prosperity, but not at the expense of national security'.[179] This was the third transaction blocked under the national security regime since the national security provisions came into effect on 12 March 2009,[180] among a very small number of transactions subject to a national security review (the statistics show that between March 2009 and March 2016 from a total of 4,359 notifications and 112 applications, only eight were assessed on national

[175] S §800.302(f)(7) of the CFIUS regulation provides that: '§800.302 Transactions that are not covered control transactions. (f) Examples: (7) Example 7. Same facts as the example in paragraph (f)(6) of this section, except that Corporation X, a U.S. business, has developed important technology in connection with the production of armoured personnel carriers. Corporation A seeks to negotiate an agreement under which it could be licensed to manufacture using that technology. Assuming no other relevant facts, neither the proposed acquisition of technology pursuant to that license agreement, nor other actual acquisition, is a covered control transaction.' See also Paul Marquardt, Chase D Kaniecki, and Nathanael Kurcab, 'CFIUS Blocks Joint Venture Outside the United States, Releases 2018–2019 Data, and Goes Electronic', Cleary Gottlieb (3 June 2020).

[176] Michelle Lally and others, 'Proposed Acquisition of Aecon by CCCI Blocked on National Security Grounds' (Osler, 24 May 2018) https://www.osler.com/en/resources/cross-border/2018/proposed-acquisition-of-aecon-by-ccci-blocked-on-national-security-grounds accessed 15 September 2023.

[177] Government of Canada, 'Annual Report: 2018-2019', Innovation, Science and Economic Development Canada, https://www.ic.gc.ca/eic/site/ica-lic.nsf/eng/h_lk81126.html#Toc528931169 (accessed 6 July 2021).

[178] Lally and others (n 176).

[179] 'Canada Blocks Chinese Takeover of Aecon on National Security Grounds' (Reuters, 23 May 2018) https://www.reuters.com/article/us-aecon-group-m-a-canada-idUSKCN1IO3F2 (accessed 15 September 2023.

[180] Government of Canada, 'Annual Report: 2018-2019', Innovation, Science and Economic Development Canada, See Statistical Information on National Security Review in 2017–2018, https://www.ic.gc.ca/eic/site/ica-lic.nsf/eng/lk81226.html (accessed 3 March 2022); see also 'Annual Report: 2015-2016', https://www.ic.gc.ca/eic/site/ica-lic.nsf/eng/h_lk81199.html#p4 (accessed 3 March 2022).

security grounds; the latest report also shows that between 2016–17 and 2019–20, just 21 orders for review were issued).[181] Yet even if the number of transactions that trigger a national security review in Canada remains low, stakeholders need to be aware that the Canadian government is willing to apply strict controls when necessary and block transactions deemed indispensable. Thus, after reviewing the development and main features of assessing mergers based on national security grounds, the next section focuses on other non-competition related issues that could also inform the analysis of transactions.

8.5 Other Non-Competition Law-Related Issues

The debate about the role of competition law in contributing to the goals of other policy areas has intensified in recent years. The European Commission, for instance, has stated that in fighting climate change and protecting the environment, competition could complement regulation and taxation, having launched a consultation process to that end inquiring how the current antitrust and merger rules could contribute to the European Green Deal most effectively.[182] National governments are also engaged in trying to integrate competition law and sustainability. As an illustration, the Austrian legislator is currently debating a legislative proposal aimed at including environmental considerations into the competition regime by noting that: 'consumers shall also be considered to be allowed a fair share of the resulting benefit if the improvement of the production or distribution of goods or the promotion of technical or economic progress contributes to an ecologically sustainable or climate-neutral economy'.[183] In the UK, the Competition and Markets Authority (CMA), after launching a consultation,[184] has published a guidance for business making environmental claims on goods and services, which sets out some principles seeking to ensure that they are truthful, unambiguous, fair, meaningful and substantiated.[185] Notably, the CMA has stated that around 50 per

[181] Government of Canada, 'Annual Report: 2018-2019', Innovation, Science, and Economic Development Canada, see Statistical Information on National Security Review in 2017–18, https://www.ic.gc.ca/eic/site/ica-lic.nsf/eng/lk81226.html (accessed 3 March 2022); see also 'Annual Report: 2015-2016', https://www.ic.gc.ca/eic/site/ica-lic.nsf/eng/h_lk81199.html#p4 (accessed 3 March 2022); 'Annual Report 2019-2020', https://www.ic.gc.ca/eic/site/ica-lic.nsf/eng/lk81227.html#Toc528931169 (accessed 3 March 2022).

[182] European Commission, 'Competition Policy contributing to the European Green Deal', https://competition-policy.ec.europa.eu/about/green-gazette/conference-2021_en accessed 15 September 2023. During the launch of the European Green Deal in December 2019, Margrethe Vestager, Executive Vice-President of the European Commission, stressed that '[a]ll EU actions and policies will have to contribute to the European Green Deal objective' adding that 'every one of us—including competition enforcers—will be called on to make our contribution to that change'. See Margrethe Vestager, 'Competition and Sustainability' (GCLC Conference on Sustainability and Competition Policy, Brussels, 24 October 2019) https://wayback.archive-it.org/12090/20191129200524/https://ec.europa.eu/commission/commissioners/2014-2019/vestager/announcements/competition-and-sustainability_en accessed 15 September 2023.

[183] §2 Cartel and Competition Law Amendment Act 2021 (the Austrian equivalent to art 101 para 3 TFEU). See Victoria HSE Robertson, 'The Austrian Competition Law Amendment 2021: A Preview', D'Kart (28 April 2021), https://www.d-kart.de/en/blog/2021/04/28/the-austrian-competition-law-amendment-2021-a-preview/ accessed 15 September 2023.

[184] CMA, 'CMA Guidance on Environmental Claims on Goods and Services' (CMA 146, 20 September 2021), https://assets.publishing.service.gov.uk/government/uploads/system/uploads/attachment_data/file/1018820/Guidance_for_businesses_on_making_environmental_claims_.pdf accessed 15 September 2023.

[185] ibid.

cent of consumers in the UK make their purchases based on environmental considerations, and that over 40 per cent of the claims made online regarding environmental benefits of products and services seemed to be misleading, which appears to be a business strategy to attract such an important pool of consumers.[186] Similarly, the CMA has indicated that as the UK has committed to become carbon neutral by 2050, the role of competition law and consumer protection law is crucial to achieve this target.[187] Likewise, some other jurisdictions have produced draft guidelines and working papers exploring the interplay between competition law and sustainability, whereby the Hellenic Competition Authority has clearly indicated that competition law can address sustainability issues when assessing mergers and acquisitions.[188]

In the same vein, academics have been calling attention to the environmental crisis that we are facing on a global level and how competition law could be a key tool to respond to this issue.[189] International organizations have also started to debate this topic. In December 2020, the OECD, for the first time, hosted a roundtable where the intersection between competition law and sustainability goals was explored,[190] and the ICN is leading a project on 'sustainable development and competition policy', which emerged as a relevant topic for competition agencies and other stakeholders.[191]

The debate centres around two specific issues. Firstly, the scope of sustainability involves environmental, economic, and societal dimensions from which a wide range of goals and objectives can derive, such as biodiversity, clean energy, gender equality, poverty reduction, zero pollution, clean and secure energy, and sustainable cities and communities, among others.[192] This scope could be seen as an advantage given that it provides some flexibility by allowing the incorporation of a diverse set of factors that could be seen as part of a framework of assessing sustainability within the competition law framework but at the same time, it could turn out to be an unclear concept

[186] ibid 5.

[187] ibid 2–3.

[188] See *Autoriteit Consument* and Markt (ACM) (2021), Guidelines on Sustainability Agreements—Opportunities within Competition Law (second draft), https://www.acm.nl/sites/default/files/documents/second-draft-version-guidelines-on-sustainability-agreements-oppurtunities-within-competition-law.pdf accessed 15 September 2023. Hellenic Competition Commission (HCC) (2020), Competition Law and Sustainability, https://www.epant.gr/en/enimerosi/competition-law-sustainability.html accessed 15 September 2023.

[189] Simon Holmes, 'Climate Change, Sustainability, and Competition Law' (2020) 8(2) Journal of Antitrust Enforcement 354; Cristina Volpin, 'Competition Enforcement and Sustainability: The Odd Couple', in Ioannis Kokkoris and Claudia Lemus (eds), *Research Handbook on the Law and Economics of Competition Enforcement* (Edward Elgar 2022) 448; Suzanne Kingston, *Greening EU Competition Law and Policy* (CUP 2012); Julian Nowag, 'Competition Law's Sustainability Gap? Tools for an Examination and a Brief Overview', Lund University Legal Research Paper Series, October 2019; Julian Nowag, *Environmental Integration in Competition and Free-Movement Laws* (OUP, 2016); Klaudia Majcher and Viktoria HSE Robertson, 'The Twin Transition to a Digital and Green Economy: Doctrinal Challenges for EU Competition Law', https://ssrn.com/abstract=3778107 accessed 15 September 2023; Giorgio Monti, 'Four Options for a Greener Competition Law', 11 Journal of European Competition Law and Practice, 124 (2020).

[190] OECD, 'Sustainability and Competition', https://www.oecd.org/daf/competition/sustainability-and-competition.htm accessed 15 September 2023.

[191] Hungarian Competition Authority (Gazdasági Versenyhivatalt, GVH), 'Sustainable Development and Competition Law—Survey Report' (2021) Special Project for the 2021 ICN Annual Conference https://www.gvh.hu/pfile/file?path=/en/gvh/Conference/icn-2021-annual-conference/sustainability_survey_REPORT_3rdEd_2021_09_30_final_PUBLIC.pdf1&inline=true accessed 15 September 2023.

[192] European Commission, 'European Green Deal', COM (2019) 640 final; Council Decision (EU) 2016/1841 of 5 October 2016 on the conclusion, on behalf of the EU, of the Paris Agreement adopted under the United Nations Framework Convention on Climate Change [2016] OJL282/1.

difficult to contain, measure, and apply.[193] Secondly, a fundamental issue that attracts significant attention is whether competition law should incorporate or protect these non-economic sustainable concerns or, in other words, to what extent the scope of competition law leaves room for the analysis of issues which fall beyond the traditional analysis of the effects on prices, quality, diversity, and innovation, often been used to measure the consumer welfare impact.[194] In this regard scholarship is divided into those who consider that antitrust law, particularly merger control laws, should focus more on promoting welfare through competition and less on attaining other goals through competition enforcement. Thomas refers to a hypothetical scenario where a merger in which the preferences of the consumers point to a product or service that is detrimental to a societal goal, like the environment. He argues that it would be unreasonable to approve transactions just because they involve environmentally friendly products, even if consumers have not embraced them due to other interests or priorities. Put differently, it would be difficult to defend a decision to block a merger just because it involves a product that does not safeguard the environment but is wanted by customers.[195] In such a scenario, he adds that neither the firms nor the consumer welfare should be used to replace or to correct the consumer's choices even if they seem to be inadequate.[196] His argument goes that it is difficult to strike a balance between competition law and societal goals, given the vagueness of the latter, which turns the quantification of harm or benefits into a complex exercise that can potentially compromise the transparency of the antitrust reasoning and therefore its legality.[197]

At the other end of the spectrum, some advocates propose a new system of competition law that focuses not just on the use of competition law to protect non-economic goals like the environment but also to correct conduct that damages it.[198] According to this view, competition law and non-economic goals rather than being mutually exclusive can serve to complement each other.[199] To exemplify how these two areas can coexist and be complementary at the same time, commentators in the field of merger control have referred to the *Aurubis/Metallo* acquisition in which the European Commission opened an in-depth investigation, that included the analysis

[193] Michael Jacobs, 'Sustainable Development as a Contested Concept' in Andrew Dobson (ed), *Fairness and Futurity: Essays on Environmental Sustainability and Social Justice* (OUP, 1999).

[194] Giancarlo Piscitelli and Anna Gerbrandy, 'The Sustainability Dilemma in Competition Law' (2018) 8 ECDPM Great Insights Magazine https://ecdpm.org/great-insights/civil-society-business-same-direction/sustainability-dilemma-competition-law/ accessed 15 September 2023; Anne C Witt, *The More Economic Approach to EU Antitrust Law* (Hart 2016); Pinar Akman, '"Consumer Welfare" and Article 82 EC: Practice and Rhetoric' (2009) 32 World Competition 71.

[195] Thomas (n 49). The literature refers to this phenomenon as the eco-paradox, which refers to the situation in which consumers are aware of the importance of protecting the environment from potential harm, but do not always choose the best alternative. See Stanislas Martin and Umberto Berkani, 'Competition Law and Sustainable Development: Opportunities with Constant Law', in Gürkaynak G, 'Sustainable Development: What Role for Competition Policy?' (Concurrences, 3 November 2020) https://www.gurkaynak.av.tr/docs/de6e1-article-99291.pdf accessed 15 September 2023.

[196] Thomas (n 49).

[197] ibid.

[198] Tomaso Ferrando and Claudio Lombardi, 'EU Competition Law and Sustainability in Food Systems: Addressing the Broken Links' (Fair Trade Advocacy Office, February 2019) 35, https://drive.google.com/file/d/1KXn3LMm9SuFmrPyD0U_wkOH5UZrf4uVa/view accessed 15 September 2023.

[199] Piscitelli and Gerbrandy (n 194); Ariel Ezrachi, 'Sponge', 5 Journal of Antitrust Enforcement 49 (2017).

of the implications of the merger in the copper scrap market, where the merger parties were involved, not just in terms of the price effects but also in relation to the environmental impact of the transaction by looking at the incentives to invest and innovate in the treatment and recovery of scrap copper.[200]

Another case that has been used to support the argument is the 'Kip van Morge' ('Chicken of Tomorrow'), where the Dutch authority was able to establish the anti-competitiveness of an agreement by quantifying its impact in terms of price increase and thus the harm to consumer welfare and quantifying the benefit of the agreement to the environment and animal welfare. The Dutch authority showed that it was possible to monetize a non-economic factor and to align environmental goals with competition law.[201] The European Commission has also integrated the environmental benefits of some agreements against a price increase, finding that '[t]he use of cleaner facilities will result in less air pollution, and consequently in direct and indirect benefits for consumers from reduced negative externalities'.[202] It has also been found that the reduction in polluting emissions was 'more than seven times greater than the increased purchase costs of more-energy efficient washing machines'.[203] These findings reveal that competition authorities can assess the trade-off between potential prices effects vis-a-vis transactions that contribute to sustainability objectives.

Nonetheless, it is important to bear in mind that even if the consumer welfare standard appears to be flexible enough to incorporate sustainable aims, more precisely environmental ones, a limitless expansion of its scope entails some risks.[204] Among them, the possibility that competition authorities could be overwhelmed by having to analyse large amounts of evidence, the increased chances of types I and II antitrust errors, the excessive room for discretion and the difficulty in attaining convergence among competition authorities, particularly, in relation to cross-border transactions.[205] In addition, stakeholders lacking enough guidance about how antitrust authorities will measure the claimed benefits of sustainable initiatives through mergers or agreements (eg, in terms of scope—areas, population, impact—and short-term vs long-term results, etc), might refrain from materializing them if there are fears that this will result in an antitrust violation. For this reason, efforts to provide more clarity, such as the draft guidelines designed by the Dutch agency[206] are welcome, as they assist undertakings to

[200] *Aurubis/Metallo Group Holding* (Case M.9409) Commission Decision C(2020) 2752 final [2019], https://ec.europa.eu/competition/mergers/cases/decisions/m9409_3908_3.pdf accessed 15 September 2023.

[201] Piscitelli and Gerbrandy (n 194).

[202] European Commission, Decision of 12 December 1994, *Philips/Osram*, IV/34.252, para 27 http://data.europa.eu/eli/dec/1994/986/oj accessed 15 September 2023.

[203] European Commission, Decision of 24 January 1999, *CECED*, IV.F.1/36.718, para 56 http://data.europa.eu/eli/dec/2000/475/oj accessed 15 September 2023.

[204] Kokkoris and Skourtis (n 57).

[205] Lucas Peeperkorn, 'Competition and Sustainability: What Can Competition Policy Do?' [2020] (4) Concurrences 40; Lucas Peeperkorn, 'European Union', in Simon Holmes, Dirk Middelschulte, and Martijn Snoep (eds), *Competition Law, Climate Change & Environmental Sustainability* (Concurrences 2021) 413; Maarten-Pieter Schinkel and Leonard Treuren, 'Green Antitrust: Friendly Fire in the Fight Against Climate Change' in Simon Holmes, Dirk Middelschulte, and Martijn Snoep (eds), *Competition Law, Climate Change and Environmental Sustainability* (Concurrences 2021) .

[206] *Autoriteit Consument* and Markt (ACM) (2021), *Guidelines on Sustainability Agreements - Opportunities within Competition Law (second draft)*, para 40–41, https://www.acm.nl/sites/default/files/documents/sec

delineate their sustainable projects according to what the authority expects from them with regard to the nature of the initiatives, what they are supposed to achieve, in which timeframe, and whether it would be likely that the initiative might deliver the alleged benefits.[207]

Likewise, as Monti has shown, some ways can be explored to reunite the tension between economic and non-economic goals, such as investing more effort and resources in advancing a cost-benefit analysis in environmental economics, revisiting existing guidelines aimed at incorporating sustainability considerations, and developing theories of harm through decision-making, which would be more compelling once the courts have the opportunity to review them.[208] In short, given the current pressing environmental difficulties experienced at a global scale, it is vital to try to address them through multiple means with competition law being one of them, so an attempt to oppose its application altogether, given the aforementioned challenges, may not seem to be a viable option any longer. The initiatives of the Dutch competition authority and the European Commission have illustrated that environmental considerations can be part of antitrust assessment and can be covered by the consumer welfare standard. Hence, with more clarity and certainty, it is likely that the reconciliation process between competition and sustainability goals can be reinforced.

Nowadays, scholarship is also devoting more time to inquiring whether wealth and income inequality should be a competition law concern.[209] For instance, some scholars have been studying how the mergers in the US health sector have enlarged the gap between socio-economic groups to the detriment of the vulnerable ones. Thus, the study carried out by Stavroulaki has revealed that disadvantaged groups, more prone to suffer from obesity and alcohol addiction, as well as minorities, more likely to suffer from cancer, diabetes or Covid, face higher barriers to access better health protection.[210] According to her, this calamity has been provoked by the approval of vertical mergers between insurers and drug suppliers, in which data plays a significant role, by allowing discrimination against those identified as unprofitable customers who then need to pay higher prices for their higher risks.[211] Indeed, the health care system in the US is so deficient, that President Joe Biden in his most recent executive order on promoting competition in the American economy has encouraged the DOJ and the FTC to review their merger guidelines. According to the White House report, the ten largest

ond-draft-version-guidelines-on-sustainability-agreements-oppurtunities-within-competition-law.pdf accessed 15 September 2023.

[207] ibid.

[208] Giorgio Monti, 'Four Options for a Greener Competition Law' (2020) 11(3–4) Journal of European Competition Law and Practice 124 .

[209] Carl Shapiro, 'Antitrust in a Time of Populism' (2018) 61 International Journal of Industrial Organization 714; Joseph Stiglitz, *The Price of Inequality: How Today's Divided Society Endangers Our Future* (WW Norton 2012).

[210] Theodosia Stavroulaki, 'Mergers That Harm Our Health' (2022) 19(1) Berkeley Business Law Journal 89, 7–8.

[211] ibid 10. Khan and Vaheesan have examined the rising concentration levels in the health care system in the US, indicating that a lenient antitrust approach has created market failures, has been inadequate to preserve a competitive market, and has eventually led to high inequality. See Lina M Khan and Sandeep Vaheesan, 'Market Power and Inequality: The Antitrust Counterrevolution and Its Discontents' (2017) 11 Harvard Law and Policy Review 235, 268.

healthcare systems now control a quarter of the market, and during the last two decades, over 150 rural hospitals have been closed due to unchallenged mergers, resulting in higher prices for patients deprived of convenient and affordable healthcare plans.[212]

In Europe, a similar concern was raised by seventeen scholars who warned the European Commission about the harm that the Google/Fitbit operation would represent in terms of discrimination and exploitation of consumers in the healthcare and health insurance sectors.[213] They were alarmed by the enormous combination of health data between the merging parties leading to additional market power in these markets and the subsequent ability to increase prices, decrease quality, build a more comprehensive patient profile, and based on this choose to selectively cover good risks and unravel bad ones.[214] Despite this warning, the European Commission approved the deal subject to some conditions, giving rise to a great deal of criticism.[215] In this context, it seems that transactions taking place in the health sector need thorough scrutiny, as vulnerable or unprofitable patients require additional protection. *Ex ante* merger control could prevent widespread inequalities. Future research assessing the effectiveness of the imposed measures in the Google/Fitbit merger will shed light on whether the alleged concerns were well grounded and whether the imposed conditions effectively addressed them.

An important aspect that needs highlighting is that while the body of literature assumes that there is an interrelation between effective competition and inequality, the number of studies exploring the validity of such an assumption remains limited.[216] The current research focuses on specific sectors, such as the one conducted by Stavroulaki on the health sector mentioned earlier, which limits the possibility of deriving more general implications. Another research that is noteworthy is the one conducted by Zac, which uses the US as a case study, focusing on two main aspects: market power and effects on prices in essential product markets and monopsony effect in labour markets.[217]

[212] White House, 'Executive Order on Promoting Competition in the American Economy' (Fact Sheet, 9 July 2021) https://www.whitehouse.gov/briefing-room/statements-releases/2021/07/09/fact-sheet-executive-order-on-promoting-competition-in-the-american-economy/ accessed 15 September 2023. The executive order indicates that increased concentration and decreased competition has widened 'racial, income, and wealth inequality'.

[213] Marc Bourreau and others, 'Google/Fitbit Will Monetise Health Data and Harm Consumers' (September 2020) Centre for Economic Policy Research Policy Insight 107 https://cepr.org/publications/policy-insight-107-googlefitbit-will-monetise-health-data-and-harm-consumers accessed 15 September 2023.

[214] ibid; see also Zhijun Chen and others, 'Data-Driven Mergers and Personalization' (2020) ISER Discussion Paper No 1108 https://ssrn.com/abstract=3725312 accessed 15 September 2023.

[215] See European Commission, 'Mergers: Commission Clear Acquisition of Fitbit by Google, Subject to Conditions' IP/20/2484 (17 December 2020) https://ec.europa.eu/commission/presscorner/detail/en/ip_20_2484 accessed 15 September 2023.

[216] Amit Zac and others, 'Competition Law and Income Inequality: A Panel Data Econometric Approach' (2021) CCLP Discussion Paper (21 May 2021) 2 https://ssrn.com/abstract=3402436 accessed 15 September 2023; Amit Zac, 'Competition Law and Economic Inequality: A Comparative Analysis of Text Similarity Using General Synthetic Control Method' (2020) Working Paper CCLP(L) 53 https://ssrn.com/abstract=3703633 accessed 15 September 2023.

[217] In relation to labour markets, see Jose Azar and others whose study suggests that in concentrated markets, the labour market power seems to increase. See Azar J and others, 'Concentration in US Labor Markets: Evidence from Online Vacancy Data' (2020) 66 Labour Economics 101886. The following studies show a decline in real increases in wages: Lawrence Mishel and Ross Eisenbrey, 'How to Raise Wages: Policies That Work and Policies That Don't' (2015) 45(1) Stetson Law Review 43, 45; James Uguccioni, Andrew Sharpe, and Alexander Murray 'Labour Productivity and the Distribution of Real Earnings in Canada, 1976–2014' (2016) Centre for the Study of Living Standards.

His finding is that the wording of the US antitrust laws has led to economic inequality, and building on this, he asserts that countries with similar competition law text might eventually show similar levels of high inequality.[218] Similarly, another study has shown a correlation between competition law indicators and income and wage inequality metrics, recognizing that further research would be advisable.[219] In this context, there is suitable evidence about the effects of lax merger control in the health sector in the US and the subsequent high levels of inequality, joined by a good number of suggestions that link competition law frameworks and inequality, and some studies signalling that in concentrated markets, there is a tendency to observe a wage decline. This bulk of research should be used to build on more theoretical and empirical evidence, to encourage the review of past transactions aimed at extracting practical lessons to inform the assessment of future transactions and to enrich the debate on the role of competition law in fostering greater equality.

8.6 Conclusion

Protectionism is not new. Time after time, governments have felt compelled to intervene in the markets, especially in times of crisis, war, or pandemics. Even if there have been periods in which governments have tried to retreat from intervening and allow the markets to function freely, as during the 1990s, it is almost inevitable that they find a reason to embrace policies oriented to protect their domestic economies. In this chapter, we have sought to better understand how merger control has been used as a protectionist measure. We have seen how some geopolitical tensions and the Covid-19 pandemic have prompted governments to try to align business interests with national strategic ones. We have also seen how governments have been adopting or reinforcing rules to control foreign investment in a synchronized fashion. These rules are often broad in scope, enforced by governmental bodies equipped with heavy powers, sometimes developed through unclear procedures, resulting in largely discretionary decisions. Lastly, despite being effective in deterring investments from foreign countries, we have seen how these rules failed to offer the required levels of transparency, predictability, and certainty that should inform these types of interventions.

This protectionism resurgence has permeated other spheres, and merger control is expected to be responsive to them. It is supposed to protect jobs, improve labour standards, deliver fair wages for ordinary people, be involved with climate change issues, and reduce inequality. Although it would be unreasonable to avoid these demands, it seems unlikely that merger control can solve all of them. This chapter has shown that more research efforts and discussions among policy- and decision-makers are required to reconcile the tensions between competition and non-competition goals. The chapter has also discussed the risks of using merger rules to accomplish a wider number of goals.

[218] Zac (n 216) 21–22.
[219] Zac and others (n 216) 30.

Among them are growing worries that politicians, who are more prone to regulatory capture, will be involved with the merger review process, risking the independence of the competition authorities and making merger enforcement less credible, less predictable, and less easy to administer.

9
Concluding Remarks

9.1 The Growing Tension Between Competition and Non-Competition Interests in Merger Control

Protectionism is not new in trade and investment. Governments have felt compelled to intervene in the economy, especially, in times of crisis, war or pandemics. Even if there have been periods in which governments have tried to retreat from intervening and allow the markets to function freely, as during the 1990s, it is almost inevitable that they find a reason to embrace policies oriented to protect their domestic economies. In this book, we have sought to understand better how national security considerations apply to merger control and mergers and acquisitions (M&A) and foreign direct investment (FDI) more broadly. We have seen how some geopolitical tensions and the Covid-19 pandemic have prompted governments to try to align business interests with national strategic ones and industrial policy. We have also seen how governments have been adopting or reinforcing rules to control foreign investment in a synchronized manner. These rules are often broad in scope, enforced by governmental bodies equipped with extensive powers, and sometimes developed through unclear procedures, resulting in largely discretionary decisions. Lastly, despite being effective in deterring investments from foreign entities/countries, we have seen how these rules, failed to offer the required levels of transparency, predictability, and certainty that should inform these types of interventions.

This book has shown that a constructive dialogue between policymakers and companies involved in FDI is required to reconcile the recurring issues in some jurisdictions or the teething ones in others The book has also discussed the risks of using national security to accomplish a wider number of goals, especially when done in a non-transparent manner. Among them are growing worries that politicians, who are more prone to regulatory capture, will be involved with the national security (and, in some countries, the merger control assessment) process, risking the independence of the relevant agencies and, at times, unjustifiably making enforcement less credible, less predictable, and less easy to administer.

9.2 Some Concluding Thoughts on the EU Regime

The analysis has revealed that the views around the implications of the European Union (EU) FDI scheme are divided and that it is still too early to predict the trajectory.

Nonetheless, it appears important that both the Commission and the Member States carefully deal with FDI under the national security prism, as they will either facilitate or obstruct FDI inflow and outflow, considering that reciprocity plays a key role in this type of negotiation. Equally, the Member States must apply the FDI rules in accordance with the EU principles and laws; otherwise, the predominance of nationalism and protectionism goals could undermine the trust of the proceedings, provoking undesirable consequences at a national and international level and outing the Single Market imperative at risk. Indeed, the extent to which Member States can obstruct FDI transactions without infringing the EU law is still unclear. In addition, Member States should be willing to cooperate, adopt rigorous standards of review, and try to reach similar approaches, as this is the best way to make this FDI framework enforceable. As for the investment community, they need to thoroughly analyse their FDI plans, examining not just the sector and the activities that the investment relates to but also the Member States in which the transaction might have an impact. Also, with time, the EU and the Member States will identify specific procedural challenges of the Regulation and address them and, therefore, improve the underlying infrastructure of the cooperation mechanism.

9.3 Some Concluding Thoughts on the UK Regime

The NSIA is expected to present new challenges for investors willing to focus on the United Kingdom (UK) economy. Careful consideration and a proactive approach would be essential to mitigate the concerns associated with the new regime.

Overall, the regime is broadly in line with many of those administered by countries around the world (the United States (US), EU, China, Russia, South Africa, India, and Japan, but also Canada, Australia, France, and Italy), so international investors are expected to be familiar with the rationale, the notification requirement, and the assessment process of such regimes.

While the Investment Security Unit (ISU) is actively consulting with practitioners and companies in respect of the notification requirements, further guidelines are expected to be developed soon, shedding some light on the operation of the new review system. In the coming months, we should expect secondary implementing legislation to be passed, providing important details of the new regime. At the time of writing, several key regulations have already been published, including:

- guidance on the intended use of the call-in power;[1]
- regulations settling the definitions of the seventeen core sectors;[2]

[1] UK Department for Business, Energy, and Industrial Strategy (BEIS), 'National Security and Investment Act 2021: Draft statement for the purposes of s 3' July 2021; the statement setting out how the Secretary of State expects to exercise the power to give a call-in notice.

[2] Draft Regulations laid before Parliament under s 63(5) of the National Security and Investment Act 2021 for approval by resolution of each House of Parliament: 'The National Security and Investment Act 2021 (Notifiable Acquisition) (Specification of Qualifying Entities) Regulations 2021'.

- guidance on how the NSI Act could affect people or acquisition outside the UK;[3]
- guidance on how the new Act will work alongside other regulators and codes, including the Enterprise Act 2002, the CMA, and the Takeover Code;[4]
- guidance on how to prepare for the new rules;[5]

while others are due to be published soon prior to the Act's commencement day:

- regulations determining the precise manner of mandatory and voluntary notification;
- regulations specifying the form and content of information required to be submitted under the mandatory and voluntary notifications.

Finally, it remains to be seen how the UK government will find in practice the fine balance between enabling sufficient control over FDI raising national security concerns and avoiding deterring investment when reviewing transactions.

9.4 Some Concluding Thoughts on the US Regime

The first part of the US chapter focused on national security concerns, showing a spectrum of CFIUS's decisions in diverse industries, including telecommunications, food, finance, defence, and technology. Among the cases, the US government has shown its determination to safeguard US industries from risks to US national security raised by acquisitions of US domestic assets by foreign acquirers.

In the assessment of the CFIUS regime, the chapter discussed how the scope of this agency has expanded to the point where almost any foreign person or entity is now potentially within its regulatory reach. In spite of its increased powers, the transparency of the process appears to remain restricted, a shortfall that has been subject to criticism among the parties and scholars. Some M&A transactions have been blocked, while the parties have withdrawn others after clear signs of opposition and long waiting assessment periods. The chapter has shown that even if the number of transactions that have been blocked remains relatively low, the assessment process would be improved if the parties and the public were provided with a more detailed perspective of the CFIUS rationale for its decisions.

[3] BEIS, 'How the National Security and Investment Act Could Affect People or Acquisitions Outside the UK' (updated 4 January 2022) https://www.gov.uk/government/publications/check-if-an-acquisition-outside-the-uk-will-be-in-scope-of-the-national-security-and-investment-act/check-if-an-acquisition-of-an-entity-or-asset-outside-the-uk-that-you-are-involved-in-could-be-assessed-by-the-government-for-national-security-risks 20 July 2021.

[4] BEIS Guidance 'The National Security and Investment Act alongside regulatory requirements' published on 20 July 2021.

[5] BEIS, Guidance 'National Security and Investment Act: Prepare for new rules about acquisitions which could harm the UK's national security', Published 20 July 2021. Also, see Guidance: 'National Security and Investment Act: Guidance for the higher education and research-intensive sectors'.

In FDI initiatives that raise national security concerns, the parties must be able to predict the outcomes of the authorities' assessment and proactively decide whether they wish to proceed and with what expected mitigation measures. To conclude, more transparency, accountability, and efficiency in the merger review process across all regulated sectors in the US would be advisable and welcome.

9.5 Some Concluding Thoughts on the Chinese Regime

The chapter discussed the role of national security interests within China's FDI screening regime. It highlighted the specificities of the Chinese framework and showed that the line between industrial policy and national security appears blurred in the Chinese context, which has implications both for the substantive and procedural aspects of the national security review. China is not an exception to this blurred line concerning the balance between industrial and national security strategies, as this book has clearly illustrated.

As we analysed in this book, today, there is no clear boundary between industrial policy and national security and FDI policy. Perhaps it is not always clear whether a specific industry or sector falls under the scope of the national security review. What is clear, however, is that we should expect more national security reviews by the Chinese authorities in the future.

9.6 Some Concluding Thoughts on the Regimes in Japan, India, Russia, and South Africa

This chapter has portrayed to what extent some nations have embraced adopting FDI rules as a tactic to defend their sovereignty. Just as the gradual use of economic sanctions has become an economic weapon, imposing restrictions on entry grounded on national security concerns is part of the arsenal.[6] The Russian government has been reluctant to relinquish a commanding role in the economy. The adoption of unrestricted FDI rules has been crucial to protect not just its commanding position in the strategic natural resources industry, Russia's main source of hard currency, but also a vast array of sectors. The economic sanctions imposed on Russia after its invasion of Ukraine have elicited the adoption of stricter FDI rules targeting those countries that have deployed them.

Like Russia, India has also developed new national security rules for FDI screening to target specific land border countries. In its efforts to encourage foreign investments, the Indian government has created a screening mechanism. Under the new screening mechanism, the government enjoys full discretion to decide on national security issues in relation to FDI; it applies at times unclear national security or national interest

[6] Nicholas Mulder, *The Economic Weapon* (Yale University Press 2022).

considerations, applicants are not involved in the review process, and, if a proposal is rejected, the Indian government will not inform of the reasons for rejection.

Japan has also established a screening regime and recently adopted FDI measures to counteract the Covid-19 blow. It lowered the threshold for pre-transaction approval from 10 per cent to 1 per cent, designated business sectors as core (eg, weapons) or non-core (eg, electricity) according to the degree they affect national security and exempted some from mandatory notification. Although the business community welcomes such an exemption , some concerns persist. Investors need to keep in mind strict filing times and be ready to accept a wide array of recommendations to address national security, public order, public safety, or smooth management of the Japanese economy issues raised by their proposals or abandon them. The meaning of these issues is uncertain, as is the whole review process. More worryingly, adopting unclear national security concerns without proper oversight can reinforce Japan's resistance towards foreign investors for decades.

The strengthening of FDI rules has echoed across South Africa, too. This is at odds with South Africa's efforts for decades to attract investors. Contrary to what we have seen in Russia, India, and Japan, whose interventions in foreign takeovers have been crafted to protect their national security, in South Africa, traditionally, high levels of crime have deterred foreign investors. Now that the pandemic seems to have receded, South Africa faces a precarious economic situation with pressing social problems increasing. Therefore, it is no surprise that the South African government has not yet implemented the reform sought to intervene in foreign takeovers on national security grounds since 2018. The real question for the government is not whether they can control inward FDI but at what price for the economy and the country. A further question is how to reconcile two policies that clash: on the one hand, the protection of the legal rights of foreign investors and, on the other, the broader social priorities of the South African economy. A particularly complex relationship indeed.

9.7 A Final Critical Thought!

This book has provided an extensive critical account of the national security considerations that major countries consider in FDI assessment, particularly in M&A transactions. As this book has stated, the line between intrusive policies and independent review of foreign M&As and FDI is now blurring. A number of additional restrictions were imposed during the pandemic to keep domestic firms safe. While the pandemic has retreated, governments have proven reluctant to surrender all the powers conferred by these FDI rules. Governments and enforcement agencies have become accustomed to using restrictions on FDI based on national security concerns as an effective way to deal with geostrategic concerns and as an indirect means to promote unclear and non-transparent, in some cases, industrial strategy. However, it is also likely that they come to learn that they have interfered with free trade at their peril. This protectionism resurgence has also permeated other spheres, the most important being merger control enforcement. Even though the book does not engage with merger control in depth, FDI through M&A activity frequently raises concerns about merger control. There have been increasing calls for merger control to protect jobs, improve labour standards, deliver fair wages for ordinary people, to be involved with climate change issues, and reduce inequality. Although it would be unreasonable to avert these demands, it seems unlikely that merger control can solve all of them.

Concerns have also been raised in relation to the interplay between FDI screening mechanisms and international investment agreements. Generally, screening mechanisms avoid explicit discrimination based on investor origin, but enforcement of such mechanisms can be at odds with the provisions of international investment agreements and can lead to litigation.[7]

One major concern of mine relates is that applying unrestricted rules could undermine the logic behind legitimate intervention. Damaging the business community's credibility is a high price in a world where trade and investment create mutual benefit.

The real test lies ahead! And it will be an exciting one!

[7] Philip McCalman et al, 'Screening of Chinese Investments Intensifies' (International Institute for Sustainable Development – Investment Treaty News, 26 December 2022) https://www.iisd.org/itn/en/2022/12/26/screening-of-chinese-investments-intensifies1-phillip-mccalman-laura-puzzello-tania-voon-andrew-walter/ accessed 15 September 2023.

Bibliography

Books

Andenas M and Wooldridge F, *European Comparative Company Law* (CUP 2009)
Barnard C, *The Substantive Law of the EU: The Four Freedoms* (OUP 2016)
Bhorat A and others (eds), *The Oxford Companion to the Economics of South Africa* (OUP 2014)
Bosco D and Gal MS (eds), *Challenges to Assumptions in Competition Law* (Edward Elgar 2021)
Clarke HD, Goodwin M, and Whiteley P, *Brexit: Why Britain Voted to Leave the European Union* (CUP 2017)
Coates K, *Competition Law and Regulation of Technology Markets* (OUP 2011)
Collins WD (ed), *Issues in Competition Law and Policy* (ABA Section of Antitrust Law 2008)
Dabbah EM, *International and Comparative Competition Law* (CUP 2010)
De Luca N, *European Company Law* (CUP 2017)
Dobson A (ed), *Fairness and Futurity: Essays on Environmental Sustainability and Social Justice* (OUP 1999)
Doern B and Wilks S, *Comparative Competition Policy* (OUP 1996)
Dowdle MW, Gillespie J, and Maher I (eds), *Asian Capitalism and the Regulation of Competition* (CUP 2013)
Drexl J, Kerber W, and Podszun R (eds), *Competition Policy and the Economic Approach* (Edward Elgar 2011)
Drexl J and others (eds), *Competition Policy and Regional Integration in Developing Countries* (Edward Elgar 2012)
Emch A and Ng W (eds), *Wang Xiaoye: The Pioneer of Competition Law in China – Liber Amicorum* (Concurrences 2019)
Epstein RA and Greve MS (eds), *Competition Laws in Conflict: Antitrust Jurisdiction in the Global Economy* (American Enterprise Institute Press 2004)
Estrin S and Meyer KE (eds), *Investment Strategies in Emerging Markets* (Edward Elgar 2004)
Erzrachi A, *EU Competition Law: An Analytical Guide to the Leading Cases* (3rd edn, Hart 2012)
Ezrachi A, *Research Handbook on International Competition Law* (Edward Elgar 2012)
Falck O, Gollier C, and Woessmann L (eds), *Industrial Policy for National Champions* (MIT Press 2011)
Feintuck M, *The 'Public Interest' in Regulation* (OUP 2004)
Fox EM and Trebilcock MJ (eds), *The Design of Competition Law Institutions: Global Norms, Local Choices* (OUP 2012)
Gerber DJ, *Law and Competition in Twentieth-Century Europe: Protecting Prometheus* (OUP 2001)
Gerber DJ, *Global Competition: Law, Markets, and Globalization* (OUP 2010)
Herring EP, *Public Administration and the Public Interest* (McGraw-Hill 1936)
Holmes S, Middelschulte D, and Snoep M (eds), *Competition Law, Climate Change & Environmental Sustainability* (Concurrences 2021)
International Bar Association, *EC Merger Control: Ten Years On – Papers from the EC Merger Control 10th Anniversary Conference held in Brüssels in September 2000 under the auspices of the European Commission Directorate General for Competition and the International Bar Association* (International Bar Association 2000)
Jones G, *Multinational Companies and Global Capitalism* (OUP 2005)
Kidron M, *Foreign Investment in India* (OUP 1965)
Kingston S, *Greening EU Competition Law and Policy* (CUP 2012)
Kokkoris I, *US Merger Control: Public Interest Considerations in US Merger Control* (OUP 2024)

Kokkoris I and Lemus C (eds), *Research Handbook on the Law and Economics of Competition Enforcement* (Edward Elgar 2022)
Kokkoris I and Levy N (eds), *Research Handbook on Global Merger Control* (Edward Elgar 2023)
Lenihan AT, *Balancing Power Without Weapons: State Intervention into Cross-Border Mergers and Acquisitions* (CUP 2018)
Lianos I and Geradin D (eds), *Handbook of Competition Law: Enforcement and Procedure* (Edward Elgar 2013)
Lianos I and Geradin D (eds), *Handbook of Competition Law: Substantive Aspects* (Edward Elgar 2013)
Malone D, Mohan CR, and Raghavan S, *The Oxford Handbook of Indian Foreign Policy* (OUP 2015)
Mason AT, *Brandeis: A Free Man's Life* (Viking Press 1946)
Mason M, *American Multinationals and Japan: The Political Economy of Japanese Capital Controls, 1899–1980* (Harvard University Press 1992)
Mitnick BM, *The Political Economy of Regulation* (Columbia University Press 1980)
Mulder N, *The Economic Weapon* (Yale University Press 2022)
Navarro E and others, *Merger Control in the EU* (2nd edn, OUP 2005)
Nowag J, *Environmental Integration in Competition and Free-Movement Laws* (OUP 2016)
Nowak M and Ricci LA (eds), *Post-Apartheid South Africa: The First Ten Years* (International Monetary Fund 2005)
Panagariya A, *India: The Emerging Giant* (OUP 2013)
Sauvant KP (ed), *Investing in the United States: Is the US Ready for FDI from China?* (Edward Elgar 2009)
Schuck PH (ed), *Foundations of Administrative Law* (OUP 1994)
Schmidtchen D, Albert M, and Voigt S (eds), *The More Economic Approach to European Competition Law* (Mohr Siebeck 2007)
Smith A, *An Inquiry into the Nature and Causes of the Wealth of Nations* (first published 1776, OUP 2008)
Smith AD, *Nationalism and Modernism: A Critical Survey of Recent Theories of Nations and Nationalism* (Routledge 1998)
Stiglitz J, *The Price of Inequality: How Today's Divided Society Endangers Our Future* (WW Norton 2012)
Wish R and Bailey D, *Competition Law* (7th edn, OUP 2012)
Witt AC, *The More Economic Approach to EU Antitrust Law* (Hart 2016)
Wolf C and others, *China's Expanding Role in Global Mergers and Acquisitions Markets* (RAND Corporation 2011)
Wolff M, *Fire and Fury* (Little Brown 2018)

Journal Articles

Agarwal S and others, 'Inconsistent Regulators: Evidence from Banking' (2014) 129 Quarterly Journal of Economics 889
Ahrend R, 'Foreign Direct Investment into Russia – Pain Without Gain? A Survey of Foreign Direct Investors' (2000) 9 Russian Economic Trends 26
Aiginger K and Rodrik D, 'Rebirth of Industrial Policy and Agenda for the Twenty-First Century' (2020) 20 Journal of Industry, Competition and Trade 189
Akman P, '"Consumer Welfare" and Article 82 EC: Practice and Rhetoric' (2009) 32 World Competition 71
Alexiadis P, Sependa E and Vlachos L, 'Merger Control: "Around the World in 80 Days: Management of the Merger Review Process of Global Deals"' (2018) 19 Business Law International 201
Archibald J and Zucker J, 'Exon-Florio "Safe Harbour" Threatened (2007) 68 The European Lawyer 14
Atkinson RD, 'U.S. Trade Policy at a Turning Point' [2021] The International Economy 16
Azar J and others, 'Concentration in US Labor Markets: Evidence from Online Vacancy Data' (2020) 66 Labour Economics 101886

Baer W, 'Import Substitution and Industrialization in Latin America: Experiences and Interpretations' (1972) 7(1) Latin American Research Review 95

Barkow RE and Huber PW, 'A Tale of Two Agencies: A Comparative Analysis of FCC and DOJ Review of Telecommunications Mergers' [2000] University of Chicago Legal Forum 29

Benston GJ, 'Savings Banking and the Public Interest' (1972) 4 Journal of Money, Credit and Banking 133

Bogran A and Clark HR, 'Foreign Direct Investment in South Africa' (1999) 27 Denver Journal of International Law and Policy 337

Bonaime A, Gulen H, and Ion M, 'Does Policy Uncertainty Affect Mergers and Acquisitions?' (2018) 129 Journal of Financial Economics 531

Boycko M, Shleifer A, and Vishny RW, 'Privatizing Russia' (1993) 2 Brookings Papers on Economic Activity 139

Brandenburger R and Matelis J, 'The 2010 U.S. Horizontal Merger Guidelines: A Historical and International Perspective' (2011) 25(3) Antitrust Magazine

Brodley JF, 'The Economic Goals of Antitrust: Efficiency, Consumer Welfare, and Technological Progress' (1987) 62 New York University Law Review 1020

Buch-Hansen H, 'The Political Economy of Regulatory Change: The Case of British Merger Control' (2012) 6 Regulation and Governance 101

Bruno RL, Campos NF, and Estrin S, 'The Effect on Foreign Direct Investment of Membership in the European Union' (2021) 59 Journal of Common Market Studies 802

Cabral L, 'Merger Policy in Digital Industries' (2021) 54 Information Economics and Policy 100866

Cartlidge H and Broderick D, 'BSkyB/ITV: Competition Appeal Tribunal Dismisses BSkyB's Appeal' (2009) 17 Utilities Law Review 47

Chen C, 'A National Security Study of the Shuanghui-Smithfield Case' [2017] DEStech Transactions on Social Science, Education and Human Science

Clark HR and Bogran A, 'Foreign Direct Investment in South Africa' (1999) 27(3) Denver Journal of International Law & Policy 339

Crane DA, 'Substance, Procedure, and Institutions in the International Harmonization of Competition Policy' (2009) 10 Chicago Journal of International Law 143

Curtin T, 'Achieving "The Franchise": The Comcast - NBC Universal Merger and the New Media Marketplace' (2010) 19 CommLaw Conspectus 149

Davidow J and Stevens PS, 'Antitrust Merger Control and National Security Review of Foreign Acquisitions in the United States' (1990) 24 Journal of World Trade 39

Davison LM, 'Envisaging the Post-Brexit Landscape: An Articulation of the Likely Changes to the EU–UK Competition Policy Relationship' (2018) 39 Liverpool Law Review 99

Decker C and others, 'Competition Law Enforcement and Household Inequality in the United Kingdom' (2022) 18(4) Journal of Competition Law & Economics 905

Eisenberg GS, 'The Policy and Law of Foreign Direct Investment in the New South Africa' (1994) 28 Journal of World Trade 5

Esplugues C, 'Towards a Common Screening System of Foreign Direct Investment on National Interest Grounds in the European Union' (2018) 11 Culture, Media and Entertainment Law

Ezrachi A, 'The Role of Voluntary Frameworks in Multinational Cooperation over Merger Control (2004) 36 George Washington International Law Review 433

Ezrachi A, 'Sponge' (2017) 5 Journal of Antitrust Enforcement 49

Faku EM, 'The Regulatory and Policy Variables Influencing FDI in South Africa' (2022) 22 Journal of Public Affairs e2689

Felix D, 'Import Substitution and Late Industrialization: Latin America and Asia Compared' (1989) 17(9) World Development 1455

Fox E, 'Mergers in Global Markets: GE/Honeywell and the Future of Merger Control' (2002) 23 University of Pennsylvania Journal of International Law 457

Fullerton L and Alvarez M, 'Convergence in International Merger Control' (2012) 26 Antitrust 20

Gadocha PM, 'Assessing the EU Framework Regulation for the Screening of Foreign Direct Investment – What Is the Effect on Chinese Investors?' (2020) 6 Chinese Journal of Global Governance 57

Galloway J, 'The Pursuit of National Champions: The Intersection of Competition Law and Industrial Policy' (2007) 28(3) European Competition Law Review 172

Galloway J, 'Convergence in International Merger Control' (2009) 5(2) Competition Law Review 179

Gerard DMB, 'Protectionist Threats against Cross-Border Mergers: Unexplored Avenues to Strengthen the Effectiveness of Article 21 EUMR' (2008) 45 Common Market Law Review 23

Gidadhubli RG, 'Yukos Affair: Putin Attacks Russia's Oil Barons' (2003) 38 Economic and Political Weekly 4949

Giebe T and Lee M, 'Competitors in Merger Control: Shall They Be Merely Heard or Also Listened To?' (2020) 49 European Journal of Law and Economics 431

Gilbert AS, 'System of Enforcement: the United Kingdom – the Monopolies Commission' (1963) 6 International and Comparative Law Quarterly Supplementary Publication 57

Goyder DG, 'Monopolies and Mergers Act, 1965' (1965) 28 Modern Law Review 693

Gribbin JD, 'Recent Antitrust Developments in the United Kingdom' (1975) 20 Antitrust Bulletin 377

Grundmann S and Moslein F, 'Golden Shares-State Control in Privatized Companies: Comparative Law, European Law and Policy Aspects' (2004) 1 European Banking & Financial Law Journal (EUREDIA)

Harker M, 'Cross-Border Mergers in the EU: The Commission v the Member States' (2007) 3 European Competition Journal 503

Heath JB, 'United Kingdom: Monopolies and Mergers Bill Foreign Antitrust Section' (1965) Antitrust Bulletin 175

Heyer K, 'Consumer Welfare and the Legacy of Robert Bork' (2014) 57(S3) Journal of Law & Economics S19

Hirschman AO, 'The Political Economy of Import-Substituting Industrialization in Latin America' (1968) 82(1) The Quarterly Journal of Economics 1

Holloway S, 'International Merger Control: Globalization or Global Failure' (2006) 34 Denver Journal of International Law and Policy 353

Holmes S, 'Climate Change, Sustainability, and Competition Law' (2020) 8(2) Journal of Antitrust Enforcement 354

Hovenkamp H, 'Is Antitrust's Consumer Welfare Principle Imperiled?' (2009) 45(1) Journal of Corporation Law 65

Husisian G, 'The future of CFIUS reviews under the Trump administration' (2017) 23(2) International Trade Law & Regulation 68

Jenny F, 'Substantive Convergence in Merger Control: An Assessment' (2015) 1(1) Concurrences 21

Jessop B, 'The Crisis of the National Spatio-Temporal Fix and the Tendential Ecological Dominance of Globalizing Capitalism' (2000) 24(2) International Journal of Urban and Regional Research 323

Kamiski T, 'Sovereign Wealth Fund Investments in Europe as an Instrument of Chinese Energy Policy' (2017) 101 Energy Policy 735

Kampouridi I, 'Arguments for the EU-US Convergence and against Global Merger Control Regime' (2015) 38(1) World Competition 107

Khan LM, 'Amazon's Antitrust Paradox' (2017) 126 Yale Law Journal 710

Khan LM, 'The New Brandeis Movement: America's Antimonopoly Debate' (2018) 9 Journal of European Competition Law & Practice 131

Khan LM and Vaheesan S, 'Market Power and Inequality: The Antitrust Counterrevolution and Its Discontents' (2017) 11 Harvard Law & Policy Review 235

Kidd B, 'The Campaign against Sport in South Africa' (1988) 43 International Journal 643

Kolasky WJ, 'The FCC's Review of the Bell Atlantic/NYNEX and SBC/Ameritech Mergers: Regulatory Overreach in the Name of Promoting Competition' (2001) 68(3) Antitrust Law Journal 771

Kransdorff M, 'Tax Incentives and Foreign Direct Investment in South Africa' (2010) 3(1) Consilience 68

Kress JC, 'Modernizing Bank Merger Review' (2020) 37 Yale Journal on Regulation 435

Kryda GM, 'The Competition Criterion in British Merger Control Policy' (2002) 30(2) Policy Studies Journal 252

Kumar N, 'Liberalisation and Changing Patterns of Foreign Direct Investments' (2005) 40(14) Economic and Political Weekly 1459

Kumar R, 'Nationalisation by Default: The Case of Coal in India' (1981) 16(17) Economic and Political Weekly 757
Lao M, 'Ideology Matters in the Antitrust Debate' (2014) 79 Antitrust Law Journal 649
Lee C, 'The Stories Merger Documents Tell: The US, EU, Asia, Brazil, Mexico, and South Africa Perspectives' (2018) 39(4) European Competition Law Review 161
Levy N, Waksman A, and Sheridan L, 'Global Merger Control – Where to Now?' (2020) 8 Journal or Antitrust Enforcement 319
Lyons B, Reader D, and Stephan A, 'UK Competition Policy Post-Brexit: Taking Back Control While Resisting Siren Calls' (2010) 5(3) Journal of Antitrust Enforcement 347
Majcher K and Robertson VHSE, 'Protecting Personal Data and the Environment: Doctrinal Challenges for EU Competition Law in our Day and Age' (2022) 47(5) European Law Review 622
Malinauskaite J, 'Development of Merger Control in Slovakia and Slovenia' (2012) 23(3) European Business Law Review 375
Mayer J, 'South Africa's Reformed Investment Regime as a Model for Developing Countries' (2022) 25(4) Lewis and Clark Review 1247
Mebratie AD and Bedi AS, 'Foreign Direct Investment, Black Economic Empowerment and Labour Productivity in South Africa' (2013) 22 (1) Journal of International Trade and Economic Development 94
Metaxas G and Armengod H, 'EC Merger Regulation and the Status of Ancillary Restrictions: Evolution of the European Commission's Policy' (2005) 9 European Competition Law Review 500
Meunier S, '"Beggars Can't Be Choosers": The European Crisis and Chinese Direct Investment in the European Union' (2014) 36(3) Journal of European Integration 283
Mishel L and Eisenbrey R, 'How to Raise Wages: Policies That Work and Policies That Don't' (2015) 45(1) Stetson Law Review 43
Mohamed S, 'National Interest Limiting EU Cross-Border Bank Mergers' (2000) 21 European Competition Law Review 248
Monti G, 'Four Options for a Greener Competition Law' (2020) 11(3–4) Journal of European Competition Law and Practice 124
Moran TH, 'Toward a Multilateral Framework for Identifying National Security Threats Posed by Foreign Acquisitions: With Special Reference to Chinese Acquisitions in the United States, Canada, and Australia' (2014) 7(1) China Economic Journal 39
Moss DL, 'Antitrust versus Regulatory Merger Review: The Case of Electricity in Review of Industrial Organization' (2008) 32 Review of Industrial Organization 241
Nolan P, 'China and the Global Business Revolution' (2002) 26(1) Cambridge Journal of Economics 119
Orbach B, 'The Antitrust Consumer Welfare Paradox' (2011) 7(1) Journal of Competition Law & Economics 133
Orbach B, 'How Antitrust Lost Its Goal' (2013) 81 Fordham Law Review 2253
Otero-Iglesias M and Weissenegger M, 'Motivations, Security Threats and Geopolitical Implications of Chinese Investment in the EU Energy Sector: The Case of CDP Reti' (2020) 26 European Journal of International Relations 594
Parisi JJ, 'International Regulation of Mergers: More Convergence, Less Conflict' (2005) 61 NYU Annual Survey of American Law 509
Pass CL and Sparkes JR, 'Control of Horizontal Mergers in Britain' (1980) 14(2) Journal of World Trade 135
Pass CY, 'Horizontal Mergers and the Control of Market Power in the UK' (1972) 17(3) Antitrust Bulletin 811
Payne RJ, 'Japan's South Africa Policy: Political Rhetoric and Economic Realities' (1987) 86 African Affairs 167
Peeperkorn L, 'Competition and Sustainability: What Can Competition Policy Do?' (2020) 4 Concurrences 40
Peng V, 'Astroturf Campaigns: Transparency in Telecom Merger Review' (2016) 49 University of Michigan Journal of Law Reform 525
Piilola A, 'Assessing Theories of Global Governance: A Case Study of International Antitrust Regulation' (2003) 39 Stanford Journal of International Law 207

Power V, 'Gun-Jumping in European Union Merger Control: The Law and Practice' (2020) 22 Irish Journal of European Law 66

Pryke S, 'Economic Nationalism: Theory, History and Prospects' (2012) 3(3) Global Policy 281

Rowley CK, 'Mergers and Public Policy in Great Britain' (1968) 11 Journal of Law & Economics 75

Salop SC, 'Question: What Is the Real and Proper Antitrust Welfare Standard? Answer: The True Consumer Welfare Standard' (2010) 22 Loyola Consumer Law Review 336

Schneider E, 'Germany's Industrial Strategy 2030, EU Competition Policy and the Crisis of New Constitutionalism: (Geo-)Political Economy of a Contested Paradigm Shift' (2023) 28(2) New Political Economy 241

Schneiderman D, 'Promoting Equality, Black Economic Empowerment, and the Future of Investment of Rules' (2009) 25(2) South African Journal of Human Rights 246

Schwartz DC and Mammen JK, 'The Role of CFIUS in International Business Transactions' [2017] International Business Law Journal 115

Seabright P, 'National and European Champions – Burden or Blessing?' (2005) 6(2) CESifo Forum 52

Serdar Dinc I and Erel I, 'Economic Nationalism in Mergers and Acquisitions' (2013) 68 Journal of Finance 2471

Shapiro C, 'Antitrust in a Time of Populism' (2018) 61 International Journal of Industrial Organization 714

Shapiro C and Farrell J, 'Antitrust Evaluation of Horizontal Mergers: An Economic Alternative to Market Definition' (2010) 10(1) BE Journal of Theoretical Economics 0000102202193517041563

Singh J, 'Economic Reforms and Foreign Direct Investment in India: Policy, Trends and Patterns' (2010) 8 IUP Journal of Financial Economics 61

Singh S and Turan N, 'Classified Routes of Foreign Direct Investment in India' (2013) 4(4) International Journal of Research in Commerce & Management 55

Smith BW and Biddle LR, 'Is the Bank Merger Regulatory Review Process Ripe for Change?' (2005) 18 Bank Accounting & Finance 9

Sosnovskikh S, 'Industrial Clusters in Russia: The Developments of Special Economic Zones and Industrial Parks' (2017) 3 Russian Journal of Economics 174

Spencer BJ and Brander JA, 'International R&D Rivalry and Industrial Strategy' (1983) 50(4) 702 Review of Economic Studies

Stavroulaki T, 'Mergers That Harm Our Health' (2022) 19(1) Berkeley Business Law Journal 89

Stephan A, 'Did Lloyds/HBOS Mark the Failure of an Enduring Economics-Based System of Merger Regulation?' (2011) 62(4) Northern Ireland Law Quarterly 539

Stine AC and Gorman ED, 'Ebbing the Tide of Local Bank Concentration: Granting Sole Authority to the Department of Justice to Review the Competitive Effects of Bank Mergers' (2012) 62 Syracuse Law Review 405

Stucke ME, 'Reconsidering Antitrust's Goals' (2012) 53 Boston College Law Review 551

Sunstein CR, 'Interest Groups in American Public Law' (1985) 38 Stanford Law Review 29

Swanepoel C and Fliers PT, 'The Fuel of Unparalleled Recovery: Monetary Policy in South Africa between 1925 and 1936' (2021) 36(2) Economic History of Developing Regions 213

Thakor AV, 'The Financial Crisis of 2007–2009; Why Did It Happen and What Did We Learn' (2015) 4(2) Review of Corporate Finance Studies 155

Tingley D and others, 'The Political Economy of Inward FDI: Opposition to Chinese Mergers and Acquisitions' (2015) 8(1) Chinese Journal of International Politics 27

Titi C, 'International Investment Law and the European Union: Towards a New Generation of International Investment Agreements' (2015) 26(3) European Journal of International Law 639

Tramont BN and Power TM, 'Too Little Restraint: How the FCC Expands Its Reach through Unenforceable and Unwieldy Voluntary Agreements' (2000) 53 Federal Communications Law Journal 49

Trybus M, 'The EC Treaty as an Instrument of European Defence Integration: Judicial Scrutiny of Defence and Security Exceptions' (2002) 39(6) Common Market Law Review 1347

Vaheesan S, 'The Twilight of the Technocrats' Monopoly on Antitrust?' (2018) 127 Yale Law Journal Forum 980

Vanderver T, 'Competition and British Merger Regulation' (1970) 11 Harvard International Law Journal 126

Weir C, 'The Implementation of Merger Policy in the U.K. 1984–1990 Foreign Antitrust' (1993) 38 Antitrust Bulletin 943

Weiss JR and Stern ML, 'Serving Two Masters: The Dual Jurisdiction of the FCC and the Justice Department over Telecommunications Transactions' (1998) 6 CommLaw Conspectus 206

Werden GJ, Froeb LM, and Tschantz S, 'The Effects of Merger Efficiencies on Consumers of Differentiated Products' (2005) 1(2) European Competition Journal 245

Williams M, Abu Alrub A, and Aga M, 'Ecological Footprint, Economic Uncertainty and Foreign Direct Investment in South Africa: Evidence from Asymmetric Cointegration and Dynamic Multipliers in a Nonlinear ARDL Approach' (2022) 12(2) SAGE Open

Wu Z, 'Perspectives on the Chinese Anti-Monopoly Law' (2008) 75 Antitrust Law Journal 73

Wu Z, 'China's Approach of Anti-Monopoly Regulation: Historical Review and Outlook'(2022) 16 Tsinghua University Law Journal 4

Yallapragada RR and Paruchuri MR, 'Foreign Direct Investment in India: A Lost Opportunity' (2003) 30 Southwestern Economic Review 27

Yoo CS, 'Merger Review by the Federal Communications Commission: Comcast-NBC Universal' (2014) 45(3) Review of Industrial Organization 295

Zhang H and Den Bulcke D, 'China's Direct Investment in the European Union: A New Regulatory Change?' (2014) 12 Asia Europe Journal 159

Zwartkruis W and Jong B, 'The EU Regulation on Screening of Foreign Direct Investment: A Game Changer?' (2020) 31(3) European Business Law Review 447

Book Chapters

Aghion P, 'Some Thoughts on Industrial Policy and Growth', in Falck O, Gollier C, and Woessmann L (eds), *Industrial Policy for National Champions* (MIT Press 2011)

Arvanitis A, 'Foreign Direct Investment in South Africa: Why Has It Been so Low', in Nowak M and Ricci LA (eds), *Post-Apartheid South Africa: The First Ten Years* (International Monetary Fund 2005)

Black A, 'The Evolution and Impact of Foreign Direct Investment into South Africa since 1994', in Bhorat A and others (eds), *The Oxford Companion to the Economics of South Africa* (OUP, 2014)

Bonakele T, 'South Africa: Jurisdictional, Substantive, and Policy Issues Including a Focus on Digital Markets', in Kokkoris I and Levy N (eds), *Research Handbook on Global Merger Control* (Edward Elgar 2023)

Budzinski O and Stohr A, 'Public Interest Considerations in European Merger Control Regimes', in Bosco D and Gal MS (eds), *Challenges to Assumptions in Competition Law* (Edward Elgar 2021)

Dolmans M, Mostyn H, and Todd PF, 'Competition Enforcement: Is the Abuse Toolbox Adequate?' in Kokkoris I and Lemus C (eds), *Research Handbook on the Law and Economics of Competition Enforcement* (Edward Elgar 2022)

Fagan DN, 'The US Regulatory and Institutional Framework for FDI', in Sauvant KP (ed), *Investing in the United States: Is the US Ready for FDI from China?* (Edward Elgar 2009)

First H, Fox EM, and Hemli DE, 'The United States. The Competition Law System and the Country's Norms', in Fox EM and Trebilcock MJ (eds), *The Design of Competition Law Institutions: Global Norms, Local Choices* (OUP 2012)

Fountoukakos K, Roberts V, and Allen R, 'Addressing National Security Concerns in the Merger Context', in Kokkoris I and Lemus C (eds), *Research Handbook on the Law and Economics of Competition Enforcement* (Edward Elgar 2022)

Gal MS and Wassmer IF, 'Regional Agreements of Developing Jurisdictions: Unleashing the Potential', in Drexl J and others (eds), *Competition Policy and Regional Integration in Developing Countries* (Edward Elgar 2012)

Gelb S and Black A, 'Foreign Direct Investment in South Africa', in Estrin S and Meyer KE (eds), *Investment Strategies in Emerging Markets* (Edward Elgar 2004)

Han W, Yin R, and Xiong Z, 'Standalone Hold Separate Orders as Remedies in Chinese Merger Control', in Emch A and Ng W (eds), *Wang Xiaoye: The Pioneer of Competition Law in China - Liber Amicorum* (Concurrences 2019)

Jacobs M, 'Sustainable Development as a Contested Concept', in Dobson A (ed), *Fairness and Futurity: Essays on Environmental Sustainability and Social Justice* (OUP 1999)

Johnson M and Fanton I, 'The Economic of Merger Control in a Dynamic World: A Focus on the Relevant Counterfactual', in Kokkoris I and Lemus C (eds), *Research Handbook on the Law and Economics of Competition Enforcement* (Edward Elgar 2022)

Kirchner C, 'Goals of Antitrust and Competition Law Revisited' in Schmidtchen D, Albert M, and Voigt S (eds), *The More Economic Approach to European Competition Law* (Mohr Siebeck 2007)

Kokkoris I, 'EU Merger Control and National Security Assessment: A Moving Target', in Kokkoris I and Levy N (eds), *Research Handbook on Global Merger Control* (Edward Elgar 2023)

Kokkoris I and Skourtis A, 'Is Consumer Welfare Still Fit for Purpose in the EU Competition Regime?', in Kokkoris I and Lemus C (eds), *Research Handbook on the Law and Economics of Competition Enforcement* (Edward Elgar 2022)

Kovacic WE, 'Towards a Domestic Competition Network' in Epstein RA and Greve MS (eds), *Competition Laws in Conflict: Antitrust Jurisdiction in the Global Economy* (American Enterprise Institute Press 2004)

Lianos I, 'Competition Law Remedies in Europe', in Lianos I and Geradin D (eds), *Handbook of Competition Law: Enforcement and Procedure*' (Edward Elgar 2013)

Lianos I, 'Some Reflections on the Question of the Goals of EU Competition Law', in Lianos I and Geradin D (eds), *Handbook of Competition Law: Substantive Aspects* (Edward Elgar 2013)

Lowe P, Kidane A, and Burnside A, 'Industrial Policy and EU Merger Control: Finding the Right Tools' in Kokkoris I and Levy N (eds), *Research Handbook on Global Merger Control* (Edward Elgar 2023)

Motta M and Ruta M, 'Mergers and National Champions', in Falck O, Gollier C, and Woessmann L (eds), *Industrial Policy for National Champions* (MIT Press 2011)

Ordover JA, 'Coordinated Effects' in Collins WD (ed), *Issues in Competition Law and Policy* (ABA Section of Antitrust Law 2008)

Peeperkorn L, 'European Union', in Holmes S, Middelschulte D, and Snoep M (eds), *Competition Law, Climate Change & Environmental Sustainability* (Concurrences 2021)

Pitofsky R, 'EU and US Approaches to International Mergers – View from the US Federal Trade Commission', in *EC Merger Control: Ten Years On – Papers from the EC Merger Control 10th Anniversary Conference held in Brussels in September 2000 under the auspices of the European Commission Directorate General for Competition and the International Bar Association* (International Bar Association 2000)

Reader D, 'UK Merger Control: Finely Tailored but Time for a New Suit?', in Rodger B, Whelan P, and MacCulloch A (eds), *The UK Competition Regime: A Twenty-Year Retrospective* (OUP 2021)

Schinkel M-P and Treuren L, 'Green Antitrust: Friendly Fire in the Fight against Climate Change', in Holmes S, Middelschulte D, and Snoep M (eds), *Competition Law, Climate Change & Environmental Sustainability* (Concurrences 2021)

Sokol D and Blumenthal W, 'Merger Control: Key International Norms and Differences', in Ezrachi A, *Research Handbook on International Competition Law* (Edward Elgar 2012)

Thomas S, 'Normative Goals in Merger Control – Why Merger Control Should Not Attempt to Achieve "Better" Outcomes than Competition', in Kokkoris I and Lemus C (eds), *Research Handbook on the Law and Economics of Competition Enforcement* (Edward Elgar 2022)

Venit JS and Kolasky WJ, 'Substantive Convergence and Procedural Dissonance in Merger Review', in Evenett SJ, Lehmann A, and Steil B, *Antitrust Goes Global: What Future for Transatlantic Cooperation?* (Royal Institute of International Affairs – Brookings Institution 2000)

Volpin C, 'Competition Enforcement and Sustainability: The Odd Couple', in Kokkoris I and Lemus C (eds), *Research Handbook on the Law and Economics of Competition Enforcement* (Edward Elgar 2022)

Werden GJ, 'Unilateral Effects of Horizontal Mergers I: Basic Concepts and Models' in Collins WD (ed), *Issues in Competition Law and Policy* (ABA Section of Antitrust Law 2008)

Werden GJ, 'Consumer Welfare and Competition Policy: Foundations and Limitations' in Drexl J, Kerber W, and Podszun R (eds), *Competition Policy and the Economic Approach* (Edward Elgar 2011)

Zheng W, 'State Capitalism and the Regulation of Competition in China' in Dowdle MW, Gillespie J, and Maher I (eds), *Asian Capitalism and the Regulation of Competition* (CUP 2013)

Working Papers

ABA Section of Antitrust Law, 'Review of Foreign Acquisitions under the Exon-Florio Provision' (1992) https://books.google.gr/books?id=BzIs-MrWIwQC&pg=PP3&lpg=PP3&dq=ABA+Section+of+Antitrust+Law,+'Review+of+Foreign+Acquisitions+under+the+Exon-Florio+Provision'&source=bl&ots=bYQSljm0nY&sig=ACfU3U1NsLDxlvaII2qaP41ARoh62mVVJg&hl=en&sa=X&ved=2ahUKEwiq-p6fvfm accessed October 2023

Barbiero F and Darvas Z, 'In Sickness and Health: Protecting and Supporting Public Investment in Europe' (2014) Bruegel Policy Contribution No 2/2014

Bergsman J, Broadman HG, and Drebenstov V, 'Improving Russia's Foreign Direct Investment Policy Regime' (2001) https://ssrn.com/abstract=288774

Bourreau M and others, 'Google/Fitbit Will Monetise Health Data and Harm Consumers' (September 2020) Centre for Economic Policy Research Policy Insight 107 https://cepr.org/publications/policy-insight-107-googlefitbit-will-monetise-health-data-and-harm-consumers accessed 16 August 2023

Carril-Caccia F and Pavlova E, 'Foreign Direct Investment and its Drivers: A Global and EU Perspective' (2018) European Central Bank Economic Bulletin, Issue 4/2018 https://www.ecb.europa.eu/pub/economic-bulletin/articles/2018/html/ecb.ebart201804_01.en.html accessed 16 August 2023

Chen Z and others, 'Data-Driven Mergers and Personalization' (2020) ISER Discussion Paper No 1108, https://ssrn.com/abstract=3725312

CUTS Centre for Competition, Investment & Economic Regulation and Institute for Global Dialogue, 'Investment Policy in South Africa: An Agenda for Action' (2003) https://cuts-ccier.org/pdf/Investment_Policy_in_South_Africa.pdf

Ding G, 'The CNOOC Bid for Unocal and US National Security: Was the Political Outcry in Congress Justified?' (2016) https://sites.duke.edu/djepapers/files/2016/10/Ding.pdf accessed 16 August 2023

Falck O and Heblich S, 'Do We Need National Champions? If So, Do We Need a Champions-Related Industrial Policy? An Evolutionary Perspective' (2007) Jena Economic Research Paper No 2007-088 https://ssrn.com/abstract=1029668

Gardella A, Rimarchi M, and Stroppa D, 'Potential Regulatory Obstacles to Cross-Border Mergers and Acquisitions in the EU Banking Sector' (February 2020) European Banking Authority Staff Paper Series, No 7 https://www.eba.europa.eu/sites/default/documents/files/document_library/844126/Potential%20obstacles%20M&A.pdf accessed 16 August 2023

Ezrachi A, 'EU Competition Law Goals and the Digital Economy' (2018) Oxford Legal Studies Research Paper No 17, https://ssrn.com/abstract=3191766

Haucap J, 'Merger Effects on Innovation: A Rationale for Stricter Merger Control?' (2017) DICE Discussion Paper No 268, https://www.econstor.eu/bitstream/10419/168579/1/898417104.pdf

Harris JM, 'Writing New Rules for the US-China Investment Relationship' (2017) https://www.cfr.org/sites/default/files/report_pdf/Discussion_Paper_Harris_China_OR.pdf

Heyer K, 'Welfare Standards & Merger Analysis: Why Not the Best?' (2006) US Department of Justice EAG Discussion Paper 06-8 https://www.justice.gov/atr/welfare-standards-and-merger-analysis-why-not-best accessed 20 June 2023

Hoffmann J and Johannsen G, 'EU-Merger Control & Big Data – On Data-specific Theories of Harm and Remedies' (2019) Max Planck Institute for Innovation and Competition Research Paper No 19-05, https://ssrn.com/abstract=3364792

Hoshi T and Kiyota K, 'Potential for Inward Foreign Direct Investment in Japan' (2019), NBER Working Paper No w25680 https://www.sciencedirect.com/science/article/abs/pii/S0889158318301370 accessed 20 May 2023

Hovenkamp HJ, 'Merger Policy and the 2010 Merger Guidelines (2010) U Iowa Legal Studies Research Paper No 10-34 https://papers.ssrn.com/sol3/papers.cfm?abstract_id=16932461 accessed June 2023

Koehler M, 'Merger Control as Barrier to EU Banking Market Integration' (2009) Centre for European Economic Research Discussion Paper No 7 https://ftp.zew.de/pub/zew-docs/dp/dp07082.pdf accessed 5 June 2023

Kovacic WE, Mavroidis PC, and Neven DJ, 'Merger Control Procedures and Institutions: A Comparison of the EU and US Practice' (2014) Robert Schuman Centre for Advanced Studies Working Paper No 476 https://scholarship.law.columbia.edu/faculty_scholarship/2372/ accessed 5 June 2023

Kozuka S, 'Foreign Direct Investment, Public Interest and Corporate Governance: Japan's Recent Experience' (2010) https://ssrn.com/abstract=1731425

Lyons B, Reader D, and Stephan A, 'UK Competition Policy Post-Brexit: In the Public Interest?' (2016) Social Science Research Network ID SSRN Scholarly Paper 2864461 4 https://papers.ssrn.com/sol3/papers.cfm?abstract_id=2864461 accessed 10 May 2022

Marcos F, 'When Competition Is the Last Concern: The Battle for the Control of ENDESA' (2012) IE Law School Working Paper AJ8-189 https://papers.ssrn.com/sol3/papers.cfm?abstract_id=2165451 accessed 10 May 2022

Mariniello M, Neven D, and Padilla J, 'Antitrust, Regulatory Capture, and Economic Integration' (July 2015) Bruegel Policy Contribution 2015/11 https://www.bruegel.org/sites/default/files/wp_attachments/pc_2015_11_.pdf accessed 16 August 2023

Naudé W, 'Industrial Policy: Old and New Issues' (September 2010) WIDER Working Paper 2010/106 https://www.wider.unu.edu/publication/industrial-policy accessed 16 August 2023

Neven DJ and Roller L-H, 'The Scope of Conflict in International Merger Control' (2000) Social Science Research Center Berlin Discussion Paper FS IV 00-14 https://d-nb.info/1191653951/34

Nowag J, Competition Law's Sustainability Gap? Tools for an Examination and a Brief Overview (2019) Lund University Legal Research Paper Series https://papers.ssrn.com/sol3/papers.cfm?abstract_id=348496430 accessed September 2022

Paprzycki R, 'What Caused the Recent Surge of FDI into Japan?' (2004) Hi-Stat Discussion Paper 31 https://ssrn.com/abstract=885983

Paprzycki R and Fukao K, 'The Extent and History of Foreign Direct Investment in Japan' (2005) Hi-Stat Discussion Paper 84 https://ssrn.com/abstract=886000

Patil A, 'Impact of FDI on Indian Economy' (2017) https://ssrn.com/abstract=3000756

Petit N, 'Competition Cases Involving Platforms: Lessons from Europe' (2018) https://ssrn.com/abstract=3285277

Popovich A, 'Investing in Emerging Markets: Finding Out how Political Risk Influences FDI in Russia' (2007) https://ssrn.com/abstract=996414

Rajput A, 'Protection of Foreign Investment in India and International Rule of Law: Rise or Decline?' (2017) KFG Working Paper Series No 10 https://ssrn.com/abstract=3135261

Reader D, 'Accommodating Public Interest Considerations in Domestic Merger Control: Empirical Insights' (2016) https://papers.ssrn.com/abstract=2736917

Schill SW, 'The European Union's Foreign Direct Investment Screening Paradox: Tightening Inward Investment Control to Further External Investment Liberalization' (2019) Amsterdam Law School Legal Studies Research Paper No 2019-17 https://papers.ssrn.com/sol3/papers.cfm?abstract_id=3434475 accessed 15 May 2023

Seaman J, Huotari M, and Otero-Iglesias M, 'Chinese Investment in Europe. A Country-Level Approach' (December 2017) European Think-tank Network on China (ETNC) https://merics.org/sites/default/files/2020-04/171216_ETNC%20Report%202017_0.pdf accessed 16 August 2023

Singh K, 'Foreign Direct Investment in India: A Critical Analysis of FDI from 1991–2005' (2005) https://ssrn.com/abstract=822584

Tarr D and Volchkova N, 'Russian Trade and Foreign Direct Investment Policy at the Crossroads' (2010) World Bank Policy Research Working Paper 5255 https://elibrary.worldbank.org/doi/abs/10.1596/1813-9450-5255

Uguccioni J, Sharpe A and Murray A, 'Labour Productivity and the Distribution of Real Earnings in Canada, 1976–2014' (2016) Centre for the Study of Living Standards http://www.csls.ca/reports/csls2016-15.pdf accessed 2 February 2023

Vande Walle S, 'Remedies in EU Merger Control – an Essential Guide' (2021) https://ssrn.com/abstract=3782333

Zac A, 'Competition Law and Economic Inequality: A Comparative Analysis of Text Similarity Using General Synthetic Control Method' (2020) Working Paper CCLP(L) 53 https://ssrn.com/abstract=3703633

Zaytsev SY, 'Diagnostics of FDI Inflow in Russia: Theoretical and Practical Issues' (2015) https://ssrn.com/abstract=2591399

Zettelmeyer J, 'The Return of Economic Nationalism in Germany' (March 2019) Peterson Institute for International Economics Policy Briefs 19-4, https://www.piie.com/publications/policy-briefs/return-economic-nationalism-germany accessed 16 August 2023

Reports

American Bar Association Section of Antitrust Law, 'Assessment of Global Competition Agency Implementation of ABA Best Practices for Antitrust: Procedure Report by the Procedural Transparency Task Force' (2019) https://www.americanbar.org/content/dam/aba/administrative/antitrust_law/comments/april-2019/sal-procedural-transparency-2019-04-29.pdf accessed 16 August 2023

Cabral L and others, 'The EU Digital Markets Act: A Report from a Panel of Economic Experts' (2021) https://dx.doi.org/10.2760/139337

Committee on Foreign Investment in the United States (CFIUS), Annual Report to Congress (various years) https://home.treasury.gov/policy-issues/international/the-committee-on-foreign-investment-in-the-united-states-cfius/cfius-reports-and-tables accessed 16 August 2023

Council for Promotion of Foreign Direct Investment in Japan – Working Group for Revising Regulations and Administrative Procedures, Final Report (24 April 2017) http://www.invest-japan.go.jp/policy/simplify_regulations_and_procedures/compilation_report_en.pdf accessed 16 August 2023

European Commission, The EU Digital Markets Act: A Report from a Panel of Economic Experts (2021) https://publications.jrc.ec.europa.eu/repository/bitstream/JRC122910/jrc122910_external_study_report_-_the_eu_digital_markets_act.pdf

European Commission, Reflection Paper on Harnessing Globalisation (2017) https://ec.europa.eu/info/publications/reflection-paper-harnessing-globalisation_en

European Competition Network, 'Public Interest Regimes in the European Union: Differences and Similarities in Approach' (2016) Final Report of the EU Merger Working Group https://ec.europa.eu/competition/ecn/mwg_public_interest_regimes_en.pdf accessed 16 August 2023

German Federal Ministry for Economic Affairs and Energy, 'Made in Germany: Industrial Strategy 2030' (February 2019) https://www.bmwi.de/Redaktion/EN/Dossier/industrial-strategy-2030.html accessed 16 August 2023

German Federal Ministry for Economic Affairs and Energy and French Ministry of Economy and Finance, 'Franco-German Manifesto for a European Industrial Policy Adapted to the 21st century' (2019) https://www.bmwk.de/Redaktion/DE/Downloads/F/franco-german-manifesto-for-a-european-industrial-policy.pdf accessed 16 August 2023

German Federal Ministry for Economic Affairs and Energy, French Ministry of Economy and Finance and Polish Ministry of Entrepreneurship and Technology, 'Modernising EU Competition Policy' (4

July 2019) https://www.bmwi.de/Redaktion/DE/Downloads/M-O/modernising-eu-competition-policy.pdf?__blob=publicationFile&v=4 accessed 16 August 2023

Hungarian Competition Authority (Gazdasági Versenyhivatalt, GVH), 'Sustainable Development and Competition Law – Survey Report' (2021) Special Project for the 2021 ICN Annual Conference https://www.gvh.hu/pfile/file?path=/en/gvh/Conference/icn-2021-annual-conference/sustainability_survey_REPORT_3rdEd_2021_09_30_final_PUBLIC.pdf1&inline=true accessed 16 August 2023

ICN, 'Implementation of the ICN Recommended Practices for Merger Notification and Review Procedures' (2005) https://www.internationalcompetitionnetwork.org/wp-content/uploads/2018/05/MWG_ImplementationRPsMergerNotification.pdf accessed 16 August 2023

ICN, 'Competition Enforcement and Consumer Welfare: Setting the Agenda' (2011) https://www.internationalcompetitionnetwork.org/wp-content/uploads/2019/11/SP_CWelfare2011.pdf accessed 16 August 2023

ICN Merger Working Group: Analytical Framework Sub-group, 'The Analytical Framework for Merger Control' (1st ICN Annual Conference, London, 2002) https://centrocedec.files.wordpress.com/2015/07/analytical-framework-for-merger-control-2002.pdf accessed 16 August 2023

ICN, Project on Merger Guidelines (3rd ICN Annual Conference, Seoul, April 2004), https://www.internationalcompetitionnetwork.org/wp-content/uploads/2018/05/MWG_MergerGuidelinesReport.pdf accessed 16 August 2023

ICN, Merger Remedies Review Project (4th ICN Annual Conference, Bonn, June 2005), https://www.uni-goettingen.de/de/document/download/b1dcf3398b09292b5ae557095337f655.pdf/ICN_Remedies_StudyFINAL5-10.pdf accessed 16 August 2023

Innovation, Science and Economic Development Canada (ISED), Investment Canada Act: Annual Report (various years) https://ised-isde.canada.ca/site/investment-canada-act/en/investment-canada-act/archives accessed 16 August 2023

Japanese Government, National Security Strategy of Japan (December 2022) https://www.mod.go.jp/j/approach/agenda/guideline/pdf/security_strategy_en.pdf accessed 16 August 2023

Japanese Ministry of Finance, Number of the Prior-notification under the Foreign Exchange and Foreign Trade Act for FY 2021 (10 June 2022) https://www.mof.go.jp/english/policy/international_policy/fdi/20220610.html accessed 16 August 2023

Kowalski P and others, 'State-Owned Enterprises: Trade Effects and Policy Implications' (2013) OECD Trade Policy Paper No 147, http://dx.doi.org/10.1787/5k4869ckqk7l-en accessed 16 August 2023

Mor F and Browning S, 'Contested Mergers and Takeovers' (2018) Commons Library Briefing No 5374 https://researchbriefings.files.parliament.uk/documents/SN05374/SN05374.pdf accessed 16 August 2023

Organisation for Economic Cooperation and Development (OECD), 'Foreign Direct Investment for Development: Maximising Benefits, Minimising Costs' (2002) https://www.oecd.org/investment/investmentfordevelopment/1959815.pdf accessed 16 August 2023

Organisation for Economic Cooperation and Development (OECD), 'Competition Law and Policy in Russia: An OECD Peer Review' (2004) http://www.oecd.org/dataoecd/10/60/32005515.pdf accessed 16 August 2023

Organisation for Economic Cooperation and Development (OECD), 'Regulatory Environment for Foreign Direct Investment: Preliminary inventory for selected African countries' (2005) https://www.oecd.org/investment/investmentfordevelopment/34783838.pdf accessed 16 August 2023

Organisation for Economic Cooperation and Development (OECD), 'Vertical Mergers' (2007) DAF/COMP(2007)21, https://www.oecd.org/daf/competition/mergers/39891031.pdf accessed 16 August 2023

Organisation for Economic Cooperation and Development (OECD), Benchmark Definition of Foreign Direct Investment (BMD4) (4th edn, 2008) https://www.oecd.org/investment/fdibenchmarkdefinition.htm accessed 16 August 2023

Organisation for Economic Cooperation and Development (OECD), Roundtable on Cross-Border Merger Control: Challenges for Developing and Emerging Economies – Background Note (2011) DAF/COMP/GF(2011)1 https://one.oecd.org/document/DAF/COMP/GF(2011)1/en/pdf accessed 16 August 2023

Organisation for Economic Cooperation and Development (OECD), 'Remedies in Merger Cases' (2012) DAF/COMP(2011)13, http://www.oecd.org/daf/competition/RemediesinMergerCases2011.pdf accessed 16 August 2023

Organisation for Economic Cooperation and Development (OECD), 'Market Definition' (2012) DAF/COMP(2012)19, http://www.oecd.org/daf/competition/Marketdefinition2012.pdf accessed 16 August 2023

Organisation for Economic Cooperation and Development (OECD), 'Report on Country Experiences with the 2005 OECD Recommendation on Merger Review' (2013) https://www.oecd.org/daf/competition/ReportonExperienceswithMergerReviewRecommendation.pdf accessed 16 August 2023

Organisation for Economic Cooperation and Development (OECD), Public Interest Considerations in Merger Control – Background Note (2016), DAF/COMP/WP3(2016)3 https://one.oecd.org/document/DAF/COMP/WP3(2016)3/En/pdf accessed 16 August 2023

Organisation for Economic Cooperation and Development (OECD), Public Interest Considerations in Merger Control – Note by the United States (2016) DAF/COMP/WP3/WD(2016)10 http://www.oecd.org/officialdocuments/displaydocument/?cote=DAF/COMP/WP3/WD(2016)10&docLanguage=En accessed 16 August 2023

Organisation for Economic Cooperation and Development (OECD), Public Interest Considerations in Merger Control – Note by Australia (2016) DAF/COMP/WP3/WD(2016)1 https://one.oecd.org/document/DAF/COMP/WP3/WD(2016)1/En/pdf accessed 26 August 2021

Organisation for Economic Cooperation and Development (OECD), Public Interest Considerations in Merger Control – Note by Canada (2016) DAF/COMP/WP3/WD(2016)2 https://www.oecd.org/officialdocuments/publicdisplaydocumentpdf/?cote=DAF/COMP/WP3/WD(2016)2&docLanguage=En accessed 16 August 2023

Organisation for Economic Cooperation and Development (OECD), Public Interest Considerations in Merger Control – Note by Japan (2016) DAF/COMP/WP3/WD(2016)4 https://www.oecd.org/officialdocuments/publicdisplaydocumentpdf/?cote=DAF/COMP/WP3/WD(2016)4&docLanguage=En accessed 16 August 2023

Organisation for Economic Cooperation and Development (OECD), Public Interest Considerations in Merger Control – Note by New Zealand (2016) DAF/COMP/WP3/WD(2016)7 https://www.oecd.org/officialdocuments/publicdisplaydocumentpdf/?cote=DAF/COMP/WP3/WD(2016)7&docLanguage=En accessed 16 August 2023

Organisation for Economic Cooperation and Development (OECD), Public Interest Considerations in Merger Control – Note by the European Union (2016) DAF/COMP/WP3/WD(2016)11 https://one.oecd.org/document/DAF/COMP/WP3/WD(2016)11/En/pdf accessed 16 August 2023

Organisation for Economic Cooperation and Development (OECD), Public Interest Considerations in Merger Control – Executive Summary of the Roundtable (2017) DAF/COMP/WP3/M(2016)1/ANN5/FINAL https://one.oecd.org/document/DAF/COMP/WP3/M(2016)1/ANN5/FINAL/en/pdf accessed 16 August 2023

Organisation for Economic Cooperation and Development (OECD), Public Interest Considerations in Merger Control – Note by South Africa (2016) DAF/COMP/WP3/WD(2016)13 https://www.oecd.org/officialdocuments/publicdisplaydocumentpdf/?cote=DAF/COMP/WP3/WD(2016)13&docLanguage=En accessed 16 August 2023

Organisation for Economic Cooperation and Development (OECD), FDI Regulatory Restrictiveness Index (2018) https://www.oecd.org/investment/fdiindex.htm accessed 16 August 2023

Organisation for Economic Cooperation and Development (OECD), 'A Policy Maker's Guide to Privatisation' (March 2019) https://doi.org/10.1787/ea4eff68-en accessed 16 August 2023

Organisation for Economic Cooperation and Development (OECD), 'Sustainability and Competition' (2020) https://www.oecd.org/daf/competition/sustainability-and-competition-2020.pdf accessed 16 August 2023

Organisation for Economic Cooperation and Development (OECD), 'Ownership and Governance of State-Owned Enterprises: A Compendium of National Practices' (2021) https://www.oecd.org/corporate/ownership-and-governance-of-state-owned-enterprises-a-compendium-of-national-practices.htm accessed 16 August 2023

Organisation for Economic Cooperation and Development (OECD), The Relationship between FDI screening and Merger Control Reviews – Note by Hungary (2022) DAF/COMP/WD(2022)104 https://one.oecd.org/document/DAF/COMP/WD(2022)104/en/pdf accessed 16 August 2023

UK Centre for the Protection of National Infrastructure, 'Geography and Ownership Risks for Users' (2022) https://www.cpni.gov.uk/data-centre-geography-and-ownership-risks-users accessed 16 August 2023

UK Department for Business, Energy & Industrial Strategy (BEIS), 'National Security and Investment Act 2021: Annual Report 2022' https://www.gov.uk/government/publications/national-security-and-investment-act-2021-annual-report-2022

UK House of Commons, Foreign Affairs Committee, 'Striking the balance: Protecting national security through foreign investment legislation' (Sixth Report of Session 2019–21, 19 January 2021) https://committees.parliament.uk/publications/4319/documents/43959/default/ accessed 16 August 2023

United Nations Conference on Trade and Development (UNCTAD), *World Investment Report 2001: Promoting Linkages* https://unctad.org/system/files/official-document/wir2001_en.pdf accessed 16 August 2023

United Nations Conference on Trade and Development (UNCTAD), 'Investment and Technology Policies for Competitiveness: Review of Successful Country Experiences' (2003) https://unctad.org/system/files/official-document/iteipc20032_en.pdf accessed 16 August 2023

United Nations Conference on Trade and Development (UNCTAD), *World Investment Report 2016: Investor Nationality – Policy Challenges*, https://unctad.org/system/files/official-document/wir2016_en.pdf accessed 16 August 2023

United Nations Conference on Trade and Development (UNCTAD), *World Investment Report 2021: Investing in Sustainable Recovery*, https://unctad.org/system/files/official-document/wir2021_en.pdf accessed 16 August 2023 accessed 16 August 2023

United Nations Conference on Trade and Development (UNCTAD), *World Investment Report 2022: International Tax Reforms and Sustainable Investment*, https://unctad.org/system/files/official-document/wir2022_en.pdf accessed 16 August 2023

United Nations Conference on Trade and Development (UNCTAD), 'The evolution of FDI screening mechanisms: Key trends and features' (2023) Investment Policy Monitor No 25 https://unctad.org/publication/evolution-fdi-screening-mechanisms-key-trends-and-features accessed 16 August 2023

Other Sources

De Gucht K, 'EU-China Investment: A Partnership of Equals' (Bruegel Debate: China Invests in Europe – Patterns Impacts and Policy Issues, Brussels, 7 June 2012) https://ec.europa.eu/commission/presscorner/detail/en/SPEECH_12_421

Fingleton J, 'Mergers and the Public Interest: A Wolf in Sheep's Clothing?' (2018) https://fingleton.com/wp-content/uploads/2018/10/John-Fingleton-Mergers-and-the-public-interest-a-wolf-in-sheeps-clothing-Oct-2018.pdf

Gao Y and Han W, 'The Chinese Anti-Monopoly Commission of the State Council Publishes Anti-Monopoly Guidelines on Platform Economy' (e-Competitions 7 February 2021)

Han W and Gao Y, 'The Chinese National People's Congress Amends the National Competition Law Act, in the First Update in Fifteen Years and Includes a New Grading System for Merger Control' (e-Competitions, 24 June 2022)

Han W and Li L, 'The New Anti-Monopoly Law of the People's Republic of China: Changes and Remaining Issues' *Competition Policy International* (7 August 2022) https://www.competitionpolicyinternational.com/the-new-anti-monopoly-law-of-the-peoples-republic-of-china-changes-and-remaining-issues/

Hatton C, Byrne BR, and Lichy A, 'The EU's FDI Proposal. What Does It Mean and How Will It Interact with EU Merger Control?' *Competition Policy International* (10 April 2018) https://www.competitionlawinsight.com/regulatory/the-eus-fdi-proposal--1.htm

Huang Y and Wu B, 'China's Fair Competition Review: Introduction, Imperfections and Solutions' *CPI Antitrust Chronicle* (March 2017) https://www.competitionpolicyinternational.com/wp-content/uploads/2017/03/CPI-Huang-Wu.pdf

Jackson JK, 'The Committee on Foreign Investment in the United States (CFIUS)' (Congressional Research Service, 3 July 2018) RL33388

Martin S and Berkani U, 'Competition Law and Sustainable Development: Opportunities with Constant Law', in Gürkaynak G, *Sustainable Development: What Role for Competition Policy?* (Concurrences, 3 November 2020) https://www.gurkaynak.av.tr/docs/de6e1-article-99291.pdf accessed 16 August 2023

Mizukoshi M, Hirano Y, and Sukada K, 'Japan: Foreign Direct Investment Regulations' *Global Competition Review* (6 December 2022) https://globalcompetitionreview.com/guide/foreign-direct-investment-regulation-guide/second-edition/article/japan

Nyaly X, Lloyd K and Avivi L, 'Merger Control in South Africa: Overview' (Thomson Reuters – Practical Law, 1 February 2022) https://uk.practicallaw.thomsonreuters.com/2-504-5969

Piscitelli G and Gerbrandy A, 'The Sustainability Dilemma in Competition Law' (2018) 8 ECDPM Great Insights Magazine https://ecdpm.org/great-insights/civil-society-business-same-direction/sustainability-dilemma-competition-law/

Reader DM, 'Revisiting the Role of the Public Interest in Merger Control' (Doctoral Thesis, University of East Anglia 2015)

STA Law Firm, 'A Guide to Foreign Direct Investment in India' (2020) https://www.stalawfirm.com/public/uploads/downloads/A_Guide_to_Foreign_Direct_Investment_in_India.pdf

Valentine J, Sholem M, and Morgan D, 'The UK's National Security & Investment Act' (2021) XI(132) National Law Review https://www.natlawreview.com/article/uk-s-national-security-investment-act

Vickers B, 'An Overview of South Africa's Investment Regime and Performance' (2001) Institute for Global Dialogue Global Insight No 16 https://igd.org.za/global-insight/url=https://igd.org.za/publication/gi-16/?wpdmdl=8108&refresh=64df48e90bb241692354793 accessed 16 August 2023

Viktorov A and Kovtunova O, 'The Foreign Investment Regulation Review: Russia' (2021) The Law Reviews https://thelawreviews.co.uk/title/the-foreign-investment-regulation-review/russia accessed 12 April 2022

Xueref-Poviac E and others, 'The Evolving Concept of National Security' *Global Competition Review* (6 December 2022) https://globalcompetitionreview.com/guide/foreign-direct-investment-regulation-guide/second-edition/article/the-evolving-concept-of-national-security

Index

For the benefit of digital users, indexed terms that span two pages (e.g., 52–53) may, on occasion, appear on only one of those pages.

Cases are cited where they receive significant discussion in the text.

Tables and figures are indicated by *t* and *f* following the page number